PERFORMANCE STUDIES

What reviewers said of the first edition:

"Replete with photographs, diagrams and a steady stream of offset excerpts from other primary sources, the book is both visually beautiful and innovatively formatted. It is commendable as well for the genuinely serious attention it gives to basic pedagogical concerns. This attention carries over into the book itself which is not only marked by generally lucid and jargon-free prose but which is also complemented by bionotes (complete with reference to major works) on virtually every author mentioned in the text. To say that Schechner's book is reader-friendly is a bit of an understatement. It is one of those rare academic publications that is attentive to both the beginning and advanced scholar and to both student and teacher . . . it marks the coming of age of performance studies . . . as an acknowledged field of study . . ."

Theatre Journal

"Through his writings, I always discover new ways of looking at performance, and through performance at the world at large. His thoughts always renew my desire to change the world."

Guillermo Gómez-Peña, performance artist and writer, San Francisco

"An appropriately broad-ranging, challenging, and provocative introduction, equally important for practising artists as for students and scholars of the performing arts."

Phillip Zarrilli, University of Exeter

"Exactly what I have longed for. It provides linkages between concepts, gives historical perspective, and explains theoretical ideas in a language accessible to undergraduate students. It will be required reading."

Takahashi Yuichiro, Dokkyo University, Hyogo

The publication of *Performance Studies: An Introduction* was a defining moment for the field. In this completely updated second edition, Schechner opens with a discussion of important developments in the discipline and closes with a chapter on "Global and Intercultural Performances" which is completely rewritten in the light of the post-September 11th world. Fully revised, with new examples, biographies, source material and photographs, this landmark textbook provides a lively and accessible overview of the full range of performance for undergraduates at all levels and beginning graduate students in performance studies, theatre, performing arts, and cultural studies. Among the topics discussed are the performing arts and popular entertainments, rituals, play and games, and the performances of everyday life. Supporting examples and ideas are drawn from the social sciences, performing arts, poststructuralism, ritual theory, ethology, philosophy, and aesthetics.

User-friendly, with a special text design, it also includes the following features:

- numerous extracts from primary sources giving alternative voices and viewpoints
- biographies of key thinkers
- student activities to stimulate fieldwork, classroom exercises and discussion
- key readings for each chapter
- more than 20 line drawings and 206 photographs drawn from private and public collections around the world.

Richard Schechner is a pioneer of Performance Studies. A scholar, theatre director, editor, and playwright he is University Professor of Performance Studies at the Tisch School of the Arts at New York University and Editor of *TDR: The Journal of Performance Studies*. He is the author of *Public Domain*, *Environmental Theater*, *The End of Humanism*, *Performance Theory*, *Between Theater and Anthropology*, *The Future of Ritual*, and *Over, Under, and Around*. His books have been translated into Spanish, Korean, Chinese, Japanese, Serbo-Croatian, German, Italian, Hungarian, and Bulgarian. He is the general editor of the Worlds of Performance series published by Routledge and the co-editor of the Enactments series published by Seagull Books.

PERFORMANCE STUDIES

An introduction

Second edition

Richard Schechner

NEW YORK AND LONDON

First published 2002 in the USA and Canada
by Routledge
270 Madison Ave, New York, NY 10016

Reprinted 2003 (twice)

Second edition published 2006 by Routledge

Simultaneously published in the UK
by Routledge
2 Park Square, Milton Park, Abingdon, Oxon OX14 4RN

Reprinted 2006, 2007 (twice)

Routledge is an imprint of the Taylor & Francis Group, an informa business

Designed and typeset in Perpetua and Benguiat Gothic by
Keystroke, Jacaranda Lodge, Wolverhampton
Printed and bound in Great Britain by
TJ International Ltd, Padstow, Cornwall

The figures have been reproduced by kind permission of their rights holders and sources. Routledge has made every effort to trace copyright holders and to obtain permission to publish illustrated material. Any omissions brought to our attention will be remedied in future editions.

Library of Congress Cataloging in Publication Data
Schechner, Richard, 1934–
Performance studies: an introduction / Richard Schechner.—
2nd ed.
p. cm.
Includes bibliographical references and index.
1. Theater—Anthropological aspects. 2. Rites and ceremonies.
3. Performing arts. I. Title.
PN2041.A57S34 2006
792.01—dc22 2005030245

British Library Cataloguing in Publication Data
A catalogue record for this book is available from the British Library

ISBN10: 0–415–37245–3 (hbk)
ISBN10: 0–415–37246–1 (pbk)

ISBN13: 978–0–415–37245–9 (hbk)
ISBN13: 978–0–415–37246–6 (pbk)

To

Barbara Kirshenblatt-Gimblett

Peggy Phelan

Diana Taylor

PERFORMANCE

Usually people say that a truly artistic show will always be unique,
impossible to be repeated: never will the same actors,
in the same play, produce the same show.
Theatre is Life.

People also say that, in life, we never really do anything
for the first time, always repeating
past experiences, habits, rituals, conventions.
Life is Theatre.

Richard Schechner, with his sensibility and intelligence,
leads us to explore the limits between Life and Theatre,
which he calls Performance. With his knowledge,
he allows us to discover other thinkers,
stimulating us to have our own thoughts.

Augusto Boal

CONTENTS

PREFACE TO FIRST EDITION

Whoever cannot seek
the unforeseen sees nothing,
for the known way
is an impasse.

Heraclitus, Fragment 7
(Brooks Haxton, translator)

No one knows better than an editor that writing a book is a collective effort. There are a lot of people I want to thank. Foremost is Professor Carol Martin, my wife, whose supportive critical and organizational skills helped me keep this work coherent and focused. Carol knows me very well. No one can speak to me in as direct and forceful a manner (and live to tell what happened next). No one has been more helpful in making this book into a reality.

Next is Professor Henry Bial, who wrote the short bio-notes and subject definitions that enliven almost every page of this book. He wrote the first drafts of the "Talk About" and "Perform" and helped select the suggested readings that end each chapter. Henry also read every word more than once, making constructive comments, keeping my spirits up during the weeks when I thought Sisyphus had it easy. Henry is also editing a companion performance studies reader that, along with this book, gives to students and their teachers the basis for a compact course in performance studies.

Then, my children: Sam MacIntosh Schechner and Sophia Martin Schechner. I know that usually "the family" are thanked last, but that's not the way it is with me. I have not only jabbered the ideas of this book with them but have witnessed performance-in-action through their growth and development. Sam is now a professional editor and writer in his own right and Sophia a poet, painter, and equestrian of formidable talent.

I want to thank my editors at Routledge, first Talia Rodgers, who commissioned this book (and waited years for me to earn my advance). Talia has always been enthusiastic and supportive, not only of this project but of so much else that is fine at Routledge. Along with her far-reaching vision Talia has a very clear editor's eye for what's what. And then Moira Taylor, Senior Textbook Development Editor and the Project Manager for this book. Moira has educated me in constructing a textbook, for which I cannot thank her enough. Talia, Moira, and their colleagues at Routledge have worked from instigation to completion, advising, cajoling, and insisting. I feel supported also by a team of readers, designers, and sales personnel – including cover designer Sutchinda Rangsi-Thompson and production editor Ruth Bourne. Altogether, I felt part of a team effort. Writing can be a woeful, solitary occupation, but producing a book is something else again.

My colleagues at the Department of Performance Studies, Tisch School of the Arts, sustained me in several ways. Professors Barbara Kirshenblatt-Gimblett and Diana Taylor read portions of the book and offered detailed, clear suggestions, many of which I took. I turn porcupine when criticized, but after a little while, I am grateful to friends who tell me in plain English what I need to do to make my work better. My other colleagues – Professors Peggy Phelan, Barbara Browning, José Muñoz, Fred Moten, and Ngũgĩ wa Thiong'o, and more recently, Anna Deavere Smith and André Lepecki – have also helped by creating a department where ideas come first, internecine war has been abolished, and intellectual, artistic, and personal diversity are cherished and practiced. Believe it or not, most of our faculty meetings are fun, some downright stimulating.

Nor could this book have been completed without the efforts of the home office, the contributing editors, and those whose work appears in *TDR: The Journal of Performance Studies*. I especially want to thank Associate Editor Mariellen Sandford, my long-time partner at *TDR*, who worked extra hard so that I had both the time and peace of mind necessary for writing. Also the student editors during the final year of work on this book: Jennifer Chan, Cathlyn Harris, Alice Reagan, and Sara Brady. The entire *TDR* community deserves thanks. I am in regular contact with the Contributing Editors, as active and broad-ranging a group of persons as one could ever hope to work with: Philip Auslander, Eugenio Barba,

John Bell, Augusto Boal, Guillermo Gómez-Peña, Barbara Kirshenblatt-Gimblett, Rebecca Schneider, William H. Sun, Diana Taylor, Ngũgĩ wa Thiong'o, Tadashi Uchino, and Susanne Winnacker. No wonder that some of their work is featured in this book. Also, reading submissions and editing accepted manuscripts helps keep me abreast of the field.

Writing a textbook demands feedback from people who are expert in the field. In performance studies, this encompasses many different kinds of persons, approaches, and specialties. In writing this book I have benefited greatly during its development from the comments of reviewers in North America and the UK, including Baz Kershaw, Head of Drama, University of Bristol; Colin Counsell, Programme Director, Theatre Studies, University of North London; Simon Shepherd, Director of Programmes, Central School of Speech and Drama, London; Rebecca Schneider, Department of Theater, Film, and Dance, Cornell University; and Sally Harrison-Pepper, School of Interdisciplinary Studies, Miami University, Ohio.

In writing this kind of prefatory memorandum, I fear I've omitted persons who are absolutely crucial. So in that spirit let me thank most wholeheartedly the Forgotten Colleagues, whoever you may be.

Finally, what kind of book is this? To whom is it addressed? How might it be useful? All the effort of my writing and the team at Routledge is to make an accessible and useful textbook suitable for any course in performance studies wherever it may be taught in the world. What this means in practical terms is that *Performance Studies: An Introduction* will be used primarily as a textbook in departments of, or programs in, performance studies, theatre, communications, speech, cultural studies, and the like. Already there is a significant worldwide interest in performance studies. I want this book to help those already involved in performance studies and to stimulate others to become involved. As I emphasize in the text that follows, performance studies is unsettled, open, diverse, and multiple in its methods, themes, subjects, arts, and persons.

The reference list at the end of the text includes every writing I have consulted or cited, as well as key writings of persons who are mentioned in the text. Some of these writings are ancient, some very contemporary – the range is from classics to newspaper articles and internet sites. There are some discrepancies between dates of first publication or composition given in the main body of the book and the dates given in the reference list. For the most part, in compiling the reference list I selected editions and translations that I feel are readable and available. My goal is to provide an extensive, if not comprehensive, set of writings that in some way characterizes the field of performance studies as I am in the process of envisioning it.

My hope is that this book will stimulate the growth of many new courses in performance studies. Not only courses concerning one or another aspect of performance studies, but broad-ranging courses that serve as an "introduction." An introduction to what? Well, life. My goal is nothing less than making performance studies a method of analysis, a way to understand the world as it is becoming, and a necessary tool for living.

Richard Schechner
Hanover, New Hampshire
July 2001

PREFACE TO SECOND EDITION

This second edition is different from the first in many instances – but it also incorporates much of the first edition. The Preface to the first edition remains intact – please consult it for the full panoply of "thank yous." Here, I will be brief, thanking only those who made the second edition possible.

First, Professor Carol Martin, my wife. Also my children, Sam MacIntosh Schechner and Sophia Martin Schechner.

Then, my editors at Routledge, Talia Rodgers, publisher of the Theatre and Performance Studies division and Moira Taylor, Senior Textbook Development Editor. Without their tireless efforts this book would not exist.

Thanks to my colleagues in NYU's Department of Performance Studies, especially Barbara Kirshenblatt-Gimblett and Diana Taylor, who are good friends, intellectual companions, and clear-eyed critics.

And I want to thank *TDR*'s editors and staff – in particular my long-time partner, Associate Editor Mariellen Sandford. During the months that I was working on the second edition, Mariellen served as *TDR*'s Acting Editor, giving me the time to accomplish what I needed to get done. Ditto for my colleagues at East Coast Artists, Christine Witmer and Jeanne Finestone especially.

What's new in this edition? All of the bio-boxes, readings, and end-of-chapter assignments and exercises have been upgraded. There are new boxes bringing the book up to date. I have thoroughly revised every chapter, and especially the final chapter, "Global and Intercultural Performances". The book is substantially longer and, I hope, better for the added material, discussion, and analysis.

I want this book to be useful to those already involved in performance studies while stimulating others to become involved. As I emphasize in the text that follows, performance studies remains unsettled, open, diverse, and multiple in its methods, themes, subjects arts, and persons. I hope this book will lead to new courses in performance studies. Not only courses concerning one or another aspect of performance studies, but broad-ranging courses serving as an "introduction" – but to what? Well, to life. My goal is nothing less than making performance studies a method of analysis, a way to understand the world in its ceaseless becoming, and a necessary tool for living.

Richard Schechner
New York City
October 2005

1 WHAT IS PERFORMANCE STUDIES?

Introducing this book, this field, and me

The book you hold in your hand is "an" introduction to performance studies. There will be others, and that suits me just fine. The one overriding and underlying assumption of performance studies is that the field is open. There is no finality to performance studies, either theoretically or operationally. There are many voices, themes, opinions, methods, and subjects. As I will show in Chapter 2, anything and everything can be studied "as" performance. But this does not mean performance studies as an academic discipline lacks specific subjects and questions that it focuses on. Theoretically, performance studies is wide open; practically, it has developed in a certain way, which I will discuss in this chapter.

Nor does openness mean there are no values. People want, need, and use standards by which to live, write, think, and act. As individuals and as parts of communities and nations people participate and interact with other people, other species, the planet, and whatever else is out there. But the values that guide people are not "natural," transcendent, timeless, God-given, or inalienable. Values belong to ideology, science, the arts, religion, politics, and other areas of human endeavor and inquiry. Values are hard-won and contingent, changing over time according to social and historical circumstances. Values are a function of cultures, groups, and individuals. Values can be used to protect and liberate or to control and oppress. In fact, the difference between what is "liberty" and what is "oppression" depends a lot on where you are coming from.

This book embodies the values, theories, and practices of a certain field of scholarship as understood by one particular person in the eighth decade of his life. This person is a Jewish Hindu Buddhist atheist living in New York City, married, and the father of two children. He is a university professor in the Performance Studies Department of New York University and the Editor of *TDR: The Journal of Performance Studies*. He directs plays, writes essays and books, lectures, and leads workshops. He has traveled and worked in many parts of the world. Who I am is not irrelevant. I will be leading you on a journey. You ought to know a little about your guide.

Because performance studies is so broad-ranging and open to new possibilities, no one can actually grasp its totality or press all its vastness and variety into a single book. My points of departure are my own teaching, research, artistic practice, and life experiences. But I am not limited by these. I will offer ideas far from my center, some even contrary to my values and opinions.

The boxes

Before going on, I want to point out a feature of this book. My text includes no quotations, citations, or notes. Ideas are drawn from many sources, but the written voice is my own. I hope this gives the reader a smoother ride than many scholarly texts. At the same time, I want my readers to hear many voices. The boxes offer alternative and supplementary opinions and interruptions. The boxes open the conversation in ways I cannot do alone. The boxes are hyperlinks enacting some of the diversity of performance studies. I want the effect to be of a seminar with many hands raised or of a computer desktop with many open windows.

What makes performance studies special

Performances are actions. As a discipline, performance studies takes actions very seriously in four ways. First, behavior is the "object of study" of performance studies. Although performance studies scholars use the "archive" extensively – what's in books, photographs, the archaeological record, historical remains, etc. – their dedicated focus is on the "repertory", namely, what people do in the activity of their doing it. Second, artistic practice is a big part of the performance studies project. A number of performance studies scholars are also practicing artists working in the avant-garde, in community-based performance, and elsewhere; others have mastered a variety of non-Western and Western traditional forms. The relationship between studying performance and doing performance is integral. Third, fieldwork as "participant observation" is a much-prized method adapted from anthropology and put to new uses. In anthropological fieldwork, participant observation is a way of learning about cultures other than that of the fieldworker. In anthropology, for the most part, the "home culture" is Western, the "other" non-Western. But in performance studies, the "other" may be a part of one's own culture (non-Western or Western), or even an aspect of one's own behavior. That positions the performance studies fieldworker at a Brechtian distance, allowing for criticism, irony, and personal commentary as well as sympathetic participation. In this active way, one performs fieldwork. Taking a critical distance from the objects of study and self invites revision, the recognition that social circumstances – including knowledge itself – are not fixed, but subject to the "rehearsal process" of testing and revising. Fourth, it follows that performance studies is actively involved in social practices and advocacies. Many who practice performance studies do not aspire to ideological neutrality. In fact, a basic theoretical claim is that no approach or position is "neutral." There is no such thing as unbiased. The challenge is to become as aware as possible of one's own stances in relation to the positions of others – and then take steps to maintain or change positions.

Performances – as I will show in some detail in Chapter 2 – occur in many different instances and kinds. Performance must be construed as a "broad spectrum" or "continuum" of human actions ranging from ritual, play, sports, popular entertainments, the performing arts (theatre, dance, music), and everyday life performances to the enactment of social, professional, gender, race, and class roles, and on to healing (from shamanism to surgery), the media, and the internet. Before performance studies, Western thinkers believed they knew exactly what was and what was not "performance." But in fact, there is no historically or culturally fixable limit to what is or is not "performance." Along the continuum new genres are added, others are dropped. The underlying notion is that any action that is framed, presented, highlighted, or displayed is a performance. Many performances belong to more than one category along the continuum. For example, an American football player spiking the ball and pointing a finger in the air after scoring a touchdown is performing a dance and enacting a ritual as part of his professional role as athlete and popular entertainer.

As a method of studying performances, the relatively new discipline of performance studies is still in its formative stage. Performance studies draws on and synthesizes approaches from a wide variety of disciplines including performing arts, social sciences, feminist studies, gender studies, history, psychoanalysis, queer theory, semiotics, ethology, cybernetics, area studies, media and popular culture theory, and cultural studies. But "performance studies is more than the sum of its inclusions" (**see Kirshenblatt-Gimblett box 1**). Performance studies starts where most limited-domain disciplines end. A performance studies scholar examines texts, architecture, visual arts, or any other item or artifact of art or culture not in themselves, but as players in ongoing relationships, that is, "as" performances. I will develop this notion of "as" performance in Chapter 2. Briefly put, whatever is being studied is regarded as practices, events, and behaviors, not as "objects" or "things." This quality of "liveness" – even when dealing with media or archival materials – is at the heart of performance studies. Thus, performance studies does not "read" an action or ask what "text" is being enacted. Rather, one inquires about the "behavior" of, for example, a painting: how, when, and by whom was it made, how it interacts with those who view it, and how the painting changes over time. The artifact may be relatively stable, but the performances it creates or takes part in can change radically. The performance studies scholar examines the circumstances in which the painting was created and exhibited; she looks at how the gallery or building displaying the painting shapes its reception. These and similar kinds of performance studies questions can be asked of any behavior, event, or material object. Of course, when performance studies deals with behavior – artistic, everyday, ritual, playful, and so on – the questions asked are closer to how performance theorists have traditionally approached theatre and the other performing arts. I discuss and apply this kind of analysis more fully in every chapter of this book.

Barbara Kirshenblatt-Gimblett (birthdate not disclosed): American performance theorist specializing in the aesthetics of everyday life, Jewish performance, and folklore. She was the founding chair of NYU's Department of Performance Studies from 1981 to 1993. Author of *Destination Culture* (1998).

In performance studies, questions of embodiment, action, behavior, and agency are dealt with interculturally. This approach recognizes two things. First, in today's world, cultures are always interacting – there are no totally isolated groups. Second, the differences among cultures are so profound that no theory of performance is universal: one size cannot fit all. Nor are the playing fields where cultures

Barbara Kirshenblatt-Gimblett

Performance studies is more than a sum of its inclusions

Performance studies starts from the premise that its objects of study are not to be divided up and parceled out, medium by medium, to various other disciplines – music, dance, dramatic literature, art history. The prevailing division of the arts by medium is arbitrary, as is the creation of fields and departments devoted to each.

To study performance, as an artform that lacks a distinctive medium (and hence uses any and all media), requires attending to all the modalities in play. This distinguishes performance studies from those that focus on a single modality – dance, music, art, theatre, literature, and cinema. For this and other reasons, performance studies is better equipped to deal with most of the world's artistic expression, which has always synthesized or otherwise integrated movement, sound, speech, narrative, and objects.

A provisional coalescence on the move, performance studies is more than the sum of its inclusions. While it might be argued that "as an artform, performance lacks a distinctive medium" (Carroll 1986: 78), embodied practice and event is a recurring point of reference within performance studies. What this means, among other things, is that presence, liveness, agency, embodiment, and event are not so much the defining features of our objects of study as issues at the heart of our disciplinary subject. While some may address these issues in relation to plays performed on a stage, others may address them in relation to artifacts in a museum vitrine.

We take our lead from the historical avant-garde and contemporary art, which have long questioned the boundaries between modalities and gone about blurring them, whether those boundaries mark off media, genres, or cultural traditions. What they found interesting – Chinese opera, Balinese barong, circus – we find interesting.

Such confounding of categories has not only widened the range of what can count as an artmaking practice, but also gives rise to performance art that is expressly not theatre; and art performance that dematerializes the art object and approaches the condition of performance.

1999, adapted by Kirshenblatt-Gimblett from "Performance Studies," a report written for the Rockefeller Foundation, www.nyu.edu/classes/bkg/ps.htm

interact level. The current means of cultural interaction – globalization – enacts extreme imbalances of power, money, access to media, and control over resources. Although this is reminiscent of colonialism, globalization is also different from colonialism in key ways. Proponents of globalization promise that "free trade," the internet, and advances in science and technology are leading to a better life for the world's peoples. Globalization also induces sameness at the level of popular culture – "world beat" and the proliferation of American-style fast foods and films are examples. The two ideas are related. Cultural sameness and seamless communications make it easier for transnational entities to get their messages across. This is crucial because governments and businesses alike increasingly find it more efficient to rule and manage with the collaboration rather than the opposition of workers. In order to gain their collaboration, information must not only move with ease globally but also be skillfully managed. The apparent victory of "democracy" and capitalism goes hand in hand with the flow of controlled media. Whether or not the internet will be, finally, an arena of resistance or compliance remains an open question. Those resisting the "new world order" are stigmatized as "terrorists," "rogue states," and/or "fundamentalists." I further discuss these rhetorical and performative strategies in Chapter 8.

Performance studies adherents explore a wide array of subjects and use many methodologies to deal with this contradictory and turbulent world. But unlike more traditional academic disciplines, performance studies is not organized into a unitary system. These days, many artists and intellectuals know that knowledge cannot be easily, if at all, reduced to a singular coherence. In fact, a hallmark of performance studies is the exposition of the tensions and contradictions driving today's world. No one in performance studies is able to profess the whole field. This is because performance studies has a huge appetite for encountering, even inventing, new kinds of performing and ways of analyzing performances while insisting that cultural knowledge can never be complete (**see Geertz box**). If performance studies were an art, it would be avant-garde.

As a field, performance studies is sympathetic to the avant-garde, the marginal, the offbeat, the minoritarian, the subversive, the twisted, the queer, people of color, and the formerly colonized. Projects within performance studies often act on or act against settled hierarchies of ideas, organizations, and people. Therefore, it is hard to imagine performance studies getting its act together or settling down, or even wanting to.

Clifford Geertz

The pitfalls of cultural analysis

Cultural analysis is intrinsically incomplete. And, worse than that, the more deeply it goes the less complete it is. It is a strange science whose most telling assertions are its most tremulously based, in which to get somewhere with the matter at hand is to intensify the suspicion, both your own and that of others, that you are not quite getting it right. But that, along with plaguing subtle people with obtuse questions, is what being an ethnographer is like.

1973, *The Interpretation of Cultures*, 29

Multiple literacies and hypertexts

Some people complain that literacy is declining not only in terms of basic reading skills, but also in what people read and how they write. The universality of television plus the growing global availability of the internet gives speech and visual communication a strong lift over conventional literacy. This affects all strata of culture from the ways ordinary people communicate to the art of writing. Few novelists in the early twenty-first century write epic "big" novels such as **Leo Tolstoy**'s *War and Peace* or even hyper-literate works such as **James Joyce**'s (*Ulysses* or *Finnegans Wake*. Life is lived very fast, with lots of fast-forward and stop-action. Events and "stars" come and go before we can really take them in. A sensational act is almost immediately displayed on the world media stage. **Andy Warhol** was on the right track when he predicted that "in the future everyone will be world-famous for fifteen minutes." The fleeting archive of our epoch is inscribed more in the CD or DVD, music video, or hyperlinked email than it is in a considered piece of literature.

Leo Tolstoy (1828–1910): Russian author, social thinker, and mystic. Novels include *War and Peace* (1863–69) and *Anna Karenina* (1875–77).

James Joyce (1882–1941): Irish author of *Ulysses* (1922) and *Finnegans Wake* (1939), novels that experiment with language while celebrating the imaginations and peregrinations of Dubliners. Joyce was a big influence on his one-time assistant, Samuel Beckett.

Andy Warhol (1928?–87): American artist and filmmaker. Leader of the Pop Art movement in the 1960s and 1970s. Warhol appropriated images from American popular culture – Campbell's soup cans, Marilyn Monroe – and repositioned them as high art.

Another way of understanding what's happening is to regard our time as witnessing an explosion of multiple literacies. People are increasingly "body literate," "aurally literate," "visually literate," and so on. Films come at all levels of sophistication, as do recorded musics. Email is a burgeoning of letter-writing. Not the elegant handwritten correspondence of eighteenth- and nineteenth-century Europe and Europeanized America, but a rapid part-words-part-pictures hypertextual communication. People not only gab on their cell phones, they converse via instant messaging, and learn to read each other's body languages and moods across cultures. Sometimes playful, sometimes dangerous, people travel actually or virtually to faraway places – communicating and hooking up across ethnic, national, linguistic, religious, and gender boundaries. Webcams and chatrooms flourish. Operating at many levels and directions simultaneously demands multiple literacies. These multiple literacies are "performatives" – encounters in the realm of doing, of pursuing a throughline of action. A shift is occurring, transforming writing, speaking, and even ordinary living into performance. Exactly how this transformation is being accomplished and what it might mean is a principal concern of this book. A world of multiple performatives is the turf of performance studies. Or to put it another way, the academic discipline of performance studies has emerged as a response to an increasingly performative world.

Traditional literacy is being forced to the extremes – a low-level pulp-and-tabloid literacy and a high-level specialized literacy. What is being squeezed is mid-level, or ordinary, literacy. The ability to read, write, and calculate above a basic standard is probably declining in so-called "advanced" societies. Whether literacy will ever be achieved globally is open to question. Computers are taking over basic tasks. For example, a clerk in a store simply swipes a bar-coded item past the scanner, enters the amount of money proffered, and waits for the computerized cash register to read out how much to give in change. Efficient voice-recognition programs transcribe speaking into writing. Already the software exists so that a person speaks in one language and her words are spoken or typed in another. Many web pages offer to translate the content into several languages. At least at the level of basic comprehensible communication, the curse of the Tower of Babel is history.

What is gaining in importance is hypertext, in the broadest meaning of that word. Hypertext combines words, images, sounds, and various shorthands. People with cell phones talk, of course. But they also take photos and use the keypads to punch out messages that combine letters, punctuation marks, and other graphics. A different kind of freedom of speech is evolving, even more rapidly in the so-called "developing world" than in Europe or North America. In China – the world's largest market – more than 350 million people own cell phones as of 2005. More than 100 million Chinese have access to the internet. The Chinese government wants to control what's being disseminated, but can't effectively do so because the origination points of messages cannot be monitored. The number of people using hypertext communications is growing exponentially – not only in China, but everywhere. Email, cell phones, blogs, instant messaging, and wi-fi are transforming what it means to be literate. Book reading is supplemented and to some degree supplanted by a range of ideas, feelings, requests, and desires that are communicated in many different ways. People are both readers and authors. Identities are revealed, masked, fabricated, and stolen. This kind of communicating is highly performative. It encourages senders and receivers to use their imaginations, navigating and interpreting the dynamic cloud of possibilities surrounding each message.

High-level literacy is fast becoming the specialty of academics who master one or more specialized knowledges. Some of these knowledges – in cybernetics, biotechnology, medicine, weapons research, and economics – are having a huge impact on the world. Whole industries are devoted to "translating" high-level research into marketable applications. At the same time, many academics do not feel the need to address a broad public or to explain exactly what the bases for the new knowledges are. Unfortunately, this is true of performance studies too. For example, performance studies scholars who "read" pop culture may not write in ways that ordinary people – those who practice pop culture – find accessible. A chasm has opened separating the scholars from those they write about.

Performance studies here, there, and everywhere

Performance studies is gaining in importance and acceptance. The name itself is trendy – leading some departments to call themselves "performance studies" with little or no revamping of the curriculum. This is to be expected because performance studies is noncanonical which means it is extremely difficult to define or pin down. The discipline is conceived, taught, and institutionalized in a number of different ways. Broadly speaking, there are two main brands, New York University's and Northwestern University's. NYU's performance studies is rooted in theatre, the social sciences, feminist and queer studies, postcolonial studies, poststructuralism, and experimental performance. NU's is rooted in oral interpretation, communications, speech-act theory, and ethnography (**see Jackson box**). But over time, these two approaches have moved toward each other sharing a common commitment to an expanded vision of "performance" and "performativity" – two terms that I will unpack in this book. But there's a lot more to performance studies than a tale of two departments.

Increasingly, new performance studies departments, programs, and courses are being created, some of them ambitious and far-reaching, others a renaming without revising the curriculum (**see Websites, emails, and advertisements box, Maxwell box, and Kennesaw box**). Sometimes performance studies is practiced under a different name, as in the Department of World Arts and Cultures of the University of California Los Angeles. There are many schools where performance studies is a thin wedge – a single course or two being "tried out." But the trend is clear. More performance studies departments, programs, and courses are on the way. Even if many professing performance studies work in non-performance studies environments, they form a strong and increasingly influential cohort reshaping a broad range of fields and disciplines.

Shannon Jackson

The genealogy of performance studies at Northwestern

The development of Northwestern's Department of Performance Studies proceeds from a different direction [than NYU's]. To some, its narrative is less often recounted. To others, of course, it is the only one that matters. [. . .] The Department of (Oral) Interpretation had a decades' long existence in a very different institutional milieu – that is, inside a School of Speech, one that also housed distinct departments of Communication Studies, Radio/TV/ Film, and Theatre. Thus, unlike the progenitors at NYU who broke from a prior institutional identity as Theatre, Northwestern's department had considered itself something other than Theatre for its entire institutional existence. Oral Interpretation was most often positioned as an aesthetic subfield within Speech, Communication, and/or Rhetoric. Its proponents drew from a classical tradition in oral poetry to argue for the role of performance in the analysis and dissemination of cultural texts, specializing in the adaptation of print media into an oral and embodied environment. Northwestern was unusual for devoting an entire department to this area. Most of that faculty's colleagues and former graduate students would find themselves in the oral interpretation slot of a larger Communication department – in the Midwest, the South, the Southwest, the West, and on the East Coast. This made for a dispersed kind of institutional network. It also meant that the decision to shift nomination and orientation to Performance Studies occurred within that network rather than exclusively within a department. The division within the National Communication Association was renamed Performance Studies [in 1985], and field practitioners around the country followed suit. [. . .] If these two stories [NYU's, Northwestern's] show that institutional contexts differently constitute disciplinary identity, they also imply that the history of a discipline changes depending upon where one decides to begin. One way to resituate this two-pronged story of a late twentieth-century formation is to cast Performance Studies as the integration of theatrical and oral/rhetorical traditions.

2004, "*Professing Performance*," 9–10

Websites, emails, and advertisements

A performance studies panoply of places, programs, and possibilities

University of Wales, Aberystwyth, UK Performance Studies focuses on the live arts – dance, theatre, performance art, ritual and popular entertainment – and employs performance as an optic through which to examine a variety of representational practices, thereby widening understanding of performance as both a vital artistic practice and as a means to understand historical, social and cultural processes. Performance Studies provides an innovative, integrating, interdisciplinary and intercultural perspective on the continuum of human action, from theatre and dance to public ceremonies, virtual performance and the performance of everyday life.

www.aber.ac.uk/~psswww/pf/general/introduction.htm

Brown University, Providence, RI, USA We do not consider our program a "hybrid" as we do not consider theatre or performance studies to be "pure," or at least we consider the best performance studies to lean at all times toward hybridity. Here at Brown, we study theatre and a variety of performance genres, as well as "performativity" and "performance in everyday life," in global, historical, practical and theoretical perspective. In many courses we employ a performance studies methodology. We are Theatre AND Performance Studies because we offer a variety of classes in Performance Studies and teach Performance Studies as both a methodology of inquiry applicable to theatre studies and as a subject matter of "performance" beyond the confines of "theatre proper." However, we consider the borders to at all times be extremely fluid, and we are not interested in rigorously parsing theatre studies and performance studies, but in continuing to let them co-inform each other.

Email from Rebecca Schneider and John Emigh

performancestudies.org lists 42 colleges and universities with performance studies programs. Most of these are in the UK or the USA, with several in Australia, Canada, Germany, and South Africa.

www.psi-web.org (Performance Studies international) lists members in the above countries plus Israel, Venezuela, Switzerland, Serbia, France, Italy, Finland, Slovenia, and Japan.

Queen Mary College, University of London, UK We are effectively a Drama Department within a School of English and Drama. We don't offer an explicit PS program pathway, but I would say that PS is integrated across our undergraduate and MA curricula. PS is also integrated in the work of many of our PhD students, so it is hard to specify how many are "doing" PS in particular. We have about 150 students in our BA program, about 10 in our MA, and about 10 (and growing) doing PhDs.

Email from Jen Harvie

National University of Singapore, Singapore To have my course, "Cultural Performance in Asia: Ritual and Theatricality," accepted, I had to make the argument that the field of performance studies was a growing one, and that the critical perspectives it offered intersected particularly fruitfully with a range of cultural and performative practices in the region. My course description: "What is the form and function of theatricality in contemporary Asian society? The module seeks to answer this question by investigating a range of live events, including religious rituals, firework displays, tourist performances, and parades. In recent years, these collective practices of symbolic action and meaning-making that prioritize the live over the mediated have become known as 'cultural performance.' The methodological perspectives of Performance Studies – anthropology, ethnography, critical theory, aesthetics – will be deployed to contextualize ritual and theatricality as integral to the practices of spectacle and display that contribute so arrestingly to social reality in urban Asia."

Email from Paul Rae supplemented by
http://ap3.fas.nus.edu. sg:8000/appl/web9/mod_offered/sem1/TS4217.htm

De Montfort University, Leicester, UK For over two decades the subjects within Performance Studies have worked with a number of professional practitioners [. . .]. Performance Studies researchers are engaged in projects as diverse as the multicultural performance of Tara Arts, Brecht in Berlin and postmodern dance in New York. These provide links with major artists and scholars nationally and internationally. Many of the faculty are practising performers themselves [. . .] all are scholars and researchers. We are an exciting community – forward looking, original and welcoming.

www.dmu.ac.uk/faculties/humanities/pa/ patext.jsp?ComponentID=6695&SourcePageID=6704

Arizona State University West, Phoenix, Arizona, USA At ASUW, my department, Interdisciplinary Arts and Performance, offers 6–8 PS courses (most of which I teach on a rotating basis, although others have taught some). Students are required to take 2 PS courses and generally take 3–4. Since it is only me, only a few students focus in PS as a major, that gives me maybe 3 students a year.

Email from Arthur Sabattini

University of Limerick, Limerick, Ireland We are making progress on the performance-based doctoral program and we are about to embark on the development of a new undergraduate program in Voice and Movement. We would like to ground this program in Performance Studies.

Email from Helen Phelan

Georgetown University, Washington, DC, USA I recently left the Performance Studies Department at UNC Chapel Hill to come to Georgetown University, where we are developing an undergraduate major in theatre and performance studies, with plans to introduce a graduate program in the coming years. Our curriculum includes courses in adaptation and performance of literature, performance art, performance ethnography, intercultural and political performance, and so forth.

Email from Derek Goldman

University of California-Berkeley, California, USA We have placed "performance studies" at the academic center of all our majors' activities, alongside the unrivaled training in dance and choreography, and in acting, directing, design, and technical theatre we provide. In the past decade, graduate study in the field of drama, theater, and performance studies has undergone an energetic renovation, and "performance" itself has become critical to scholarship and research across the humanities. At the same time, this disciplinary ferment has demanded a much higher degree of specialization, and of scholarly rigor from Ph.D. candidates seeking academic careers at the college and university level. The Graduate Group Ph.D. in Performance Studies at Berkeley is at the cutting edge of this epistemic shift. Currently, Ph.D. students are working on subjects that range from postcolonial theatricality to the performance of medicine, from puppets and performing objects to contemporary Shakespearean acting; from the discourses of Latino/a theater to feminist geography in contemporary drama.

http://ls.berkeley.edu/dept/theater/GraduateProgram/index-grad.html

Critical Studies in Performance at UCLA with courses in transnational/intercultural critique, historiography/historical research, staging identity/identification, performance theory. Study with an interdisciplinary faculty in the new Center for Performance Studies

Advertisement in *TDR*, fall 2005

Concordia University, Montreal, Quebec, Canada Concordia University is instituting a minor in Performance Studies (undergraduate) and will be starting an interdisciplinary MFA in performing arts in the next few years, untitled as yet; it probably won't be called "Performance Studies," but I'll be involved with creating it, so it will have PS elements, for sure. It's why they hired me.

Email from Mark Sussman

A Rose by Any Other Name There are three institutions which have been quite strong on PS in the UK – University College Northampton, Plymouth, and University of Wales, Aberystwyth – but there are a number of courses which are developing – de Montfort University, for example. There is now an A-level in Performance Studies – when I queried this to find out how it was different from the previous A-level in Performing Arts – I was told that it was effectively a re-branding with no significant change in content. Aberystwyth is holding to the name! Trying to work out what's in a name though is difficult in itself – we tried to find out if there were people whose work wasn't officially described as performance studies but who would self-describe their work in that way – but we didn't really get any response to that question. I think all of the Performance Studies courses in the UK are linked to drama/theatre studies/dance courses – rather than social science courses.

Email from Franc Chamberlain

University of Chicago, Illinois, USA Here at the University of Chicago we have a hybrid: a nascent Committee on Theater & Performance Studies. As you surely know, the University offers degrees through departments and "committees" – like the Committee on Social Thought or the Committee on Cinema & Media Studies. We leach our faculty from the humanities (e.g., language departments, cinema/media studies, music/ethnomusicology) and the social sciences (e.g., anthropology, politics).

We currently offer a full B.A. program; a graduate program would be a few years down the road.

Email from David Levin

University of Bristol, Bristol, UK For the past 6 years I've run a 1 yr full time MA in Cultural Performance in partnership with Welfare State International in which the students spend a semester at Bristol looking at scholarly and creative approaches to CP, then a semester with WSI in Cumbria combining the company's workshop/education program with advanced creative innovation training and a practical dissertation project. I think it's the only one of its kind in Europe, or maybe even anywhere.

Email from Baz Kershaw

Roehampton University, London, UK Performance Studies takes as it object performance in a myriad of cultural forms, from traditional concerns with drama, dance and theatrical representation, to wider questions of ritual practice, social role, and the performativity of cultural identity. Its focus on the critique and problematization of traditional forms of knowledge provides a new interdisciplinary framework through which to approach the materiality of performance practice in a range of theatrical, and quasi-theatrical, situations.

The MA/MRes Performance Studies programs have an identity and profile distinct from existing provision in the field. Their particular research and critical agendas stage a timely intervention in the international direction of the discipline. The perspectives they mobilize, and their engagement with questions of performance and space, ethics, cultural politics and critical practices, provide a unique and stimulating program of study for the student who wishes to address the discipline at its cutting edge.

Roehampton is at the forefront of introducing Performance Studies into the British academy. Roehampton has a strong presence in Performance Studies publishing, and staff are consolidating the University's growing international reputation as a place of innovation, agenda-setting and leadership in Performance Studies.

www.roehampton.ac.uk/pg/ps/

Ian Maxwell

What is performance studies at the University of Sydney?

At the Department of Performance Studies we set out from the premise that performance is not limited to those forms traditionally marked as being "artistic," and that any theory of performance must, accordingly, be generalizable to a wide range of performative practices, across and between cultures, history, and conventional social categories.

Performance Studies focuses on theatre, spectacle, dance and ritual and draws on disciplines including anthropology, history, sociology, semiotics, architecture, and theatre studies among others. We examine how cultural performances are linked to everyday interactions. Performance Studies includes such diverse topics as Brazilian carnival, Sydney's Mardi Gras, post-modern and avant-garde performance, popular music as well as what you might think of as more "conventional" theatre, dance and drama.

Some Performance Studies students move into professional theatre and dance, but the aim of our course is to provide a theoretical background which provides students, whatever they end up doing, with insights into how and why people behave the way they do in a range of complex social exchanges. [. . .] European theatre and dance traditions are situated in relation to performance traditions emanating from other cultures, and we are constantly exploring possibilities of engaging with performance practice in ways that neither marginalise the work of the professional actor nor displace the critical and theoretical perspective that is fundamental to an academic discipline.

Essential to Performance Studies as it is being developed at the University of Sydney is collaboration with practising artists across many performance genres, and in these collaborative projects the students' task is to observe, document, analyse and theorise about the performance practices they witness. [. . .] Students acquire hands-on experience with documentation of both rehearsal process and performance; they undertake the detailed analysis of performance (both live and recorded) and current ethnographic practice is used to explore modes of writing about performance.

2005, www.arts.usyd.edu.au/departs/perform/about_us/profile.shtml

Kennesaw State University, Georgia, USA

"Performance studies: Living, looking, learning"

"Performance Studies," the new addition to the name in Kennesaw State University's Department of Theatre and Performance Studies, celebrates the program's diverse educational and artistic objectives, positions the university with the best contemporary schools of the arts, and gives students broader scholastic, personal, and professional choices.

But what is "Performance Studies"?

Imagine, if you will, a powerful link:

- A link between cultural anthropology, sociology, drama, oral interpretation of literature, literary criticism, folklore, mythology, and psychology;
- A link between the creative process of making art and the critical process of analyzing performances, both those staged performances, such as plays in which a trained artist applies a skill, and community events, those ritual-like performances of everyday life;
- A link between 'performing' our professional and social roles, telling a joke or a folktale, and staging community spectacles such as parades, circuses, sports, weddings, the Olympics, and public hangings, all of which follow a set order that combines the visual and the auditory and conveys meaning. [. . .]

Providing such a link is a major undertaking, but the change in name not only describes what the KSU curriculum has featured for several years but also documents what the Kennesaw State University College of the Arts stands for. The Department of Theatre and Performance Studies [. . . teaches] performance as an art form, as a field of study, and as a method of inquiry (or a way of knowing).

2005, "What is Performance Studies?"
www.kennesaw. edu/theatre/NEWS_EVENTS/What-Is-TPS.html

Is performance studies an independent field?

Even with the updated nomenclature, is performance studies truly an independent field? Can it be distinguished from theatre studies, cultural studies, and other closely allied fields? One can construct several intellectual histories explaining the various specific outlooks of performance studies as practiced by different schools of thought. In this book, I am developing my own version of the "NYU School of Performance Studies." But even my present and former colleagues at NYU have different versions of this story (**see Kirshenblatt-Gimblett box 2, Taylor box, and Phelan box**). The narrative outlining how performance studies developed at NYU concerns interactions among Western and Asian philosophies, anthropology, gender studies, feminism, the aesthetics of everyday life, race theory, area studies, popular entertainments, queer theory, and postcolonial studies. These interactions have been heavily inflected by an ongoing contact with the avant-garde – both the Euro-American "historical avant-garde" (from symbolism and surrealism through to Dada and Happenings) to the more current avant-gardes being practiced in many parts of the world. Many students, and some professors, of performance studies at NYU are also practicing artists – in performance art, dance, theatre, and music. Preponderantly, their approach has been experimental – to stretch the limits of their arts in ways analogous to how performance studies stretches the limits of academic discourse.

Barbara Kirshenblatt-Gimblett

NYU's Department of Performance Studies

When I was recruited in 1980 the then Graduate Drama Department at NYU's School of the Arts was adrift. At first, I thought I was an unlikely candidate for chair. I had a PhD in folklore, not theatre. I studied performance in everyday life, not on the stage. Soon I realized there was no mistake. A mark of NYU's seriousness in making the transformation to performance studies was hiring a chair who did not come from drama or theatre. I brought a performance perspective to the study of culture that was remarkably aligned with what was emerging as performance theory and in a broad range of experimental and popular performance. By having someone who was not a theatre scholar chair, the faculty was ensuring a more radical break between the former Graduate Department of Drama and emerging Department of Performance Studies.

At the time that I was being recruited, the department consisted of four men – Richard Schechner, Brooks McNamara, Michael Kirby, and Theodore Hoffman. The department had never had a woman on the faculty. There were more than 400 MA and PhD students on the books, some of them deceased.

The idea for performance studies that I encountered had been developing in the context of contemporary experimental performance, with links to the historical avant-garde. Schechner, Kirby, and McNamara were themselves active in the off off Broadway movement. Performance studies would let them align their artistic practice with their pedagogy. This meant abandoning a traditional curriculum in European and American drama and theatre. EuroAmerican theatre would thenceforth find its place within an intercultural, intergeneric, and interdisciplinary intellectual project as one of many objects of study. Taking their lead from the historical avant-garde and contemporary experimental performance, they determined that Western theatre and the dramatic text would not be at the center of the new Performance Studies curriculum, though it continues to play an important role. [. . .]

Over the 12 years of my chairing (1980–92), we developed a rich Performance Studies curriculum that came to include dance research, thanks to Marcia Siegel, and feminist theory, thanks to Peggy Phelan. We placed greater emphasis on theory across the curriculum than had previously been the case. We raised academic and admission standards, reduced and transformed our student body so that everyone was full-time, increased financial aid, restructured requirements, and increased the pace and likelihood of completing the degree. We created a Performance Studies Archive. And, on our tenth anniversary, we organized the first Performance Studies international conference.

2001, personal correspondence

Diana Taylor

Performance studies: a hemispheric focus

My particular investment in performance studies derives less from what it is than what it allows us to do. What I want performance studies to do is provide a theoretical lens for the sustained historical analysis of performance practices – the Americas being my special area of interest. The many definitions of the word "performance," as everyone has noted more or less generously, result in a complex, and at times contradictory, mix. For some it is a process, for others the "result" of a process. For some it is that which disappears, while others see it as that which remains as embodied memory. As the different uses of the term rarely engage each other, "performance" has a history of untranslatability. Ironically, the word is stuck in the disciplinary boxes it defies, denied the universality and transparency that some claim it promises its objects of analysis. These many points of "untranslatability," of course, are what make the term and the practices so culturally revealing. While performances may not give us access and insight into another culture, they certainly tell us a great deal about our desire for access and the politics of our interpretations.

"Performance" has no equivalent in Latin America. Translated simply but nonetheless ambiguously as masculine ("el performance") or feminine ("la performance"), it usually refers to performance art. Nonetheless, scholars and artists have started to use the term to refer more broadly to social dramas and embodied practices. What this "performance studies" approach allows us to do is crucial: rethink cultural production and expression from a place other than the written word which has dominated Latin American thought since the conquest. While writing was used before the conquest – either in pictogram form, hieroglyphs or knotting systems – it never replaced the performed utterance. Writing was a prompt to performance, a mnemonic aid, not a separate form of knowing. With the conquest, the legitimation of writing over other epistemic and mnemonic systems assured that colonial power could be developed and enforced without the input of the great majority of the population – the indigenous and marginal populations without access to systematic writing. While some scholars engage in "indigenismo" by focusing on oral traditions, the schism does not lie between the written and spoken word but rather between discursive and performative systems.

Western culture, wedded to the word, whether written or spoken, enables language to usurp epistemic and explanatory power. Performance studies allows us to take seriously other forms of cultural expression as both praxis and episteme. Performance traditions also serve to store and transmit knowledge. Performance studies, additionally, functions as a wedge in the institutional understanding and organization of knowledge. In the United States, departments of Spanish and Portuguese limit themselves to "language and literature" to the exclusion of much else. In Latin American institutions, "departamentos de letras" assure a similar schism between literary and embodied cultural practice. The resulting exclusions of many forms of embodied knowledge from analysis effect their own performance of erasure.

Performance is as much about forgetting as about remembering, about disappearing as about re-appearing. A "hemispheric" focus indicates just how much "America," as the U.S. likes to think of itself, has forgotten about America, whose name, territory, and resources it has fought so hard to dominate. Domination by culture, by "definition," by claims to "originality" and "authenticity," functions in tandem with military and economic supremacy. Though a-historical in much of its practice, performance studies can allow us to engage in a sustained historical analysis of performance practices. That's what I'm asking it to do.

2001, personal communication

Diana Taylor (1950–): leading theorist of Latin American performance and founding director of the Hemispheric Institute of Performance and Politics. Taylor chaired NYU's Performance Studies Department from 1996 to 2002. Her books include *Theatre of Crisis: Drama and Politics in Latin America* (1991), *Disappearing Acts: Spectacles of Gender and Nationalism in Argentina's 'Dirty War'* (1997), and *The Archive and the Repertoire* (2003).

Peggy Phelan

Another history, another future of performance studies

One potent version of the history of performance studies is that the field was born out of the fecund collaborations between Richard Schechner and Victor Turner. In bringing theatre and anthropology together, both men saw the extraordinarily deep questions these perspectives on cultural expression raised. If the diversity of human culture continually showed a persistent theatricality, could performance be a universal expression of human signification, akin to language? [. . .] Was "theatre" an adequate term for the wide range of "theatrical acts" that intercultural observation was everywhere revealing? Perhaps "performance" better captured and conveyed the activity that was provoking these questions. Since only a tiny portion of the world's cultures equated theatre with written scripts, performance studies would begin with an intercultural understanding of its fundamental term, rather than enlisting intercultural case studies as additives, rhetorically or ideologically based postures of inclusion and relevance.

This is the story that surrounded me when I first began teaching in the Department of Performance Studies [. . .] in 1985. I was immediately fascinated by the idea that two men gave birth. [. . .]

When I first began reading Turner's and Schechner's work I was struck by its generosity and porousness, its undisguised desire to be "taken up." [. . .] But I was also a little suspicious of their ease, their sense that all could be understood if we could only see widely and deeply enough. [. . .] As the institutionalization of performance studies spread throughout the eighties (sometimes under other names) in the United States and internationally, the openness of the central paradigm sometimes made it seem that performance studies was (endlessly?) capable of absorbing ideas and methods from a wide variety of disciplines. [. . .]

But institutionalization is hardly ever benign, and one could easily tell the story of the consolidation of the discipline of performance studies in a much less flattering manner. Many people (including some of my own inner voices), did tell me such stories, but I'll use the conditional here to muffle echoes and because I love the guilty. To wit: one could accuse the discipline of practicing some of the very colonialist and empire-extending arts it had critiqued so aggressively. One could argue that performance studies was a narrow, even small-minded, version of cultural studies. One could say that performance studies had so broad a focus precisely because it had nothing original to say. One could suggest that the famous "parasitism" of J. L. Austin's linguistic performative was actually a terrific description of performance studies itself. One could even argue that the whole discipline was created as a reactionary response to the simulations and virtualities of postmodernism; a discipline devoted to live artistic human exchange could easily be taken up by the universities in the eighties precisely because its power as a vital form of culture exchange had been dissipated. A new discipline just in time to commemorate a dead art would be in keeping with the necrophilia of much academic practice.

But each of these (conditional) claims misses what I believe are the most compelling possibilities realized by performance studies. While theatre and anthropology certainly played a central role in the generative disciplines of performance studies, other "points of contact" have also had exceptional force in the field. [. . . W]e must begin to imagine a post-theatrical, post-anthropological age. [. . .]

Thinking of performance in the expanded field of the electronic paradigm requires that we reconsider the terms that have been at the contested center of performance studies for the past decade [since 1988]: simulation, representation, virtuality, presence, and above all, the slippery indicative "as if." The electronic paradigm places the "as if" at the foundation of a much-hyped "global communication," even while it asks us to act "as if" such a network would render phantasmatic race, class, gender, literacy, and other access differentials. [. . .]

The electronic paradigm as an epistemic event represents something more than a new way to transmit information; it redefines knowledge itself into that which can be sent and that which can be stored. Performance studies [. . .] is alert to the Net's potential to flatten and screen that which we might want most to remember, to love, to learn. We have created and studied a discipline based on that which disappears, art that cannot be preserved or posted. And we know performance knows things worth knowing. As the electronic paradigm moves into the center of universities, corporations, and other systems of power-knowledge, the "knowing" that cannot be preserved or posted may well generate a mourning that transcends the current lite Luddite resistance to technology.

1998, "Introduction" to *The Ends of Performance*, 3–5,8

Peggy Phelan (birthdate not disclosed): American feminist scholar, chair of NYU's Department of Performance Studies from 1993 to 1996, and a founder of Performance Studies international. Author of *Unmarked* (1993), *Mourning Sex* (1997), and *Art and Feminism* (2001, with Helena Reckitt).

The philosophical antecedents to performance studies include questions addressed in ancient times, in the Renaissance, and in the 1950s to 1970s, the period immediately before performance studies came into its own. Early philosophers both in the West and in India pondered the relationship between daily life, theatre, and the "really real." In the West, the relationship between the arts and philosophy has been marked, according to the Greek philosopher **Plato**, by "a long-standing quarrel between poetry and philosophy." The ancient Greek felt that the really real, the ideal, existed only as pure forms. In his *Republic* (*c.* 370 BCE), Plato argued that ordinary realities are but shadows cast on the wall of the dark cave of ignorance. (One wonders if shadow puppetry, so popular in Asia from ancient times, was known to Plato.) The arts – including the performing arts – imitate these shadows and are therefore doubly removed from the really real. As if this weren't enough, Plato distrusted theatre because it appealed to the emotions rather than to reason, "watering the growth of passions which should be allowed to wither away." Plato banned poetry, including theatre, from his ideal republic. It was left to Plato's student **Aristotle** to redeem the arts. Aristotle argued that the really real was "indwelling" as a plan or potential, somewhat like a genetic code. In the *Poetics*, Aristotle reasoned that by imitating actions, and by enacting the logical chain of consequences flowing from actions, one might learn about these indwelling forms. Far from wanting to avoid the emotions, Aristotle wanted to arouse, understand, and purge their deleterious effects.

Plato (*c.* 427– *c.* 347 BCE): Greek philosopher, the advocate of reason, restraint, and logic over excess and passion. Plato developed the dialogical or dialectical style of discourse – reasoning by means of dialogue and the confrontation of opposites. Ironically, Plato's dialogues are extremely theatrical and he was very passionate about the life of the mind.

Aristotle (384–322 BCE): Greek philosopher, student of Plato. Aristotle published numerous philosophical treatises, including the *Poetics* (*c.* 335 BCE), where he outlines the principles of Greek tragic drama. Aristotle's ideas have profoundly influenced European and European-derived performance theory.

Indian philosophers had a different idea altogether. Writing at roughly the same time as the Greeks, they felt that the whole universe, from ordinary reality to the realm of the gods, was *maya* and *lila* – illusion, play, and theatre on a grand scale. The theory of maya–lila asserts that the really real is playful, ever changing, and illusive. What is "behind" maya–lila? On this, Indian philosophers had several opinions. Some said that nothing was beyond maya–lila. Others proposed realities too awesome for humans to experience. When Arjuna, the hero-warrior of the *Mahabharata*, asks Krishna in the *Bhagavad Gita* section of the epic to show his true form, the experience is terrifying in the extreme. Still other philosophers proposed the existence of *brahman*, an absolute unity-of-all which a person can enter through meditation, yoga, or living a perfected life. At the achievement of *moksha*, or release from the cycle of birth–death–rebirth, a person's individual *atman* (the absolute within) becomes one with *brahman* (the universal absolute). But for most people most of the time, reality is maya–lila. The gods also enter the world of maya–lila. The gods take human form, as Krishna does in the performance of Raslila (Krishna's dance with adoring female cow-herders and with his favorite lover, Radha) or as Rama does in the performance of Ramlila (when Vishnu incarnates himself as Rama to rid the world of the demon Ravana). Raslila and Ramlila are performed today. Hundreds of millions of Indian Hindus believe in these enacted incarnations – where young boys temporarily become gods. Notions of maya–lila are discussed more fully in Chapter 4.

In Renaissance Europe the widely accepted notion that the world was a great theatre called the *theatrum mundi* was well put in **William Shakespeare**'s *As You Like It* when Jaques says, "All the world's a stage | And all the men and women merely players; | They have their exits and their entrances; | And one man in his time plays many parts" (2, 7: 139–42). Hamlet, in his instructions to the players, had a somewhat different opinion, more in keeping with Aristotle's theory of mimesis: "[. . .] the purpose of playing, whose end, both at the first and now, was and is, to hold, as 't were, the mirror up to nature; to show virtue her own feature, scorn her own image, and the very age and body of the time his form and pressure" (3, 2: 21–25). To people living in the theatrum mundi everyday life was theatrical and, conversely, theatre offered a working model of how life was lived.

The most recent variation on the theatrum mundi theme emerged shortly after World War II and continues to the present. In 1949, **Jacques Lacan** delivered his paper "The Mirror Stage," an influential psychoanalytic study proposing that infants as young as six months recognize themselves in the

William Shakespeare (1564–1616): playwright, poet, and actor generally regarded as the greatest writer in the English language. Among his 38 plays are *Hamlet*, *King Lear*, *Othello*, *The Merchant of Venice*, *Macbeth*, *Measure for Measure*, *As You Like It*, *Henry V*, *A Midsummer Night's Dream*, *Romeo and Juliet*, and *The Tempest*.

mirror as "another" (**see Lacan box**). In 1955, **Gregory Bateson** wrote "A Theory of Play and Fantasy." Bateson emphasized the importance of what he termed "metacommunication," the message that tells the receiver that a message of a certain kind is being sent – social communications exist within a complex of frames. Bateson's ideas were elaborated on by **Erving Goffman** in a series of works about performing in everyday life, the most influential of which is his 1959, *The Presentation of Self in Everyday Life*. At roughly the same time, philosopher **J. L. Austin** developed his notion of "performativity." Austin's lectures on the performative were published posthumously in 1962 as *How to Do Things with Words*. According to Austin, performatives are utterances such as bets, promises, namings, and so on that actually do something, that perform. A little later, in France, **Jean-François Lyotard, Gilles Deleuze, Michel Foucault, Jean Baudrillard, Pierre Bourdieu, Jacques Derrida, Guy Debord**, and **Félix Guattari** proposed what were then radical new ways to understand history, social life, and language. Many of these ideas retain their currency even today. I discuss performativity, postmodernism, simulations, and poststructuralism in Chapter 5.

Jacques Lacan

The mirror stage

The child [. . . from the age of six months can] already recognize as such his own image in a mirror. [. . .] This act [. . .] immediately rebounds [. . .] in a series of gestures in which he experiences in play the relation between the movements assumed in the image and the reflected environment, and between this virtual complex and the reality it reduplicates – the child's own body, and the persons and things, around him. [. . .] We understand the mirror stage *as an identification*, in the full sense that analysis gives to this term: the transformation that takes place in the subject when he assumes an image. [. . .] The *mirror* stage is a drama whose internal thrust is precipitated from insufficiency to anticipation – and which manufactures for the subject, caught up in the lure of spatial identification, the succession of fantasies that extends from a fragmented body-image to a form of its totality that I shall call orthopaedic – and, lastly, to the assumption of the armor of an alienating identity, which will mark with its rigid structure the subject's entire mental development. [. . . Later in life while free associating in psychoanalysis] he ends up by recognizing that this being has never been anything more than his construct in the imaginary and that this construct disappoints all his certainties. For in this labor which he undertakes to reconstruct *for another*, he rediscovers the fundamental alienation that made him construct it *like another*, and which has always destined it to be taken from him *by another*.

1977, *Écrits*, 1, 4, 42

Jacques Lacan (1901–81): French structuralist psychoanalyst who theorized the development of an alienated self in terms of interactions among the Imaginary, the Symbolic, and the Real. His works include *Écrits* (1977) and *The Four Functions of Psychoanalysis* (1978).

Gregory Bateson (1904–80): British-born anthropologist, cyberneticist, and communications theorist. Major works include *Naven* (1936), *Steps to an Ecology of Mind* (1972) and *Mind and Nature* (1979).

Erving Goffman (1922–82): Canadian-born anthropologist who studied the performances and rituals of everyday life. His books include *The Presentation of Self in Everyday Life* (1959), *Behavior in Public Places* (1963), *Interaction Ritual* (1967), and *Frame Analysis* (1974).

J. L. Austin (1911–60): English philosopher and linguist. His influential Harvard lectures on the concept of the "performative" were posthumously published as *How to Do Things with Words* (1962).

Jean-François Lyotard (1924–98): French philosopher. Major works include *The Postmodern Condition* (1984), *The Differend* (1988), and *Peregrinations: Law, Form, Event* (1988).

Gilles Deleuze (1925–95): French poststructuralist philosopher who collaborated with **Félix Guattari (1930–92)**. Together they wrote *Anti-Oedipus* (1977) and *A Thousand Plateaus* (1987).

Michel Foucault (1926–84): French philosopher-historian who analyzed and criticized prison systems, psychiatry, and medicine. Foucault explored the relationships connecting power and knowledge. Among his works are *Madness and Civilization* (1965), *The Order of Things* (1970), *The Archaeology of Knowledge* (1972), *Discipline and Punish* (1977), and *The History of Sexuality* (1978).

Jean Baudrillard (1929–): French cultural theorist known for his work on simulations. His books include *Simulations* (1983), *The Illusion of the End* (1994), and *Selected Writings* (2001).

Pierre Bourdieu (1930–2002): French sociologist who worked extensively in Algeria before becoming a professor at the Collège de France in Paris. Among his many books are *Outline of a Theory of Practice* (1972, Eng. 1977), *Practical Reason: On the Theory of Action* (1994, Eng. 1998), *Acts of Resistance* (1988), and *Masculine Domination* (2001).

Jacques Derrida (1930–2004): Algerian-born French philosopher who pioneered the literary and cultural theory of deconstruction. Among his many books: *Of Grammatology* (1976), *Writing and Difference* (1978), *Limited Inc* (1988), *Who's Afraid of Philosophy?* (2002), and *On Touching* (with Peter Dreyer, 2005).

Guy Debord (1931–94): French writer and filmmaker, founder of the Situationists (1957–72), a revolutionary group of artists and writers who came to prominence during the Paris riots of May 1968. Author of *The Society of the Spectacle* (1994).

My own role in the formation of performance studies goes back to the mid-1960s. My 1966 essay "Approaches to Theory/Criticism" was a formulation of an area of study I called "the performance activities of man" (*sic*): play, games, sports, theatre, and ritual. "Actuals," published in 1970, related rituals in non-Western cultures to avant-garde performances. Both of these essays are in *Performance Theory* (2003). In 1973, as guest editor of a special *TDR* issue on "Performance and the Social Sciences," I outlined seven "areas where performance theory and the social sciences coincide":

1 Performance in everyday life, including gatherings of every kind.
2 The structure of sports, ritual, play, and public political behaviors.
3 Analysis of various modes of communication (other than the written word); semiotics.
4 Connections between human and animal behavior patterns with an emphasis on play and ritualized behavior.
5 Aspects of psychotherapy that emphasize person-to-person interaction, acting out, and body awareness.
6 Ethnography and prehistory – both of exotic and familiar cultures (from the Western perspective).
7 Constitution of unified theories of performance, which are, in fact, theories of behavior.

I saw these nodes connected to each other either as a "fan" or a "web" (**see figure 1.1**). In 1977, the first edition of *Performance Theory* appeared, revised and expanded in 1988 and again in 2000. I published *Between Theater and Anthropology* in 1985 and *The Future of Ritual* in 1993. I also co-edited several books as well as serving twice as editor of *TDR* (1962–69, 1986–present). I related my theories to my artistic work and research activities in various parts of the world, and to my growing sense of the broad spectrum of performance (**see figures 1.2 and 1.3**).

The Victor Turner connection

This network of ideas and practice was nourished by my relationship with anthropologist **Victor Turner**. Though we knew each other's work earlier, Turner and I met in 1977 when he invited me to participate in a conference he was organizing on "Ritual, Drama, and Spectacle." The conference was so successful, and the chemistry between Turner and me so positive, that we joined to plan a "World Conference on Ritual and Performance," which developed into three related conferences held during 1981–82. The first focused on the performances of the Yaquis of northern Mexico and the US Southwest; the second on the work of **Suzuki Tadashi**. The culminating meeting took place in New York from 23 August to 1 September 1982. Attending were artists and scholars from the Americas, Asia, Europe, and Africa. All in all, 74 participated, 49 at the New York conference – only

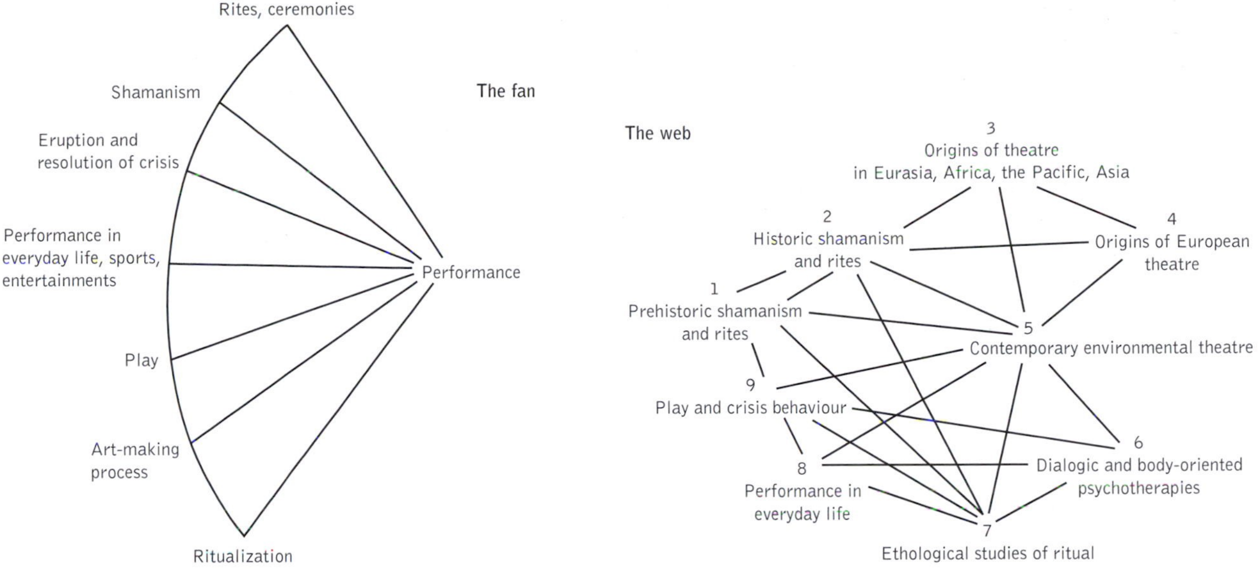

fig 1.1. Performance can be graphically configured as either a fan or a web. This open fan depicts an orderly panorama ranging from "ritualization" on one end through the "performances of everyday life" in the center to "rites and ceremonies" at the other end. Ritualization is an ethological term; rites and ceremonies are uniquely human.

The web depicts the same system more dynamically – and therefore more experientially. Each node interacts with all the others. It's no accident that I place my "contemporary environmental theatre" in the center. This arbitrary and subjective positioning expresses my life practice. Others might place something else at the center. In actual fact, there is no center – one ought to imagine the system as in continuous motion and realignment. Furthermore I place historical events alongside speculations and artistic performances. This method is similar to that of Indigenous Australians who credit dreams with a reality maybe even stronger than awake-time events. My method is also similar to the classic theatre exercise wherein "as if" = "is".

Drawing: "Fan" and "Web" from p. ii of Performance Theory, 1977 and all subsequent editions.

Victor and **Edith Turner**, **Phillip Zarrilli**, and I were at all three meetings. Turner exulted in the meetings as utopian gatherings (**see Turner box**). *By Means of Performance* (1990) was edited from the proceedings of the three episodes of the World Conference.

Victor Turner (1917–83): Scottish-born anthropologist who theorized notions of liminality and social drama. Major works include *Forest of Symbols* (1967), *The Ritual Process* (1969), *Dramas, Fields, and Metaphors* (1974), and *From Ritual to Theatre* (1982). Turner collaborated with his wife **Edith Turner (1921–)** on projects. Among Edith Turner's writings are *Experiencing Ritual* (1992) and *The Hands Feel It* (1996).

Suzuki Tadashi (1939–): Japanese founding artistic director of the Suzuki Company of Toga, with whom he has directed a number of influential works including *The Trojan Women* and *Dionysus*. He advocates an intensely physical approach to actor training which he outlines in *The Way of Acting* (1986).

Phillip Zarrilli (1947–): American-born director, writer, and actor trainer. A Professor of Performance Practice at Exeter University, Zarrilli has developed a psychophysical acting process drawing on Asian martial, medical, and meditation practices. His books include *When the Body Becomes All Eyes* (1998), *Kathakali Dance Drama* (2000), and *Acting (Re) Considered* (editor, 2nd edition, 2002).

What made Turner's conferences so special was that they were extended get-togethers of relatively few people, lasting from five days to two weeks. Participants had plenty of time to trade ideas, view performances, tell stories, and socialize. These conferences very much shaped my ideas about what performance studies could become. In my courses at NYU, I invited many of those who were at one or another of the conferences to lecture or guest teach. Friends reached out to friends. Tilting performance studies toward anthropology – which was particularly strong in the 1970s and 1980s – is linked to working with Turner and the people he introduced me to; other possibilities for performance studies have since come strongly into play.

fig 1.2. A selection of performances directed by Richard Schechner.

YokastaS Redux, Saviana Stanescu and Richard Schechner. The Yokastas strike a pose. From the left: Phyllis Johnson, Jennifer Lim, Daphne Gaines, Rachel Bowditch. East Coast Artists, New York, 2005. Photograph by Ryan Jensen.

Cherry Ka Bagicha (The Cherry Orchard), Anton Chekhov. Act 2, Dunyasha flirting with Yepikhodov. With the Repertory Company of the National School of Drama, New Delhi, 1982. Photograph by Richard Schechner.

Ma Rainey's Black Bottom, August Wilson. Act 2, Ma Rainey (seated, played by Sophie Mcina), her girl Dussie Mae, played by Baby Cele, and her nephew, Sylvester. Grahamstown Festival, Republic of South Africa, 1992. Photograph by Richard Schechner.

Three Sisters, Anton Chekhov. Act 2, Vershinin, played by Frank Wood, orating about the future. With East Coast Artists, New York 1997. Photograph by Richard Schechner.

The Oresteia, Aeschylus (in Chinese). Agamemnon, played by Wu Hsing-kuo, steps on the purple carpet. With the Contemporary Legend Theatre, Taipei, 1995. Photograph by Richard Schechner.

Victor Turner

By their performances shall ye know them

Cultures are most fully expressed in and made conscious of themselves in their ritual and theatrical performances. [. . .] A performance is a dialectic of "flow," that is, spontaneous movement in which action and awareness are one, and "reflexivity," in which the central meanings, values and goals of a culture are seen "in action," as they shape and explain behavior. A performance is declarative of our shared humanity, yet it utters the uniqueness of particular cultures. We will know one another better by entering one another's performances and learning their grammars and vocabularies.

1980, from a Planning Meeting for the World Conference on Ritual and Performance, quoted in "Introduction" to Richard Schechner and Willa Appel (eds), *By Means of Performance* (1990), 1.

After Turner's death in 1983, I convened another conference in his style – a 1990 meeting on "intercultural performance" attended by about 20 artists and scholars at the Rockefeller Foundation's villa in Bellagio, Italy. Many of the participants were closely associated with what was by then being called the "emerging field of performance studies." The three conferences – stretching over 15 years – were important as field-defining events, as means of dissemination, and as prototypes for the yet-to-be-convened "Points of Contact" conferences of the Centre for Performance Research in Wales and the annual conferences of Performance Studies international (PSi).

The Centre for Performance Research and PSi

From 1980, when the NYU Graduate Drama Department morphed into the Department of Performance Studies, the first such in the world, performance studies developed rapidly. I resumed editorship of *TDR* in 1986, subtitling it "*The Journal of Performance Studies*." In Wales in 1988, **Richard Gough** founded the Centre for Performance Research (CPR). The CPR convened a series of conferences entitled "Points of Contact" (named after the introduction to my *Between Theater and Anthropology*) and in 1996 launched its own journal, *Performance Research*. In 1990, what was planned as a modest, graduate-student-led conference celebrating the tenth anniversary of NYU's performance studies department attracted 110 people, 43 from outside the USA. The conveners of the conference playfully dubbed it PSi, Performance Studies international, and the name stuck (**see Performance Studies international box**). In 1993, members of ATHE (American Theatre in Higher Education) formed a performance studies "focus group" sponsoring performance studies panels and, more recently, a two-day "pre-conference" as part of ATHE's annual meeting. In 1995, the first annual PSi conference – "The Future of the Field" – brought 550 people to NYU. *The Ends of Performance* (1998, Peggy Phelan and Jill Lane, editors) is based on the 1995 conference. In 1996, PSi met at NU. After that, and continuing in the twenty-first century, the movable feast of PSi's annual meetings have been served up in the UK, Germany, New Zealand, Singapore, and the USA. PSi became an official organization in 1997 with Richard Gough its first president and Adrian Heathfield serving as of 2005.

Richard Gough: (1956–): founder and director of the Centre for Performance Research (CPR) of Aberystwyth, Wales and first president of PSi. Gough organized a series of conferences, "Points of Contact," in the 1990s which helped define performance studies. He is a founding editor of the journal *Performance Research*.

Northwestern's brand of performance studies

It was no accident that the second annual PSi conference took place in 1996 at Northwestern University in Evanston, Illinois. NU's brand of performance studies, which took its present shape during the 1980s, emerged from speech communications, oral interpretation (the performance of literature other than dramas), rhetoric (debate and public speaking), and urban anthropology. Adherents of the NU approach take a very broad view of what constitutes "text"

fig 1.3. A photographic array of some examples of the "broad spectrum of performance."

Ritual:
Masked performer during carnival in Guinea-Bissau, 1980s. Photograph by Eve L. Crowley. Photograph courtesy of Richard Schechner.

Ritual:
Girl receiving Eucharist from a priest at Grand Bay, Mauritius, First Holy Communion. Photograph by Perry Joseph/ArkReligion.com. Reproduced with permission.

Play:
Sam and Kate Taylor and their cousin Bridget Caird playing "dress up" in New Zealand, 1979. Photograph by Moira Taylor.

Sports:
New Zealand Crusaders' Justin Marshall runs between South Africa Cats' Wikus van Heerden and Trevor Hall during his 100th Super 12 rugby match at Jade Stadium, Christchurch, New Zealand, April 2005. AP/Photopress, Ross Land. Copyright EMPICS. Reproduced with permission.

Popular Entertainment:
Woodstock Festival of music, 1968. Photograph by Ken Regan.

Performing Arts: Theatre
Peter Brook's 1970 production of Shakespeare's *A Midsummer Night's Dream*, Royal Shakespeare Theatre. On the swings, Alan Howard as Oberon and John Kane as Puck. Below, Sara Kestelman as Titania and David Waller as Bottom. Copyright 1970 David Farrell. Courtesy of the Shakespeare Birthplace Trust.

Performing Arts: Dance
Azuma Katsuko performing kabuki dance, Japan, 1980s. Photograph by Torben Huss. Photograph courtesy of Eugenio Barba.

Performance in Everyday Life:
One city partnership meeting at Djangoly Innovation Centre. Copyright John Birdsall. Reproduced with permission.

Performance Art
Performance View Poetry Project at Saint Marks Church, 1985. Karen Finley performing *Don't Hang the Angel*. Photograph by Dona Ann McAdams.

Political Performance:
Students in a sitdown demonstration confronting the National Guard at the University of California, Berkeley, 1969. Copyright Hulton-Deutsch Collection/ Corbis.

Performance Studies international (PSi)

Artists and scholars from throughout the world

PSi is a professional association founded in 1997 to promote communication and exchange among scholars and practitioners working in the field of performance. We seek to create opportunities for dialogue among artists and academics in a variety of disciplines whose concerns converge in the still-evolving areas of live art and performance.

PSi is actively committed to creating a membership base of artists and scholars from throughout the world. We recognize that while performance studies as a field encourages conversations across disciplinary boundaries, professionals in various parts of the world often wish for greater opportunities to exchange research and information about performance with others who share their interests and expertise. PSi is a network of exchange for scholars and practitioners working in diverse locations, both disciplinary and geographic. We act as a crucible for new ideas and forms in performance discourse and practice, often testing the relation between the two. As a professional organization, PSi is committed to encouraging the development of both emerging and established artists and scholars.

2005, "PSi Mission," http://psi-web.org/mission.html

(**see Stern and Henderson box**). In the 1980s, two historians of performance studies felt it was "too early" to claim a paradigm shift from oral interpretation and theatre to performance studies (**see Pelias and VanOosting box**). But by the start of the new millennium the shift was well established.

Impetus for the shift came strongly from **Dwight Conquergood**, the chair of Performance Studies at NU from 1993–99 and a major theorist, ethnographer, and filmmaker. Conquergood argued for a performance-based rather than text-based approach combining scholarly research with artistic training and practice (**see Conquergood box 1**). In the mid-1990s Conquergood called for performance studies adherents to "rethink" five areas of study (see **Conquergood box 2**). Conquergood's program remains at the core of the NU approach to performance studies.

Dwight Conquergood (1949–2004): American ethnographer and performance theorist. Chair of Northwestern University's Department of Performance Studies during a decisive, formative period, 1993–99. Through his teaching, ethnographic work, and lecturing, Conquergood was instrumental in shaping the NU brand of performance studies. Co-director (with Taggart Siegel) of the video documentary *The Heart Broken in Half* (1990).

The "inter" of performance studies

Performance studies resists fixed definition. Performance studies does not value "purity." It is at its best when operating amidst a dense web of connections. Academic disciplines are most active at their ever-changing interfaces. In terms of performance studies, this means the interactions between theatre and anthropology, folklore and sociology, history and performance theory, gender studies and psychoanalysis, performativity and actual performance events – and more. New interfaces will appear as time goes on, and older ones will disappear. Accepting "inter" means opposing the establishment of any single system of knowledge, values, or subject matter. Performance studies is open, multivocal, and self-contradictory. Therefore, any call for a "unified field" is, in my view, a misunderstanding of the very fluidity and playfulness fundamental to performance studies.

At a more theoretical level, what is the relation of performance studies to performance proper? Are there any limits to performativity? Is there anything outside the purview of performance studies? I discuss these questions in Chapters 2 and 5. For now, let me say that the performative occurs in places and situations not traditionally marked as "performing arts," from dress-up and drag to certain kinds of writing and speaking. Accepting the performative as a category of theory makes it increasingly difficult to sustain a distinction between appearances and reality, facts and make-believe, surfaces and depths. Appearances are

Carol Simpson Stern and Bruce Henderson

A whole field of human activity

The term performance incorporates a whole field of human activity. It embraces a verbal act in everyday life or a staged play, a rite of invective played in urban streets, a performance in the Western traditions of high art, or a work of performance art. It includes cultural performances, such as the personal narrative or folk and fairy tales, or more communal forms of ceremony – the National Democratic Convention, an evensong vigil march for people with AIDS, Mardi Gras, or a bullfight. It also includes literary performance, the celebration of individual genius, and conformity to Western definitions of art. In all cases a performance act, interactional in nature and involving symbolic forms and live bodies, provides a way to constitute meaning and to affirm individual and cultural values.

1993, *Performance*, 3

Ronald J. Pelias and James VanOosting

A magical renaming that opens doors

The term "performance studies" as a disciplinary title enjoys increasing currency, often used in place of the more familiar label, "oral interpretation." [. . .]

Performance studies calls into question the privilege of academic authority by including all members of a speech community as potential artists, all utterances as potentially aesthetic, all events as potentially theatrical, and all audiences as potentially active participants who can authorize artistic experience. By rejecting canonical security and exclusionary conventions, performance studies practitioners eschew artistic imperialism in favor of aesthetic communalism. These claims, then, yield an ideology that is racially democratic and counterelitist. [. . .]

[T]he move to performance studies institutionalizes what oral interpretation sanctioned as experimentation. [. . .] While positioned squarely within the field of speech communication, [the name] "performance studies" suggests clear links to theatre, ethnography and folklore, popular culture, and contemporary literary criticism. However, the new nomenclature is hardly arbitrary or mercenary; it is justified by the long evolutionary development of oral interpretation. [. . .] Performance studies, thus, is an act of magical renaming, a stage of evolutionary development, and a revisionist reading. But does the name change point to a paradigm shift? It is too early to say.

1987, "A Paradigm for Performance Studies," 219, 221, 228–29

actualities – neither more nor less so than what lies behind or beneath appearances. Social reality is constructed through and through. In modernity, what was "deep" and "hidden" was thought to be "more real" than what was on the surface (Platonism dies hard). But in postmodernity, the relationship between depths and surfaces is fluid; the relationship is dynamically convective.

Ethical questions

Many who practice performance studies resist or oppose the global forces of capital. Fewer will concede that these forces know very well – perhaps even better than we do – how to perform, in all the meanings of that word. The interplay of efficiency, productivity, activity, and

Dwight Conquergood

Performance studies at Northwestern

What is really radical about theatre, performance, and media studies at NU is that we embrace both written scholarship and creative work, texts and performance. [. . .] Printed texts are too important and powerful for us to cede that form of scholarship. But it is not enough. We also engage in creative work that stands alongside and in metonymic tension with conventional scholarship. We think of performance and practical work as a supplement to – not substitute for – written scholarship. [. . .]

Speaking from my home department, we sometimes refer to the three A's of performance studies: artistry, analysis, activism. Or to change the alliteration, a commitment to the three C's of performance studies: creativity, critique, and community. By community, I mean citizenship and civic struggles for social justice. Theatre, performance, and media studies at NU all struggle to forge a unique and unifying mission around the triangulation of these three perspectives on performance and creative work:

1. Accomplishment (the making of art and culture; creativity; embodiment; the work of imagination; artistic process and form; knowledge that comes from doing, participatory understanding, practical consciousness, performing as a way of knowing).
2. Analysis (the interpretation of art and culture; critique; thinking about and with performance; performance as an optic, a metaphor or theoretical model for understanding culture; knowledge that comes from contemplation and comparison – concentrated attention and contextualization as a way of knowing).
3. Application (activism, the connection to community; social contexts and articulations; action research; artistic and research projects that reach outside the academy and are rooted in an ethic of reciprocity and exchange; knowledge that is tested by practice within a community – social commitment, collaboration, and contribution/intervention as a way of knowing: praxis).

The ongoing challenge of our collaborative agenda is to refuse and supersede the deeply entrenched division of labor, apartheid of knowledges, that plays out inside the academy as the difference between thinking and doing, interpreting and making, conceptualization and creativity. The division of labor between theory and practice, abstraction and embodiment, is an arbitrary and rigged choice, and like all binarisms it is booby-trapped. It's a Faustian bargain. If we go the one-way street of abstraction, then we cut ourselves off from the nourishing ground of participatory experience. If we go the one-way street of practice, then we drive ourselves into an isolated cul de sac, a practitioner's workshop or artist's colony. Our radical move is to turn, and return, insistently, to the crossroads.

1999, from a talk at the "Cultural Intersections" conference, Northwestern University.

Dwight Conquergood

The Five areas of performance studies

1. *Performance and Cultural Process.* What are the conceptual consequences of thinking about culture as a verb instead of a noun, a process instead of product? Culture as an unfolding performative invention instead of reified system, structure, or variable? What happens to our thinking about performance when we move it outside of aesthetics and situate it at the center of lived experience?

2. *Performance and Ethnographic Praxis.* What are the methodological implications of thinking about fieldwork as the collaborative performance of an enabling fiction between observer and observed, knower and known? How does thinking about fieldwork as performance differ from thinking about fieldwork as the collection of data? [. . .]

3. *Performance and Hermeneutics.* What kinds of knowledge are privileged or displaced when performed experience becomes a way of knowing, a method of critical inquiry, a mode of understanding? [. . .]

4. *Performance and Scholarly Representation.* What are the rhetorical problematics of performance as a complementary or alternative form of "publishing" research? What are the differences between reading an analysis of fieldwork data, and hearing the voices from the field interpretively filtered through the voice of the researcher? [. . .] What about enabling people themselves to perform their own experience? [. . .]

5. *The Politics of Performance.* What is the relationship between performance and power? How does performance reproduce, enable, sustain, challenge, subvert, critique, and naturalize ideology? How do performances simultaneously reproduce and resist hegemony? How does performance accommodate and contest domination?

1991, "Rethinking Ethnography," 190

Jon McKenzie

Performance is a new subject of knowledge

[. . . P]*erformance will be to the 20th and 21st centuries what discipline was to the 18th and 19th, that is, an onto-historical formation of power and knowledge* [italics in original]. [. . .] Like discipline, performance produces a new subject of knowledge, though one quite different from that produced under the regime of panoptic surveillance. Hyphenated identities, transgendered bodies, digital avatars, the Human Genome Project – these suggest that the performative subject is constructed as fragmented rather than unified, decentered rather than centered, virtual as well as actual. Similarly, performative objects are unstable rather than fixed, simulated rather than real. They do not occupy a single, "proper" place in knowledge; there is no such thing as the thing-in-itself. Instead, objects are produced and maintained through a variety of socio-technical systems, overcoded by many discourses, and situated in numerous sites of practice. While disciplinary institutions and mechanisms forged Western Europe's industrial revolution and its system of colonial empires, those of performance are programming the circuits of our postindustrial, postcolonial world. More profoundly than the alphabet, printed book, and factory, such technologies as electronic media and the Internet allow discourses and practices from different geographical and historical situations to be networked and patched together, their traditions to be electronically archived and played back, their forms and processes to become raw materials for other productions. Similarly, research and teaching machines once ruled strictly and linearly by the book are being retooled by a multimedia, hypertextual metatechnology, that of the computer.

2001, *Perform Or Else*, 18

Jere Longman

Genetically altered athletes

Genes serve as a script that directs the body to make proteins. It seems fantastic today to think that injecting a gene could result in more fast-twitch muscle fibers, enabling a sprinter to run 100 meters in six seconds instead of just under 10. Or injecting a gene that could increase oxygen-carrying capacity so that a marathoner could run 26.2 miles in one and a half hours instead of just over two. Some scientists and Olympic committee members think genetic engineering in sports is a decade away. Some believe it may appear in two years. Still others believe crude forms might already be in use, at great health risk to athletes. [. . .] Instead of repeatedly ingesting pills or taking injections, an athlete may be able, with a single insertion of genetic material, to sustain bulked-up muscle mass or heightened oxygen-carrying capacity for months or even years. Such genetic manipulation would be extremely difficult, if not virtually impossible to detect [. . .].

2001, "Someday Soon, Athletic Edge May Be from Altered Genes"

entertainment – in a word, performance – informs and drives countless operations. In many key areas of human activity "performance" is crucial to success. The word crops up in apparently very different circumstances. These divergent uses indicate a basic overall similarity at the theoretical level. Performance has become a major site of knowledge and power (**see McKenzie box**). In relation to this relatively new situation, many ethical questions remain nakedly open. The most important concern "intervention" – biologically, militarily, culturally. When, if ever, ought force be used to "save" or "protect" people – and why say yes to Kosovo and no to the Sudan? Who has the right and/or the responsibility to say yes or no? What about genetic intervention? Who can be against preventing or curing diseases and increasing crop yields? But what about cloning? Or modifying human traits? What constitutes a "disease" and what traits are "bad"? The nineteenth and twentieth centuries saw some very nasty things done under the aegis of a eugenic "improvement" of the human species. What about genetically engineering "super athletes" (**see Longman box**)? In terms of art and scholarship, what, if any, ought to be the limits to creativity and cultural borrowings? I take up some of these questions in Chapter 8.

Conclusion

Performance studies came into existence within, and as a response to, the radically changing intellectual and artistic circumstances of the last third of the twentieth century. As the twenty-first century unfolds, many people remain dissatisfied with the status quo. Equipped with ever more powerful means of finding and sharing information – the internet, cell phones, sophisticated computing – people are increasingly finding the world not a book to be read but a performance to participate in. Paradoxically, this textbook is a book about the world becoming less of a book. Performance studies is an academic discipline designed to answer the need to deal with the changing circumstances of the "glocal" – the powerful combination of the local and the global. Performance studies is more interactive, hyper-textual, virtual, and fluid than most scholarly disciplines. At the same time, adherents to performance studies face daunting ethical and political questions. What limits, if any, ought there to be to the ways information is gathered, processed, and distributed? Should those with the means intervene in the interest of "human rights" or must they respect local cultural autonomy at whatever cost? Artists and scholars are playing increasingly decisive roles in addressing these ethical and political questions. One goal of this textbook is to help you think about and act on these questions.

TALK ABOUT

1. Clifford Geertz wrote, "Cultural analysis is intrinsically incomplete. And, worse than that, the more deeply it goes the less complete it is" (*Interpretation of Cultures*, p. 29). Is this true of your own department in relation to performance studies? What is the "place" of performance studies in your department?
2. How might performance studies help to deal with some of the problems facing the world, such as threats to

the environment, the oppression and exploitation of people, overpopulation, and war?

PERFORM

1. Form a circle. Each person speaks her/his name. Continue until everyone in the class knows everyone else's name.
2. Someone walks across the room. Someone else describes that action. The person walks across the room again, "showing" what previously they were just "doing." What were the differences between "walking" and "showing walking?"

READ

Bell, John. "Performance Studies in an Age of Terror." *TDR* 47, 2 (2003): 6–9.

Conquergood, Dwight. "Performance Studies: Interventions and Radical Research." *TDR: The Drama Review* 46.2 (2002): 145–57.

Jackson, Shannon. "Professing Performance: Disciplinary Genealogies." *The Performance Studies Reader*, Henry Bial, ed.: 32–42. London and New York: Routledge, 2004.

Kirshenblatt-Gimblett, Barbara. "Performance Studies." *The Performance Studies Reader*, Henry Bial, ed.: 43–55. London and New York: Routledge, 2004.

McKenzie, Jon. "The Liminal Norm." *The Performance Studies Reader*, Henry Bial, ed.: 26–31. London and New York: Routledge, 2004.

Pelias, Ronald J., and James VanOosting. "A Paradigm for Performance Studies." *Quarterly Journal of Speech* 73 (1987): 219–31.

Schechner, Richard. "Performance Studies: The Broad Spectrum Approach." *The Performance Studies Reader*, Henry Bial, ed.: 7–9. London and New York: Routledge, 2004.

Worthen, W. B. "Disciplines of the Text/Sites of Performance." *The Performance Studies Reader*, Henry Bial, ed.: 10–25. London and New York: Routledge, 2004.

2 WHAT IS PERFORMANCE?

What is "to perform"?

In business, sports, and sex, "to perform" is to do something up to a standard – to succeed, to excel. In the arts, "to perform" is to put on a show, a play, a dance, a concert. In everyday life, "to perform" is to show off, to go to extremes, to underline an action for those who are watching. In the twenty-first century, people as never before live by means of performance.

"To perform" can also be understood in relation to:

- Being
- Doing
- Showing doing
- Explaining "showing doing."

"Being" is existence itself. "Doing" is the activity of all that exists, from quarks to sentient beings to supergalactic strings. "Showing doing" is performing: pointing to, underlining, and displaying doing. "Explaining 'showing doing'" is performance studies.

It is very important to distinguish these categories from each other. "Being" may be active or static, linear or circular, expanding or contracting, material or spiritual. Being is a philosophical category pointing to whatever people theorize is the "ultimate reality." "Doing" and "showing doing" are actions. Doing and showing doing are always in flux, always changing – reality as the pre-Socratic Greek philosopher **Heraclitus** experienced it. Heraclitus aphorized this perpetual flux: "No one can step twice into the same river, nor touch mortal substance twice in the same condition" (fragment 41). The fourth term, "explaining 'showing doing'," is a reflexive effort to comprehend the world of performance and the world as performance. This comprehension is usually the work of critics and scholars. But sometimes, in Brechtian theatre where the actor steps outside the role to comment on what the character is doing, and in critically aware performance art such as **Guillermo Gómez-Peña**'s and **Coco Fusco**'s *Two Undiscovered Amerindians Visit the West* (1992), a performance is **reflexive**. I discuss this sort of performance in Chapters 5, 6, and 8.

Heraclitus of Ephesus (*c.* 535–475 BCE): Greek philosopher credited with the creation of the doctrine of "flux," the theory of impermanence and change. You can't step into the same river twice because the flow of the river insures that new water continually replaces the old.

Guillermo Gómez-Peña (1955–): Mexican-born bi-national performance artist and author, leader of La Pocha Nostra. His works include both writings *Warrior for Gringostroika* (1993), *The New World Border* (1996), *Dangerous Border Crossers* (2000), and *Ethno-Techno Writings on Performance, Activism, and Pedagogy* (2005, with Elaine Peña) – and performances: *Border Brujo* (1990), *El Naftazeca* (1994), *Border Stasis* (1998), *Brownout: Border Pulp Stories* (2001), and *Mexterminator vs the Global Predator* (2005).

Coco Fusco (1960–): Cuban-born interdisciplinary artist based in New York City. Collaborated with Guillermo Gómez-Peña on the performance *Two Undiscovered Amerindians Visit the West* (1992). Other performances include: *Dolores from 10h to 22h* (2002, with Ricardo Dominguez) and *The Incredible Disappearing Woman* (2003, with Ricardo Dominguez). Fusco is the author of *English is Broken Here* (1995), *Corpus Delecti: Performance Art of the Americas* (2000), *The Bodies That Were Not Ours* (2001), and *Only Skin Deep* (2003, with Brian Wallis).

reflexive: referring back to oneself or itself.

Performances

Performances mark identities, bend time, reshape and adorn the body, and tell stories. Performances – of art, rituals, or ordinary life – are "restored behaviors," "twice-behaved behaviors," performed actions that people train for and rehearse (**see Goffman box**). That making art involves training and rehearsing is clear. But everyday life also involves years of training and practice, of learning appropriate culturally specific bits of behavior, of adjusting and performing one's life roles in relation to social and personal circumstances. The long infancy and childhood specific to the human species is an extended period of training and rehearsal for the successful performance of adult life. "Graduation" into adulthood is marked in many cultures by initiation rites. But even before adulthood some persons more comfortably adapt to the life they live than others who resist or rebel. Most people live the tension between acceptance and rebellion. The activities of public life – sometimes calm, sometimes full of turmoil; sometimes visible, sometimes masked – are collective performances. These activities range from sanctioned politics through to street demonstrations and other forms of protest, and on to revolution. The performers of these actions intend to change things, to maintain the status quo, or, most commonly, to find or make some common ground. A revolution or civil war occurs when the players do not desist and there is no common ground. Any and all of the activities of human life can be studied "as" performance (I will discuss "as" later in this chapter). Every action from the smallest to the most encompassing is made of twice-behaved behaviors.

What about actions that are apparently "once-behaved" – the Happenings of **Allan Kaprow**, for example, or an everyday life occurrence (cooking, dressing, taking a walk, talking to a friend)? Even these are constructed from behaviors previously behaved. In fact, the everydayness of everyday life is precisely its familiarity, its being built from known bits of behavior rearranged and shaped in order to suit specific circumstances. But it is also true that many events and behaviors are one-time events. Their "onceness" is a function of context, reception, and the countless ways bits of behavior can be organized, performed, and displayed. The overall event may appear to be new or original, but its constituent parts – if broken down finely enough and analyzed – are revealed as **restored behaviors**. "Lifelike" art – as Kaprow calls much of his work – is close to everyday life. Kaprow's art slightly underlines, highlights, or makes one aware of ordinary behavior – paying close attention to how a meal is prepared, looking back at one's footsteps after walking in the desert. Paying attention to simple activities performed in the present moment is developing a Zen consciousness in relation to the daily, an honoring of the ordinary. Honoring the ordinary is noticing how ritual-like daily life is, how much daily life consists of repetitions.

Allan Kaprow (1927–2006): American artist who coined the term "Happening" to describe his 1959 installation/performance *18 Happenings in 6 Parts*. Author of *Assemblage, Environments and Happenings* (1966), *Essays on the Blurring of Art and Life* (2003, with Jeff Kelley), and *Childsplay* (2004, with Jeff Kelley).

restored behavior: physical, verbal, or virtual actions that are not-for-the-first time; that are prepared or rehearsed. A person may not be aware that she is performing a strip of restored behavior. Also referred to as twice-behaved behavior.

Erving Goffman

Defining performance

A "performance" may be defined as all the activity of a given participant on a given occasion which serves to influence in any way any of the other participants. Taking a particular participant and his performance as a basic point of reference, we may refer to those who contribute to the other performances as the audience, observers, or co-participants. The pre-established pattern of action which is unfolded during a performance and which may be presented or played through on other occasions may be called a "part" or a "routine." These situational terms can easily be related to conventional structural ones. When an individual or performer plays the same part to the same audience on different occasions, a social relationship is likely to arise. Defining social role as the enactment of rights and duties attached to a given status, we can say that a social role will involve one or more parts and that each of these different parts may be presented by the performer on a series of occasions to the same kinds of audiences or to an audience of the same persons.

1959, *The Presentation of Self in Everyday Life*, 15–16

There is a paradox here. How can both Heraclitus and the theory of restored behavior be right? Performances are made from bits of restored behavior, but every performance is different from every other. First, fixed bits of behavior can be recombined in endless variations. Second, no event can exactly copy another event. Not only the behavior itself – nuances of mood, tone of voice, body language, and so on, but also the specific occasion and context make each instance unique. What about mechanically, digitally, or biologically reproduced replicants or clones? It may be that a film or a digitized performance art piece will be the same at each showing. But the context of every reception makes each instance different. Even though every "thing" is exactly the same, each event in which the "thing" participates is different. The uniqueness of an event does not depend on its materiality solely but also on its interactivity – and the interactivity is always in flux. If this is so with regard to film and digitized media, how much more so for live performance, where both production and reception vary from instance to instance. Or in daily life, where context cannot be perfectly controlled. Thus, ironically, performances resist that which produces them.

Which leads to the question, "Where do performances take place?" A painting "takes place" in the physical object; a novel takes place in the words. But a performance takes place as action, interaction, and relation. In this regard, a painting or a novel can be performative or can be analyzed "as" performance. Performance isn't "in" anything, but "between." Let me explain. A performer in ordinary life, in a ritual, at play, or in the performing arts does/shows something – performs an action. For example, a mother lifts a spoon to her own mouth and then to a baby's mouth to show the baby how to eat cereal. The performance is the action of lifting the spoon, bringing it to mother's mouth, and then to baby's mouth. The baby is at first the spectator of its mother's performance. At some point, the baby becomes a co-performer as she takes the spoon and tries the same action – often at first missing her mouth and messing up her lips and chin with food. Father videotapes the whole show. Later, maybe many years later, the baby is a grown woman showing to her own baby a home video of the day when she began to learn how to use a spoon. Viewing this video is another performance existing in the complex relation between the original event, the video of the event, the memory of parents now old or maybe dead, and the present moment of delight as mother points to the screen and tells her baby, "That was mommy when I was your age!" The first performance "takes place" in between the action of showing baby how to use the spoon and baby's reaction to this action. The second performance takes place between the videotape of the first performance and the reception of that first performance by both the baby-now-mother and her own baby (or anyone else watching the videotape). What is true of this "home movie" performance is true of all performances. To treat any object, work, or product "as" performance – a painting, a novel, a shoe, or anything at all – means to investigate what the object does, how it interacts with other objects or beings, and how it relates to other objects or beings. Performances exist only as actions, interactions, and relationships.

Bill Parcells wants you to perform

A 1999 full-page advertisement in *The New York Times* selling the Cadillac Seville car features American legendary football coach **Bill Parcells** staring out at the reader (**see figure 2.1**). One of Parcells' eyes is in shadow, the darkness blending into the background for the stark large white-on-black text:

IF YOU WANT TO IMPRESS
B I L L P A R C E L L S
Y O U H A V E T O
P E R F O R M

Bill Parcells (1941–): American football coach. Winner in 1987 and 1991 of two Superbowls with the New York Giants.

Underneath a photograph of a Seville, the text continues in smaller type, "Great performers have always made a big impression on Bill Parcells. That explains his strong appreciation for Seville [. . .]."

The ad conflates performing in sports, business, sex, the arts, and technology. Parcells excels as a football coach. By making demands upon his players he motivates them and they respond on the field with winning performances. Parcells' excellence derives from his drive, his ability to organize, and his insistence on careful attention to each detail of the game. His stare has "sex appeal" – his penetrating gaze is that of a potent man able to control the giants who play football. He combines mastery, efficiency, and beauty. At the same time, Parcells displays an understated flash; he

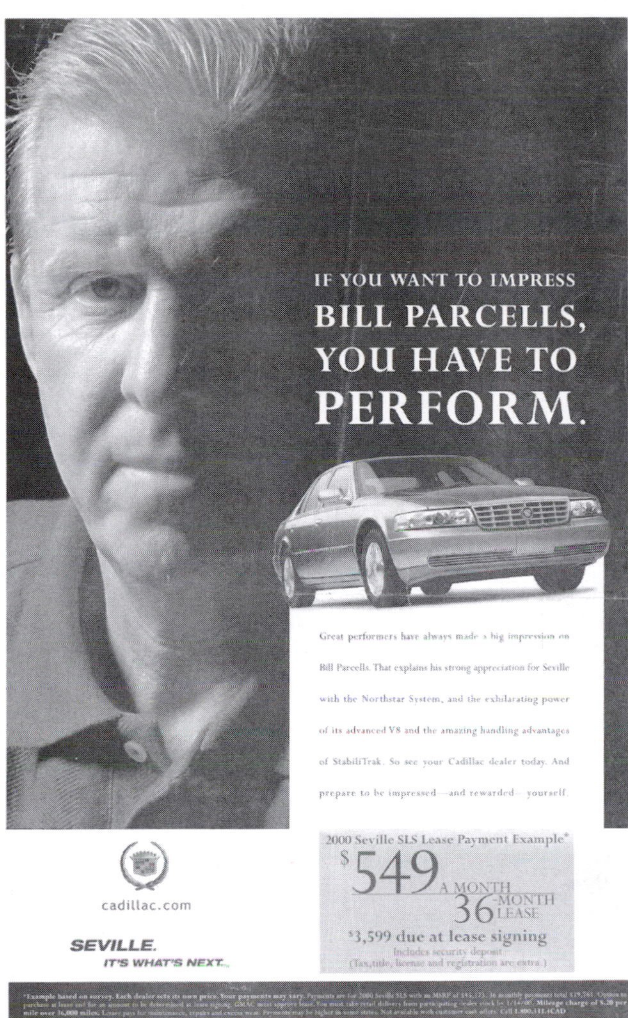

fig 2.1. Football coach Bill Parcells in an advertisement for Cadillac automobiles that appeared in *The New York Times* in 1999. Photograph courtesy of General Motors Corporation.

knows he is playing to the camera and to the crowds. All of this informs the ad, which tries to convince viewers that the Cadillac, like Parcells, is at the top of its game, sexy and powerful, well made down to the last detail, dependable, the leader in its field, and something that will stand out in a crowd.

Eight kinds of performance

Performances occur in eight sometimes separate, sometimes overlapping situations:

1 in everyday life – cooking, socializing, "just living"
2 in the arts
3 in sports and other popular entertainments
4 in business
5 in technology
6 in sex
7 in ritual – sacred and secular
8 in play.

Even this list does not exhaust the possibilities (**see Carlson box**). If examined rigorously as theoretical categories, the eight situations are not commensurate. "Everyday life" can encompass most of the other situations. The arts take as their subjects materials from everywhat and everywhere. Ritual and play are not only "genres" of performance but present in all of the situations as qualities, inflections, or moods. I list these eight to indicate the large territory covered by performance. Some items – those occurring in business, technology, and sex – are not usually analyzed with the others, which have been the loci of arts-based performance theories. And the operation of making categories such as these eight is the result of a particular culture-specific kind of thinking.

Marvin Carlson

What is performance?

The term "performance" has become extremely popular in recent years in a wide range of activities in the arts, in literature, and in the social sciences. As its popularity and usage has grown, so has a complex body of writing about performance, attempting to analyze and understand just what sort of human activity it is. [. . .] The recognition that our lives are structured according to repeated and socially sanctioned modes of behavior raises the possibility that all human activity could potentially be considered as "performance," or at least all activity carried out with a consciousness of itself. [. . .] If we consider performance as an essentially contested concept, this will help us to understand the futility of seeking some overarching semantic field to cover such seemingly disparate usages as the performance of an actor, of a schoolchild, of an automobile.

1996, *Performance: A Critical Introduction*, 4–5

It is impossible to come at a subject except from one's own cultural positions. But once I began writing this book, the best I could do is to be aware of, and share with the reader, my biases and limitations. That having been noted, designating music, dance, and theatre as the "performing arts" may seem relatively simple. But as categories even these are ambiguous. What is designated "art," if anything at all, varies historically and culturally. Objects and performances called "art" in some cultures are like what is made or done in other cultures without being so designated. Many cultures do not have a word for, or category called, "art" even though they create performances and objects demonstrating a highly developed aesthetic sense realized with consummate skill.

Not only making but evaluating "art" occurs everywhere. People all around the world know how to distinguish "good" from "bad" dancing, singing, orating, storytelling, sculpting, fabric design, pottery, painting, and so on. But what makes something "good" or "bad" varies greatly from place to place, time to time, and even occasion to occasion. The ritual objects of one culture or one historical period become the artworks of other cultures or periods. Museums of art are full of paintings and objects that once were regarded as sacred (and still may be by pillaged peoples eager to regain their ritual objects and sacred remains). Furthermore, even if a performance has a strong aesthetic dimension, it is not necessarily "art." The moves of basketball players are as beautiful as those of ballet dancers, but one is termed sport, the other art. Figure skating and gymnastics exist in both realms (**see figure 2.2**). Deciding what is art depends on context, historical circumstance, use, and local conventions.

Separating "art" from "ritual" is particularly difficult. I have noted that ritual objects from many cultures are featured in art museums. But consider also religious services with music, singing, dancing, preaching, storytelling, speaking in tongues, and healing. At a Christian evangelical church service, for example, people go into trance, dance in the aisles, give testimony, receive anointment and baptism. The gospel music heard in African-American churches is closely related to blues, jazz, and rock and roll. Are such services art or ritual? Composers, visual artists, and performers have long made works of fine art for use in rituals. To what realm does **Johann Sebastian Bach**'s *Mass in B Minor* and his many cantatas or **Wolfgang Amadeus Mozart**'s *Mass in C Minor* belong? Church authorities in medieval Europe such as **Amalarius**, the Bishop of Metz, asserted that the Mass was theatre equivalent to ancient Greek tragedy (**see Hardison box**). More than a few people attend religious services as much for aesthetic pleasure and social interactivity as for reasons of belief. In many cultures, participatory performing is the core of ritual practices. In ancient Athens, the great theatre festivals were ritual, art, sports-like competition, and popular entertainment simultaneously. Today, sports are both live and media entertainment featuring competition, ritual, spectacle, and big business.

fig 2.2. Ice skater Denise Biellmenn does a triple toe-loop as seen in a time-lapse photograph, n.d. Photograph by Alberto Venzago. Copyright Camera Press, London.

Johann Sebastian Bach (1685–1750): German composer, choir director, and organist. His polyphonic compositions of sacred music place him among Europe's most influential composers.

Wolfgang Amadeus Mozart (1756–91): Austrian composer whose vast output and range of compositions including operas, symphonies, and liturgical music.

Amalarius of Metz (780–850): Roman Catholic bishop and theologian, author of several major treatises on the performance of liturgical rites, including *Eclogae de ordine romano* (*Pastoral Dialogues on the Roman Rite*) (814) and *Liber officialis* (Book of the Service) (821).

As noted, some sports are close to fine arts. Gymnastics, figure skating, and high diving are recognized by the Olympics. But there are no quantitative ways to determine winners as there are in racing, javelin throwing, or weight lifting. Instead, these "aesthetic athletes" are judged qualitatively on the basis of "form" and "difficulty." Their performances are more like dancing than competitions of speed or strength. But with the widespread use of slow-motion photography and replay, even "brute sports" like football, wrestling, and boxing yield an aesthetic dimension that is more apparent in the re-viewing than in the swift, tumultuous action itself. An artful add-on is the taunting and victory displays of athletes who dance and prance their superiority.

For all that, everyone knows the difference between going to church, watching a football game, or attending one of the performing arts. The difference is based on function, the circumstance of the event within society, the venue, and the behavior expected of the players and spectators. There is even a big difference between various genres of the performing arts. Being tossed around a mosh pit at a rock concert is very different from applauding a performance of the American Ballet Theatre's *Giselle* at New York's Metropolitan Opera House. Dance emphasizes movement, theatre emphasizes narration and impersonation, sports emphasize competition, and ritual emphasizes participation and communication with transcendent forces or beings.

O. B. Hardison

The medieval Mass was drama

That there is a close relationship between allegorical interpretation of the liturgy and the history of drama becomes apparent the moment we turn to the Amalarian interpretations. Without exception, they present the Mass as an elaborate drama with definite roles assigned to the participants and a plot whose ultimate significance is nothing less than the "renewal of the whole plan of redemption" through the re-creation of the "life, death, and resurrection" of Christ. [. . .] The church is regarded as a theatre. The drama enacted has a coherent plot based on conflict between a champion and an antagonist. The plot has a rising action, culminating in the passion and entombment. At its climax there is a dramatic reversal, the Resurrection, correlated with the emotional transition from the Canon of the Mass to the Communion. Something like dramatic catharsis is expressed in the gaudium [joy at the news of the Resurrection] of the Postcommunion. [. . .]

Should church vestments then, with their elaborate symbolic meanings, be considered costumes? Should the paten, chalice, sindon, sudarium, candles, and thurible be considered stage properties? Should the nave, chancel, presbyterium, and altar of the church be considered a stage, and its windows, statues, images, and ornaments a "setting"? As long as there is clear recognition that these elements are hallowed, that they are the sacred phase of parallel elements turned to secular use on the profane stage, it is possible to answer yes. Just as the Mass is a sacred drama encompassing all history and embodying in its structure the central pattern of Christian life on which all Christian drama must draw, the celebration of the Mass contains all elements necessary to secular performances. The Mass as the general case – for Christian culture, the archetype. Individual dramas are shaped in its mold.

1965, *Christian Rite and Christian Drama in the Middle Ages*, 39–40, 79

In business, to perform means doing a job efficiently with maximum productivity. In the corporate world, people, machines, systems, departments, and organizations are required to perform. At least since the advent of the factory in the nineteenth century, there has been a merging of the human, the technical, and the organizational. This has led to an increase in material wealth – and also the sense that individuals are just "part of the machine" (**see figure 2.3**). But also this melding of person and machine has an erotic quality. There is something sexual about high performance in business, just as there is a lot that's businesslike in sexual performance. Sexual performance also invokes meanings drawn from the arts and sports. Consider the range of meanings attached to the phrases "performing sex," "How did s/he perform in bed?" and being a "sexual performer." The first refers to the act in itself and the second to how well one "does it," while the third implies an element of either going to extremes or of pretending, of putting on a show and therefore maybe not really doing it at all.

Restoration of behavior

Let us examine restored behavior more closely. We all perform more than we realize. The habits, rituals, and routines of life are restored behaviors. Restored behavior is living behavior treated as a film director treats a strip of film. These strips of behavior can be rearranged or reconstructed; they are independent of the causal systems (personal, social, political, technological, etc.) that brought them into existence. They have a life of their own. The original "truth" or "source" of the behavior may not be known, or may be lost, ignored, or contradicted – even while that truth or source is being honored. How the strips of behavior were made, found, or developed may be unknown or concealed; elaborated; distorted by myth and tradition. Restored behavior can be of long duration as in ritual performances or of short duration as in fleeting gestures such as waving goodbye.

Restored behavior is the key process of every kind of performing, in everyday life, in healing, in ritual, in play, and in the arts. Restored behavior is "out there," separate from "me." To put it in personal terms, restored behavior is "me behaving as if I were someone else," or "as I am told to do," or "as I have learned." Even if I feel myself wholly to be myself, acting independently, only a little investigating reveals that the units of behavior that comprise "me" were not invented by "me." Or, quite the opposite, I may experience being "beside myself," "not myself," or "taken over" as in trance. The fact that there are multiple "me"s in every

fig 2.3. Charlie Chaplin turning, and being turned by, the wheels of industry in *Modern Times*, 1936. The Kobal Collection.

person is not a sign of derangement but the way things are. The ways one performs one's selves are connected to the ways people perform others in dramas, dances, and rituals. In fact, if people did not ordinarily come into contact with their multiple selves, the art of acting and the experience of possession trance would not be possible. Most performances, in daily life and otherwise, do not have a single author. Rituals, games, and the performances of everyday life are authored by the collective "Anonymous" or the "Tradition." Individuals given credit for inventing rituals or games usually turn out to be synthesizers, recombiners, compilers, or editors of already practiced actions.

Restored behavior includes a vast range of actions. In fact, all behavior is restored behavior – all behavior consists of recombining bits of previously behaved behaviors. Of course, most of the time people aren't aware that they are doing any such thing. People just "live life." Performances are marked, framed, or heightened behavior separated out from just "living life" – restored restored behavior, if you will. However, for my purpose here, it is not necessary to pursue this doubling. It is enough to define restored behavior as marked, framed, or heightened. Restored behavior can be "me" at another time or psychological state – for example, telling the story of or acting out a celebratory or traumatic event. Restored behavior can bring into play non-ordinary reality as in the Balinese trance dance enacting the struggle between the demoness Rangda and the Lion-god Barong (**see figure 2.4**). Restored behavior can be actions marked off by aesthetic convention as in theatre, dance, and music. It can be actions reified into the "rules of the game," "etiquette," or diplomatic "protocol" – or any other of the myriad, known-beforehand actions of life. These vary enormously from culture to culture. Restored behavior can be a boy not shedding tears when jagged leaves slice the inside of his nostrils during a Papua New Guinea initiation; or the formality of a bride and groom during their wedding ceremony. Because it is marked, framed, and separate, restored behavior can be worked on, stored and recalled, played with, made into something else, transmitted, and transformed.

As I have said, daily life, ceremonial life, and artistic life consist largely of routines, habits, and rituals: the recombination of already behaved behaviors. Even the "latest," "original," "shocking," or "avant-garde" is mostly either a new combination of known behaviors or the displacement of a behavior from a known to an unexpected context or occasion. Thus, for example, nakedness caused a stir in the performing arts in the 1960s and early 1970s. But why the shock? Nude paintings and sculptings were commonplace. At the other end of the "high art–low art" spectrum, striptease was also common – and erotic. But the naked art in museums were representations presumed to be non-erotic; and striptease was segregated and gender-specific: female strippers, male viewers. The "full frontal nudity" in productions such as *Dionysus in 69* (1968) or *Oh! Calcutta* (1972) caused a stir because actors of both genders were undressing in high-art/live-performance venues and these displays were sometimes erotic. This kind of nakedness was different than naked bodies at home or in gymnasium shower rooms.

fig 2.4. The lion god Barong ready to do battle against the demon Rangda in Balinese ritual dance theatre, 1980s. Photograph Jim Hart, Director of TITAN Theatre School, Norway.

At first, this art could not be comfortably categorized or "placed." But it didn't take long before high-art naked performers were accommodated in many genres and venues, from ballet to Broadway, on campuses and in storefront theatres. Even pornography has gone mainstream, further blurring genre boundaries (**see Lanham box**). Of course, in many cultures nakedness is the norm. In others, such as Japan, it has long been acceptable in certain public circumstances and forbidden in others. Today, no one in most global metropolitan cities can get a rise out of spectators or critics by performing naked. But don't try it in Kabul – or as part of kabuki.

Restored behavior is symbolic and reflexive (**see Geertz box**). Its meanings need to be decoded by those in the know. This is not a question of "high" versus "low" culture. A sports fan knows the rules and strategies of the game, the statistics of key players, the standings, and many other historical and technical details. Ditto for the fans of rock bands. Sometimes the knowledge about restored behavior is esoteric, privy to only the initiated. Among Indigenous Australians, the outback itself is full of significant rocks, trails, water

Robert Lanham

BurningAngel.com

Known informally as alt-porn, this genre attempts embellish pornography with a hip veneer by offering soft- to hard-core erotica next to interviews with members of appropriately cool and underground bands. The form first surfaced in 2001, when the West Coast web site SuicideGirls began to offer erotic photos of young women online. Later the site added interviews of artists and celebrities (from Woody Allen to Natalie Portman to the current hot band, Bloc Party) and then soft-core videos online. Imitators like fatalbeauty.com, brokendollz.com and more than a dozen others soon followed.

Joanna Angel, 24, started BurningAngel in 2002 as a hard-core alternative to such sites. [. . .] The first "BurningAngel.com: The Movie" was released for sale online on April 1 [2005] and sells for $20. Shot on a shoestring budget of $4,000, the film, which stars Ms. Angel (her stage name), is a series of hard-core sex scenes strung together without benefit of a plot. It burnishes its hipster credentials by incorporating music by the Brooklyn band Turing Machine and Tim Armstrong of Rancid. Interviews with bands like Dillinger Escape Plan and My Chemical Romance are interspersed with the sex.

"Some people make music, others paint, I make porn," she [Ms. Angel] said. Still, Ms. Angel is in no way a pioneer in her field; there seem to be plenty of women who, rather than struggle to get published in *The Paris Review* or written up in *ArtNews*, have instead channeled their creative ambitions into erotica.

2005, "Wearing Nothing but Attitude," 15.

Clifford Geertz

Human behavior as symbolic action

Once human behavior is seen as [. . .] symbolic action – action which, like phonation in speech, pigment in painting, line in writing, or sonance in music, signifies – the question as to whether culture is patterned conduct or a frame of mind, or even the two somehow mixed together, loses sense. [. . .] Behavior must be attended to, and with some exactness, because it is through the flow of behavior – or more precisely, social action – that cultural forms find articulation. They find it as well, of course, in various sorts of artifacts, and various states of consciousness; but these draw their meaning from the role they play [. . .] in an ongoing pattern of life [. . .].

1973, *The Interpretation of Cultures,* 10, 17

holes, and other markings that form a record of the actions of mythical beings. Only the initiated know the relationship between the ordinary geography and the sacred geography. To become conscious of restored behavior is to recognize the process by which social processes in all their multiple forms are transformed into theatre. Theatre, not in the limited sense of enactments of dramas on stages (which, after all, is a practice that, until it became very widespread as part of colonialism, belonged to relatively few cultures), but in the broader sense outlined in Chapter 1. Performance in the restored behavior sense means never for the first time, always for the second to nth time: twice-behaved behavior.

Caution! Beware of generalizations

I want to emphasize: Performances can be generalized at the theoretical level of restoration of behavior, but as embodied practices each and every performance is specific and different from every other. The differences enact the conventions and traditions of a genre, the personal choices made by the performers, directors, and authors, various cultural patterns, historical circumstances, and the particularities of reception. Take wrestling, for example. In Japan, the moves of a sumo wrestler are well determined by long tradition. These moves include the athletes' swaggering circulation around the ring, adjusting their groin belts, throwing handfuls of salt, eyeballing the opponent, and the final, often very brief, grapple of the two enormous competitors (**see figure 2.5**). Knowing spectators see in these carefully ritualized displays a centuries-old tradition linked to Shinto, the indigenous Japanese religion. By contrast, American professional wrestling is a noisy sport for "outlaws" where each wrestler flaunts his own raucous and carefully constructed identity (**see figure 2.6**). During the matches referees are clobbered, wrestlers are thrown from the ring, and cheating is endemic. All this is spurred on by fans who hurl epithets and objects. However, everyone knows that the outcome of American wrestling is determined in advance, that the lawlessness is play-acting – it's pretty much "all a show." Fans of sumo and fans of World Wrestling Federation matches know their heroes and villains, can tell you the history of their sport, and react according to accepted conventions and traditions. Both sumo and what occurs under the banner of the World Wrestling Federation are "wrestling;" each enacts the values of its particular culture.

What's true of wrestling is also true of the performing arts, political demonstrations, the roles of everyday life (doctor, mother, cop, etc.), and all other performances. Each genre is divided into many sub-genres. What is American theatre? Broadway, off Broadway, off off Broadway, regional theatre, community theatre, community-based theatre, college theatre, and more. Each sub-genre has its own particularities – similar in some ways to related forms but also different. And the whole system could be looked at from other perspectives – in terms, for example, of comedy, tragedy, melodrama, musicals; or divided according to professional or amateur, issue-oriented or apolitical, and so on. Nor are categories fixed or static. New genres emerge,

fig 2.5. Japanese sumo wrestlers grappling in the ring. The referee in ritual dress is in the left foreground. Photograph by Michael MacIntyre. Copyright Eye Ubiquitous/Hutchison Picture Library.

fig 2.6. (above) "The Road Warriors" professional American wrestlers posing with their manager. Copyright Superstar Wrestling. (right) Wahoo McDaniel displaying himself for his admiring fans. Copyright www.pwbts.com.

others fade away. Yesterday's avant-garde is today's mainstream is tomorrow's forgotten practice. Particular genres migrate from one category to another.

Take jazz, for example. During its formative years at the start of the twentieth century, jazz was not regarded as an art. It was akin to "folk performance" or "popular entertainment." But as performers moved out of red-light districts into respectable clubs and finally into concert halls, scholars increasingly paid attention to jazz. A substantial repertory of music was archived. Particular musicians' works achieved canonical status. By the 1950s jazz was regarded as "art." Today's popular music includes rock, rap, and reggae, but not "pure jazz." But that is not to say that rock and other forms of pop music will not someday be listened to and regarded in the same way that jazz or classical music is now. The categories of "folk," "pop," and "classical" have more to do with ideology, politics, and economic power than with the formal qualities of the music.

"Is" and "as" performance

What is the difference between "is" performance and "as" performance? Certain events are performances and other events less so. There are limits to what "is" performance. But just about anything can be studied "as" performance. Something "is" a performance when historical and social context, convention, usage, and tradition say it is. Rituals, play and games, and the roles of everyday life are performances because convention, context, usage, and tradition say so. One cannot determine what "is" a performance without referring to specific cultural circumstances. There is nothing inherent in an action in itself that makes it a performance or disqualifies it from being a performance. From the vantage of the kind of performance theory I am propounding, every action is a performance. But from the vantage of cultural practice, some actions will be deemed performances and others not; and this will vary from culture to culture, historical period to historical period.

Let me use the European tradition as an example to explain in more detail how definitions operate within contexts. What "is" or "is not" performance does not depend on an event in itself but on how that event is received and placed. Today the enactment of dramas by actors "is" a theatrical performance. But it was not always so. What we today call "theatre" people in other times did not. The ancient Greeks used words similar to ours to describe the theatre (our words derive from theirs), but what the Greeks meant in practice was very different from what we mean. During the epoch of the tragedians **Aeschylus**, **Sophocles**, and **Euripides**, the enactment of tragic dramas was more a ritual infused with competitions for prizes for the best actor and the best play than it was theatre in our sense. The occasions for the playing of the tragedies were religious festivals. Highly sought-after prizes were awarded. These prizes were based on aesthetic excellence, but the events in which that excellence was demonstrated were not artistic but ritual. It was Aristotle, writing a century after the high point of Greek tragedy as embodied performance, who codified the aesthetic understanding of theatre in its entirety – in all of its "six parts," as the philosopher parsed it. After Aristotle, in Hellenic and Roman times, the entertainment-aesthetic aspect of theatre became more dominant as the ritual-efficacious elements receded.

Aeschylus (*c.* 525–*c.* 456 BCE): Greek playwright and actor, regarded as the first great tragedian. Surviving works include *The Persians* (*c.* 472 BCE) and *The Oresteia* (458 BCE).

Sophocles (*c.* 496–*c.* 406 BCE): Greek playwright, credited with introducing the third actor onto the stage of tragedy. Surviving plays include *Oedipus the King* (*c.* 429 BCE), *Electra* (date uncertain), and *Antigone* (*c.* 441 BCE).

Euripides (*c.* 485–*c.* 405 BCE): Greek playwright whose surviving works include *Medea* (431 BCE), *Hippolytus* (428 BCE), *The Trojan Women* (415 BCE), and *The Bacchae* (*c.* 405 BCE).

Skipping forward more than a millennium to medieval Europe, acting written dramas on public stages was "forgotten" or at least not practiced. But there was not a scarcity of performances. On the streets, in town squares, in churches, castles, and mansions a wide range of popular entertainments and religious ceremonies held people's attention. There were a multitude of mimes, magicians, animal acts, acrobats, puppet shows, and what would later become the *commedia dell'arte*. The Church offered a rich panoply of feasts, services, and rituals. By the fourteenth century the popular entertainments and religious observances joined to form the basis for the great cycle plays celebrating and enacting the history of the world from Creation through the Crucifixion and Resurrection to the Last Judgment. These we would now call "theatre," but they were not named that at the time. The anti-theatrical prejudice of the Church disallowed any such designation. But then, in the fifteenth and sixteenth centuries the revolution in thought and practice called the Renaissance began. Renaissance means "rebirth" because the humanists of the day thought they were bringing back to life the classical culture of Greece and Rome. When **Andrea Palladio** designed the Teatro Olimpico (Theatre of Olympus) in Vicenza, Italy, he believed he was reinventing a Greek theatre – the first production in the Olimpico was Sophocles' *Oedipus* – not pointing the way to the modern proscenium theatre which the Olimpico did.

Andrea Palladio (1508–80): Italian architect who worked in Vicenza and Venice designing villas and churches. Palladio's Teatro Olimpico, completed four years after his death, is the only remaining example of an indoor Renaissance theatre. Author of *I Quattro Libri dell' Architettura* (1570, *The Four Books on Architecture*, 1997).

Take another leap to the last third of the nineteenth century. The notion of theatre as an art was by then well established. In fact, so well founded that counter-movements called "avant-garde" erupted frequently as efforts among radical artists to disrupt the status quo. Onward into and throughout the twentieth century, each new wave attempted to dislodge what went before. Some of yesterday's avant-garde became today's establishment. The list of avant-garde movements is long, including realism, naturalism, symbolism, futurism, surrealism, constructivism, Dada, expressionism, cubism, theatre of the absurd, Happenings, Fluxus, environmental theatre, performance art . . . and more. Sometimes works in these styles were considered theatre, sometimes dance, sometimes music, sometimes visual art, sometimes multimedia, etc. Often enough, events were attacked or dismissed as not being art at all – as were Happenings, an antecedent to performance art. Allan Kaprow, creator of the first Happening, jumped at this chance to make a distinction between "artlike art" and "lifelike art" (**see Kaprow box**). The term "performance art" was coined in the 1970s as an umbrella for works that otherwise resisted categorization.

The outcome is that today many events that formerly would not be thought of as art are now so designated. These kinds of actions are performed everywhere, not just in the West. The feedback loop is very complicated. The work of a Japanese dancer may affect a German choreographer whose dances in turn are elaborated on by a Mexican performance artist . . . and so on without definite national or cultural limits. Beyond composed artworks is a blurry world of "accidental" or "incidental" performance. Webcams broadcast over the internet what people do at home. Television frames

Allan Kaprow

Artlike art and lifelike art

Western art actually has two avantgarde histories: one of artlike art, and the other of lifelike art. [. . .] Simplistically put, artlike art holds that art is separate from life and everything else, while lifelike art holds that art is connected to life and everything else. In other words, there's art at the service of art, and art at the service of life. The maker of artlike art tends to be a specialist; the maker of lifelike art, a generalist. [. . .]

Avantgarde artlike art occupies the majority of attention from artists and public. It is usually seen as serious and a part of the mainstream Western art-historical tradition, in which mind is separate from body, individual is separate from people, civilization is separate from nature, and each art is separate from the other. [. . .] Avantgarde artlike art basically believes in (or does not eliminate) the continuity of the traditionally separate genres of visual art, music, dance, literature, theatre, etc. [. . .]

Avantgarde lifelike art, in contrast, concerns an intermittent minority (Futurists, Dadas, guatai, Happeners, fluxartists, Earthworkers, body artists, provos, postal artists, noise musicians, performance poets, shamanistic artists, conceptualists). Avantgarde lifelike art is not nearly as serious as avantgarde artlike art. Often it is quite humorous.

It isn't very interested in the great Western tradition either, since it tends to mix things up: body with mind, individual with people in general, civilization with nature, and so on. Thus it mixes up the traditional art genres, or avoids them entirely – for example, a mechanical fiddle playing around the clock to a cow in the barnyard. Or going to the laundromat.

Despite formalist and idealist interpretations of art, lifelike art makers' principal dialogue is not with art but with everything else, one event suggesting another. If you don't know much about life, you'll miss much of the meaning of the lifelike art that's born of it. Indeed, it's never certain if an artist who creates avantgarde lifelike art is an artist.

1983, "The Real Experiment," 36, 38

the news as entertainment. Public figures need to be media savvy. Is it by accident that an actor, **Ronald Reagan**, became president of the USA and that a playwright, **Vaclav Havel**, became president of the Czech Republic, while another actor and playwright, **Karol Jozef Wojtyla**, became pope? Performance theorists argue that everyday life is performance – courses are offered in the aesthetics of everyday life. At present, there is hardly any human activity that is not a performance for someone somewhere. Generally, the tendency over the past century has been to dissolve the boundaries separating performing from not-performing, art from not-art. At one end of the spectrum it's clear what a performance is, what an artwork is; at the other end of the spectrum no such clarity exists.

Ronald Reagan (1911–2004): fortieth president of the United States (1981–89) and Governor of California (1967–75), Reagan was a broadcaster, movie actor, and public speaker before entering electoral politics. Known as the "Great Communicator," Reagan's self-deprecating quips and relaxed manner on camera endeared him to millions despite his conservative and often bellicose policies.

Vaclav Havel (1936–): Czech playwright who was the last president of Czechoslovakia (1989–92) and the first of the Czech Republic (1993–2003). A fierce defender of free speech and leader of the "Velvet Revolution" of 1989 overturning Communist rule, Havel's often political plays include *The Memorandum* (1965), *Protest* (1978), and *Redevelopment* (1978).

Karol Jozef Wojtyla, Pope John Paul II (1920–2005): Polish actor and playwright who in 1978 became pope. During World War II, Wojtyla was a member of the Rhapsodic Theatre, an underground resistance group. Ordained as a priest in 1945, Wojtyla continued to write for and about the theatre. His theatrical knowledge served him well as a globe-trotting, media-savvy pontiff. See his *Collected Plays and Writings on Theater* (1987).

Maps "as" performance

Any behavior, event, action, or thing can be studied "as" performance. Take maps, for example. Everyone knows the world is round and maps are flat. But you can't see the whole world at the same time on a globe. You can't fold a globe and tuck it in your pocket or backpack. Maps flatten the world the better to lay out territories on a table or tack them to a wall. On most maps, nations are separated from each other by colors and lines, and cities appear as circles, rivers as lines, and oceans as large, usually blue, areas. Nation-states drawn on maps seem so natural that when some people picture the world they imagine it divided into nation-states. Everything on a map is named – being "on the map" means achieving status. But the "real earth" does not look like its mapped representations – or even like a globe. People were astonished when they saw the first photographs taken from space of the white-flecked blue ball Earth (**see figure 2.7**). There was no sign of a human presence at all.

Nor are maps neutral. They perform a particular interpretation of the world. Every map is a "projection," a specific way of representing a sphere on a flat surface. On maps, nations do not overlap or share territories. Boundaries are definite. If more than one nation enforces its claim to the same space, war threatens, as between Pakistan and India over Kashmir, or Palestine and Israel over Jerusalem. The most common projection in use today is derived from the Mercator Projection, developed in the sixteenth century by the Flemish geographer-cartographer **Gerardus Mercator** (**see figure 2.8**).

fig 2.7. The Americas and Hurricane Andrew as photographed by a weather satellite in 1992. Image source NASA.

Gerardus Mercator (1512–94): Flemish geographer-cartographer whose basic system of map-making is still practiced today. His actual name was Gerhard Kremer, but like many European scholars of his day, he Latinized his name.

The Mercator Projection distorts the globe wildly in favor of the northern hemisphere. The further north, the relatively bigger the territory appears. Spain is as large as Zimbabwe, North America dwarfs South America, and Europe is one-fourth the size of Africa. In other words, Mercator's map enacts the world as the colonial powers wished to view it. Although times have changed since the sixteenth century, the preponderance of world economic and military power remains in the hands of Europe and its North American inheritor, the USA. Perhaps it won't be this way in another century or two. If so, a different projection will be in common use. Indeed, satellite photography allows a detailed re-mapping of the globe. There are also maps showing the world "upside down," that is, with south on top; or drawn according to population, showing China and India more than four times the size of the USA. The Peters Projection developed in 1974 by **Arno Peters** is an "area accurate" map showing the world's areas sized correctly in relation to each other (**see figure 2.9**). No longer is Greenland the same size as Africa when in fact Africa is fourteen times larger than Greenland. But the Peters map has its own inaccuracies. It is not correct in terms of shape – the southern hemisphere is elongated, the northern squashed. Making a flat map of a round earth means that one must sacrifice either accurate shape or size. If the Peters map looks "unnatural," then you know how much the Mercator Projection – or any other map – is a performance.

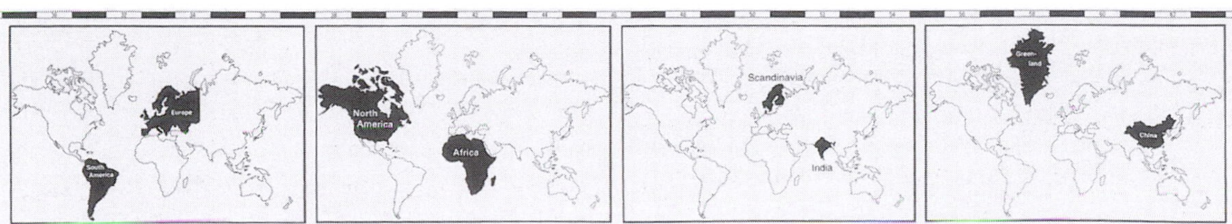

fig 2.8. A contemporary version of the Mercator Projection map of the world. Copyright Worldview Publications.

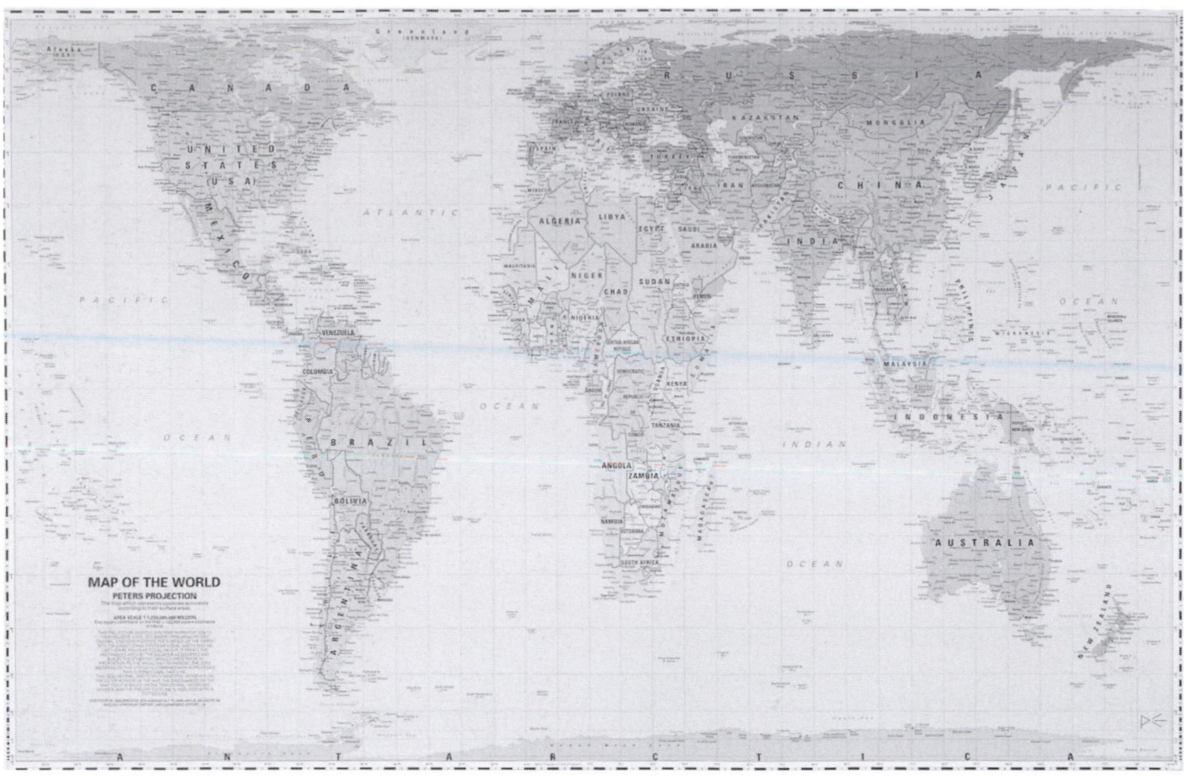

fig 2.9. The Peters Projection "area accurate" world map. Copyright Oxford Cartographers.

Arno Peters (1916–2002): German historian. Developed in 1974 an area-accurate world map, known as the Peters Projection.

One of the meanings of "to perform" is to get things done according to a particular plan or scenario. Mercator's maps proved very helpful for navigating the seas because straight lines on the projection kept to compass bearings. Mercator drew his maps to suit the scenarios of the mariners, merchants, and military of an expansionist, colonizing Western Europe. Similarly, the authors of the new maps have scenarios of their own which their maps enact. Interpreting maps this way is to examine map-making "as" performance. Every map not only represents the Earth in a specific way, but also enacts power relationships.

It's not just maps. Everything and anything can be studied "as" any discipline of study – physics, economics, law, etc. What the "as" says is that the object of study will be regarded "from the perspective of," "in terms of," "interrogated by" a particular discipline of study. For example, I am composing this book on a Dell Dimension 4100 desktop computer. If I regard it "as physics," I would examine its size, weight, and other physical qualities, perhaps even its atomic and subatomic qualities. If I regard it "as mathematics," I would delve into the binary codes of its programs. Regarding it "as law" would mean interpreting networks of patents, copyrights, and contracts. If I were to treat the computer "as performance," I would evaluate the speed of its processor, the clarity of its display, the usefulness of the pre-packaged software, its size and portability, and so on. I can envision Bill Parcells staring out at me telling me how well my computer performs.

Make belief and make-believe

Performances can be either "make-belief" or "make-believe." The many performances in everyday life such as professional roles, gender and race roles, and shaping one's identity are not make-believe actions (as playing a role on stage or in a film most probably is). The performances of everyday life (which I will discuss in more detail in Chapters 5 and 6) "make belief" – create the very social realities they enact. In "make-believe" performances, the distinction between what's real and what's pretended is kept clear. Children playing "doctor" or "dress-up" know that they are pretending.

On stage, various conventions – the stage itself as a distinct domain, opening and closing a curtain or dimming the lights, the curtain call, etc. – mark the boundaries between pretending and "being real." People watching a movie or a play know that the social and personal worlds enacted are not those of the actors but those of the characters. Or do they? This distinction was first challenged by the avant-garde and later further eroded by the media and the internet.

make-believe performances maintain a clearly marked boundary between the world of the performance and everyday reality. **make-belief** performances intentionally blur or sabotage that boundary.

Public figures are often making belief – enacting the effects they want the receivers of their performances to accept "for real." When an American president signs an important piece of legislation, or makes a grave announcement of national importance, his handlers often stage the event in the Oval Office of the White House where the president can perform his authority. Behind him is an array of VIPs, including the vice-president. A large presidential seal provides an appropriately patriotic foreground (**see figure 2.10**). At other times, the national leader may wish to appear as a friend or a good neighbor talking informally with "fellow citizens" (**see figure 2.11**).

fig 2.10. In a formally arranged "photo op," President George W. Bush smiles from behind his stage prop, the Seal of the President, as he is cheered by fellow Republicans at a party fundraiser in Paradise Valley, Arizona, 12 October 2004. Photograph J. Scott Applewhite/AP. Copyright EMPICS.

By now, everyone knows these kinds of activities are meticulously staged. Today's American presidency – at least its public face – is a totally scripted performance. The president's words are written by professional speechwriters, the backdrops and settings carefully designed for maximum effect, the chief executive himself well rehearsed. Teleprompters insure that the president will appear to be speaking off the cuff while he is actually reading every word. Each detail is choreographed, from how the president makes eye contact (with the camera, with the selected audience at a town meeting), to how he uses his hands, dresses, and is made up. The goal of all this is to "make belief" – first, to build the public's confidence in the president, and second, to sustain the president's belief in himself. His performances convince himself even as he strives to convince others.

Arguably, the president is an important personage by virtue of his position of authority. But with the exponential growth of media, hordes of citizens have jumped into the make-belief business. Some are hucksters selling everything from cooking utensils and firm buttocks to everlasting salvation. Others are venerable network "anchors," familiar voices and faces holding the public in place amidst the swift currents of the news. Still others are "pundits," experts – economists, lawyers, retired generals, etc. – whose authority is reaffirmed if not created by their frequent appearances. Then come the "spin doctors," employed by politicians and corporations to turn bad news into good. As for the producers behind the scenes, their job is to make certain that whatever is going on is dramatic enough to attract viewers. The greater the number watching, the higher the revenues from sponsors. Some news is inherently exciting – disasters, wars, crimes, and trials. But media masters have learned how to dramatize the stock market and the weather. How to build the "human interest" angle into every story. The producers know that the same information is available from many different sources, so their job is to develop attractive sideshows. Paradoxically, the result is a public less easy to fool. With so many kinds of performances on view, many people have become increasingly sophisticated and suspicious deconstructors of the theatrical techniques deployed to lure them.

fig 2.11. British Prime Minister Tony Blair acts the part of a "man of the people" in an "informal meeting" with some "ordinary citizens." Of course, such meetings are carefully planned, staged, and photographed. Photo: Andrew Burman. Copyright *The Independent*. Reproduced with permission.

Blurry boundaries

Let's return to Mercator's map. The world represented there is one of neatly demarcated sovereign nation-states. That world no longer exists, if it ever did (in Mercator's day the European nations were frequently at war with each other over who controlled what). Today national boundaries are extremely porous, not only to people but even more so to information and ideas. The newest maps can't be drawn because what needs to be represented are not territories but networks of relationships. Mapping these takes fractals or streams of numbers continually changing their shapes and values. The notion of fixity has been under attack at least since 1927, when **Werner Heisenberg** proposed his "**uncertainty principle**" and its accompanying "Heisenberg effect". Few people outside of a select group of quantum physicists really understood Heisenberg's theory. But "uncertainty" or "indeterminacy" rang a bell. It has proven to be a very appropriate, durable, and powerful metaphor affecting thought in many disciplines including the arts. Music theorist and composer **John Cage** often used indeterminacy as the basis for his music, influencing a generation of artists and performance theorists.

Werner Heisenberg (1901–76): German physicist, winner of the Nobel Prize for Physics in 1932 for his formulation of quantum mechanics which is closely related to his uncertainty principle.

uncertainty principle: a tenet of quantum mechanics proposed by Werner Heisenberg in 1927 which states that the measurement of a particle's position produces uncertainty in the measurement of the particle's momentum, or vice versa. While each quantity may be measured accurately on its own, both cannot be totally accurately measured at the same time. The uncertainty principle is closely related to the Heisenberg effect which asserts that the measurement of an event changes the event.

John Cage (1912–92): American composer and music theorist whose interests spanned using indeterminacy to make art, Zen Buddhism, and mushrooms. Author of *Silence: Selected Lectures and Writings* (1961) and *A Year from Monday* (1967). His many musical compositions include *Fontana Mix* (1960) and *Roaratorio* (1982).

Boundaries are blurry in different ways. On the internet, people participate effortlessly in a system that transgresses national boundaries. Even languages present less of a barrier than before. Already you can log in, write in your own language, and know that your message will be translated into the language of whomever you are addressing. At present, this facility is available in only a limited number of languages. But the repertory of translatables will increase. It will be routine for Chinese-speakers to address Kikuyu-speakers or for someone in a remote village to address a message to any number of people globally. Furthermore, for better or worse, English has become a global rather than national language. At the United Nations, 120 countries representing more than 97 percent of the world's populations choose English as their medium for international communication.

The dissolution of national boundaries is occurring in relation to manufactured objects as well as with regard to politics and information. If, for example, you drive an American or Japanese or Swedish or German or Korean car, you may believe it came from the country whose label it displays. But where were the parts manufactured? Where was the car assembled, where designed? The brand name refers to itself, not to a place of origin. Japanese cars are made in Tennessee and Fords roll off assembly lines in Canada, Europe, and elsewhere. Mexico is a major assembly point for many cars. And what about your clothes? Look at the labels of the clothes you are wearing right now. Do your dress, pants, shoes, and blouse come from the same country? Do you even know where they were stitched or by whom and at what wage or under what working conditions?

But more than cars and clothes are transnational. Cultures are also blurring. Globalization is accelerating. Airports are the same wherever you travel; standardized fast food is available in just about every major city in the world. American television and movies are broadcast everywhere. But the USA itself is increasingly intercultural in both its populations and its living styles. The profusion of international arts festivals and the hosts of artists touring all parts of the world are a major means of circulating styles of performing. "World beat" music combines elements of African, Asian, Latin American, and Euro-American sounds. New hybrids are emerging all the time. People are arguing whether or not all this mixing is good or bad. Is globalization the equivalent of Americanization? Questions of globalization and intercultural performance are taken up in Chapter 8.

The functions of performance

I have touched on what performance is and what can be studied as performance. But what do performances accomplish? It is difficult to stipulate the functions of performance. Over time, and in different cultures, there have been a number of proposals. One of the most inclusive is that of the Indian sage **Bharata**, who felt that performance was a comprehensive repository of knowledge and a very powerful vehicle for the expression of emotions (**see Bharata box**). The Roman poet-scholar **Horace** in his *Ars poetica* argued that theatre ought to entertain and educate, an idea taken up by many Renaissance thinkers and later by the German playwright and director **Bertolt Brecht**.

Bharata

The functions of Natya
(Dance–Music–Theatre)

I [The god Brahma] have created the Natyaveda to show good and bad actions and feelings of both the gods and yourselves. It is a representation of the entire three worlds and not only of the gods or of yourselves. Now dharma [duty], now artha [strategies], now kama [love], now humor, now fights, now greed, now killing. Natya teaches right to people going wrong; it gives enjoyment for those who are pleasure seekers; it chastises those who are ill-behaved and promotes tolerance in the well-behaved. It gives courage to cowards, energy to the brave. It enlightens people of little intellect and gives wisdom to the wise. Natya provides entertainment to kings, fortitude to those grief stricken, money to those who want to make a living, and stability to disturbed minds. Natya is a representation of the ways of the world involving various emotions and differing circumstances. It relates the actions of good, bad, and middling people, giving peace, entertainment, and happiness, as well as beneficial advice, to all. It brings rest and peace to persons afflicted by sorrow, fatigue, grief, or helplessness. There is no art, no knowledge, no learning, no action that is not found in natya.

1996 [second century BCE–second century CE], *The Natyasastra*, chapter 1

Bharata (*c.* second century BCE–*c.* second century CE): Indian sage, the putative author of *The Natyasastra*, the earliest and still very influential South Asian theoretical and practical treatise on all aspects of traditional Indian theatre, dance, playwriting, and to a lesser extent, music.

Horace (65–68 BCE): Roman poet whose *Ars poetica* (*The Art of Poetry*, 1974) offers advice on the construction of drama. His basic instruction that art should both "entertain and educate" is very close to Brecht's ideas on the function of theatre.

Bertolt Brecht (1898–1956): German playwright, director, and performance theorist. In 1949 he and actress Helene Weigel (1900–71), his wife, founded the Berliner Ensemble. Major works include The *Threepenny Opera* (1928), *The Rise and Fall of the City of Mahagonny* (1930), *Mother Courage and her Children* (1941), Galileo (1943), *The Good Woman of Szechwan* (1943), and *The Caucasian Chalk Circle* (1948 Eng; 1954 Ger.) The dates refer to stage premieres. Many of his theoretical writings are anthologized in English, in *Brecht on Theatre* (1964).

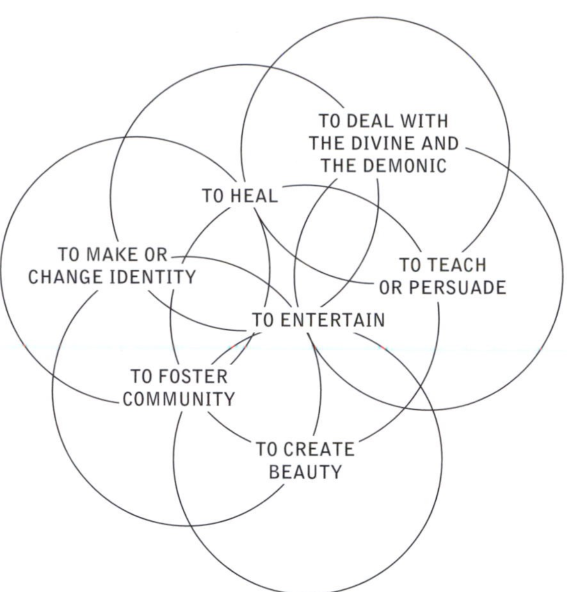

fig 2.12. The seven interlocking spheres of performance. Drawing by Richard Schechner.

Putting together ideas drawn from various sources, I find seven functions of performance:

1 to entertain
2 to make something that is beautiful
3 to mark or change identity
4 to make or foster community
5 to heal
6 to teach, persuade, or convince
7 to deal with the sacred and/or the demonic.

These are not listed in order of importance. For some people one or a few of these will be more important than others. But the hierarchy changes according to who you are and what you want to get done. Few if any performances accomplish all of these functions, but many performances emphasize more than one.

For example, a street demonstration or propaganda play may be mostly about teaching, persuading, and convincing – but such a show also has to entertain and may foster community. Shamans heal, but they entertain also, foster community, and deal with the sacred and/or demonic. A doctor's "bedside manner" is a performance of encouragement, teaching, and healing. A charismatic Christian church service heals, entertains, maintains community solidarity, invokes both the sacred and the demonic, and, if the sermon is effective, teaches. If someone at the service declares for Jesus and is reborn, that person's identity is marked and changed. A state leader addressing the nation wants to convince and foster community – but she had better entertain also if she wants people to listen. Rituals tend to have the greatest number of functions, commercial productions the fewest. A Broadway musical will entertain, but little else. The seven functions are best represented as overlapping and interacting spheres, a network (**see figure 2.12**).

Whole works, even genres, can be shaped to very specific functions. Examples of political or propaganda performances are found all over the world. El Teatro Campesino of California, formed in the 1960s in order to support Mexican migrant farmworkers in the midst of a bitter strike, built solidarity among the strikers, educated them to the issues involved, attacked the bosses, and entertained. Groups such as Greenpeace and ACTUP use performance militantly in support of a healthy ecology and to gain money for AIDS research and treatment. "Theatre for development" as practiced widely since the 1960s in Africa, Latin America, and Asia educates people in a wide range of subjects and activities, from birth control and cholera prevention to irrigation and the protection of endangered species. **Augusto Boal**'s Theatre of the Oppressed empowers "spectactors" to enact, analyze, and change their situations.

Augusto Boal (1931–): Brazilian director and theorist, founder of Theatre of the Oppressed. His books include *Theatre of the Oppressed* (1985), *Games for Actors and Non-Actors* (1980, Eng. 1992), *Legislative Theatre* (1998), and his autobiography, *Hamlet and the Baker's Son* (2001).

Boal's Theatre of the Oppressed is based to some degree on Brecht's work, especially his *Lehrstücke* or "learning plays" of the 1930s such as *The Measures Taken* or *The Exception and the Rule* (**see figure 2.13**). During China's Cultural Revolution (1966–75), which she helped orchestrate, **Jiang Qing** produced a series of "model operas" carefully shaped

fig 2.13. *The Measures Taken*, by Bertolt Brecht and Hans Eisler, a Lehrstück or "teaching play" – a play with a clear message. At the Berlin Philharmonnie, 1930. Copyright Bertolt Brecht Archive, Berlin.

to teach, entertain, and put forward a new kind of community based on the values of Chinese Communism as Jiang interpreted them. These theatre and ballet pieces employed both traditional Chinese performance styles modified to suit the ideological purposes of the Cultural Revolution and elements of Western music and staging (**see figure 2.14**). The utopian vision of the model operas contradicted the terrible fact of the millions who were killed, tortured, and displaced by the Cultural Revolution. But by the turn of the twenty-first century, the model operas were again being performed, studied, and enjoyed for their entertainment value, technical excellence, and artistic innovations (**see Melvin and Cai box**).

Jiang Qing (1914–91): Chinese Communist leader, wife of Chairman Mao Zedong (1893–1976). As Deputy Director of China's Cultural Revolution (1966–76), Jiang Qing sought to redefine all forms of artistic expression in strict adherence to revolutionary ideals. She oversaw the development of "model operas" and "model ballets," versions of Chinese traditional performance genres that made heroes of peasants and workers instead of aristocrats. After the Cultural Revolution, she was tried as one of "The Gang of Four." She died in prison.

fig 2.14. *The Red Lantern*, one of five "model operas" performed in China during the Cultural Revolution (1966–76). Copyright David King Collection.

Sheila Melvin and Cai Jindong

The model operas

"The Communist Party of China is like the bright sun," sang Granny Sha, her face glowing through wrinkles of sorrow as she told of abuse at the hands of a "poisonous snake, bloodsucker" landlord in Kuomintang-ruled China. Her words, soaring and elongated in the lyrical gymnastics of Beijing Opera, were punctuated by a roar of applause from the audience in the Yifu theatre here. [. . .] While the scene on stage closely resembled Cultural Revolution-era performance, the audience members – mostly middle-aged and stylishly dressed, casually taking cell phone calls, slurping Cokes and licking ice cream bars as the opera proceeded – were decidedly Shanghai 2000. [. . .] As the number of performances increases, so do attempts to analyze the artistic value of this genre created expressly to serve politics. "Naturally, this is sensitive," said Wang Renyuan, a Nanjing-based professor who wrote a book on the music in model operas. "We oppose the Cultural Revolution now, so of course products from then are also criticized. But model operas were very special, and we can't just ignore them. If we say that the Cultural Revolution was politics raping art, then we shouldn't still be doing this today. Criticize the Cultural Revolution, criticize Jiang Qing, but why can't we analyze model operas artistically?" [. . .]

Most intellectuals, even those who detest the genre, are willing to concede that if people want to watch model operas, they should have that right. "I don't want to watch them," said Mr. Luo Zhengrong, the composer.

"I don't want to hear them. But they were created well, and if they didn't have a political purpose, they wouldn't exist. The fact is there's a market for them. If there wasn't a market, they wouldn't be performed."

2000, "Why this Nostalgia for Fruits of Chaos?" 1, 31

Entertainment means something produced in order to please a public. But what may please one audience may not please another. So one cannot specify exactly what constitutes entertainment – except to say that almost all performances strive, to some degree or other, to entertain. I include in this regard both fine and popular arts, as well as rituals and the performances of everyday life. What about performances of avant-garde artists and political activists designed to offend? Guerrilla theatre events disrupt and may even destroy. These are not entertaining. However, "offensive" art usually is aimed at two publics simultaneously: those who do not find the work pleasant, and those who are entertained by the discomfort the work evokes in others.

Beauty is hard to define. Beauty is not equivalent to being "pretty." The ghastly, terrifying events of kabuki, Greek tragedy, Elizabethan theatre, and some performance art are not pretty. Nor are the demons invoked by shamans. But the skilled enactment of horrors can be beautiful and yield aesthetic pleasure. Is this true of such absolute horrors as slavery, the Shoah, or the extermination of Native Americans? **Francisco de Goya y Luciente**'s *The Disasters of War* show that nothing is beyond the purview of artistic treatment (**see figure 2.15**). Philosopher **Susanne K. Langer** argued that in life people may endure terrible experiences, but in art these experiences are transformed into "expressive form" (**see Langer box**). One of the differences between "art" and "life" is that in art, we do not experience the event itself but its representation. Langer's classical notions of aesthetics are challenged today, an epoch of simulation, digitization, performance artists, and webcam performers who "do" the thing itself in front of our very eyes. A considerable amount of postmodern art does not offer viewers objects or actions for contemplation.

Francisco de Goya y Luciente (1746–1828): Spanish artist. Often referred to simply as "Goya." His series of etchings titled *The Disasters of War* chronicled the Peninsular Wars (1808–14) among Spain, Portugal, and France.

Susanne K. Langer (1895–1985): American philosopher and aesthetician. Her major works include *Philosophy in a New Key* (1942), *Feeling and Form* (1953), and *Problems of Art* (1957).

Susanne K. Langer

Every good art work is beautiful

A work of art is intrinsically expressive; it is designed to abstract and preset forms for perception – forms of life and feeling, activity, suffering, selfhood – whereby we conceive these realities, which otherwise we can but blindly undergo. Every good work of art is beautiful; as soon as we find it so, we have grasped its expressiveness, and until we do we have not seen it as good art, though we may have ample intellectual reason to believe that it is so. Beautiful works may contain elements that, taken in isolation, are hideous. [. . .] The emergent form, the whole, is alive and therefore beautiful, as awful things may be – as gargoyles, and fearful African masks, and the Greek tragedies of incest and murder are beautiful. Beauty is not identical with the normal, and certainly not with charm and sense appeal, though all such properties may go to the making of it. Beauty is expressive form.

1953, *Feeling and Form*, 395–96

fig 2.15. From Goya's *Disasters of War*, 1810–14. From www.napoleonguide.com/goya18.html.

Conclusion

There are many ways to understand performance. Any event, action, or behavior may be examined "as" performance. Using the category "as" performance has advantages. One can consider things provisionally, in process, and as they change over time. In every human activity there are usually many players with different and even opposing points of view, goals, and feelings. Using "as" performance as a tool, one can look into things otherwise closed off to inquiry. One asks performance questions of events: How is an event deployed in space and disclosed in time? What special clothes or objects are put to use? What roles are played and how are these different, if at all, from who the performers usually are? How are the events controlled, distributed, received, and evaluated?

"Is" performance refers to more definite, bounded events marked by context, convention, usage, and tradition. However, in the twenty-first century, clear distinctions between "as" performance and "is" performance are vanishing. This is part of a general trend toward the dissolution of boundaries. The internet, globalization, and the ever-increasing presence of media is saturating human behavior at all levels. More and more people experience their lives as a connected series of performances that often overlap: dressing up for a party, interviewing for a job, experimenting with sexual orientations and gender roles, playing a life role such as mother or son, or a professional role such as doctor or teacher. The sense that "performance is everywhere" is heightened by an increasingly mediatized environment where people communicate by fax, phone, and the internet, where an unlimited quantity of information and entertainment comes through the air.

One way of ordering this complex situation is to arrange the performance genres, performative behaviors, and performance activities into a continuum (**see figure 2.16**). These genres, behaviors, and activities do not each stand alone. As in the spectrum of visible light, they blend into one another; their boundaries are indistinct. They interact with each other. The continuum is drawn as a straight line to accommodate the printed page. If I could work in three dimensions, I would shape the relationships as more of an overlapping and interlacing spheroid network. For example, though they stand at opposite ends of the straight-line

(a) **PLAY–GAMES–SPORTS–POP ENTERTAINMENTS–PERFORMING ARTS–DAILY LIFE–IDENTITY CONSTRUCTIONS–RITUAL**

(b) **GAMES–SPORTS–POP ENTERTAINMENTS–PERFORMING ARTS–DAILY LIFE–IDENTITY CONSTRUCTIONS**
PLAY AND RITUAL

fig 2.16. The performance continuum showing the range, unity, and comprehensivity of performance. In 2.16a the continuum is depicted as a continuous range. In 2.16b "play" and "ritual" are shown as underlying, supporting, and permeating the whole range.

fig 2.17. All of these performance genres integrate dance, theatre, and music.

A kathakali performer in Kerala, India, in a heroic role displaying vigor and energy. Copyright Performing Arts Library.

Yaqui Deer Dancer, New Pascua, Arizona, 1980s. Photograph by Richard Schechner.

Makishi mask performer, Zambia. Photograph courtesy of Richard Schechner.

continuum, playing and ritualizing are closely related to each other. In some ways, they underlie all the rest as a foundation.

With regard to figure 2.16: games, sports, pop entertainments, and performing arts include many genres each with their own conventions, rules, history, and traditions. An enormous range of activities comes under these banners. Even the same activity – cricket, for example – varies widely. Cricket at a test match is not the same as that played on a neighborhood oval. And cricket in the Trobriand Islands, where it was changed into a ritual encounter between towns featuring dancing as much as hitting and fielding, and with the home team always winning, is something else again. The fact that the ritualized cricket match shown in Jerry W. Leach's and Gary Kildea's *Trobriand Cricket* (1973) was staged for the cameras adds another layer of performative complexity. Despite all complicating factors, certain generalizations can be made. Even though genres are distinct, and no one would confuse the Superbowl with *Les Sylphides*, both ballet and football are about movement, contact, lifting, carrying, falling, and rushing to and fro. In many cultures, theatre, dance, and music are so wholly integrated that it is not possible to place a given event into one or the other category. Kathakali in India, a Makishi performance in Zambia, and the Deer Dance of the Yaquis are but three examples among many that integrate music, dance, and theatre (**see figure 2.17**).

The terms on the right side of figure 2.16 – daily life and identity constructions – are relatively fluid when compared to the strict governance on the left side. But that is not to say that there are no limits. Even the most apparently casual social interaction is rule-guided and culture-specific. Politeness, manners, body language, and the like all operate according to known scenarios. The specifics of the rules differ from society to society, circumstance to circumstance. But there is no human social interaction that is not "lawful," that is not rule-bound.

In the remaining chapters of this book I explore these matters in more detail. Chapter 3 deals with ritual, and Chapter 4 with play. Chapter 5 concerns performativity, the extension of the idea of performance into all areas of human life. Chapter 6 concerns the different kinds of performing – from everyday life to theatre to trance. Chapter 7 is about performance processes – generating, presenting, and evaluating performances; and about how performers train, rehearse, warm up, perform, and cool down. Chapter 8 examines globalization and its relationship to intercultural performances. It is neither possible nor advisable to fence these topics off from each other – so although each chapter develops a basic theme, there is also a good deal of overlap and interplay among the chapters.

TALK ABOUT

1. Pick an action not usually thought to be a performance. For example, waiting on line at a supermarket checkout counter, crossing the street at a busy intersection, visiting a sick friend. In what ways can each of these be analyzed "as" a performance?
2. Select a sports match, a religious ritual, an everyday life occurrence, and a performing art. Discuss their similarities and differences "as" performances with regard to venue, function, audience involvement, event structure, and historical-cultural context.

PERFORM

1. Observe an everyday encounter of people you do not know. Intervene in the encounter yourself with a definite goal in mind. Afterwards, discuss how your intervention changed the performances of the others. Did they welcome or resent your invention? Why?
2. In small groups, take turns reproducing for your group a bit of behavior that you ordinarily do only in private. How did the behavior change when you were self-consciously performing for others?

READ

Carlson, Marvin. "What is Performance?" *The Performance Studies Reader*, Henry Bial, ed.: 68–73. London and New York: Routledge, 2004.

Gabler, Neal. "Life the Movie." *The Performance Studies Reader*, Henry Bial, ed.: 74–75. London and New York: Routledge, 2004.

Geertz, Clifford. "Blurred Genres: The Refiguration of Social Thought." *The Performance Studies Reader*, Henry Bial, ed.: 64–67. London and New York: Routledge, 2004.

Goffman, Erving. "Performances: Belief in the Part One Is Playing." *The Performance Studies Reader*, Henry Bial, ed.: 59–63. London and New York: Routledge, 2004.

Kaprow, Allan. "Art which Can't Be Art (1986)." *Essays on the Blurring of Art and Life*, Allan Kaprow and Jeff Kelley: 219–22. Berkeley, Calif.: University of California Press, 2003.

Phelan, Peggy. "Marina Abramovic: Witnessing Shadows." *Theatre Journal* 56, 4 (2004): 569–77.

Schechner, Richard. "Restoration of Behavior." *Between Theater and Anthropology*: 35–116. Philadelphia, Pa.: University of Pennsylvania Press, 1985.

Taylor, Diana. "Translating Performance." *Profession* 2002, 1 (2002): 44–50.

3 RITUAL

Ritual, play, and performance

Performances – whether in the performing arts, sports, popular music, or everyday life – consist of ritualized gestures and sounds. Even when we think we're being spontaneous and original, most of what we do and utter has been done and said before – by us even. Performing arts frame and mark their presentations, underlining the fact that artistic behavior is "not for the first time" but enacted by trained persons who take time to prepare and rehearse. A performance may feature highly stylized behavior such as in kabuki, kathakali, ballet, or the dance-dramas of Indigenous Australians. Or it may be congruent to everyday behavior as in naturalism. A performance may be improvised – but as in jazz or contact improvisation dance, most improvisations consist of arranging and moving through known materials.

In Chapter 2, I pointed out that performances consist of twice-behaved, coded, transmittable behaviors. This twice-behaved behavior is generated by interactions between ritual and play. In fact, one definition of performance is: Ritualized behavior conditioned and/or permeated by play.

Rituals are collective memories encoded into actions. Rituals also help people (and animals) deal with difficult transitions, ambivalent relationships, hierarchies, and desires that trouble, exceed, or violate the norms of daily life. Play gives people a chance to temporarily experience the taboo, the excessive, and the risky. You may never be Oedipus or Cleopatra, but you can perform them "in play." Ritual and play lead people into a "second reality," separate from ordinary life. This reality is one where people can become selves other than their daily selves. When they temporarily become or enact another, people perform actions different from what they do ordinarily. Thus, ritual and play transform people, either permanently or temporarily. Rituals that transform people permanently are called "rites of passage." Initiations, weddings, and funerals are rites of passage – from one life role or status to another. In play, the transformations are temporary, bounded by the rules of the game or the conventions of the genre. The performing arts, sports, and games combine ritual and play. In this chapter, I consider ritual and in the following chapter, play.

Varieties of ritual

Every day people perform dozens of rituals. These range from religious rituals to the rituals of everyday life, from the rituals of life roles to the rituals of each profession, from the rituals of politics and the judicial system to the rituals of business or home life. Even animals perform rituals.

Many people equate ritual with religion, with the sacred. In religion, rituals give form to the sacred, communicate doctrine, open pathways to the supernatural, and mold individuals into communities. But secular public life and everyday life are also full of ritual. Great events of state often combine sacred and secular ritual, as in the coronations, inaugurations, or funerals of leaders. Less marked, the rituals of everyday life can be intimate or even secret; sometimes these are labeled as "habits," "routines," or "obsessions." But all rituals – sacred or secular, public or hidden – share certain formal qualities (**see Rappaport box**). Performing rituals seems to go back to the very earliest periods of human cultural activity. Numerous cave and burial sites dating back 20,000–30,000 years before the present show a ceremonial care with handling the dead as well as wall paintings and sculptings that seem to be of ritual significance. Nor has this need to deal ritually with the big events of life diminished. Present-day life throughout the world is saturated with ritual observances. To specify only a few of the myriad of religious rituals: the Passover Seder of the Jews, the five daily prostrations toward Mecca of Muslims, the Roman Catholic Eucharist, the waving of a camphor flame at the climax of a Hindu *puja*, the dances, songs, and utterances of a person possessed by an *orixa* of Umbanda or Candomble – and too many more to list even a small fraction (**see figure 3.1**). Religious rituals are as various as religion itself.

Nor is religion limited to the normative practices of the "world religions" – Islam, Buddhism, Christianity, Hinduism, and Judaism. There are many local, regional, and sectarian variations of the world religions. There are Shaman, Animist, Pantheist, and New Age religions. Most people, even if they don't openly admit it, actually follow more than one religion. A devout Christian may carry in her pocket a "good luck charm" or regularly consult her horoscope. Diasporic,

Roy A. Rappaport

The obvious aspects of ritual

I take ritual to be a form or structure, defining it as the performance of more or less invariant sequences of formal acts and utterances not encoded by the performers. [. . .] No single feature of ritual is peculiar to it. It is in the conjunction of its features that it is unique. [. . .] Rituals tend to be stylized, repetitive, stereotyped, often but not always decorous, and they also tend to occur at special places and at times fixed by the clock, calendar, or specified circumstances. [. . .] Performance is the second *sine qua non* of ritual. [. . .] Performance is not merely a way to express something, but is itself an aspect of that which it is expressing. [. . .R]itual not only communicates something but is taken by those performing it to be "doing something" as well. [. . .] However, that which is done by ritual is not done by operating with matter and energy [. . .] in accordance with the laws of physics, chemistry, or biology. The efficacy of ritual derives [. . .] from "the occult." The occult differs from "the patent" in that the patent can be known in the last resort by sensory experience, and it conforms to the regularities of material cause. The occult cannot be so known and does not so conform.

1979, *Ecology, Meaning, and Religion*, 175–78.

formerly colonized and missionized peoples combine the religions of their homelands with what was imposed on them. When under stress, people who ordinarily would not do so seek out healers and seers.

Sacred and secular

Rituals are frequently divided into two main types, the sacred and the secular. Sacred rituals are those associated with, expressing, or enacting religious beliefs. It is assumed that religious belief systems involve communicating with, praying, or otherwise appealing to supernatural forces. These forces may reside in, or be symbolized by, gods or other superhuman beings. Or they may inhere in the natural world itself – rocks, rivers, trees, mountains – as in Native American and Native Australian religions (**see figure 3.2**). Secular rituals are those associated with state ceremonies, everyday life, sports, and any other activity not specifically religious in character.

But this neat division is spurious. Many state ceremonies approximate or include religious ritual, with the State playing the role of the transcendent or godly other. Hitler and his Nazi party were particularly adept at this kind of quasi-religious performance of the State. The great party rallies at Nuremberg in the 1930s were secular-sacred ritual performances of party-state power (see Chapter 6 for more discussion of the Nazi rallies). The Memorial Day observance at the US Arlington National Cemetery is a secular-sacred state ritual. On the other side of the coin, many religious rituals include activities that are decidedly worldly or non-transcendent, such as the masking, playing, drinking, and sexuality of **Carnival** (**see figure 3.3**). Additionally, many, perhaps most, rituals are both secular and sacred. A wedding, for example, is the performance of a state-sanctioned contract, a religious ceremony, and a gathering of family and friends. The rituals of a typical American wedding are both secular and sacred. Secular wedding rituals include "cutting the cake," "throwing the bridal bouquet," "the first dance with the bride," and so on (**see figure 3.4**). Sacred wedding rituals include clergy performing the ceremony and prayers. Some weddings are officiated by a judge or a ship's captain – in these cases state rituals are performed. Sometimes, the sacred portion of a wedding is separated from the secular by having the wedding ceremony in a temple or church and the party elsewhere. Mixing the secular with the sacred is common to many observances, celebrations, and life-passage events such as birthday parties, job-related celebrations honoring years of service or retirement, and the numerous holidays punctuating the calendar.

Carnival: period of feasting and revelry which precedes the start of Lent on Ash Wednesday. The term "Carnival" includes, but is not limited to, Mardi Gras celebrations.

fig 3.1. Religious rituals of various faiths.

Muslims praying outside the Registan complex of mosques in Samarakand, 1996. Photograph by Shamil Zhumatov. Copyright Reuters.

An Animist Ndembu woman in trance, possessed by a spirit during a girl's initiation rite, Zambia 1985. Copyright Edith Turner, Victor and Edith Turner Collection, Center for the Study of World Religions at Harvard Divinity School Image Bank.

Reinhard Bonnke, German evangelist at the Elim/AoG conference. Photograph by David Butcher/ArkReligion.com. Reproduced with permission.

Worship of the Hindu goddess Durga during Durga Puja, Calcutta, 1980s. Photograph by Richard Schechner.

fig 3.2. Uluru, sacred to Indigenous Australians, is the world's largest monolith, with a height of 318 meters and a circumference of 8 kilometers. This same formation is called "Ayer's Rock" by non-Native Australians. Photograph courtesy of Ernest Bial.

fig 3.3. Trinidad Carnival combines the secular and the sacred, the ecstatic and solemn, the celebratory and the erotic.

A line of young people "wining" – rotating the hips and rubbing up close to one another – during Carnival in Port of Spain, Trinidad, 1990s. Photograph by Pablo Delano.

Maskers "bloody" and ecstatic celebrate Carnival in Trinidad, 1990s. Photograph by Jeffrey Chock.

fig 3.4. Bob and Joy Hall "cutting the cake," one of the secular rituals of a traditional British or American wedding. Wanganui, New Zealand, 1970. Photograph by Moira Taylor.

Richard A. Gould

Ritual is an inseparable part of the whole

The daily life of the Aborigines is rewarding but routine. There is a kind of low-key pace to the everyday round of living. In their ritual lives, however, the Aborigines attain a heightened sense of drama. Sharp images appear and colors deepen. The Aborigines are masters of stagecraft and achieve remarkable visual and musical effects with the limited materials at hand. [. . .] Gradually I experienced the central truth of Aboriginal religion: that it is not a thing by itself but an inseparable part of a whole that encompasses every aspect of daily life, every individual and every time – past, present, and future. It is nothing less than the theme of existence, and as such constitutes one of the most sophisticated and unique religious and philosophical systems known to man.

1969, *Yiwara*, 103–04

Anna Halprin (1920–): American dancer and choreographer. A pioneer in the use of expressive arts for healing and ritual-making. Her work in the 1960s had a profound influence on postmodern dance. Halprin continues to explore the uses of the arts in/as therapy – see her *Returning to Health with Dance, Movement, and Imagery* (2002, with Seigmar Gerken).

Many cultures do not enforce a rigid separation between the sacred and the secular. Sometimes there is no separation whatsoever. To those Native Australians who continue to live traditionally, every thing and every place has a sacred quality to it (**see Gould box**). This idea of the sacredness of the ordinary is a major theme of New Age religions and of some performance art. Dancer-choreographer-ritualizer **Anna Halprin** works with many different kinds of groups to locate and consciously perform the rituals of everyday life – eating, sleeping, greeting, touching, moving – and to invent new rituals that "honor" the body and the Earth. For example, Halprin's 1987 *Planetary Dance*, a two-day "dance ritual," consisted of groups of dancers in 25 countries moving in synchrony to make a "wave" of dance circling the Earth. The dance was repeated in 1994.

Structures, functions, processes, and experiences

Rituals and ritualizing can be understood from at least four perspectives:

1 Structures – what rituals look and sound like, how they are performed, how they use space, and who performs them.
2 Functions – what rituals accomplish for individuals, groups, and cultures.
3 Processes – the underlying dynamic driving rituals; how rituals enact and bring about change.
4 Experiences – what it's like to be "in" a ritual.

These four aspects of ritual have been explored from many angles by ethologists, neurologists, anthropologists, and archaeologists. All of these approaches are relevant to performance studies. Throughout this book, I will be referring to them. In brief: Ethologists study the continuities between animal and human rituals – particularly how rituals are used to control and redirect aggression, to establish and maintain hierarchy, to determine access to mates, and to mark and defend territory. Neurologists investigate what effects certain ritual practices have on the brain. Performing actions rhythmically and repetitively can put people into trance. While in trance, people are "possessed," "swept away," or have "out of body experiences." I will discuss trance performing in Chapter 6. Anthropologists observe, describe, and theorize living ritual practices. Archaeologists are forensic anthropologists who reconstruct extinct societies by reasoning from surviving evidence ranging from bones, ruins, pottery shards, and midden heaps to artworks and implements, weapons, and tools.

How ancient are rituals?

The evidence shows that human ritual practices go back many thousands of years. The paintings and sculptings found in caves such as Lascaux and Altamira in today's France and Spain date from as recent as 9,000 BCE to as far back as 30,000 years ago. Archaeologists studying this cave "art" surmise that rituals were probably performed in association with the paintings and sculptings. (I put quotation marks around the word "art" because no one knows for sure what the makers of these works thought of them or meant them to be or do.) Some paintings are abstract patterns, others are stenciled handprints. Many are reasonably accurate representations of animals such as bison, horses, boar, and deer. A few depict dancing humans wearing masks. Taken both individually and as a whole, these works speak to modern humans across a great expanse of time. But what exactly are they saying to us today? Even more important, what were they saying to the people who made them? The "art" probably was a repository of group memory, desire, and imagination. At least some of the cave spaces were used for performances: there are footprints preserved in clay indicating dancing. Whatever the caves were, they were not art galleries in the modern sense – they are hard to access and even with torches the paintings and sculptings are difficult to illuminate clearly. Probably the caves were sites of hunting magic, initiations, and other kinds of performed rituals – behavior that concretely embodied the "as if" (**see Montelle box**). The paintings and sculptings were more likely to be "action works" – items executed to get some result – than visual art designed for viewing in a mood of appreciation or reflection as in a museum. Still, we today can appreciate the power and beauty of the "art" – and this argues for a continuity of human consciousness and aesthetic design from prehistoric times to the present. That is, not only were the "artists" who made the works in the caves fully human biologically, they were our contemporaries culturally as well. I will discuss the cave performances again in Chapter 7.

Eleven themes relating ritual to performance studies

From the vast literature on ritual, I suggest eleven themes especially relevant to performance studies:

1 ritual as action, as performance
2 human and animal rituals
3 rituals as liminal performances
4 communitas and anti-structure
5 ritual time/space
6 transportations and transformations
7 social drama
8 the efficacy–entertainment dyad
9 origins of performance
10 changing or inventing rituals
11 using rituals in theatre, dance, and music

During the remainder of this chapter, I will explore these themes.

Rituals as action, as performance

The relationship between "ritual action" and "thought" is complex (**see Bell box**). The idea that rituals are performances was proposed nearly a century ago. **Émile Durkheim** theorized that performing rituals created and sustained "social solidarity." He insisted that although rituals may communicate or express religious ideas, rituals were not ideas or abstractions, but performances enacting known patterns of behavior and texts. Rituals don't so much express ideas as embody them. Rituals are thought-in/as-action. This is one of the qualities that makes ritual so theatre-like, a similarity Durkheim recognized (**see Durkheim box**).

Yann-Pierre Montelle

Paleoperformance: theatricality in the caves

Upper Paleolithic cave users laid out the paradigmatic foundations for a social process which has remained characteristic of our species to the present: the subjunctive world of the self-consciously constructed "as if." [. . .] Theatricality finds its first tangible evidence in the deep caves of the Upper Paleolithic, at least 17,000 years ago. [. . .] Pleistocene use of caves and iconography can be found in the Americas, Europe, Australia, China, India, Central Asia, and the Middle East. This global phenomenon helps confirm the emergence and ubiquity of theatricality on a worldwide scale. [. . .] The undeniable sense of *mise-en-scène* and the degree of planning indicate that the cave was a sophisticated place where "otherness" was explored, explained, and contained. It was also a place where societal segregation took place in order to guarantee stability and survival. Knowledge was variably disseminated during initiatory procedures that were carefully choreographed. [. . .] Evidence shows that two levels of communication were put in place. The exoteric, or visible, body of information was manufactured and shared with the intent of creating and solidifying networks of cooperation and alliances between neighboring and incoming bands. The esoteric, or invisible (less visible), body of information was a restricted knowledge transmitted to specific individuals through an initiatory procedure – this in order to enforce autonomy *vis à vis* the neighboring bands, and to facilitate the distribution of labor and instill specific knowledge within the members of a resident band. The degree of visibility and invisibility in these systems of information suggests that the "passing on" and sharing of knowledge, both externally and internally, were mediated by a rigid and ideological structure. It is at the junctions between components of this controlled repartition of cognition that theatricality emerges.

2004, *Paleoperformance*, 2–3, 5, 20, 183–4

Émile Durkheim

Ritual and theatre

We have already had occasion to show that they [rites performed by Native Australians] are closely akin to dramatic representations. [. . .] Not only do they employ the same processes as real drama, but they also pursue an end of the same sort: being foreign to all utilitarian ends, they make men forget the real world and transport them into another where their imagination is more at ease; they distract. They sometimes even go so far as to have the outward appearance of a recreation: the assistants may be seen laughing and amusing themselves openly. [. . .] Art is not merely an external ornament with which the cult has adorned itself in order to dissimulate certain of its features which may be too austere and too rude; but rather, in itself, the cult is something aesthetic.

1965 [1915], *The Elementary Forms of the Religious Life*, 424, 426–27

Catherine Bell

Ritual structure

[R]itual is to the symbols it dramatizes as action is to thought; on a second level, ritual integrates thought and action; and on a third level, a focus on ritual performances integrates our thought and their actions.

1992, *Ritual Theory, Ritual Practice*, 32

Émile Durkheim (1858–1917): French social scientist. One of the founding theorists of anthropology, sociology, and psychology. Author of *The Elementary Forms of the Religious Life* (1911, Eng. 1915).

Arnold van Gennep also recognized the theatrical dynamics of ritual. In his study of the "rites of passage," Gennep proposed a three-phase structure of ritual action: the preliminal, liminal, and postliminal. He pointed out that life was a succession of passages from one phase to another and that each step along the way was marked by ritual (**see Gennep box**). In the 1960s, Victor Turner developed Gennep's insight into a theory of ritual that has great importance for performance studies. Later in this chapter, I will discuss Gennep's and Turner's work. But first I need to explain ritual from an evolutionary perspective.

Arnold van Gennep (1873–1957): French ethnographer and folklorist who analyzed rituals that change a person's status in society. Gennep's notion of the liminal has been very influential. Author of *The Rites of Passage* (1908, Eng. 1960).

Arnold van **Gennep**

The rites of passage

The life of an individual in any society is a series of passages from one age to another and from one occupation to another. [. . .] Life comes to be made up of a succession of stages with similar ends and beginnings: birth, social puberty, marriage, fatherhood, advance-ment to a higher class, occupational specialization, and death. For every one of these events there are ceremonies whose essential purpose is to enable the individual to pass from one defined position to another which is equally well defined.

1960 [1908], *The Rites of Passage*, 3

Human and animal rituals

All animals, including *Homo sapiens*, exist within the same ecological web subject to the same evolutionary processes. But animals are not all alike. Homologies and analogies must be put forward cautiously. It is not correct to call the abdominal waggle and footwork of honeybees communicating to other bees the whereabouts of nectar "dances" in the human sense. The bees cannot improvise, change the basic patterns of movement, or express their feelings. Bees don't have feelings in any human understanding of that word. Where everything is genetically determined, where there is no learning, where no improvisation is possible, where error and/or lying cannot occur, art is not. So what are the bees doing? They are communicating by means of a system of movements. This kind of communication suggests a connection, one of very many, linking human and animal rituals.

Charles Darwin not only proposed the evolutionary development of species in terms of anatomy but also in terms of behavior. In his 1872 *The Expression of the Emotions in Man and Animals*, Darwin theorized that the similarities in behavior between humans and animals indicated an evolutionary development of feelings and the expression of emotions. Darwin's idea led **Julian Huxley** to assert that human and animal rituals are related through evolution. This idea has been developed by many ethologists, sociobiologists, and ritual theorists (**see Lorenz box, d'Aquili et al. box, and Wilson boxes**).

Charles Darwin (1809–82): English naturalist who developed the theory of evolution by natural selection. In addition to his landmark *The Origin of Species* (1859), Darwin also wrote the increasingly influential *The Expression of the Emotions in Man and Animals* (1872).

Julian Huxley (1887–1975): English biologist, author of *Evolution: The Modern Synthesis* (1942) and *Essays of a Humanist* (1964) among many other works.

Konrad Lorenz (1903–89): Austrian ethologist, winner (with Karl von Frisch and Nikolaas Tinbergen) of the 1973 Nobel Prize in medicine. His books include *On Aggression* (1963, Eng. 1966) and *The Foundations of Ethology* (1978, Eng. 1981).

E. O. (Edward Osborne) Wilson (1929–): American entomologist and pioneer of sociobiology. His works include *Sociobiology* (1975), *On Human Nature* (1978), and *Consilience* (1998).

Konrad **Lorenz**

Ritualization in animals and humans

[Julian] Huxley discovered the remarkable fact that certain movement patterns lose, in the course of phylogeny, their original specific function and become purely "symbolic" ceremonies. He called this process ritualization and used this term without quotation marks;

in other words, he equated the cultural processes leading to the development of human rites with the phylogenetic processes giving rise to such remarkable "ceremonies" in animals. From a purely functional point of view this equation is justified, even bearing in mind the difference between the cultural and phylogenetic processes. [. . .]

The triple function of suppressing fighting within the group, of holding the group together, and of setting it off, as an independent entity, against other, similar units, is performed by culturally developed ritual in so strictly analogous a manner as to merit deep consideration. [. . .]

The formation of traditional rites must have begun with the first dawning of human culture, just as at a much lower level phylogenetic rite formation was a prerequisite for the origin of social organization in higher animals. [. . .] In both cases, a behavior pattern by means of which a species in the one case, a cultured society in the other, deals with certain environmental conditions, acquires an entirely new function, that of communication. The primary function may still be performed, but it often recedes more and more into the background and may disappear completely so that a typical change of function is achieved. Out of communication two new equally important functions may arise, both of which still contain some measure of communicative effects. The first of these is the channeling of aggression into innocuous outlets, the second is the formation of a bond between two or more individuals. [. . .] The display of animals during threat and courtship furnishes an abundance of examples, and so does the culturally developed ceremonial of man. [. . .] Rhythmical repetition of the same movement is so characteristic of very many rituals, both instinctive and cultural, that it is hardly necessary to describe examples. [. . .]

This "mimic exaggeration" results in a ceremony which is, indeed, closely akin to a symbol and produces that theatrical effect that first struck Sir Julian Huxley as he watched his Great Crested Grebes. [. . .] There is hardly a doubt that all human art primarily developed in the service of rituals and that the autonomy of "art for art's sake" was achieved only by another, secondary step of cultural progress.

1966, *On Aggression*, 54–55, 72–74

Eugene G. d'Aquili, Charles D. Laughlin Jr., and John McManus

The biological foundations of ritual

We may say then that the primary biological function of ritual behavior is cybernetic: ritual operates to facilitate both intraorganismic and interorganismic coordination. Such coordination is necessary to form coherent, corporate responses, with common motive and drive, for the completion of some effect or task that could not be completed by conspecifics acting alone. Human ceremonial ritual is not a simple institution unique to man but rather a nexus of variables shared by other species. [. . .] One may trace the evolutionary progression of ritual behavior from the emergence of formalization through the coordination of formalized communicative behavior and sequences of ritual behavior to the conceptualization of such sequences and the assignment of symbols to them by man.

1979, *The Spectrum of Ritual*, 33, 36–37

Edward O. Wilson

Tribalism, religion, ritual

The shamans and priests implore us, in somber cadence, Trust in the sacred rituals, become part of the immortal force, you are one of us. As your life unfolds, each step has mystic significance that we who love you will mark with a solemn rite of passage, the last to be performed when you enter that second world free of pain and fear.

If the religious mythos did not exist in a culture, it would be quickly invented, and in fact it has been everywhere, thousands of times through history. Such inevitability is the mark of instinctual behavior in any species. That is, even when learned it is guided toward certain states by emotion-driven rules of mental development. To call religion instinctive is not to suppose any particular part of its mythos is untrue, only that its sources run deeper than ordinary habit and are in fact hereditary, urged into birth through biases in mental development encoded in the genes. [. . .] There is a hereditary selective advantage to membership in a powerful group united by devout belief and purpose. Even when individuals subordinate themselves and risk death in common cause, their genes are more likely to be transmitted to the next generation than are those of competing groups who lack equivalent resolve.

1998, *Consilience*, 257–58.

The evolutionary scheme of ritual can be depicted as a "ritual tree" (**see figure 3.5**). Animals with simple nervous systems, such as insects and fish, enact genetically fixed rituals. Further up the evolutionary ladder, mammal and bird species – dogs and parrots, for example – elaborate on what is genetically given. These animals are able to learn, mimic, and improvise. Much closer to humans are the non-human primates. Chimpanzees and gorillas perform in ways quite like humans but with nowhere near the complexity, diversity, or cognitive qualities of humans. In terms of ritual, humans have developed ritual into elaborate and sophisticated systems divisible into three main categories: social ritual, religious ritual, and aesthetic ritual. As noted earlier, these are not locked out from each other, but often overlap or converge.

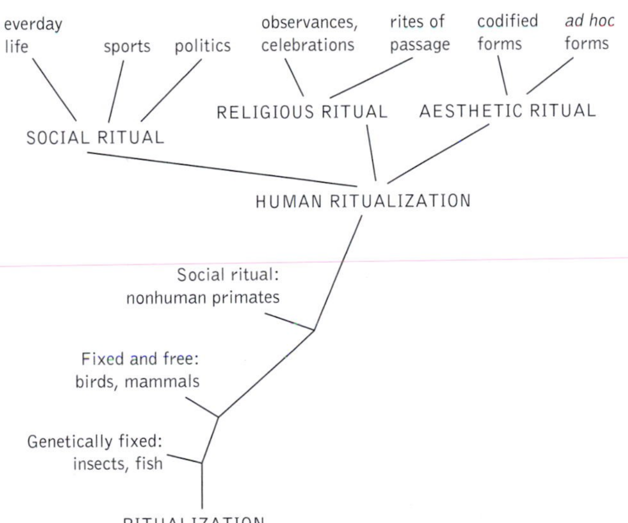

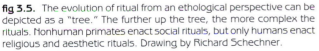

fig 3.5. The evolution of ritual from an ethological perspective can be depicted as a "tree." The further up the tree, the more complex the rituals. Nonhuman primates enact social rituals, but only humans enact religious and aesthetic rituals. Drawing by Richard Schechner.

To glimpse just how close some of the higher primates are to humans, one must turn both to field studies and to laboratory experiments, especially those concerning language acquisition and use. From the field, **Jane Goodall** described a performance by a juvenile male chimpanzee in the Gombe Stream Reserve in Tanzania in which a young animal challenged the alpha male not by means of combat, but through ritual display (**see Goodall box 1**). Not long after his show, "Mike" replaced "Goliath" as the troupe's alpha male. Note that the animals Goodall observed were not trained or tamed. Goodall gave them names for identification purposes only. Where does ritual come in? Like so many other encounters among animals concerning dominance, mating, territory, and food, Mike's challenge was played out as a ritual, as symbolic display, not as the "real thing," deadly combat. Goodall observed other performances by chimpanzees that she thought were very like human theatre (**see Goodall box 2**).

Jane Goodall (1934–): British ethologist, known for her research among the chimpanzees in Tanzania's Gombe Stream National Park. Her books include *In the Shadow of Man* (1971) and *The Chimpanzees of Gombe: Patterns of Behavior* (1986).

Jane Goodall

Chimpanzee ritual challenge

All at once Mike [a young male chimp] calmly walked over to our tent and took hold of an empty kerosene can by the handle. Then he picked up a second can and, walking upright, returned to the place where he had been sitting. Armed with his two cans Mike continued to stare toward the other males. After a few minutes he began to rock from side to side. At first the movement was almost imperceptible, but Hugo and I were watching him closely. Gradually he rocked more vigorously, his hair slowly began to stand erect, and then softly at first, he started a series of pant-hoots. As he called, Mike got to his feet and suddenly he was off, charging toward the group of males, hitting the two cans ahead of him. The cans, together with Mike's crescendo of hooting, made the most appalling racket: no wonder the erstwhile peaceful males rushed out of the way. Mike and his cans vanished down a track, and after a few moments there was silence. [. . .]

After a short interval that low-pitched hooting began again, followed almost immediately by the appearance of the two rackety cans with Mike closely behind them. Straight for the other males he charged, and once more they fled. This time, even before the group could reassemble, Mike set off again; but he made straight for Goliath [the alpha male] – and even he hastened out of Mike's way like all the others. Then Mike stopped and sat, all his hair on end, breathing hard.

1971, *In the Shadow of Man*, 122–23

Jane Goodall

Chimpanzee theatre

At about noon the first heavy drops of rain began to fall. The chimpanzees climbed out of the tree and one after the other plodded up the steep grassy slope toward the open ridge at the top. There were seven adult males in the group [. . .], several females, and a few youngsters. At that moment the storm broke. The rain was torrential, and the sudden clap of thunder, right overhead, made me jump. As if this were a signal, one of the big males stood upright and as he swayed and swaggered rhythmically from foot to foot I could just hear the rising crescendo of his pant-hoots above the beating of the rain. Then he charged flat-out down the slope toward the trees he had just left. He ran some thirty yards, and then, swinging round the trunk of a small tree to break his headlong rush, leaped into the low branches and sat motionless.

Almost at once two other males charged after him. One broke off a low branch from a tree as he ran and brandished it in the air before hurling it ahead of him. The other, as he reached the end of his run, stood upright and rhythmically swayed the branches of a tree back and forth before seizing a huge branch and dragging it farther down the slope. A fourth male, as he too charged, leaped into a tree and, almost without breaking his speed, tore off a large branch, leaped with it to the ground, and continued down the slope. As the last two males called and charged down, so the one who had started the whole performance climbed from his tree and began plodding up the slope again. The others, who had also climbed into trees near the bottom of the slope, followed suit. When they reached the ridge, they started charging down all over again, one after the other, with equal vigor.

The females and youngsters had climbed into the trees near the top of the rise as soon as the displays had begun, and there they remained watching throughout the whole performance. As the males charged down and plodded back up, so the rain fell harder, jagged forks or brilliant flares of lightning lit the leaden sky, and the crashing of the thunder seemed to shake the very mountains.

My enthusiasm was not merely scientific as I watched, enthralled, from my grandstand seat on the opposite side of the narrow ravine, sheltering under a plastic sheet. [. . .] I could only watch, and marvel at the magnificence of those splendid creatures. With a display of strength and vigor such as this, primitive man himself might have challenged the elements.

1971, *In the Shadow of Man*, 52–53

George Schaller, who studied the mountain gorilla in Uganda, also underscores similarities between human and non-human primates. Schaller shows how cheering, stomping, waving, and throwing things by involved fans at sports events is very much like what gorillas do (**see Schaller box**) (**see figure 3.6**). Recent studies confirm that sports fans are involved to such a degree that they undergo both physiological and psychological changes (**see McKinley box**). Enthusiastic, even violent displays are not infrequent at football games and wrestling matches. In sports such as golf and tennis, impulses to full-fledged emotional displays are dampened by the traditions of the game. But the situation is not static. In recent years, tennis fans (and players) have become more demonstrative, if not rowdy.

George B. Schaller (1933–): American ethologist, author of *The Mountain Gorilla* (1963) and *The Serengeti Lion* (1972).

fig 3.6. The expressive displays of humans and the great apes can be very similar.

Liverpool football fans displaying, Wembley Stadium, London. Copyright Popperfoto.

A mountain gorilla displaying, Congo (Zaire). Photograph by D. Parer and E. Parer Cook. Copyright Ardea, London Ltd.

George Schaller

Gorillas and sports fans

Various aspects of the chest-beating display sequence are present in the gibbon, orangutan, chimpanzee, and man, although the specificity is sometimes lacking.

[. . .] Man behaves remarkably like a chimpanzee or a gorilla in conflicting situations. Sporting events are ideal locations for watching the behavior of man when he is generally excited and emotionally off-guard. A spectator at a sporting event perceives actions which excite him. Yet he cannot participate in them directly, nor does he want to cease observing them. The tension thus produced finds release in chanting, clapping of hands, stamping of feet, jumping up and down, throwing of objects. This behavior is sometimes guided into a pattern by the efforts of cheerleaders who, by repeating similar sounds over and over again, channel the displays into a violent, synchronized climax. The intermittent nature of such behavior, the transfer of excitement from one individual to the next, and other similarities with the displays of gorillas are readily apparent.

1963, *The Mountain Gorilla*, 235

James C. McKinley Jr.

Root, root, root for the home team!

It has long been assumed that ardent sports fans derive excitement and a sense of community from rooting for a big-time team. But a growing body of scientific evidence suggests that for some fans, the ties go much deeper. [. . .]

One theory traces the roots of fan psychology to a primitive time when human beings lived in small tribes, and warriors fighting to protect tribes were true genetic representatives of their people, psychologists say.

In modern society, professional and college athletes play a similar role for a city in the stylized war on a playing field, the theory goes. Even though professional athletes are mercenaries in every sense, their exploits may re-create the intense emotions in some fans that tribal warfare might have in their ancestors. It may also be these emotions that have in large part fueled the explosion in the popularity of sports over the last two decades. [. . .]

Some recent studies suggest that some fans experience physiological changes during a game or when shown photos of their team. A study in Georgia has shown, for instance, that testosterone levels in male fans rise markedly after a victory and drop just as sharply after a defeat. The same pattern has been documented in male animals who fight over a mate: biologists theorize that mammals may have evolved this way to ensure quick resolutions to conflicts.

James Dabbs, a psychologist at Georgia State University, tested saliva samples from different groups of sports fans before and after important games. In one test, Dr. Dabbs took saliva samples from 21 Italian and Brazilian men in Atlanta before and after Brazil's victory over Italy in soccer's 1994 World Cup. The Brazilians' testosterone rose an average of 28%, while the Italians' levels dropped 27%. [. . .]

Among zealous male and female fans, Dr. Hillman's study found, the levels of arousal – measured by heart rate, brain waves, and perspiration – was comparable to what the fans registered when shown erotic photos or pictures of animal attacks, he said. [. . .]

Edward Hirt of Indiana University has demonstrated that an ardent fan's self-esteem tends to track a team's performance. [. . . M]en and women who were die-hard fans were much more optimistic about their sex appeal after a victory. They were also more sanguine about their ability to perform well at mental and physical tests, like darts and word games, Dr. Hirt found. When the team lost, that optimism evaporated. [. . .]

In most cases, this deep attachment to a team can be healthy, studies have shown. Daniel Wann, a psychologist at Murray State University in Kentucky, has done several studies showing that an intense interest in a team can buffer people from depression and foster feelings of self-worth and belonging.

2000, "It Isn't Just a Game: Clues to Rooting," 1–7

And not only sports events. Large-scale rhythmic formations of many kinds – marching, movement choirs, hymn singing, disco dancing, and parades, to name some of many – are examples of the same kind of group behavior. Only a few of these allow for individual expression. Mass demonstrations and rallies, religious revivals, the streets of Tehran crowded with people chanting their support for or opposition to the mullahs, party conventions in the UK and USA, the gathering of a million people in Beijing's Tiananmen Square – all trade in the same emotional currency (**see figure 3.7**). When **mood displays** are ritualized into mass actions, individual expression is discouraged or prohibited and replaced by exaggerated, rhythmically coordinated, repetitive actions and utterances. Aggression is evoked and channeled for the benefit of the sponsor, team, corporation, politician, party, religion, or state.

mood display: an ethological term indicating how an animal communicates through movements, postures, sounds, and faces that it is happy, angry, sad, etc.

But what exactly happens to ordinary behavior when it is ritualized? Are there any patterns? Is there a non-ideological system to ritual? Ethologists say that rituals are the result of a process that over millions of years evolved behaviors that

fig 3.7. The People's Liberation Army on parade in Tiananmen Square, Beijing, 1951. Copyright AP/Wide World Photographs.

have an "adaptive advantage." In other words, rituals help animals survive, procreate, and pass on their genes. All rituals share certain qualities:

- some ordinary behaviors (movements, calls) are freed from their original functions;
- the behavior is exaggerated and simplified; movements are often frozen into postures; movements and calls become rhythmic and repetitive;
- conspicuous body parts for display develop, such as the peacock's tail and the moose's horns. In humans, these are artificially provided – uniforms, costumes, masks, sound-makers, etc.;
- the behavior is "released" (performed) on cue according to specific "releasing mechanisms" (stimuli releasing conditioned responses).

One can see similarities to "restoration of behavior." As in restored behavior, rituals are "strips of behavior" that are repeated regardless of their "origins" or original functions. The movements, utterances, and postures of human rituals are often ordinary actions that have been exaggerated, simplified, and then repeated. Humans have not developed conspicuous body parts, but are extremely skilled at masks, costumes, makeup, jewelry, scarification, cosmetic surgery, and other ways to modify the body either temporarily or permanently. The "important parts" of the human body have been replicated in untold, often highly exaggerated, representations. Exactly what is "important" varies culturally, though there are some favorites – phallus, breasts, buttocks, and face.

These qualities of ritual enhance its functions. From an ethological perspective, the functions are to reduce deadly fighting within a group, to determine and maintain hierarchy, to enhance group cohesion, to mark out and protect territory, to share food, and to regulate mating. Ethologists argue that these functions carry over into human cultures, where they are overlaid by beliefs, ideologies, and cognition ("we do this because"). In other words, human rituals accomplish the same tasks as animal rituals – but in addition, human rituals are meaningful. Exactly what those meanings are depends both on the specific ritual practice and on the specific culture, religion, society, or kin group.

Are ethologists begging the question? Do they call some animal behavior "ritual" because it looks like what people do? Are those female and juvenile chimps sitting in the trees watching the big males perform really spectators in any human sense? Are the chimps at the theatre? Or was Goodall projecting? Is there really a link connecting human behavior with the behavior of other animals analogous to the evolutionary development of body structure? This is not an easy question to settle.

In both animals and humans rituals arise or are devised around, and to regulate, disruptive, turbulent, dangerous, and ambivalent interactions. In these areas faulty communications can lead to violent or even fatal encounters. Rituals enhance clear communications because they are overdetermined, redundant, exaggerated, and repetitious. Ritual's insistent **metamessage** is, "You get the message, don't you?!" This message is both imploring and problematic. Is God listening? Is the trance real? Was that a miracle or a hoax?

metamessage: a message that refers back to itself. For example, a message that says, "This is a message." A metamessage of prayer would be praying in such a way that everyone knows, "Now I am praying." The idea is based on Gregory Bateson's notion of "metacommunication," which I will discuss in Chapter 4.

Human rituals go beyond animal ritualization in two key regards. Human rituals mark a society's calendar. Human rituals transport persons from one life phase to another. Animals are not conscious of puberty, Easter, Ramadan, marriage, or death as "life passages." Animals do not wonder about life after death or reincarnation. Animals don't take oaths of fealty, or exchange gifts on a birthday. Human rituals are bridges across life's troubled waters.

Rituals as liminal performances

Everywhere people mark the passing from one life stage to another – birth, social puberty (which may occur before or after the biological changes associated with the onset of adolescence), marriage, parenthood, social advancement, job specialization, retirement, and death. As I pointed out earlier, Gennep noted that these rites of passage move through three phases – the preliminal, liminal, and postliminal. The key phase is the liminal – a period of time when a person is "betwixt and between" social categories or personal identities (**see Turner box 1**). During the liminal phase, the work of rites of passage takes place. At this time, in specially marked spaces, transitions and transformations occur. The liminal phase fascinated Turner because he recognized in it a possibility for ritual to be creative, to make new situations, identities, and social realities.

Victor Turner

Liminality

Liminal entities are neither here nor there; they are betwixt and between the positions assigned and arrayed by law, custom, convention, and ceremonial. As such, their ambiguous and indeterminate attributes are expressed by a rich variety of symbols in the many societies that ritualize social and cultural transitions. Thus, liminality is frequently likened to death, to being in the womb, to invisibility, to darkness, to bisexuality, to the wilderness, and to an eclipse of the sun or moon. Liminal entities, such as neophytes in initiation or puberty rites, may be represented as possessing nothing. [. . .] Their behavior is normally passive or humble; they must obey their instructors implicitly, and accept arbitrary punishment without complaint. It is as though they are being reduced or ground down to a uniform condition to be fashioned anew and endowed with additional powers to enable them to cope with their new stations in life. Among themselves, neophytes tend to develop an intense comradeship and egalitarianism.

1969, *The Ritual Process*, 95

During the liminal phase of a ritual two things are accomplished: First, those undergoing the ritual temporarily become "nothing," put into a state of extreme vulnerability where they are open to change. Persons are stripped of their former identities and positions in the social world; they enter a time-place where they are not-this-not-that, neither here nor there, in the midst of a journey from one social self to another. For the time being, they are powerless and identityless. Second, during the liminal phase, persons are inscribed with their new identities and initiated into their new powers. There are many ways to accomplish the transformation. Persons may take oaths, learn lore, dress in new clothes, perform special actions, be scarred, circumcised, or tattooed. The possibilities are countless, varying from culture to culture, group to group, ceremony to ceremony. As I will explain later in this chapter, the workshop-rehearsal phase of performance composition is analogous to the liminal phase of the ritual process.

At the conclusion of the liminal phase of a ritual, actions and objects take on, and radiate, significances in excess of their practical use or value. These actions and objects are symbolic of the changes taking place. The "I do" and exchange of rings at a wedding, the snipping of an eight -day-old Jewish boy's foreskin in a circumcision, the handful of earth thrown on the coffin at a funeral, the giving of a diploma at a graduation, the placing of a red cap on a new-made cardinal's head – each signifies a change in status, identity, or what-have-you. Each marks the transformation that is taking place.

But liminality need not require pomp or the use of valuables in order to signify. In Hindu India, the corpse is wrapped in plain cloth, carried on a wooden pallet to the burning grounds, and set ablaze. The body must be consumed, the skull cracked open to release the atman, the ashes scattered. Only then, when all the rituals have been performed, can the self fly free from the body – to final release or on its way to another reincarnation. The Zoroastrian Parsis of Mumbai expose their dead atop the Doongarwadi, the Tower of Silence, where vultures swiftly consume the flesh and smaller bones. Bones too large for the birds are buried or crushed to dust.

Limens, lintels, and stages

A **limen** is a threshold or sill, a thin strip neither inside nor outside a building or room linking one space to another, a passageway between places rather than a place in itself. In ritual and aesthetic performances, the thin space of the limen is expanded into a wide space both actually and conceptually. What usually is just a "go-between" becomes the site of the action. And yet this action remains, to use Turner's phrase, "betwixt and between." It is enlarged in time and space yet retains its peculiar quality of passageway or temporariness. Architecturally, the empty space of a limen is bridged at the top by a lintel, usually made of lumber or stone. This provides reinforcement. Conceptually, what happens within a liminal time–space is "reinforced," emphasized.

limen: literally a threshold or sill, an architectural feature linking one space to another – a passageway between places rather than a place in itself. A limen is often framed by a lintel, which outlines the emptiness it reinforces. In performance theory, "liminal" refers to "in-between" actions or behaviors, such as initiation rituals.

This conceptual-architectural detail remains visible in the design of many proscenium theatres. The front frame of a proscenium stage, from the forestage to a few feet behind the curtain, is a limen connecting the imaginary worlds performed onstage to the daily lives of spectators in the house. The house is permanently decorated, while the stage is often fully dressed in settings indicating specific times and places. But most of the world's stages are empty spaces, to use **Peter Brook**'s phrase (**see figure 3.8**). An empty theatre space is liminal, open to all kinds of possibilities: a space that by means of performing could become anywhere. The orchestra circle of the ancient Greek amphitheatre was unadorned and empty except for the altar of Dionysus at its center. The noh stage is made of smoothed *hinoki*, Japanese cypress. The only decorations are a painting of bamboo to the side and a backdrop painting of a large pine tree – the Yogo Pine at the Kasuga Shrine in Nara – where each year since the fourteenth century *Okina*, the "first" noh play, is performed. Under every noh stage large hollow earthen jugs are positioned so that when the actors stamp on the wooden stage a deep reverberation swells. The Elizabethan stage was likewise simple and empty, hardly more than "two boards and a passion." The dancing ground of an African village and the temporary erection of a screen for Javanese *wayang kulit* (shadow puppets) are both liminal spaces ready to be populated by imagined realities. Illusionistic stage sets, so familiar in the West since the nineteenth century, are actually the exception to the rule. The spaces of film, television, and computer monitors are more traditional. Apparently full of real things and people, they are actually empty screens, populated by shadows or pixels.

Peter Brook (1925–): British director who, after heading the Royal Shakespeare Company, moved to Paris in 1970 where he founded the International Centre for Theatre Research. Among Brook's many productions are Peter Weiss' *Marat/Sade* (1964), *A Midsummer's Night Dream* (1970), *The Mahabharata* (1985), *Don Giovanni* (1998), and *Tierno Bokar* (2004). His books include *The Empty Space* (1968), *The Shifting Point* (1987), *The Open Door* (1995), and *The Threads of Time* (1998).

Turner realized that there was a difference between what happens in traditional cultures and in modern cultures. With industrialization and the division of labor, many of the functions of ritual were taken over by the arts, entertainment, and recreation. Turner used the term **"liminoid"** to describe ritual-like types of symbolic action that occurred in leisure activities. If the liminal includes "communication of sacra" and "ludic recombinations and inversions," the liminoid includes the arts and popular entertainments (**see figure 3.9**). Generally, liminoid activities are voluntary, while liminal rites are obligatory.

liminoid: Victor Turner's coinage to describe symbolic actions or leisure activities in modern or postmodern societies that serve a function similar to rituals in pre-modern or traditional societies. Generally speaking, liminoid activities are voluntary, while liminal activities are required. Recreational activities and the arts are liminoid.

Turner felt that the counter-culture of the 1960s was in part an attempt to recuperate the force and unity of traditional liminality. Shortly before his death in 1983, Turner recognized that the counter-culture had moderated into the New Age with its alternative religions and medicines, concerns for ecology, and increasing tolerance of different sorts of non-traditional lifestyles. Turner was an optimist, if not an outright utopian. He predicted that "the liberated and disciplined body itself, with its many untapped resources for pleasure, pain, and expression," would lead the way to a better world.

The decades since Turner's death indicate that his utopianism was unjustified. As we move deeper into the twenty-first century, sacred and secular rituals, staged in central, symbolically loaded places – major avenues, civic centers, cathedrals, stadiums, and capitols – reinforce officialdom and mainstream values. Various fundamentalisms – Christian, Islamic, Jewish, Hindu, and even Buddhist (in Sri Lanka) – attract adherents by the hundreds of millions. Liminoid artistic and social activities take place at the margins

fig 3.8. The empty space of performance in different cultures.

The Greek theatre at Epidaurus, 4th–2nd centuries BCE. This theatre, still in use, holds up to 17,000 spectators. Copyright Ancient Art and Architecture Collection.

The interior of the Swan Theatre as drawn in Elizabethan times by Johannis de Witt. Notice how close the audience is to the performers. Copyright British Museum.

A Bira village dancing ground in Congo (Zaire), 1950s. Here ordinary space is transformed into a performance arena by the action taking place. The women are performing a *maipe* ritual dance. Photograph by Colin Turnbull. Photograph courtesy of Richard Schechner.

Paul Claudel's *La Femme et son Ombre* (*A Woman and Her Shadow*) as performed by Izumi Yoshio, left, and Izumi Yasutake in Nagoya, 1972. Performing in an empty space emphasizes the performers, not the scenery. Photograph by Tanaka Masao. Photograph courtesy of Karen Brazell.

Scene 8 of Bertolt Brecht's *Mother Courage and Her Children*, with The Performance Group, directed by Richard Schechner, in the New School Gymnasium, New Delhi, 1976. Stephen Borst as The Chaplain threatens Jim Griffiths as The Cook. The surrounding audience focuses the otherwise empty space. Photograph by Pablo Bartholomew. Photograph courtesy of Richard Schechner.

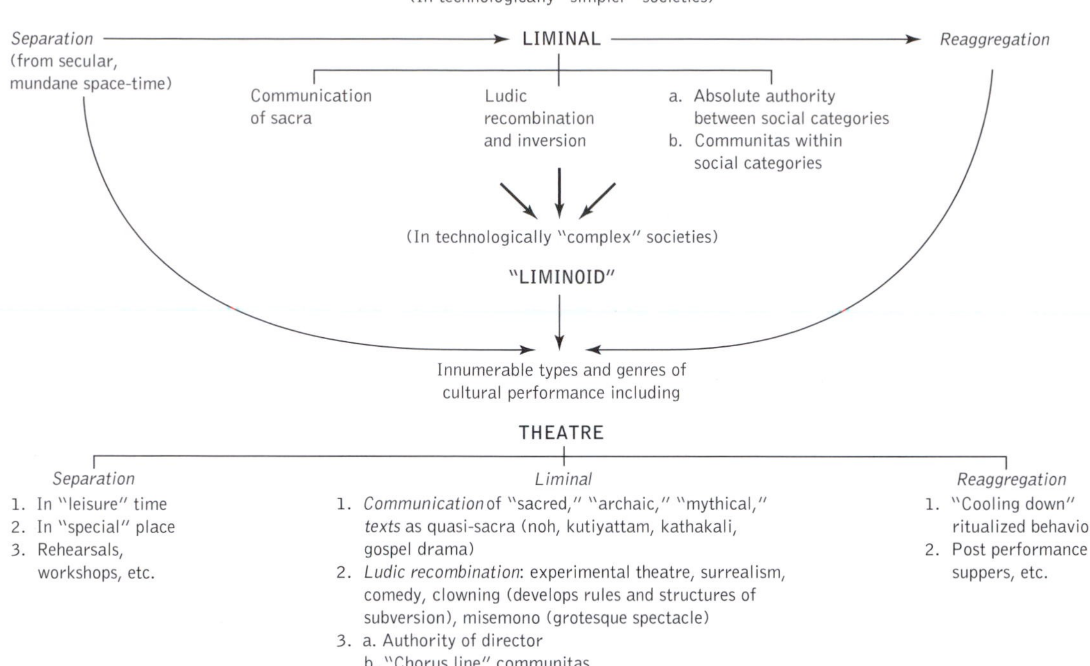

fig 3.9. Victor Turner's diagram of the ritual process in relationship to the liminal, liminoid, and theatre. Figure from *On the Edge of the Bush: Anthropology as Experience*, by Victor Turner. Copyright The Arizona Board of Regents. Reprinted by permission of the University of Arizona Press.

and in the creases of established cultural systems, off the beaten track in "bad" neighborhoods, and in remote rural areas. The internet pulls these distant and disparate venues and tendencies together, allowing for unity and dispersal at the same time. The question remains whether or not official cultures – by means of regulation, commercialization, and globalization – will reign in the vibrancy and diversity of the internet. Struggles over "intellectual property" indicate that the internet will not be as free – in all senses of that word – as it has been. And even the vaunted freedom of the internet is a double-edged sword. Freedom of speech has spawned a plethora of hate sites whose goal is to shut down the very liberties the sites depend on. These issues will be explored further in Chapter 8.

Communitas and anti-structure

Rituals are more than structures and functions; they are also among the most powerful experiences life has to offer. While in a liminal state, people are freed from the demands of daily life. They feel at one with their comrades; personal and social differences are set aside. People are uplifted, swept away, taken over. Turner called this liberation from the constraints of ordinary life "anti-structure" and the experience of ritual camaraderie "communitas" (**see Turner box 2**).

"Communitas" is a complex term. As Turner defined it, communitas comes in several varieties, including the "normative" and the "spontaneous." Normative communitas is what happens during communion in an Episcopal or Roman Catholic service. The congregation is united "in Christ" by the Eucharist. However, not every congregant may feel "in Christ" at that moment. The communitas is "official," "ordained," "imposed." Spontaneous communitas – Turner's favorite – is different, almost the opposite. Spontaneous communitas happens when a congregation or group catches fire in the Spirit. It can also be secular, as when a sports team is playing so well that each player feels inside the others' heads.

Spontaneous communitas abolishes status. People encounter each other directly, "nakedly," in the face-to-face intimate encounter that **Martin Buber** called the dialogue of "I–you" (*ich–du*). Once, during a theatre workshop I was leading, we reached a state of high spontaneous communitas. A man looked deeply and at length at each of the ten or so of us standing in a circle. "There's a little bit of you in each of me," he said. I never knew whether he intended to say what he said or its opposite – but he truly expressed the feeling in the circle at that moment.

Victor Turner

A total, unmediated relationship

In liminality, communitas tends to characterize relationships between those jointly undergoing ritual transition. The bonds of communitas are anti-structural in the sense that they are undifferentiated, equalitarian, direct, extant, nonrational, existential, I-Thou relationships. Communitas is spontaneous, immediate, concrete – it is not shaped by norms, it is not institutionalized, it is not abstract. [. . .] In human history, I see a continuous tension between structure and communitas, at all levels of scale and complexity. Structure, or all that which holds people apart, defines their differences, and constrains their actions, is one pole in a charged field, for which the opposite pole is communitas, or anti-structure [. . .] representing the desire for a total, unmediated relationship between person and person, a relationship which nevertheless does not submerge one in the other but safeguards their uniqueness in the very act of realizing their commonness. Communitas does not merge identities; it liberates them from conformity to general norms, though this is necessarily a transient condition if society is to continue to operate in an orderly fashion. [. . .]

1974, *Dramas, Fields, and Metaphors*, 274

In the workshop, village, office, lecture-room, theatre, almost anywhere people can be subverted from their duties and rights into an atmosphere of communitas. [. . .] Is there any of us who has not known this moment when compatible people – friends, congeners – obtain a flash of lucid mutual understanding on the existential level, when they feel that all problems, not just their problems, could be resolved, whether emotional or cognitive, if only the group which is felt (in the first person) as "essentially us" could sustain its intersubjective illumination? [. . .]

In industrial societies, it is within leisure, and sometimes aided by the projections of art, that this way of experiencing one's fellows can be portrayed, grasped, and sometimes realized.

1982, *From Ritual to Theatre*, 45–48

Martin Buber (1878–1965): Jewish philosopher and Zionist. Buber was born in Austria, raised in the Ukraine, and was teaching in Frankfurt, Germany, when Nazism forced him in 1938 to emigrate to Israel where he became the first president of the Israeli Academy of Science and Humanities. Author of many books, including: *I and Thou* (1922, Eng. 1937), *Eclipse of God* (1952), and *The Origin and Meaning of Hasidism* (1960).

Spontaneous communitas rarely "just happens." It is generated by the ritual process. Across a ritual limen, inside of a "sacred space/time," spontaneous communitas is possible. Those in the ritual are all treated equally, reinforcing a sense of "we are all in this together." People wear the same or similar clothing; they set aside indicators of wealth, rank, or privilege. Formal titles are done away with; sometimes even first names are not used. Instead, people call each other "sister," "brother," "comrade," "you," or some other generic term. In workshops (liminoid experiences), I encourage people to give themselves new names. More than once, a new name sticks: a transformation takes place.

Ritual experiences are not always pleasant or fun. It can be terrifying to encounter group forces and face memories, demonic or divine. When in the *Bhagavad Gita* Arjuna glimpses Krishna in his true form, the unmatched warrior turns to jelly. It is not "good" or "evil" that frightens Arjuna, but coming face to face with the Absolute: "I see no end, or middle, or beginning to your totality [. . .] I am thrilled and yet my mind trembles with fear at seeing what has not been seen before." Initiation rites are often frightening for the neophytes who are taken to strange and forbidding locations where they are forced through ordeals, some of which may be painful or bloody. Even a celebratory ritual occasion such as a wedding can be very scary to the bride and groom, and, for the parents, a time of high anxiety mixing sadness and joy.

Ritual time/space

Because rituals take place in special, often sequestered places, the very act of entering the "sacred space" has an impact on participants. In such spaces, special behavior is required. One must remove one's shoes before entering a mosque or a Hindu temple. In the synagogue men are asked to wear *yarmulkas* (skull caps) and *talisem* (prayer shawls). In some parts of the world, it is customary for women in Roman Catholic churches to cover their heads. When the sacred space is a natural place – a sacred tree, cave, or mountain, for example – one approaches and enters the space with care. But ordinary secular spaces can be made temporarily special by means of ritual action. Dance and yoga classes often require a careful preparation of the space and special clothes for the participants. When I lead a performance workshop, daily life is left behind. Once participants enter the workshop space, there is no socializing. We begin by changing into our work clothes – plain shirts and loose pants. No shoes, jewelry, or timepieces. Without watches, duration is defined by our mutual experiences. Each session begins with a careful and silent cleaning of the floor. The simple actions of sweeping and mopping transport the participants to a different place mentally and emotionally. These rites of entry create communitas even before the exercises begin.

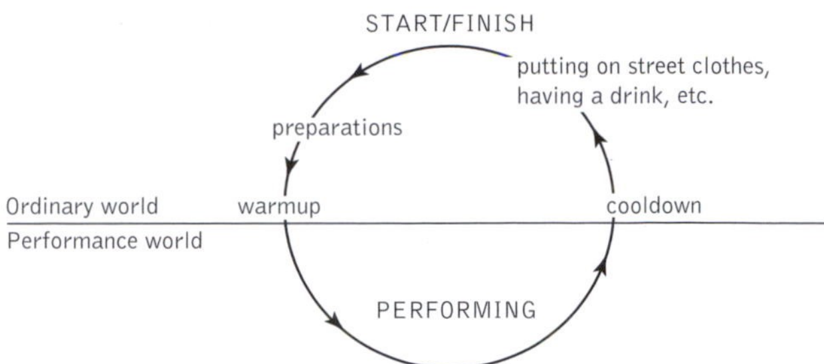

fig 3.10. A "transportation performance" from the point of view of a performer. A performer leaves her daily world and by means of preparations and warm-ups enters into performing. When the performance is over, the performer cools down and re-enters ordinary life. For the most part, the performer is "dropped off" where she entered. She has been "transported" – taken somewhere – not "transformed" or permanently changed. Drawing by Richard Schechner.

Transportations and transformations

Liminal rituals are transformations, permanently changing who people are. Liminoid rituals, effecting a temporary change – sometimes nothing more than a brief communitas experience or a several-hours-long playing of a role – are transportations. In a transportation, one enters into the experience, is "moved" or "touched" (apt metaphors), and is then dropped off about where she or he entered. **Figure 3.10** is a model of a transportation performance from the point of view of a performer in a dance, play, or sports contest; or even a deeply religious person at a church service or an adherent of the Afro-Brazilian Candomble religion in trance.

In transportation performances, a person can fall into a trance, speak in tongues, handle snakes, "get happy" with the Spirit – or perform many other actions that result in experiencing overwhelmingly powerful emotions. But no matter how strong the experience, sooner or later, most people return to their ordinary selves. At the Institutional Church of God in Christ in Brooklyn, New York, I have seen women go into trance and dance, speak in tongues, and tremble with the Spirit at 11 o'clock in the morning, while by 1 in the afternoon they are chatting and joking in the church kitchen as they prepare the "fellowship lunch." In a suburb of Rio de Janeiro I witnessed a young Brazilian man being seized by an *orixa* (god) of Candomble, sing, speak in an African language, dance, and yank others into trance with him. After four hours of intense performing, the orixa left his body, he came back to himself, and he served supper to the many neighbors assembled in his mother's home, which was also her *terrero* (sacred place).

These examples are more complex than they may at first appear. The entranced Brooklyn women and the Candomble *filho de santo* (initiated medium), at the moment of their decisive life-changing experience – not at the time I saw them – were transformed. The women had "declared for Christ" and were "twice born." The man became a Candomble filho de santo. But once they were transformed, they were enabled to participate in any number of transportation performances. The two kinds of performing are not mutually exclusive, but they do occur with different frequencies. A person is transformed only a few times in life, if ever. However, a person may experience transportations on an almost daily basis.

Transportations occur not only in ritual situations but also in aesthetic performances. In fact, this is where all kinds of performances converge. Actors, athletes, dancers, shamans, entertainers, classical musicians – all train, practice, and/or rehearse in order to temporarily "leave themselves" and be fully "in" whatever they are performing. In theatre, actors onstage do more than pretend. The actors live a double negative. While performing, actors are not themselves, nor are they the characters. Theatrical role-playing takes place between "not me . . . not not me." The actress is not Ophelia, but she is not not Ophelia; the actress is not **Paula Murray Cole**, but she is not not Paula Murray Cole. She performs in a highly charged in-between space-time, a liminal space-time. Spectators help by not reminding Cole who she "really is" in her ordinary life. But during the curtain call, they applaud Cole, not Ophelia. Or rather they applaud Cole's ability to perform Ophelia.

Paula Murray Cole (1964–): American actor, co-head of East Coast Artists education program. Cole is a master teacher of the rasaboxes technique of emotional training. With ECA, Cole has worked with Schechner on several productions, including Chekhov's *Three Sisters* (1997) and *Hamlet* (1999).

Of course, it's not so simple. Many actors train hard in order to believe in the actuality of whom and what they are representing. And from the mid-1950s, happeners and performance artists have explored many different ways of performing themselves. But even someone so insistent on performing his own life as **Spalding Gray** played a character called "Spalding", a persona who was a framed and edited version of the "real" Spalding. Gray developed his life-narratives by tape recording early in-process appearances, listening to the recordings, and editing his text. By the time Gray appeared onstage at Lincoln Center, his apparently casual self-presentation was honed in every detail, including slips and "mistakes." The audience enjoyed "Spalding" as presented by Gray.

Spalding Gray (1941–2004): American monologist, author, and actor. A member of The Performance Group (1970–80) and then The Wooster Group (1980–2004). His autobiographical performances began with the ensemble works, *Three Places in Rhode Island* (1975–80). In his monologues, Gray wryly told the story of his life – from his childhood through his acting career to his experiences as family man. Many of his monologues are published, including: *Swimming to Cambodia* (1985), *Sex and Death to the Age of 14* (1986), *Morning, Noon, and Night* (1999), and *Life Interrupted* (2005).

There are performers – actors as well as musicians – who improvise, for whom each instance is "original." But even in these cases, the restoration of behavior applies. A careful comparison of a number of instances would reveal strips of behavior repeated regularly as well as recurring patterns of presentation (timing, tone of voice, gestures). It is the manipulation of these repetitions that give each performer her or his own style.

Transformation performances bring together two kinds of performers – those who are being transformed and those who manage the transformation. Rites of passage such as initiations are transformation performances. Every initiation rite is a system worked by those who are being transported, the initiators, on those who are being transformed, the initiates. Let me make this clear by looking at a specific example of an initiation rite.

Asemo's initiation

In the 1950s, Asemo was a boy of the Gahuku people living in Susaroka, a settlement in the mountainous highlands of Papua New Guinea. Asemo's initiation is described in detail by **Kenneth E. Read** in *The High Valley*. Read tells how Asemo, then about ten years old, was abruptly snatched from his mother's house and secluded along with his age-mates in the bush for two weeks, where they underwent extreme ordeals such as forced vomiting and nose-bleeding. During this phase of the initiation, the boys were literally being emptied, prepared to receive the knowledge of their tribe.

Kenneth E. Read (1917–95): Australian anthropologist specializing in Papuan New Guinea cultures. His books include *The High Valley* (1965) and *Return to the High Valley* (1986).

After two weeks, the tired, bedraggled boys were brought back to the village. Riding on the shoulders of the men, they ran a gauntlet of women wielding stones, wood, an axe or two, and even bows and arrows. The attacks were "ritualized," but severe nonetheless, terrifying the boys. Read writes, "There was no mistaking the venom in the assault of the women," which "teetered on the edge of virtual disaster." On the edge, but not over: the attack was contained within its performative boundaries, much the way a bloody hockey game barely but reliably remains a game.

Next, the boys were taken back to the bush for six more weeks of indoctrination and training. They were in a liminal time–space during the process of being transformed into Gahuku men. Read was not allowed to witness the details of this education. But the outcome made it clear that what happened during the six weeks was enough to make a real change in Asemo. The day Asemo and his age-mates returned to Susaroka was a time of feasting and dancing (**see figure 3.11**). This time the women did not attack the men, but greeted them with a "rising chorus of welcoming calls." The newly conferred men, the initiates, danced without the assistance or protection of the older men (**see Read box**).

fig 3.11. Men and newly initiated boys – one can be seen in the center – dancing on the final day of Asemo's initiation. Photograph by Kenneth E. Read.

Kenneth E. Read

Asemo transformed

They moved unsteadily under the ungainly decorations, and I failed to see the splendid stirring change that had been apparent to their elders' eyes. But dignity touched them when they began to dance, a slow measure based on the assertive stepping of the men but held to a restrained, promenading pace by the weight [of their headdresses . . .] For a moment I was one with the crowd of admirers. [. . .] Asemo was in the front rank of the dancers, his legs moving in unison with his age-mates, his face, like theirs, expressionless, his eyes fixed on some distant point only he could see.

1965, *The High Valley*, 177

Read wrote in 1965 that he felt he had seen the last Gahuku initiation rite. If that was so, then this signals a big shift in the basis of Gahuku society. That is because the initiation rites didn't merely "mark" a change – as, say, graduation ceremonies in Western-style schools do. Asemo's initiation, taken as an eight-week whole, was the machine that transformed Asemo from a boy into a Gahuku man. This status – whatever its personal meanings and effects, whatever private styles it accommodates – is at its heart social, public, and objective. It did not determine what kind of Gahuku man Asemo became, or even how he felt about it, any more than a wedding ceremony determines what kind of husband the groom will be. But definite acts were performed that forever made Asemo into a Gahuku man. These acts were not symbolic of a change accomplished elsewhere. The ritual acts were themselves the system of transformation.

All the same, the men training Asemo and his cohort were not transformed. They had been transformed earlier in life, at the time of their own initiations. At Asemo's initiation their job was to see that Asemo and his age-mates were properly instructed and made it through. They were the boys' teachers, guides, models, protectors, tormentors, and elders. They were the transporters of those who were transformed. The relationship between transporters and transformers is depicted in **figure 3.12**. The transporters were experienced performers. They shared in the bleeding, vomiting, gauntlet-running, and dancing. But when the performance was over, the previously initiated Gahuku men re-entered ordinary life approximately where they left it. If any change occurred among them, it was subtle: some achieved more respect, or lost it, through performing what was required of them.

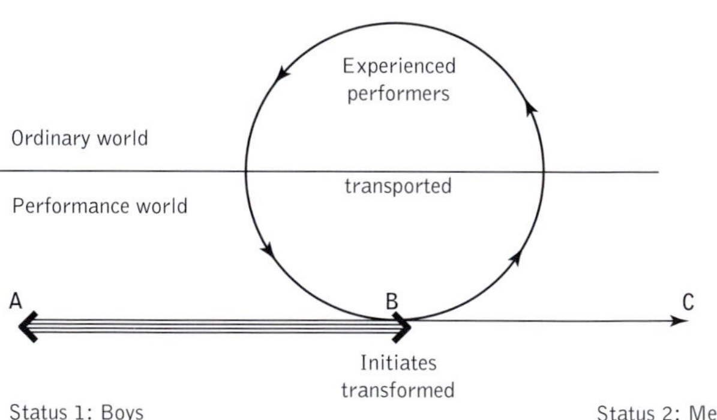

fig 3.12. The transportation-transformation system works like a printing press. At point B – where the "press" meets the "paper" – permanent impressions are imprinted by the transporters on the transformed. In Asemo's case, the already initiated men, all experienced performers, temporarily leave their ordinary lives and enter a performance world where they lead the boys through their initiation. During the initiation period, Asemo and his cohorts move from point A to point B again and again. Each ordeal or instruction makes a permanent impression on them. Finally, at the conclusion of the initiation period they enter the village dancing – for the first time as men, C. Drawing by Richard Schechner.

Social drama

One of Turner's most fruitful yet problematic ideas was his theory of social drama (**see Turner box 3**). Every social drama develops in four phases, one following the other: Breach—Crisis—Redressive Action—Reintegration or Schism.

A breach is when a particular event breaks open an incipient situation that when activated threatens the stability of a social unit – family, corporation, community, nation, etc. A crisis is a widening of the breach into increasingly open or public displays. There may be several successive crises, each more public and threatening than the last. Redressive action is what is done to deal with the crisis, to resolve or heal the breach. Often enough, at this phase of a social drama, every crisis is answered by a redressive action which fails, evoking new, even more explosive crises. Reintegration is the resolution of the original breach in such a way that the social fabric is knit back together. Or a schism occurs.

Take, for example, the great social drama of sixteenth-century Europe called the Protestant Reformation. The conflict in this social drama was between the established Church of Rome and rebels such as **Martin Luther** and **John Calvin**. The decisive breach – that which let loose the great crisis in Christendom of the Reformation – was Luther nailing his **"95 Theses"** to the door of Wittenberg's Castle Church on 31 October 1517. Each attempt by Rome to redress, appease, or suppress the Protestants failed. Year by year, the Protestants grew stronger. Crisis by crisis, the breach widened, generating a schism yet to be healed. Other examples of social dramas are the ongoing conflicts in Northern Ireland or between the Palestinians and the Israelis. Social dramas can be extremely long-lived, bitter, and intractable. On the other hand, some social dramas are resolved relatively swiftly, at least on the surface. The long-festering conflict in the USA over slavery led to the secession of eleven southern states and the Civil War (1861–65). The war resolved the crisis in favor of the Union who enforced reintegration by arms. The underlying situation was the inability of slave states and free states to agree on the future of slavery and therefore on the future of the Union. The crisis erupted when the Confederates attacked Fort Sumter, South Carolina, in April 1861. The Civil War that followed was one portion of the redressive action. The surrender of the Confederate army at Appomattox, Virginia in 1865 signaled the start of reintegration. However, the end of the war did not settle the matter. Questions of equality, civil liberties, racism, and economic justice brought to the fore in the Civil War era are still in the process of being resolved. The redressive action and reintegration phases are still going on, as evidenced by affirmative action, civil rights legislation, and litigation.

Victor Turner

Social dramas

Social dramas are units of aharmonic process, arising in conflict situations. Typically, they have four main phases of public action. [. . .] These are: 1. Breach of regular, norm-governed social relations. [. . .] 2. Crisis during which [. . .] there is a tendency for the breach to widen. [. . .] Each public crisis has [. . .] liminal characteristics, since it is a threshold between more or less stable phases of the social process, but it is not a sacred limen, hedged around by taboos and thrust away from the centers of public life. On the contrary, it takes up its menacing stance in the forum itself and, as it were, dares the representatives of order to grapple with it. [. . .] 3. Redressive action [ranging] from personal advice and informal mediation or arbitration to formal judicial and legal machinery, and, to resolve certain kinds of crisis or legitimate other modes of resolution, to the performance of public ritual. [. . .] Redress, too, has its liminal features, its being "betwixt and between," and, as such, furnishes a distanced replication and critique of the events leading up to and composing the "crisis." This replication may be in the rational idiom of a judicial process, or in the metaphorical and symbolic idiom of a ritual process. [. . .] 4. The final phase [. . .] consists either of the reintegration of the disturbed social group or of the social recognition and legitimization of an inseparable schism between contesting parties.

1974, *Dramas, Fields, and Metaphors*, 37–41

Martin Luther (1483–1546) and **John Calvin (1509–64):** the two most important leaders of the Protestant Reformation. Luther, a German, challenged the authority of the pope and the corruption of the Roman Catholic Church. Calvin, a Frenchman, put forward his ideas on reform in *The Institutes of the Christian Religion* (1536). Luther's famous **"95 Theses"** of 1517 protested the selling of indulgences: "when the penny jingles into the money-box, gain and avarice can be increased" (Thesis 28); and "The assurance of salvation by letters of pardon is vain, even though the commissary, nay, even though the pope himself, were to stake his soul upon it" (Thesis 52).

These brief applications of Turner's theory expose its weaknesses. The theory reduces and flattens out events. The precise details, the ups and downs, the nuances and differences that make cultural analysis interesting and enlightening are pressed into sameness. Any conflict can be analyzed "as" social drama – but what new insights does such an analysis yield? The one advantage to the theory is that it is helpful in distilling very complicated circumstances into manageable units. As a teaching device, the social drama theory has its good points. One can select a starting point and a finishing point, framing a set of social or historical events so that a cluster of occurrences that may at first appear inchoate become manageable "as" drama. It makes closure appear inevitable. Such framing is always arbitrary.

What Turner's theory does is twist worlds of difference into the shape of a Western aesthetic genre, the drama. The progression from breach and crisis through redressive action to reintegration/schism is the underlying scheme of the Greek tragedies, the Elizabethan theatre, and modern realist drama. It is what Aristotle meant when he wrote "plot is the soul of tragedy" and "every tragedy has a beginning, middle, and end." This is the theatre Turner was most familiar with. However, this diachronic structure is not so apparent in the theatre of the absurd or other counter-dramatic, non-narrative pieces, such as **Samuel Beckett**'s *Waiting for Godot* or even Brecht's *Mother Courage and her Children* with its episodic plot, each scene comprising a small drama in itself. It doesn't apply at all to many Happenings or performance art. Nor is it present in the extended, episodic works of many non-Western cultures. Peter Brook was roundly criticized in the 1980s for turning the *Mahabharata* into a Western-style drama. Similarly, Turner can be taken to task for turning all the world's conflicts into Western-style dramas. Perhaps today's world of terrorism, guerrilla warfare, prolonged civil wars, and economic espionage are better modeled by performance art or the seemingly endless episodes of the *Mahabharata*. It may be that life mirrors art as much as the other way round – and that social theorists need to choose very carefully what aesthetic genres they use as models.

Samuel Beckett (1906–89): Irish-born playwright and novelist who spent most of his adult life residing in France. His works for the stage include *Waiting for Godot* (1953), *Endgame* (1957), and *Happy Days* (1961). Beckett won the Nobel Prize for Literature in 1969.

Turner integrated his social drama theory into his theory of ritual process (**see figure 3.13**). During the redressive action phase of a social drama, people turn to: political process (from legislation to war), the legal process (from arbitration to formal trials), and the ritual process. The ritual process employs a wide range of devices – divination, sacrifice, and, in Turner's words, the "ludic deconstruction and recombination of familiar cultural configurations." In other words, art. But exactly how art helps resolve social conflict Turner does not make clear.

What is more useful than the social drama model is noting the very fluid relationship between aesthetic processes and social processes, including aesthetic and social dramas. This relationship can be depicted as a horizontal numeral 8 or infinity symbol (**see figure 3.14**). This model depicts an ongoing and never-ending process whereby social dramas affect aesthetic dramas and vice versa. That is to say, the visible actions of any given social drama are informed, shaped, and guided by aesthetic principles and performance/rhetorical devices. Reciprocally, a culture's visible aesthetic practices are informed, shaped, and guided by the processes of social interaction (**see Turner box 4**). The politician, activist, lawyer, or terrorist all use techniques of performance – staging, ways of addressing various audiences, setting, etc. – to present, demonstrate, protest, or support specific social actions – actions designed to maintain, modify, or overturn the existing social order. Reciprocally, artists draw on actions performed in social life, "real events," not only as materials to be enacted but as themes, rhythms, and models of behavior and representation. As figure 3.14 indicates with its arrows, there is a positive feedback flow between social and aesthetic drama. This model demands that each social drama, each aesthetic drama (or other kind of performance), be understood in its specific cultural and historical circumstances. The word "drama" is used not to assert Western hegemony, but as a cipher representing any kind of specific cultural enactment. Another way of putting this relationship is to say that every performance – aesthetic or social – is both efficacious and entertaining. That is, each event proposes something to get done and each event gives pleasure to those who participate in it or observe it. Let me give a concrete example of what I mean.

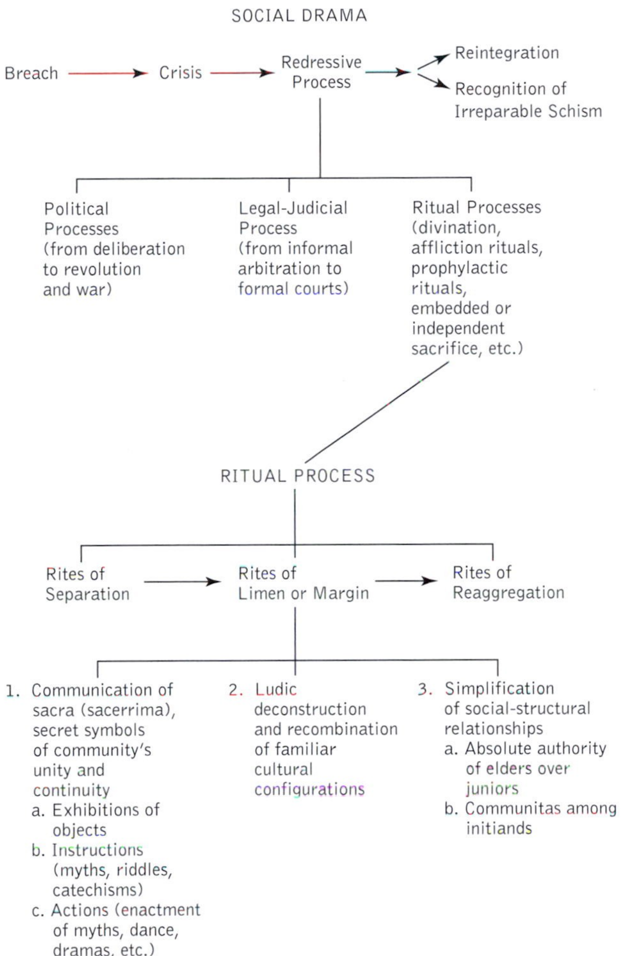

fig 3.13. Victor Turner's diagram of the relationship between social drama and the ritual process. Figure from *On the Edge of the Bush: Anthropology as Experience*, by Victor Turner. Copyright The Arizona Board of Regents. Reprinted by permission of the University of Arizona Press.

Victor Turner

Social drama/aesthetic drama

Notice that the manifest social drama feeds into the latent realm of stage drama; its characteristic form in a given culture, at a given time and place, unconsciously, or perhaps preconsciously, influences not only the form but also the content of the stage drama of which it is the active or "magic" mirror. The stage drama, when it is meant to do more than entertain – though entertainment is always one of its vital aims – is a metacommentary, explicit or implicit, witting or unwitting, on the major social dramas of its social context (wars, revolutions, scandals, institutional changes). Not only that, but its message and its rhetoric feed back into the latent processual structure of the social drama and partly accounts for its ready ritualization. Life itself now becomes a mirror held up to art, and the living now perform their lives, for the protagonists of a social drama, a "drama of living," have been equipped by aesthetic drama with some of their most salient opinions, imageries, tropes, and ideological perspectives. Neither mutual mirroring, life by art, art by life, is exact, for each is not a planar mirror but a matricial mirror; at each exchange something new is added and something old is lost or discarded. Human beings learn through experience, though all too often they repress painful experiences, and perhaps the deepest experience is through drama not through social drama or stage drama (or its equivalent) alone but in the circulatory or oscillatory process of their mutual and incessant modification.

1985, *On the Edge of the Bush*, 300–301

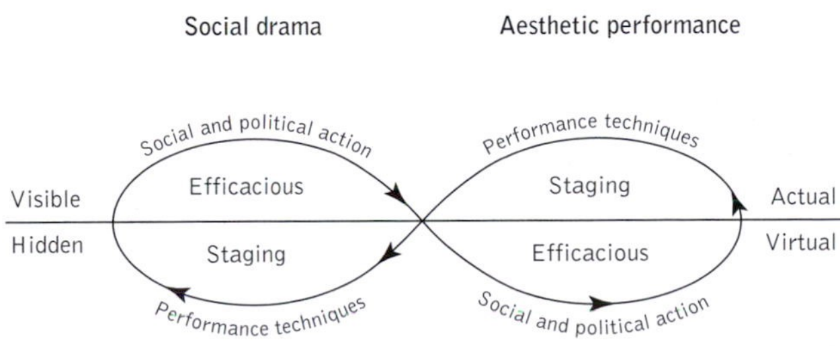

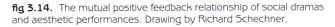

fig 3.14. The mutual positive feedback relationship of social dramas and aesthetic performances. Drawing by Richard Schechner.

The pig-kill dancing at Kurumugl

In March 1972 at the "Council Grounds" in the vicinity of Kurumugl, a village in the Papua New Guinea highlands, I observed a two-day pig-kill celebration. The performance I saw was in danger of tipping over into actual combat. The dances and songs were adapted from combat movements and war chants. The armed dancers dressed partly for battle and partly for dancing (**see figure 3.15**). The first day consisted

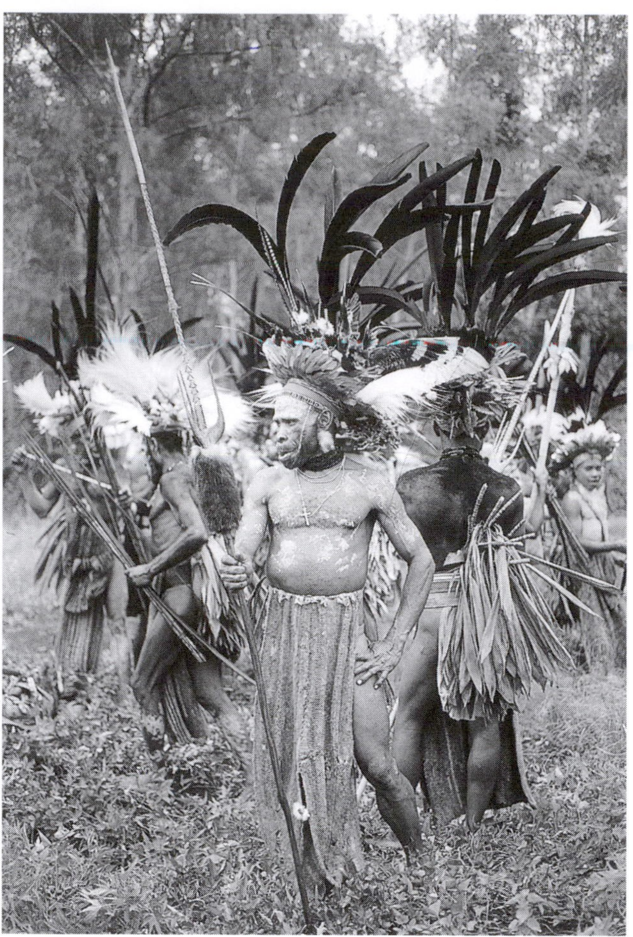

fig 3.15. Men dressed for dancing at Kurumugl, Papua New Guinea Highlands, 1972. Photograph by Richard Schechner.

of setting up house in long rectangular huts and digging cooking pits. The second day began with the slaughter of about 200 pigs. As each owner killed his animal he melodically orated a speech saying how hard it was to raise the pig, who it was promised to, what a fine animal it was, etc. These recitatives were applauded with laughs and roars, as they often were full of jokes and obscene invective. Then the pigs were gutted, butchered in halves, and lowered into the pits to roast over hot rocks. The guts were hung in nets over the ovens and steamed. Bladders were blown into balloons for children to play with. A festive scene.

As the cooking started, the men retired to their huts to get ready. I went inside with one who set up a mirror and applied blue, red, and black pigment to his arms, face, and torso. He painted half his nose red, the other half blue. I asked him what the patterns meant. He said he chose them because he liked the way they looked. When he was done he emerged, his casual air evaporating as he literally thrust his chest forward and up, gave a long whooping call, put on his four-foot long peacock and cassowary feather headdress, and displayed himself.

He was costumed not for a fictional role in a play, but for a life role – displaying his strength, his power, his wealth, and his position in the group. He joined his comrades, whose costumes were like his, amalgams of traditional–local and new–imported: bones and sunglasses, cigarette holders and homemade pipes, khaki shorts under grass skirts. But despite what a purist might call intrusions, a traditional ritual of "payback" was being enacted. The pig-kill at Kurumugl was very like the *kaiko* that anthropologist **Roy A. Rappaport** witnessed in 1963 – a traditional performance enacted regularly at least since the beginning of the twentieth century. As at the kaiko, the dances at Kurumugl were adapted from military moves (**see Rappaport box**).

Roy A. Rappaport (1926–97): American anthropologist who analyzed the ritual performances of the Tsembaga of Papua New Guinea. He also developed a general theory of ritual. His books include *Pigs for the Ancestors* (1968), *Ecology, Meaning, and Religion* (1979), and *Ritual and Religion in the Making of Humanity* (1999).

Roy A. Rappaport

From fighting to dancing

The visitors approach the [village] gate silently, led by men carrying fight packages [full of materials to give a warrior courage and improve his chances of killing an enemy], swinging their axes as they run back and forth in front of their procession in the peculiar crouched fighting prance. Just before they reach the gate they are met by one or two of those locals who have invited them and who now escort them over the gate. Visiting women and children follow behind the dancers and join the other spectators on the sidelines. There is much embracing as the local women and children greet visiting kinfolk. The dancing procession charges to the center of the dance ground shouting the long, low battle cry and stamping their feet, magically treated before their arrival [. . .] to enable them to dance strongly. After they charge back and forth across the dance ground several times, repeating the stamping in several locations while the crowd cheers in admiration of their numbers, their style, and the richness of their finery, they begin to sing.

1968, *Pigs for the Ancestors*, 187

The visitors approaching the Council Grounds came not as friends to a party but as invaders seizing what they were owed. As the invaders – armed with fighting spears – danced their assault on the Council Grounds, they were repelled by armed campers – men plus about twenty fully armed women dancing their defense of the meat. The invaders launched vigorous assaults dozens of times. A valuable peanut field was trampled to muck. Each assault was met by a determined counter-attack. But foot by foot, the invaders penetrated to the heart of the Council Grounds, to the pile of meat and the altar of jawbones and flowers at its center. Once the invaders reached the meat they merged with their "enemies" forming one whooping, chanting, dancing doughnut of warriors. They danced around the meat for nearly an hour.

I was pinned against a tree, between warriors and meat. Then suddenly the dancing stopped. Orators plunged into the meat, pulling out a leg or a flank, shouting-singing things like (in pidgin English), "This pig I give you in payment for the pig you gave my father three years ago! Your pig was scrawny, no fat on it at all! But my pig is enormous, with tons of fat, and lots of good meat – see! see! – much better than what you gave my father! My brothers and I will remember that we are giving you today better than what you gave us. If we call you to help us in a fight, you must come! You owe us bigtime!"

Sometimes the speechifying rose to song. Insults were hurled back and forth. The fun in orating, and the joking, teetered on the edge. Participants did not forget that not so long ago they were blood enemies. After more than an hour of orating, the meat was distributed. Hoisted onto sleds, the booty was carried shoulder-high as whole families, with much singing, departed with their share. This meat found its way by means of the network of ritual obligations to places far from Kurumugl and to many who were not present that day at the Council Grounds.

Instead of a secret raiding party there were dancers; instead of taking human victims, they took meat. Instead of entering enemy territory on the sly as would occur in war, the whole performance took place on the Council Grounds, a no man's land. And instead of doubt about the outcome, everyone knew what was going to happen. A ritualized social drama – as war in the highlands had been – had been transformed into something approaching an aesthetic drama.

What are the differences between social and aesthetic dramas? Aesthetic dramas create symbolic times, spaces, and characters; the outcome of the story is predetermined by the drama. Aesthetic dramas are fictions. Social dramas have more variables, their outcomes are in doubt, and they are like games. Social dramas are "real," they happen "here and now." But aspects of social dramas, as with aesthetic dramas, are pre-arranged, foreknown, and rehearsed. The celebration at Kurumugl was somewhere between a social and an aesthetic drama.

Figure 3.16 diagrams what happens at a successful pig-kill celebration. The transformations "above the line" convert dangerous encounters into mostly benign aesthetic and economic performances. Those "below the line" show how the situation existing between groups is changed by the ritual. The pig-kill and dancing at the Council Grounds managed a complicated and potentially dangerous exchange of goods and obligations with a minimum of danger and a maximum of pleasure. This success was due to performing. Performing was the way the participants achieved "real results." The dancing, orating, and giving out meat did not mark or "represent" the results, but created the results they celebrated. Those at the Council Grounds performed in two senses: they put on a show, and they got something done.

As "above-line right-side" activities in figure 3.16 grow in importance, the entertainment value of the event increases relative to its efficacy value. Maybe the first times groups gathered at the Council Grounds, they danced so that they might exchange pigs to fulfill social obligations. But over time, they came to the grounds and exchanged pigs so that they could dance. Or at least the motives for the gathering blurred. It was not only that creditors and debtors changed positions, but also that people wanted to show off, dance, and have a good time. It was not only to "perform results" that the dances were staged, but because people enjoyed the sing-sing (festive celebration) for its own sake.

war parties human victims battledress combat	. . .	transformed into	. . .	dancing groups pig meat costumes dancing
two groups debtors creditors	. . .	become	. . .	one group creditors debtors

fig 3.16. At a successful pig-kill celebration a set of transformations is effected. Those transformations "above the line" change potentially lethal encounters into aesthetic and economic performances. Those "below the line" depict the changes wrought by the ritual performance.

The efficacy–entertainment dyad

Efficacy and entertainment are not binary opposites. Rather, they are the poles of a continuum (**see figure 3.17**). The basic polarity is between efficacy and entertainment, not ritual and theatre. Whether one calls a specific performance "ritual" or

EFFICACY/RITUAL ←→	ENTERTAINMENT/PERFORMING ARTS
Results	For fun
Link to transcendent Other(s)	Focus on the here and now
Timeless time – the eternal present	Historical time and/or now
Performer possessed, in trance	Performer self-aware, in control
Virtuosity downplayed	Virtuosity highly valued
Traditional scripts/behaviors	New and traditional scripts/behaviors
Transformation of self possible	Transformation of self unlikely
Audience participates	Audience observers
Audience believes	Audience appreciates, evaluates
Criticism discouraged	Criticism flourishes
Collective creativity	Individual creativity

fig 3.17. The efficacy/ritual-entertainment/aesthetic performance dyad. Although typeset as a binary, the figure ought to be read as a continuum. There are many degrees leading back forth from "results" to "fun," from "collective creativity" to "individual creativity," and so on.

"theatre" depends mostly on context and function. A performance is called one or the other because of where it is performed, by whom, in what circumstances, and for what purpose. The purpose is the most important factor determining whether a performance is ritual or not. If the performance's purpose is to effect change, then the other qualities under the heading "efficacy" in figure 3.17 will also be present, and the performance is a ritual. But if the performance's purpose is mostly to give pleasure, to show off, to be beautiful, or to pass the time, then the performance is an entertainment. The fact is that no performance is pure efficacy or pure entertainment.

Origins of performance: If not ritual, then what?

Performance doesn't originate in ritual any more than it originates in one of the aesthetic genres. Performance originates in the creative tensions of the binary efficacy–entertainment. Think of this figure not as a flat binary, but as a braid or helix, tightening and loosening over time and in specific cultural contexts. Efficacy and entertainment are not opposites, but "dancing partners," each depending on and in continuous active relationship to the other.

No "first performance" will ever be identified either specifically or in terms of genre. That has not stopped Western scholars since the end of the nineteenth century trying to prove that the performing arts originated in ritual. The first scholars to propose such an origin were influenced by several factors. Early European and American anthropologists derived their theories from the observations of colonists, missionaries, and adventurers who wrote reports about so-called "primitive peoples" in Africa, Native America, Australia, and elsewhere performing rituals using dance, music, and theatre. In one of the distortions of social Darwinism, "primitive peoples" were thought to be still "living in the stone age," their practices evidence of how all peoples once lived. If these "primitives" performed rituals but had not yet "reached the level" of the aesthetic performing arts in the West, then this indicated that the arts originated in/as ritual. Second, a particular group of scholars centered at Cambridge University – **Jane Ellen Harrison, Gilbert Murray**, and **Francis Cornford** – believed they found in ancient Greek tragedy evidence of a "primal ritual" or *sacer ludus* (sacred game) re-enacting the sacrifice–rebirth of a god (**see Murray box**). Third, medievalists traced the origins of Renaissance theatre to church ritual.

Jane Ellen Harrison (1850–1928), Gilbert Murray (1866–1957), and **Francis Cornford (1874–1943):** British classicists based at Cambridge and Oxford Universities in the early part of the twentieth century who proposed several influential theories on the relationship of ritual to theatre. Their works included Harrison's *Themis: A Study of the Social Origins of Greek Religion* (1912), Cornford's *The Origins of Attic Comedy* (1914), and Murray's *Five Stages of Greek Religion* (1925).

Gilbert Murray

The ritual origins of Greek tragedy

The following note presupposes certain general views about the origin and essential nature of Greek Tragedy. It assumes that tragedy is in origin a Ritual Dance, a Sacer Ludus [. . .] Further, it assumes in accord with the overwhelming weight of ancient tradition, that the dance in question is originally or centrally that of

Dionysus, performed at his feast, in his theatre. [. . .] It regards Dionysus in this connection as an "Eniautos-Daimon," or vegetation God, like Adonis, Osiris, etc., who represents the cyclic death and rebirth of the earth and the world, i.e., for practical purposes, of the tribe's own lands of the tribe itself. It seems clear, further, the Comedy and Tragedy represent different stages in the life of this Year Spirit.

1912, "Excursus on the Ritual Forms Preserved in Greek Tragedy," 341

But each of these arguments is spurious. There is no such thing as "primitive" peoples. Social Darwinism mistakenly assumes a hierarchy of cultures. Difference does not prove superiority. The "primal ritual" of the Cambridge Anthropologists (as Harrison, Cornford, and Murray were called) is provable only if one uses circular reasoning. The primal ritual exists because of remnants of it in Greek tragedy; Greek tragedy contains remnants of a primal ritual; therefore there must be such a ritual. As for the origins of modern European theatre in the Mass or other church celebrations such as the cycle plays of the fourteenth to sixteenth centuries, doubtlessly these great civic and religious events influenced what was to become Renaissance theatre. But it is also true that the medieval period enjoyed many popular entertainments as well as a variety of "private" or indoor theatricals, dances, and musical performances. All of these impacted the Renaissance performing arts. The medieval epoch was full of performing arts, both within, nearby, and separate from the Church.

The fact is that at any given point in time, in every part of the world and in every culture, people were and are making dances, music, and theatre. They are using performances for a variety of purposes, including entertainment, ritual, community-building, and socializing. These functions can be summarized as the dynamic tension between efficacy and entertainment. The desire to imagine a "first performance" tells us more about what scholars of a certain culture desire than about what may have actually happened.

Theoretically, the "first performance" is a situation, not an event or a genre. Performance originates in the need to make things happen and to entertain; to get results and to fool around; to show the way things are and to pass the time; to be transformed into another and to enjoy being oneself; to disappear and to show off; to embody a transcendent other and to be "just me" here and now; to be in trance and to be in control; to focus on one's own group and to broadcast to the largest possible audience; to play in order to satisfy a deep personal, social, or religious need; and to play only under contract for cash. The shift from ritual to aesthetic performance occurs when a participating community fragments into occasional, paying customers. The move from aesthetic performance to ritual happens when an audience of individuals is transformed into a community. The tendencies to move in both these directions are present in all performances.

Changing rituals or inventing new ones

Rituals provide stability. They also help people accomplish change in their lives, transforming them from one status or identity to another. But what about rituals themselves? They give the impression of permanence, of "always having been." That is their publicly performed face. But only a little investigation shows that as social circumstances change, rituals also change (**see Drewal box**). Sometimes the change is accomplished informally as ritual practitioners – shamans, Hindu priests, tribal elders – adjust their performances to suit new circumstances. Introducing newer technology sometimes subtly and sometimes more obviously changes the ritual. Electric lighting, microphones, and more recently the use of the internet have all resulted in changes in the performance of rituals. In other circumstances, official changes are introduced to bring rituals into line with new social realities. Thus Vatican II, meeting in Rome from 1962 to 1965 with the stated purpose of bringing the Church more into harmony with the modern world, actually deeply changed Roman Catholic rituals. The liturgy was reformed in order to bring ordinary people closer to the service. Latin was replaced by the vernacular as the language of the Mass. Non-priests were given more of a chance to participate in services. On the other hand, many ingrained practices of the Church were retained, including priestly celibacy (in theory at least).

But rituals may also be invented – both by official culture and by individuals. In fact, one sleight of hand of official culture is to make relatively new rituals and the traditions they embody appear old and stable. Such an appearance helps support official culture's claim to tradition and to assert that the status quo provides social stability. It is no accident that dictatorships thrive on state ceremony, much of it concocted to suit the needs of a particular regime. To a large degree, the

Margaret Thompson Drewal

Revising rituals

Practitioners of Yoruba religion are aware that when ritual becomes static, when it ceases to adjust and adapt, it becomes obsolete, empty of meaning, and eventually dies out. They often express the need to modify rituals to address current social conditions. Sometimes change is the result of long deliberations, oftentimes it is more spontaneous. Many revisions are not particularly obvious, unless the observer is thoroughly familiar with the ritual process by having followed a number of its performances, much in the same way a critic follows the productions of a dance or theatre piece.

1992, *Yoruba Ritual*, 8

emergence of the idea of a "nation" from the eighteenth century onward was buttressed by new rituals enacting national consciousness. Designating and singing a "national anthem," "saluting the flag," and even the pomp surrounding the British monarchy are not anywhere near as old or set as they appear to be (**see Hobsbawm box**). Schools are hotbeds of invented rituals pertaining to sororities and fraternities, "school spirit," and the awarding of degrees at graduation. A set order of behavior and annual repetition rather quickly ritualizes behavior such as hazings and initiations, academic processions, and cheers at sports matches (**see figure 3.18**). The fact that the student population turns over every few years helps establish new rituals swiftly. In real life a generation takes 20 or 30 years to turn over; at college it is four years.

fig 3.18. An academic procession at New York University in the 1990s. These kinds of processions are secular ritual celebrations. The music, pace of marching, kinds of robes, insignia, and hats worn by the participants indicate the school, degree, and other particulars fixed by the tradition. Photo courtesy New York University.

Eric Hobsbawm

Inventing traditions

Nothing appears more ancient, and linked into an immemorial past, than the pageantry which surrounds British monarchy in its public ceremonial manifestations. Yet [. . .] in its modern form it is the product of the late 19th and 20th centuries. [. . .] "Invented tradition" is taken to mean a set of practices, normally governed by overtly or tacitly accepted rules and of a ritual or symbolic nature, which seek to inculcate certain values and norms of behavior by repetition, which automatically implies continuity with the past. In fact, where possible, they normally attempt to establish continuity with a suitable historic past. A striking example is the deliberate choice of the Gothic style for the 19th-century rebuilding of the British Parliament and the equally deliberate decision after World War II to rebuild the parliamentary chamber on exactly the same basic plan as before. [. . .]

To establish the clustering of "invented traditions" in western countries between 1870 and 1914 is relatively easy. [These include] Bastille Day and the Daughters of the American Revolution, May Day, [. . .] the Olympic Games, the Cup Final, and the Tour de France as popular rites, and the institution of flag worship in the U.S.A. [. . .] Moreover, the construction of formal ritual spaces, already consciously allowed for in German nationalism, appears to have been systematically undertaken even in countries which had hitherto paid little attention to it. [. . .] New constructions for spectacle and de facto mass ritual such as sports stadia, outdoor and indoor, [. . .] and the use of such buildings as the Sportspalast in Berlin or the Vélodrome d'Hiver in Paris [. . .] anticipate the development of formal spaces for public mass ritual (Red Square from 1918 [in Moscow, Tiananmen Square from 1949 in Beijing]).

1983, *The Invention of Tradition*, 1–2, 303, 305

Individual artists, especially since the 1960s, have taken to inventing rituals. Anna Halprin calls some of her performances "rituals," as do many other artists (**see figure 3.19 and Halprin box**). The impulse behind these claims is an attempt to overcome a sense of individual and social fragmentation by means of art. This need is exacerbated by the fact that certain groups feel excluded by organized religion. Gay Roman Catholics, for example, are not able to worship openly as gay people in the Church; similarly Islam, Orthodox Judaism, and many fundamentalist Protestant churches are homophobic. Many heterosexuals also feel excluded for various reasons. But these exclusions do not diminish people's love of and need for ritual. The need to build community is fostered by ritual. And if official rituals either do not satisfy or are egregiously exclusive, new rituals will be invented, or older rituals adapted, to meet felt needs.

Using rituals in theatre, dance, and music

Not only have rituals been invented wholesale, but older rituals have long provided grist for the artistic mill or have been used as a kind of popular entertainment. There is a long history of importing "authentic rituals" and showing them at colonial expositions, world's fairs, and amusement parks. Some of these presentations have had significant impact on Western theatre and dance – even when they were spurious. At the turn of the twentieth century, modern dance pioneer **Ruth St. Denis** saw "Indian dancing" at Coney Island's "Hindu Village." The Village was installed at the famous amusement park because of the great success of Little Egypt's "nautch dance" at the 1893 Chicago Exposition. What St. Denis saw was vaguely connected to Indian *sadir nac*, itself related to ritual temple dancing – later reconstructed in India as *bharatanatyam*. Whatever St. Denis saw in the Hindu Village propelled her toward leading a revolution in modern dance. St. Denis and her partner **Ted Shawn** counted as their students and company members **Martha Graham** and **Doris Humphrey**, both major modern dancers–choreographers who themselves had many influential students. Similarly, what French performance theorist **Antonin Artaud** made of the Balinese ritual dancers he saw in Paris's 1931 Colonial Exposition changed the history of modern Western theatre (**see figure 3.20**).

fig 3.19. Dancer and ritual-maker Anna Halprin takes a vehement step leading a line of performers during a workshop, 1990s. Photograph by Jay Grayam. Photograph courtesy of Anna Halprin.

Anna Halprin

The transforming power of dance

In these large group dances I noticed an exceptional phenomenon occurring, time and time again. When enough people moved together in a common pulse with a common purpose, an amazing force, an ecstatic rhythm, took over. People began to move as if they were parts of a single body, not in uniform motion but in deeply interrelated ways. This recurrence of spatial and interrelated movement is no accident. It is an external version of the geometry and biology of our inner life – our bodies extended in space. People form circles. They make processions. Spirals. Entrances and exits. They orient themselves in space by using the four directions. They create a central axis. [. . .] In these archetypal movements people seemed to be tracing out the forms and patterns of a larger organism, communicating with and being moved by a group body-mind or spirit. [. . .] Had I discovered something new? Of course not! This large-scale group movement is an ancient phenomenon in dance. [. . .] What was exciting was that we were learning how to generate this same tribal spirit and energy, this same sense of group ritual with people whose culture contains little of such tradition in dance performances. We were learning how to return to performers and spectators power which in this culture had often been taken from them and placed in the hands of scientific experts and official artists. [. . .] More and more, in both workshops and public rituals, I encouraged people to work with their own lives as material, to use real-life issues so that the transforming power of dance would have the opportunity to effect real-life changes for them.

1995, *Moving Toward Life*, 228–29

Ruth St. Denis: (1879–1968): American dancer and choreographer who along with **Ted Shawn (1891–1972)** founded the Denishawn Dance Company in 1915. Among Denishawn's students and dancers were Martha Graham, Doris Humphrey, Charles Weidman, and Louis Horst. St Denis specialized in "oriental" dances, including the Indian *Radha* (1906), the Japanese *O-Mika* (1913), and the Chinese *Kuan Yin* (1916).

Martha Graham (1894–1991): American modern dancer and choreographer. Graham choreographed more than 170 group and solo productions including *Primitive Mysteries* (1931), *Appalachian Spring* (1944), and *Seraphic Dialogue* (1955).

Doris Humphrey (1895–1958): American dancer and choreographer. Humphrey's major works include *Life of the Bee* (1929), *The Shakers* (1930), and *Song of the West* (1940–42).

Antonin Artaud (1896–1948): French actor, director, theorist, and poet. Author of *The Theatre and its Double* (1938; Eng. 1958).

Sufi Mevlevi dancers – "whirling dervishes" – have appeared many times on concert stages. When I saw them perform in 1972 at the Brooklyn Academy of Music, spectators were admonished in writing, "The program is a religious ceremony. You are kindly requested to refrain from applause." The BAM audience was reminded that what they had paid money to see as entertainment retained enough of its ritual aura to require a change in conventional theatre response. Or, perhaps slyly, the spectators were being told that they were getting their money's worth of something "authentic." But it's not only in the West that such reframing occurs. I have seen Bengali and other Indian folk-ritual put on stage before "high-art" audiences in Calcutta, New Delhi, and Mumbai. Similarly, in China, Mexico, and Cuba I have witnessed rituals reframed as aesthetic performances. This kind of reframing is taking place all around the world. That is because "First World" and "Third World" people exist cheek-by-jowl in many countries. Tourist shows draw on locals as well as foreigners for audiences. The distinction is no longer mostly "East/West" or "North/South" but increasingly "center/margin," "metropolis/outlying areas," and "tourist/local."

The reshaping of ritual materials into new "original works" is also widespread. **Jerzy Grotowski** synthesized rituals from several cultures to make his final performance, fig 3.20.

Several of the Balinese dancers Artaud saw at the Colonial Exposition of 1931 in Paris. The structure appears to be a Balinese temple, but it actually is the replica of one constructed for the Exposition. Photograph courtesy of Nicola Savarese.

PARTICIPATION NÉERLANDAISE A L'EXPOSITION COLONIALE INTERNATIONALE DE PARIS

PROGRAMME

DE LA MUSIQUE ET DES DANSES

EXÉCUTÉES

PAR UN GROUPE DE DANSEURS ET DANSEUSES DE L'ILE DE BALI

SOUS LA DIRECTION DU

TJOKORDE GDE RAKE SOEKAWATI

Instruments et joueurs de gong.

AU PENDOPO (THÉATRE) DU PAVILLON DE LA HOLLANDE

coquemer

The program of the performance Artaud saw. The picture is of a Balinese gamelan orchestra with the caption, "Instruments and players of the gong." The rest of the text reads, "Participation of the Netherlands in the International Colonial Exposition of Paris. Program of music and dances performed by a group of men and women dancers from the island of Bali under the direction of Tjokorde Gde Rake Soekawati. At the Pendopo (theatre) of the Holland Pavilion." Program courtesy of Nicola Savarese.

Action (**see Osinski box**). Versions of *Action* are still being performed by Grotowski's designated artistic heir, **Thomas Richards**. **Philip Glass**'s *Symphony No. 5* fuses Australian Aboriginal and African music with Glass's own distinct style. The sung texts come from more than 20 different cultures and epochs, ranging over 3,000 years, from the Rig Veda, the Bible, and the Qur'an to Hawaiian, Zuni, and Mayan myths, Persian poetry, Chinese philosophy, and the Tibetan *Book of the Dead*. Glass's self-stated ambition was to create a "spiritual human history" from Creation to the future, a millennial version equal to one of the great Masses of Bach or Mozart. But, distinct from these earlier artists, Glass wanted to compose music that was not "localized" in the Christian tradition. This desire for cultural transcendence – or is it hybrid synthesis? – is a powerful, if problematic, outgrowth of globalization and cosmopolitanism. Using rituals to make new aesthetic performances is not a practice of European and Euro-American artists only. African-American choreographer **Ralph Lemon**, Indian theatre director **Ratan Thiyam**, and Taiwanese choreographer **Lin Hwai-Min** are three among many artists importing and/or reshaping rituals in their productions (**see figure 3.21**). I will examine globalization, hybridity, and intercultural performance in Chapter 8.

Jerzy Grotowski (1933–99): Polish theatre director, performer trainer, and theorist. Founding director of the Polish Laboratory Theatre (1959–84), with which he explored environmental theatre staging, scenic and textual montage, and connections between ritual and theatre. After 1965, Grotowski investigated the links between ancient and modern rituals and the interior life of what he called the "doer," the performer. His theatre works include Stanislaw Wyspianski's *Akropolis* (1962), Christopher Marlowe's *Doctor Faustus* (1963), Calderón de la Barca's *The Constant Prince* (1965) and a work based on the New Testament, *Apocalypsis cum Figurus* (1969). Grotowski is the author of *Towards a Poor Theatre* (1968) and author/subject of *The Grotowski Sourcebook* (1997), edited by Lisa Wolford and Richard Schechner.

Thomas Richards (1962–): American actor whom Grotowski designated his "artistic heir." At present, Richards heads the Grotowski Workcenter in Pontedera, Italy, where he works closely with Mario Biagini. The artistic output of the Workcenter includes: *One Breath Left* (1998), *Dies Iræ: My Preposterous Theatrum Interioris Show* (2005), and the *Tracing Roads Across* project (2003–06). Richards is the author of *At Work with Grotowski on Physical Actions* (1995).

Zbigniew Osinski

Creating a ritual by means of theatre

Every day the ritual [of action or actions] is evoked anew. Always the same and yet each time not just the same. This ritual is [. . .] not just a theatre creation, or an imitation or reconstruction of any of the familiar rituals. [. . .] Nor is it a synthesis of rituals which, in Grotowski's opinion, would be impossible in practice. [. . .] Grotowski's work [. . .] has elements related concomitantly to several traditions which are archetypal. These elements are set into a composition [. . .]. Grotowski defines the technical difference between a theatre production and a ritual in relation to "the place of montage." In the production, the spectators' minds are the place of montage. In the ritual, the montage takes place in the minds of the doers. The connection with old initiation practices is very subtle, and the basic duty of each doer is to do everything well. This should be understood in a tangible, almost physical sense. The body must respond properly and precisely, and must not pump up emotions and expression. Therefore, Grotowski would not ask anyone, "Do you believe?" but "You must do well what you do, with understanding."

[. . .] The Action is evoked and accomplished each day in its totality. Sometimes it is executed every few days if the technical work on details or the search for some elements from scratch takes up too much time. The theatre functions in relation to the spectators who come to see a production. Here, the logic and clarity of the Actions are essential and – through these Actions – the process of participants bringing them to life. There is no place for spectators as such.

1997, "Grotowski Blazes the Trails," 391–92

Philip Glass (1937–): American composer whose innovative compositions include collaborations with Robert Wilson, *Einstein on the Beach* (1976) and *White Raven* (1991) and David Henry Hwang, *1000 Airplanes on the Roof* (1988) and *The Voyage* (1992) as well as an opera trilogy based on the works of Jean Cocteau – *Orphée* (1993), *La Belle et la Bête* (1994), and *Les Enfants Terribles* (1996). Glass has composed the scores for many films including: *The Truman Show* (1992), *The Hours* (2002), *The Fog of War* (2003), and *Going Upriver: The Long War of John Kerry* (2004).

fig 3.21. A scene from *Uttar Priyadarshi* – a "meditation on war and peace" – as performed in the USA in 2000 by the Chorus Repertory Theatre of Manipur, India, directed by Ratan Thiyam. This performance combines Buddhist ritual, Manipuri music and dance, and Thiyam's own invention. Photograph by Ratan Thiyam. Photograph courtesy of Erin Mee.

Ralph Lemon (1952–) American dancer and choreographer, known for highly emotional dances, often involving mixed media. Dance works include *Joy* (1989), *Persephone* (1991), and *The Geography Trilogy* (1997–2004).

Ratan Thiyam (1948–): Manipuri-Indian founder-director of the Chorus Repertory Theatre. Major productions include Thiyam's play *Chakravyuha* (1986) and *Uttar Priyadarshi* (1996), concerning the life of the Indian Buddhist King Ashoka (second century, BCE).

Lin Hwai-Min (1949–): Taiwanese choreographer and dancer. In 1973, he founded Cloud Gate Dance Theatre, Taiwan's foremost modern dance company. His works include: *Dream of the Red Chamber* (1983), *Nine Songs* (1995), *Moonwater* (1998), *Bamboo Dream* (2001), and the *Cursive* trilogy (2001, 2003, 2005).

Conclusion

Human ritual is of a piece with animal ritual. Rituals are used to manage potential conflicts regarding status, power, space, resources, and sex. Performing rituals helps people get through difficult periods of transition and move from one life status to another. Ritual is also a way for people to connect to a collective, to remember or construct a mythic past, to build social solidarity, and to form or maintain a community. Some rituals are liminal, existing between or outside daily social life; other rituals are knitted into ordinary living. During their liminal phase, ritual performances produce communitas, a feeling among participants that they are part of something greater than or outside of their individual selves. On a larger scale, ritual plays an essential role in social dramas, helping to resolve crises by bringing about either the reintegration needed to heal or allowing a schism needed to form a new community. In either case, ritual is necessary for closure. If social dramas are "big productions," the rituals of everyday life sometimes hardly make a ripple. We perform waking-up rituals, mealtime rituals, greeting rituals, parting rituals, and so on, in order to smooth out and moderate most of our ongoing social life. Understanding how these rituals operate gives us an insight into basic human interactions.

Although the belief is widespread that the performing arts originated in or as rituals, there is no historical or archaeological evidence to prove this assertion. More probably from the very earliest times the entertainment qualities of performance were as present as the ritual elements. Instead of thinking of the oppositional binary "ritual or art," one should think of a spectrum or a dynamic braid. Every performance both entertains and ritualizes. The questions one ought to ask are to what degree does a performance entertain, give pleasure, is made so that it is beautiful; and to what degree is a performance efficacious, made in order to accomplish something, please or appeal to the gods, mark or celebrate an important event or life milestone such as birth, puberty, marriage, or death? Although specific performances tend to emphasize one or the other, entertainment or efficacity, all performances are actually to some degree both entertaining and efficacious.

Artists of many cultures have long made art used in rituals – church music, altar pieces and devotional paintings, temple icons, masks, religious dances and dramas, and so on. Furthermore, at first influenced by colonialism and later by globalization, artists have drawn on the rituals of many cultures for use in their own new works. Some artists have investigated not just specific rituals but the ritual process itself in order to synthesize existing rituals or invent new rituals. In the not-so-distant past, colonial exhibitors brought rituals from "faraway" places as entertainments and exotic curiosities. This practice continues today under the rubric of "international festival." These festivals occur in many parts of the world, not just in Europe or North America.

Not only artists, but also governments, sports teams, schools, and other entities invent rituals. These rituals are often passed off as venerable and traditional when, in fact, they are of recent vintage. National anthems, pledges to the flag, the carrying of the Olympic torch (and many other aspects of the modern Olympic games), and sorority or fraternity initiations are some examples of invented rituals. In fact, rituals and the ritual process enact a tension between new/old, conservative/innovative. Although many rituals are long-lasting and protective of the status quo, many others evolve and change – and promote change. The ritual process itself encourages innovation by opening up a space and time for anti-structure, a setting aside of restraints, a suspension of social rules or the temporary adherence to an alternative set of rules. Sometimes rituals change formally through the work of councils, assemblies of ritual specialists, or state authorities. But often, in many cultures and in widely variant situations, rituals evolve by means of changes introduced by individuals at a local level.

TALK ABOUT

1. Consider your day. Describe some ordinary rituals you do. Do you also take part in, or witness, any sacred or official rituals? What are the similarities/differences between these two kinds of rituals? Do you consider both kinds to be "performances"? Why or why not?
2. Have you experienced communitas during an event that was not a ritual – for example, a concert, sports event, or party? Would analyzing the event that led to your experiencing communitas "as" a ritual add to your understanding of what you experienced?

PERFORM

1. Go to a synagogue, mosque, or church *not of your own faith*. Insofar as you can without feeling dishonest, participate in the rituals. What effect does this participation have on you? Did you feel you were "playing a role" as in the theatre? Or did you experience something else?
2. Invent a ritual. Then perform it. Then teach it to others and perform it with them. Is what you did "really" a ritual? If so, why; if not, why not?

READ

Bell, Catherine. "Performance and Other Analogies." *The Performance Studies Reader*, Henry Bial, ed.: 88–96. London and New York: Routledge, 2004.

d'Aquili, Eugene D., Charles D. Laughlin Jr., and John McManus. "The Spectrum of Ritual." *The Spectrum of Ritual*, Eugene D. d'Aquili, Charles D. Laughlin Jr. and John McManus, eds: 36–41. New York: Columbia University Press, 1979.

Faber, Alyda. "Saint Orlan: Ritual as Violent Spectacle and Cultural Criticism." *The Performance Studies Reader*, Henry Bial, ed.: 108–14. London and New York: Routledge, 2004.

Mason, Michael Atwood. "'The Blood that Runs Through the Veins': The Creation of Identity and a Client's Experience of Cuban-American *Santeria Dilogun* Divination." *The Performance Studies Reader*, Henry Bial, ed.: 97–107. London and New York: Routledge, 2004.

Santino, Jack. "Performative Commemoratives, the Personal, and the Public: Spontaneous Shrines, Emergent Ritual." *Journal of American Folklore* 117 (2004): 363–72.

Turner, Victor. "Liminality and Communitas." *The Performance Reader*, Henry Bial, ed.: 79–87. London and New York: Routledge, 2004.

4 PLAY

The joker in the deck

Playing, like ritual, is at the heart of performance. In fact, performance may be defined as ritualized behavior conditioned/permeated by play. How and why this is so is the subject of this chapter. Ritual has seriousness to it, the hammerhead of authority. Play is looser, more permissive – forgiving in precisely those areas where ritual is enforcing, flexible where ritual is rigid. To put it another way: restored behavior is playful; it has a quality of not being entirely "real" or "serious." Restored behavior is conditional; it can be revised. Playing is double-edged, ambiguous, moving in several directions simultaneously. People often mix bits of play – a wisecrack, a joke, a flirtatious smile – with serious activities in order to lighten, subvert, or even deny what is apparently being communicated. "I was just kidding" reflexively claims that the "for real" action was in fact a performance. This claim in favor of playing points to the kind of performing associated with the arts, with creativity, with childhood. It is not a claim that stands up well to the technical or business applications of performance.

Play is very hard to pin down or define. It is a mood, an activity, a spontaneous eruption. Sometimes it is rule-bound, sometimes very free. It is pervasive. Everyone plays and most people also enjoy watching others play – either formally in dramas, sports, on television, in films; or casually, at parties, while working, on the street, on playgrounds (**see figure 4.1**). Play can subvert the powers that be, as in parody or carnival, or it can be cruel, amoral power, what Shakespeare's Gloucester meant when he cried out, "As flies to wanton boys, are we to the gods, | They kill us for their sport" (*King Lear*, 4, 1: 38–39).

Victor Turner called play the "joker in the deck," meaning it was both indispensable and untrustworthy (**see Turner box**). Indeed, in Western thought, play has been both valued and suspect (**see Spariosu box 1**). From the **Enlightenment** through the nineteenth century, a strong effort was made to rationalize play, to control its anarchic expressions, to channel it into numerous rule-bound, site-specific games and various official displays enacted as public, civic, military, or religious spectacle. An effort was made to assign specific places for playing and to limit playtime to after work or Sundays (and then, when the working week shrank, to the weekend or "days off"). For any society depending upon industry, maintaining the measured regularity of the assembly line is necessary for the creation of wealth. Play has to be kept off the line as much as possible. But the best laid plans. . . . People keep playing furiously, if not always publicly. The more historians learn of rapidly industrializing Victorian Britain, for example, the more they discover secret gardens of play. Drunkenness was endemic on the job and off; workers played hooky to gamble and whore; lunchtime dime theatres drew crowds of child laborers. These and other practices played havoc with the official doctrine of orderly production. Maintaining discipline in the factories was a major undertaking.

A change in how play was regarded began at the turn of the twentieth century, and it has accelerated ever since. Play returned as a category of creative thought and action. Notions of the **unconscious** in psychology and literature, theories of relativity and uncertainty (or indeterminacy) in physics, and game theory in mathematics and economics are examples of play taken seriously. In the visual arts,

fig 4.1. Some of the varieties of play and playing. The actual diversity and range is endless: what is depicted here is but a small sample.

A school playground in Northhamptonshire, UK, 1988. Photograph by Brunskill. Copyright Popperfoto.

fig 4.1. (Continued)

Canada's doubles team Frederic Niemeyer (right) and Daniel Nestor return the ball to Venezuela's doubles team José de Armas and Yohny Romero in a Davis Cup semifinal, Valencia, Venezuela May 2005. AP Photo/Leslie Mazoch. Copyright EMPICS. Reproduced with permission.

"War Games" – during the Second World War. Notice the playful sign, "You are now crossing the Rhine River through courtesy of E Co . . ." Photograph from *After the Battle Magazine*.

Victor Turner

The joker in the deck

Playfulness is a volatile, sometimes dangerously explosive essence, which cultural institutions seek to bottle or contain in the vials of games of competition, chance, and strength, in modes of simulation such as theatre, and in controlled disorientation, from roller coasters to dervish dancing. [. . .] Most definitions of play involve notions of disengagement, of free-wheeling, of being out of mesh with the serious "bread-and-butter," let alone "life-and-death" processes of production, social control, "getting and spending," and raising the next generation. [. . .] Play can be everywhere and nowhere, imitate anything, yet be identified with nothing. [. . .] Play is the supreme bricoleur of frail transient constructions, like a caddis worm or a magpie's nest. [. . .] Its metamessages are composed of a potpourri of apparently incongruous elements. [. . .] Yet, although "spinning loose" as it were, the wheel of play reveals to us (as Mihaly Csikszentmihalyi has argued [1975]) the possibility of changing our goals and, therefore, the restructuring of what our culture states to be reality.

1983, "Body, Brain, and Culture," 233–34

playing with ordinary reality – inventing new ways to look at things – led to cubism and then abstract expressionism. Various avant-gardes disrupted, parodied, and playfully subverted official culture. Play is intrinsically part of performing because it embodies the "as if," the make-believe. Much recent thinking on play accords it an important place in human and animal life. In Indian philosophy, play is the very ground of existence.

Mihai Spariosu

Return of the repressed

Although Plato and Aristotle convert heroic and tragic poetry into "fiction" or "literature," subordinating it to the serious and moral truth of metaphysics, the ancient agon between the poets and the philosophers comes back again and again to haunt Western thought. Whenever prerational values attempt to regain cultural supremacy, what has been repressed under the name of "literature" or "art" as mere play and illusion also reasserts its claim to knowledge and truth, that is, its claim to power. Faced with this challenge or threat, the modern philosophers may react in two ways: they either reenact the Platonic suppression of prerational values, relegating them again to the realm of "mere" art and play (the case of Kant); or they wholeheartedly embrace these values, turning literature or art into an effective weapon against their own philosophical opponents (the case of the artist-metaphysicians [Nietzsche, Heidegger, Derrida]).

1989, *Dionysus Reborn*, 162

Enlightenment: European philosophical movement originating in the eighteenth century but continuing to the present championing rationality, empirical reasoning, the rule of law both natural and human, and universal ethical, political, aesthetic, and scientific values.

unconscious: as theorized by Sigmund Freud (1856–1939), thoughts, feelings, impulses, or memories of which we are not aware, and over which we have no or little control. The unconscious manifests itself in dreams, as slips of the tongue, forgetting, compulsive behavior, and the like.

What is play? What is playing?

Is playing different than "play"? Do the activities called "playing" directly correspond to the phenomenon called "play"? What do playing baseball, playing poker, playing around with your boy/girlfriend, playing a role in a play, playing the fool, letting some play into your fishing line, and playing out an idea have in common? Are fantasy, dreaming, and daydreaming kinds of interior playing? Is playing always fun? Is it always guided by rules or can it be unpredictable? Is playing prerational, rational, arational, or irrational? How has the idea of playing figured in Western and non-Western philosophies and cosmologies? Do animals play in the same way as humans do? Do adults play in the same way as infants and children do? What are the connections between ritual and playing (**see Handelman box 1**)? Between art and playing? Between the earliest human cultures and playing? Is war a kind of playing? These questions do not exhaust what can be asked. There are more questions than can be answered – and this is a significant aspect of the whole "problem" of play and playing.

Don Handelman

Complementarity of play and ritual

Ritual and play are shadow images of one another in the kinds of messages they transmit to the social order. They are analogous states of cognition and perception, whose messages are complementary for the resolution of the ongoing, immoral, deviant, domain of ordinary reality.

1977, "Play and Ritual: Complementary Frames of Metacommunication," 190

If the dichotomies dividing play from work, serious business, and ritual are too rigid and culture-bound; if it is wrong to fence children's play off from adult play; if playing need be neither voluntary nor fun; if play is characterized both by flow – losing oneself in play – and reflexivity – the awareness that one is playing; if ethological and semiotic studies show that play's functions include learning, regulating hierarchy, exploration, creativity, and communication; if psychoanalysis links playing with fantasy, dreaming, and the expression of desires; if the "in between" and "as if" time-space of playing is the source of cultural activities including arts, sciences, and religions . . .can we ever really understand something so complex?

You might regard the writing I am doing at this moment as a game played in order to bring the multiple possibilities of play and playing under the aegis of rational thought. Indeed, a principal task of scholarly writing is to find discipline within or impose it on seemingly anarchic phenomena.

This tension between the orderly and the unpredictable – the rational rule of law (human or other) versus the throw of the dice – is irresolvable. But it is comprehensible as the struggle between two kinds of playing. The first kind of playing is where all players accept the rules of the game and are equal before the law. The second kind of playing is Nietzschean, where the gods (fate, destiny, luck, indeterminacy) change the rules of the game at any time, and therefore, where nothing is certain.

Some qualities of playing

Playing is a genetically based lifelong activity of humans and a number of other animals. Playing consists of play acts, the basic physical units of playing and gaming. Though it is not easy to separate play from games, one can say that generally games are more overtly structured than playing. Games are rule-bound, occur in designated places ranging from stadiums to card tables, have definite outcomes, and engage players who are clearly marked (sometimes with uniforms). Play can take place anywhere at any time engaging any number of players who may abide by or unexpectedly change the rules. Most play acts are governed by rules that the players agree to play by. Games from tennis and chess to improvisational theatre and war games are governed by rules that control the moment-to-moment playing. But there are also many play acts with no articulated or published rules, or with rules that change during playing, as in fantasy or "kidding around." Sometimes playing is anti-structural, with the main fun being how one can get around the rules or subvert them.

Adult playing is different from children's in terms of the amount of time spent playing and the shift from mostly "free" or "exploratory" play to rule-bound playing. However, some adults arrange their work so that they may continue to play in much the same ways that children do. Artists are not the only adults who are given leave to "play around." Researchers in science and industry, and even some business people, are able to integrate play into their work. Both child play and adult play involve exploration, learning, and risk with a payoff in the pleasurable experience of "flow" or total involvement in the activity for its own sake. Playing creates its own multiple realities with porous boundaries. Playing is full of creative world-making as well as lying, illusion, and deceit. Play is performance (when it is done openly, in public) and performative when it is more private, even secret – a strategy or reverie rather than a display. This interiority separates play from ritual, which is always be enacted. Games – a special kind of playing – depend on more fixed, solid boundaries. In the card game of blackjack, having an ace and a face card is a sure winner (**see figure 4.2**). In baseball, the umpire shouts "You're out!" and the player leaves the field; being "offside" draws a penalty in football.

Playing can be physically and emotionally dangerous. Because it is, players need to feel safe, seeking special play spaces and play times. The perils of playing are masked by asserting that playing is "fun," "voluntary," "ephemeral," or a "leisure activity." These are modern Western beliefs. In fact, much of the fun of playing, when there is fun, is in playing with fire, going in over one's head, engaging in "deep play," to use **Jeremy Bentham**'s term as developed by **Clifford Geertz**. In deep play, the risks to the player outweigh the potential rewards. I will have more to say about deep play when later in this chapter I discuss its close relation, "dark play."

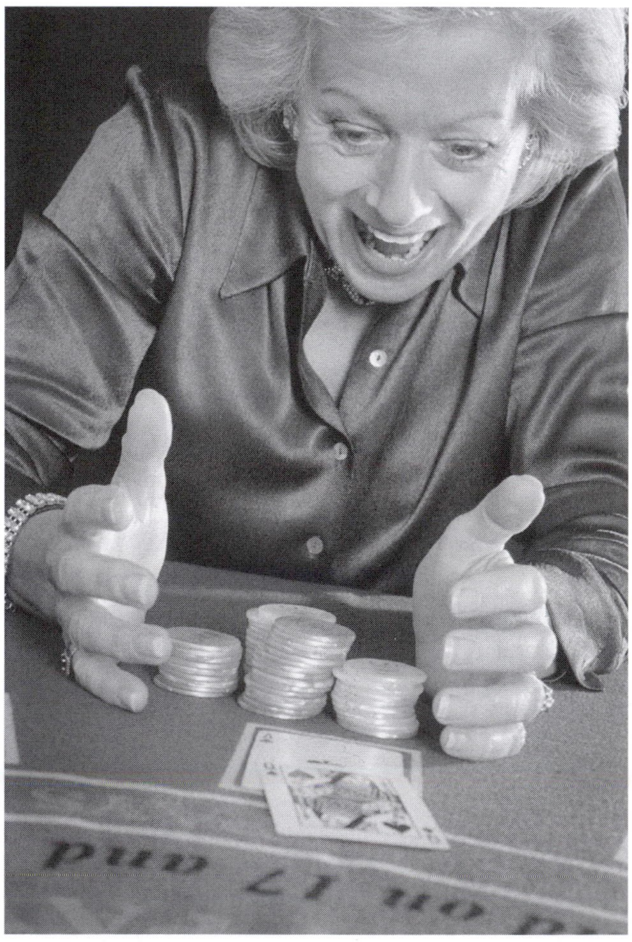

fig 4.2. A happy gambler raking in her chips after winning at blackjack. Copyright image 100/Alamy.

Jeremy Bentham (1748–1832): English philosopher and social reformer whose theory of utilitarianism asserted that the best society was the one that provided "the greatest good for the greatest number." Bentham proposed *The Panopticon* (1791), a plan for prisons, hospitals, insane asylums, and schools where all the inhabitants could be continuously and simultaneously observed. His most influential work, *Introduction to the Principles of Morals and Legislation* (1789), focused on the ethics of law, language, and government.

Clifford Geertz (1926–): American anthropologist, innovator of interpretive anthropology, an approach that treats cultural activities as comprehensible texts. Author of many books, including *The Interpretation of Cultures* (1973), *Negara: The Theatre State in Nineteenth Century Bali* (1980), *Local Knowledge* (1983), and *Available Light* (2000).

Seven ways to approach play

I offer seven interrelated ways to approach play and playing not as a definitive list, but as a strategy for organizing the inquiry into play.

1 Structure: What are the relationships among the events constituting a play act? How, for example, how does an "at bat" fit into the structure of an inning in baseball; and how does each inning relate to the shape of the entire game? Each play act consists of many sub-acts, distinct behavioral units that fit together into a coherent whole. A coherent sequence of play acts forms a game.
2 Process: Over time, how are play acts generated and what are their phases of development? Again, to use baseball as an example, how do the strategies of play change as the game progresses; or how do the score, weather, injuries, and so on affect emerging strategies of play? Process and structure should be considered as a related pair.
3 Experience: What are the feelings and moods of the players and the observers? How do these affect playing? What are the different experiences of players, spectators, scholarly observers, directors, organizers, and so on? How do differing feelings and moods change over the course of play, affecting the playing itself? Are spectator sports more affected by the "home field advantage" than informal games or more intimate playing (make-believe, riding a swing or seesaw, erotic foreplay)? How does one determine whether the play has been "good" or not?
4 Function: What purposes do play acts serve? How do they affect individual and community learning, growth and creativity, distribute and express aggression, act out myths, fantasies, or values . . . or any number of other possible "uses" play has? What are the economic consequences of any particular play act or genre of play?
5 Evolutionary, species, and individual development of play: What is the relationship of human play to animal play? What are the differences between child play and adult play? What is the relationship between playing and individual creativity? What is the relationship between play and culture – especially creativity, the arts, and religion?
6 Ideology: What political, social, and personal values does any specific playing enunciate, propagate, criticize, or subvert – either knowingly or unconsciously? Are these values the same for all players, spectators, and observers? And if there are differences, how are these expressed and negotiated?
7 Frame: How do players, spectators, and so on know when play begins, is taking place, and is over? How is the message "now I am playing" broadcast and received? And what about "dark" or risky play, where the message "this is play" is intentionally omitted or disguised, such as in con games or in Augusto Boal's **Invisible Theatre**? Is "I want to stop playing" the same as "I am finished playing?"

Invisible Theatre: a performance technique developed by Augusto Boal where an action is staged in a public place for an "audience" of bystanders who do not know that what they are witnessing is a theatrical performance. An Invisible Theatre event almost always has a political meaning.

The rest of this chapter is an investigation of these seven ways to approach play and playing. However, these ways cannot be separated out from each other as sharply as I have done in the list. Many of these ways overlap each other. Therefore, the discussion will move among these seven rather than discuss each one after the other.

Types of playing

Roger Caillois classifies play and games into four categories:

1 Agon or competition. Games where there are winners and losers. The outcome is determined by the skills and/or strength of the players. Examples: races, weightlifting, chess.

2 Alea or chance. Games where fate, luck, or grace determine the winner. Examples: dice, roulette.
3 Mimicry or simulation. Playing within an imaginary, make-believe, or illusory world. Examples: theatre, children's make-believe play.
4 Ilinx or dizziness. Playing to induce a disorienting experience or state of mind. Examples: spinning, roller-coaster rides, getting "crazy drunk."

Roger Caillois (1913–78): French sociologist, play theorist, and anti-fascist. Founding editor of *Diogenes* published under the auspices of the United Nations. Author of *Man, Play, and Games* (1958, Eng. 1979).

This division is useful if one realizes that actual playing and gaming more often combine categories than keep them distinct. For example, poker involves both agon and alea, with more than a touch of mimicry thrown in (the famous "poker face" worn by the best players). Greek tragedies draw power and pathos from a combination of alea and agon – fate and conflict – while the stage performances of the dramas are mimicries. "Musical chairs" and "ring around the rosy" combine ilinx and agon. Carnival masquerading combines all four categories. And so on. Caillois himself recognized this, pointing out that horse racing combines agon, alea, and mimicry.

Caillois emphasized the reciprocity between any given society and the games it plays (**see Caillois box 1**). Most play theorists agree that play both expresses and drives social life. The disagreements come over what kinds of playing are preferable. Professional athletes and gamblers play for money. Business people and politicians exploit gaming techniques. Playing "mind games" in order to control other people is a social skill. Scams, stings, and con games are endemic. Some theorists, such as **Brian Sutton-Smith** see playing as largely a means of exercising power (**see Sutton-Smith box 1**). Caillois and others prefer the disinterested play of "gentleman amateurs," which they regard as a mark of high culture. The darker kinds of play Caillois calls "corruptions" evidencing a decline in "civilization." Caillois is imagining (or proposing) a golden age when people with time to spare play by the rules. In this Utopia, violent, irruptive ecstasy is rare and strictly governed; there is little reliance on chance or fate because people live rationally. Plato was the first in the West to imagine such a world. In China, **Confucius** proposed a similarly rational code for living.

Roger Caillois

A society is the games it plays

[There is] a truly reciprocal relationship between a society and the games it likes to play. There is indeed an increasing affinity between their rules and the common characteristics and deficiencies of the members of the groups. These preferred and widely diffused games reflect, on the one hand, the tendencies, tastes, and ways of thought that are prevalent, while, at the same time, in educating and training the players in these very virtues or eccentricities, they subtly confirm them in their habits and preferences. Thus, a game that is esteemed by a people may at the same time be utilized to define the society's moral or intellectual character, provide proof of its precise meaning, and contribute to its popular acceptance by accentuating the relevant qualities.

1979 [1958], *Man, Play, and Games*, 82–83

Brian Sutton-Smith

Play and power

Considerations of play and power come under various names, such as warfare, hegemony, conflict, competition, glory, manliness, contest, and resistance. Some of these are quite ancient terms historically, preceding the modern rhetorics of progress, the imaginary, and the self. [. . .] In modern times, however, the concept of power has also been applied in play theory to solitary play: the child plays because he enjoys the power of being a cause, or because he doesn't have power and in play is seeking empowerment as a kind of compensation or wish fulfillment. On the social play level, the general idea of the power rhetoric is that play or games or sports or athletics that have to do with some kind of contest and reflect a struggle for superiority between two groups (two people, two communities, two tribes, two social classes, two ethnic groups, two or more nations) exist because they give some kind of representation or expression to the existing real conflict between these groups. Whichever side wins the game or contest is said to bring glory to its own group, bonding the members together through their common contestive identity. Furthermore the two groups typically have in common their enthusiasm for this kind of contest, which may thus unite rather than divide them.

1997, *The Ambiguity of Play*, 75

Brian Sutton-Smith (1924–): New Zealand-born folklorist and play theorist. Author of numerous works on play, including *Play and Learning* (1979), *Toys as Culture* (1986), and *The Ambiguity of Play* (1997).

Confucius (551–479 BCE): Chinese moral philosopher and poet. Confucianism – a code of conduct based on his teachings – was the official religion of China until 1911, and is still widely practiced.

Play acts, play moods

In any given play situation there may be both players and observers. The observers may be actively involved in the play – as fans or avid followers of the game; or they may be more disinterested witnesses. There are also professional watchers, the referees and judges who make sure that the playing is going by the rules or who determine who wins, who loses. It is possible to be playing from the perspective of the observers but not be playing, or at least not be in a play mood, from another point of view. The roaring Romans in the Coliseum delighted in the gladiatorial games as play, while the gladiators themselves were not playing. Modern bullfights resemble the gladiatorial games, with the odds fixed strongly in favor of the matador (**see figure 4.3**). The bull is not playing, the matador is both playing and not playing, and the spectators are enjoying the blood sport. Indeed, professional sports present a particularly complex situation. A lot of hype goes into convincing fans that the players are in it "for the love of the game." Probably many players enjoy playing at a professional level. But clearly money and stardom also count for a lot. Furthermore, the players on the field are only the most visible parts of an extremely elaborate network of managers, owners, and media joined to real estate, government, and corporate interests. At what level does the play stop and something else begin? At all levels of professional sports, playing is implicated with other activities.

Hindsight can transform a serious event into play. Watching home movies, for example. Or television programs like *Candid Camera*. The popularity at the turn of the millennium of "reality television," as well as access to hundreds of webcams streaming over the internet, are variations on the candid camera theme. Who is playing in these situations? And when does the playing take place? The

fig 4.3. A bullfight at Pamplona, Spain, 1997. Spanish bullfighter Pepin Liria executes a pass while on his knees – this is called a "larga cambiada." Copyright Reuters.

playing is relocated to the playback; or if the program is live, the players are more like athletes engaged in a contest. With the webcams, the playing is more or less "unconscious," the delight voyeuristic. In a scam, sting, or practical joke the targets are part of a play event, but do not know it; the other participants must keep up the illusion of seriousness; the audience (friends, the police) use the event either as an occasion for amusement or as evidence. In the case of a scam, it is important to the perpetrators that there be no audience, ever.

Play acts often serve multiple, contradictory purposes simultaneously. What's fun for the cat is not for the mouse. Among the Aztecs and Mayans of Mesoamerica, ball-playing fulfilled many functions. People played ball just for fun and to show off skills. The hard rubber ball, which was knocked without touching it with the hands, ranged in size from about 8 inches in diameter among the Aztecs to 18 inches in the Mayan game (**see figure 4.4**). Often there were large bets riding on a game with valuable textiles wagered (the Mayans and Aztecs did not have money as such). Sometimes the ball game was a matter of life and death. Captives especially were forced to play – and lose both the game and their lives. Such ritual games built community solidarity and confirmed the superiority of ruling deities and kings, even as it brought death to those selected for sacrifice.

If play acts themselves are not necessarily fun, neither are the processes that generate play acts always playful. Sports training and practicing often involve hours of grueling effort proving the adage, "no pain, no gain." Filming a motion picture is more tedious work, involving lots of boring repetition and waiting, than it is play. On the other hand, sometimes the processes involved in preparing can be more enjoyable than the outcome. Many people report that workshops and rehearsals are a lot more playful and satisfying than the finished products. Thus there is no necessary relationship between process and product. Either, both, or neither may be playful.

Moods are especially labile, shifting suddenly and totally. Observe a children's playground. A kid can be laughing one minute, crying the next, angry the next, and laughing again a moment later. All of these moods are part of the playing. Or the playing can go over the edge, in humans as with animals. In the midst of a hotly contested match, play can suddenly turn venomous and deadly. Only in well-organized games – which constitute a minority of play acts – is the situation always under control. And even in such well-managed situations, an injury to a player or spectator, or a fight on the field or in the stands, can suddenly break the play mood. Once the wounded player is carried from the field, or order restored, play resumes.

Though it is not easy to separate play from games, as noted earlier, generally games are highly structured events with clearly marked players playing in/on specified places, fields, or boards. Games have established agreed-on rules that guarantee an orderly progression to definite outcomes. Even one person can play a game – such as a crossword puzzle or solitaire; or one can compete against an imaginary or programmed opponent as in computer chess or pinball.

fig 4.4. A Mayan ballgame as depicted on a cylindrical vessel, 600–800 CE. The illustration is a "roll out" – the cylinder has been photographically extended into a flat plane. Note the large size of the ball. Four ball players are shown. Photograph by Justin Kerr.

Games can range from single instances to "seasons" that take months to complete. The Olympic Games renew themselves every four years. **James P. Carse** divides games into "finite" and "infinite" (**see Carse box**). A finite game moves toward resolution, while the goal of an infinite game is to keep on playing. Cultures are infinite games. The ultimate infinite game is the open-ended play that sustains existence.

James P. Carse (1932–): American theologian, author of *Death and Existence* (1980), *Finite and Infinite Games* (1986), and *Breakfast at the Victory: The Mysticism of Ordinary Experience* (1994).

James P. Carse

Finite and infinite games

There are at least two kinds of games. One could be called finite, the other infinite. A finite game is played for the purpose of winning, an infinite game for the purpose of continuing play. [. . .] The rules of a finite game are the contractual terms by which the players can agree on who has won. [. . .] The rules of an infinite game must change during the course of play. [. . .] The rules of an infinite game are changed to prevent anyone from winning the game and to bring as many persons as possible into the play. [. . .] To be serious is to press for a specified conclusion. To be playful is to allow for possibility whatever the cost to oneself. [. . .] Since culture is itself a poiesis, all of its participants are poietai – inventors, makers, artists, storytellers, mythologists. They are not, however, makers of actualities, but makers of possibilities. The creativity of culture has no outcome, no conclusion. It does not result in art works, artifacts, productions. Creativity is a continuity that engenders itself in others.

1986, *Finite and Infinite Games*, 3, 9, 19, 67

Flow, or experiencing playing

What about the experience of playing? There are play faces, play moods, and play experiences. The faces can be mapped from the outside; the moods can be read by someone skilled in understanding body languages, gestures, and facial displays. It is much harder to get at the player's "experience," which is a private occurrence, varying enormously from one person to the next. Several people can participate in the same event, even behave identically, and yet have wildly different experiences.

In the early 1970s, **Mihaly Csikszentmihalyi** studied the experience of playing in a wide range of people, from chess players to surgeons, rock climbers to rock dancers. The term he gave to what people felt when their consciousness of the outside world disappeared and they merged with what they were doing is **"flow"** (**see Csikszentmihalyi box**). By now, "flow" has entered popular language: To "go with the flow" means not only to do what everyone else is doing, but to merge with whatever activity one is engaged in. Players in flow may be aware of their actions, but not of the awareness itself. What they feel is close to being in trance (see Chapter 6) and the "oceanic" experience of rituals (see Chapter 3). Flow occurs when the player becomes one with the playing. "The dance danced me." At the same time, flow can be an extreme self-awareness where the player has total control over the play act. These two aspects of flow, apparently contrasting, are essentially the same. In each case, the boundary between the interior psychological self and the performed activity dissolves.

Mihaly Csikszentmihalyi (1934–): American psychologist, an expert on flow and its relation to experience and creativity. Author of *Beyond Boredom and Anxiety* (1975), *Flow: The Psychology of Optimal Experience* (1990), *Creativity, Flow, and the Psychology of Discovery and Invention* (1996), and *Good Business Leadership, Flow, and the Making of Meaning* (2003).

flow: the feeling of losing oneself in the action so that all awareness of anything other than performing the action disappears. A gambler "on a roll" or an athlete playing "in the zone" are experiencing flow.

Mihaly Csikszentmihalyi

Flow – the optimal state of inner experience

Flow – the state in which people are so involved in an activity that nothing else seems to matter; the experience itself is so enjoyable that people will do it even at great cost, for the sheer sake of doing it. [. . .] The flow experience is not just a peculiarity of affluent, industrialized elites. It was reported in essentially the same words by old women from Korea, by adults in Thailand and India, by teenagers in Tokyo, by Navajo shepherds, by farmers in the Italian Alps, and by workers on the assembly line in Chicago. [. . .]

The optimal state of inner experience is one in which there is order in consciousness. This happens when psychic energy – or attention – is invested in realistic goals, and when skills match the opportunities for action. [. . .] "Flow" is the way people describe their state of mind when consciousness is harmoniously ordered, and they want to pursue whatever they are doing for its own sake. In reviewing some of the activities that consistently produce flow – such as sports, games, art, and hobbies – it becomes easier to understand what makes people happy. [. . .]

If we were to interpret the lives of animals with a human eye, we would conclude that they are in flow most of the time because their perception of what has to be done generally coincides with what they are prepared to do. [. . .] Animals' skills are always matched to concrete demands because their minds, such as they are, only contain information about what is actually present in the environment in relation to their bodily states, as determined by instinct. So a hungry lion only perceives what will help it to find a gazelle, while a sated lion concentrates fully on the warmth of the sun.

1990, *Flow: The Psychology of Optimal Experience*, 4–6, 227–28

In the flow state, action follows upon action according to an internal logic that seems to need no conscious intervention by the actor. He experiences it as a unified flowing from one moment to the next, in which he is in control of his actions, and in which there is little distinction between self and environment, between stimulus and response, or between past, present, and future. Flow is what we have been calling "the autotelic experience."

1975, *Beyond Boredom and Anxiety*, 35–36

Understanding flow tells us something important about the difference between whatever a particular play act or game may mean and the experience of playing. Or being fully engaged in any activity, for that matter: acting in a play, selling automobiles, experimenting in a laboratory. Whatever the meaning, the players themselves, if they are in flow, are focused on the immediate demands of the activity. Baseball may be interpreted as a perilous journey of a Ulysses-like hero, the batter hitting the ball in order to venture into dangerous enemy territory where he is safe only when standing on one of three tiny islands (the bases), and successful only when he arrives back home. Or baseball may be seen as a romantic idealization of an open, verdant space, the "ball park," sculpted out of the brick and asphalt of a crowded city. Or a demonstration of the tensions between individual prowess and team effort. Baseball may be any number of things on the meaning level. But while the game is being played, for the players, baseball is about pitching, hitting, catching, and running – and the experience of performing these actions (**see figure 4.5**).

fig 4.5. American baseball's "perilous journey" – the batter tries to get to a safe base, or even hit a home run, at Shea Stadium, New York, 2001. Photograph by Henry Bial.

Transitional objects, illusions, and culture

There is another way to understand the experience of playing. Psychoanalyst **D. W. Winnicott** thought that playing was a very special experience of trust that had its origins in the "potential space" between baby and mother. This space is both an actual playground and the conceptual arena where human culture originates. Experiencing this potential space starts when an infant first senses the difference between "me" and "not me." At birth and for some weeks after, the baby cannot make such a distinction. To the newborn, mother's breasts are "part of" the baby. As a baby suckles, the nipple is inside the baby's mouth; the breast gives warm, good-tasting, life-sustaining milk (**see figure 4.6**). Touching and sucking build a somatic–emotional bridge bonding mother and baby into a new liminal organism. This sucking and fondling precedes even intense mutual gazing. For a few days after birth, an infant's eyes don't focus, but the mouth works splendidly even before birth – as we know from photographs of fetuses sucking the thumb in utero. But even as the mother's breasts are "me" to the suckling infant, they are also "not me." The thumb is always there, but not the breast. The baby cries when hungry yet the breast is absent. The crying signifies something is missing. When the breast arrives, along with the familiar-smelling/feeling mother, the baby quiets and feeds, once more feeling complete. Babies deprived of this early experience suffer a lack that persists into adulthood.

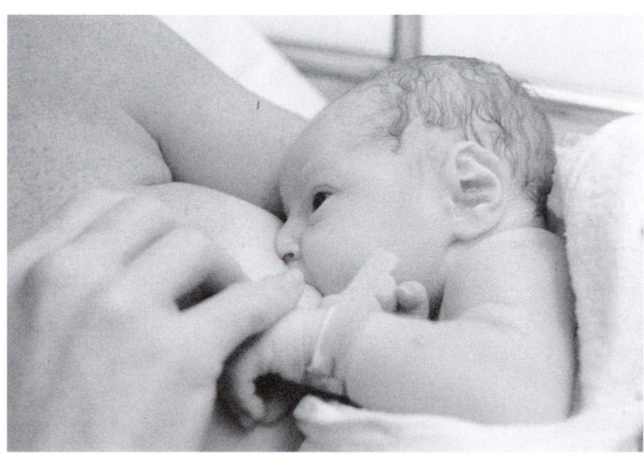

fig 4.6. An infant nursing begins the journey from self to other – hopefully establishing with mother a safe liminal "transitional space." Photograph by Richard Schechner.

D. W. Winnicott (1896–1971): English psychoanalyst and developmental psychologist specializing in the relationship between mother and child as the basis for culture, art, and religion. Works include *The Child and the Family* (1957) and *Playing and Reality* (1971).

Mother's breasts are, in Winnicott's term, "transitional objects" – parts of the body-person that belong solely neither to the mother nor to the baby. The mutual fondling and then gazing are "transitional phenomena." Not too long after birth, the baby begins to find or invent more transitional objects – fist, fingers, thumb, a pacifier, the corner of a "security blanket." These become players in an ever-more complicated set of transitional phenomena. Soon enough there are favorite toys and other objects which the baby much values and needs. These are used to construct what Winnicott calls a "neutral space" of unchallenged illusion. Over time, as the baby begins to play in ways that adults recognize, the time spent playing increases. Almost any object, space, or span of time can be used "in play." And for the playing child within this liminal play world, anything can become something else. The first years of life are a period of protean creativity. Toy manufacturers try to convince anxious parents that this or that product is the "right toy" for their child. Indeed, when the infant becomes a toddler, she is susceptible to advertising. But in terms of biosocial process, toys are made by the imagination, not by Mattel.

Winnicott locates the origins of creativity and illusion in playing. He writes that the satisfaction of playing is a feeling that comforts and sustains a person throughout life. Winnicott asserts that the satisfying experience of playing is inherent in art and religion. Indeed, Winnicott theorizes that the transitional experience first explored between mother and baby is the foundation for the vast superstructure of culture (**see Winnicott box**). Winnicott's position is similar both to Turner's theory of liminality and the Indian philosophy of *maya–lila* (to be discussed later in the chapter).

The ethological approach to play

Winnicott expressed a psychoanalytic theory based on certain biological assumptions. This can be looked at in another way – returning to matters raised in Chapter 3 with regard to ritual. Whatever the human cultural aspects of play, there are also ethological aspects. Ethologically, play and ritual are closely related. Just as human ritual has roots in nonhuman animal behavior, so play has been observed in many species. Ethologists note three types of play: locomotor (running, jumping, tumbling, etc.), object (playing with things), and social (chasing, play-fighting, etc.). Of course, these different kinds of play are often combined. Everyone has seen a dog play with a bone or stick, monkeys chase each other or swing from branch to branch, a cat playing with a ball of yarn or a mouse – the doomed rodent an unwilling playmate in a feline version of "dark play". From an ethological perspective, playing happens when there is sufficient metabolic energy, low stress, a need for stimulation, and the intelligence to support complex sequences of somewhat improvised behavior (**see Burghardt box 1**).

D. W. Winnicott

Playing and the location of cultural experience

Of every individual who has reached to the stage of being a unit with a limiting membrane and an outside and an inside, it can be said that there is an inner reality to that individual, an inner world that can be rich or poor and can be at peace or in a state of war. This helps, but is it enough?

My claim is that if there is a need for this double statement, there is also a need for a triple one: the third part of the life of a human being [. . .] is an intermediate area of experiencing, to which inner reality and external life both contribute.

[. . .] I am here staking a claim for an intermediate state between a baby's inability and his growing ability to recognize and accept reality. I am therefore studying the substance of illusion, that which is allowed to the infant, and which in adult life is inherent in art and religion, and yet becomes the hallmark of madness when an adult puts too powerful a claim on the credulity of others, forcing them to acknowledge a sharing of illusion that is not their own. We can share a respect for illusory experience, and if we wish we may collect together and form a group on the basis of the similarity of our illusory experiences. This is a natural root of grouping among human beings. [. . .]

[W]hereas inner psychic reality has a kind of location in the mind or in the belly or in the head or somewhere within the bounds of the individual personality, and whereas what is called external reality is located outside those bounds, playing and cultural experience can be given a location if one uses the concept of the potential space between the mother and the baby. [. . .]

The place where cultural experience is located is in the potential space between the individual and the environment (originally the [transitional] object). The same can be said of playing. Cultural experience begins with creative living first manifest in play. [. . .]

The potential space between baby and mother, between child and family, between individual and society or the world, depends on experience which leads to trust. It can be looked on as sacred to the individual in that it is here that the individual experiences creative living.

1971, *Playing and Reality*, 2–3, 53, 100, 103

Gordon M. Burghardt

When do animals play?

Four main factors appear to underlie play in animals [. . .] (1) there is sufficient metabolic energy (both energy stores and the capacity for sustained vigorous activity). (2) The animals are buffered from serious stress and food shortages [. . .]. (3) There is a need for stimulation to elicit species typical behavioral systems to reach an optimal level of arousal for physiological functioning (e.g., there is a susceptibility to boredom). (4) There is a life-style that involves complete sequences of behavior in varying conditions, including diverse and unpredictable environmental and/or social resources (e.g., generalist species should play more with objects than those with more rigid, specialized behavioral repertoires). Play in all species, then, including humans, will be most prevalent when there are excess resources along with appropriate evolved motivational, physiological, and ecological systems.

2005, *The Genesis of Animal Play*, 172

The more "freely" the members of a species play, the closer they are to humans, and the more recognizably "playful" their activities appear. Bees, ants, and fish are rich in ritual but poor in play. But "poor" does not mean totally absent. Recent investigations by ethologists indicate that play occurs abundantly in mammals and birds, and surprisingly often among reptiles and fish – even octopuses and some insects play (**see Burghardt box 2**). In terms of the relationship between ritual and play, ritual contributes the set patterns and repetitions, the systems, to performance; play contributes exploratory behavior, creativity, and world-making. Only a few reptiles, some birds, more mammals, and all primates play. As we might expect, the play of monkeys, gorillas, and especially chimpanzees most resembles human play. But are humans alone in displaying a verifiable "aesthetic sense" – a designed presentation of self – in playing? Some keen observers of animal behavior feel that some birds and certainly a number of mammal species show off to themselves, their playmates, and their audiences.

Gordon M. Burghardt (1941–): American ethologist and psychologist, editor of the *Journal of Comparative Psychology*, and past president of the Animal Behavior Society. His books include: *Foundations of Comparative Ethology* (1985), *The Cognitive Animal* (2002, co-edited with Colin Allen and Marc Bekoff), and *The Genesis of Animal Play* (2005).

Gordon M. Burghardt

Even the octopuses do it

The study of octopus object play by experienced students of cephalopod behavior is so far the most convincing evidence we have for play in invertebrates. If these findings are valid, then the roots of the biological ability to evolve and perform playful acts go back over a billion years! [. . .] The comparative evidence shows that play is not limited to some or even all placental mammals, but is found in a wide range of animals, including marsupials, birds, turtles, lizards, fish, and invertebrates. [. . .] The field of molecular genetics has begun to pay attention to the interaction of specific genes with the development and life history processes in the expression of many traits of animals. Underlying the grand biological diversity in the world is a surprisingly conservative genetic toolkit. Traits that were thought to have arisen completely independently in animals separated by hundreds of millions of years, such as eyes in flies and mice, are controlled by similar genes [. . .]. Thus although play arose many times in evolution, it may have been the result of common evolutionary contexts that activated a suite of retained homeotic hox genes which, although they may have other functions, could be repeatedly co-opted in the service of playlike traits.

2005, *The Genesis of Animal Play*, 379, 382, 384–85

Ethologists identify five functions of playing in primates, including humans:

1 Education and/or practice for the young. Nonhuman and human primates lead very complex social lives. Young primates need to learn so much because their behavior is not genetically fixed. "Culture" – social practices specific to a given group passed on through learning – is not a human monopoly.
2 An escape from, remedy for, or alternative to stress.
3 A source of information about the environment and those who live in it.
4 A means for the young to find their place within the group's hierarchy and for adults to keep or change their places in the hierarchy.
5 Muscular exercise.

Not all play theorists agree on these functions, or even with the functional approach. Sutton-Smith argues that functional studies are driven by a rationalist desire to prove that "play works." However, I find the functional explanations useful.

It is also interesting to note that playing in primates – although said to be the locus of "creativity" – is unoriginal at the level of behavior. To extrapolate from the work of several ethologists, it seems that playing "borrows" behaviors from contexts where their purpose is clear – such as fighting or mating – redeploys them, makes a show of them, and uses them for no apparent purpose (**see Loizos box**). In fact, this lack of purpose is a key indicator that playing is going on. Thus a sequence of play includes rearrangements of "not-play" actions that are fragmented, reordered, exaggerated, and repeated. The creativity of play comes in the new ways already-known behaviors are reorganized, made into new sequences. Some individual movements within a play sequence may never be completed, and this incomplete element may be repeated over and over. Seen this way, play is a very cogent example of "restored behavior."

Caroline Loizos

Primate playing including people

One of [play's] immediately noticeable characteristics is that it is behavior that borrows or adopts patterns that appear in other contexts where they achieve immediate and obvious ends. When these patterns appear in play they seem to be divorced from their original motivation and are qualitatively distinct from the same patterns appearing in their originally motivated contexts. [. . .] The fundamental similarity [. . .] between human and animal play [. . .] lies in the exaggerated and uneconomical quality of the motor patterns involved. Regardless of its motivation or its end-product, this is what all playful activity has in common; and it is possible that it is all that it has in common, since causation and function could vary from species to species.

1969, "Play Behavior in Higher Primates: A Review," 228–29

In animals, a play sequence may be broken off by the introduction of different activities such as eating and then resumed later with full intensity as if the break in the action had not occurred. This "time out" quality, as in human sports or games, is extremely important. It demonstrates how play acquires an independence, how it forms its own make-believe world. Although playing is made up of behavior taken from highly functional activities, it becomes an end in itself without direct functional consequences. The pleasure in playing is autotelic, coming not from what it "earns" but from enjoying the actions in themselves. Furthermore, playing is a way to perform safely and without consequences actions that in other contexts would determine hierarchy, mating rights, or even life itself. Playing is "playing around." As noted, the behavior building blocks of play are structurally very close to those of ritual. Does this make play a sub-category of ritual? Or is it the other way round?

The message, "This is play"

How does a person signal, "I am playing"? It is easy enough when play takes the form of games performed according to accepted rules. But despite the enormous popularity of rule-bound games, much playing is not formal. And even formal games are often played informally, as in "sandlot baseball," where players twist the rules to meet contingencies. More pervasive still are bursts of microplay that can erupt anywhere, anytime, even in the midst of work (**see Handelman box 2**). So how do people know when someone is "just playing" or that now is the time to "pull a fast one"? Although it's not possible to answer this question definitively, humans probably signal, "This is play" by overplaying or underplaying, or by culturally specific signals like a smirk or the winking of an eye (**see figure 4.7**).

fig 4.7. A wink is more than a blink – it's a signal, a metacommunication. Photograph of Sophia Martin Schechner by Richard Schechner.

Gregory Bateson theorized that an animal wanting to play "metacommunicates" that intention – says, in effect, "I am playing" or "I want to play." A **metacommunication** is a signal that frames other signals contained within or after it. Let me explain using "Bateson's dog" as my example. You are playing with Bateson's dog, who shows his teeth, snarls, and nips you – even exaggerating the action of nipping you by not letting go and growling. But you are not afraid. That is because Bateson's dog has metacommunicated that he is only playing. The dog is saying, "I could really bite you, but I am not biting you. My nipping tells you the opposite of what a bite would tell you. A bite would tell you, 'I hate you; I am angry with you.' But my nip tells you, 'I love you; I am at ease with you.'" The dog metacommunicates the message, "What I am doing now is playing with you. My playing refers to my 'not playing'; my 'not hurting' you refers to the fact that I could hurt you, but choose not to. My choosing not to is proof that I am playing." Within the play frame or during playtime, everything, even what would be negative or harmful, is positive and good (**see Bateson box**).

metacommunication: a signal that tells receivers how to interpret the communication they are receiving. For example, winking an eye or holding up crossed fingers while speaking indicates to the listener that the speaker's words are not to be taken seriously.

Don Handelman

Banana time

So a serious discussion about the high cost of living could be suddenly transformed into horseplay or into a prank; or a worker might utter a string of "oral autisms." The expression of themes was thus temporary, somewhat idiosyncratic excursions into the reality of play; and each protagonist experimented in his own way, and to some extent at his own pace, with these transitions from the reality of work to that of expressive behavior.

1976, "Rethinking 'Banana Time,'" 442

Extend this to the performing arts. It is easy enough to see how comedy and farce, circus and stand-up comedians, music and dance are playful. But why is tragedy playful? Why are violent videogames playful? Because these arts and entertainments refer to that which, if real, would be painful. We can empathize with that pain, or pull the trigger of that videogame gun without "really doing" what we would be doing if we were not playing. This is consonant with the Stanislavskian "as if." It is also consistent with my own theory of performing as the enactment of a double negative, the "not . . . not."

The question remains: given the functions of play, does viewing tragedies or playing violent videogames dull people to pain, or train them to administer it? There is a contradiction between ethological theory, which indicates play is practice and training, and Batesonian theory, which asserts play is a way around violence, a way to express aggression without doing harm. To the contrary, the Batesonian argument goes, such playing does good by clearly outlining the play frame and keeping the performance inside it. Bateson's dog "promises" not to really bite. At present, there is no resolution to this contradiction. Those who see harm in violent entertainments argue that teenagers especially are unable to keep the play frame intact, that they "actually" kill while intending to "just play." The arguments on both sides are ideologically loaded.

Gregory Bateson

Playful nips and bites

[T]he statement "This is play" looks something like this: "These actions in which we now engage do not denote what those actions for which they stand would denote." [. . .] Not only does the playful nip not denote what would be denoted by the bite for which it stands, but, in addition, the bite itself is fictional. Not only do the playing animals not quite mean what they are saying but, also, they are usually communicating about something which does not exist. At the human level, this leads to a vast variety of complications and inversions in the fields of play, fantasy, and art. [. . .]

Finally, in the dim region where art, magic, and religion meet and overlap, human beings have evolved the "metaphor that is meant," the flag which men will die to save, and the sacrament that is felt to be more than "an outward and visible sign, given to us." [. . .] We face then two peculiarities of play: (a) that the messages or signals exchanged in play are in a certain sense untrue or not meant; and (b) that that which is denoted by these signals is nonexistent. These two peculiarities sometimes combine strangely to reverse a conclusion reached above. It was stated that the playful nip denotes the bite, but does not denote that which would be denoted by the bite. But there are other instances where an opposite phenomenon occurs. A man experiences the full intensity of subjective terror when a spear is flung out at him out of the 3D screen or when he falls headlong from some peak created in his own mind in the intensity of nightmare. At the moment of terror there was no questioning of "reality," but still there was no spear in the movie house and no cliff in the bedroom.

1972, *Steps to an Ecology of Mind*, 180, 182–83

Bateson's *Othello*

In Act 5, Scene 2 of Shakespeare's *Othello*, the Moor murders Desdemona, his wife. Three actions occur simultaneously:

- Othello murders Desdemona.
- Two actors play a scene.
- Spectators experience a theatre piece.

On the first level, there is no playing. In a jealous rage, Othello commits murder. Othello does not send any message to Desdemona that he is just playing. Nor does Desdemona play at terror while pleading for her life (**see figure 4.8**).

Playing enters the scene on the second level. To play effectively, the actors have to communicate to each other that everything they do onstage is part of the play in both senses of the word: they are enacting Shakespeare's drama; they are playing with each other and not really murdering. How do they do this? They rehearse. They work out all the details. By the time of the public performance, they follow a score of restored behavior that both actors know and have practiced together. This reinforces the play frame, signaling during every performance, both to themselves and to the spectators, "We are just playing."

To use Bateson's words,

> These actions in which we now engage [acting in a theatre] do not denote what those actions for which they stand would denote [murdering an innocent but presumed adulterous wife]. Not only does the playful nip not denote what would be denoted by the bite for which it stands, but, in addition, the bite itself is fictional [the murder is a stage action].

It is the fiction, the skill of the acting and writing – not what the fiction stands for, the murdering of an innocent wife – that wins the audience's applause. Othello, Desdemona, Iago, and the rest of the characters may be condemned, admired, or pitied; what happens to them may move an audience to tears. But it is the actors who take the bows, the playwright who is celebrated.

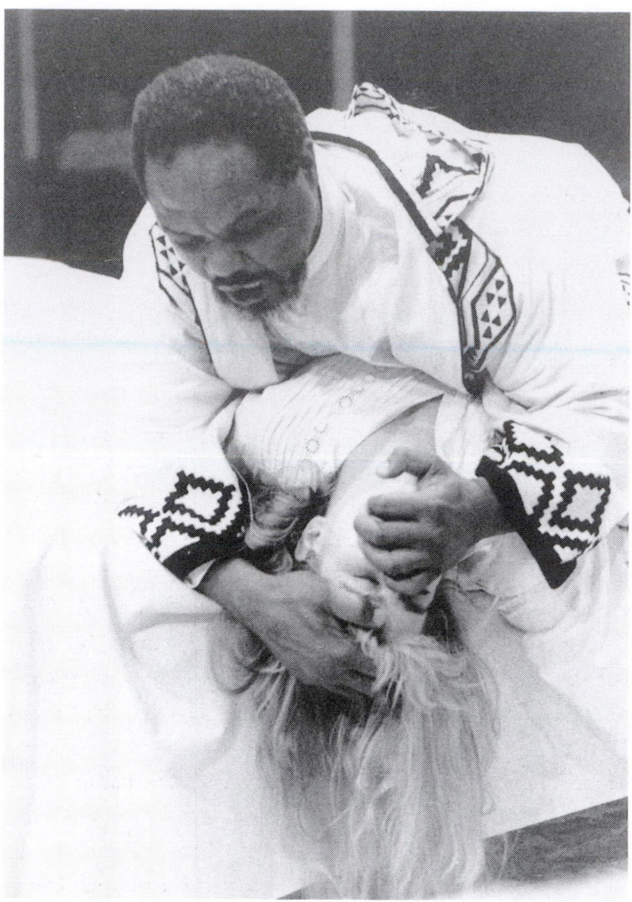

fig 4.8. Othello, played by Willard White, murdering Desdemona, played by Imogen Stubbs, 1989. Copyright Shakespeare Centre Library.

On the third level, what spectators experience – the nip – is Shakespeare's *Othello*, and the bite is how the play resonates in each spectator's life. This is both an individual and a collective experience. Audiences share subtle but unmistakable cues. A rapt audience creates a special kind of focused silence. Levels two and three interact. The audience receives Shakespeare's play by means of its performance. If the acting is bad, the spectators stop paying attention; there is coughing and whispering, maybe even booing. But no matter how involved or displeased, no one jumps onto the stage to stop the murder. Sometimes a play is stopped because the spectators are outraged by what they are seeing. At other times, people walk out. In these cases, the performance is rejected at levels two or three, never at level one. Some people may object to a performance at level one, believing that certain subjects or actions are not suitable for artistic representation. Two very different examples of the "unrepresentable" would be the Shoah and snuff pornography. But despite objections, probably just about everything doable or imaginable has been shown as art or as entertainment, that is, "in play."

At level three, if the actors were to depart from the score in a big way – if Othello pushed down smotheringly hard on the pillow, if Desdemona poked a finger in Othello's eye – the scene would be destroyed as play. Even less extreme, if one of the actors felt the other was no longer playing, or not playing according to the agreed-on score, the stage show would be disrupted. Many arguments erupt backstage over just that kind of thing. "You lost it; you were totally out of control!" But no matter how "out of control," no actors playing a death scene ever lost it to such a degree that they stopped playing and performed "for real." The same cannot be said for police enacting the life role of "cop."

What about audience participation, public meetings, Boal's Forum Theatre, or other performances whose metacommunication is that the playing includes or even demands a blurring of the boundaries separating audience and performers, stage and house? By naming participants "spect-actors," Boal signals that the Theatre of the Oppressed is most effective when the boundary between spectators and actors is blurred or entirely effaced. Boal's message to spectators is, "This is play, and you must play with us!" During the 1960s and 1970s, signals and rules governing audience participation were often vague or deliberately ambivalent, creating both exciting theatre and confusion onstage and off.

Playing blood rites

There are "for real" performances that are difficult to categorize as either play or ritual. Trance performing presents an intriguing example. While in trance, performers are "being played with" rather than playing. While in trance, a person is possessed by a being or force that takes them over. However, even in trance, performers are not out of control. They perform within defined conventions. In the Balinese Rangda-Barong trance drama, the dancers turn their *krisses* (8-inch-long daggers) against their own breasts, pressing the krisses with such force that the knife blades bend. But the trance dancers rarely draw blood (**see figure 4.9**). The Balinese say, "If a person hurts himself, the trance is not real." I will discuss trance performances in more detail in Chapter 6.

fig 4.9. A Balinese dancer in trance turns his *kris* (ceremonial knife) against his own body – but he does not hurt himself. Photograph courtesy of Eugenio Barba.

In some performances, drawing blood is essential. From gladiatorial contests to bullfighting and boxing, the show of blood is inextricably part of the game. Many rituals depend on blood. The Passion of Christ is a blood sacrifice erected on the typical Roman capital punishment of crucifixion, while the Communion is a sharing of flesh and blood. Among the Aztecs, tearing out the still-beating heart was at the center of their ritual performances. In Europe, from the Middle Ages to the French Revolution, executions were elaborate, carnivalesque ritual shows. Many executions featured well-prepared final speeches by the condemned, sometimes including confessions, followed by long hours of painful and humiliating suffering – all eagerly enjoyed by multitudes of spectators (**see Chute box and Merback box**).

Public executions continue today in various parts of the world. Executions in the USA must be witnessed by designated official viewers – transforming the State's ultimate punishment into a performance. But far from all executions are so neatly regulated. From 1882 to 1968, 4,742 Americans – the overwhelming preponderance of them African-Americans – were lynched. Too often, lynchings were festive occasions attended by hundreds of people, many with cameras. People turned these souvenir snapshots into postcards and mailed them. *Without Sanctuary* (2000) was first an exhibit and then a book containing some of these post-cards (http://withoutsanctuary.org/). When the Americans invaded Iraq in 2003, journalists "embedded" within combat units made video broadcasts that looked and sounded like action movies. After the fall of Baghdad, the Iraqi insurgency struck back with suicide bombings, kidnappings, and executions – distributing videotapes of beheadings designed not only to warn and terrify but also to gloat.

Marchette Chute

Performing public executions in Elizabethan London

Another source of public entertainments was executions, and the criminals knew what was expected of them by the public. They went to their death like actors, delivering final speeches from the scaffolds, and a hanging at Wapping was made especially impressive because the chief performer wore breeches of crimson taffeta. When there was an important mass execution, like that which followed the Babington Conspiracy in 1586, the government made the scaffold high and railed off the place to keep horsemen away so "the people might plainly see the execution." The idea of the government was to imprint on the popular mind the horrors of treason and the ghastly death to which it led, but the Londoners treated the occasion like an especially interesting day at the theatre. "There was no lane, street, alley or house in London [. . .] out of which there issued not some of each age and sex, insomuch that the ways were pestered with people so multiplied, as they thronged and overran one another for haste, contending to the place of death for the advantage of the ground where to stand, see and hear."

1949, *Shakespeare of London*, 67–68

Mitchell Merback

The spectacle of executions in medieval Europe

Before the execution ever took place, spectators were presented with an array of symbols communicating vital information about the criminal and his or her deeds.

[. . .] In Germany the formal handing over of the convict to the executioner was treated as a spectacle: while repeating the sentence of death, the officiating judge or town clerk would hold up a wand of office, colored white, red or black (depending on local tradition), break it with great aplomb, cast the bits down on the convict's feet and announce the condemned's now broken bond with humanity. [. . .] After sentencing a bell might toll, and then continue until the moment of death. Clothing conveyed the convict's status at a glance: nobles might wear their livery, while infamous characters were often stripped to the waist. [. . .]

What did spectators come to see? It has often been said that for ordinary people executions, though intended to be terrifying, actually offered an experience that was emotionally comforting: the reassurance that comes with seeing a bona fide sinner confess his crimes, show contrition, receive absolution, endure a painful ordeal and find redemption on the other side. If such an unfortunate wretch can be thus saved, the reasoning goes, so can a sinner like me. [. . .] Except in cases where heinous criminals, outsiders and infamous characters of various stripes became the object of intense collective hatred, the community insisted that the spectacle be edifying, not as a lesson in the majesty of the law but as a drama of Christian repentance, purification, and salvation.

1999, *The Thief, the Cross, and the Wheel*, 138, 144

Philosophies of play

The early view of play allied it with power. Those with the most power – the gods, mythic heroes, kings – acted with absolute freedom, creating their own rules as they went along, indulging their unconstrained desires. These beings played on a big scale. Their playing was world-making, either cosmically or socially. A basic theme of ancient Greek tragedy is the struggle between the unconstrained power of "free play" and the "rule of law," or behavior governed by rules that every being had to obey. To whom did such unconstrained power belong – to the gods, royals, heroes, nature? There was as yet no dominion of human law – a system of constraints more powerful than any individual yet not divine. This dialectical tension between power and law is strong throughout Western philosophy and history, up to the present.

About a century after the high point of ancient Greek tragic theatre, the reigning philosophers of the Western tradition, Plato and Aristotle, established rationality as the dominant system of thought. Plato wanted a city, and Aristotle a science, governed by known, universal, and generally accepted rules or laws. These laws had to be obeyed by people, gods, and nature itself. Free play was replaced by rule-governed games. Free play, *paidia*, was subsumed under, or governed by, rule-bound behavior, *ludus* (**see Caillois box 2**). Caillois uses the Greek word *paidia* (related to the word for "child") to mean a spontaneous burst of play, turbulent and unconstrained. On the other hand, the Latin *ludus* means a game governed by rules. This useful distinction between paidia and ludus is overlooked by many theorists, who depend solely on variations of ludus – ludic, illusion, delusion, ludicrous, etc.

Roger Caillois

Paidia and ludus

[Play] can be placed on a continuum between two opposite poles. At one extreme an almost indivisible principle, common to diversion, turbulence, free improvisation, and carefree gaiety is dominant. It manifests a kind of uncontrolled fantasy that can be designated by the term paidia. At the opposite extreme, this frolicsome and impulsive exuberance is almost entirely absorbed or disciplined by a complementary, and in some respects inverse, tendency to its anarchic and capricious nature: there is a growing tendency to bind it with arbitrary, imperative, and purposely tedious conventions [. . .]. I call this second component ludus.

1979 [1958], *Man, Play, and Games*, 13

Mihai I. Spariosu

Nietzsche and prerational play

Nietzsche's philosophical project can be seen as a return to Hellenic prerational values, and his critique of modern culture as being carried out from the point of view of these values. [. . .] If Nietzsche's doctrine of eternal return can be traced back to Heraclitus, that of the Will to Power can be traced back to the archaic principle of might makes right, and that of the Übermensch to the epic and tragic hero. Furthermore, Nietzsche's oracular, gnomic, and dithyrambic style bears a strong family resemblance to that of lyric and tragic poetry, suggesting a reversion to a prerational mentality. Consequently, to a predominantly rational mode of thinking Nietzsche will appear as a paradoxical, ambiguous, multidimensional thinker. But viewed from the prerational perspective, his philosophical project loses its paradoxical and ambiguous quality, offering instead a far-ranging critique of modern rational values.

1989, *Dionysus Reborn*, 69

But just because Plato threw the poets out of his Republic did not mean that paidia was forever banished. In the nineteenth century, themes from pre-Socratic Greek philosophy were taken up by **Friedrich Nietzsche** (**see Spariosu box 2**) and further developed in the twentieth century as a scientific theory by Werner Heisenberg in the "uncertainty principle" and as a cultural theory by Jacques Derrida in "deconstruction." "Free play" in many guises – from Dada to performance art, from the unconscious to indeterminacy – has regained much of its power, if not its divine status. But the question is far from settled. It probably never can be settled because the struggle is not over data or interpretation, but over basic worldviews.

The rationalists hold that the cosmos is an objective entity, existing outside of, and without dependence on, human consciousness. This cosmos, often called "nature," is governed by its own orderly systems that may not yet, or ever, be wholly understood by humans but which exist, as it were, "in the mind of God," or as "natural laws." As part of nature, humans are also governed by natural law. The job of science is to discover the laws of nature, to confirm them through experiment and observation, and to systematize them into axioms and theories in human form, principally as mathematics. Two examples of this "scientific method" are **Isaac Newton**'s "three laws motion" (of inertia, of action and reaction, and of acceleration proportional to force) and **Albert Einstein**'s famous equation, $e = mc^2$ (energy equals mass times the speed of light squared).

Friedrich Nietzsche (1844–1900): German philosopher whose ideas and writings continue to influence philosophical, political, and aesthetic theory. Among his many writings are *The Birth of Tragedy* (1872), *Thus Spake Zarathustra* (1883–85), and *Beyond Good and Evil* (1886).

Isaac Newton (1642–1727): English mathematician and scientist, author of the *Principia* (1687) and inventor of calculus (independently devised by Gottfried Wilhelm Leibniz, (1646–1716). Newton's "laws" of gravity and thermodynamics went unchallenged until the advent of quantum mechanics in the twentieth century.

Albert Einstein (1879–1955): German-born physicist who emigrated to the USA in 1933 after Hitler came to power. Winner in 1921 of the Nobel Prize in Physics, Einstein is best known for his special and general theories of relativity.

The opposing view holds that the cosmos is a multiverse consisting of dynamic, emergent, multiple, uncentered processes that are always changing, existing as relational systems that can be known only probabilistically; and that these probabilities are the results of an ongoing and unfinishable negotiation between human consciousness-imagination and whatever is "out there" (if anything). There may even be billions of universes existing simultaneously (**see Waldrop box**).

If the world is a game – a metaphor not only of Western thought, but widespread in many cultures – do its rules exist outside or only within specific playfields and playtimes? Are there universal characteristics of play, as **Johan Huizinga** claims, or is play culture-specific (**see Huizinga box 2**)? Does playing the game change the rules, as Heisenberg asserts? Are the consistency and universality which rationality seeks only temporary and local? This make-up-the-rules-as-you-go-along is what Nietzsche called the "will-to-power." Nietzsche believed artists and children played in this way (**see Nietzsche box**). The creation of "illusory" worlds may in fact be humankind's main preoccupation (**see Sutton-Smith box 2**).

Johan Huizinga (1872–1945): Dutch historian and play theorist. Author of one of the most enduringly influential treatises on play, *Homo Ludens* (1938, Eng. 1944).

M. Mitchell Waldrop

Multiple universes

An analysis of localized inflation ["black holes"] suggests that empty space may be spawning universes by the billions, without us ever knowing; was our own universe created this way? What would happen if we could somehow reproduce the conditions of the Big Bang in the modern universe? More precisely, what would happen if a sample of matter were somehow compressed into a tiny region of ultrahigh density and temperature – say 10^{24}K? In one solution, for example, the outside universe simply crushes the hot region into a standard black hole. However, there is a much more interesting solution in which the hot region does indeed inflate – but in a totally different direction that is perpendicular to ordinary space and time. It becomes a kind of aneurysm bulging outward from the side of our familiar universe. In fact, it quickly pinches off and becomes a separate universe of its own. [. . .]

This newborn cosmos [could then] expand to a scale of billions of light-years, producing galaxies, stars, planets, and even life.

1987, "Do-It-Yourself Universes," 845–46

Johan Huizinga

The formal characteristics of play

Summing up the formal characteristics of play we might call it a free activity standing quite consciously outside "ordinary" life as being "not serious," but at the same time absorbing the player intensely and utterly. It is an activity connected with no material interest, and no profit can be gained by it. It proceeds within its own proper boundaries of time and space according to fixed rules and in an orderly manner. It promotes the formation of social groupings which tend to surround themselves with secrecy and to stress their difference from the common world by disguise or other means. The function of play [. . .] can largely be derived from two basic aspects under which we meet it: as a contest for something or a representation of something. These two functions can unite in such a way that the game "represents" a contest, or else becomes a contest for the best representation of something.

1970 [1938], *Homo Ludens*, 13

Friedrich **Nietzsche**

God's play, child's play, artists' play

In this world only play, play as artists and children engage in it, exhibits coming-to-be and passing away, structuring and destroying, without any moral additive, in forever equal innocence. And as children and artists play, so plays the ever-living fire. It constructs and destroys, all in innocence. Such is the game that the aeon plays with itself. Transforming itself into water and earth, it builds towers of sand like a child at the seashore, piles them up and tramples them down. From time to time it starts the game anew. An instant of satiety – and again it is seized by its need, as the artist is seized by his need to create. Not hybris but the ever self-renewing impulse to play calls new worlds into being. The child throws its toys away from time to time – and starts again in innocent caprice. But when it does build, it combines and joins and forms its structures regularly, conforming to inner laws. Only aesthetic man can look thus at the world [. . .].

1962 [c. 1870], *Philosophy in the Tragic Age of the Greeks*, 62

Brian **Sutton-Smith**

Play and human achievement

Given that there is nothing more characteristic of human achievement than the creation of illusory cultural and theoretical worlds, as in music, dance, literature, and science, then children's and gamblers' full participation in such play worlds can be seen not as a defect, or as compensation for inadequacy, but rather as participation in a major central preoccupation of humankind. The modern computer-age habit of calling these "virtual worlds" rather than illusory worlds highlights this move toward a more positive, if narrower, epistemological attitude about their function.

1997, *The Ambiguity of Play*, 54

Heisenberg discovered that the act of observing very small particles (quanta of matter-energy) changes what is being observed. Although the mathematics is beyond me, the underlying theory and its implications can be simply stated. In the world of subatomic phenomena, ordinary commonsense causality does not function. Instead, one can only state the "probability" that a group of subatomic particles/waves will act in a certain way, be in a certain position, at a certain time (**see Heisenberg box and Northrup box**).

Werner **Heisenberg**

Particles, waves, and uncertainty

The electron may have been practically at rest before the observation. But in the act of observation at least one light quantum of the X-ray must have passed the microscope and must first have been deflected by the electron. Therefore, the electron has been pushed by the light quantum, it has changed its momentum and its velocity, and one can show that the uncertainty of this change is just big enough to guarantee the validity of the uncertainty relations. [. . .]

Actually, we need not speak of particles at all. For many experiments it is more convenient to speak of matter waves [. . . which is] much nearer to the truth than the particle picture. [. . .] The two pictures are of course mutually exclusive, because a certain thing cannot at the same time be a particle (i.e., substance confined to a very small volume) and a wave (i.e., a field spread out over a large space), but the two complement each other. By playing with both pictures, by going from the one picture to the other and back again, we finally get the right impression of the strange kind of reality behind our atomic experiments. [. . .] The knowledge of the position of a particle is complementary to the knowledge of its velocity or momentum. If we know the one with high accuracy we cannot know the other with high accuracy; still we must know both for determining the behavior of the system. [. . .] A real difficulty in understanding this interpretation arises, however, when one asks the famous question: But what happens "really" in an atomic event? [. . . W]hat one deduces from an observation is a probability function, a mathematical expression that combines statements about possibilities or tendencies with statements about our knowledge of facts. So we cannot completely objectify the results of an observation, we cannot describe what "happens" between this observation and the next.

1958, *Physics and Philosophy*, 47–50

F. S. C. Northrup

The uncertainty principle

In quantum mechanics [. . .] the very act of observing alters the object being observed when its quantum numbers are small. [. . .] The introduction of the concept of probability into the definition of state of the object of scientific knowledge in quantum mechanics rules out [. . .] *in principle* and not merely in practice due to the imperfections of human observation and instruments, the satisfying of the condition that the object of the physicist's knowledge is an isolated system. Heisenberg shows also that the including of the experimental apparatus and even of the eye of the observing scientist in the physical system which is the object of the knower's knowledge does not help, since, if quantum mechanics be correct, the states of all objects have to be defined in principle by recourse to the concept of probability.

1958, "Introduction" to Heisenberg, *Physics and Philosophy*, 24

uncertainty principle were revolutionary. Heisenberg overturned classical Newtonian physics. If at a fundamental level, "nature" cannot be fixed outside of probability, then there is no physical solidity, no fundamental material substance. The "what is" of the universe is not founded on certainty but on a kind of gaming, a throw of the subatomic dice. It was this that so infuriated Einstein. He insisted that God does not play dice (**see Einstein box**).

Albert Einstein

God does not play dice

You believe in the God who plays dice, and I in complete law and order in a world which exists, and which I, in a wildly speculative way, am trying to capture. [. . .] Even the great initial success of the quantum theory does not make me believe in the fundamental dice-game [. . .].

1971, *The Born–Einstein Letters*, 180–81

It might seem that such a theory is of small consequence to everyday life, and indeed commonsense causality is not affected by the uncertainty principle. If I throw a stone at a window and the glass breaks, I can determine the instant when the stone shattered the pane of the glass. But from a philosophical point of view, quantum mechanics and the

Einstein (and God) aside, the uncertainty principle underlies much of contemporary thinking. When translated into philosophy, it appears as Derridean deconstruction, perhaps the most playful – if also very difficult to understand – speculation (**see Wilson box**). According to Derrida, there is no center because the center is not a fixed place but a function (**see Derrida box**). All authority is subverted, "displaced," opening spaces for all kinds of radical free play. Derrida's writing not only inaugurates a discourse on decentering, but enacts it with plentiful wordplay, punning, and double meanings. Derrida's thought ramifies beyond philosophy into politics and aesthetics, as well as into cultural, literary, and performance theory. I will discuss deconstruction more fully in Chapter 5.

R. Rawdon Wilson

Play and deconstruction

[T]hough it may not be possible adequately to define the concept, Derrida seems to make it clear that free play is limitless, unlimited by any irreducible signified or transcendental concept that cannot be further decomposed, and it manifests itself in the process of indefinite substitution. Play, considered as free play, lies beyond stable, centered structures, makes them untenable, decenters them, and deprivileges them.

1990, *In Palamedes' Shadow*, 16

Jacques Derrida

Where there is no center, all is playing

It was necessary to begin thinking that there was no center, that the center could not be thought in the form of a present-being, that the center had no natural site, that it was not a fixed locus but a function, a sort of nonlocus in which an infinite number of sign-substitutions came into play. This was the moment when language invaded the universal problematic, the moment when, in the absence of a center or origin, everything became discourse – provided we can agree on this word – that is to say, a system in which the central signified, the original or transcendental signified, is never absolutely present outside a system of differences. The absence of the transcendental signified extends the domain and the play of signification infinitely.

1978, *Writing and Difference*, 280

Artists may not follow Heisenberg literally, but they understand him metaphorically. Arts, once the home of strict choreography, precise scores, and fixed mise-en-scènes have for some time been open to chance processes, unpredictable eruptions from the unconscious, and improvisation. Of course, there are multiple causes that brought these operations into play during the past century. Improvisation, for example, is fundamental to African performing arts and rituals (**see Drewal box**). From the seventeenth century, African cultures became better known in Europe and the Americas as a consequence of slavery and colonialism. But however Africa arrived, its impact has been enormous. In the arts, painters such as **Pablo Picasso** took the basics of cubism from African art, and African music from ragtime and jazz to rock and roll and hip-hop reshaped first Western and then world pop music. Freud's investigations into "dream work," the unconscious, and creativity also had an enormous impact on the arts. Seen this way, Heisenberg's uncertainty principle was part of a larger movement in Western thought broadening the basis of creativity and expression. A theory that changed physics was adapted to the arts. Among many examples of performances based on uncertainty are the chance musical compositions and lectures of John Cage, the Fluxus group of New York, Happenings, and the "manifestations" of Dada artists (**see figure 4.10**). The outflow from this kind of thinking continues to affect performance art, music, theatre, dance, and the visual arts in the twenty-first century.

Margaret Thompson Drewal

Improvisation, play, and ritual

Whenever improvisation is a performative strategy in ritual, it places ritual squarely within the domain of play. It is indeed the playing, the improvising, that engages people, drawing them into the action, constructing their relationships, thereby generating multiple and simultaneous discourses always surging between harmony/disharmony, order/disorder, integration/ opposition, and so on.

1992, *Yoruba Ritual*, 7–8

Pablo Picasso (1881–1973): Spanish visual artist, inventor of the cubist style of painting, as illustrated by *Les Demoiselles d'Avignon* (1907). Picasso's long artistic career spanned eight decades and featured innovations in a number of styles and media.

fig 4.10. Chance or indeterminate performances can take many forms, ranging from electronic music presented in a concert hall to a barely noticed "action" blending in to everyday life.

John Cage looking over the shoulder of David Tudor as they prepare a concert of "chance" music. Royal Festival Hall, 1972. Copyright Hulton-Deutsch Collection/Corbis.

Fluxus artist Ben Vautier sweeping a street in Nice, France, 1960s. Photograph courtesy of Richard Schechner.

The bias against play

The other side of the coin is the deep-seated Western bias against play. From Plato to the Puritans, the playful has been considered frivolous, unimportant, and even sinful. Playing is a major distraction tempting people away from work, which is the "real business" of living. Plato wanted to banish the players, especially poets, playwrights, and actors, from his ideal Republic. Shockingly, he almost succeeded. Adults are supposed to play only during "time off" (from work) in specially designated places and according to well-defined rules. If the playing is regarded as risky, sexual, and subversive to work values or the authority of the state, whole neighborhoods are fenced off and designated a "red-light" district. The color red symbolizes both something hot and "stop." Or special days are designated for playing – holidays, time off, and vacation. But every Mardi Gras is followed by Ash Wednesday, each binge by a confession. It is no accident that red-light districts are full of con artists, prostitutes, cross-dressers (who are fantasy role-players), actors, and musicians. In many cities, the railroad station, the theatre district, and the red-light district are cheek by jowl. People want to come and go efficiently from where they can play or watch others play.

In fact, the theatre has only relatively recently, and still perilously, been accorded middle-class status in the West. In Germany, the *Stadt-Theater* (municipal theatre) tradition started by the aristocracy was soon adopted by the increasingly wealthy and culture-hungry middle class. The German model was widely imitated throughout Europe and in the USA, where it was dubbed the "regional theatre" movement.

fig 4.11. Times Square, New York – then and now, except that "then" is removed in space rather than time.

The "new" 42nd Street, featuring Disney's *The Lion King*, directed by Julie Taymor. Photograph by Richard Schechner.

The way 42nd Street used to look before "development." This picture was taken in 2001 a few blocks away on 8th Avenue on a block not yet developed. As of 2005, the block looks the same. Photograph by Richard Schechner.

But America's largest and most famous theatre district is New York's Broadway, located near Times Square. Commencing in the early 1990s, Times Square and West 42nd Street were transformed from an "adults-only" district into a "family-oriented" neighborhood dominated by Disney, MGM, the Ford Motor Company, and other mega-corporations. But only a few blocks north of the "new Times Square," remnants of the "old Times Square" remain in place (**see figure 4.11**).

The performing arts have traditionally been ambivalent with regard to "morality," with one foot in church, the other barely out of bed: from sacred music to whorehouse jazz, from magisterial displays of royalty to the strutting of Restoration epoch actresses and their rakes, from the long-legged grace of the prima ballerina to the sexually available girls of the corps de ballet displayed backstage to the men of means who could afford to purchase access to them (**see figure 4.12**).

Other cultures have not been so ambivalent. In India, music, dance, sex, and religion were long associated with each other (until British Victorian values imposed by colonialism took hold). *Devadasis*, well-trained temple dancers whose name means "servants of god," performed in front of the *murtis* or icons of the gods. Devadasis were available on a regulated basis for sex with priests, princes, and important patrons of the temples – who were also patrons of the arts. The children of such unions were brought up to be dancers and musicians. In most of India, the devadasis were outlawed in the 1930s after a fierce campaign against them led by both Indian reformers and the British. A few devadasis continued to dance into the 1970s. Several classical Indian dance forms – *bharatanatyam* and *odissi* among them – originated in devadasi dancing (**see figure 4.13**).

Maya–lila

India may be more receptive to a playful mix of categories because playing is a fundamental ingredient of Indian philosophy, worldview, and aesthetics. The idea that the universe may be a cosmic dice game, that meaning is a "play of signification," that the "will to power" and the uncertainty principle operate at all levels of natural, animal, and human life and experience has been a persistent theme in India for about 2,500–3,000 years. *Maya* and *lila* are Sanskrit words meaning "illusion" and "play." The concepts embedded in these two words are hard to pin down because – as with the Greek *mimesis*, *praxis*, and *katharsis* – key terms in Aristotle's theory of tragedy – there is an enormous library of commentary, contradictory interpretations, and changing emphasis over historical time. The earliest meaning of maya was "real," derived from its root "ma" – "to make" (**see O'Flaherty box**). But it was not long before maya became identified with the creative force as such, both divine and artistic; and with powers of transformation – the making of something out of something else, or out of nothing.

maya–lila: an Indian philosophical concept of existence as play where boundaries separating "real" and "illusion," "true" and "false," are continuously shifting and are wholly permeable. The notion that life is a game, a dream, a sport, a drama.

fig 4.12. Edgar Degas' *Rehearsal of the Ballet*, 1876, depicts an old man supervising the young dancers while another man gazes. The painting romanticizes the access to women performers that men of privilege and money enjoyed. Photograph by E. G. Schemp. Copyright The Nelson-Atkinson Museum of Art, Kansas City, Missouri. (Purchase: The Kenneth A. and Helen F. Spencer Foundation Acquisition Fund, F-73-30).

But in India, as elsewhere, artists were suspect, slippery characters. And the gods were much like artists – sometimes to be admired, sometimes to be distrusted and feared. Therefore, maya soon began to expand its meanings to include "illusion," "not real," "false," "unsubstantial," "deceitful." It has kept these multiple meanings. "All life is maya," an Indian will say, meaning that nothing is reliable, everything is just show. But he may also mean that living is extremely unpredictable, unreliable, subject to sudden shifts, fundamentally playful, but not necessarily fun. And he may imply that all experienced reality is constructed. The ultimate absolute – the brahman beyond all knowing – is without shape or form, unmanifest, uncreated: the categorical opposite of maya.

Lila is a more ordinary word meaning "play," "sport," or "drama." In Indian terms, the gods in their lila made a world of maya: when the gods play, the world comes into existence; but this world, however substantial it appears, is not fixed or reliable. It is ultimately governed by desire and chance. But desire and chance as the gods play it. From the human standpoint, the gods' lilas range from the capricious to the awesome. Annually, in north India a cycle play recounting the life of Vishnu's seventh avatar (incarnation) Rama is called Ramlila – the lila or play of Rama. At Ramnagar, across the sacred Ganga river from the holy city of Banaras (also called Varanasi and Kashi), the Ramlila takes 31 days to enact and draws ardently reverential crowds of up to 75,000 persons (**see figure 4.14**). At the core of the Ramlila experience is

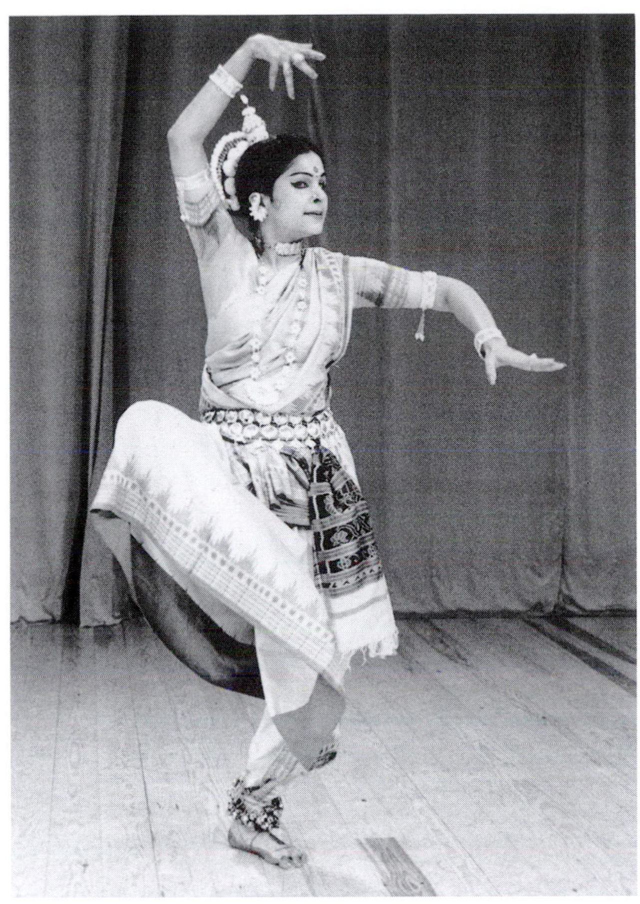

fig 4.13. Indian dancer Sanjukta Panigrahi (1944–97) in a classic stance of odissi, 1990s. Photograph courtesy of Eugenio Barba.

the belief that when they appear in their full costumes and enact the story of Rama, five pre-adolescent boys are actually the gods Rama, his wife Sita, and Rama's three brothers (**see figure 4.15**). The presence of the divine is a lila that at moments dissolves maya, revealing an absolute reality, who is Sita-Rama. The gods-as-boys/boys-as-gods is the lila of Vishnu and Lakshmi who take on the human form of Rama and Sita. The 31-day play is the specific human lila (theatre) in which the divine lila takes place. The lesser incorporates the greater; the absolute appears in the heart of illusion. If this is dizzying, that is because the relationship of maya to lila is paradoxical.

Ramlila is not the only lila of India. The deities often manifest themselves both in regularly scheduled performances and in unpredictable ways. The Khumbmela – a festival that takes place every twelve years – attracts millions of people. The Khumbmela at Allahabad in 2001 brought up to 60 million to the *triveni* – the spot where the Ganga and Jamuna rivers – both sacred – are joined by the invisible

Wendy Doniger O'Flaherty

Maya and the real illusion

[*Maya* originally] meant only what was real; through its basis in the verbal root *ma* ("to make") it expressed the sense of "realizing the phenomenal world" [. . .] In the *Rig Veda*, to "measure out" the universe was to create it, to divide it into its constituent parts, to *find* it by bringing it out of chaos. [. . .] Magicians do this; artists do it; gods do it. But according to certain Indian philosophies, every one of us does it every minute of our lives.

This concept of *maya* as a kind of artistic power led gradually to its later connotation of magic, illusion, and deceit. [. . .] It often means not merely bringing something into existence [. . .] but manipulating the existent forces of nature or invoking the power to create and achieve the marvelous. Thus *maya* first meant making something that was not there before; then it came to mean making something that was there into something that was not really there. The first describes the universe in the Vedic world-view; the second, the universe in the Vedantic world-view. [. . .] In both cases *maya* can often best be translated as "transformation." [. . .] A similar cluster of meanings radiates from it [*maya*] as from the English derivatives of the Latin word for play (*ludo*) – de-lusion, il-lusion, e-lusive, and so forth – and from the word "play" itself – play as drama, as swordplay or loveplay, as the play of light that causes mirages, as the double image implicit in word-play. [. . .] These word clusters delineate a universe full of beauty and motion that enchants us all. All Indian philosophies acknowledge that *maya* is a fact of life – the fact of life; but some (the *moksha*-oriented [those who seek liberation from the wheel of birth–death–rebirth] regard it as a negative fact, to be combated, while others (*samsara*-oriented [those who enjoy this world as it is] regard it as a positive fact, to be embraced.

1984, *Dreams, Illusions, and Other Realities*, 117–19

fig 4.14. Enormous crowds gather for some of the episodes of the 31-day long Ramlila of Ramnagar, north India, 1997. Photograph by Sam Schechner.

Saraswati river descending from heaven. Among the multitudes were many sages, *rishis*, and *sadhus* claiming to be avatars. The porosity of the boundaries between the human and the divine, combined with the ubiquity of maya-lila, make such manifestations inevitable. Raslila and Krishnalila – large-scale public enactments of the life of Krishna, Vishnu's sixth avatar – are more like Ramlila: carefully staged large-scale public enactments. What happens at Ramlila, Raslila, and Krishnalila is not make-believe. Different orders of reality converge in the lilas. The young boys who are the *swarups* (forms of the gods) of Rama or Krishna not only enact but also embody the gods. Like temple *murtis* (paintings, statues, or other divine manifestations), they do not represent the gods, but are inhabited by them. Yet at the same time the boys remain children. If a swarup giggles, forgets his lines, falls asleep, or jokes with a friend, the spectators are not taken aback. The people say: "Cannot the god play? Is not this Bala Krishna [boy Krishna], full of mischief and sleep?" Rama is more "serious," a warrior and teacher – yet inhabiting a pre-adolescent boy whose voice has not yet deepened. At Ramlila, people come to just look at him and his wife, Sita, mother of the world. Or to touch their feet, accept a lotus blossom from their hands (**see figure 4.16**). These devotees are face to face with gods, with boys, with maya–lila.

In a maya–lila world, the material universe is a playground. Everything that happens is part of Brahma's day or Vishnu's playing or Shiva's *tandava* dancing or dice game (**see Handelman and Shulman box**). According to one Indian version of the cosmos, Shiva's throw of the dice activates the universe – or even more: the universe is a dice game, always at risk, a play of chance, always in motion.

fig 4.15. Young boys become the *swarups* or "form of the gods" during Ramlila. The swarups are garlanded, crowned, adored, and worshipped, 1997. Photograph by Sam Schechner.

fig 4.16. A devotee touching the foot of Sita during the Ramlila of Ramnagar, 1977. Photograph by Richard Schechner.

Don Handelman and David Shulman

Siva's cosmic dice game

Siva often plays dice with the goddess – his consort, Parvati. Almost invariably, he loses to her. [. . .] Sometimes she becomes angry when he refuses to pay up, or even to acknowledge that he has lost; this stubborn stance may then lead to further conflict – aggressive acts by one or both partners, sulking, quarrels, separations, even curses hurled in rage. Or, still in a playful spirit, the goddess might cover Siva's eyes with her hands, thereby enveloping the universe itself in catastrophic darkness.

Nothing [. . .] is as rich in consequence as a game. Perhaps we should say *the* game. The dice match is in some sense equal to the cosmos, both a condensed expression of its process and a mode of activating and generating that process. If one is God, there is, finally, no other game. All the more shocking, then, is the fact that he must lose. No wonder that he is sometimes more than a little reluctant to play.

The dice throws, as is well known, correlate with the four *yugas*, the cosmic ages in their recursive, devolutionary sequence. Thus, time itself proceeds out of this divine game. Without the game, there would be no time, perhaps no space as well (for the dice also model the cardinal directions in horizontal alignment and in relation to the vertical vector of the zenith) – in short, no world as we know it: language, sexual differentiation and identity, self-knowledge – all these, too, [. . .] are part of the generative cycles of the game.

1997, *God Inside Out: Siva's Game of Dice*, 4–6

The dice-game universe is a function of the dynamics of chance interacting with a supreme god's unbridled will. In the *Mahabharata*, one of the two great Sanskrit epics (the *Ramayana* is the other), the initiating action is a dice game where Yudhisthira loses everything – his wealth, his kingdom, and even his wife's clothing. In another origin/end of the world myth, Shiva's tandava dance – awakening and radiating *shakti*, a combined female–male energy – brings the universe into existence. At the end of time, when Brahma sleeps, Shiva dances existence into extinction. After eons, as Brahma awakens, Shiva starts dancing again, and the universe is created again, the same but different. For Indians, believing that the cosmos is a dance, a dream, a gamble – maya–lila – is not softheaded. Did Einstein know Shiva played dice?

In a maya–lila world, experience and reality are multiple, a plenitude of performed, transformable, non-exclusive events or play-worlds. If all realities and experiences shape each other, are networks of flexible constructs, transformations, dreams of dreams, unsettled relationships, what then of "ordinary play" – children playing tag or make-believe, grownups knocking a golf ball across the countryside, a rapt audience listening to a Brahms symphony? These kinds of things – adjusted to suit specific cultures – happen in India, and everywhere else. But the Indians and others who have not lost their unrational abilities are more tuned to sudden, delightful, or shocking transformations, the appearance of scary or farcical demons in the midst of an all-night performance, or a glimpse of the Absolute that Krishna reveals to Arjuna in the *Bhagavad Gita* (**see Vyasa box**). It was the *Gita* that **J. Robert Oppenheimer**, head of the scientific team that developed the atomic bomb, quoted on 16 July 1945 as he witnessed the world's first nuclear explosion: "If the light of a thousand suns were to rise in the sky at once [. . .]. I am time grown old, creating world destruction."

Vyasa

The absolute Krishna

Listen [Krishna tells Arjuna] as I recount for you in essence the divine powers of myself. Endless is my extent. [. . .] I am the beginning, middle, and end of creations. [. . .] I am indestructible time, the creator facing everywhere at once. [. . .] I am death the destroyer of all, the source of what will be, the feminine powers: fame, fortune, speech, memory, intelligence, resolve, patience. [. . .] I am the great ritual chant, the meter of sacred song, [. . .] I am the dice game of gamblers, [. . .] I am the epic poet Vyasa among sages, the inspired singer among bards.

1986 [*c.* 200 BCE], *The Bhagavad Gita*, 91–94

J. Robert Oppenheimer (1904–67): American nuclear physicist and director of the Manhattan Project, the team that developed and detonated the first atomic bomb in the New Mexico desert on 16 July 1945. From 1947 to 1952, Oppenheimer was chairman of the General Advisory Committee of the Atomic Energy Commission. Accused of being a Communist sympathizer, Oppenheimer lost his security clearance in 1953. In 1947 he became director of the Institute for Advanced Studies which he led until his retirement in 1966.

Although binary models are tricky because they split into two opposing sides a world of nuances and continua, they can also be useful if used cautiously. I offer one here, contrasting the difference between maya–lila and the Western rational understandings of play (**see figure 4.17**).

Contrasting Attitudes Towards Play and Playing

Maya–Lila	Rationalist
Unending cycles of creating/destroying	Single creation
Multiple realities	Single reality
How the universe is	Make-believe
Playing is on a par with religion, art	Playing is on a par with art, but not as important as religion or as real as science
Creative–destructive	Creative
Everywhere	In playgrounds or other special places
Free	Rule bound
For everyone	For children mostly
All the time	After work
Fundamental	Recreational
Female–Male combined	Childlike, pre-sexual
Extremely powerful	Little power
Celebrates the erotic as the divine energy	Represses the erotic as "bad"

fig 4.17. Maya–lila is more volatile, creative–destructive, all-encompassing, and transformative than the rationalist view of play. In the West, especially since the Enlightenment, playing has been isolated, located in "after work," "recreation," or in childhood. However, in recent decades, partly because the world is more global, non-rationalist notions of playing have re-emerged in the West.

Deep play, dark play

In theatrical terms, maya–lila is an interweaving of the performer and the role. Is the role "real"? And if we can safely say of aesthetic performance – of Hamlet or Shakuntala or the Black Swan – that the role is not real, what of ritual performances such as the appearance of a pope in full regalia to bless the believers or the manifestation of an Afro-Brazilian orixa who "mounts" the body of a dancer in deep trance? In rituals there is no "suspension of disbelief." Rather there is "deep play" as understood by Geertz (**see Geertz box**).

Clifford Geertz

Deep play

Bentham's concept of "deep play" is found in his *The Theory of Legislation*. By it he means play in which the stakes are so high that it is, from his utilitarian standpoint, irrational for men to engage in it at all. For if a man whose fortune is a thousand pounds (or ringgits [Balinese money]) wagers five hundred of it on an even bet, the marginal utility of the pound he stands to win is clearly less than the marginal disutility of the one he stands to lose. In genuine deep play, this is the case for both parties. They are both in over their heads. Having come together in the search of pleasure they have entered into a relationship which will bring the participants, considered collectively, net pain rather than net pleasure. [. . . D]espite the force of Bentham's analysis men do engage in such play, both passionately and often, and even in the face of law's revenge. For Bentham and those who think as he does (nowadays mainly lawyers, economists, and a few psychiatrists), the explanation is [. . .] that such men are irrational – addicts, fetishists, children, fools, savages, who need only to be protected against themselves. But for the Balinese, though naturally they do not formulate it in so many words, the explanation lies in the fact that in such play, money is less a measure of utility, had or expected, than it is a symbol of moral import, perceived or imposed. [. . .] In deep ones [play], where the amounts of money are great, much more is at stake than material gain: namely, esteem, honor, dignity, respect – in a word, though in Bali a profoundly freighted word, status.

1973, *The Interpretation of Cultures*, 432–33

Geertz is writing about why some Balinese make ruinous bets on cockfights. Geertz's insight into deep play has broad implications. Deep play applies to mountain-climbing, high-speed auto-racing, and many other activities where there is very high risk physically, fiscally, and/or psychologically. Deep play involves such high stakes that one wonders why people engage in it at all. As Geertz explains it, deep playing draws the whole person into what amounts to a life-and-death struggle expressing not only individual commitment (to the irrational even more than to the rational), but also cultural values. Deep play is all absorbing – and closely related to what I call "**dark play**."

dark play: "playing with fire," "breaking the rules," "getting away with murder." Playing that emphasizes risk, deception, and sheer thrill.

"Playing in the dark" means that some of the players don't know they are playing – like in a con game or when rats run a maze or when the gods or fate or chance lay traps to catch people in. Dark play is connected to maya–lila. Dark play involves fantasy, risk, luck, daring, invention, and deception. Dark play may be entirely private, known to the player alone. Or it can erupt suddenly, a bit of microplay, seizing the player(s) and then as quickly subsiding – a wisecrack, burst of frenzy, delirium, or deadly risk. Dark play subverts order, dissolves frames, and breaks its own rules – so much so that the playing itself is in danger of being destroyed, as in spying, double-agentry, con games, and stings. Unlike carnivals or ritual clowns whose inversions of established order are sanctioned by the authorities, dark play is truly subversive, its agendas always hidden. Dark play rewards its players by means of deceit, disruption, and excess. In my courses on play, I invite students to write examples of dark play from their own lives. Here are four responses (used with permission):

1 *Female*: When I am feeling especially depressed or angry about the world and my life, I play a form of Russian Roulette with New York City traffic. I cross streets without pausing to see if it is safe to do so or not. [. . .] At the time of playing there is a thrill in abandoning precautions and in toying with the value of life and death.

2 *Female*: Sometimes I'll be in a bar with friends and some guy will hit on me. If I don't want anything to do with him, I ignore him. But if he persists, then I'll speak in my made-up language. Some guys get the hint. Others will try to understand me or ask me very loudly and very slowly, "WHERE ARE YOU FROM?" as if I'd suddenly understand them. When that happens, I'll engage a friend in my game. We'll converse in the made-up language until the guy gets so frustrated he leaves. The language sounds real. I've been practicing it ever since I was a kid.

3 *Male*: When I was 15 years old, together with three friends, I spent some nights in a youth hostel, a seventeenth-century castle, in a small fishing village in Holland. One night, the four of us discovered a trapdoor in the ceiling of the bathroom. We were convinced that this led to the roof of the castle. We saw many signs stating that the roof was off limits. For us, those signs were orders to get to the roof. We sneaked out of the dorm, went through the trapdoor and found some stairs. It was pitch dark, we could only find our way by touch. When we got to the roof, a very strong wind was blowing. We yelled into the storm, screamed obscenities, and cursed the hostel managers who made us all pray before each meal. We cursed the clouds, the Virgin Mary, the village. We yelled at the fishing boats we knew were out on the sea. "Go down, go down!" one of us yelled. "Sink boats, sink!" It became a chant. "Sink, boats, sink!" Just before dawn we were back in the dorm. We felt proud as hell. At 8 a.m. we were thrown out of the hostel. In a café, tired, sleepy but still excited, we drank our coffee. A local newspaper lay on the table. The headline said, "Two Fishermen Drown When Boat Sinks." One of us began to cry. I did not believe then, and do not believe now, and will never believe that we caused this accident. But it had an effect. For the next couple of days we did not play; hardly joked.

4 *Female*: I was 16 years old and on vacation at Yosemite with my father. I climbed out over the guardrail to get a better view of the waterfall. When I realized that my father was crying for me to come back, I went to the very edge and did an arabesque. I continued balancing on one leg until he got onto his knees, crying, begging for me to come back. Ten years later, in the Sierra Nevada range, I repeated the same act in front of my husband who shouted at me to think of our daughter as a motherless child. My initial inspiration for dancing on the edge was in both cases the thrill of the beauty and the danger of the dance. My father's and husband's anxiety sharpened the experience for me – the further I got away from them the closer I came to communion with some Other.

Leaving aside psychological interpretations of motives, personal gains, anxieties, desires played out, and so on, what do these examples show?

First, they subvert the metacommunicative message "this is play" that Gregory Bateson posited as necessary for play to begin, continue, and thrive. Second, in dark play, as in Boal's Invisible Theatre, some of the players do not know that a game is being played. The drivers of vehicles in New York City, the guys trying to decipher a "foreign" language in a bar, the fishermen caught in a storm – none of these knew they were players in a game. These "non-knowing players" –

innocents, dupes, butts, victims – are essential to the playing. In the third example, the chanting boys had no idea that their play might have an effect – and the author, a convinced rationalist, is certain that there was no connection between the curses and the sinking fishing boat. Still, the coincidence – always a key mark of fate – draws tears from one of the boys, their vacation was temporarily dampened, and the author still protests he has no such superpower.

The final example is complicated. This scene was played twice, ten years apart, testing first the love of a father and then of a husband. Still later, the dark-player provided me with a photograph of the re-enactment (**see figure 4.18**). The scene was played, replayed, documented, and now made public. At each iteration it becomes more of a performance. It is a test of love, but also a mocking of love; laughing at it, taunting it. The two life roles, husband and father, were conflated and devalued. The men were manipulated into begging the dancer to stop playing. The father shed tears; the husband reminded the dancer of her serious responsibilities as a mother. None of this brought the dancer back from the edge – in fact, quite the opposite: it heightened the "thrill of the beauty and the danger of the dance." The more the men were terrified, the more ecstatic the dancer. All anxiety left her and spilled into them. What was important to her was dancing on the edge. Liberated, she relished her spiritual experience. In having power over herself, she gained power over the two "patriarchal males" in her life (up to that point). And giving me the photo for this book? A final trump card sending the message to those who know and remember, a secret few.

Why do people create and enact dark play? Are children innocent of such play? Sutton-Smith offers examples of what

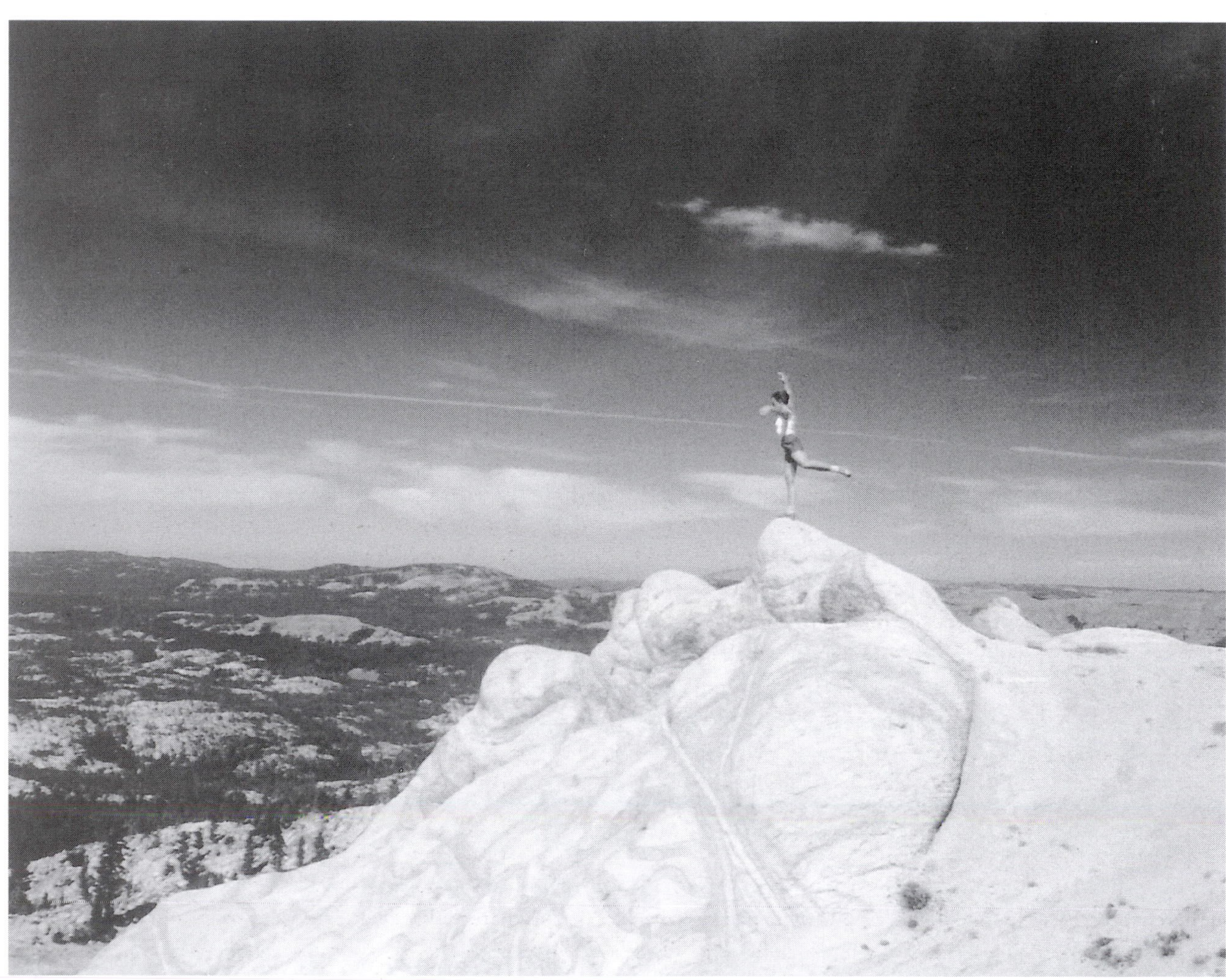

fig 4.18. An episode of dark play re-enacted on a rock at Yosemite National Park, USA. Photograph courtesy of the performer, name withheld.

he calls the "masks of play" – play that conceals its purposes, even its existence. Children no less than adults engage in this kind of play. In school, camp, prison, and church – wherever the eyes of authority gaze down on them – kids find ways around the rules. They make April Fool's jokes, play in the toilet, whisper, doodle, make faces, mock adults, and so on. They form clubs, gangs, and cliques. They even develop careful strategies in order to shoot up a school.

All these activities – the pleasant, the provocative, and the terrifying – can be understood as playing, as ways of establishing autonomous social orders and hierarchies, of exploring or exploding the limits of power, of resisting the adult world that apparently so dominates them. Some of these children grow up to be spies, police, terrorists, colonels, con-men, and crooks – all with sensible reasons for making dark play. But why do others engage in it? Assuming a new or alternative identity, even briefly, is very important. Masking, cloaking one's ordinary self just to get away from the humdrum, is also important. Much role-playing over the internet is this kind of dark play. Sometimes a person puts herself at risk to test her luck, to prove her value, to enact a special destiny. In life-risk play such as crossing the street without looking, one's "immortality" is tested. In dancing on the edge, one leaves behind the mundane, hears it screaming and begging, and soars toward a "communion with some Other." In disguise-play such as talking in an invented language, alternative selves are given license. The gratification and thrill of dark play involves everything from physical risk-taking to inventing new selves to engaging one's inner self to communion with the Other. There is something excitingly liberating about this kind of playing.

In dark play sometimes even the acknowledged players are not sure if they are playing or not. What begins as a game, as a gesture of bravado, can quickly get out of hand. More than a few have died on a dare. Survivors may claim they were "just fooling around." On the other hand, actions that were not play when they were performed become play retroactively when the events are retold. What happened does not change, but when a person recounts a "narrow escape," for example, what was deadly serious in the doing becomes playful in the retelling.

Conclusion

In this chapter, I've examined play "as" performance, and play "is" performance. When animals and humans play, they exaggerate and show off in order to impress playmates as well as non-players who are watching (this is true of chimpanzees, gorillas, and monkeys as well as of humans). In most kinds of play, in order to play successfully, all the players must agree to play. Players send metacommunicative messages that say, "We are playing." In some ways, play is very much like ritual and theatre. Play is often an orderly sequence of actions performed in specified places for known durations of time. Much playing is narrational, with winners and losers, conflict, and the arousal and display of emotion. But there is also playing that is less formal-bursts of microplay that can lessen the tensions in a room or relieve the boredom of routinized work. Some play is "dark," making fun of people, deceiving them, or leading them on. One group of play theorists sees playing as the foundation of human culture, art and religion especially. Others regard play as an ambivalent activity both supporting and subverting social structures and arrangements. However one looks at it, play and playing are fundamentally performative.

TALK ABOUT

1. Anonymously write out your dark-play experiences. Put the papers in the middle of a table and select several at random to read out loud. How do these examples fit the theories of Geertz and Bateson? What happens when the metamessage "this is play" is subverted?
2. What is the relationship between flow, discussed in this chapter, and communitas, discussed in Chapter 2?

PERFORM

1. Teach a group from the class how to play a game you used to play as a child. Don't theorize, but rather convey only what's required to play the game. After playing, discuss the structure of the game. Does it have a beginning, middle, and end? How do you know when to stop? Are the rules stable? Or are they obscure and subject to change? What signals are used to send the message "this is play"? Did the group find the game enjoyable? Why or why not?
2. Using Augusto Boal's Invisible Theatre technique, prepare a brief scene. Perform your scene in a public place without letting on that it is "theatre." Have a designated observer or observers note how the scene is received by people. Afterwards, discuss the reactions. Was what you performed theatre? If not, why not? What was it if not theatre?

READ

Ancelet, B. J. "Falling apart to stay together: deep play in the Grand Marais Mardi Gras." *Journal of American Folklore* 114, 452 (2001).

Bateson, Gregory. "A Theory of Play and Fantasy." *The Performance Studies Reader*, Henry Bial, ed.: 121–31. London and New York: Routledge, 2004.

Csikszentmihalyi, Mihaly. "A Theoretical Model for Enjoyment." *Beyond Boredom and Anxiety*: 35–54. San Francisco, Calif.: Jossey-Bass, 1975.

Handelman, Don. "Play and Ritual: Complementary Frames of Meta-Communication." *International Conference on Humour and Laughter: It's a Funny Thing, Humour*, Antony J. Chapman and Hugh Foot, eds: 185–92. Oxford and New York: Pergamon Press, 1977.

Huizinga, Johan. "The Nature and Significance of Play as a Cultural Phenomenon." *The Performance Studies Reader*, Henry Bial, ed.: 117–20. London and New York: Routledge, 2004.

Sutton-Smith, Brian. "The Ambiguity of Play: Rhetorics of Fate." *The Performance Studies Reader*, Henry Bial, ed.: 132–38. London and New York: Routledge, 2004.

5 PERFORMATIVITY

A term hard to pin down

Performativity is everywhere – in daily behavior, in the professions, on the internet and media, in the arts, and in language. It and its sister term, "performative", are very difficult to pin down. These words have acquired a wide range of meanings. Sometimes they are used precisely, but often they are used loosely to indicate something that is "like a performance" without actually being a performance in the orthodox or formal sense. "Performative" is both a noun and an adjective. The noun indicates a word or sentence that does something (I will explain this shortly). The adjective inflects what it modifies with performance-like qualities, such as "performative writing" (**see Phelan box**). "Performativity" is an even broader term, covering a whole panoply of possibilities opened up by a world in which differences are collapsing, separating media from live events, originals from digital or biological clones, and performing onstage from performing in ordinary life. Increasingly, social, political, economic, personal, and artistic realities take on the qualities of performance. In this sense, performativity is similar to what I called "as" performance in Chapter 2.

Performativity is a major underlying theme of this book. In performance studies, performativity points to a variety of topics, among them the construction of social reality including gender and race, the restored behavior quality of performances, and the complex relationship of performance practice to performance theory. Some of these topics are covered in other chapters; some will be dealt with here. To understand performativity you need to grasp certain key terms, theories, (no longer oppositional) binaries, and artistic practices:

- Austin's performative
- Searle's speech acts
- Reality TV and beyond
- Postmodernism
- Simulation
- Poststructuralism/deconstruction
- Constructions of gender
- Constructions of race
- During, before, and after performance art

> Peggy **Phelan**
>
> ***Performative writing***
>
> Performative writing is different from personal criticism or autobiographical essay, although it owes a lot to both genres. Performative writing is an attempt to find a form for "what philosophy wishes all the same to say." Rather than describing the performance event in "direct signification," a task I believe to be impossible and not terrifically interesting, I want this writing to enact the affective force of the performance event again, as it plays itself out in an ongoing temporality made vivid by the psychic process of distortion (repression, fantasy, and the general hubbub of the individual and collective unconscious), and made narrow by the muscular force of political repression in all its mutative violence. [. . .]
>
> Performative writing is solicitous of affect even while it is nervous and tentative about the consequences of that solicitation. Alternately bold and coy, manipulative and unconscious, this writing points both to itself and to the "scenes" that motivate it.
>
> 1997, *Mourning Sex*, 11–12

Austin's performative

The concept of the performative was explored by linguistic philosopher J. L. Austin in lectures delivered in 1955 at Harvard University (posthumously edited and published as *How to Do Things with Words*). Austin coined the word "performative" to describe utterances such as, "I take this woman to be my lawful wedded wife" or "I name this ship the *Queen Elizabeth*" or "I apologize," or "I bet you ten dollars it will rain tomorrow" (**see Austin box 1**). In these cases, as Austin notes, "To *say* something is to *do* something." In uttering certain sentences people perform acts. Promises, bets, curses, contracts, and judgments do not describe or represent actions: they are actions. Performatives are an integral part of "real life." As many have found out too late, even if the heart says "no," once the tongue says "yes" the performative binds. But not quite. The words usually need to be corroborated by actions. "I bet 100 dollars" in poker is followed by chips pushed to the center of the table. The "I do" uttered at a wedding is ratified by an exchange of rings and the signing of licenses. The christening of a ship is finalized by smashing a champagne bottle against the bow. In an American court, a witness swears "to tell the truth, the whole truth, and nothing but the truth" by uttering this performative while placing a hand on the Bible (or comparable text). Other societies do likewise.

J. L. Austin

The performative

The term [. . .] "performative" is derived, of course, from "perform" [. . .]: it indicates that the issuing of the utterance is the performing of an action. [. . .] The uttering of the words is, indeed, usually a, or even the, leading incident in the performance of the act [. . .].

1962, *How to Do Things with Words*, 6–8

J. L. Austin

Theatre the parasite

[A] performative utterance will [. . .] be in a peculiar way hollow or void if said by an actor on the stage, or if introduced in a poem, or spoken in soliloquy. [. . .] Language in such circumstances is in special ways – intelligibly – used not seriously, but in ways parasitic upon its normal use – ways which fall under the doctrine of etiolations of language. All this we are excluding from consideration. Our performative utterances [. . .] are to be understood as issued in ordinary circumstances.

1962, *How to Do Things with Words*, 22

Does the need to have performative utterances backed up by actions point to a weakness or incompleteness in the performatives themselves? Are all performatives tainted by association with the theatre – where words are "true" and therefore effective only within the bounds of convention? – Austin reasoned that performatives uttered under false circumstances were "unhappy" or "infelicitous." If a person is lying about who she is, then she is playing a role – and anything done in that role is suspect. A bigamist in a society that disallows multiple mates does not really marry even though he may sincerely proclaim "I do" and his "wife" believe she is his one and only. Austin carried this reasoning further when he argued that all performatives uttered in theatre were unhappy. Characters swear, bet, and marry; but, being fictions, none of what they do "really" happens. According to Austin, the performative utterances of characters are "parasitic [. . .] etiolations of language" (**see Austin box 2**). But Austin's neat division separating authentic from parasitic performatives cannot stand up to scrutiny.

Austin did not understand, or refused to appreciate, the unique power of the theatrical as imagination made flesh. Recalling the maya–lila notion of reality, what happens on stage has emotional and ideological consequences for both performers and spectators. The characters are real within their own domain and time. Both actors and audiences identify with the characters, shed real tears over their fate, and become deeply involved with them. Insofar as the characters partake of their special reality, their performative utterances are efficacious. Furthermore, at least on the erotic side, many actors have fallen in love with their stage lovers only to find out, when the play is over or the movie wrapped, that what was sworn with such passion passes into nothing. One might call this evaporation of stage life "Austin's revenge," unhappy as the real life outcomes so often are. But however brief or long-lasting, the aesthetic reality is neither the same nor the opposite of ordinary daily reality. It is its own realm, an intermediary, liminal, transitional, maya–lila time–space. What the "as if" provides is a time–space where reactions can be actual while the actions that elicit these reactions are fictional. This maya–lila time–space is one where effects are much greater than their causes. Or, more precisely, where the causes issue from one domain of reality – that of artistic production – while the effects happen in another domain, that of emotional response. Spectators are carried away only so far. People allow a watchdog with half an open eye to drowse in the corner of their minds, barely growling that what they are laughing at, or frightened by, or weeping over is "only a play." The situation is paradoxical, and uniquely human. It demands the ability to keep two contradictory realities simultaneously in play. Accomplishing this is a stupendous emotional and intellectual achievement. In his own way, Austin, like Plato, distrusted the poets, fearing and denigrating their utterances, if not banning them outright.

Within a few years of Austin, Jacques Derrida and other poststructuralists invited artists back into the game. The poststructuralists stood Austin's argument on its head. Slyly – because he sabotaged his own reasoning by making it unresolvedly paradoxical – Derrida insisted that all utterances are infelicitous: speech in the theatre is a "determined modification" of a "general iterability" (**see Derrida box 1**). That is, meaning cannot be permanently fixed: every utterance is a repetition – just as stage speech is the repetition of a script. But Derrida's "iterability" is not the parroting of a known script, but a quality inherent in language and therefore embedded in thought, in the personal-cultural construction of reality. Meaning is not singular, original, or locatable. Meaning is not owned by the speaker, the spectator, or even the circumstance. Meaning – and all and every meaning is contingent, temporary – is created in process through the complex interaction of all speakers – players – and their specific personal-cultural circumstances. By 1972, when Derrida wrote "Signature, Event, Context," Austin's "performative" had been taken up by a number of thinkers – its use expanded exponentially. Given the collapse of the boundaries segregating individual categories that marks the postmodern period, it is not surprising that Austin's term took off on its own (**see Parker and Sedgwick box**).

Andrew Parker and Eve Kosofsky Sedgwick

Defining "performative"

[. . . W]hile philosophy and theatre now share "performative" as a common lexical item, the term has hardly come to mean "the same thing" for each. Indeed, the stretch between theatrical and deconstructive meanings of "performative" seems to span the polarities of, at either extreme, the extroversion of the actor, the introversion of the signifier. [. . . I]n another range of usages, a text like [Jean-François] Lyotard's *The Postmodern Condition* uses "performativity" to mean an extreme of something like efficiency – while, again, the deconstructive "performativity" of Paul de Man or J. Hillis Miller seems to be characterized by the dislinkage precisely of cause and effect between the signifier and the world. At the same time, it's worth keeping in mind that even in deconstruction, more can be said of performative speech acts than that they are ontologically dislinked or introversively nonreferential. [. . . The performative is marked by] the torsion, the mutual perversion, as one might say, of reference and performativity.

1995, "Introduction: Performativity and Performance," 2–3

Jacques Derrida

Successful performatives are impure

For, ultimately, isn't it true that what Austin excludes as anomaly, exception, "non-serious," citation (on stage, in a poem, or a soliloquy) is the determined modification of a general citationality – or rather, a general iterability – without which there would not even be a "successful" performative? So that – a paradoxical but unavoidable conclusion – a successful performative is necessarily an "impure" performative [. . .]?

1988 [1972], "Signature, Event, Context," in *Limited Inc.*, 17

Searle's speech acts

One of the first to develop Austin's conception of the performative was **John R. Searle**, who in the 1960s asserted that the basic unit of communication was the "speech act." Searle located speech acts in the realm of behavior, as doings on at least three levels: (1) the uttering of sounds formed into words and sentences; (2) words and sentences that refer to

John R. Searle (1932–): American philosopher who was a student of J. L. Austin at Oxford University in the 1950s. Searle developed Austin's ideas in *Speech Acts* (1969) and *Expression and Meaning* (1979). His more recent work includes *The Construction of Social Reality* (1995), *Mind, Language, and Society: Philosophy in the Real World* (1998), *Rationality in Action* (2001), and *Mind: A Brief Introduction* (2004).

things and events or predict; (3) words and sentences that state, question, command, promise, and so on. He insisted that speech acts be studied within specific contexts – not simply as formal structures but as organized systems just as chess or baseball are not only rule-bound activities but fully developed games played by the rules (**see Searle box**). Searle argued that people constructed their realities largely by means of speech acts; and they communicated these realities to each other by means of speech acts. Yet, like Austin before him, Searle separates "normal real world talk" from "parasitic forms of discourse such as fiction, play acting, etc."

Searle and Austin took this position because they didn't recognize that art can be a model for rather than, or in addition to, being a mirror of or escape from life. But even well before the 1960s, many artists and theorists were fascinated by the collapsing distinctions between "fiction" and "reality." Certain artistic work both explored and helped bring about the erosion of the real–fictional boundary. From **Luigi Pirandello** and **Nikolai Evreinov** to John Cage, Allan Kaprow, and many of today's performance artists, this interplay of realities has increasingly become a central theme in performance art, film and TV, the internet, experimental theatre, the visual arts, and popular entertainment. Perhaps this is so because of the increasing sophistication of both digital and genetic cloning. The very idea of "original" has been successfully sabotaged. The previously fictional is more real, and the previously real is more fictional. Both categories appear at the very least inaccurate, and perhaps totally outmoded. To what degree is "reality television" real, to what degree packaged? But the same question can be asked of a presidential press conference, a classified intelligence report, or even a medical diagnosis sent forward to a health maintenance organization for approval and reimbursement.

Luigi Pirandello (1867–1936): Italian playwright and novelist who explored the ambiguous interface between the stage and ordinary life. His many plays include *Right You Are (If You Think You Are)* (1917), *Six Characters in Search of an Author* (1921), and *Henry IV* (1922).

Nikolai Evreinov (1879–1953): Russian visionary theatre director who wanted to dissolve the boundaries separating the stage event from the audience. In 1920, Evreinov staged *The Storming of the Winter Palace* using 10,000 performers including units of the Red Army and the Baltic Fleet many of whom had taken part in the real event in 1917. None of Evreinov's books have been translated into English. See Spencer Golub, *Evreinov: The Theatre of Paradox and Transformation* (1984).

John R. Searle

Speech acts

[S]peaking a language is engaging in a rule-governed form of behavior. To put it more briskly, talking is performing acts according to rules. [. . .] The unit of linguistic communication is not, as has generally been supposed, the symbol, word or sentence, or even the token of the symbol, word or sentence, but rather the production or issuance of the symbol or word or sentence in the performance of the speech act. To take the token as a message is to take it as a produced or issued token. More precisely, the production or issuance of a sentence token under certain conditions is a speech act, and speech acts [. . .] are the basic or minimal units of linguistic communication. [. . . A] theory of language is part of a theory of action, simply because speaking is a rule-governed form of behavior. Now, being rule-governed, it has formal features which admit of independent study. But a study purely of those formal features, without a study of their role in speech acts, would be [. . .] as if baseball were studied only as a formal system of rules and not as a game.

1969, *Speech Acts*, 16–17

Reality TV and beyond

Popular films of the late 1990s, such as *Wag the Dog*, *The Truman Show*, *Ed TV*, and *The Blair Witch Project* explore the very porous membrane separating the "real" from the "staged." The movies are fictions about dissolving the differences between the real and the fictional. Reality television goes much further. *Survivor* first aired in May 2000. Years later, it remains one of the most popular American television shows (**see *Survivor* box**). It's very premise is to erase the distinctions between the real and the staged. *Survivor* contestants are drawn from the public (not stars) and marooned somewhere remote and exotic. Each week the group votes on who to throw out until there is only one person left, The Survivor – winner of a million-dollar prize. *Survivor*'s motto is "Outwit, Outplay, Outlast" – a succinct summation of market-driven capitalism. By August, 2000, more than 30 million viewers tuned in, and many millions still do. *Survivor* clones, spin-offs, websites, and merchandising outlets are thriving. This kind of programming obviously appeals to a broad public.

From the official *Survivor* website

Outwit, outplay, outlast

Deprived of basic comforts, exposed to the harsh natural elements, your fate at the mercy of strangers . . . who would you become? For 39 days, 20 strangers will be stranded together and forced to carve out a new existence, using their collective wits to make surviving in their rugged environment a little easier. Day by day, the harsh elements and threatening indigenous animals will test the endurance of the Survivors. Each three days of island life will result in a one-hour SURVIVOR episode. The Survivors must form their own cooperative society, building shelter, gathering and catching food, and participating in contests for rewards. Those who succeed in the day-to-day Challenges will be rewarded with things to make life on the Island more bearable. Those who fail must do without. On the last day of each three-day cycle, the Survivors must attend Tribal Council. At this meeting, each person votes secretly to send one fellow Survivor home. The person with the most votes must leave their tribe immediately. Week by week, one by one, people are voted off, until at the end of the final episode, only two Survivors remain. At that point, the seven most recently eliminated Survivors will return to form the final Tribal Council and decide who will be Sole Survivor and win one million dollars.

2005, www.cbs.com/primetime/survivor11/

What are they getting? The thrill of the real, sexiness, typecasting, unpredictability, and the amateur status of the contestants – the "that could be me!" factor? Cameras are always rolling, even if manned by the contestants. The *Survivor* website informs us that the CBS camera crew lives in tents near the contestants' camp, roughing it, too. The film is edited in the network studio facilities to ensure a high level of drama and the expurgation of "inappropriate" material. Contestants know that if a real emergency arises, they will be evacuated. *Survivor* is "real" within the frame and control of the CBS network. Because their own votes determine who the final survivors would be, tensions rise as the weeks go by. What *Survivor* contestants are enacting is not improvised theatre, exactly; nor is it real life, exactly. This same kind of reality duplicity (both a doubling and a lie) infuses related TV shows such as *Peoples' Court* or *Divorce Court*. The combination of voyeurism and "that could be me!" is taken up by the thousands of webcam sites. The difference is that many webcam sites are not regulated either by the government or by big business. The sites play directly to the market, displaying and selling what is desired. What is desired is often precisely what is ordinarily repressed. Thus it is no surprise that a high proportion of webcam sites are pornographic.

Sometimes "real real life" rivals if not exactly pre-empts fabricated real life. That happened in 2001 when Dr. Ronald S. Shemenski, age 59, was the only physician stationed at the Rothera Research Station, Antarctica. Shemenski diagnosed himself with a serious gall-bladder problem. A made-to-order media event was at hand. Brave pilots volunteered to fly from southern Chile to Antarctica in wintery darkness, land on the snow, rest briefly, and evacuate the ailing medic. Millions watched this "real-life" survivor narrative. Shemenski himself told CBS News hours after arriving in Chile, "If I had my druthers, I'd be at the Pole. But the window of opportunity to get me out was now. I couldn't sit around and wait." Once in a hospital in the USA, Shimenski was found to have earlier suffered a heart attack – so he had his arteries unclogged prior to having his gall bladder removed. Because Shemenski-type opportunities come only once in a blue moon, media producers will keep serving new *Survivor* look-alikes until public interest in the genre diminishes.

Sponsoring and exploiting "real-life" adventures to gain market share and increase revenues is not new. The genre developed hand-in-glove with the growth of newspapers, magazines, and other media that sprang up to create and then satisfy an appetite for vicarious excitement. In the nineteenth century there was the additional thrill of participating in the "fruits" of colonialism. Take, for example, the manufactured expedition into central Africa of British adventurer **Henry Morgan Stanley**, assigned by *The New York Herald* to find "missing" explorer **David Livingstone**. After months of looking, Stanley located Livingstone in 1871 at Ujiji on Lake Tanganyika. At the moment of first meeting, Stanley tells us he spoke the famous one-liner, "Dr. Livingstone, I presume." But did he, actually? We have only Stanley's word for it. Stanley's expedition was cooked up and exploited by the *Herald*, who owned and published

Stanley's account. The colonial practice of entering the "exotic," "primitive," or "unknown" (to the West) continues to this day under the auspices of such organizations as the National Geographic Society. Because treating human societies in the manner of the nineteenth- to mid-twentieth-century adventurers is no longer appropriate, attention has refocused on wildlife and the challenges of "nature" – the life cycle of a pride of lions on the Serengeti, the perils of scaling Mt. Everest, or the challenge of raising dinnerware unbroken from the *Titanic*. The impulse remains the same, while vastly improved technology allows for better "on-the-scene" participation by distant viewers.

Henry Morgan Stanley (1841–1904): English travel writer and explorer who conducted a highly publicized (and successful) search through central Africa in 1870–71 to find fellow English explorer **David Livingstone (1813–73)**.

fig 5.1. "Live from Trafalgar Square," as the earthcam.com site proclaims. The image changes every few seconds. The shot above was taken at 5:41 p.m., 17 June 2005. Earthcam.com offers hundreds of live shots from all over the world. Of course, there are a godzillion other webcam sites.

The news programs about the Shemenski rescue had a lot in common with the Stanley–Livingstone story and with *Survivor* and similar entertainment programs. The Shemenski story suited our times: condensed, episodic, and visual. News came via airplane and satellite, rather than through trekking and hand-delivered manuscripts. There was the "human interest" side of things, controlled reports of dangers and progress, a growing tension about the outcome, and a happy ending. *Survivor* has all this plus the thrill of a sports-like elimination contest. Not "real sports," but rather more like professional wrestling with its over-stuffed heroes and villains cheered and jeered by deliriously excited fans. Over time, *Survivor* viewers pick their favorites to love, pity, admire, and hate. Is the contest real or rigged? We know that the outcome of a stage drama is settled before the curtain rises. The public expects sports to be untampered with – although steroid use gives some athletes unfair advantage over others and the scandals that regularly occur suggest that cheating in sports is structural and endemic, not occasional.

The fact is, the tons of money in play on television, and the fierce struggle among networks for viewer share, have eroded the walls once separating "entertainment," "news," and "sports." It's all entertainment now – ironically, that's where "reality" is located. What is true of TV is doubly so on the internet, where 24-hour webcams broadcast a continuous stream of "reality." Earthcam.com is but one of many sites bringing viewers real time webcams from many locations all over the world (**see figure 5.1**). At earthcam, the topics range from arts, sports, entertainment, and gambling casino surveillance to traffic, animals, and a category called "weird and bizarre." Websites have fewer taboos than broadband or even cable television. Sex and nakedness are big attractions. But almost anything will do. The prototype of this genre of entertainment was the month-long broadcast of the ongoing lives of the Loud family of southern California in 1971. People asked then, and the question remains salient, does the presence of the camera change behavior or convert someone's home from a "real-life" venue into a "theatre"? It is a sociological application of Heisenberg's indeterminacy principle where the observation affects the outcome. The Louds and *Survivor* are managed by the networks. But the little guy is in on the action too. Starting in the mid-1990s there arose a profusion of internet sites such as *JenniCam* – the creation of Jennifer Ringley who in 1996 at the age of 20 decided to install a camera in her dorm room at Dickinson College in Pennsylvania. *JenniCam* ran through 2003, bringing millions of viewers sometimes funny, sometimes intimate views of Ringley (**see figure 5.2 and Ringley box**). Ringley scandalized many when she had sex on camera with the fiancé of a friend – and the friend found out about it when she tuned into *JenniCam*. *JenniCam* is no more, but thousands of similar sites are thriving. Although Ringley said she was not an actress or entertainer, she advertised the *JenniShow* on her site, a bi-weekly video webcast hosted by Jenni herself. Viewers sent emails to Jenni, who read them during the show. Many of these "real-life" sites are "subscriber only" – you have to pay to watch – converting "just living life" into a business.

Sometimes others are paid to watch us, even if we do not want to be watched, using surveillance cameras installed by

fig 5.2. Jenni makes a face for the camera – her webcams were always turned on – and viewers had to subscribe to follow Jenni around her domicile. As Jenni said on her homepage, "JenniCam is not suitable for children."

Jennifer Ringley

JenniCam

JenniCam is, to put it simply, a sort of window into a virtual human zoo. My name is Jennifer Ringley, and I am not an actor, or dancer, or entertainer. I am a computer geek with the good fortune to be able to work from home. I design, code, and administer this website and manage the company that keeps the site alive.

[. . .] The "JenniCam" is a series of cameras located throughout the house Dex and I live in, cameras that take images of my house all day long, every day. [. . .] So feel free to watch, or not, as you desire. I am here to be loved or hated. I am here simply to be me.

2001, from www.jennicam.org

corporations and police. The panopticon was first proposed as a means for guards to surveil prisons. Does the ubiquity of the looking eye make the world into one vast prison (as Hamlet believed Denmark to be)? Viewing the output of these cameras – sometimes even broadcasting footage on television or over the internet – converts ordinary or illicit actions into "performances for the camera." Almost anyone can avail themselves of a "photo op" once reserved for stars and politicians. Where will the line separating private from public be drawn? Can it be drawn anywhere? The line is disappearing, if it has not already vanished. These are situations addressed, but by no means resolved, by theories of performativity.

Postmodernism

Performativity as understood by performance studies is part of, or closely related to, postmodernism. One of the decisive qualities of postmodernism is the application of the "performance principle" to all aspects of social and artistic life. Performance is no longer confined to the stage, to the arts, and to ritual. An early authority on postmodernism, Jean-François Lyotard, argued that power depends on the optimization of performance (in the business and technical senses), a kind of performativity that is self-legitimating (**see Lyotard box**). Theorist **Linda Hutcheon** takes the opposite position. Focusing not on business, government, or technology but on postmodern art, Hutcheon sees artists continuing the subversive project of the historical avant-garde by undermining the basic principles of bourgeois liberalism (**see Hutcheon box**). **Fredric Jameson** believes that in postmodern times "the market has become a substitute for itself and fully as much a commodity as any of the items it includes within itself" (**see Jameson box**). These views are not easily reconcilable with each other – but this ability to embrace contradiction and eclecticism is a hallmark of the postmodern.

Jean-François Lyotard

Performativity and power

This is how legitimation by power takes shape. Power is not only good performativity, but also effective verification and good verdicts. It legitimates science and the law on the basis of their efficiency, and legitimates this efficiency on the basis of science and law. It is self-legitimating, in the same way a system organized around performance maximization seems to be. Now it is precisely this kind of context control that a generalized computerization of society may bring. The performativity of an utterance, be it denotative or prescriptive, increases proportionally to the amount of information about its referent one has at one's disposal. Thus the growth of power, and its self-legitimation, is now taking the route of data storage and accessibility, and the operativity of information.

The relationship between science and technology is reversed. [. . .] Research funds are allocated by States, corporations, and nationalized companies in accordance with this logic of power growth. Research sectors that are unable to argue that they contribute even indirectly to the optimization of the system's performance are abandoned by the flow of capital and doomed to senescence. The criterion of performance is explicitly invoked by the authorities to justify their refusal to subsidize certain research centers.

1984, *The Postmodern Condition*, 47

Linda Hutcheon (1947–): Canadian literary critic, cultural theorist, and Professor of English at the University of Toronto. Among her books: *A Theory of Parody* (1985), *A Poetics of Postmodernism* (1988), and *The Politics of Postmodernism* (2002).

Linda Hutcheon

Postmodern human-made truths

Postmodern art similarly asserts and then deliberately undermines such principles as value, order, meaning, control, and identity that have been the basic premises of bourgeois liberalism. Those humanistic principles are still operative in our culture, but for many they are no longer seen as eternal and unchallengeable. The contradictions of both postmodern theory and practice are positioned within the system and yet work to allow its premises to be seen as fictions or as ideological structures. This does not necessarily destroy their "truth" value, but it does define the conditions of that "truth." Such a process reveals rather than conceals the tracks of the signifying systems that constitute our world – that is, systems constructed by us in answer to our needs. However important the systems are, they are not natural, given, or universal. The very limitations imposed by the postmodern view are also perhaps ways of opening new doors: perhaps now we can better study the interrelations of social, aesthetic, philosophical, and ideological constructs. In order to do so, postmodernist critique must acknowledge its own position as an ideological one.

1988, *A Poetics of Postmodernism*, 13

Fredric Jameson (1934–): Marxist cultural critic and Professor of Comparative Literature at Duke University. Author of *The Political Unconscious* (1981), *Postmodernism or the Cultural Logic of Late Capitalism* (1991), and *A Singular Modernity* (2002).

Fredric Jameson

What is postmodernism?

So, in postmodern culture, "culture" has become a product in its own right; the market has become a substitute for itself and fully as much a commodity as any of the items it includes within itself: modernism was still minimally and intentionally the critique of the commodity and the effort to make it transcend itself. Postmodernism is the consumption of sheer commodification as a process. [. . .] Culturally, the precondition [of postmodernism] is to be found [. . .] in the enormous social and psychological transformations of the 1960s. [. . . The] economic preparation of postmodernism or late capitalism began in the 1950s, after the wartime shortages of consumer goods and spare parts had been made up, and new products and new technologies (not least those of the media) could be pioneered. On the other hand, the psychic habitus of the new age demands the absolute break, strengthened by a generational rupture, achieved more properly in the 1960s. [. . .] As the word itself suggests, this break is most often related to notions of the waning or extinction of the hundred-year-old modern movement (or to its ideological or aesthetic repudiation). Thus abstract expressionism in painting, existentialism in philosophy, the final forms of representation in the novel, the films of the great auteurs, or the modernist school of poetry [. . .] all are now seen as the final, extraordinary flowering of a high-modernist impulse which is spent and exhausted with them.

[The] fundamental feature of [. . .] postmodernism [is] the effacement [. . .] of the older (essentially high-modernist) frontier between high culture and so-called mass or commercial culture, and the emergence of new kinds of texts infused with the forms, categories, and contents of that very culture industry so passionately denounced by all the ideologues of the modern [. . .].

Nor should the break in question be thought of as a purely cultural affair: indeed, theories of the postmodern – whether celebratory or couched in the language of moral revulsion and denunciation – bear a family resemblance to all those more ambitious sociological generalizations which, at much the same time, bring us the news of the arrival and inauguration of a whole new type of society, most famously baptized "postindustrial society" [. . .] but often also designated consumer society, media society, information society, electronic society or high tech, and the like.

1991, *Postmodernism, Or, The Cultural Logic of Late Capitalism*, x, xx, 1, 2–3

It is not easy to summarize postmodernism because it means one thing to dancers, several other things to cultural critics and philosophers, and still something else to architects. Defining and theorizing the postmodern began in the turbulent 1960s with attacks on the "master narratives" of modernism: the nation-state, natural law, rational logic, patriarchal authority, mandatory coherence, and beginning-middle-and-end stories. But after the deconstruction of the master narratives, then what? Fragmentation, pastiche, relativism, local truths, delight in contradictions?

On the one hand, the media rush in with a host of "temporary master narratives." Pundits galore pontificate about the day's events, especially political and economic news. Anchors intone, while reporters sensationalize ordinary life. The arts themselves take a back seat because ordinary life is framed so "artistically." Authored dramas are relegated to public networks or less-viewed specialty channels. Widely watched news channels propagate tug-the-heart human-interest stories even as they make the ups and downs of the stock market into a soap-opera cliffhanger. Instead of this resulting in a single narration or even a coherent bundle of narrations, the media throw the public hundreds of fragmented stories and compressed dramas.

Compression and fragmentation are the order of the day. Television commercials are 15- or 30-second mini-dramas, exquisite from the technical point of view, emotional and convincing – but ultimately empty except in stimulating the urge to buy. One commercial follows another and a suite of commercials are succeeded by programs that require short attention spans. Only sports viewing and re-runs of movies demand a relatively long attention span. Surfing the internet brings users into contact with multiple texts and links, most animated by hyperactive banner ads blinking or beeping their insistent calls for interaction. "See me, click me, buy me," they intone.

Recognizing, analyzing, and theorizing the convergence and collapse of clearly demarcated realities, hierarchies, and categories is at the heart of postmodernism. Such a convergence or collapse is a profound departure from traditional Western performance theory. From Plato and Aristotle forward, theorists have agreed that theatre "imitates," "reflects," "represents," or "expresses" individual actions and social life. As Hamlet told the Players, the purpose of theatre is "to hold the mirror up to nature." Representational art of all kinds is based on the assumption that "art" and "life" are not only separate but of different orders of reality: life is primary, art secondary. But developments in photography, film, and digital media overturned traditional theories. Questions arose concerning exactly what was an "original" – even if there could be such a thing as an original.

Before photography, there was "nature" and there was "painting." Copies could be made of paintings, but these constituted either authorized reproductions or forgeries. With the advent of photography came the negative (which was not the photo but that from which the "positive" or photograph was made). How could either a negative or a positive made from the negative be an original? And if a particular positive was an original, which one – the first made from the negative or the best from a technical point of view? A question that was relatively easy with regard to painting became very troubled in photography. **Walter Benjamin**, writing about "the work of art in the age of mechanical reproduction," took up this problem. If there were no original, there could be no "presence," no "unique existence," and no "aura" surrounding the artwork (**see Benjamin box**). This demystification of art – and by implication of all cultural products, including the State and religion – was not at all bad. It created the possibility for a transfer of power from elites to the masses.

But Benjamin had no sense of the further complications introduced by digital media and bio-technology. If

Walter Benjamin

Authenticity, presence, aura

In principle, a work of art has always been reproducible. Manmade artifacts can always be imitated by man. Replicas were made by pupils in practice of their craft, by masters for diffusing their works, and finally, by third parties in the pursuit of gain. Mechanical reproduction of a work of art, however, represents something new. [. . .]

Even the most perfect reproduction of a work of art is lacking in one element: its presence in time and space, its unique existence at the place where it happens to be. This unique existence of the work of art determined the history to which it was subject throughout the time of its existence. This includes the changes which it may have suffered in physical condition over the years as well as the various changes in its ownership. [. . .]

The authenticity of a thing is the essence of all that is transmissible from its beginning, ranging from its substantive duration to its testimony to the history which it has experienced. Since the historical testimony rests on the authenticity, the former, too, is jeopardized by reproduction [. . .]. And what is really jeopardized when the historical testimony is affected is the authority of the object.

One might subsume the eliminated element in the term "aura" and go on to say: that which withers in the age of mechanical reproduction is the aura of the work of art. This is a symptomatic process whose significance points beyond the realm of art. One might generalize by saying: the technique of reproduction detaches the reproduced object from the domain of tradition. By making many reproductions it substitutes a plurality of copies for a unique existence.

1969 [1936], *Illuminations*, 218, 220–21

reproduction threatens the "authority of the object," think how much greater the threat to that authority when there is no original at all. Digital images are not present, emit no aura, and cannot be authenticated. That is because these images are actually binary codes capable of generating any number of identical images or anything else specified by the program. Cloning is roughly the same idea applied to biology. In all these cases – the painting, photo, digital image, clone – "nature" still exists as separate from, or at least prior to, whatever comes after. But instead of the "after" being a variation on the "before" – like but not identical – the after is identical to the before. In a world populated by digital codes and clones, the classic distinctions between "nature" and "art," "original" and "copy," are getting more difficult to make. It is not only changes in philosophical theories that blur the boundaries. "Integration" is a powerful movement at the highest levels of global centralized power. Big business long ago moved in to control the means of information production. On the margins dissident individuals can put up what they want on their own websites or blogs. But the "means of digital production" are owned and controlled by a very few – the "military–industrial complex" combining with the "scientific–technological elite" American president **Dwight D. Eisenhower** warned against in his 1961 farewell address (**See Eisenhower box**). Experimental artists sometimes resist and sometimes abet these extremely powerful combines. Some of the most creative performance artists are pushing the envelope, experimenting with "cyborg" bodies (amalgams of the biological, the mechanical, and the digital). I will discuss these experiments at the end of this chapter.

Walter Benjamin (1892–1940): German Marxist essayist and intellectual who committed suicide on the border between France and Spain while fleeing from the Nazis. His very influential writings – including *Illuminations* (1968), *Understanding Brecht* (1973), and *Reflections* (1986) – were collected after his death.

Dwight D. Eisenhower (1890–1969): thirty-fourth president of the United States (1952–60) and Supreme Commander in Europe during World War II of the armies of the Western powers. As president, Eisenhower was what today would be called a "moderately conservative Republican."

Dwight D. Eisenhower

Beware the military–industrial complex and the scientific–technological elite

Until the latest of our world conflicts [World War II], the United States had no armaments industry. [. . .] But now [. . .] we have been compelled to create a permanent armaments industry of vast proportions. [. . .] This conjunction of an immense military establishment and a large arms industry is new in the American experience. The total influence–economic, political, even spiritual – is felt in every city, every state house, every office of the Federal government. We recognize the imperative need for this development. Yet we must not fail to comprehend its grave implications. Our toil, resources and livelihood are all involved; so is the very structure of our society.

In the councils of government, we must guard against the acquisition of unwarranted influence, whether sought or unsought, by the military-industrial complex. The potential for the disastrous rise of misplaced power exists and will persist. We must never let the weight of this combination endanger our liberties or democratic processes. We should take nothing for granted. Only an alert and knowledgeable citizenry can compel the proper meshing of huge industrial and military machinery of defense with our peaceful methods and goals, so that security and liberty may prosper together.

Akin to, and largely responsible for the sweeping changes in our industrial–military posture, has been the technological revolution during recent decades. [. . .] In this revolution, research has become central; it also becomes more formalized, complex, and costly. [. . .] In the same fashion, the free university, historically the fountainhead of free ideas and scientific discovery, has experienced a revolution in the conduct of research. Partly because of the huge costs involved, a government contract becomes virtually a substitute for intellectual curiosity. For every old blackboard there are now hundreds of new electronic computers.

The prospect of domination of the nation's scholars by Federal employment, project allocations, and the power of money is ever present and is gravely to be regarded. Yet, in holding scientific research and discovery in respect, as we should, we must also be alert to the equal and opposite danger that public policy could itself become the captive of a scientific–technological elite.

1999 [1961], "Farewell Address to the American People," 1035–40

Simulation

What Benjamin was leaning toward, but what he did not possess the theoretical tools to explore, was "simulation." With simulation representation ends, and reproduction takes over. Biological reproduction until recently was the province of nature – tinkered with by means of breeding and horticulture. But with the knowledge of genetics exploding exponentially, clones and genetically engineered plants are becoming evermore common occurrences. In the realm of the arts and information technology, digital "copies" are not copies at all, but clones. Jean Baudrillard foresaw this in the early 1980s (**see Baudrillard box 1**). Simulation as a concept continues to evolve in the twenty-first century. At the level of popular culture, simulation is closely related to "reality" television and "real life" internet sites.

A simulation is neither a pretense nor an imitation. It is a replication of . . . itself as another. That makes simulations perfect performatives. A cloned sheep or a U2 song distributed digitally over the internet is not a copy but an "original" in a theoretically infinite series; or it is a "copy" in a theoretically infinite series. There is no difference between "copy" and "original." The decision about whether to call a specific sequence of digitized data an original or a copy is a matter of ideology, not of any difference between the so-called original and the so-called copy. One can determine the "first" in chronological and even legal terms, as the courts have done; but this determination depends on knowledge outside the simulation. There is nothing inherent in the code that tells whether it was first, fifth, or nth.

Jean Baudrillard

The phases of imaging

These are the successive phases of the image:

- it is the reflection of a basic reality
- it masks and perverts a basic reality
- it masks the absence of a basic reality
- it bears no relation to any reality whatever: it is its own pure simulacrum.

In the first case, the image is a good appearance – the representation is of the order of sacrament. In the second, it is an evil appearance – of the order of a spell. In the third, it plays at being an appearance – it is of the order of sorcery. In the fourth, it is no longer in the order of appearance at all, but of simulation.

1983, *Simulations*, 11–12

Katie Hafner

Death and life on the internet

On May 14 [2001], Kaycee Nicole Swenson, an effervescent 19-year-old, died from complications surrounding leukemia, which she had been battling for nearly two years. From her home in Kansas, Kaycee, an unyieldingly optimistic high school basketball star, had chronicled her remissions and relapses in her on-line diary, or Weblog, which she had dubbed "Living Colours."

For nearly a year thousands of people went to the site to follow her travails. Many came to feel as if they knew her, and a few talked with her regularly on the phone. Some sent her gifts. Others with cancer spoke of her as an inspiration. [. . .] Hundreds of people [. . .] were crushed by the news of her death. "So many people reached out to this beautiful girl who was so positive in the face of adversity," said Saundra Mitchell, a screenwriter in Indianapolis.

But Ms. Mitchell was one of the first to cast doubt on what turned out to be an intricately detailed fabrication. A few days after the death announcement, Debbie Swenson, a 40-year-old homemaker, confessed to having invented the life and death of Kaycee. Ms. Swenson, who has two teenage children and lives in Peabody, Kan., a small town about 50 miles northeast of Wichita, had posed as Kaycee's mother. [. . .]

Ms. Swenson said that she believed the Kaycee character had been more helpful than harmful. "A lot of people have problems," she said. "I know I helped a lot of people in a lot of different ways." She could be right. So compelling was Ms. Swenson's creation that powerful online connections were made among those who believed in the Kaycee persona and among those who pulled it apart.

2001, "A Beautiful Life, an Early Death, a Fraud Exposed," 1–2, 5

A simulation is not the enactment of a fiction, as when an actress plays Ophelia. Nor is it a hoax such as the last days of Kaycee Nicole Swenson who died in May, 2001 of complications arising from her long fight against leukemia. Thousands followed Kaycee's blog, sent her gifts, and wept when they learned of her death (**see Hafner box**). A convincing simulation is the presence of an appearance (where there is no original) or a replication so perfect it is indistinguishable from an original. It is possible, of course, to progress from pretending to acting to performing to simulating. As Baudrillard points out, a person pretending to be sick knows she is not really sick, but someone simulating sickness actually produces the symptoms of the illness and in so doing "is" sick (**see Baudrillard box 2**). Once the symptoms appear, there is no way to distinguish someone who is "sick" from someone who is sick. The quotation marks can be added only extrinsically (by knowing that a simulation is taking place). Phenomenologically, the distinction between real and feigned disappears – but in a peculiar way. In the simulated illness, and like cases, the imaginary causes the actual. As I will point out in the next chapter, this is not so different from what shamans do. The shaman does not feign the illness she suffers in sympathy with the patient – the shaman simulates the illness so thoroughly that she gets sick herself – and then cures the patient and in so doing, cures herself (or the other way round).

Émile Maximilien Paul Littré (1801–81): French philologist best known for his dictionary of the French language, commonly called "the Littré."

Jean Baudrillard

Feigning to have what one doesn't

To dissimulate is to pretend not to have what one has. To simulate is to feign to have what one hasn't. One implies a presence, the other an absence. But the matter is more complicated, since to simulate is not simply to feign: "Someone who feigns an illness can simply go to bed and make believe he is ill. Someone who simulates an illness produces in himself some of the symptoms" (**[Émile Maximilien Paul] Littré**). Thus, feigning or dissimulating leaves the reality principle intact: the difference is always clear, it is only masked; whereas simulation threatens the difference between the "true" and "false," "real" and "imaginary." Since the simulator produces "true" symptoms, is he ill or not? He cannot be treated objectively either as ill, or as not ill.

1983, *Simulations*, 5

This process can be outlined as:

real life → pretending → acting on stage → simulating → real life

On the page, the progression moves from left to right, but actually the system loops back into itself with the extreme right, "real life," equal to the extreme left, "real life." The shaman – or any performer similarly self-convinced – performs with such intensity and conviction that she transcends the pretense that first characterizes her performance. One pretends, then acts, then simulates, then arrives back at real life. A kind of experiential mobius strip is performed. Is this second real life "real life" and not real life? How can one tell? This can be a legal-ethical question as much as a philosophical one, as can be seen in the simulated child pornography case argued before the US Supreme Court in 2001 (**see Liptak box**). The Supreme Court ruled in 2002 that simulated child pornography was protected free speech because no real children were exploited. However, since 1994, in the UK "indecent pseudo-photographs" of children are prohibited just as if they are actual.

Adam Liptak

Is simulated sex too real?

In the science-fiction thriller *The Matrix*, Keanu Reeves confronts a future in which computer-generated virtual reality is not only indistinguishable from ordinary experience but also has powerful real-world consequences. Last Monday [22 January 2001], the Supreme Court announced that it would follow Mr. Reeves into the virtual realm by agreeing to hear a case concerning whether uncannily realistic digital simulations of children involved in sexual activity should have real-world consequences of up to 30 years in prison.

The federal law in question criminalizes the creation or possession of fake but sometimes startlingly exact images of children in sexual settings. The Supreme Court will decide whether the law is constitutional and whether, as the American Civil Liberties Union put it in a friend-of-the-court brief, "there is a real difference between touching children sexually and touching computer keys to create images."

The question is a variation on one that has often been before the courts in the digital era: do perfect replicas require different rules? So far, in contexts like the controversy over Napster and the banning of computer code allowing decryption of DVD's, the courts have tended to answer yes. In other words, the better the simulation, the more likely it is to be illegal. [. . .]

Neither the courts nor the experts foresaw the quality of modern digital simulations and the ease with which they can be distributed over the World Wide Web.

2001, "When Is a Fake too Real? It's Virtually Uncertain," 3

There are many different kinds of simulations – for example, the elaborately designed entertainment environments at the various Disney parks simulating Mexico, China, Italy, and other locales (**see figure 5.3 and Baudrillard box 3**). But, finally, Disney and the like are mainly simulations of simulations: movie sets open to the public, populated by actors, and designed to stimulate consumers. In fact, some of the most popular sites are simulations of movie sets, or even working movie sets, as at Universal Studios in Orlando, Florida. Here entrepreneurs designed simulating machines that simulate simulating machines. But who's fooled? Somewhat more sophisticated simulations are restored villages such as Colonial Williamsburg or Plimoth Plantation that not only claim to look like what the sites once "really were," but employ trained "interpreters" to enact historical persons who once lived there (**see figure 5.4**). Here the purpose is to trade on a national nostalgia in the garb of education. But only children are fooled – and even they not for long.

fig 5.3. Disneyworld in Florida features sanitized and commercialized versions of Mexico, China, Italy, and other nations. The structures are mostly façades, suitable for photographing, leading to interiors that contain restaurants and stores.

Mexico

China

Italy

Jean Baudrillard

Disneyland is simulated

Disneyland is a perfect model of all the entangled orders of simulation. To begin with it is a play of illusions and phantasms: Pirates, the Frontier, Future World, etc. This imaginary world is supposed to be what makes the operation successful. But what draws the crowds is undoubtedly much more the social microcosm, the miniaturized and religious reveling in real America, in its delights and drawbacks. [. . .]

The objective profile of America, then, may be traced throughout Disneyland, even down to the morphology of individuals and the crowd. All its values are exalted here, in miniature and comic strip form. Embalmed and pacified. [. . .] Disneyland is there to conceal the fact that it is the "real" country, all of the "real" America, which is Disneyland [. . .]. Disneyland is presented as imaginary in order to make us believe that the rest is real, when in fact all of Los Angeles and the America surrounding it are no longer real, but of the order of the hyperreal and of simulation. It is no longer a question of a false representation of reality (ideology), but of concealing the fact that the real is no longer real [. . .].

1983, *Simulations*, 23–25

fig 5.4. A view of Plimoth Plantation, where "it is always 1627" (as the Plantation's website announces). Plimoth is a reconstruction of the Pilgrim settlement in Massachusetts. A reconstruction rather than restoration because none of the original structures survive and the Plantation is near but not exactly at the spot where the Pilgrims lived in the seventeenth century. Photograph from the 1980s by Richard Schechner.

The most effective and influential twenty-first-century simulations take place at the level of corporate operations, military war games, and scientific experiments. Here simulations are replacing actual events because simulations are cheaper and more controllable than real life, yielding reliable information about real life or having known effects on real life. Japan, barred by its post-Second World War constitution from fielding an army, wages simulated war instead. In an exercise conducted on Mt. Fuji in 2000, 300 Japanese soldiers engaged 100 invading enemy. Commanders watched the battle over closed-circuit television, monitoring every move and exchange of fire. The soldiers were actually on the mountain, but everything else – small arms, artillery, mines, and mortars – was controlled by the computer program. "This was one of the most overwhelming exercises of my career," an officer said. "When you see your soldiers being killed and injured one right after the other, it adds a sense of realism to the drill." The US Army also uses simulations extensively, but keeps its work under wraps.

The internet site of the National Simulation Center at Fort Leavenworth, Kansas – https://nsc.leavenworth.army.mil/new/nscstart.aspx – is open only to those with security clearances. The page that greets viewers shows a photo of three combat-ready soldiers moving through what appears to be an Iraqi or Afghan urban landscape – the picture is titled "Modeling and Simulation Support Center" and the caption reads, "Operation Enduring Freedom" "Operation Iraqi Freedom" (**see figure 5.5**). There is no way to tell whether the photo is real or a simulation – though given the site, I assume it is a simulation. The Federal Bureau of Investigation concludes the training of its agents on the FBI's own movie set, simulating situations that the agents may find themselves in (**see Colborn-Roxworthy box**). The government is far from the only entity interested in

fig 5.5. Homepage of National Simulation Center. Is the photograph of actual combat or is it a simulation? Photo at: https://nsc.leavenworth.army.mil/new/nscstart.aspx

simulations. Private firms offer a wide variety of courses in simulation theory and practice for both industry and the military (**see Distributed Simulation Technology box**). If the simulated can seem real, the opposite is also true – the real can appear to be simulated. Many commentators noted that real wars – as fought by the US against Iraq in 1992 and again starting in 2002, or the bombing of Yugoslavia in 1999 – are like videogames, with "smart bombs," missiles launched from distances of hundreds of miles, and damages "assessed" (scored) by satellite observation.

Emily Colborn-Roxworthy

The performance paradigm in Hogan's Alley

They wink from the pages of trade magazines and quip in the columns of major newspapers, throwing into high relief the increasing confluence of performance and governance in the contemporary U.S. They are role-players whom the Federal Bureau of Investigation (FBI) hires to train new agents at their Academy in Quantico, Virginia. "I've been poked, prodded, cuffed, arrested, and shot at," one of the role-players, professional actor Frank Robinson Jr., told an observing reporter in Training magazine. [. . .]

The last 90 hours of the FBI Academy's 16-week training program for new agents looks more like a movie production every day, owing both to the drama and presence of professional actors, who now make up 25 percent of the contracted role-players, and the surreal stage set where the scenarios take place, Hogan's Alley. The FBI began construction of this mock city in 1986 [. . .] replicating architectural designs from the 1920s to the present. [. . .] By having office personnel on the grounds of Hogan's Alley, the FBI Academy produced ample traffic "to create realistic tactical concerns for trainees," as those in character circulate among those just playing themselves. [. . .]

The puzzling yet tantalizing phenomenon of realism in FBI role-playing can best be parsed by examining it along the three performance axes Jon McKenzie identifies in *Perform Or Else: From Discipline to Performance.* Building on Michel Foucault's thesis in *Discipline and Punish,* McKenzie marks World War II as a turning point in the historical shift from a disciplinary to a performative locus of power and knowledge. [. . .] McKenzie [. . .] notes the "excessive" nature of the performance paradigm, which promotes overlapping and competition, as opposed to the "repressive" nature of the discipline paradigm. The excessiveness of the new paradigm can be observed in three seemingly distinct realms of performance, which McKenzie encourages critics to recognize as embedded and interrelated: bureaucratic or organizational performance, which hinges on the criterion of "efficiency;" technical and technological performance, which trumpets "effectiveness;" and, finally, performance studies' usual area of inquiry, cultural performance, focused since the mid-1950s on "efficacy." McKenzie's elevation of performance as the organizing principle of postwar U.S. (and increasingly, world) business, politics, and art certainly seems correct when applied to law enforcement. Agencies like the FBI have been relying on performance rhetoric and performance strategies from the start of World War II, but after 9/11 the reliance on the performance paradigm has increased exponentially.

2004, "Role-Play Training at a 'Violent Disneyland'," 81–83

Distributed Simulated Technology, Inc.

Military simulation techniques and technology

Students will be provided with a comprehensive overview of simulation architecture, theory and usage. Upon completion of this course, students are aware of the variety of simulations in the military world and are prepared to continue further into the simulation world. [. . .]

Power of Simulation lecture describes the evolution of simulation in the military and the categories of military simulations. This lecture will also describe how the military uses simulation as well as the advantages and disadvantages.

Systems Architecture lecture identifies the major components, their functionality and interfaces. This lecture also describes synthetic environment, scenario generation and exercise management.

Interoperability lecture defines interoperability and its importance in the field of military simulation. This lecture describes the protocols used in military simulation to insure interoperability and what it means to be HLA compliance. Several architectures will be discussed such as JSIMS and OneSAF.

Event Management lecture describes the role of events and objects in simulations and provides several techniques for managing them.

Time Management lecture extends the idea of managing events to the idea of managing and synchronizing time within a simulation. Simulation time is driven by events; the two ideas are closely related.

Physical Modeling lecture provides an outline for physical modeling along with several examples from virtual and constructive simulations.

Environmental Modeling lecture explores the techniques used to represent the virtual environment and the difference between static and dynamic environments. The standardization of the environmental modeling is also discussed.

Behavioral Modeling lecture describes the modeling of human reasoning, military decision making and the use of agents in a simulation. Military applications are reviewed as well as a survey of techniques for modeling behavior.

Multi-Resolution Modeling lecture describes the use of multiple levels of model resolution to obtain information at different levels of details and as mechanism for tying simulations together.

VV&A describes verification, validation, accreditation and certification of military simulations. It also describes the VV&A process, categories and techniques.

Future of simulation is reviewed including product design, distributed learning, simulation in the entertainment industry and resources that can be used when you return to your job. [. . .]

This class takes place over a three day period [. . .] $1295.

2005, www. simulation.com/training/Military_Sim/ military_sim.html

Simulations are the bread and butter of experimental science. Before, after, and sometimes in place of actual laboratory or observational experimentation, computer simulations generate useful data. A five-year (2001–05) search of the archives of *Science*, the journal of the American Association for the Advancement of Science, brings up 1,317 articles using simulations across the whole range of scientific inquiry from genetics, climatology, and molecular biology to astronomy, medicine, earthquake prediction, and lots more. The rise of simulation is tightly joined to the increasing speed, reduced size, multimedia abilities, and number-crunching power of computers – computers that each year "perform better" than the year before. The result is a conjunction of commercial, military, scientific, and academic operations where the "performance principle" is a concatenation of theatre, knowledge, and power. Who controls these operations? The dominant players are corporate executives, university officials, military brass, and government bureaucrats. The workers proposing theories and experiments, crunching the numbers, devising specific simulations and as-if experiences, and turning the results into knowledge are professors, soldiers, scientists, and a few artists. What's done with this knowledge, who owns it, who gets to decide how to "apply" it, remains highly contested. Increasingly, however, the workers are losing control over what use is made of the their experiments' outputs. At the level of popular entertainment and art, simulations, virtual realities, and cyborgs (the human–machine interface) may end up in video arcades or at art shows. I will discuss some of this later in the chapter. I note now that this same technology, the fruit of high-level simulation experiments, is also being used to locate targets and guide "smart bombs" to these targets. But the smart weapons are dumb robots ethically, only as good as the men who deploy them, and that's not good enough to avoid killing civilians by the thousands.

Simulation is important to the arts – especially with regard to works that occupy a liminal area between what is socially–legally acceptable and what is beyond the pale. Increasingly, the off-limits signposts are being moved outward. Performance and visual artists are showing works that include surgery, body parts, and even cannibalism. I will discuss some of this work in later chapters. Here, I want to concentrate on how sex is publicly performed. In contemporary Western culture, the "erotic" is permitted (if not wholly welcomed) while the "pornographic" is scorned (if not fully proscribed). But distinguishing the two is not easy. Sex in art is implied or simulated while sex in pornography at least pretends to be explicit. In *Jacobellis* v. *Ohio*, a 1964 case decided by the US Supreme Court, Justice Potter Stewart famously opined that although it was difficult to define pornography in the legal sense, "I know it when I see it." For the US Supreme Court, to be pornographic, the sex has to be hardcore, real, and only about itself. But these are no longer reliable determinators. In Michael Winterbottom's film *9 Songs* (2004), actors Margo Stilley and Kieran O'Brien have sex on camera. When asked whether *9 Songs* was pornography, Winterbottom replied, à la Potter Stewart: "You watch 10 porn films and then watch *9 Songs*, it's pretty clear the difference." Really? According to Winterbottom, the theme of *9 Songs* is to show sex in itself with little intervening plot (**see Rodrick box**). But doesn't the presence of the film crew, the careful arrangement of shots, the use of a script or at least a scenario (Winterbottom mostly eschews scripts), and the knowledge that the product will be marketed "as" a

Stephen Rodrick

When "real sex" on camera is a simulation

Margo Stilley and Kieran O'Brien, the stars of *9 Songs*, met only three days before they first had sex on film. There was a quick get acquainted session and a slightly longer screen test. [. . .] On the first day of filming in the fall of 2003, they met again at a hotel in London. First, they helped [filmmaker Michael] Winterbottom and his two-man crew haul equipment up to a suite. Then everyone had a cup of tea. A few minutes later, the two actors got naked.

"We shot a scene where Margo and I were just kissing and taking our clothes off," O'Brien recalls. "It wasn't until after lunch that we had sex." When he first met Stilley and O'Brien before filming, Winterbottom told them that *9 Songs* would be shot without a script [. . .] and little would be explained about their characters, Lisa and Matt, except that she is an American student in London and he is a scientist. The only real break from sex would be the occasional rock concert. [. . .]

As would happen throughout the shoot, Winterbottom left little to chance. "He really mapped out everything," O'Brien says. "The order he wanted me to take off my clothes, her clothes, whether my socks stayed on or not. He had specific ideas of how he wanted our bodies to move. Sometimes, he would start us and then stop and say, 'Let's try this from a slightly different angle,' and then take 15 minutes to reset the shot. I wondered if he remembered the delicate machinery of the male sex organ." [. . .] As the shooting dragged on [for 30 days], Stilley found it increasingly difficult to see *9 Songs* as just a job. "The only way I could do it was to be Lisa on and off this set. I'd answer the phone as Lisa. My friends thought I was crazy. But it was the only way I could deal with that feeling of, "Oh, God, what kind of person am I becoming that I'm getting used to this?"

2005, "Michael Winterbottom Gets Naked," 25.

fiction put whatever happens – however "real" – in quotation marks? What assured Stilley and O'Brien that they were making art and not porn while they fucked was that they knew Winterbottom's movie was destined for independent film theatres, not porn houses. Most of Winterbottom's films are similar to *9 Songs*, "real" without being either home movies or documentaries. They are shot with the camera angles, lighting, and rhythm of an independent filmmaker known for his artistry. At the same time, Winterbottom drives his actors so that neither they nor Winterbottom (or, finally, the viewers) can reliably distinguish between themselves and their characters – if, indeed, there are any characters. This kind of hyperrealism is in line with **cinema verité** and more akin to webcams than to fiction films. Is this an emerging mode of simulated reality – or of its identical opposite, real simulation?

cinema verité – literally "truth film" or "true film" – is a style of filmmaking originating in France in the 1960s. Cinema verité artists use hand-held cameras to film real people on location in unrehearsed situations. Cinema verité output may be documentaries or art films. Some better-known cinema verité filmmakers are **Jean-Luc Godard**, **Jean-Pierre Rouch**, **Frederick Wiseman**, **the Maysles brothers (David and Albert)**, and **Donn Pennebaker**. Not only are cinema verité filmmakers still working, their techniques continue to influence filmmaking.

Jean-Luc Godard (1930–): French filmmaker who brought cinema verité techniques from the documentary realm into fiction films. Among Godard's many works: *A bout de souffle* (*Breathless*, 1960), *Une femme mariée* (*A Married Woman*, 1964) *Alphaville* (1965), *Nouvelle Vague* (*New Wave*, 1990), *Liberté et patrie* (*Liberty and Homeland*, 2002), and *Paris, je t'aime* (*Paris, I Love You*, 2005)

Jean-Pierre Rouch (1917–2004): French filmmaker and anthropologist. Among his more than 100 films: *Moi, un Noir* (*Me, a Black*, 1959), *Les Maîtres Foux* (*The Mad Masters*, 1954), *Chronique d'un été* (*Chronicle of a Summer*, 1961), *La Chasse au lion* (*The Lion Hunters*, 1957–64), and *Dionysus* (1984).

Frederick Wiseman (1930–): American filmmaker whose stark made-for-TV documentaries include *Titicut Follies* (1967), *High School* (1968), *Hospital* (1969), *Juvenile Court* (1973) – and on through a long list – to *Domestic Violence* (2001), *Domestic Violence 2* (2002), and *The Garden* (2005).

Maysles brothers (David, 1932–87 and Albert, 1926–): American filmmakers whose work comprises a broad range of subjects including *What's Happening: The Beatles in the USA* (1964), *Salesman* (1968), *Gimme Shelter* (1970), and *Abortion: Desperate Choices* (1992, with Susan Froemke and Deborah Dickson). First the brothers and later Albert with other collaborators have documented the works of Christo and Jean-Claude from *Christo's Valley Curtain* (1974) through *Running Fence* (1978) and *Umbrellas* (1995, with Henry Corra and Graham Weinbren) to *The Gates* (in process 2005, with Antonio Ferrera).

Donn Pennebaker (1925–): American filmmaker whose works on electioneering and pop culture include *Primary* (1960), *Don't Look Back* (1967), *Monterey Pop* (1967), *The War Room* (1993), and *Elaine Stritch at Liberty* (2004).

Poststructuralism/deconstruction

Postmodernism and poststructuralism are the bases for academic theories of performativity. Postmodernism and poststructuralism can only be understood if they are examined in relation to each other. Postmodernism is a practice in the visual arts, architecture, and performance art. Poststructuralism, a.k.a. "deconstruction," is an academic response to postmodernism. Taken together, they constitute practices and theories of performativity. But these practices and theories are not consistently applied or understood across disciplines. The uses of performativity in business, science, and the military are often at odds with how artists and academics understand and use performativity. The first wave of scholars and artists – those who devised poststructuralism and practiced postmodernism – were vehemently anti-authoritarian. They elaborated Austin's ideas of performativity in ways that were philosophically, politically, and aesthetically anti-authoritarian. Today's poststructuralists and postmodernists continue this work of subverting the established order of things. But the matter doesn't end there. What's happened is that the ideas of poststructuralism and the techniques of performativity – simulation especially – have been eagerly taken up by business, science, and the military, eager to enhance their control over knowledge; anxious to acquire more power. How the contradiction between the performance studies/cultural studies intellectuals and artists and the power brokers will be resolved is not certain. The universities are sites of this contradiction. While many faculty fly the banner of subversive poststructuralism/postmodernism, boards of trustees and governors

– the ultimate university authorities – take steps to rationalize and corporatize the system, bringing it more and more in line with big business, big science, and big government.

Poststructuralism, a discourse in cultural, linguistic, and philosophical circles, began in France in the 1960s both as a revolt against "structuralism" and in sympathy with the radical student movement that culminated in the strikes and insurrections of 1968. Poststructuralism has never totally lost touch with its radical beginnings, though (as we will see) this has also proven to be a burden as the rest of the world moves on.

Structuralism, closely associated with the "structural linguistics" of **Ferdinand de Saussure** and **Roman Jakobson**, and led in the 1960s and 1970s by **Claude Lévi-Strauss**, took as its main program the discovery of universal unconscious structures of language, mind, and culture (**see Lévi-Strauss box and Ehrmann box**). The structuralists often worked by analyzing cultural practices both "diachronically" (over time) and "synchronically" (as a single structural unit). A favorite device of the structuralists was using "binary oppositions" to map the dialectical tensions of a system. The poststructuralists deplored both the structuralists' desire to universalize and their use of binary oppositions. The poststructuralists argued that these reduced complex situations to over-simplified models. Furthermore, the poststructuralists felt that structuralism buttressed the status quo socially, politically, and philosophically. Poststructuralists opposed all notions of universals, originals, or firsts. To poststructuralists, every act, every utterance, every idea, is a performative.

Ferdinand de Saussure (1857–1913): Swiss linguist, whose posthumously published *Course in General Linguistics* (1916, Eng. 1959) lays the foundation of structural linguistics, as well as of structuralism more generally.

Roman Jakobson (1896–1982): Russian-born linguist. Author of *Fundamentals of Language* (1956), *Studies in Verbal Art* (1971), and *Main Trends in the Science of Language* (1973).

Claude Lévi-Strauss (1908–): French anthropologist, the doyen of structuralism. Among his many books are: *The Elementary Structures of Kinship* (1949, Eng. 1969), *Structural Anthropology* (1958, Eng. 1963), *The Savage Mind* (1962, Eng. 1966), and *The Raw and the Cooked* (1964, Eng. 1969), and *Look, Listen, Read* (1997).

Claude Lévi-Strauss

The universal of structuralism

If, as we believe to be the case, the unconscious activity of the mind consists in imposing forms upon content, and if these forms are fundamentally the same for all minds – ancient and modern, primitive and civilized (as the study of the symbolic function, expressed in language, so strikingly indicates) – it is necessary and sufficient to grasp the unconscious structure underlying each institution and each custom, in order to obtain a principle of interpretation valid for other institutions and other customs, provided of course that the analysis is carried far enough.

1963, *Structural Anthropology*, 21

Jacques Ehrmann

What is structuralism?

What is structuralism? Before being a philosophy, as some tend to see it, it is a method of analysis. Even as such its many facets and different uses make it a subject of various interpretations, debate, even polemics. No simple or single definition applies to it except in very general terms. One could say a structure is a combination and relation of formal elements which reveal their logical coherence within given objects of analysis. Although structuralism can hardly be subsumed in some overall formula, or be given any label which will identify it for public consumption, we can say it is first of all, when applied to the sciences of man, a certain way of studying language problems and the problems of languages.

1966, "Introduction" to special issue of *Yale French Studies* on Structuralism, 7

Poststructuralists regard each phenomenon as part of an endless stream of repetitions with no "first voice" of ultimate authority (**see Foucault box 1**). In their insistence on process, poststructuralists are Heraclitean and Nietzschean – everything is in flux. The flux of experience and history is the battleground for an ongoing power struggle. Who has the authority to speak in the "father's voice" – except there is no father. Just as the Wizard of Oz proves to be an illusion, a magic show manipulated by an ordinary man, so do the great icons of societal power. (An insight that **Jean Genet** expressed as early as 1956 in *The Balcony*.) Unstable "iteration" – repetition, but not quite exactly – replaces stable representation. But by the turn of the new millennium, this idea ran smack into the practice of digital and biological cloning. Thus, on the one hand, postmodern repetition and recombination; on the other, poststructuralist *différance* (to be discussed soon).

Although their discourse is principally about language and takes the form of essays and books, poststructuralists entertain a very broad view of what constitutes language. "There is nothing outside the text," Derrida wrote. But the "text" in Derrida's theory is all of human culture. "Writing," as Derrida has it, comprises an all-inclusive array of cultural expressions and social practices. By "writing", Derrida means more than graphic inscription and literature. He means entire systems of "inscribed" power: laws, rituals, traditions, hierarchies, politics, economic relations, science, the military, and the arts (**see Derrida box 2**). Derrida views cultures as constructed sets of relations, historically founded and always contested. Inscribed power performs its privileges by means of established authorities – police, courts, the military, priesthood, scientists, teachers, and critics. It's no accident that in English the word "authority" includes the word "author." The writing produced by the authorities is not "transparent" – a windowpane through which one sees the "true," the "real," or the "natural." All writing enacts agendas of power. Writing doesn't serve power, but the other way around: who writes performs authority. Yet all authority, whatever its proclamation of eternity and universality, is temporary: "inalienable rights," "the 1,000-year Reich," "all roads lead to Rome," "I am the resurrection and the life" – no "writing" is either first or final.

Michel Foucault

A secret origin, an already-said

We must renounce two linked, but opposite themes. The first involves a wish that it should never be possible to assign, in the order of discourse, the irruption of a real event; that beyond any apparent beginning, there is always a secret origin – so secret and so fundamental that it can never be quite grasped in itself. Thus one is led inevitably [. . .] towards an ever-receding point that is never itself present in any history; this point is merely its own void; and from that point all beginnings can never be more than recommencements or occultation (in one and the same gesture, this and that). To this theme is connected another according to which all manifest discourse is secretly based on an "already-said"; and that this "already-said" is not merely a phrase that has already been spoken, or a text that has already been written, but a "never-said," an incorporeal discourse, a voice as silent as a breath, a writing that is merely the hollow of its own mark. It is supposed therefore that everything that is formulated in discourse was already articulated in that semi-silence that precedes it, which continues to run obstinately beneath it, but which it covers and silences. The manifest discourse, therefore, is really no more than the repressive presence of what it does not say; and this "not-said" is a hollow that undermines from within all that is said. The first theme sees the historical analysis of discourse as the quest for and the repetition of an origin that eludes all historical determination; the second sees it as the interpretation of "hearing" an "already-said" that is at the same time a "not-said." We must renounce all those themes whose function is to ensure the infinite continuity of discourse and its secret presence to itself in the interplay of a constantly recurring absence. We must be ready to receive every moment of discourse in its sudden irruption; in that punctuality in which it appears, and in that temporal dispersion that enables it to be repeated, known, forgotten, transformed, utterly erased, and hidden, far from all view, in the dust of books. Discourse must not be referred to the distant presence of the origin, but treated as and when it occurs.

1972, *The Archeology of Knowledge*, 25

Jean Genet (1910–86): French playwright and novelist – formerly a thief and prostitute – whose works include *The Maids* (1948, Eng. 1954), *Our Lady of Flowers* (1948, Eng. 1949), *The Thief's Journal* (1949, Eng. 1959), *The Balcony* (1956, Eng. 1958), *The Blacks* (1958, Eng. 1960), and *The Screens* (1961, Eng. 1962).

Jacques Derrida

"Writing" and "deconstruction"

If we take the notion of writing in its currently accepted sense – one which should not – and that is essential – be considered innocent, primitive, or natural, it can only be seen as a means of communication [. . .] extending enormously, if not infinitely, the domain of oral or gestural communication. [. . .]

Once men are already in the state of "communicating their thoughts," and of doing it by means of sounds [. . .], the birth and progress of writing will follow a line that is direct, simple, and continuous. [. . .]

The representational character of the written communication – writing as picture, reproduction, imitation of its content – will be the invariant trait of all progress to come. [. . .] Representation, of course, will become more complex, will develop supplementary ramifications and degrees [. . .].

A written sign is proffered in the absence of the receiver. How to style this absence? [. . .T]his distance, divergence, delay, this deferral [*différance*] must be capable of being carried to a certain absoluteness of absence if the structure of writing, assuming that writing exists, is to constitute itself. [. . .] My communication must be repeatable – iterable – in the absolute absence of the receiver [. . .]. Such iterability – (iter, again, probably comes from itara, other in Sanskrit, and everything that follows can be read as the working out of the logic that ties repetition to alterity) structures the mark of writing itself, no matter what particular type of writing is involved [. . .]. A writing that is not structurally readable – iterable – beyond the death of the addressee would not be writing. [. . .]

The possibility of repeating and thus of identifying the marks is implicit in every code, making it into a network that is communicable, transmittable, decipherable, iterable for a third, and hence for every possible user in general. To be what it is, all writing must, therefore, be capable of functioning in the radical absence of every empirically determined receiver in general. And this absence is not a continuous modification of presence, it is a rupture in presence. [. . .] What holds for the receiver holds also, for the same reason, for the sender or producer. To write is to produce a mark that will constitute a sort of machine which is productive in turn, and which my future disappearance will not, in principle, hinder in its functioning, offering things and itself to be read and to be rewritten. [. . .]

[T]he traits that can be recognized in the classical, narrowly defined concept of writing are generalizable. They are valid not only for all orders of "signs" and for all languages in general but moreover, beyond semiotic-linguistic communication, for the entire field of what philosophy would call experience, even the experience of being: the above-mentioned "presence." [. . .]

Every sign, linguistic or nonlinguistic, spoken or written (in the current sense of this opposition), in small or large units, can be cited, put between quotation marks; in so doing it can break with every given context, engendering an infinity of new contexts in a manner which is absolutely illimitable. This does not imply that the mark is valid outside of a context, but on the contrary that there are only contexts without any center or absolute anchoring. [. . .]

We are witnessing not an end of writing that would restore [. . .] a transparency or an immediacy to social relations; but rather the increasingly powerful historical expansion of a general writing, of which the system of speech, consciousness, meaning, presence, truth, etc., would be only an effect, and should be analyzed as such. [. . .]

Deconstruction cannot be restricted or immediately pass to a neutralization: it must, through a double gesture, a double science, a double writing – put into practice a reversal of the classical opposition and a general displacement of the system. [. . .] Deconstruction does not consist in moving from one concept to another, but in reversing and displacing a conceptual order as well as the nonconceptual order with which it is articulated.

1988, *Limited Inc.*, 3, 5, 7–9, 12, 21

That is because behind every writing are other writings. New writing tries to erase or co-opt what came before, but is never wholly successful. To Derrida, cultures are **palimpsests** of official and counter-hegemonic graffiti. Every writing is a power struggle (**see Derrida box 3**). Even simple binaries such as "day/night," "white/black," "man/ woman" inscribe power. In Western languages, by reading the term on the left first we perform its authority over the term on the right. To reverse terms is to perform a new power relation: "black/white" is different than "white/black." From this perspective, history is not a story of "what happened" but an ongoing struggle to "write," or claim ownership, over historical narratives. Yet every narrative, no matter how elegant or seemingly total, is full of holes, what Derrida calls "aporia" – open spaces, absences, and contradictions. Nothing can be totally erased. These aporias leak various pasts and alternatives into the present order of things.

palimpsest: a document or artwork that has been repeatedly written or drawn on, then partly erased, then written or drawn on again, so that the previous writings leave a still visible trace on the writing surface. Thus a palimpsest contains and expresses its own history of being inscribed on.

The authorities – "those who author" – attempt to make the present take on the appearance of being the outcome of an inevitable process (fate, destiny, historical necessity). But this ineluctable continuity – a knowable past that determines a stable present leading to an inevitable future – is a fiction. The past is full of holes; the present is provisional, the future not known. All historical narratives are haunted by what/who is erased, threatened by what/who demands representation. The struggle to write history, to represent events, is an ongoing performative process full of opinion and other subjectivities (**see Blau box**).

hegemonic: exerting dominance or control, usually by or on behalf of the state, religious body, corporation, or other established power.

Jacques Derrida

Writing and power never work separately

Fostering the belief that writing fosters power (one can, in general, and one can write if occasioned to), that it can ally itself to power, can prolong it by complementing it, or can serve it, the question suggests that writing can come [*arriver*] to power or power to writing. It excludes in advance the identification of writing as power or the recognition of power from the onset of writing. It auxiliarizes and hence aims to conceal the fact that writing and power never work separately, however complex the laws, the system, or the links of their collusion may be. [. . .]

Writing does not come to power. It is there beforehand, it partakes of and is made of it. [. . .] Hence, struggles for powers set various writings up against one another [*les luttes pour les pouvoirs opposent des écritures*].

1998 [1979], *Scribble (writing-power)*, in *The Derrida Reader*, 50

Herbert Blau

Nothing can keep subjectivity out

If the pressure felt by historians from poststructuralism and "the linguistic turn" pushed one or another to mockery or disdain for "discourse about discourse about discourse," even the most recidivist empiricist would acknowledge that as the past is experienced, thought through, felt, then reexamined, not even **cliometrics** or microhistory can keep out subjectivity, or the encroachment of language on how history is conceived. As for what actually happened, there are still historicists [. . .] who remain attached to some reasonable facsimile of a scientific hermeneutic, wanting to stay with the facts, but knowing at the same time that the writing of history occurs through the questions asked about it, with unavoidable special interests from contentious points of view, from which – with documents, texts, archives, objects, and objective commitment too – they know they're not exempt. Axiom: fact is fact, depending on how you look at it, or as mirrored in the mind.

2004, "Thinking History, History Thinking," 257

cliometrics: the application of methods developed in other fields – anything from economics and statistics to performance studies and psychology – to the study of history.

In order to call attention to the unstable, performative quality of writing, Derrida coined the word ***différance*** (French), meaning "difference" + "deferral" – otherness plus a lack of fixed or decided meaning. Because writing is always a contested system of erasing as well as composing, meaning cannot "be" once and for all. Meaning is always performed: Always in rehearsal, its finality forever deferred, its actuality only provisional, played out in specific circumstances. This "playing out" is related to Nietzsche's "will-to-power" (see Chapter 4). As play acts, performatives are not "true" or "false," "right" or "wrong." They happen. Furthermore, writing in the poststructuralist sense consists of "iterations" – quotations, repetitions, and citations. Derrida emphasizes that language in general and speech acts in particular depend on an active estrangement, an encounter with "otherness."

This is very close to Brecht's ***Verfremdungseffekt*** (alienation effect). In Brechtian theatre, the actor stands beside herself and beside the events enacted – doing and showing at the same time (**see figure 5.6**). The Brechtian performer is not lost in the role, or entirely empathetic with the situation (I will discuss Brechtian acting more thoroughly in Chapter 6). Brecht argued that art is not a mirror held up to nature but a hammer with which to shape it.

différance: a noun coined by Jacques Derrida emphasizing the double meaning of the French verb *différer* – "to differ" and "to defer." Différance – a difference and a deferral – marks the slippage between a word as such and what the word refers to. Différance has entered English and is used without quotation marks.

Verfremdungseffekt: Bertolt Brecht's term, difficult to translate, meaning the effect of "alienation" or "estrangement" from a theatrical role. Using the Verfremdungseffekt, Brecht wanted to make the familiar appear strange and the strange appear familiar. The Verfremdungseffekt demands a measure of detachment from the action – positioning the actor "next to" instead of "in" the role. While "next to," the actor can express her own, or the playwright's, opinions on the character and on what is being performed.

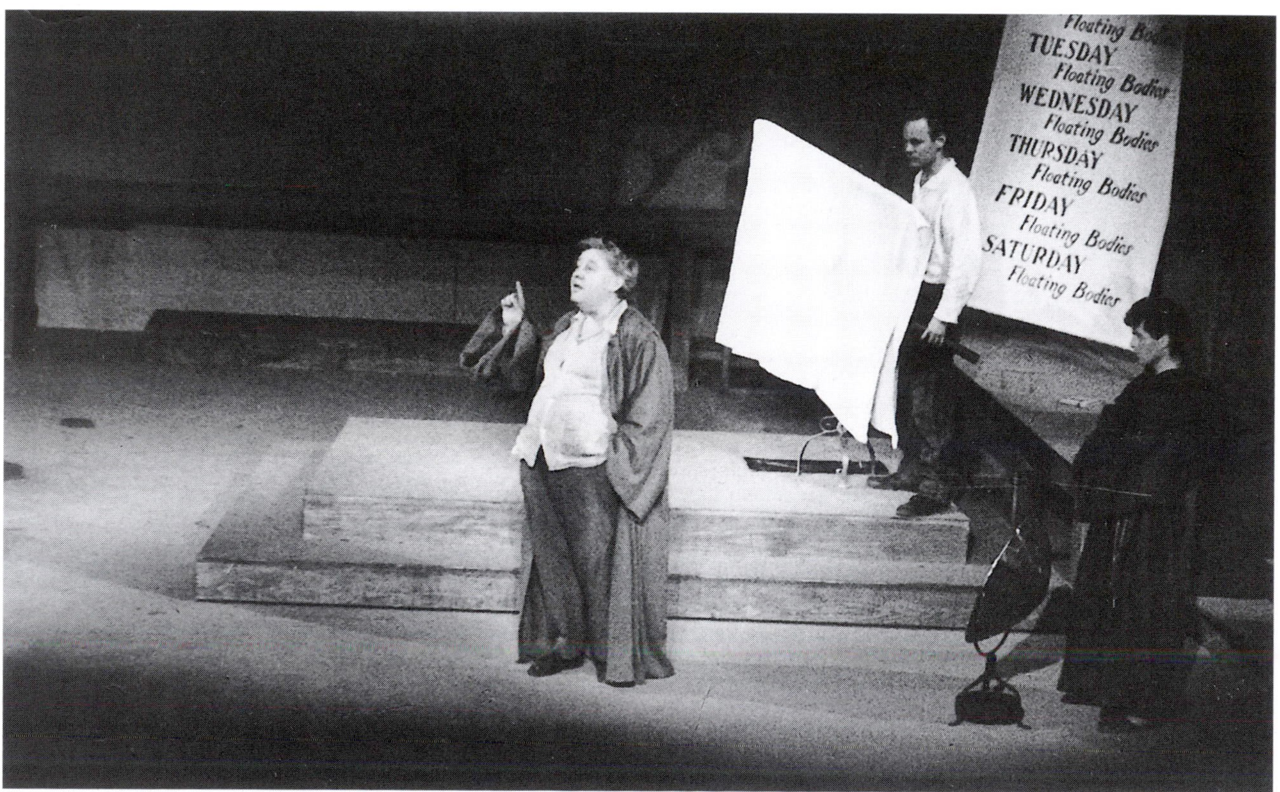

fig 5.6. Charles Laughton, an actor Bertolt Brecht admired for his ability to play the character and stand beside character, performing in Brecht's *The Life of Galileo* in the Beverly Hills Coronet Theatre, 1947. Photograph by Ruth Berlau. Copyright the Bertolt Brecht Archive, Berlin.

The diffusion of poststructuralism

From the 1980s onward, poststructuralism spread far beyond France. For English-speakers, the most influential French poststructuralists are Michel Foucault, Jacques Derrida, Giles Deleuze, and Félix Guattari. Very important as well, though not strictly speaking poststructuralists, are Jean Baudrillard, Guy Debord, Pierre Bourdieu, and Jacques Lacan. In the UK and North America, poststructuralism drew on and soon enough merged with theories of the performative conceived by Austin and richly elaborated by **Judith Butler** – whose ideas I will have more to say about later in this chapter. Many adherents of the poststructuralist approach were drawn to the "**Frankfurt School**" – a group of thinkers including **Theodor Adorno**, **Max Horkheimer**, **Herbert Marcuse**, and **Jürgen Habermas**. These Marxist critical theorists found allies in Walter Benjamin and Bertolt Brecht. Adherents of the Frankfurt School developed a fruitful convergence of poststructuralist, Marxist, and Freudian thought. This in turn fed a wide range of theories and "studies" – gender, cultural, postcolonial, race, queer, and performance. What unites this diverse and sometimes self-contradictory collation is both an identification with the **subaltern** – the marginalized – the discriminated against – and a desire to sabotage, if not directly overthrow, the existing order of things.

Judith Butler (1956–): American philosopher and queer theorist whose work has concentrated on developing a theory of gender performativity. Her books include *Gender Trouble* (1990), *Bodies that Matter* (1993), and *Excitable Speech* (1997).

The Frankfurt School: a group of philosophers and critical theorists originating in Germany between the world wars, who apply Left thinking to a wide range of social, cultural, political, ideological, and aesthetic questions. Among the members and adherents of the Frankfurt School are Horkheimer, Adorno, Marcuse, Benjamin, Brecht, and Habermas. The Institute for Social Research (the Frankfurt School's formal name) was established in 1922 at the University of Frankfurt. When the Nazis shut the Institute down in the 1930s because many of its members were both Marxists and Jews, the Institute's director, Max Horkheimer, led a wholesale emigration to the USA. In 1950, Horkheimer and Adorno returned to Frankfurt to re-start the Institute. The Frankfurt School deeply influenced the radical social and political thought of the 1960s and beyond, including cultural studies and performance studies.

Theodor Adorno (1903–69): German philosopher concerned with the relationship between art and politics. Fleeing the Nazis, Adorno taught at Oxford, Princeton, and the University of California, Berkeley before returning to Frankfurt in 1950 to join Horkheimer in restarting the Institute for Social Research. Adorno's books include *Prisms* (1967), *Dialectic of Enlightenment* (with Max Horkheimer, 1972), *The Philosophy of Modern Music* (1973), and *The Authoritarian Personality* (1982).

Max Horkheimer (1895–1973): German philosopher and critical theorist, director of the Institute for Social Research at Frankfurt University. After leaving Germany in 1934, Horkheimer taught at Columbia University and the University of California. Returning to Germany in 1950, he not only worked with Adorno in restarting the Institute but also served as rector of Frankfurt University, 1951–53. Author of *Eclipse of Reason* (1947), *Critical Theory: Selected Essays* (1972), *Dialectic of Enlightenment* (with Theodor Adorno, 1972), and *Between Philosophy and Social Science* (1993).

Herbert Marcuse (1898–1979): German-born philosopher and a founding member of the Frankfurt School. Marcuse emigrated to America in 1934, taught at Columbia University, became a US citizen in 1940, and served during World War II as an intelligence analyst for the US Army. After the war he resumed teaching with his final post being at the University of California. A radical Freudian Marxist, Marcuse's thought had a great impact on the student movements of the 1960s and '70s. His books include: *Eros and Civilization* (1955), *One Dimensional Man* (1964), *Negations: Essays in Critical Theory* (1968), and *Towards a Critical Theory of Society* (2001).

Jürgen Habermas (1929–): German philosopher who studied with Adorno and Horkheimer. Habermas headed the Institute for Social Research 1983–93. Habermas's books include: *Theory and Practice* (1974), *The Theory of Communicative Action* (2 vols, 1984–87), *The Future of Human Nature* (2003), *Philosophy in a Time of Terror* (with Jacques Derrida and Giovanna Borradori, 2003).

subaltern: literally, subordinate, of low rank. Often used to indicate the oppressed or marginalized status of persons or groups in the Third World.

The core operation of poststructuralism is "decentering," an attack on every kind of **hegemony**, authority, and fixed system – philosophical, sexual, political, artistic, economic, artistic. Poststructuralists subvert the First Performative of Western and Islamic cultures, God's Utterances in *Genesis*,

"God said . . . and there was!" (Derrida, though French, grew up Jewish in Arab Algeria. His early cultural experiences are Semitic, European, and colonial.) Poststructuralists also undercut Aristotle's notion of a First Cause. On these originary Spoken Presences, Derrida pours acidic puns and ironies. Derrida's attacks are consonant with Foucault's renunciation of the "secret origin" and the "already-said." Foucault wanted to undermine the idea that history proceeded as a continuous smooth stream of causes and effects. He proposed instead seeking the "ruptures" and "transformations" that throw up "new foundations" (**see Foucault box 2**). The poststructuralists challenge not so-called facts, but how knowledge itself is manufactured, performed, and written (in the Derridean sense). As a consequence, the term "performative" now includes everything from doable acts of the body, to imaging of all kinds (painterly, photographic, digital), and writing as such.

Michel **Foucault**

Threshold, rupture, break, mutation, transformation

And the great problem [. . .] is not how continuities are established, how a single pattern is formed and preserved, how for so many different, successive minds there is a single horizon, what mode of action and what substructure is implied by the interplay of transmissions, resumptions, disappearances, and repetitions, how the origin may extend its sway well beyond itself to that conclusion that is never given – the problem is no longer one of tradition, of tracing a line, but one of division, of limits; it is no longer one of lasting foundations, but one of transformations that serve as new foundations, the rebuilding of foundations. What one is seeing, then, is the emergence of a whole field of questions, some of which are already familiar, by which this new form of history is trying to develop its own theory: how is one to specify the different concepts that enable us to conceive of discontinuity (threshold, rupture, break, mutation, transformation)? By what criteria is one to isolate the unities with which one is dealing; what is a science, what is an *œuvre* [work]? What is a theory? What is a concept? What is a text? How is one to diversify the levels at which one may place oneself, each of which possesses its own divisions and form of analysis? [. . .] In short, the history of thought, of knowledge, of philosophy, of literature seems to be seeking, and discovering, more and more discontinuities [. . .].

1972, *The Archeology of Knowledge*, 5–6

Problems with poststructuralism

Despite its highly developed political consciousness and its analysis of, and sympathy for, the marginalized and disempowered, poststructuralism is not a mass movement with a direct impact on the vast majority of people. Poststructuralists are mostly sequestered in the ivory tower, the "tenured radical" phenomenon. The authorities both within academia and outside it don't worry much about poststructuralists disrupting the status quo. In fact, an ironclad status quo has developed within poststructuralism. Ironically, poststructuralism is ruled by the works of (mostly dead) authors. The writings and ideas of the poststructuralist canon are continually recycled inside a closed hermeneutical system (**see Butt box**).

The causes of this situation are not difficult to locate. Once the "disturbances" of the 1960s were snuffed out, many defeated radicals returned to, or took refuge in, academia. There they won in theory what they could not in the streets. Addressing other like-minded professors and their students, poststructuralist writing grew complex and arcane, cleaving a bigger and bigger space between the movement and the larger public. Even as the range of subjects studied expanded – including all aspects of popular culture – direct contact with ordinary people – even professionals and other academics – decreased. Upon graduation, most students left poststructuralism behind. The few who continued to hold the torch became young professors. What had started as an effort to change society ended as an academic "tradition" dependent on the aforementioned canon of anti-canonical authors. These authors continue to inform, if not wholly drive, cultural studies and performance studies. Given this situation of more or less self-imposed isolation, neither corporate boards, government, nor university officials messed with what was happening. Why bother? Unlike the disruptions of the 1960s, the new radicals keep their activities mostly confined to "discourse" – writings, seminars, petitions, artworks, well-regulated protests, and so on. These are all cultural products that make the universities appear "liberal" and open to the

Gavin Butt

When theory constrains rather than enables

When referring to "theory" [. . .] we usually invoke a melange of theoretical paradigms and perspectives which have now come to be dominant in the Western humanities: semiotics, deconstruction, psychoanalysis, and post-structuralism. But the problem seems to arise when such hermeneutic tools – originally deployed to critique various forms of power and authority within cultural and artistic representations – have come to be credited with a kind of authority *of their own*. The final paradoxical twist comes about when a body of work renowned for its deconstruction of authorial value comes to be accredited with precisely such forms of authority. What does the [. . .] student do in order to substantiate his argument about, for example, the representation of masculinity in contemporary art? Answer: he cites the proper name Derrida (or similar), and the authority of his body (of work) [. . .]. It is precisely in this way that post-structural theory (perhaps above all) has come to operate both as criticism's chief enabler whilst simultaneously marking its limit point [. . .] working to constrain the production of new concepts and/or methods [. . .].

2005, "The Paradoxes of Criticism," 4

widest diversity of opinion. An increasingly totalizing global system can easily tolerate or even exult in displaying the products of its liberalism – as long as the radicals remain in their proper places. In fact, the more liberal the academic system, the more easily it keeps radical impulses within known bounds. Meanwhile, at the level of governance, power is increasingly centralized in deans, presidents, and boards of trustees. Universities – public as well as private – are increasingly adopting the corporate management style. Absorbed into academia with its strict rules of tenure and promotion, or tormented by the insecurities of part-time adjunct positions, the revolution of thinking envisioned by the poststructuralists has largely been reduced to and transformed into performative play.

Furthermore, while the Right was forming think tanks and developing policy papers designed to impact government and business, the radical Left took up permanent residence as outsiders, the opposition – an "alternative" lacking strategies to move back to the center of social decision-making (**see Lakoff box**). Thus, even traditional moderate Left parties, such as British Labour or the US Democrats, moved further and further to the Right. Even when egregious policies – such as the second American invasion of Iraq in 2003 or the failure of the USA to ratify the 1997 Kyoto Accords on global warming – gave the Left opportunities for mass movements, only relatively few people could be mobilized. Far fewer than the millions who opposed the Vietnam war in the 1960s–'70s – a sizable number of whom were willing to risk jail through acts of civil disobedience. Why was this so? In a way, ironically, the performative replaced performance. The internet had become the global forum. People blogged and petitioned rather than putting bodies in the streets. When people did demonstrate – against the invasion of Iraq or the meetings of the World Trade Organization, for example – the police were well able to control the situations. The near absolute freedom of internet expression led to lots of excellent ideas and analyses that had little effect on policies. The many opinions served more to blow off steam than to form a united front. With regard to the Iraq war, even when it was clear that the Bush administration had lied about weapons of mass destruction and later authorized torturing prisoners; and even as American troops and Iraqis were dying and public opinion was turning against the war, George W. Bush was re-elected, his war program intact.

Am I being too critical? Or nostalgic about actions the Left no longer considers appropriate or effective? The '60s–'70s brought many thousands of bodies into the streets, while the new millennium works by means of digital imaging, the internet, cloning, and related phenomena. These are the performatives of the Left. But not only the Left. Fundamentalists of all stripes are not averse to using the most advanced technologies – even as they also employ direct action, which is what terrorism, suicide bombs, ethnic cleansings, honor rapes, and the rest are. I will discuss these difficult matters in terms of interculturalism and globalization in Chapter 8. For now I ask: Hasn't much of the post-structuralist program been accomplished? Isn't there more

George Lakoff

How the Right got it right

Back in the 1950s conservatives hated each other. [. . .] A group of conservative leaders [. . .] started asking what the different groups of conservatives had in common and whether they could agree to disagree in order to promote a general conservative cause. They started magazines and think tanks [the Heritage Foundation, the Olin Institute at Harvard, and others]. These institutes have done their job very well. People associated with them have written more books than the people on the left have, on all issues. The conservatives support their intellectuals. They create media opportunities. They have media studios down the hall in institutes so that getting on television is easy. Eighty percent of the talking heads on television are from the conservative think tanks. Eighty percent. [. . .] In 2002 four times as much money was spent on research by the right as by the left, and they got four times as much media time. They get what they pay for. This is not an accident. Conservatives, through their think tanks, figured out the importance of framing, and they figured out how to frame every issue. They figured out how to get those frames out there, how to get their people in the media all the time. They figured out how to bring their people together. [. . .] They work out their differences, agree to disagree, and when they disagree, they trade off. The idea is, *This week he'll win on his issue. Next week, I'll win on mine.* Each one may not get everything he wants, but over the long haul, he gets a lot of what he wants.

Nothing like this happens in the progressive world, because there are so many people thinking that what each does is *the right* thing. It is not smart. It is self-defeating.

2004, *Don't Think of an Elephant*, 15–16

acceptance of diversity in European and North American cultures? Haven't women, gays, people of color, Muslims, Hindus, Animists, and Jews gotten further in these societies than ever before? Aren't unpopular opinions heard more often? Haven't school curriculums been thoroughly revised and expanded? How many AIDS walks, Gay Pride parades, Trinidad-style Carnivals, and many other manifestations of minoritarian and multi-cultural values and desires are there? Community-based performances give voice to those who were not previously heard. Much of this can be credited to the long-term impact of poststructuralism. But be careful about confusing "tolerance" and "good management" with actual change. In the United States, at least, the diversity of behavior and opinion has not yet been tested against a serious economic recession or depression. In Europe, when minorities rise above a certain number, or move out of their enclaves, the "native" population resists. It's easy to be "generous" when times are good. It takes hard times to bring out the need for scapegoats.

Hard times need not be economic. They can also be psychological, an induced state of mind. The events of 9/11 reinvigorated American xenophobia, dubbed "homeland security." For those old enough to remember, the War on Terror resembles the Cold War. The threats then and now were/are real – Soviet and American missiles were armed and aimed (mostly not yet disarmed); terrorist bombs are exploding and more horrific biological and nuclear attacks are possible. During the Cold War leaders on both sides aggravated and exploited the mutual hostility. From the late 1940s, US ideological zealots hunted for communists or communist "sympathizers" in the arts, government, education, and entertainment. Many people were "character assassinated" and/or blacklisted, losing their jobs and often their friends. Ever-increasing defense expenditures fattened the military-industrial complex. Even as the Soviets promised to bury the West, citizens of the **NATO** alliance were put on notice that the Cold War would go on indefinitely because the USSR was a ruthless, "godless enemy." The demon of the War on Terror is, if anything, worse than godless – Al Qaeda worships the wrong god. For its part, Al Qaeda regards the West, and the USA especially, as the Great Satan, the ultimate infidel. As during the Cold War, the ideological enemies need each other, cooking their core followers a repast of fear and hatred.

NATO: the North Atlantic Treaty Organization (NATO) was created in 1949 as a military alliance among ten European nations plus the USA and Canada designed to confront and "contain" the Soviet Union whose forces during and after World War II had occupied Eastern Europe. In 1952, Greece and Turkey joined NATO and by 2004 – fifteen years after the end of the Cold War – ten Eastern European nations, former Soviet satellites, had been admitted to NATO. NATO's core provision is that an attack on any member nation would be regarded as an attack on all. This clause of the treaty was invoked in 2001 in response to 9/11. Previously, in 1995 and 1999, NATO forces intervened in the civil wars of the former Yugoslavia (Bosnia, Croatia, Herzegovina, Kosovo, and Serbia).

Constructions of gender

If history is an open project, and social reality the interplay of conflicting performatives, how does this affect circumstances thought to be fixed biologically or by unshakable traditions – gender and race, for example? Is a person "woman" or "man," "of color" or "white," because genetics say so or because of social arrangements? This is not a question of how people are treated or how much power they have. A revolution, or other engine of change, could result in women or people of color taking power without shaking the supposedly inherent differences between the sexes and the races. The "performative inquiry" includes but also seeks beyond changes wrought by social action. The performative inquiry asks, "What constitutes individual identity and social reality? Are these constructed or given? And if constructed, out of what?" The questions are begged, of course: once one deems gender and race (plus all other social realities) "performative," the answer is that these consist not of naturally determined operations but of something built and enforced by means of "performance" in the senses I used to describe that word in Chapter 2. Even "nature" is not natural, or prior, but a humanly constructed concept designed (consciously or unconsciously) to accomplish human ends. This argument could be, and has been, applied to many areas of human activity. Here I will explore it as it pertains to gender and race.

Judith Butler develops the assertion of French existential writer **Simone de Beauvoir** that "One is not born, but, rather, *becomes* a woman" (**see Butler box 1**). That is, one's biological sex ("female" or "male") is raw material shaped through practice into the socially constructed performance that is gender ("woman" or "man"). Of course, these binaries are much too simple, but for the moment let us stick with them. Each individual from an early age learns to perform gender-specific vocal inflections, facial displays, gestures, walks, and erotic behavior as well as how to select, modify, and use scents, body shapes and adornments, clothing, and all other gender markings of a given society. These differ widely from period to period and culture to culture – indicating

Judith Butler

Gender is performative

[T]he body is a historical situation, as Beauvoir has claimed, and is a manner of doing, dramatizing, and reproducing a historical situation. [. . .]

The act that gender is, the act that embodied agents are inasmuch as they dramatically and actively embody and, indeed, wear certain cultural significations, is clearly not one's act alone. Surely, there are nuanced and individual ways of doing one's gender, but that one does it, and that one does it in accord with certain sanctions and proscriptions, is clearly not a fully individual matter. [. . .] The act that one does, the act that one performs, is, in a sense, an act that has been going on before one arrived on the scene. Hence, gender is an act which has been rehearsed, much as a script survives the particular actors who make use of it, but which requires individual actors in order to be actualized and reproduced as reality once again. [. . .]

Gender reality is performative, which means, quite simply, that it is real only to the extent that it is performed. [. . .] If gender attributes [. . .] are not expressive but performative, then these attributes effectively constitute the identity they are said to express or reveal. The distinction between expression and performativeness is quite crucial, for if gender attributes and acts, the various ways a body shows or produces its cultural signification, are performative, then there is no preexisting identity by which an act or attribute might be measured; there would be no true or false, real or distorted acts of gender, and the postulation of a true gender identity would be revealed as a regulatory fiction. That gender reality is created through sustained social performances means that the very notions of an essential sex, a true or abiding masculinity or femininity, are also constituted as part of the strategy by which the performative aspect of gender is concealed. [. . .]

Gender reality is performative, which means, quite simply, that it is real only to the extent that it is performed.

1988, "Performative Acts and Gender Constitution," 521, 524–28

Simone de Beauvoir (1908–86): French feminist, existentialist philosopher, and novelist. Her best-known non-fiction text is *The Second Sex* (1949, Eng. 1953), which called for an end to the myth of "the eternal feminine." Other works include *The Mandarins* (1954, Eng. 1960) and *Force of Circumstance* (1963, Eng. 1965).

strongly that gender is constructed (**see Acting the part of a woman box**). To perform these "successfully" situates a person securely within a given social world. To refuse to perform one's assigned gender is to rebel against "nature."

As Butler points out, there are "nuanced" and "individual ways" of playing one's gender, but whatever these are, a person performs her or his gender in accordance with already inscribed performatives. Butler very specifically compares gender roles to rehearsed theatrical performances that follow known scripts which survive the particular actors of the moment. In this Butler is applying the "all the world's a stage" metaphor enunciated by Shakespeare and explored in our own time by Erving Goffman and his many followers. Where Butler makes her own contribution is in her application of notions drawn from poststructuralism's theory of performatives. Butler argues that gender as performed in contemporary Western societies enacts a normative heterosexuality that is a major tool for enforcing a patriarchal, phallocentric social order (**see Butler box 2**). Thus, Butler politicizes non-heterosexual (queer, gay, lesbian, drag, etc.) sexuality positioning these in opposition to the hegemonic social order. In other words, to become gay is to enact a radical politics along the lines of "the personal is the political."

This is made strikingly clear in the heated argument over gay marriage. Those enforcing "compulsory heterosexuality" want marriage to be defined as "between a man and a woman." They recognize that any other definition profoundly alters society. Behind the opposition to gay marriage is the belief that marriage is foremost about generating children. Because same gender couples cannot bear each other's children, the compulsory heterosexual crowd brands these couples as "unnatural" and/or "sinful." Never mind that this argument fails when gay couples adopt or, if lesbian, bear children. The circumstances under which children are generated – that is, what constitutes a "family" – is a decisive social question because the family in many cultures is the vehicle for distributing wealth from one generation to

Acting the part of a woman

1860, Anonymous

Some ladies walk so as to turn up their dresses behind, and I have seen a well-dressed woman made to look very awkward by elevating her shoulders slightly and pushing her elbows too far behind her. Some hold their hands up to the waist, and press their arms against themselves as tightly as if they were glued there. Others swing them backward and forward as a businessman walking along the street. Too short steps detract from dignity very much, forming a mincing pace; too long steps are masculine.

1860, *Complete Rules of Etiquette and Usages of Society*, 3–4

2001, Cara Birnbaum in Cosmopolitan

How do you work everything from tone of voice to body language to dazzle anyone instantly – from a hot stud to a cold-as-ice job interviewer? [. . .] It's crucial that your nonverbal cues, including gestures and posture, work overtime to put you in the best possible light. [. . .] To score some guy candy: Subtly tilt your head and pivot your body whenever he does. If he pauses to loosen his tie, stop for a second to moisten your lips. It's all about showing him you're enchanted enough to be tracking his every move. [. . .] Start by adjusting your voice so that it matches his energy level. If his tones are enthusiastic, enthuse back. If he sounds mellow, you should too. It will only take a few minutes for a man to make up his mind that you're just like him. Once you've established that, you can be yourself.

2001, "How to Wow Anyone You Meet," 148–49

Judith Butler

Compulsory heterosexuality

To guarantee the reproduction of a given culture, various requirements, well established in the anthropological literature of kinship, have instated sexual reproduction within the confines of a heterosexually-based system of marriage which requires the reproduction of human beings in certain gendered modes which, in effect, guarantee the eventual reproduction of that kinship system. As Foucault and others have pointed out, the association of a natural sex with a discrete gender and with an ostensibly natural "attraction" to the opposing sex/gender is an unnatural conjunction of cultural constructs in the service of reproductive interests. Feminist cultural anthropology and kinship studies have shown how cultures are governed by conventions that not only regulate and guarantee the production, exchange, and consumption of material goods, but also reproduce the bonds of kinship itself, which require taboos and a punitive regulation of reproduction to effect that end.

[. . .] My point is simply that one way in which this system of compulsory heterosexuality is reproduced and concealed is through the cultivation of bodies into discrete sexes with "natural" appearances and "natural" heterosexual dispositions. [. . .] The contention that sex, gender, and heterosexuality are historical productions which become conjoined and reified as natural over time has received a good deal of critical attention not only from Michel Foucault, but Monique Wittig, gay historians, and various cultural anthropologists and social psychologists in recent years. [. . .]

The transformation of social relations becomes a matter, then, of transforming hegemonic social conditions rather than individual acts that are spawned by these conditions. [. . .] Just as within feminist theory the very category of the personal is expanded to include political structures, so there is a theatrically based and, indeed, less individually oriented view of acts that goes some of the way in defusing the criticism of act theory as "too existentialist."

1988, "Performative Acts and Gender Constitution," 524–25

another. However, increasingly in a globalized world of markets, wealth moves by means other than inheritance. And as the exchange of wealth by means of marriage and childbearing loses its primacy, new kinds of families are imagined and performed. Gay marriage is one of these new kinds of family.

Those advocating gay marriage usually don't cite global markets and inheritance. Generally, they pursue two lines of thought – the "gay gene" and "lifestyle." If there is a gay gene, homosexuality is natural for a certain fraction of any population. If being gay is a lifestyle choice, genetics are irrelevant. Of course, both these arguments can be true – and that is precisely where the social construction of gender comes into play. Some genetically predisposed homosexuals will repress their gayness and live straight lives; and some genetically predisposed heterosexuals will decide to live gay lives. Thus, genetics as such is a red herring. What counts is both how people actually perform their lives and what laws and conventions govern and guide them. To legalize gay marriage – as in Canada, Spain, Holland, and Belgium – is to detach "family" from a narrow definition. Some families will procreate, others not; some will be same sex and others not. As for gender, people of the same sex can be, and often are, of different genders.

What about those who refuse to perform their assigned heterosexual gender roles? It is to be at the least an "oddball," maybe an actor or dancer. Or, if the refusal is more radical, to be "queer," or "butch" or "femme," a "drag queen," bisexual or transsexual – or any other gender possibility that is outside hetero-orthodoxy. Butler and others who adhere to her point of view believe that gender is "real" only insofar and in the specific ways it is performed. She also makes the very important distinction between performing against the dominant code in a theatre and doing so in the street. Much more is permitted onstage than off. Offstage there are no conventions of the theatre to protect a drag queen from ridicule or worse (**see figure 5.7**). Even remaining in the closet, being "quietly gay," as it were, is no protection against attacks ranging from stares and verbal abuse to murder. Unorthodox gender performatives are not merely affronts to patriarchy; they challenge long-standing Western philosophical distinctions between appearance and reality. If one

fig 5.7. A drag queen poses at Wigstock in New York. Photograph by Brad Rickerby. Copyright Reuters.

wears and can to some degree change what one "really is," then what about the existence of a settled identity or an indwelling eternally abiding soul?

Constructions of race

If gender is performed, what about race? Does one "become" black, white, brown, red, or yellow in the same way that one becomes a woman or man? Does skin color, hair, a set of facial or bodily features, or any single attribute, or combination of attributes, indicate that a person belongs to one race or another? Are there any dependable markers of race? Skin color and all other "racial features" are extremely variable across populations. Added to this, cosmetics and cosmetic surgery can effectively modify how one looks. Race is akin to ethnicity, a human cultural feature. As a cultural feature, race matters. But the importance of race as a cultural category cannot be sustained by its often purported basis in "nature." Visible marks of race are unreliable. To take "blacks" and "whites" as an instance, many so-called "whites" have darker skin than many so-called "blacks." Other visible markers such as hair texture, eye and nose shape, and so on are also unreliable – not only in relation to "black" and "white" but also with regard to other groups. Jews have sometimes been designated as a race with specific facial characteristics (big noses, thick lips, dark eyes), sometimes as a religious group with no particular racial markers. But what about under the skin? Biologists and anthropologists agree that race has no basis in genetics or biology (**see Marshall box**).

Because race is a cultural construct, racial identifications change in reaction to culture-specific historical forces. For example, throughout much of US history, people were placed in, and placed themselves in, very definite racial categories. But with the numbers of multiracial and multicultural children growing, and the influx of millions of people from Latin America and Asia, the categories began to collapse. In the 2000 US census, more people than ever before identified themselves as "multicultural" or refused to categorize themselves racially. Even the shift in nomenclature is important. As late as the 1970s words such as "black," "Negro," or "colored" were in general use. But today one speaks mostly of "African-Americans," pointing to culture and geography rather than color. Other groups that formerly were identified by color are also now marked by nationality or ethnicity ("Chinese" or "Japanese," not "yellow;" "Native American," not "red;" "Indian" or "South Asian," not brown). Contrarily, however, the term "people of color" designates everyone who is not "white." Thus, despite moves to downplay visible markers, racial categories defined by how people look remain in wide use. Race may not be real scientifically, but it is strongly operative culturally.

In addition, specific stereotyped looks and behaviors are associated with certain groups. The stereotypes often disparage "the Other" as inferior or, oppositely, too powerful. Sometimes, particularly in relation to Jews, the hated group is felt to be both inferior and too powerful. Frequently, stereotypes jumble race, ethnicity, religion, and nationality. Stereotypes abound, aimed at just about every group, including "red necks," white rural American southerners and "WASPs," white Anglo-Saxon Protestants. Nor is being victimized an inoculation against disparaging others. Targeted groups turn around and target other groups. The whole matter is further complicated when certain stereotypes are embraced by those they are meant to stigmatize, transforming the would-be attack into a positive cultural expression. For example, many African-Americans enjoy the racialized humor

Eliot Marshall

There is no such thing as race

Genetic diversity appears to be a continuum, with no clear breaks delineating racial groups. Last year, the U.S. Office of Management and Budget (OMB) completed a contentious 4-year review of the racial and ethnic categories that will be used to define the U.S. population in federal reports, including the 2000 census. It finally settled on seven groupings: American Indian or Alaska Native; Asian; Black or African American; Native Hawaiian (added after OMB received 7000 postcards from Hawaiians) or Other Pacific Islander; White; Hispanic or Latino; and Not Hispanic or Latino. The categories could have enormous implications – from the distribution of government resources to political districting to demographic research. But as far as geneticists are concerned, they're meaningless.

"Ridiculous" is the word cultural anthropologist John Moore of the University of Florida, Gainesville, uses to describe such racial typing. This view is based on a growing body of data that indicates, as Moore says, that "there aren't any boundaries between races." Geneticist Kenneth Kidd of Yale University says the DNA samples he's examined show that there is "a virtual continuum of genetic variation" around the world. "There's no place where you can draw a line and say there's a major difference on one side of the line from what's on the other side." If one is talking about a distinct, discrete, identifiable population, Kidd adds, "there's no such thing as race in [modern] Homo sapiens." Indeed, the American Anthropological Association urged the government last year to do away with racial categories and, in political matters, let people define their own ethnicity. [. . .]

Anthropologists have long objected to the stereotypes that are used to classify human populations into racial groups. But the most potent challenge to such groupings has come from genetic studies of human origins. The field was "transformed" in the late 1980s, says anthropologist Kenneth Weiss of Pennsylvania State University in University Park, by an analysis of variations in mitochondrial DNA (mtDNA) begun by Rebecca Cann of the University of Hawaii, Manoa, Mark Stoneking of Penn State, and the late Allan Wilson of the University of California, Berkeley. These researchers reported that diversity in mtDNA genes was two to three times greater in Africa than in Europe or the rest of the world. Assuming that the rate of change in mtDNA was fairly constant, they concluded that Africans' mtDNA was older than that of non-Africans, and that modern humans originated from a small population that emerged from Africa and migrated around the globe.

1998, "DNA Studies Challenge the Meaning of Race," 654

of **Eddie Murphy**, buy tickets to Blaxploitation movies, and elevate rapsters into superstars. With regard to rap and hip-hop, there are strong feelings both for and against. For some, hip-hop and rap are explosively robust manifestations of youthful African-American culture. For others, the music is violent, racist, sexist, and gynophobic. This division of opinion is not wholly along racial or gender lines. And if this were not enough of a complication, there's also a lot of crossing over. **Eminem** is visibly white, but his music and presentation of self are black. I will discuss hip-hop more thoroughly in Chapter 8. In fact, "black style" dominates mainstream American pop music and is a strong influence on other areas of American culture. But this does not inhibit African-Americans from adopting elements of "white culture." There is in the USA no dominant racial "way to be" comparable to what Butler terms "compulsory heterosexuality." Instead, there is an enormous amount of cultural-racial mixing.

Eddie Murphy (1961–): American actor and comedian. Films include *48 Hours* (1982), *Beverly Hills Cop* (1984), *Coming to America* (1988), *Shrek* (2001, voice only), *The Haunted Mansion* (2003), and their sequels.

Eminem (1972–): American rap artist, born Marshall Mathers. CDs/DVDs include *Infinite* (1996), *The Real Slim Shady* (2000), *The Slim Shady Show* (2001), *Mosh or Die* (2004), *The Anger Management Tour* (2005), and *Ass Like That* (2005).

Adrian Piper (1948–): conceptual artist and philosopher whose work in numerous media, including live performance, focuses on issues of race, racism, and racial stereotyping. *Adrian Piper: A Retrospective* (1999) is a comprehensive overview of her artworks. Many of Piper's writings are published in the two-volume collection *Out of Order, Out of Sight: Selected Writings in Meta-Art and Art Criticism 1967–1992* (1996). Among Piper's artworks – live performances, videos, and installations – are *Streetworks* (1970), *The Mythic Being* (1975–76), *My Calling Card #1 and #2* (1986–90), *Cornered* (1988), *Self-Portrait 2000* (2001), and *Shiva Dances* (2004),

Immanuel Kant (1724–1804): German philosopher, author of the *Critique of Pure Reason* (1781/87), *Critique of Practical Reason* (1788), and *Critique of Judgment* (1790) as well as numerous other seminal philosophical works.

Adrian Piper theorizes race both in her writings and in performance. Piper, a philosopher specializing in **Immanuel Kant**, is also a conceptual artist whose performance art and installations focus on racism, racial stereotyping, and xenophobia. One of her best-known works is *Cornered* (1988), a video installation that begins with Piper, dressed in dark clothes, a string of pearls around her neck, seated in the corner of a room at a table, hands folded, looking directly at the camera (**see figure 5.8**). The TV set on which Piper's image appears is itself placed in the corner of the gallery with an overturned table in front of it. The set-up suggests both being cornered (that is, trapped) and some kind of violent overturn. After a pause, the light-skinned Piper begins, "I'm black. Now let's deal with this social fact and the fact of my stating it, together." Piper's inaugural challenge is a "speech act," a performative. She goes on, "If I don't tell you who I am, then I have to pass for white. And why should I have to do that? The problem with passing for white is not just that it's based on sick values, which it is. It's also that it creates a degrading situation in which I may have to listen to insulting remarks about blacks made by whites who mistakenly believe there are no blacks present. That's asking a bit much. I'm sure you'll agree." Assuming

fig 5.8. *Cornered*, a video installation, 1988. Copyright Adrian Piper Research Archive 2005. Collection: Museum of Contemporary Art, Chicago.

a white spectator, for the next 14 minutes Piper, earnestly but with cutting irony, dissects the emotional impact, social practices, and legalities of racism in America.

In *Cornered*, Piper never raises her voice. She develops her points with impeccable logic. She does not speak directly of enslavement, lynchings, and segregation or give graphic examples of American racism. Her anger is understated. Presenting herself in a manner that confounds stereotyping, Piper dissects what constitutes racial identity. She asserts that according to commonly accepted beliefs that race is "in the blood," everyone in the USA has between 5 and 20 percent black ancestry. "Most purportedly white Americans are in fact black. [. . .] The chances are really quite good that you are, in fact, black. What are you going to do about it?" Sarcastically, Piper invites the putative white viewer to tell friends and employers that s/he is black. Or, Piper suggests, why not take advantage of "affirmative action" programs designed to assist blacks? Or stay silent or discredit the research or dismiss *Cornered* as just another "art experience." Piper corners the viewer, concluding the 16-minute piece with the challenge, "Now that you have this information about your black ancestry, whatever you do counts as a choice. [. . .] So, what are you going to do?" In *Cornered* and many other of her works, Piper probes the shifting ground that barely supports socially constructed racial categories. Take, for example, the Angry Art "calling card" Piper gives to people who make racist remarks or let them pass unchallenged when made by others (**see figure 5.9**). When someone who "looks" black "acts" white, or vice versa, the person may be accused of "passing" – pretending or performing a self that one has no legitimate claim to given the racist constructions of contemporary Euro-American society (**see Piper box**). But as Piper points out, the very concept of racial classification is an instrument of racism. Race, like gender, is constructed.

Dear Friend,

I am black.

I am sure you did not realize this when you made/laughed at/agreed with that racist remark. In the past, I have attempted to alert white people to my racial identity in advance. Unfortunately, this invariably causes them to react to me as pushy, manipulative, or socially inappropriate. Therefore, my policy is to assume that white people do not make these remarks, even when they believe there are no black people present, and to distribute this card when they do.

I regret any discomfort my presence is causing you, just as I am sure you regret the discomfort your racism is causing me.

fig 5.9. An "Angry Art" card Adrian Piper gives to people who make racist remarks or do not intervene when others do so, 1986. Card courtesy of Adrian Piper.

Adrian Piper

On passing and not passing

It was the New Graduate Student Reception for my class, the first social event of my first semester in the best graduate department in my field in the country. I was full of myself, as we all were, full of pride at having made the final cut [. . .]. I was a bit late, and noticed that many turned to look at – no scrutinize – me as I entered the room. I congratulated myself on having selected for wear my black velvet, bell-bottomed pantsuit (yes, it was that long ago) with the cream silk blouse and crimson vest. [. . .] The most famous and highly respected member of the faculty observed me for a while from a distance and then came forward. Without introduction or preamble, he said to me with a triumphant smirk, "Miss Piper, you're about as black as I am."

One of the benefits of automatic pilot in social situations is that insults take longer to make themselves felt. [. . .] What I felt was numb, and then shocked and terrified, disoriented, as though I'd been awakened from a sweet dream of unconditional support and approval and plunged into a nightmare of jeering contempt. [. . .] Finally, there was the groundless shame of the inadvertent impostor, exposed to public ridicule or accusation. For this kind of shame, you don't actually need to have done anything wrong. All you need to do is care about others' image of you, and fail in your actions to reinforce their positive image of themselves. Their ridicule and accusations then function to both disown and degrade you from their status, to make you as not having done wrong but as being wrong. [. . .]

And I experienced [then, and at other times] that same groundless shame, not only in response to those who accused me of passing for black but also in response to those who accused me of passing for white. This was the shame caused by people who conveyed to me that I was underhanded or manipulative, trying to hide something, pretending to be something I was not, by telling them I was black, like the art critic in the early 1970s who had treated me with the respect she gave emerging white women artists in the early days of second-wave feminism, until my work turned to issues of racial identity; she then called me to verify that I was black, reproached me for not telling her, and finally disappeared from my professional life altogether. [. . .]

But I've learned that there is no "right" way of managing the issue of my racial identity, no way that will not offend or alienate someone, because my designated racial identity itself exposes the very concept of racial classification as the offensive and irrational instrument of racism that it is. We see this in the history of classifying terms variously used to designate those brought as slaves to this country and their offspring: first "blacks," then "darkies," then "Negroes," then "colored people," then "blacks" again, then "Afro-Americans," then "people of color," now "African-Americans." Why is it that we can't seem to get it right, once and for all? The reason, I think, is that it doesn't really matter what term we use to designate those who have inferior and disadvantaged status, because whatever term is used will eventually turn into a term of derision and disparagement in virtue of its reference to those who are derided and disparaged, and so will need to be discarded for an unsullied one.

1992, "Passing for White, Passing for Black," in *Out of Order, Out of Sight*, vol. 1, 275–76, 1996

During, before, and after performance art

Piper's pieces are performance art, a grab-bag category of works that do not fit neatly into theatre, dance, music, or visual art (**see Brentano box**). The practice of performance art and the theories of performativity are closely related. Many performance artists work solo, conflating the artist and the artwork. The solo performance is a "one and only," the artist – sometimes naked literally as well as figuratively – is an "original," both creator and object created (**see Schneider box**). One of the recurring themes/actions in performance art is the construction of identity. The question performance art often asks, sometimes answered, sometimes left hanging, is, "Who is this person doing these actions?" This is very different from the question theatre asks, "Who is this character doing these actions?" Insisting that spectators regard not a character but an actual person (even if the artist embellishes that persona, as Spalding Gray did), actualizes the slogan, "the personal is the political." Or any other equivalency: "the personal is the . . ." The emphasis is on the personal: the artist/ person present performing right in your face.

"Personal is Political" is the title of a short essay written by feminist **Carol Hanisch** in 1969. Hanisch was one of the instigators of the famous 1968 "bra-burning" protest against the Miss America Pageant in Atlantic City (**see Hanisch box**). In her essay and other writings, Hanisch asserted that even the most personal situations, when fully understood and analyzed, show how society is organized in ways that disempower women. She emphasized that "consciousness raising" groups, which some feminists thought were a waste of time, actually not only exposed issues crucial to women's rights but also led to successful strategies to improve the situation. Hanisch's line of reasoning showed that "the personal" opened to many fundamental political questions. Women devised ways to operate politically both within and

Robyn **Brentano**

Performance art

The term "performance art" first appeared around 1970 to describe the ephemeral, time-based, and process-oriented work of conceptual ("body") and feminist artists that was emerging at the time. It was also applied retrospectively to Happenings, Fluxus events, and other intermedia performances from the 1960s. Over the past thirty-five years, many styles and modes of performance have evolved, from private, introspective investigations to ordinary routines of everyday life, cathartic rituals and trials of endurance, site-specific environmental transformations, technically sophisticated multimedia productions, autobiographically-based cabaret-style performance, and large-scale, community-based projects designed to serve as a source of social and political empowerment. [. . .] What has come to be called performance art [. . .] has taken myriad forms, a result of its interdisciplinary nature (drawing from painting, sculpture, dance, theater, music, poetry, cinema, and video) and disparate influences, including [. . .] the Futurists, Dadaists, Constructivists, Surrealists, Abstract Expressionism, performance and art traditions of Native American and non-European cultures, feminism, new communications technologies, and popular forms such as cabaret, the music hall, vaudeville, the circus, athletic events, puppetry, parades, and public spectacles.

1994, *Outside the Frame*, 31–32

Rebecca **Schneider**

The rise of solo performance art

We have become accustomed to posit the rise of (solo) performance art as a direct result of late capitalism and the object's famous loss of aura. When the aura of the discrete art object dissipated under the habits and pressures of indiscriminate reproduction, the aura was displaced onto the artist himself – a figure supposedly not given to duplication – i.e., there was only *one* Jackson Pollock [. . .] Thus, such a theory spins, in reaction to the commodification of art and the loss of the auratic object, emphasis shifted to the (singular) artist making that object. With the object in crisis, artists abandoned the object as site and collected under the awning of performance. Under this awning the site of the work shifted to the space between the object and the maker, the object and the viewer, the object and any given context [. . .]. This space between viewer and viewed was closely aligned with dance and theatre, where any product is more profoundly in the process, in the action, in the exchange, than in any formally discrete object. The Solo Artist *making* art became, then, the auratic object itself. The artist stepped (or danced) into the place of the object and rescued origin, originality, and authenticity in the very unrepeatable and unapproachable nature of his precise and human gesture – his solo act.

2005, "Solo Solo Solo" *After Criticism*, 33.

beyond the domestic sphere. This sphere comprised issues of sexuality, feelings, and control over their own bodies (enforcement of rape laws, abortion rights) as well as more orthodox political questions that had for decades been of importance to women from gaining the vote to equality within the workplace. The phrase "the personal is the political" caught on, becoming a well-known slogan in activist and art circles. Much feminist performance art of the 1960s–1970s was simultaneously personal, political, and sexual (**see Roth box**). In this work, feminists were concerned with many of the same situations that occupied the French postructuralists. I do not know if these feminist artists were aware of the poststructuralists; or if the French theorists knew what was going on in Los Angeles's Womanhouse or even in New York where Adrian Piper, **Martha Wilson**, and others were busy pioneering performance art. Be that as it may, the feminist practice and the poststructuralist theory go well together. Only by recognizing that identity is constructed, not given, contested, not settled, historically and politically evolving, not fixed in "nature," can personal art be regarded as political. Among the many examples of "the personal is the political" art of that period, **Carolee Schneemann**'s 1975 *Interior Scroll* stands out (**see figure 5.10**). Naked, standing legs akimbo, Schneemann reached into her vulva and pulled out a long scroll from which she read the words of a "structuralist filmmaker" who refused even to look at her films:

> [. . .] there are certain films
> we cannot look at
> the personal clutter
> the persistence of feelings
> the hand-touch sensibility
> the diaristic indulgence
> the painterly mess
> the dense gestalt
> the primitive techniques.

Carol Hanisch (1942–): American feminist and civil rights worker. In the 1960s and '70s, Hanisch was a member of New York Radical Women and Gainesville (Florida) Women's Liberation. Some of her early writings can be accessed through the Redstockings Women's Liberation Archives for Action, www.afn.org/~redstock/ and in *Feminist Revolution* (Kathie Sarachild, ed., 1978). Her more recent essays are available in *Frankly Feminist* (1997).

Martha Wilson (1947–): American performance artist and founder of Franklin Furnace, a leading New York performance art venue, from 1976 to 1990. After the Furnace lost its space, Wilson transmuted it into an internet site – www.franklin furnace.org/ – offering live art on the web. Wilson's own works include *Breast Forms Permutated* (1972), *I Make Up the Image of My Perfection/I Make up the Image of My Deformity* (1974), and *Separated at Birth* (2003).

Carol Hanisch

Trashing the instruments of female torture, 1968

On September 7, 1968, the Women's Liberation Movement protested the Miss America Pageant in Atlantic City. It was, for its time, a daring act of defiance against everything that women were supposed to be. [. . .] The Miss America Pageant telling women what to look like, what to wear, how to wear it, how to walk, how to speak, what to say (and what not to say) to be considered attractive. In short: look beautiful (no matter the cost in time and money), smile (no matter what you're feeling), and don't rock the boat. [. . .]

We did some street theater: crowning a live sheep Miss America, chaining ourselves to a large red, white, and blue Miss America dummy to point up how women are enslaved by beauty standards, and throwing what we termed "instruments of female torture" into a Freedom Trash Can. It was the latter that brought about the "bra-burner" moniker. It wasn't that we hadn't intended to burn bras – we had – but along with other "instruments of female torture" including high heels, nylons, garter belts, girdles, hair curlers, false eyelashes, make-up and *Playboy* and *Good Housekeeping* magazines. [. . .]

One of our members worked for a bridal magazine and was able to acquire a block of 16 tickets so we could continue the protest inside Convention Hall. In order not to arouse suspicion, we, too, put on dresses, high heels and make-up. Smuggling in a large banner in an oversized handbag, we took our seats in the balcony very near the stage and discovered that not only did we have an excellent view of the proceedings, but there were several burly policemen in riot gear in the wings, probably a first for the Pageant.

When the outgoing Miss America stepped to the microphone to deliver her farewell speech, it was the signal for the four of us who had volunteered to hang the banner to make our move. [. . .] We quickly dropped the banner – reading "Women's Liberation" – over the railing, tied it as securely as we could, and began shouting, "Women's Liberation," "No More Miss

America," "Freedom for Women." [. . .] The police came bounding up the stairs, took down the banner, and hustled us out of the hall, but they didn't arrest us. We returned to the Boardwalk picket line and triumphantly added our high heels to the Freedom Trash Can. [. . .]

When we read the morning papers, we knew our immediate goal had been accomplished: alongside the headline of a new Miss America being crowned was the news that a women's liberation movement was afoot in the land and that it was going to demand a whole lot more than "equal pay for equal work." We were deluged with letters, more than our small group could possibly answer, many passionately saying "I've been waiting all my life for something like this to come along." Taking the Women's Liberation Movement into the public consciousness gave some women the nudge they needed to form their own groups. They no longer felt so alone and isolated. [. . .]

Looking back, I don't believe we totally understood the depth of the Miss America Protest or what we called "the appearance issue." We had talked about it in terms of comfort, fashion dictates and how beauty competition divides women. But more importantly, we were targeting and challenging, however consciously or unconsciously, the *uniform* of women's inferior class status. After all, what really lies beneath this "appearance thing" is male prerogative and control. It's not only about sexual attractiveness vs. comfort; it's about power. [. . .]

As I write this in 1996, much of what we began to fight for nearly 30 years ago seems far out of reach. Today the Women's Liberation Movement – and the world-changing hope, truth and energy it aroused and led – has been largely replaced by wheel-spinning individual forms of struggle which can bring only token success to a few women, if that. It is crucial that women know and acknowledge that it was the power of women organized and working in groups in the Women's Liberation Movement that made our lives change for the better.

1998, "Two Letters from the Women's Liberation Movement," 197–201

Moira Roth

Women's performance art

Performance art began in the late 1960s at the same time as the women's movement. In the general context of a highly charged and theatrical decade, radical feminists employed theatre in such events as the 1968 disruption of the Miss America Pageant in Atlantic City and the nationwide WITCH (Women's International Terrorist Conspiracy from Hell) demonstrations at the same time. In feminist art circles, theatrical means – raw eggs and sanitary napkins littering pristine museum spaces – were used to protest the low percentage of women in the 1970 Whitney Museum's Biennial in New York. [. . .]

At the same time as women plunged into public battles, they also took on, within themselves, private ones. Through consciousness-raising groups, harsh feminist manifestos, poetic evocations in literature and scholarly studies, women – including many early performers – individually explored and collectively validated the substance of their lives. They re-examined and redefined the models on which they had based their self-images. As early feminists recognized that what had previously been designated (and, accordingly, often dismissed) as merely individual experience was, in actuality, an experience shared by many others, they developed the concept that "the personal is the political." It was this fresh and passionate investigation of self and of identification with other women that created the fervent supportive alliance between the first women performers and their audiences. And it was this bonding with the often all-women audiences, as much as the new personal content in the art, that accounted for the power of the early work.

1983, *The Amazing Decade*, 16–17

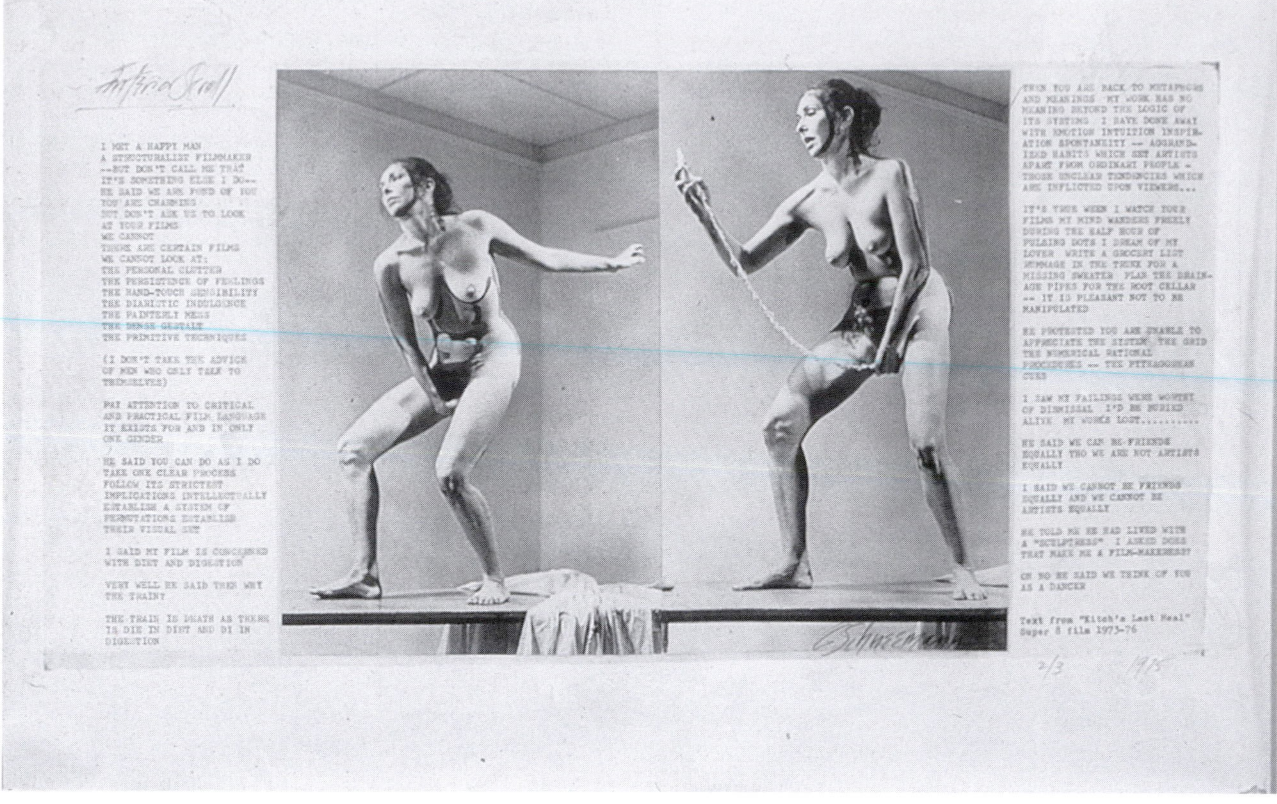

fig 5.10. Carolee Schneemann performing *Interior Scroll*, 1975.Photos of performance and scroll text (48 inches height and 72 inches width). Photograph Anthony McCall, courtesy of Carolee Schneemann.

Carolee Schneemann (1939–): American visual and performance artist. Works include *Meat Joy* (1964), *Interior Scroll* (1975), *Vulva's Morphia* (1995). She is the author of *More Than Meat Joy: Performance Works and Selected Writings* (1997).

Ironic, angry, and – given the taboos of that time – shocking, *Interior Scroll* was simultaneously personal, political, and avant-garde. Schneemann did not reject the filmmaker's estimation that her work was personal, full of touch, indulgent, messy, and "primitive." Through the gestus of her performance, Schneemann vehemently rejected his rejection, arguing on the contrary that the very qualities the male filmmaker cited in disqualifying her work from even being looked at were exactly what made her work important and new. History proved Schneemann right.

In the early days of performance art, much of the audience consisted of fellow artists who freely borrowed from each other. What took place was an extremely fertile convergence of ideas, techniques, and audiences. Some artists sought out specific audiences of women or gays or political activists of a given kind. No longer was art seen as converging on the grand places and occasions of official culture, Lincoln Center or Broadway. Performance art took place in venues not previously used for performance – roofs, beaches, swimming pools, galleries, street corners, storefronts (and many more). Performance art evolved to some degree from painting (**see Kaprow box 1**). Therefore, unlike theatre, dance, and music, much performance art was and is the work of individual artists using their own selves – bodies, psyches, notebooks, experiences – as material. The work was not shaped for large general audiences, but kept its particularity and edge. It was a fine equivalent to the quirky, difficult, and stimulating thought of people like Derrida. Over time, as so often happens with the avant-garde, much performance art went mainstream – as standup comedy, on cable TV and music videos, in the well-attended concerts of **Laurie Anderson** and the monologues of Spalding Gray to name just a few from a long list. But some performance art remains risky, political and personal. In the 1990s, the "**NEA Four**"

Allan Kaprow

Happenings

With the breakdown of the classical harmonies following the introduction of "irrational" or nonharmonic juxtapositions, the Cubists tacitly opened up a path to infinity. Once foreign matter was introduced into the picture in the form of paper [collage], it was only a matter of time before everything else foreign to paint and canvas would be allowed to get into the creative act, including real space. Simplifying the history of the ensuing evolution into a flashback, this is what happened: the pieces of paper curled up off the canvas, were removed from the surface to exist on their own, became more solid as they grew into other materials and, reaching out further into the room, finally filled it entirely. [. . .] Inasmuch as people visiting such Environments are moving, colored shapes too, and were counted "in," mechanically moving parts could be added, and parts of the created surroundings could then be rearranged like furniture at the artist's and visitors' discretion. And, logically since the visitor could and did speak, sound and speech, mechanical and recorded, were also soon to be in order. Odors followed.

1966, *Assemblage, Environments, and Happenings*, 165–66

lost US Government support because their art was deemed dangerous and decadent. Ever since, the National Endowment for the Arts has been timid in who/what it funds. This did not stop **Annie Sprinkle**, never an NEA recipient, who proclaims on her website that she is a "porn star and prostitute turned sex guru and performance artist" (www.anniesprinkle.org). Not so lucky are members of the **Critical Art Ensemble** whose *Free Range Grain* (2004), one of CAE's series on cloning, genetically altered crops, and other aspects of the bio-tech industry so outraged and frightened the authorities that CAE member Steven J. Kurtz was charged with "bioterrorism" under the Patriot Act (legislation passed in the USA in the aftermath of 9/11) (**see Schneider and McKenzie box**). When it became clear that Kurtz was not a terrorist, he was charged with mail and wire fraud in regard to how CAE obtains the biological samples it uses in its performances. As of July 2005, that felony charge remains in force.

Laurie Anderson (1947–): American performance artist, composer, and filmmaker whose pieces are ironic, political, and hi-tech. Her 1981 single, *O Superman*, reached second place on British pop charts. In 2003–04, Anderson was named NASA's "artist in residence" – to date, the one and only. Among her many performances, CDs, and publications: *United States* (1984), *Strange Angels* (1989), *Moby Dick* (1999), *Life on a String* (2001), and *Live in New York* (2002).

NEA Four: in 1990, overruling the unanimous recommendation of its own peer panel of experts, the US National Endowment for the Arts denied funding to performance artists Karen Finley, Tim Miller, Holly Hughes, and John Fleck. Caving in to the censoring and homophobic Right, the NEA declared it would not support "obscenity" and "homoerotic art" – asserting that the two were identical. This more than chilled the art world, it led to a fundamental change in US government funding for the arts. Henceforth, no grants were made to individual artists, but only to presenting institutions and not-for-profit corporations. Artists receiving government money through these channels had to sign a pledge promising not to use the money to "promote, disseminate or produce materials which in the judgment of the NEA [. . .] may be considered obscene, including, but not limited to depictions of sadomasochism, homoeroticism, the sexual exploitation of children, or individuals engaged in sex acts which, when taken as a whole, do not have serious literary, artistic, political or scientific value." Representative works of Miller, Fleck, and Hughes – as well as Peggy Phelan's analysis of the struggle over the NEA – may be read in *Offensive Plays*, a special supplement of *TDR: The Drama Review* (1991). Finley's work is collected in *A Different Kind of Intimacy* (2000). See also Holly Hughes and David Roman, eds., *O Solo Homo: The New Queer Performance* (1998) and Tim Miller, *Body Blows: Six Performances* (2002).

Annie Sprinkle (1954–): born Ellen Steinberg, Sprinkle in her own words is a "prostitute/porn star turned performance artist/sexologist [. . . who] has passionately researched and explored sexuality [. . .] in her own unique brand of sex films, photographic work, teaching workshops, and college lectures" (www.anniesprinkle.org/html/about/short_bio.html). Her books are *Post-Porn Modernist* (1998), *Hardcore from the Heart* (2001), and *Spectacular Sex* (2005).

Critical Art Ensemble: according to its website, the CAE is "a collective of five artists [. . .] dedicated to exploring the intersections between art, technology, radical politics, and critical theory" (www.critical-art.net).

Rebecca Schneider and Jon McKenzie

Performance artist, you are under arrest!

These are times marked and marred by Homeland Security measures, terrorist attacks, preemptive "just" wars, and non-denial denials regarding the legality of torture and unrecorded detentions. [. . .] To get our own bearings on the situation, we visited Mass MOCA (Massachusetts Museum of Contemporary Art) to view *Free Range Grain*, an aborted exhibition by the CAE [Critical Art Ensemble] and Beatriz da Costa. The performative exhibit was to have been part of Mass MOCA's show, *The Interventionists: Art in the Social Sphere* [. . .]. The show asked, in part: "How can artists and the public become engaged in complex sciences like biotechnology, sociology, and anthropology. Why would they want to? We think of science as a world unto itself, the realm of super-specialists, but is it a public sphere, too?" Mass MOCA's questions seemed entirely appropriate, and yet . . . one of the exhibitions was aborted. Why? The reason appears to have everything to do with policing the boundaries of the public sphere. [. . .]

On the morning of 11 May [2004], two weeks before the opening of *The Interventionist Show*, [CAE member] Steve Kurtz awoke to find that his wife had passed away in the night. If the death of a loved one was not tragic enough, Kurtz's 911 call to EMS [Emergency Medical Service] set off a long and troubling set of events. Soon Kurtz found himself surrounded by regional terrorism investigators, FBI agents, and the federal Joint Terrorism Task Force. Their suspicion: possession of illegal biological agents. [. . .] The Kurtz residence in Buffalo, New York, doubles as a studio for Critical Art Ensemble. As CAE's recent work has focused on the biotech industries, the main floor of his house contained laboratory equipment, petri dishes, and biological samples. Reportedly, it was these scientific art materials that led authorities to contact federal officials, who detained Kurtz and later arraigned him before a federal grand jury, even though state investigators declared his house safe and the suspected organisms harmless. [. . .]

What sort of work has CAE been producing that would provoke a federal case against Kurtz? [. . .] Since the early 1990s, CAE has challenged artists and activists to extend the performative matrix blown open in the 1960s by The Living Theatre, whom CAE credits with helping to break down the art/life divide. However, with the rise of virtual nomadic power, CAE argues that this matrix must be further expanded to include electronic networks [. . .]. Most recently, CAE has opened yet another critical dimension of the performative matrix, that of molecular genetics. [. . .] Arguing that the biotech industry is largely immune to both traditional and electronic forms of civil disobedience, CAE outlines an alternative form of resistance, which they call "contestational biology." [. . .] Most forms of contestational biology discussed by CAE involve participatory, pedagogical performances designed to combine everyday life experience and informed, critical reflection on the social, economic, and political dimensions of biotechnology. [. . .] *Free Range Grain* [. . .] was to have included a genetic testing laboratory in which CAE would test "organic" foods brought to the exhibit by Mass MOCA patrons, for genetically modified organisms. [. . .] What exactly is the act of terror under investigation? What else is at stake?

It's not hard to guess. Perhaps one of the reasons CAE is so dangerous in the eyes of those invested in the Patriot Act is precisely the inherent subterfuge of theatre combined with the terror of pedagogy (you know, cloaks and daggers). From its early roots in ACTUP in Florida, members of CAE have worked (1) *as a collective* [. . .]; (2) *intermedially* (no art piece is discreet – there's the performance, the book, the website, the commodity, the faux corporation); and (3) *with express political aim to expand access to "specialist" fields by tactical demystification.*

2004, "Keep Your EYES on the FRONT and WATCH YOUR BACK," 5–8.

Performance art is part of a line of the avant-garde reaching back to the turn of the twentieth century – symbolism, futurism, Dada, surrealism, and so on. The immediate source of performance art was a convergence of Happenings, postmodern dance, and pop art (**see figures 5.11 and 12**). Allan Kaprow coined the word "Happenings" to describe art events that simply happened without picture frames, plots, or any marks of orthodox visual arts, theatre, dance, or music. In 1966, Kaprow outlined the seven qualities of Happenings (**see Kaprow box 2**). In his own way, he was

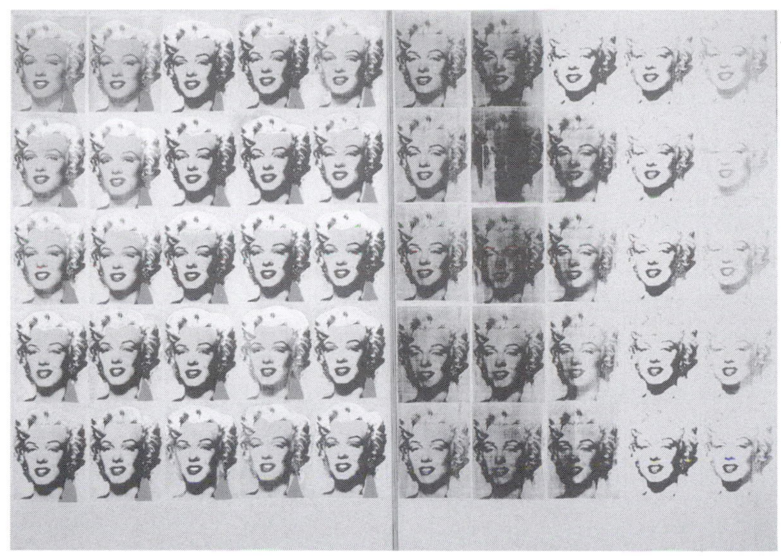

fig 5.11. *Marilyn Monroe Diptych* by Andy Warhol, 1962. Copyright © The Andy Warhol Foundation for the Visual Arts, Inc./ARS, NY and DACS London, 2005. Photography copyright Tate, London 2005.

fig 5.12. The dance collective Grand Union in performance at Judson Church, 1960s. Photograph by Michael Kirby. Photograph courtesy of Richard Schechner.

Allan Kaprow

The seven qualities of happenings

1. The line between art and life is fluid, even indistinct.
2. The themes, materials, and actions of happenings are taken from anywhere but the arts.
3. Happenings should be performed in several widely spaced locales.
4. Time, which follows closely on spatial considerations should be variable and discontinuous.
5. Happenings should be performed only once.
6. Audiences should be eliminated entirely – everyone at a Happening participates in it.
7. The composition/sequence of events is not rational or narrational, but based on associations among various parts; or by chance.

1966, *Assemblage, Environments, and Happenings*, 88–98

laying the basis for "the personal is the political." Kaprow, like **Marcel Duchamp** and Andy Warhol, wanted to demystify art, debunk the establishment that controlled museums, and make arts that could be performed by anyone. Kaprow proclaimed what he called "lifelike art" – not naturalism or any other kind of **mimesis**, but art that conformed to the processes of ordinary life. During the same period, many postmodern dancers rejected the strict codifications of both ballet and modern dance. They favored "pedestrian," or everyday, movement, let dancers speak about their own lives as they danced, and got involved in political actions (**see Banes box**).

Marcel Duchamp (1887–1968): seminal French Dada artist. Among his many works are the painting *Nude Descending a Staircase* (1912), the construction *The Bride Stripped Bare by her Bachelors, Even* (also known as the *Large Glass*) (1915–23), and his "readymades" – ordinary objects displayed as art. Duchamp's most notorious readymade is *Fountain* (1917), a urinal. Duchamp lived for many years in New York, becoming an American citizen in 1955.

mimesis: Greek word meaning "imitation." In the *Poetics* Aristotle argues that a tragedy is a "mimesis of a praxis" (an action) of great enough magnitude to have a beginning, a middle, and an end. Exactly what Aristotle meant by mimesis has been the subject of much debate over the centuries. Currently, most commentators agree that Aristotle did not mean mimesis literally but as a specific artistic process of representation.

Sally Banes

Postmodern dance

Originally reacting against the expressionism of modern dance, which anchored movement to a literary idea or musical form, the post-modernists propose [. . .] that the formal qualities of dance might be reason enough for choreography, and that the purpose of making dances might be simply to make a framework within which we look at movement for its own sake. But there are other purposes post-modernism claims for dance. One is that a dance can formulate or illustrate a theory of dance [. . .]. Another purpose, partly inspired by phenomenological philosophers and writers, is to embody different perspectives on space, time, or orientation to gravity [. . .]. The breakdown of the distinction between art and life [. . .], the clarification of individual, discrete movements, the isolation of the essential characteristics of dance, have all become valid purposes for making a dance. So has the option of making a dance for the pleasure of the dancer, whether or not the spectator finds it pleasing, or even accessible. The very question of what it means to create a dance can generate choreography: is writing a score [. . .] an act of choreography? Is dance-making an act of construction and craft or a process of decision-making? In post-modern dance, the choreographer becomes a critic, educating spectators in ways to look at dance, challenging the expectations the audience brings to the performance, framing parts of the dance for closer inspection, commenting on the dance as it progresses.

1980, *Terpsichore in Sneakers*, 15–16

What the Gravedigger knew about the performative

Discussing whether or not Ophelia's suicide bars her from heaven, the more theoretical of two Gravediggers asserts, "An act hath three branches – it is to do, to act, to perform" (*Hamlet*, 5, 1: 11). The Gravedigger divides an action into its physical attributes ("do"), its social aspects ("act"), and its theatrical qualities ("perform"). But why does he use the word "act" twice – first as an overall category and then as a subset of itself?

Any action consciously performed refers to itself, is part of itself. Its "origin" is its repetition. Every consciously performed action is an instance of restored behavior. Restored behavior enacted not on a stage but in "real life" is what poststructuralists call a "performative." It is their contention that all social identities, gender, for example, are performatives. The Gravedigger is not so much repeating himself as he is proposing a situation where the smaller ("to act") contains the larger ("an act"). He is also connecting "an act" as something accomplished in everyday life with "to act," something played on the stage. The ultimate example of "to act" is "to perform" – to be reflexive about one's acting. Shakespeare did not have Austin, Derrida, or Butler in mind when he wrote *Hamlet*. But the Gravedigger's brief disquisition shows that the notion of performativity has been around a long time.

Conclusion

Most theorists of performativity argue that all social realities are constructed. The construction of gender, race, and identity are three key examples. Social life as behaved is performed in the sense that I outlined in Chapter 2: every social activity can be understood as a showing of a doing. I write "as behaved" to underline the "liveness" of certain aspects of social life – and to circumscribe the particular region that is most important to performance studies. This broad definition of liveness includes film, television, recorded musics, telephony, and the internet. In fact as well as in theory, the live and the mediated have collapsed into each other (**see Auslander box**). These cannot be regarded as mere reproductions; because of how they are produced and received they participate in "liveness." Other parts of social life are not behaved, or at least not obviously so, such as laws, architecture, written literature, and the like. However, poststructuralist theories of performativity indicate that even these aspects of social life can be best understood "as performance." Austin's performative concerned utterances only. But those who built on Austin's ideas were soon discovering a wide range of "speech acts" and applying the theory of performativity to all areas of social life. Derrida's insistence that all human codes and cultural expressions are "writing" is a powerful example of this kind of thinking.

These theories of the performative inhabit performance art, especially works dealing with gender, race, and the assertion that the personal is the political. And just as theorists found the performative in all areas of personal and social life, so performance artists broke free from orthodox venues and styles of performance. Some performance art may take only a few seconds, while other events can take a year or more to complete. Some works occur on street corners or in storefront windows; others are dispersed to locations all around the world. In other words, just as there are no theoretical limits to performativity, so there are no practical limits to performance art.

What are the relationships between performativity, the performative, and performance proper – between what goes on at the Metropolitan Opera and what the poststructuralists posit? By far, performativity is the larger category. Many performances are clearly marked and delimited, such as formal presentations in theatres or episodes of public ceremony. Other performances are less clearly marked. Even non-performance – sitting in a chair, crossing the street, sleeping – can be made into a performance by framing these ordinary actions "as performance." If I look at what happens on the street, or at the rolling ocean, and see these "as performance," then in that circumstance they are such. This is what John Cage meant when he answered my question, "What is theatre?" with, "Just look and listen." Indeed, performances belong mostly to the eye and ear. Performatives also come in two types – the clearly marked and the more diffuse. A performative may be a specific speech act such as a promise, bet, or contract. Or it may be something difficult to

Philip **Auslander**

Mediatized and live: An impossible oscillation

Live performance has become the means by which mediatized representations are naturalized, according to the simple logic that appeals to our nostalgia for what we assumed was the im-mediate: if the mediatized image can be recreated in a live setting, it must have been "real" to begin with. This schema resolves (or rather, fails to resolve) into an impossible oscillation between the two poles of what once seemed a clear opposition: whereas mediatized performance derives its authority from its reference to the live or the real, the live now derives its authority from its reference to the mediatized, which derives its authority from its reference to the live, etc. The paradigm that best describes the current relationship between the live and the mediatized is the Baudriallardian paradigm of *simulation*: "nothing separates one pole from the other, the initial from the terminal: there is jut a sort of contraction into each other, a fantastic telescoping, a collapsing of the two traditional poles into one another: an IMPLOSION [. . .]: *this is where simulation begins.*" (1983:57). [. . .] As the mediatized replaces the live within cultural economy, the live itself incorporates the mediatized both technologically and epistemologically. The result of this implosion is that a seemingly secure opposition is now a site of anxiety, the anxiety that underlies many performance theorists' desire to reassert the integrity of the live and the corrupt, co-opted nature of the mediatized.

1999, *Liveness*, 38–39

pin down – a "concept" (as in conceptual art), the "idea of" performance suffusing an act or activity. In this sense, there is an "as if" of performativity analogous to the "as if" of theatre. In theatre, the "as if" consists of characters, places, actions, and narratives – all of which exist only as they are performed. In performativity, the "as if" consists of constructed social realities – gender, race, what-have-you – all of which are provisional, are "made up." At another level, performativity is a pervasive mood or feeling – belonging not so much to the visual–aural realm (as performances do) but to the senses of smell, taste, and touch. "I smell something funny going on," or "that's to my taste," or "I was touched by what happened" are ways of apprehending the performative.

TALK ABOUT

1. The "performative" began as a theory about utterances. It has developed into something much broader than that. Do you think that this expansion of the term makes it "unusable" or "useless"? Or do you feel that indeed much of postmodern life is lived "performatively"?
2. What are some of the political and social implications of conceiving race, gender, and other identity formations as "performatives"?

PERFORM

1. Cross-dress and go out for a "night on the town." Note how people react to you, how you feel about yourself. Come home and write a brief essay on the subject "Gender is a Social Construction: True or False?"
2. Compose a piece of "performative writing" describing a personal experience. Randomly exchange these and then act them out. Were you imitating or simulating? What is the difference?

READ

Austin, J. L. "*How to Do Things with Words*: Lecture II." *The Performance Studies Reader*, Henry Bial, ed.: 147–53. London and New York: Routledge, 2004.

Butler, Judith. "Performative Acts and Gender Constitution: An Essay in Phenomenology and Feminist Theory." *The Performance Studies Reader*, Henry Bial, ed.: 154–66. London and New York: Routledge, 2004.

Derrida, Jacques. "The Theatre of Cruelty and the Closure of Representation." *Writing and Difference*: 232–50. Chicago, Ill.: University of Chicago Press, 1978.

———. "Signature, Event, Context" (excerpt). *Margins of Philosophy*, Alan Bass, tr.: 325–27. Chicago, Ill.: University of Chicago Press, 1982.

Fabian, Johannes. "Theatre and Anthropology, Theatricality and Culture." *The Performance Studies Reader*, Henry Bial, ed.: 175–82. London and New York: Routledge, 2004.

Hanisch, Carol. "The Personal Is Political." *Feminist Revolution*, Kathie Sarachild, ed.: 204–05. New York: Random House, 1978.

Parker, Andrew, and Eve Kosofsky Sedgwick. "Introduction to *Performativity and Performance*." *The Performance Studies Reader*, Henry Bial, ed.: 167–74. London and New York: Routledge, 2004.

Searle, John. "Why Study Speech Acts?" *Speech Acts: An Essay in the Philosophy of Language*: 16–19. Cambridge: Cambridge University Press, 1969.

6 PERFORMING

The broad spectrum of performing

Performing onstage, performing in special social situations (public ceremonies, for example), and performing in everyday life are a continuum. These various kinds of performing occur in widely divergent circumstances, from solo shows before the mirror to large-scale public events and rituals, from shaman healing rituals to identity-changing trances, from theatre and dance to the great and small roles of everyday life (**see figure 6.1**). This broad spectrum of performing

fig 6.1. An array of the many different kinds of performing.

Mrs. Agnes Smith, a forewoman at an English shipbuilding yard and a mother of ten, during World War II, 1941. Copyright Imperial War Museum, London.

Lord Justice Tucker. Photograph Bassano, Camera Press, London.

A splendidly garbed Havana dancer at a party. Courtesy of Moira Taylor.

A tourist performance by Maasai warriors in Kenya. Photograph Bertrand Arthus. Copyright Ardea London Ltd.

Older persons gather in a Polish village to exchange stories, songs, and other "cultural material" as part of the work of the Gardzienice Theatre Association, 1980s. Photograph courtesy of Wlodzimierz Staniewski.

can be depicted as a continuum with each category leading to, and blending into, the next (**see figure 6.2**). There are no clear boundaries separating everyday life from family and social roles or social roles from job roles, church ritual from trance, acting onstage from acting offstage, and so on. I separate them for teaching purposes. Furthermore, a person can "jump" from one category to another – from daily life to trance, from ritual to entertainment, from one everyday life role to another. Sudden changes are common. Usually, a person knows when she is playing a role and when she is "being herself." To "be myself" is to behave in a relaxed and unguarded manner – but to another, even this kind of easy demeanor may come across as a performance. To "perform myself" means to take on the appearance (clothes, demeanor, etc.), voice, and actions of Mother or Friend, Plumber or Doctor, and so on. Some people work very hard to enact one of society's "great roles" such as Judge, Senator, or Movie Star. Others have a great role thrust on them, such as Survivor of Catastrophe, Grieving Parent, Lottery Winner, or even King. And some people work hard at being "just me," that is, at performing oneself. Most people, most of the time, know the difference between enacting a social role and playing a role onstage – wearing the clothes, making the gestures, uttering the words, and maybe even feeling the emotions of characters in a drama.

All of this is complicated both by the media and by panoptic surveillance systems. Network, cable, and satellite television are joined by the internet and thousands of surveillance cameras whose eyes are ever open, gazing down on people in stores, streets, elevators, and who knows where else. Some cameras bring us the news of the day as it happens wherever it is happening. Other cameras are deployed supposedly for our "safety," both to protect us and, failing that, to "catch criminals in the act." Some eyes in the sky spy on military deployments and industrial outputs. Other satellites are able to pinpoint the location of any given individual anyplace on the planet – if that person (or car, boat, or plane) is so equipped. The always-open lens adds a disturbing sense not only of being watched but of requiring us to be always "on," to play for the cameras knowing that our performances are being studied by people we do not know and whom we have not given permission to look. The Surveillance Camera Players of New York perform especially for spy cameras (**see Surveillance Camera Players box**). Then there are actors, athletes, politicians, and more than a few clerics – paid performers all seeking attention, adulation, re-election, and money. These types play not only for local audiences in arenas, stadiums, churches, and public halls but for the many millions tuned in around the globe. Across this very wide spectrum of performing are varying degrees of self-consciousness and consciousness of the others with whom and for whom people play. The more self-conscious a person is, the more one constructs behavior for those watching and/or listening, the more such behavior is "performing." There are exceptions. In trance performing, the possessed are sometimes unaware of their own performances.

Surveillance Camera Players

Protesting the panopticon

We're the Surveillance Camera Players, a group formed in New York City in November, 1996. We protest against the use of surveillance cameras in public places because the cameras violate our constitutionally protected right to privacy. We manifest our right by performing specially adapted plays directly in front of these cameras. We use our visibility – our public appearances, our interviews with the media, and our website – to explode the cynical myth that only those who are "guilty of something" are opposed to being surveilled by unknown eyes. We have come here today because this area is filled with unmarked surveillance cameras. If you, too, are worried about the destruction of your constitutional rights in the name of "fighting crime," we encourage you to form your own surveillance camera group. You can even use the name "Surveillance Camera Players"! Just let the message go out, Down with Big brother!

Even as we speak, the Surveillance Camera Players are out there somewhere, in the subway system beneath Times Square, performing snippets of George Orwell's *1984*, Samuel Beckett's *Waiting for Godot*, or Edgar Allan Poe's *The Raven*. This troupe of puckish performers strikes with guerrilla theatre wherever cameras lurk, using sandwich boards for subtitles, because the players play to an audience that can't hear anything – security guards who would otherwise be nodding off at their video screens, stupefied by the monotonous behavior of ordinary citizens.

2005, www.notbored.org/the-scp.html

Sacred ritual: A Korean shaman performing a ritual to bring peace for persons who drowned in a boat accident, 1981. Photograph by Du-Hyun Lee. Photograph courtesy of Richard Schechner.

Secular ritual: Members of the judiciary in England process in 1986 with a copy of Magna Carta to celebrate its signing in June 1215. It is the most important document of British constitutional history. Photograph courtesy of Moira Taylor.

Performing arts: A realistic European drama on a conventional proscenium stage, late nineteenth or early twentieth century. Photograph courtesy of Richard Schechner.

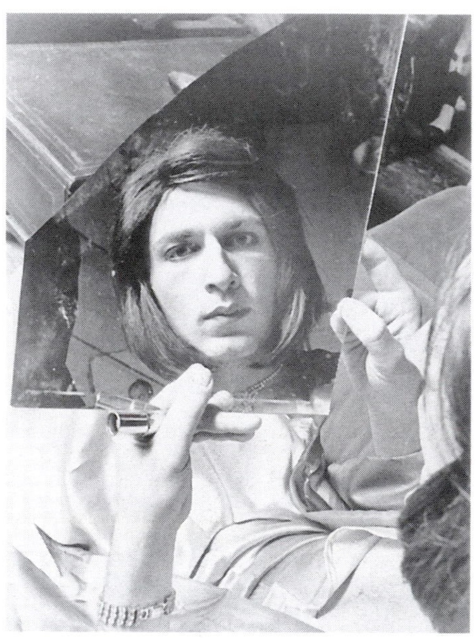

Performing arts: Ron Vawter as Irma in Jean Genet's *The Balcony* gazes in the mirror at himself as a woman. The Performance Group, 1979, production directed by Richard Schechner. Photograph by David Behl. Photograph courtesy of Richard Schechner.

PERFORMING IN EVERDAY LIFE—FAMILY AND SOCIAL ROLES—JOB ROLES—SPECTATOR SPORTS AND OT

fig 6.2. The broad spectrum of performing. Although the chart shows distinct categories, several of these categories blend into one or more of the others. There are no fixed boundaries separating, for example, "family and social roles" from "job roles" or "secular and sacred rituals" from "shamanism" or "trance."

Family role: A mother playing with her children. Copyright John Birdsall Photography, www.JohnBirdsall.co.uk. Reproduced with permission.

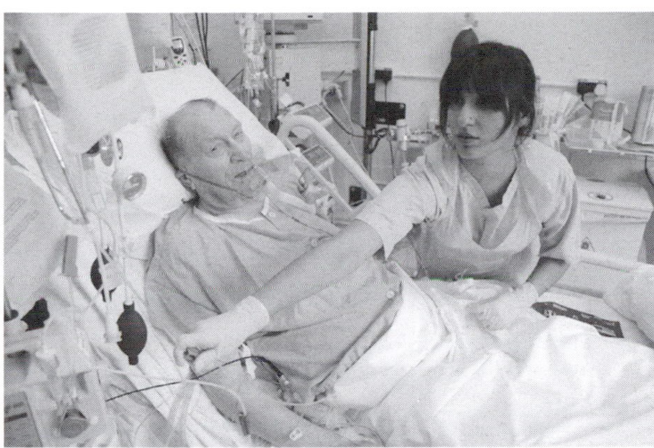

Job role: Staff nurse attending her patient in an adult intensive care unit. Copyright John Birdsall Photography, www.JohnBirdsall.co.uk. Reproduced with permission.

Popular entertainment: The British rock band Iron Maiden in concert. Some 4,700 in the audience screamed "Maiden, maiden" for two hours. POLPHOTO/EMPICS. Copyright EMPICS. Reproduced with permission.

Political/social ritual: The Japanese Prime Minister Junichiro Koizumi walks back from a meeting with children in the Delhi Public School, New Delhi, India, April 2005. AP/Photo Saurabh Das. Copyright EMPICS. Reproduced with permission.

Performing ritual: Ram Chakyar as the demoness Surpanikha in Kutiyattam, the Sanskrit theatre of Kerala, India, 1976. Photograph by Richard Schechner.

From total acting to not acting

Acting is a sub-category of performing. At one extreme is the minimal acting or even not acting of some performance art (**see figure 6.3**). At the other extreme is the total acting of shamans and the trance-possessed (**see figure 6.4**). Acting consists of focused, clearly marked and framed behaviors specifically designed for showing. At the not-acting end of the spectrum, there is no portrayal of another or of a character. The minimalist actor simply performs certain actions that are received as acting by spectators because of context. By contrast, in total acting, the "other" is so powerful that it takes over or possesses the performer.

fig 6.4. A Balinese *sanghyang dedari* performer in trance. Photograph courtesy of Richard Schechner.

fig 6.3. Performance artist Spalding Gray delivering one of his monologues. Gray appeared to be not acting. His whole presentation was studied and stable from one monologue to the next: a plaid or box-pattern shirt, simple wood table, water glass, and microphone. Photograph by Donna An McAdams. Photograph courtesy of Spalding Gray.

Performance theorist **Michael Kirby** proposed a continuum of acting passing through five nodal points (**see Michael Kirby box; see figure 6.5**):

1 nonmatrixed performing
2 symbolized matrix
3 received acting
4 simple acting
5 complex acting

Michael Kirby (1931–97): American performance historian and theorist, director, and actor. Editor of *TDR: The Drama Review* (1971–85). Author of *Happenings* (1965) and *A Formalist Theatre* (1987).

Nonmatrixed performance is doing something onstage other than playing a character – such as the work of the *koken* (stagehands) of Japanese kabuki theatre who, while the performance continues and in full view of the audience, move props and assist in onstage costume changes. Symbolized matrix performing is someone performing actions that can be understood by spectators as "belonging to" a character even though the performer always behaves "as herself." Received acting is what "extras" do – they are in costume, they may speak fragments of lines, and the audience reads them as part of the situation of a scene. But extras do very little "character acting." Simple acting involves simulation and impersonation. The performer generates a character with feelings. Some emotional work is required. In complex acting, the whole being of the performer – physical, mental, emotional – is called on at a high level of commitment. Acting becomes increasingly complex the more elements are used in con-

Michael Kirby

Not acting and acting

To act means to feign, to simulate, to represent, to impersonate. As Happenings demonstrated, not all performing is acting. [. . .] The performers in Happenings generally tended to "be" nobody or nothing other than themselves. [. . .]

There are numerous performances that do not use acting. Many, but by no means all, dance pieces would fall into this category. Several Far Eastern theatres make use of stage attendants such as the Kurombo and Koken of Kabuki. These attendants move props into position and remove them, help with on-stage costume changes, and even serve tea to the actors. Their dress distinguishes them from the actors, and they are not included in the informational structure of the narrative. [. . .]

Extras, who do nothing but walk and stand in costume, are seen as "actors." Anyone merely walking across a stage containing a realistic setting might come to represent a person in that place – and, perhaps, time – without doing anything we could distinguish as acting. [. . .] "Received actor" is only an honorary title.

If the performer does something to simulate, represent, impersonate, and so forth, he or she is acting. [. . .] Acting may be said to exist in the smallest and simplest action that involves pretense. [. . .]

Acting becomes more complex as more and more elements [including the emotions] are incorporated into the pretense.

It must be emphasized that the acting/not-acting scale is not intended to establish or suggest values. Objectively, all points on the scale are equally "good." It is only personal taste that prefers complex acting to simple acting or nonmatrixed performing to acting. The various degrees of representation and personification are "colors," so to speak, in the spectrum of human performance; artists may use whichever colors they prefer.

1987, *A Formalist Theatre*, 3, 6–7, 10, 20

NOT-ACTING **ACTING**
Nonmatrixed performing ↔ Symbolized matrix ↔ Received acting ↔ Simple acting ↔ Complex acting

fig 6.5. Figure from Michael Kirby's *A Formalist Theatre*, p 10.

structing the characterization. The difference between simple and complex acting is one of degree but not a matter of genre. Performing realistically takes training and effort, just as does performing in a clearly marked style such as *jingju* (sometimes called "Beijing opera"), a traditional Chinese genre. Realistic acting seems "easier," that is, more familiar, because it draws its basic vocabulary from everyday life. But to simulate or recreate everyday life onstage is a difficult task (**see Stanislavsky box**).

Another way to understand acting, one not so dependent on notions of impersonation, is to divide acting into five kinds according to the congruence to daily life, the kind of actions presented, the state of mind of the performer, and the importance of performing objects:

1 realistic
2 Brechtian
3 codified
4 trance
5 performing objects – masks and puppets.

These terms are somewhat arbitrary. Certainly, a single genre or actor may employ more than one kind of acting (**see Harding box**). But, arbitrary or not, the terms are a useful way to begin examining similarities and differences in performing across a range of genres and cultures.

nonmatrixed performing: actions performed onstage which do not involve role-playing.

symbolized matrix performing: onstage actions which the spectator recognizes as "belonging to" a character, even though the performer continues to behave "as herself."

Konstantin **Stanislavsky**

How hard it is to act "naturally"

In every branch of art there are first hundreds of people who wish to study it. Many come in response to the bait of "learning creatively," but having realized how much of their time they have to devote to it; how difficult it is to achieve the complete freedom of the body and all its parts; how long it takes to control then develop one's attention and to learn to transfer it entirely – at one blow – and instantly from one group of muscles to another before you even get to the psychological problems; how difficult it is to develop the sense of rhythm in oneself and change it in the most extraordinary way to the rhythm of the music before you even start on your exercises for collecting your energy and distributing it in different directions – having grasped all that, the majority of those who come to study the art of acting will leave the studio. Many of those who stay behind will also very soon leave, for the temptation to earn money by slipshod work is very great.

1961, *Stanislavsky on the Art of the Stage*, 161–62

Frances **Harding**

Acting and not-acting in Africa

[In Africa] the audience–performer relationship [is one] in which the interaction between them is a suspension of the ordinary rather than a suspension of reality and thus constitutes more of a heightening of reality in which it is recognized that ordinary people can become extra-ordinary for a period of time. [Following from this] is a preference for multilayered performances whereby any one performer may, within a single performance, be at one point "acting" and at another point "presenting the self." Neither the audience nor the performer experiences any difficulty in accommodating a movement between the two. A sustained, uninterrupted representation is not required in order to convince the spectators of the presence of an "other." It is more a case of recognizing that some people have – albeit temporarily (i.e., for the duration of the performance) – the power to move between the presentation of self and the presentation of an "other."

2004, "Presenting and Re-Presenting the Self", 198

received acting: onstage behavior in which the performer makes no attempt to impersonate a character, but is nonetheless viewed by the audience as part of the situation of a scene. "Extras" practice received acting.

simple acting: when a performer simulates the speech and behavior of a character.

complex acting: when the performer's entire physical, mental, and emotional capability is involved in the portrayal of a character.

Realistic acting

In realistic acting, the behavior onstage is based on ordinary life. This kind of acting was considered avant-garde when it was introduced in Europe in the last decades of the nineteenth century. Soon it became dominant (**see figure 6.6**). Realistic acting remains the dominant style of Western acting in everything from soap operas to the stage to movies and television. Even when the story, action, and settings are fantastic – as in *Star Wars* or *Crouching Tiger, Hidden Dragon* – the acting is realistic. Realistic acting assumes that the emotions of the characters are like those of "real people," even if the characters are dancing across treetops or living in a galaxy "far, far away." They may fight in a way no real humans ever could or pilot spaceships through a time warp across billions of light years – but when they speak, they speak ordinary language in the ordinary way. They fall in love, argue, joke, feel sad, and explode in rage in ways that are easily recognizable. Spectators need no special knowledge of a theatrical code to understand what is going on. Codified forms, from ballet to noh, and many rituals, operate from a different assumption (which I will discuss later in the chapter).

Realistic acting was part of a whole system that profoundly reformed Western theatre in the latter part of the nineteenth century. Along with realistic acting came realist

fig 6.6. Act 4 of Anton Chekhov's *Three Sisters*, directed by Konstantin Stanislavsky at the Moscow Art Theatre, 1903. Olga Knipper as Masha, M. G. Savitskaya as Olga, and N. N. Litovtseva as Irina. Copyright SCR Photograph Archive, London.

playwriting, set design, and staging. Realist theatre reached many parts of the world on the wings of colonialism and the spread of Western culture. In Japan, realistic theatre was called *shingeki* (new theatre), in China, *huaju* (spoken theatre) (**see figure 6.7**). In many places, the realist theatre was known simply as "modern theatre," akin to the rest of modernism – railroads and automobiles, telephones, and new kinds of political and economic relations. These relations were more popular and democratic, stretching across the span of social classes, but emphasizing the middle class. Realist theatre was regarded as progressive, while traditional forms represented outmoded social systems and beliefs. Most traditional theatres around the world depict the doings of gods or other supernatural beings, generals and warriors, and the aristocracy. The staging conjoins drama, dance, song, and music. Traditional forms are frequently codified. For a time, these theatres were rejected. Many revolutionaries wanted cultural as well as technical, political, and economic modernization. They wanted to bring traditional forms into line with new views of what the social order ought to be (**see Mao box**).

Of course, **realistic acting** changes as social life changes. What was "natural" in 1902 is not natural in 2006; and 2006 behavior will look unnatural when regarded by those living in 2100. This can be demonstrated if one looks at old movies made in a realist style. The acting often appears stilted and "unreal." This is both because realist acting, like all acting, is stylized (abstracted and shaped from what happens in ordinary life) and because the daily behaviors upon which realist acting is modeled change over time. Old newsreels, documentaries, and movies provide evidence of how the behavior of daily life changes from one historical period to another. One notes also, however, that certain behaviors – those of religious, judicial, and secular rituals, for example – tend to conserve themselves. This kind of acting will be discussed in the section on "codified acting."

realistic acting: acting where the behavior of the characters is modeled on everyday life. Although realistic acting is a style, the impression it gives is of actual events occurring. Realistic acting is widespread on the stage and dominant in film and television drama.

fig 6.7. A *huaju* or spoken drama play, Sun Huizhu's *Mingri Jiuyao Chu San* (*Tomorrow He'll Be Out of the Mountains*), directed by Richard Schechner at the Shanghai Peoples Art Theatre, 1989. Photograph courtesy of Richard Schechner.

Mao Zedong

The Cultural Army serves the people

In our struggle for the liberation of the Chinese people there are various fronts, among which there are the fronts of the pen and of the gun, the cultural and the military fronts. To defeat the enemy we must rely primarily on the army with guns. But this army alone is not enough, we must also have a cultural army. [. . .] The first problem is: literature and art for whom?

This problem was solved long ago by Marxists, especially by Lenin. As far back as 1905 Lenin pointed out emphatically that our literature and art should "serve [. . .] the millions and tens of millions of working people." [. . .]

Indeed literature and art exist which are for the exploiters and oppressors. Literature and art for the landlord class are feudal literature and art. Literature and art for the bourgeoisie are bourgeois literature and art. [. . .] Then literature and art exist which serve the imperialists. [. . .] With us, literature and art are for the people, not for any of the above groups. We have said that China's new culture at the present stage is an anti-imperialist, anti-feudal culture of the masses of the people under the leadership of the proletariat. [. . .]

In the last analysis, what is the source of all literature and art? Works of literature and art, as ideological forms, are products of the reflection in the human brain of the life of a given society. [. . .] The life of the people is always a mine of raw materials for literature and art, materials in their natural form, materials that are crude, but most vital, rich, and fundamental; they make all literature and art seem pallid by comparison; they provide literature and art with an inexhaustible source, their only source. [. . .] Some may ask, is there not another source in books, in the literature and art of ancient times and of foreign countries? In fact the literary and artistic works of the past are not a source but a stream; they were created by our predecessors and the foreigners out of the literary and artistic raw materials they found in the life of the people of their time and place. We must take over all the fine things in our literary and artistic heritage, critically assimilate whatever is beneficial, and use them as examples when we create works out of the literary and artistic raw materials in the life of the people of our own time and place. [. . .]

Our specialists in literature should pay attention to the wall newspapers of the masses and to the reportage written in the army in the villages. Our specialists in drama should pay attention to the small troops in the army and the villages. Our specialists in music should pay attention to the songs of the masses. Our specialists in the fine arts should pay attention to the fine arts of the masses. [. . .] On the one hand, they should help and guide the popularizers, and on the other, they should learn from these comrades and, through them, draw nourishment from the masses to replenish and enrich themselves so that their specialties do not become "ivory towers," detached from the masses and from reality, devoid of content or life. [. . .] Only by speaking for the masses can a specialist educate them and only by being their pupil can he be their teacher.

1967 [1942], *Mao Tse-Tung on Literature and Art*, 1, 10–11, 18, 22–23

In realistic acting, the actor "disappears into the role" (**see figure 6.8**). Audiences experience the characters as real, living persons. When an actor performs realistically, she is probably following basic principles laid down by **Konstantin Stanislavsky** at the turn of the twentieth century and reinforced many times since. The Russian actor and director developed techniques such as the "magic if" and "emotional recall" to help an actor identify deeply with the character – to such a degree that the actor's own self is fused with the self of the character. The goal of actor-training in realistic acting is twofold. First, to help the actor find situations in her own life that are analogous (emotionally, if not actually) to what happens to the character. Second, to be able to show these feelings in a sincere way to spectators. This last is particularly difficult, because revealing "real feelings" tends to happen only among intimates, not before several hundred strangers. Actors Studio founder **Lee Strasberg** recognized this difficulty and devised the "private moment" exercise to deal with it (**see Strasberg box 1**).

Konstantin Stanislavsky (1863–1938): Russian actor, director, and acting teacher. Co-founder in 1898 with Vladimir Nemirovich-Danchenko of the Moscow Art Theatre. In the early part of the twentieth century, Stanislavsky developed principles of actor training that continue to be extremely influential. Author of *My Life in Art* (1924), *An Actor Prepares* (1936), *Building a Character* (1949), *Stanislavsky on the Art of the Stage* (1950), and *Creating a Role* (1961).

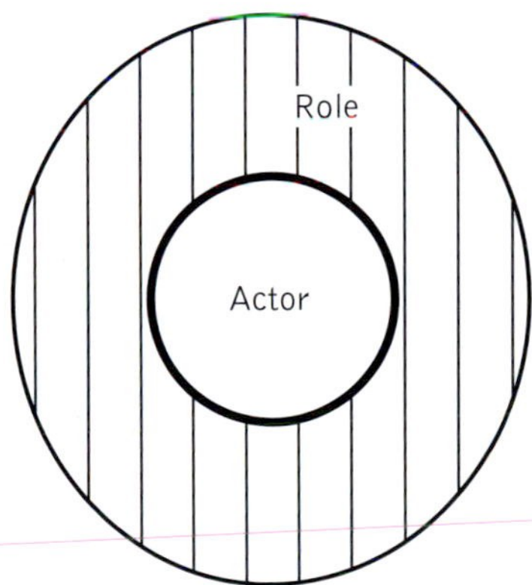

fig 6.8. In realistic acting, the actor is enclosed within the role.

Lee Strasberg

The private moment

Another recent exercise – which is very valuable, even for staging – is what I call "The Private Moment." It came from a rereading of that Stanislavsky book in which he uses the famous phrase about being "private and public." The most difficult thing for the actor is to be private in public, which means he must seem to be in a real situation while he knows full well that he is on a stage. In order to deal with this directly, I experimented with some of the people I had difficulty with. There was a great deal of inner emotion, a lot taking place which wasn't coming out because of the tension created by the audience. But how to deal with it – after all, the audience is there and you can't wipe it out. If you can concentrate, fine, but if somehow it doesn't work for you, what do you do? And then I said: you must have a moment in life when you're alone, when you behave in a way which, if anyone comes in, if you hear the door opening, you immediately stop. In other words, it is not a moment when you are simply alone, it is a moment when you are private. I thought by making use of the strong impulse and impetus of something that happens only in private, and yet placing it in public before an audience – making the actor do that – we could lick this problem of the actor's being inhibited by the audience. And it worked. [. . .]

We also found wonderful theatrical material. [. . .] We found that people have wonderfully theatrical behavior when they're private, much more so than when they are simply alone. They speak to themselves with such vividness, they argue, they tell people off. They carry on in a way which they immediately inhibit when somebody is there. So, in addition to the training effect of the Private Moment, we found that it had within itself enormous possibilities as a guide to staging certain moments – soliloquies, monologues, opera moments, moments when a person is left alone on the stage – what Stanislavsky calls the Star Pause.

1964, "Working with Live Material," 125–26

Lee Strasberg (1901–82): American acting teacher, actor, and director. In 1931, he co-founded the Group Theatre of New York – whose actors and directors had a profound influence on American theatre and movies. Strasberg taught at the Actors Studio in New York from 1949 until his death. There he developed "the Method," a system based on Stanislavsky's but which emphasized how actors could use their own personal emotional lives as the basis for developing roles. Strasberg's ideas are to some degree represented in two books: *Strasberg at the Actors Studio: Tape Recorded Sessions* (1965, with Robert H. Hethmon) and *A Dream of Passion in the Development of the Method* (1987, with Evangeline Morphos).

Realistic acting works best with realist or naturalist dramas – such as **Henrik Ibsen**'s *Hedda Gabler*, **Arthur Miller**'s *Death of a Salesman*, or **David Mamet**'s *American Buffalo*. Realistic acting is well suited to film, where close-ups and microphoning add immeasurably to the illusion of intimacy. Realistic acting does not work as well with poetic drama such as the plays of Shakespeare, **Kalidasa**, or **Federico García Lorca**. But for all its apparent "naturalness," realistic acting is a style – it is not "real life itself." If it were, no actor-training would be necessary to master this style. The existence of many schools of acting indicates clearly that realist acting is a style. Even Strasberg emphasized that realism was a style, not "life itself." He felt it was necessary for the actor to rise to the level of the play. It was a mistake to bring the play down to the experiences of the actor (**see Strasberg box 2**).

Henrik Ibsen (1828–1906): Norwegian playwright noted for his pioneering realistic dramas dealing with the personal and social interactions of middle-class characters. Among his many plays are *Peer Gynt* (1867), *A Doll's House* (1879), *Ghosts* (1881), *Enemy of the People* (1882), *Hedda Gabler* (1890), and *The Master Builder* (1891).

Arthur Miller (1915–2005): American playwright in the realist style. Among his many plays are *All my Sons* (1947), *Death of a Salesman* (1949), *The Crucible* (1953), *A View from the Bridge* (1955), *After the Fall* (1964), *The Price* (1968), *The Ride Down Mt. Morgan* (1991, revised 1999), *Broken Glass* (1994), and *Resurrection Blues* (2002). For Miller's views on theatre, see *The Theatre Essays of Arthur Miller* (1996).

David Mamet (1947–): American playwright, screenwriter, and director. Among his many plays are *American Buffalo* (1975), *Glengarry Glen Ross* (1983), *Oleanna* (1992), *The Old Neighborhood* (1997), and *Romance* (2005). His films include *House of Games* (1987), *The Spanish Prisoner* (1998), and *Wag the Dog* (1998).

Kalidasa (probably 4th or 5th century CE): the master poet-dramatist of the Indian Sanskrit tradition. His best-known play, *Shakuntala*, a tale of love lost and then regained, is still often performed. His other works include *Malavikaa and Agnimitra* and *Vikramorvashiiya (Urvashii Won Through Valor)*.

Federico García Lorca (1898–1936): Spanish poet and playwright, murdered by Falange fascists at the outset of the Spanish civil war. Lorca's plays include *Blood Wedding* (1933), *Yerma* (1934), and *The House of Bernarda Alba* (1936).

Lee Strasberg

Raising the actor to the level of the character

First, you must define the essential ingredient in a part. In other words: what would have to happen to me so that I would be Lady Macbeth? We don't say, "I'm Lady Macbeth," and then begin work. There is a formulation here which I would like to emphasize because it's one of the few things worth putting theoretically. [. . .] Generally speaking it is true that Stanislavsky would say, "Now, if you were Lady Macbeth, how would you do this? How would you behave?" And in doing this, he often made the aesthetic mistake of taking the role down to the actor.[. . .] On the other hand, [Yevgeni] Vakhtangov [1883–1922] says, "If you had to do such and such a thing [. . .], what would have to happen to you, what would motivate you to do that?" In other words he places the aesthetic intention first and then uses the technique as a way of carrying out the aesthetic intention. When that is not done, often, even in Stanislavsky's productions, the work makes the reality descend to the level of the actor, rather than helping the actor to ascend to the level of the character. You see, work on a part helps create the reality and so we must be careful to bring the actor to the reality of the play by motivating him to act as the character acts.

1964, "Working with Live Material," 129

Brechtian acting

Brechtian acting is not so much "opposed" to realistic acting as supplemental to it. Brecht was both a playwright and a director. In staging his own plays, he emphasized both the meaning of the drama and the individual agency of the actor. Brecht did not want the actor to disappear into the role. He wanted the actor to engage the role actively, to enter into a dialectical relationship with the role (**see figure 6.9**). Brecht called this Verfremdungseffekt (I discussed it briefly in chapter 5), roughly meaning "alienation" or "estrangement" (**see Willett box**). It is best to think of the Verfremdungseffekt as a way to drive a wedge between the actor, the character, the staging (including blocking, design, music, and any other production element) so that each is able to bounce off of, and comment upon, the others.

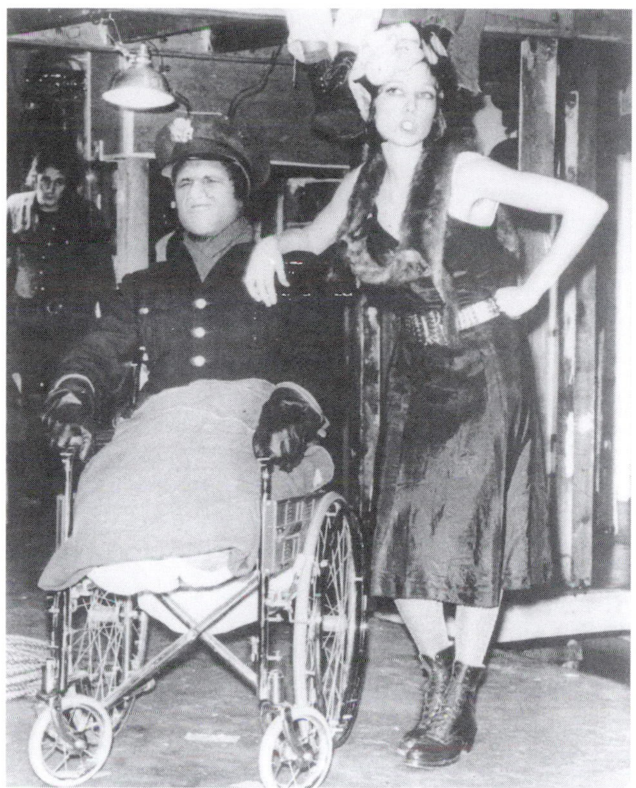

fig 6.9. Elizabeth LeCompte as Yvette and James Griffiths as the Colonel in a scene from The Performance Group's production of Bertolt Brecht's *Mother Courage and Her Children*, directed by Richard Schechner, New York, 1975. Here both LeCompte and Griffiths stand "next to" as well as "inside" the roles they play.

John Willett

Verfremdungseffekt in Brecht

With "Verfremdung" went the "Verfremdungseffekt," where "Effekt" corresponded to our own stage use of the word "effects": a means by which an effect of estrangement could be got. Both these new words have a single object: to show everything in a fresh and unfamiliar light, so that the spectator is brought to look critically even at what he has so far taken for granted. [. . .] "Verfremdung", in fact, is not simply the breaking of illusion (though that is one means to the end); and it does not mean "alienating" the spectator in the sense of making him hostile to the play. It is a matter of detachment, of reorientation: exactly what **[Percy Bysshe] Shelley** meant when he wrote that poetry "makes familiar objects to be as if they were not familiar," or **[Arthur] Schopenhauer** when he claimed that art must show "common objects of experience in a light that is at once clear and unfamiliar."

1960, *The Theatre of Bertolt Brecht*, 179

Brecht's idea of the Verfremdungseffekt, modeled on the Russian formalist notion of *priem ostranenie* (the way to make strange), was powerfully reinforced when Brecht, while in Moscow in 1935, apparently oblivious to the Stalinist terror then in full bloom, saw the great Chinese actor **Mei Lanfang** perform. At a formal banquet in his honor, in a tuxedo, and without lights, scenery, or makeup, Mei showed a *dan* (woman) role from jingju (**see Brecht box**). Mei's performance disrupted the equation "theatre = reality," confirming for Brecht the superiority of non-illusionistic theatre. Mei exemplified exactly those qualities Brecht was looking for: a distance separating actor from role; a disregard for the fourth wall; a quoting of the character played rather than any complete conversion into the character.

In **Brechtian acting**, the actor does not hide behind the attributes of the role or disappear into the role. The actor – and the playwright and director, too – takes a position to some degree outside what is being performed (**see figure 6.10**). From this more objective place, the artist can offer opinions – both directly and by means of a specific gesture (a "gestus," Brecht called it) – concerning the dilemma facing the character, the social context of the drama, and the relationship

Percy Bysshe Shelley (1772–1822): English Romantic poet whose works include the plays *The Cenci* (1819) and *Prometheus Unbound* (1820) and "Adonais" (1821), an elegy written in memory of the fellow poet, John Keats.

Arthur Schopenhauer (1788–1860): German philosopher whose most important work is *The World as Will and Representation* (1818). A pessimist, Schopenhauer believed that some relief from the pain of living could be found in music, philosophy, and art.

Mei Lanfang (1894–1961): Chinese performer of jingju and kunju, two kinds of classical sung theatre or "opera." Mei specialized in *dan* roles (women). Mei's international tours and demonstrations helped bring Chinese theatre to the attention of non-Chinese theatre practitioners and scholars.

Bertolt Brecht

Alienation effects in Chinese acting

[T]he Chinese artist never acts as if there were a fourth wall [. . .]. He expresses his awareness of being watched. This immediately removes one of the European stage's characteristic illusions. The audience can no longer have the illusion of being the unseen spectator at an event which is really taking place. [. . .] The artist's object is to appear strange and even surprising to the audience. He achieves this by looking strangely at himself and his work. As a result everything put forward by him has a touch of the amazing. Everyday things are thereby raised above the level of the obvious and automatic. [. . .] The Chinese artist's performance often strikes the Western actor as cold. That does not mean that the Chinese theatre rejects all representation of feelings. The performer portrays incidents of utmost passion, but without his delivery becoming heated. [. . .] The Chinese performer [. . .] rejects complete conversion. He limits himself from the start to simply quoting the character played. But with what art he does this!

1964 [1936], *Brecht on Theatre*, 91–94

Brechtian acting: socially and politically aware performing where the actor does not disappear entirely into the role. At certain moments, the actor – by means of gesture, song, or statement – comments on the role or the dramatic situation.

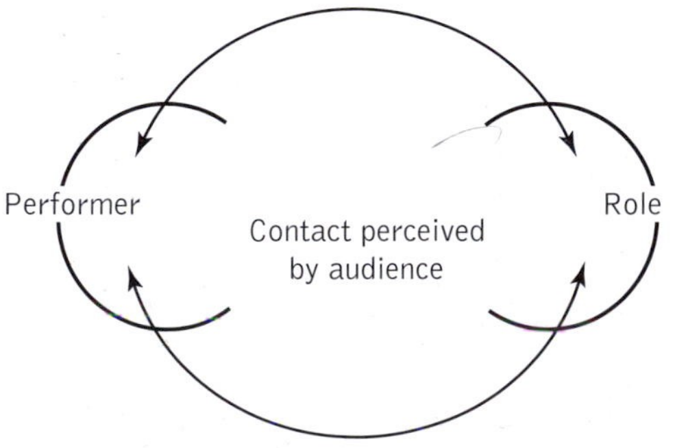

fig 6.10. In Brechtian acting, the actor takes a position to some degree outside the role, engaging the role and even criticizing the character. The audience is aware of the tension that both draws the actor to the role and separates her from the role.

of the play to the situation of the audience. The important thing is to create an art where history is not already given, a theatre not controlled by fate or destiny, but open to historical intervention and actual social change. This insistence on the ability to interrogate, intervene, and change forms the basis of Augusto Boal's Theatre of the Oppressed – a neo-Brechtian community-based theatre of social change enacted by spectators turned into actors, "spect-actors," Boal calls them (**see Boal box**).

Augusto Boal

The spect-actor rehearsing the revolution

In order to understand the poetics of the oppressed one must keep in mind its main objective: to change the people – "spectators," passive beings in the theatrical phenomenon – into subjects, into actors, transformers of the dramatic action. [. . .] The spectator delegates no power to the character (or actor) either to act or to think in his place; on the contrary, he himself assumes the protagonist role, changes the dramatic action, tries out solutions, discusses plans for change – in short, trains himself for real action. In this case, perhaps the theatre is not revolutionary in itself, but it is surely a rehearsal for the revolution. [. . .] It is not the place of the theatre to show the correct path, but only to offer the means by which all possible paths may be examined.

1985 [1974], *Theatre of the Oppressed*, 122, 141

Brechtian acting interrogates the character's actions, proposes alternative actions, and demystifies events that might otherwise appear to be "inevitable." If Stanislavsky stressed the actor's "work on oneself," urging an intense personal study and preparation, Brecht worked "in committee," collaborating with a dedicated group of colleagues. The creative team stops, reflects, uncovers contradictions, tests variations, tries out events from several points of view. Brecht's theatre was profoundly social. (Brecht was himself criticized for putting his name alone on works that belonged to the "committee," for taking too much individual credit for collective work – especially in relation to the women he so depended on, **Ruth Berlau**, **Margarete Steffin**, and **Helene Weigel**.)

Ruth Berlau (1906–74): Danish novelist, actress, and theatre director. Collaborated with Bertolt Brecht on the writing of *The Caucasian Chalk Circle* (1943–5) and *The Good Person of Szechwan* (1938–41).

Margarete Steffin (1908–41): German author who collaborated with Brecht on the writing of several of his plays including *The Round Heads and the Pointed Heads* (1931–4), *The Terror and Misery of the Third Reich* (1935–8), *Señora Carrar's Rifles* (1937), *Galileo* (1937–9), *The Good Person of Szechwan* (1938–41), and *The Resistible Rise of Arturu Ui* (1941).

Helene Weigel (1900–71): Austrian-born actor, the wife and partner of Brecht. Weigel played leading roles in a number of Brecht's plays including *The Mother* (1932) and *Mother Courage and her Children* (1949). After Brecht's death in 1956, Weigel became leader of the Berliner Ensemble.

Codified acting

For Brecht, Mei might have been demonstrating the Verfremdungseffekt, but according to his own culture, Mei was engaged in the highly formalized, centuries-old acting of jingju. Jingju is codified – its every detail set by tradition and passed down from teacher to student by means of rigorous, years-long training (**see Mei box**). **Codified acting** is based on semiotically systematized gestures, movements, songs, costumes, makeup, and dramas. In order for spectators to enjoy codified acting, they have to know what each gesture, move, costume, and melody means. One learns to read codified acting in much the same way as one learns to read a written language. Both performers and spectators have to know the specific vocabulary and grammar of a particular codified system of acting in order to fully understand what is being expressed. Unless you know the vocabulary and grammar of jingju, you can't really understand Mei's performing. The codes of ballet or noh are different from the code of jingju.

codified acting: performing according to a semiotically constructed score of movements, gestures, songs, costumes, and makeup. This score is rooted in tradition and passed down from teachers to students by means of rigorous training.

In jingju, when an actor is led onto the stage by a stagehand carrying a "wind flag," the character is understood to be caught in a windstorm. If a character exits walking on his knees, spectators understand that he is brought down by grief or terror. If an actor walks around the stage in a circle, he is presumed to have traveled many miles; if he carries

fig 6.11. In various traditional Chinese sung theatre genres, actions are conveyed to the audience by means of codified gestures, movements, and vocal patterns. This scene from *bangzi*, a north China genre, shows a group traveling by boat. The action is conveyed by the Boatman's oar and the alignment and movement of the three actors to the Boatman's left. Photograph by Isabelle Duchesne.

Mei Lanfang

The aesthetic basis of Chinese "opera"

Like all other arts, the Chinese classical opera has its own aesthetic basis. The Chinese classical operas based on singing and dance movements must follow the cadence of the music to form a certain pattern. The beautiful dance movements created by past artists are all based on gestures in real life, synthesized and accentuated to become art. And so the performing artist has a twofold task: apart from acting his role according to the development of the story, he must also remember that his job is to express himself through beautiful dance movements. [. . .]

The teacher gives us our basic training. In the beginning, naturally we have no artistic perception or judgment; we can only imitate his every sound, every gesture. After we reach a certain level, we have to concentrate on the teacher's special technique. [. . .] For example, at the time I studied the kunqu opera *The Peony Pavilion* under veteran kunqu artist, Jiao Huilan. Jiao had already long since given up the stage. My impression of him was that of a wizened old man. But when he started demonstrating gestures, I felt that the aged man wearing an old fur coat had ceased to exist. I could see only the exquisite movements of the heroine in the play.

When you develop perception, not only can you emulate your teachers – you discover things worth noticing everywhere. For instance, you observe the expression of a man sitting leisurely, those of a person who has lost his child on the road, the way a good calligraphist holds his pen, the adept movements of a woman washing clothes, and so on. [. . .] All unusual expressions or highly rhythmic movements can be grasped by a person with a sharp sense of perception, then translated into art and adapted for the stage. [. . .]

Sometimes the artist intends to absorb useful material from life, but because he cannot distinguish the good from the bad, the beautiful from the ugly, and has not studied properly the experience of past artists [. . .] he does not know what things can be adapted to the stage and what cannot.

Take for instance the character of the Monkey King. When played by a good actor, the audience feels that he is a hero, a god; on stage he looks splendid. His makeup and movements convey his heroic spirit, while at the same time he displays the characteristic agility of the monkey. That is how the character should be depicted. However, some actors playing this role do not convey the same feeling. They try hard to imitate a real monkey, bringing to the stage a lot of unbecoming gestures. Such an indiscriminate adherence to nature is a very bad tendency. Of course, an artist should be inventive in his stage art, but this originality must come through study. If he has not studied widely, if he has not properly digested past experiences, he will not be able to find the right means of expression.

1981 [1956], "Reflections on my Stage Life," 35–36, 44–45

a riding whip, he has made the trip on horseback (**see figure 6.11**). Most often, the gestures of codified acting carry specific meaning. But sometimes the codified behavior has no specific meaning. It simply is itself. This is true of much modern dance, where movements may evoke emotions in the spectators but are not directly translatable into words or situations, as in jingju or bharatanatyam (a traditional dance of Tamil Nadu, south India).

Codified acting is widespread throughout the world. There are hundreds, if not thousands, of codified systems of acting. Ballet, kathakali, gelede, jingju, and noh are codified. In fact, the notion of devising new movements, songs, costumes, and stage designs for each production is a relatively recent phenomenon, closely associated with realistic and Brechtian acting. In Asia, codified acting has been practiced and theorized for more than 2,000 years. *The Natyasastra* of Bharata (approximately second century BCE–second century CE), a Sanskrit manual of theatre, dance, and music conceived of as a single art, details with great precision how hand and eye movements, body gestures, dance steps, music, and costumes express and communicate specific emotions, dramatic situations, and character types (**see Bharata box**).

Although I am discussing codified acting in terms of the performing arts, most rituals – secular as well as sacred – some popular entertainments, and sports employ codified movements. To perform a marriage, execute a ballroom dance, or shoot a basketball requires mastering codified behavior (**see figure 6.12**). Sports matches are incomprehensible to those who don't know the codified movements of the game. Sports owe their particular power to engage players and spectators to the combination of codified and improvised behavior. The basic moves are codified, and knowing these moves allows people to get what's going on, to appreciate fine play and disparage poor play. At the same

fig 6.12. Some examples of codified performances outside of the theatre.

Ballroom dancing as shown in the Australian movie, *Strictly Ballroom*, with Paul Mercurio and Gia Carides, 1992. Copyright Kobal Collection, London.

A rabbi performing the marriage of Christine Dotterweich to Henry Bial, 1998. Photograph courtesy Henry Bial.

A basketball player at the 1996 Atlanta Olympics takes aim. Copyright Colorsport.

Bharata

Acting with a single hand; with the chest

Abhinaya [acting] done by a single hand are 24. [. . .] 1. Pataka: With thumb bent and other fingers stretched out. To convey striking, driving, joy, pride, etc. With both hands and fingers moving, it suggests rain, showering of flowers, etc. [. . .] 5. Arala: The thumb is bent, the other fingers are spread out from each other, the second finger bent like a bow. This mudra [hand gesture] is used for blessing in the case of males, and for collecting the hair in the case of women; courage, dignity of men and self-admiration by women are also suggested. [. . .] 21. Sandamsa: This mudra is Arala (no. 5) but with the change that the tips of the thumb and the second finger touch and the palm is downwards. It is of three kinds – (i) Agraja, when taking out a thorn or picking delicate flowers, (ii) Mukhaja, when flowers are picked from the stalks or when brushes (for putting collyrium on the eyes) are used, and (iii) Parsvaja, when pearls are pierced, etc. [. . .] These, says Bharata, are all mudras shown by one hand. [. . .]

Movements of the chest are of five kinds. [. . .]. 1. Abhugna: both the shoulders are drooping down and (arms) loosely held, while the back is arched outwards. It conveys or suggests agitation, fear, sorrow, touch of cold, rain falling, etc. 2. Nirbhugna: is when the breath is drawn in, the chest expands and lifts, and the back curves in. This suggests speaking truth, bragging, haughtiness, deep breath, affected indifference (by women). [. . .]

1996 [2nd century BCE–2nd century CE], *The Natyasastra*, 83, 84, 86, 87

time, individual moves are brief and flexible enough to allow variations and new combinations. A "great player" is one who knows the moves and can riff on them as an accomplished jazz musician knows a particular progression of music and is able to improvise on it.

It is important to note the differences among scored, codified, and improvised performances. Any performance – even the most naturalistic – can be "scored," all its details set and invariable. But scoring a production does not mean it is codified. Codified acting is present only when there is a known, organized, and formally transmittable semiotic system of meaning separate from everyday behavior. Of course, everyday behavior can be analyzed semiotically – all behavior "means something." In codified acting, the actors have consciously mastered a system separate from ordinary behavior. One can improvise either with new materials or with codified behavior. Improvising means working without a set score. The bits a performer uses to build an improvisation can be from everyday behavior or from codified behavior.

Mastering codified performing takes years of training. Each genre has its own vocabulary. In kathakali, young actors have their bodies massaged into "kathakali shape" (**see figure 6.13**) and practice rigorous exercises to train each part of their bodies, including the eyes (**see figure 6.14**). When he was a boy, Mei was told his eyes were too dull and inexpressive for jingju. To correct this, Mei practiced staring at a point of incense burning in a dark room, following kites as they flew high in the sky, and tracing with his eyes the soaring and wheeling of birds. Mei succeeded in earning the bright eyes for which he was renowned. Training that actually reforms the body is used in sports too. Weight-lifting, pole-vaulting, and acrobatics are codified forms demanding specifically trained and re-formed bodies. One can begin to learn realistic or Brechtian acting relatively late in life because people have "practiced" daily behavior all their lives. Training in realist performance is focused on gaining conscious control over what one already knows how to do. But to master a codified form, one must begin very young when both mind and body are flexible. Acquiring a "second body" and a "focused mind" is not easy. Each form has its own demands, whether ballet or kathakali, piano or violin, the opera or acrobatics, sprint racing or marathon running, basketball power forward or football lineman. To some degree, a person is born with the disposition toward a specific body. But for those who reach world-class levels of performance, an enormous effort and determination goes into conforming to the demands of the codified behavior of a specific genre or sport (**see Barba box 1**).

Eugenio Barba (1936–): Italian-born director and theorist, founder in 1964 of Odin Teatret of Holstebro, Denmark. The Odin features ensemble devised pieces, intensive actor training, workshops, and touring. In 1980 Barba convened the first session of ISTA – the International School of Theatre Anthropology, an ongoing intercultural investigation into performing. Barba's books include *The Floating Islands* (1979) and *Beyond the Floating Islands* (1986), both with Fernando Taviani, *A Dictionary of Theatre Anthropology: The Secret Art of the Performer* (1991, with Nicola Savarese), *The Paper Canoe* (1995), and *Land of Ashes and Diamonds* (1999).

Eugenio Barba

Lokadharmi *versus* natyadharmi

"We have two words," the Indian dancer Sanjukta Panigrahi said to me, "to describe man's behavior: *lokadharmi* stands for behavior (*dharmi*) in daily life (*loka*); *natyadharmi* for behavior in dance (*natya*)." [. . .] Certain Oriental and Occidental performers possess a quality of presence which immediately strikes the

fig 6.13. A kathakali student at the Kalamandalam, Kerala, India, receives a massage that helps shape his body to the needs of this exacting genre, 1976. Photographs by Richard Schechner.

fig 6.14. TRYPTICH. a–c
Some examples of the exercises used at the kathakali Kalamandalam, Kerala, India for training the eyes, 1976. Photograph by Richard Schechner.

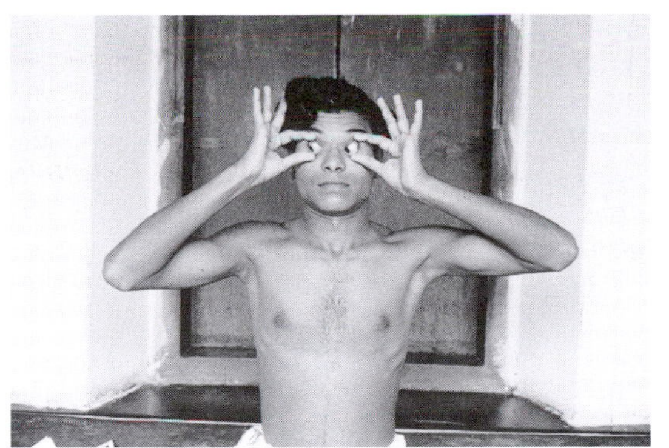

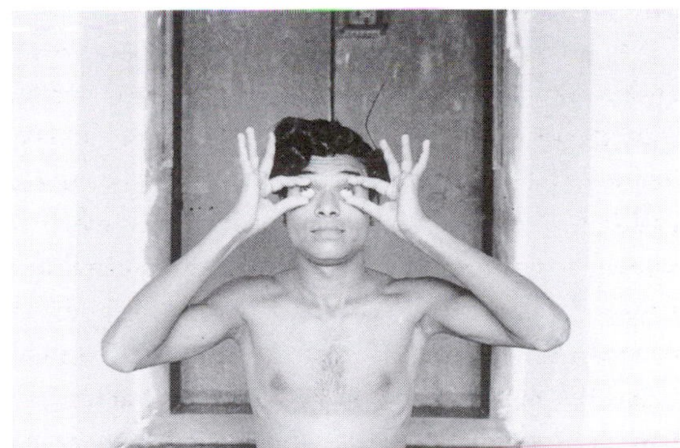

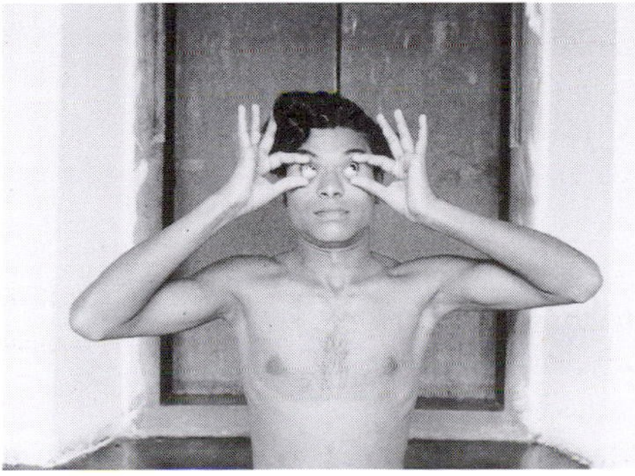

spectator and engages his attention. This occurs even when these performers are giving a cold, technical demonstration. [. . .] The way we use our daily bodies in daily life is substantially different from the way we use them in performance. We are not conscious of our daily techniques: we move, we sit, we carry things, we kiss, we agree and disagree with gestures which we believe to be natural but which are in fact culturally determined. [. . .] The first step in discovering what the principles governing a performer scenic bios, or life, might be, lies in understanding that the body's daily techniques can be replaced by extra daily techniques, that is, techniques which do not respect the habitual conditioning of the body. Performers use these extra daily techniques.

1991, *A Dictionary of Theatre Anthropology*, 9

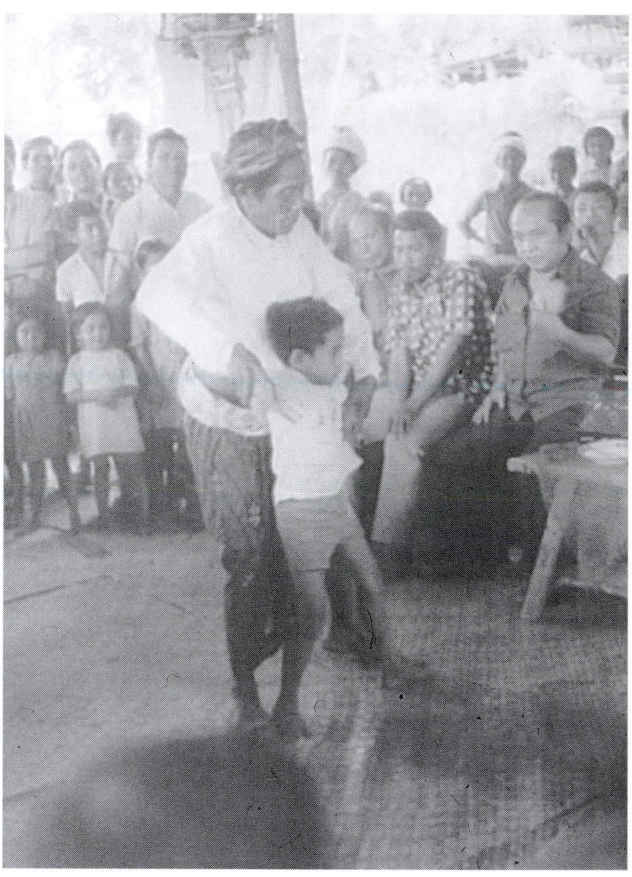

fig 6.15. A Balinese dance teacher stands behind his young pupil manipulating the student's body – literally putting the dance into the body, 1972. Photograph by Richard Schechner

The codified actor "steps into" or "puts on" a role much as it has been performed by earlier masters. The novice does not learn abstractly but directly from a teacher passing down a specific line of a tradition. In Bali, the dance teacher stands behind the student, literally manipulating the young dancer, putting the dance directly into the body (**see figure 6.15**). The results of this kind of specific learning are traditions rich in subtle variations. In noh theatre there are five families. To an outsider, a performance by the Kanze family may look just like one by the Kongo family. But connoisseurs are able to detect and appreciate differences in tempo, intensity, singing, use of the noh masks, and so on. Similarly, "ballet" is a general term for a traditional genre of dancing developed in Europe from the eighteenth century forward. But there are different styles of ballet, tied to specific choreographers and dancers. Each of these is codified. Individual dancers interpret but do not change the movement. New ballets are composed using the basic vocabulary which is codified.

In realistic or Brechtian acting there are as many ways to play a role as there are actors and directors ready to interpret it. This is true even if the drama is not realistic, as with Shakespeare. Any text can be played realistically, in Brechtian style, or according to a codified system of acting. Some might worry that codified acting is mechanical and dull. However, this is not so. As attested to by many performers and spectators, deep feelings can be expressed and shared within the strict confines of a codified form.

Codified acting and the avant-garde

Of course, the avant-garde delights in stretching all envelopes, including that of codified acting. In 1995, for example, British choreographer **Matthew Bourne** staged an all-male *Swan Lake* which was not only successful when it opened, but remains in his company's repertory as of 2005 (**see Lyall box**). It is important to note that the dancing followed the rules of ballet. It was the casting and the interpretation of the story that caused a stir. What critics and audiences alike admired was Bourne's ability to work within the strictures of ballet and come up with something exhilarating and new. Bourne's approach is not the only one. For many years, Les Ballets Trockadero de Monte Carlo has also presented an all-male *Swan Lake* – but as parody. However, even the parody demands ballet dancers with a reasonably high level of skill (**see Les Ballets Trockadero de Monte Carlo box**).

Matthew Bourne (1960–): English dancer and choreographer. Winner in 1996 of the Olivier and Tony Awards for his all-male *Swan Lake*. Additionally, his work includes *The Nutcracker* (2002), *Play Without Words* (2002), *Highland Fling* (2005), and *Edward Scissorhands* (2005).

Sarah Lyall

Matthew Bourne's all-male Swan Lake

When it opened at Sadler's Wells last year [1995], Matthew Bourne's provocative version of the most classic of classic ballets was immediately labeled the "gay Swan Lake." It was not surprising: Mr. Bourne's swans were not dainty dancers in tutus, but fierce, bare-chested men in feathery pantaloons. The result could have been a disastrous parody, a fiasco destined to make Mr. Bourne a laughingstock in London's unforgiving ballet world. But audiences and critics alike have lavished praise on the production. [. . .] Mr. Bourne studied the swans in St. James Park [in London] and showed his dancers a slow-motion videotape of an angry swan attacking a fishing boat. "Swans are not always beautiful, and they're not always gliding," he said. He strove, he said, to evoke the swannish ungainliness the birds show when, for example, they land on the water and shift their weight backward. "It's an odd, almost ugly thing, and it's very undancerly," he said.

1996, "A 'Swan Lake' with Male Swans is a Hit in London," 1–3

Les Ballets Trockadero de Monte Carlo

The Trocks in their own words

Founded in 1974 by a group of ballet enthusiasts for the purpose of presenting a playful, entertaining view of traditional, classical ballet in parody form and *en travesti*, Les Ballets Trockadero de Monte Carlo first performed in the late-late shows in Off-Off Broadway lofts. [. . .] By mid 1975, the Trocks' inspired blend of their loving knowledge of dance, their comic approach, and the astounding fact that men can, indeed, dance *en pointe* without falling flat on their faces, was being noted beyond New York. [. . .] Since those beginnings, the Trocks have established themselves as a major dance phenomenon throughout the world. They have participated in dance festivals in Holland, Madrid, New York, Paris, Spoleto, Turin, and Vienna. [. . .] The Company has appeared in over 500 cities worldwide since its beginnings. In Japan their annual summer tours have created a nation-wide cult following and a fan club. [. . .] Recent additions to the repertory include choreography by Merce Cunningham, Robert La Fosse, Meg Harper, Agnes de Mille, and Gary Pierce, a restaging in one act of *Don Quixote*, and of a lost M. Petipa ballet, *Humpback Horse*. [. . .] The comedy is achieved by incorporating and exaggerating the foibles, accidents, and underlying incongruities of serious dance. The fact that men dance all the parts – heavy bodies delicately balancing on toes as swans, sylphs, water sprites, romantic princesses, angst-ridden Victorian ladies – enhances rather than mocks the spirit of dance as an art form, delighting and amusing the most knowledgeable, as well as novices, in the audiences.

2005, "The Company History," www.trockadero.org/history.html

No theatre worker has experimented more with codified forms than Eugenio Barba and his colleagues at the International School of Theatre Anthropology. In a 1987 ISTA session in Italy, Barba spent a week investigating how **Johan Wolfgang von Goethe**'s and **Christopher Marlowe**'s versions of *Faust* could be interpreted by non-Western performers employing their own codified means of expression. Indian odissi dancer **Sanjukta Panigrahi** and Japanese buyo dancer **Azuma Katsuko** improvised scenes from *Faust* using their own specific genres of performance (**see figure 6.16**). The intention was to "destabilize" the codified forms – to stretch their limits of expressivity. The result was an intercultural clash, simultaneously invigorating and confusing (**see Pavis box**). In Chapter 8, I will discuss Barba's work and intercultural performance in more detail.

Johann Wolfgang von Goethe (1749–1832): prolific and influential German poet, novelist and playwright – first a Romantic and then a classicist. Among his many works are *The Sorrows of Young Werther* (1774), *Iphigenia in Taurus* (1787), *Torquato Tasso* (1789), *The Apprenticeship of Wilhelm Meister* (1796), and *Faust (Part 1*, 1808, Part 2, published posthumously, 1833).

Christopher Marlowe (1564–93): English playwright killed in a barroom brawl when he was 29, whose works include *The Jew of Malta* (*c.* 1589), *Edward II* (*c.* 1592), and *Dr. Faustus* (*c.* 1593).

Sanjukta Panigrahi (1932–97): Indian dancer widely regarded as the leading exponent of odissi dance. Panigrahi also collaborated with Eugenio Barba at the International School of Theatre Anthropology (ISTA) on many experiments exploring the relationship between Asian and Western performing.

Azuma Katsuko (1943–96): Japanese nihon buyo dancer. Nihon buyo is closely related to kabuki. Azuma collaborated with Eugenio Barba for a number of years at the International School of Theatre Anthropology (ISTA).

fig 6.16. Azuma Kazuko, left, and Sanjukta Panigrahi improvise a scene from the Faust plays and legend as part of Eugenio Barba's work at the International School of Theatre Anthropology, 1987. Photograph by Tony d'Urso. Photograph courtesy of Eugenio Barba.

Codified acting, ritual, charisma, and presence

Strictly speaking, performing rituals is not "acting" at all in the theatrical sense. The doer is performing but not acting. It is not acting because most rituals involve no impersonation. (Some rituals, such as shamanizing, include impersonation; this kind of ritual performing will be dealt with later in the chapter.) Persons performing rituals do prescribed actions, wear designated costumes, and in other ways enact highly codified behaviors. A Roman Catholic priest celebrating the Mass follows a strictly prescribed score that dictates what clothes (costume) he wears, where he stands in the church (set and blocking), what implements (props) he manipulates, how he interacts with the congregation (audience participation) – in short, everything said and done (mise-en-scène). The priest's performance is understood by those who know what the vestments, gestures, utterances, chalice, wafer, and church architecture mean. The Mass is similar to liturgies in other religions – not in specific detail, but in basic structure and process. Liturgies consist of sequences of publicly performed symbolic behavior expressing meanings shared by both the performers and the receivers (**see Rappaport box**). Liturgies are codified performing.

Some secular rituals, such as the coronation of a British monarch or the inauguration of an American president, are as codified as the Mass. Other secular rituals such as the signing of leases and other contracts, the christening of a ship at launch, and courtroom trials combine codified and improvised behavior. The overall shape of the event is set. Some of the core actions are performed exactly and invariably – breaking a bottle on the bow of the ship, witnessing legal documents, rising when the judge enters a courtroom. But other parts of the performance are open – even in unexpected and startling ways, as with surprise testimony in a trial.

Patrice **Pavis**

Improvising with codified acting

The Japanese dancer Katsuko Azuma and the Indian dancer Sanjukta Panigrahi belong to two totally different cultural and theatrical/choreographic worlds. [. . .] Getting these performers to work together is not self-evident, since the contrast in their presence, dynamic, and gestural representations is striking. [. . .] It is not easy to measure the distance between canonical odissi or buyo and the improvisations created by these dancers. Deviation from the codified traditional gestures does not seem to be a threat, but rather a consciously assumed risk. The director's role [. . .] is to destabilize the dancer, to unbalance her in the sense of imposing a gesture or series of gestures, an attitude foreign to the original codification. For example, Barba puts a glass bottle in Panigrahi's hands and asks her to do drunken – and therefore rhythmically distorted – mudras, to show the character's drunkenness. This process of voluntary deformation is immediately followed by re-formation, by moving to another type of codification. The dance of the drunken mudras becomes a parody of popular dance in which one dancer imitates the movements of the other, a joyful dance of two drunkards who end up synchronizing their drunkenness. This de-formation is not an elimination of the codified traditional form, but a re-formation into another kind of gesture, inspired by the tradition and which prepares for the next stages of the reelaboration.

1989, "Dancing with Faust," 39–40

Roy A. **Rappaport**

The codified liturgical order

Without performance there is no ritual, no liturgical order. [. . .] A liturgical order is an ordering of acts or utterances, and as such it is enlivened, realized, or established only when those acts are performed and those utterances voiced. [. . .] Since to perform a liturgical order, which is by definition a relatively invariant sequence of acts and utterances encoded by someone other than the performer himself, is to conform to it, authority or directive is intrinsic to liturgical order.

[. . .] This is to say that by performing a liturgical order the performer accepts, and indicates to himself and to others that he accepts, whatever is encoded in the canons of the liturgical order in which he is participating.

1979, *Ecology, Meaning, and Religion*, 192–93

Rituals are theatre-like, but they are not theatre itself. They differ in at least two ways. First, those performing rituals are not impersonating others. The ritualist is enacting a designated ritual role as himself. Second, the virtuosity of the performer as a stage presence is not as highly prized in itself as it is in theatre. The first of these differences leads to the second. The ritualist must actually be who she is designated as being, even if she cannot perform the ritual with theatrical flair. How excellently a ballet dancer elevates herself on toe, how rich a vocal range of interpretation a jingju actor displays, and so on, are at the very core of codified acting on stage. Codified art forms are to a large degree about how well the artist is able to perform – and to a lesser degree about what the performance means. But in rituals, the meaning and consequence of the ritual action as authenticated by the presence of the actual person authorized to enact the ritual are what count. This is so even if this person is feeble in voice and unsteady in gesture. In fact, sometimes the lack of theatrical virtuosity adds to the power of a ritual performance by underlining the importance of the action and of the social–sacred role of the ritual performer. John Paul II celebrating the Mass near the end of his life was all the more affecting in his weakened old age, carrying in his frail physical being the millennia-long authority of the Roman Catholic Church.

Having noted these differences, it is also true that although rituals are not reviewed in the same manner as stage performances, ritualists are frequently judged by parishioners, congregations, and adepts on the basis of stage skills. Charisma in a ritualist or political leader is "presence" in a stage or film actor. A large part of charisma–presence is not mysterious at all. It is a mastery of what Eugenio Barba calls the "pre-expressive" as well as using specific stage techniques of the body, voice, setting, timing, and mise-en-scène.

At the personal level, "private rituals" (toilet habits, erotic foreplay, ways of preparing food and eating it, etc.) are also to a large degree codified. This behavior is variously termed habit, routine, ritual, or even compulsion, depending on how one wants to regard the performer and the action. What all these terms share is their pointing to a fixed sequence of behavior.

fig 6.17. Photograph by Maya Deren from *Divine Horsemen: The Living Gods of Haiti*. Copyright 1952 Maya Deren. All rights reserved. Courtesy of McPherson & Company, Publishers.

Trance performing

Trance is a widespread, complex phenomenon – including hypnotic, psychotic, epileptic, hallucinatory, possession, ecstatic, and shamanic trances. Sometimes these mental states and behaviors overlap or are difficult to distinguish from each other. One culture's "psychosis" or "hallucination" may be another's "shamanic journey." One must guard against imposing a particular cultural opinion across a range of very different phenomena and practices. Here, I will discuss only three kinds of trance performing: possession, ecstatic, and shamanic. These are frequently intertwined with specific belief systems.

In **possession trance**, performers are taken over by non-human beings or things – gods, spirits, demons, forces, animals, or objects. While possessed, performers enact actions not of their own devising. Possession trance is very widespread, occurring in many cultures and contexts, for example: Pentecostal Christians "speaking in tongues" (glossolalia) when filled by the holy spirit; voudoun adepts mounted by the loa, Afro-Haitian "divine horsemen" (**see figure 6.17**); Candomble initiates "incorporating" the orishas, Afro-Brazilian gods; pre-adolescent Balinese girls dancing as *sanghyang dedari*, divine nymphs; *tarantismo* believers in southern Italy expelling the spider's venom by dancing to its particular music. And on through untold other examples from around the world.

Several different methods are used to induce trance: among the most common are rhythmic music, especially drumming and chanting, and the drinking or inhalation of various psychotropic substances (**see Lewis box**). Getting out of trance may involve ritual actions or simply resting. Once out of trance, the trancer may or may not remember what she said and did. Induction, cooldown, and recollection differ from culture to culture, genre to genre, even instance to instance.

I. M. Lewis

Getting into trance

As is well known, trance states can be readily induced in most normal people by a wide range of stimuli, applied either separately or in combination. Time-honored techniques include the use of alcoholic spirits, hypnotic suggestion, rapid over-breathing, the inhalation of smoke and vapors, music, and dancing; and the ingestion of such drugs as mescaline or lysergic acid and other psychotropic alkaloids. Even without these aids, much the same effect can be produced, although usually [. . .] more slowly, by such self-inflicted or externally imposed mortifications and privations as fasting and ascetic contemplation.

1971, *Ecstatic Religion*, 39

Trance performing is the opposite of Brechtian acting. Brecht asked actors to maintain a critical distance from their roles. He wanted actors at one moment to be in character and at the next to step outside the role and comment on the social situation of the character and the action. For Brecht, the ability to choose, control, change, and express an opinion about the character's situation was decisive. For a Brechtian actor, "history" took concrete shape in the immediacy of the performance being prepared for and then enacted on stage. Brecht was famous for taking as much time as necessary in rehearsals, inquiring of his actors and even of persons sitting in on rehearsals, about their opinions of the scene being worked on. Brecht wanted actors and audiences to practice a consciously politically engaged relationship to the drama. In trance performing, the performer has little or no agency; there may be no spectators, but if there are, they do not interrogate the performance. In possession trance, the trancer is "taken over" – sometimes willingly, sometimes forcibly – by powerful beings and/or forces. Trance performing is so widespread and popular because it provides the entranced and spectators alike an extraordinarily vivid "total theatre" experience. People enjoy giving themselves up to transcendent, powerful forces, melding into and/or acting along with the community, congregation, or crowd.

possession trance: occurs when performers are taken over by non-human beings or things – gods, spirits, demons, forces, animals, or objects. In possession trance performing, the possessed are like puppets; they do not control themselves or their actions. After coming out of trance, they may or may not remember what they did.

How does it feel to be "in trance"? There is no single answer. What it feels like to be in trance in Bali is different from how it feels to "fall out" in an African-American church or to be on a Native American "vision quest." In the 1930s, **Jane Belo** asked a number of Balinese what it felt like to be in trance. In one village, the trance performers were possessed by mundane beings and things – small animals, local spirits, and even brooms, pot lids, and potatoes. Belo was struck by how ordinary trance was to these people. For them, going into trance was a common, enjoyable event that both entertained them and drew the community closer together (**see Belo box**). Other Balinese trance performing is fraught with cosmic drama and risk. The widely performed Calanarong ritual confrontation between the demon Rangda and the beneficent lion Barong culminates when Rangda casts a spell on Barong's followers throwing them into deep trance. The trancers turn their krisses – long-bladed daggers – against their own breasts. The force of this sometimes bends the krisses, but the trancers are not wounded. If a trancer wounds her/himself, the villagers say that the trance was faked. Finally, the trancers fall to the ground where they lie rigid until carried off. Powerful rituals, including the sacrifice of chickens whose heads are then eaten raw, are needed to bring some of them back to ordinary reality.

Trance dancing in Bali, and probably everywhere else, does not occur accidentally. Balinese trance dancers are trained – if not in the formal way that gambuh, ballet, or buyo dancers are, then by osmosis whereby over the years they absorb what they are to do, learning very exactly the behavior expected of them.

Jane Belo (1904–68): American anthropologist and ethnographic filmmaker who collaborated with Margaret Mead and Gregory Bateson on the film, *Trance and Dance in Bali* (1951). Her books include: *Trance in Bali* (1960), *Traditional Balinese Culture Essays* (1970), and *Bali: Rangda and Barong* (1986).

The behavior that characterizes trance performing and the feats that people accomplish while in trance, although diverse, display a remarkable underlying sameness across cultures and circumstances (**see Rouget box**). This sameness indicates that trance has a neurobiological basis. However, very few brain studies of trance in the field have been made. Of the two that I found, both used as subjects Balinese men performing the Calanarong ritual (the Rangda–Barong story) that was also studied and filmed in 1937–39 by Gregory Bateson, **Margaret Mead**, and Jane Belo (*Trance in Bali*, 1951). It is difficult to study trance in vivo because participants in the rituals often do not want to be studied and if they agree it is hard to attach instruments to measure brain waves. It is easier to take blood samples before, during, and after a trance. One of the studies I consulted measured alpha, beta, and theta brain waves, the other looked at changes in blood chemistry during trance. Both studies showed significant alterations from normal (**see Two Field Studies of Trance box**).

While in trance, people are both relaxed and full of energy – a seemingly paradoxical condition. They are "taken over" and/or experience a dissolution of boundaries between self and other, inner and outer. Although not yet fully researched, neurologically, trance may be what people experience when both the frontal lobes of the brain are highly stimulated at the same time. The left lobe, the seat of logical thought and speech, controls the "ergotropic" (energy)

Jane Belo

Trance in a Balinese mountain village

A quite distinct type of trance manifestation was the group of sanghyangs performed in the mountain district around Selat, in the eastern section of Bali. These were folk plays, crude, earthy performances given without any elaborate and gilded costuming and paraphernalia but using the simple homely objects to be found around the house. [. . .] No-high-flown jargon relating to the gods [. . .] was invoked to explain why Darja suddenly would go into trance and wallow in the mud like a pig, why Darma suddenly would climb the bamboo pole and sway from it like a monkey. [. . .]

The crowd that gathered was alert and attentive, the whole spirit like that for a game in which everyone would take part. Everyone would join in the singing which directed the trancers' performance. People would call out jibes to the performers, urging them on, taunting them with phrases known to infuriate them. The crowd enjoyed this very much indeed. When the time came to bring the act to an end, a whole group would fall upon the trancer, who struggled fiercely in convulsions precipitated by the attack. Amid great excitement, everyone would fall over everyone else in a headlong rough-and-tumble. Then they would set themselves to nursing the trancer back to normal consciousness. All would then be just as intent and caring for the man who was coming back to himself as they had been a few moments before in taunting and exciting the creature he had "become."

[. . .]

[Belo's Balinese assistant "GM" talked to those who went into trance.]

GM: What is your feeling when you are first smoked [put into trance]?

DARJA: Somehow or other suddenly I lose consciousness. The people singing I hear. If people call out, calling me "Tjit – tah!" [pig call], like that, I hear it too. If people talk of other things, I don't hear it.

GM: When you're a sanghyang pig, and people insult you, do you hear it?

DARJA: I hear it. If anyone insults me I am furious.

GM: When you've finished playing, how do you feel, tired or not?

DARJA: When it's just over, I don't feel tired yet. But the next day, or the day after that, my body is sick.

[. . .]

GM: If you're a sanghyang puppy, what do you feel?

DARJA: I just feel like a puppy. I feel happy to run along the ground. I am very pleased, just like a puppy running on the ground. [. . .]

GM: And if you're a sanghyang broom, what's it like, and what do you feel?

DARMA: Like sweeping the filth in the middle of the ground. Like sweeping filth in the street, in the Village, I feel I'm being carried off by the broom, led on to sweep.

[. . .]

GM: And who enters sanghyangs, god or demons?

GOJA: Those three cannot be separated – god, demon, man – they cannot be broken off from each other.

1960, *Trance in Bali*, 201–02, 220–22

system. Stimulating the ergotropic system increases heart rate, blood pressure, and sweat. The pupils of the eyes dilate. Brainwaves are desynchronized; muscles become tense or even rigid. Hormones such as epinephrine, norepinephrine, cortisol, and thyroxine are pumped into the blood. One feels energized, aroused, and alert. The right lobe, the seat of spatial and tonal perceptions, controls the "trophotropic" (relaxation) system. Stimulating the trophotropic system decreases heart rate, lowers blood pressure, and lessens sweating. The pupils constrict, brainwaves are synchronized, muscle tone relaxes, and secretions of insulin, estrogen, and androgen increase.

Gilbert Rouget

Signs and behaviors of trance performing

[W]hat are the telltale signs of trance? [. . . T]rembling, shuddering, horripilation, swooning, falling to the ground, yawning, lethargy, convulsions, foaming at the mouth, protruding eyes, large extrusions of the tongue, paralysis of a limb, thermal disturbances (icy hands despite tropical heat; being hot despite extreme circumambient cold), insensitivity to pain, tics, noisy breathing, fixed stare, and so on. In addition, there are two signs that are difficult to categorize [. . .]: First, the subject gives the impression that he is totally engaged in his trance, that the field of his consciousness has been completely taken over [. . .]. Second (somewhat complementary to the first), once the subject has emerged from his trance, he has no recollection of it. [. . .]

As for behavioral signs [. . .] one could say that in practice they always symbolize the intensification of some particular faculty by means of an action endowed with certain extraordinary or astonishing aspects. Thus trance may be recognized, among other signs, by the fact that one can walk on burning coals without being burned, pierce one's own flesh without bleeding, bend swords one would normally be unable to curve, confront danger without flinching, handle poisonous snakes without being bitten, cure diseases, see into the future, embody a divinity, speak a language one has never learned, swoon or die of emotion, be illuminated by the Eternal, enter into contact with the dead, travel to the land of the gods, confront those gods, emit totally unhuman cries, give acrobatic displays beyond one's normal ability, bend backwards to make a perfect arc, compose poems in one's sleep, sing for days and nights on end without a break, dance without difficulty despite being crippled. Thus trance always manifests itself in one way or another as a transcendence of one's normal self, as a liberation resulting from the intensification of a mental or physical disposition, in short, as an exaltation – sometimes a self-mutilating one – of the self. [. . .] These behavioral signs can vary, needless to say, from the very spectacular to the extremely discrete, just as the symptoms listed earlier can vary from the extremely visible to the almost imperceptible.

1985, *Music and Trance*, 13–14

Margaret Mead (1901–78): American anthropologist and public intellectual who was a curator at New York's Museum of Natural History from 1926 to 1978. Mead expressed strong opinions on a wide range of subjects from sexuality, women's rights, and racism, to population control, the environment, and nuclear arms. Among her books: *Coming of Age in Samoa* (1928), *Growing Up in New Guinea* (1930), *Sex and Temperament in Three Primitive Societies* (1935), *And Keep Your Powder Dry: An Anthropologist Looks at America* (1942), and *Male and Female* (1949).

Two field studies of trance

What happens in the brain during trance?

Study 1: Brain Chemistry

For the first time, we have measured the plasma concentrations of several neuroactive substances: catecholamines, their metabolites, and neuropeptides, from subjects involved in ritual dramas under natural conditions. The results of the present study indicate that possession trances are associated with a significant increase in plasma concentrations of catecholamines and opioid peptides.

The 15 subjects later included in the trance group attacked the person playing a witch with swords [krisses, short daggers]. They threw themselves against the witch, glowered at her, staggered around for a while, and then threw themselves again. They performed these automatism-like behaviors repeatedly. They exhibited a mask-like face with their eyes fixed but unfocused. They vigorously poked their swords against their chest, abdomen, head, and face. Some of them devoured live chicks as sacrifices. Finally, they fell to the ground with stiff limbs. A few of them exhibited tremors. After a priest sprinkled a few drops of holy water on their faces and bodies and assistants patted them, they were able to stand (with assistance) and gradually returned to a normal state in a few minutes. [. . .] Without exception, all subjects in the trance group exhibited anterograde amnesia of the episode. [. . .]

The significant increase in NA [noradrenaline], DA [dopamine], and â-endorphin in the trance group raises the possibility that activation of these neuronal circuits in the CNS [central nervous system] has a role in the altered states of consciousness, memory deficits, and unusual behavior observed during possession trances. [. . .] We suggest that an increase in the plasma concentration of NA may reflect, in part, the activation of the central NA system, which may represent the physiological mechanism underlying the hyperarousal state, tensity, stenosis of consciousness, and decreased pain sensation during possession trances.

â-Endorphin is one of the major endogenous opioid peptides. â-Endorphin-producing neurons exist in a limited area of the arcuate nucleus in the hypothalamus and the commissural nucleus in the medulla oblongata [. . .]. The opioid peptidergic system in the spinal cord primarily has an analgesic function, whereas that in the brain affects the emotional state and induces a sense of well-being and euphoria. [. . .]

The results of the present study suggest that catecholamines and opioid peptides in the CNS are involved in possession trances including markedly altered states of consciousness, memory, pain sensation, and behaviors. The present study represents a strong foundation for further characterization of the neuronal mechanisms underlying possession trances.

2001, Kawai et al. "Catecholamines and Opioid Peptides Increase in Plasma in Humans during Possession Trances," 3419–23

Study 2, EEG [electroencephalogram]

The entire observation period of Subject 1, who became possessed, was categorized into two states: normal state (NS) and trance state (TS). The NS was further subdivided into 3 phases: the resting phase with eyes closed before the drama (PRE), the music-playing phase (MUSIC), and the resting phase with eyes closed after the drama (POST). The TS was subdivided into 5 phases: the first moving phase with eyes opened (MOVE-I), the first falling-down phase with eyes closed (FALL-I), the second moving phase with eyes opened (MOVE-II), the second falling-down phase with eyes closed (FALL-II) and the final phase (FINAL). The EEG data for Subject 2 (whose EEG was recorded simultaneously with that of Subject 1 but who did not become possessed) was compared phase by phase with that of Subject 1 in real time.

The raw EEG waveforms indicated that during the PRE and POST phases, Subject 1 showed a symmetrical dominant rhythm in the occipital regions with normal waxing and waning. Peak frequencies were 11 and 10.5 Hz for PRE and POST, respectively. No apparent spikes or sharp waves were observed during the 3 min PRE and POST recordings. [. . .]

Even just before TS, Subject 1 did not show any obvious rhythmic paroxysmal discharges or an electrical decremental pattern suggesting an ictal EEG. In MOVE-I and MOVE-II, it was difficult to evaluate the existence of spikes and sharp waves by a visual inspection of the raw EEG because of the extraneous artifacts. On the other hand, in FALL-I and FALL-II an occipital dominant rhythm peaking at 10.5 Hz was clearly observed without spikes, sharp waves, or generalized slow waves. 3.3.2. Power spectrum analysis of the EEG In Subject 1, a remarkable difference between NS and TS was seen in the power spectra of the spontaneous EEG as well as between the different phases within TS. [. . .]

During TS, by contrast, Subject 1 showed a distinctive increase in the power of the theta, alpha 1 and alpha 2 bands. The power of the alpha 1 band was relatively predominant during MOVE-I and MOVE-II, whereas that of the alpha 2 band was more prominent during FALL-I and FALL-II. The enhancement of the power in these frequency ranges became more prominent as time went on. [. . .]

The recorded EEG in this study showed an enhancement of the theta and alpha bands of spontaneous EEG activity, and differed from epileptic disorders and mental disorders. [. . .]

A positive correlation has been shown between the occipital alpha-EEG and the regional cerebral blood flow in the deep brain structure, including the thalamus. Therefore, we need to consider the possibility that a possession trance may be associated with a change of activity in deep-lying structures, including the thalamus.

2002, Oohashia et al. "Electroencephalographic Measurement of Possession Trance in the Field," 437–44

Of course, these opposite reactions cannot happen at the same time – the eyes can't both be dilated and constricted, brainwaves desynchronized and synchronized, muscles relaxed and rigid, and so on. Apparently, what happens is that in the first phase, either the ergotropic or the trophotropic system prevails; in the second phase, a rebound introduces the opposing system; in the third phase, the two systems are tuned or harmonized. Once "tuned," the experience is that of yogic *samadhi*, sexual orgasm, mystical rapture: trance (**see Fischer box and figure 6.18**). Although "opposites," shamanic ecstasy and yogic samadhi produce a similar feeling state. Kundalini yoga is said to lead one to an experience of perpetual orgasm. A person feels both profoundly excited and deeply calm. What "rebound" or "tuning" results in is a feeling of energy and relaxation at the same time – a perfect state of flow. A person in this state is able to do extraordinary things – prolonged dancing, walking on coals, uttering unknown languages, and more – without stress, exhaustion, or pain.

Extreme trance experiences are not everyday events, but light trance is common. You can lose yourself (an accurate description) dancing, driven by drink, drugs, and "trance" music appropriately named for its insistent, trance-inducing beat. The "other" that possesses one need not be a god or such. People are taken over by the "crowd spirit" at a sports match – or, on the dark side, by a lynch mob's murdering animus. Quieter kinds of trance include meditation and even jogging long distances at a steady pace. Although in ritual performances such as the Balinese Rangda versus Barong dance-drama or Brazilian Candomble adepts suddenly "fall into" trance, many trances happen as a more gradual intensification and focusing resulting in the "flow" experience discussed in Chapter 4. Flow might be thought of as light trance. There are many gradations of trance – only some of which "are" performances although all can be studied "as" performance.

Roland Fischer

Ergotropic and trophotropic in synchrony

In spite of the mutually exclusive relation between the ergotropic and trophotropic systems, however, there is a phenomenon called "rebound to superactivity" or trophotropic rebound which occurs in response to intense sympathetic excitation, that is, at ecstasy, the peak of ergotropic arousal. [. . .] Meaning is "meaningful" only at that level of arousal at which it is experienced, and every experience has its state-bound meaning. During the "Self"-state of highest levels of hyper or hypo arousal, this meaning can no longer be expressed in dualistic terms, since the experience of unity is born from the integration of interpretive (cortical) and interpreted (subcortical) structures. Since this intense meaning is devoid of specificities, the only way to communicate its intensity is the metaphor; hence, only through the transformation of objective signs into subjective symbol in art, literature, and religion can the increasing integration of cortical and subcortical activity be communicated.

1971, "A Cartography of the Ecstatic and Meditative States," 902

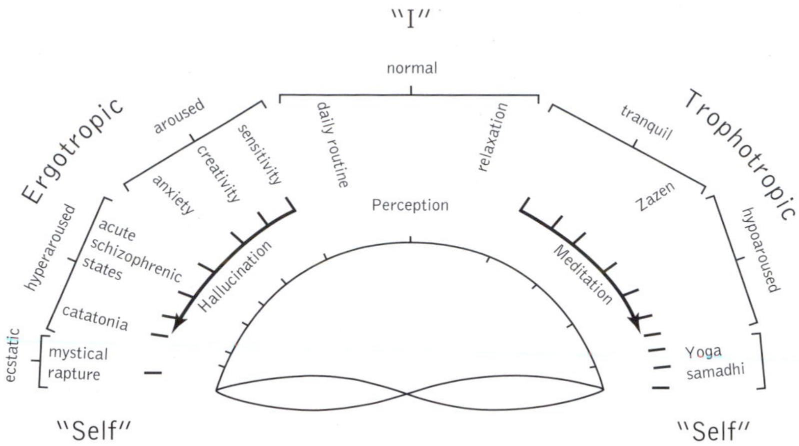

fig 6.18. Fischer's cartography of the ecstatic and meditative states. "Varieties of conscious states [are] mapped on the perception-hallucination continuum of increased ergotropic arousal (left) and a perception-mediation continuum of increasing trophotropic arousal (right). These levels of hyper and hypoarousal are interpreted by man [*sic*] as normal, creative, psychotic, and ecstatic states (left) and Zazen and samadhi (right). The loop connecting ecstasy and samadhi represents the rebound from ecstasy to samadhi, which is observed in response to intense ergotropic excitation." Fischer 1971: 898. Reproduced by permission of the American Association for the Advancement of Science. Copyright 1971 by the AAAS.

Trance performing and shamanism

In possession trance, a being enters the trancer's bodymind and takes over. In shamanic trance, the shaman, often aided by animal spirits and other helpers, leaves her body to undertake perilous journeys through human and non-human worlds. Sometimes shamans are possessed by the beings they encounter on their mystical journeys. **Shamanism** is a very ancient practice. Most scholars believe that the performances that took place in the paleolithic caves, discussed in Chapter 3, were shamanic. Shamans diagnose, exorcise and heal, divine and prophesy, avenge and hex, locate game, settle quarrels, ease childbirth, and a lot more. Shamans are also entertainers. Shamans do their work by means of drumming, dancing, singing, storytelling, magic-making, masking, and costuming (**see figure 6.19**). The exact work of a shaman will vary from culture to culture, circumstance to circumstance. Shamans enact and retain a community's knowledge. Shamans acquire knowledge through training, initiation, and practice. Sometimes shamans exchange techniques with each other. Shamans also develop close working relationships with animal spirits, animals, and other nonhuman entities. When in trance, shamans separate their souls from their bodies and, aided by their spirit helpers, venture to nonhuman worlds in pursuit of demons or in search of cures. Often, shamans perform while in trance. They may even induce trance in spectators.

fig 6.19. In 1981, Korean shaman Yu-son Kim performed the *peridegi* – a dramatic combination of singing, story telling, dance, and enactment. The goal of the peridegi is to obtain curing water from the otherworld. Yu-son Kim performed for three hours without a break. Photograph by Du-Hyun Lee. Photograph courtesy of Richard Schechner.

The word "shaman" is of Tungus (Siberian) origin. It can be argued that in a strict sense shamanism belongs solely to north central Asia – and perhaps, via the land bridge once linking Siberia to Alaska, to the Americas. But as a practice and theory, shamanism occurs all over the world. Originally a practice of hunter-gatherer peoples, shamanism is today found in agricultural, industrial, and post-industrial societies.

Archeological remains, evidence of migrations, and similarities in performance styles link the shamanism of north central Asia to practices in the Americas, India, Sri Lanka, Bali, China, Tibet, Korea, and Japan. Elements of shamanism are visible in ancient Greek rituals and Japanese Shinto and noh. What shamans do indicates that the earliest human performances were both entertaining and sacred; that any radical separation between "secular" and "sacred" is false. Because it is so widespread and ancient, some scholars believe that shamanism is the "original" theatre, while others take shamanism's ubiquity as evidence of an "evolutionary psychobiology" (**see Kirby box and Winkelman box**).

shamanism: an ancient kind of performance still practiced today by specialists in exorcism, prophecy, divination, healing, and trance. Shamans employ a rich performance toolkit that includes music, dance, masks, costumes, and objects. Although the word is of north central Asian origin, shamanism in its many varieties is practiced all over the world.

E. T. Kirby

Shamanistic origins of popular entertainments

[S]hamanistic ritual was the "great unitarian artwork" that fragmented into a number of performance arts. [. . .] Shamanist ritual occurs or has occurred virtually the world over, among the most different and distantly separated peoples or cultures, and can be traced back to prehistoric times. [. . .] At their origin, popular entertainments [ventriloquism, acrobatics, magic tricks, playing with fire, sword-swallowing, rope tricks, clowning, etc.] are associated with trance and derive from the practices of trance [. . .]. They do not seek to imitate, reproduce, or record the forms of existent social reality. Rather, the performing arts that develop from shamanist trance may be characterized as the manifestation, or conjuring, of an immediately present reality of a different order, kind, or quality, from reality itself. Shamanist illusionism, with its ventriloquism and escape acts, seeks to break the surface of reality, as it were, to cause the appearance of the super-reality that is quote "more real" than the ordinary.

1974, "The Shamanistic Origins of Popular Entertainments," 6, 14

Michael Winkelman

Shamanism: A biologically based mode of integrative consciousness

Shamans' ritual activities and experiences (e.g. soul flight, guardian spirit quest, death and rebirth) involve fundamental structures of cognition and consciousness and representations of psyche, self, and other. Shamanism involves social adaptations that use biological potentials provided by integrative altered states of consciousness (ASC) to facilitate community integration, personal development, and healing. Shamanic processes intensify connections between the limbic system and lower brain structures and project these synchronous integrative slow wave (theta) discharges into the frontal brain. These integrative dynamics enhance attention, self-awareness, learning, and memory and elicit mechanisms that mediate self, attachment, motives, and feelings of conviction. Shamanic ritual provides therapeutic effects through mechanisms derived from psychobiological dynamics of ASC, the relaxation response, effects upon serotonergic action and endogenous opioid release, and activation of the paleomammalian brain. Shamanism manipulates emotions, attachments, social bonding, sense of self, and identity, creating a primordial development of consciousness that constituted the earliest manifestations of culturally modern humans. Shamanic structures of consciousness are manifest in the universal use of ASC in religious healing, contemporary illness called spiritual emergencies, the dynamics of addiction, basic elements of contemporary spontaneous religious experiences, and the modern resurgence of neoshamanism. The basis of the shamanic paradigm in evolutionary psychology and the psychobiology of consciousness explains its widespread presence in ancient and contemporary societies. [. . .]

Shamans' ASC reflects a biologically based mode of integrative consciousness as fundamental to human nature as deep sleep, dreaming, and waking consciousness. ASC involve systematic brain discharge patterns that produce interhemispheric synchronization and coherence, an integration of brain discharges across the neuroaxis of the brain that produces a synthesis of behavior, emotion, and thought. [. . .] Shamanic ASC induction utilizes the innate capacity for music and innate brain modules associated with call and vocalization systems manifested in singing and chanting. [. . .] Calls, hoots, group enactments, and chanting involve an ancient audio-vocal communication system predating speech, an expressive system that communicates emotional states, motivates others' responses, and plays a role in managing social contact, interpersonal spacing, mate attraction, pair bonding and group cohesion.

The shaman's ASC is referred to by terms such as "soul flight" and "soul journey" and has direct homologies to modern out-of-body experiences and astral projection, reflecting experiences of traveling to and encountering entities from the spiritual or supernatural world. The biological basis of these experiences is indicated by their near universality [. . .]. Visionary experience is a natural phenomenon of the nervous system and results from disinhibition of the visual centers of the brain.

2004, "Shamanism as the Original Neurotheology," 194–95, 198–200

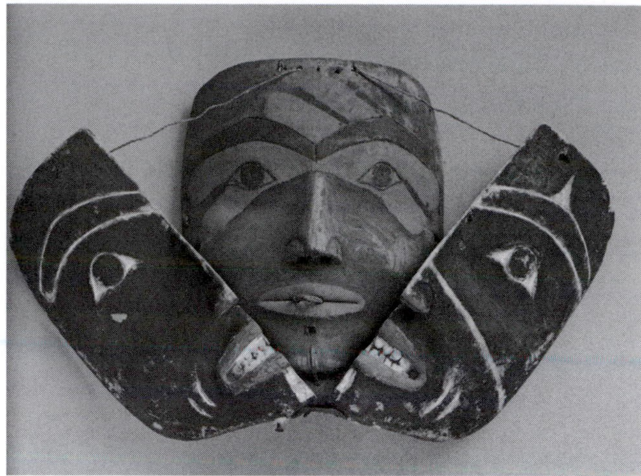

fig 6.20. A transformation mask from the Haida, Pacific coast of North America. At a climactic moment in the performance, the outer male mask springs open revealing a female mask behind, 1884–93. Photograph courtesy of the Center for Inter American Relations.

Shamans are expert performers and storytellers – masters at throwing their voices, dancing, singing, manipulating objects, and constructing spectacular costumes and masks. The shamanic ceremonies of many Native American nations were once complex dance-theatre performances. Some Haida shamans of the Pacific coast of North America featured spectacular "transformation masks" (**see figure 6.20**). At a climactic moment of a performance, the outer male mask sprang open and the interior female mask was revealed signaling the change from one being to another. Full-scale shamanic performances are infrequent these days. But elements of shamanism have been integrated into more ordinary theatre and dance – such as the *hamatsa* performance, which in recent years has been revived (**see Huntsman box**).

Not all shamans take up their calling voluntarily. Korean shamans, women called *mansins*, are expected at first to resist the call and often suffer severe illness as a result (**see Kendall box**). But once a mansin is initiated, she begins a long period of rigorous training which in many ways is very like what is demanded of any person preparing to perform a highly codified performance genre. Thus, paradoxically, even though a Korean shaman performs in a trance, the songs, gestures, and other details of her performance are codified and learned through apprenticeship. The training gives the shaman her dancing and singing. The trance gives her the necessary psychic strength to undertake the perilous journey and battle the malevolent forces (the shaman's narrative). Together these comprise the core of the shaman's performance.

Jeffrey F. Huntsman

From ritual to theatre on the American northwest coast

Native American experiences encompass a wide variety of shamanistic practices. [. . .] In some cases the shaman is in direct contact with a particular guardian or helping spirit, as is typical of the shamans of the Northwest Coast [. . .]. In other cases the experience of spirit contact is presented in symbolic terms that represent true drama and does not depend on the immediate and direct manifestation to the audience of the supernatural presence. [. . .] The moment at which shamanistic displays become drama is when the shaman begins to plan the ceremony in advance rather than giving himself or herself over completely to the paranormal state. At this point, the shaman has begun to perform according to a script. [. . .]

Some of the Northwest Coast dramas, such as the Makah Wolf Ritual (Klukwalle) [as described in 1952], show their unmistakable origins in shamanistic spirit contact. Typical of most of the Northwest Coast dramas of this type is the emphasis on the frightful danger posed by the spirit powers and the delicate balance of rationality and cooperation offered by human society. Shared by a number of contiguous peoples (many otherwise unrelated) around Vancouver, British Columbia, the Wolf Ritual has as its major function the initiation of community members into the group. The children to be initiated are "captured" by the Wolves, who are impersonated by older initiates, and "rescued" by other society members at the end of the four days the drama runs. In the process of rescue the Wolves' madness is cured through the ritual purgation of the spirit, and on the last night of the festivity, all – rescuers and defenders, the captive children, and the rampaging Wolves, now cured of their madness – celebrate their reunion with an evening of singing, dancing, and feasting.

2000, "Native American Theatre," 92–94

In certain ways, shamans are very much like stage actors: both shamans and actors play many roles using both stock and new means of expression. However, in a single performance, a shaman frequently plays multiple roles – often in conflict with each other. While possessed, the shaman's voice, movements, gestures, and even thoughts and feelings are transformed (**see Lee box**). Although many of the roles are given by tradition, the shaman is able to imbue a performance with her own singular style. A successful shaman is one who heals or placates angry spirits. Accomplishing these ends depends on the quality of the performing. A positive feedback loop rewards good acting with a high proportion of cures and appeasements.

Shamanic narratives most often center on a life-and-death struggle against powerful opponents: placating the keepers of the dead, fighting a disease, exorcising a demon, overcoming a spell that is threatening an individual or an entire community. In this drama, the shaman is the main but not only performer. Shamans-in-training or assistant shamans help. In some cases, there are animal sacrifices. The costumes are carefully constructed; there is drumming, music, and dancing. Always there is audience participation. In shamanic healing, the one afflicted by disease is passive, sometimes barely conscious. The immediate stage of the struggle is the

Laurel Kendall

The "God-Descended" shamans of Korea

A *mansin* [shaman] engages in a battle of wills with the gods from the very beginning of her career. A woman is expected to resist her calling and struggle against the inevitable, but village women say that those who resist the will of the gods to the very end die raving lunatics. [. . .] According to Yongsu's Mother,

> It's very difficult for them. They're sick and they stay sick, even though they take medicine. And there are people who get better even without taking medicine. There are some who can't eat the least bit of food; they just go hungry. There are some who sleep with their eyes open, and some who can't sleep at all. They're very weak but they get well as soon as the gods descend in the initiation *kut* [shaman ceremony]. For some people the gods descend gently, but for others the gods don't descend gently at all. So they run around like crazy women.

1987, *Shamans, Housewives, and Other Restless Spirits*, 57

Lee Du-Hyun

Guiding the dead to the Lotus Blossom Peak

[In the *chinogwi-kut*] rite performed to guide the spirit of a deceased person [a small town florist] to the other world, [. . .] the shaman plays the role of the deceased. She talks, cries, and otherwise communicates with the dead person's family. [One part] involves the acting out of a melodrama between the family of the dead man and the shaman herself who becomes a greedy messenger from hell. The shaman says, "The deceased told me 'we are so rich that we can afford to give you a huge feast.' But what poor treatment! Your goddamned dead husband made a fool of me!" The messenger (the shaman), in a rage, comes to throw away the abode of the departed spirit (the dried fish on her back). Then the members of the family, apologizing for their lack of hospitality, give the messenger some money. (This also means that the family has asked the messenger not to take the deceased to hell). After receiving the money, the messenger sings "Saje t'aryong" ("The Messenger's Song") while holding the dried fish in her left hand and shaking the brass bells with her right hand. Here is an abstract of the "Saje t'aryong": When the florist died of hypertension, the messenger came to take him to be judged. They journey to the gate of the other world, where the Ten Kings will give him judgment. The shaman (the messenger) asks these judges to allow the dead man to live on the lotus blossom peak in paradise, despite the fact that the dead man was not noted for his charity. The shaman informs the Ten Kings that if the dead man ever lives on earth again he will be extremely kind, considerate, and charitable. [. . .]

Finally, [. . .] the shaman, wearing a paper image of a spirit on her head, invokes the spirit of the deceased by singing an invocation chant in time to shamanistic music; and while dancing wildly, the entranced shaman becomes possessed by the spirit of the deceased. At that moment, tinkling her bells, she begins to recite a mournful message from the deceased. In this way, the shaman becomes the deceased. Shrieking "Oh! How awful!" or "Ahhh! How awful!" she weeps over death and falls into a faint. Supported and awakened by the family of the deceased, she (the deceased) grasps his wife, sympathizes with her by saying "What will become of you alone in the future?" and consoles the widow in her sorrow.

1990, "Korean Shamans," 149–52, 156.

body of the patient. But the bad demons may emerge into the performance space and the site of the battle may expand across a wide arena. This titanic struggle is played out by the shaman, who enacts, tells, dances, and sings what is happening, drawing the audience deeper and deeper into the reality of the performance (**see Anisimov box**).

The shaman is a link, a connector, a hero whose perilous journeys to the under- and over-worlds bring into simultaneous play several contending, overlapping, and dynamic domains: that of the individual and community the shaman serves, that of the disease or curse which is expelled but never entirely extirpated or exterminated (it may return,

A. F. Anisimov

Shaman's performance, Siberia 1931

In the middle of the tent a small fire burned. The tent was in semi-darkness. Along the sides sat the clansmen, talking softly. A pervasive feeling of expectation of something extraordinary [. . .]. Opposite the entrance the shaman sat. His pinched nervous face pale; he, silent, alert, irritable, moved his shoulders, gently swaying side to side. His face twitched, his hands trembled. [. . .]

In an improvised song of summons to the spirits, the shaman addressed his spirit helpers, calling them to his aid in the struggle against the spirit of the disease. [. . .] The shaman sent the *khargi* [the shaman's chief helper, his animal-double] to the lower world to learn the cause of the clansman's illness. The sound of the drum became thunderous, the shaman's song more agitated. [. . .]

The journey of the khargi to the other world is described in the shaman's songs in such fantastic form, so deftly accompanied by motions, imitations of spirit-voices, comic and dramatic dialogues, wild screams, snorts, noises, and the like that it startled and amazed even this far from superstitious onlooker. The tempo of the song became faster and faster, the shaman's voice more and more excited, the drum sounded ever more thunderously. The moment came when the song reached its highest intensity and feeling of anxiety. The drum moaned, dying out in peels and rolls in the swift, nervous hands of the shaman. One or two deafening beats were heard and the shaman leaped from his place. Swaying from side to side, bending in a half-circle to the ground and smoothly straightening up again, the shaman let loose such torrent of sounds that it seemed everything hummed, beginning with the poles of the tent, and ending with the buttons on the clothing. Screaming the last parting words to the spirits, the shaman went further and further into a state of ecstasy, and finally, throwing the drum into the hands of his assistant, seized with his hands the thongs connected to the tent pole then began the shamanistic dance – a pantomime illustrating how the khargi, accompanied by the group of spirits, rushed on his dangerous journey fulfilling the shaman's commands. [. . .]

Under the hypnotic influence of the shamanistic ecstasy, those present fell into a state of mystical hallucination, feeling themselves active participants in the shaman's performance.

1963, "The Shaman's Tent of the Evenks and the Origin of the Shamanic Rite," 100–02 to the same or another patient, or to the whole tribe or community), that of the dead and the keepers of the dead, that of the spirit-helpers, and that of the various regions the shaman and/or the helpers journey to. Shamanic performances are very powerful total theatre experiences (**see Shirokogoroff box**).

S. M. Shirokogoroff

The intensity of shamanic performing

The rhythmic music and singing, and later the dancing of the shaman, gradually involve every participant more and more in a collective action. When the audience begins to repeat the refrains together with the assistants, only those who are defective fail to join the chorus. The tempo of the action increases, the shaman with a spirit is no more an ordinary man or relative, but is a "placing" (i.e. incarnation) of the spirit; the spirit acts together with the audience, and this is felt by everyone. The state of many participants is now near to that of the shaman himself, and only a strong belief that when the shaman is there the spirit may only enter him, restrains the participants from being possessed in mass by the spirit. [. . .] When the shaman feels that the audience is with him and follows him he becomes still more active and this effect is transmitted to his audience. After shamanizing, the audience recollects various moments of the performance, their great psychophysiological emotion and the hallucinations of sight and hearing which they have experienced. They then have a deep satisfaction – much greater than that from emotions produced by theatrical and musical performances, literature, and general artistic phenomena of the European complex, because in shamanizing the audience at the same time acts and participates.

1935, *Psychomental Complex of the Tungus*, as quoted in I. M. Lewis, *Ecstatic Religion* (1971), 53

In shamanic performance, entertainment is integral – the efficacy of the cure or exorcism depends on the excellence of the performance. For the healing to succeed, the community's attention must be grabbed and focused; energies must be enlisted and directed. Entertainment is a crowd-gatherer and an attention-holder. The spectacle of performing validates the shaman's journey, struggle, and triumph. Persons who have grown up with electric lights, televisions, and movies may find it hard to empathize or even imagine societies submerged in frightening nightly darkness or, in the far north, months of wintery gloom. Shamanic performances combined the competition of sports, the terror of blood sacrifice, the suspense of life-and-death struggle, and the narrativity of drama and storytelling – all thrillingly incorporated into music, song, dance, costumes, and masks. Having written this, I note also its opposite. In their 1973 film, *Magical Death*, Timothy Asch and Napoleon Chagnon document a shamanic journey-struggle among the Yanomamo of the Amazon rain forest where the shamans' bodies remain in their hammocks as their spirits fly forth (see www.der.org/films/magical-death.html).

Masks, puppets, and other performing objects

What happens when actors are not people at all, but masks and puppets? A mask is more than a way to cloak the identity of the masker. A puppet is more than dead wood or flat leather animated by human actors. Masks and puppets actually constitute second beings who interact with the human actors. These performing objects are suffused with a life force capable of transforming those who play with and through them. In Japan, a noh actor will sometimes sleep next to the mask of a role he is to play so that the mask will meld with him. A Balinese performer assesses each new mask, looking for ways to let its life enter into his body (**see Emigh box**). The *chapayeka* masks of the Yaquis of Mexico and the United States are the many faces of Judas who pursue Jesus during the annual six-week long *Waehma* (*Passion Play*). Chapayeka masks possess such strong negative force that at the end of Waehma they are burned as their wearers rush into the church to renew communion with the tribe and with God (**see figure 6.21**). Because new masks are made each year, the visible aspect of Judas changes over time.

The *dhalang* of Javanese *wayang kulit* (leather puppets) is both shaman and puppeteer. He alone manipulates and gives voice to the myriad puppet characters of dramas that last for eight hours without pause. The narratives of wayang kulit are all-inclusive, spanning the mythic and the modern, the gods, demons, and humans. Improvised banter attacking local and national excesses is interwoven with set dialogues. The puppets vary also, keeping up with the times without losing touch with tradition. Puppets depict boys on motorbikes, fat

fig 6.21. At the end of the Yaqui Waehma, a Native People–Christian syncretic Lent-to-Easter performance, the Chapayekas are defeated, their masks burned. Photograph by Western Ways. Photograph courtesy of Richard Schechner.

John Emigh

The living mask

When a Balinese actor holds a new mask in his right hand, gazing upon it, turning it this way and that, making it move to a silent music, he is assessing the potential life of the mask and searching for the meeting place between himself and the life inherent in its otherness. If he is successful, then a bonding takes place that will allow him to let the potential life flow through his own body. If he finds that place of congruence between his physical and spiritual resources and the potential life of the mask, then a living amalgam is created: a character, a persona. This amalgam is at best unstable – based as it must be upon paradox, ambiguity, and illusion – but "it" moves, "it" speaks, "it" breathes, "it" is perceived – by the performer and by the audience – as having an organic integrity. If the performer fails to find such a meeting place within this field of paradox, ambiguity, and illusion, then the mask will retain its separateness: whatever its worth as an object, a "work" of art, it will at best function as a decoration, a costume element. The process begins with a respect for the mask's potential life as a separate entity and proceeds by narrowing the gap between self and other through a process of imaginative play.

1996, *Masked Performance*, 275

divine clowns, the heroes of the *Mahabharata*, and many more (**see figure 6.22**). Dhalangs are spiritually powerful people, even if they (like actors almost everywhere) are often also wanderers and outcasts. They draw their authority from the performance knowledge they embody and from the puppets. In Japanese *bunraku*, three persons manipulate each puppet – one controls the head and right arm, one the left arm, and one the feet. A chanter accompanied by a *samisen* (stringed instrument) narrates the story. But bunraku acting is not dispersed. Everything is focused on the puppets. Their presence unifies the performance.

In the political and criminal vein, masks can be used both to hide identities and to shape public opinion. For example, in March 2001, leaders of the Zapatista movement of Mexican indigenous peoples traveled from Chiapas to Mexico City to present their grievances and hopes to the Mexican Congress. At one and the same time, the Zapatistas were heroes and outlaws, rebels and citizens. Their leader, who operates under the pseudonym Subcomandante Marcos, was not present. The 23-member group was led by Commander Esther, a Mayan woman. The whole delegation wore black ski masks which they said symbolized the "facelessness of indigenous people in Mexico" (**see figure 6.23**).

Hybrid acting

Many actors do not strictly adhere to the categories I have discussed. In one and the same performance, an actor may perform realistically, use a mask, combine codified behavior with improvisation, and in other ways jump or elide the boundaries between kinds of acting. But the question remains

fig 6.22. *Wayang kulit*, Javanese shadow puppet theatre.

The view from in front of the screen watching the shadows cast by the puppets. Photograph by Richard Schechner.

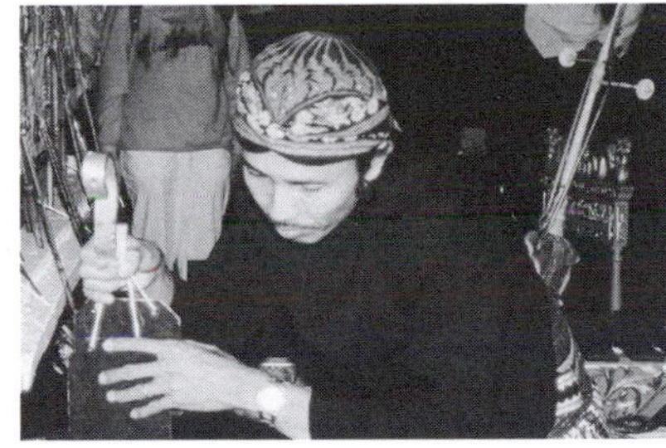

The view from behind the screen watching the dhalang manipulate the puppets. Photograph by Richard Schechner.

fig 6.23. Photo on left shows Subcomandante Marcos saluting. Photo on right shows two Zapatistas. They wear ski masks in order to symbolize the "facelessness of indigenous people in Mexico." Photos by La Voz de Azatlan.

whether hybrid acting is a melding or a quilt. For the most part, it is a quilt, moving from one kind of acting to another. It is difficult to imagine how to blend codified or trance acting with realistic acting. By definition, Brechtian acting does not blend in with other kinds of acting but can be used side by side with any kind.

But sometimes a performer is able to create a unity that draws on several kinds of acting. For example, **Anna Deavere Smith** in her celebrated one-woman performances *Fires in the Mirror* and *Twilight Los Angeles* enacts many points of view of different persons who were involved in momentous, violent events that millions of people know through the

Anna Deavere Smith (1950–): American actor, performance artist, and writer best known for her one-woman shows – *Fires in the Mirror* (1992) and *Twilight LA* (1993) – in which she embodied individual responses to the violent crises that shook their communities. Author of *Talk to Me: Listening Between the Lines* (2000) and *House Arrest* (2004).

fig 6.24. Anna Deavere Smith embodying three of the many persons in who populate *Twilight Los Angeles*, film version, 2001.

As Cornel West. Photograph by Adger W. Cowans. Photograph courtesy of Anna Deavere Smith.

As Gina Rae, also known as Queen Malkah. Photograph by Adger W. Cowans. Photograph courtesy Anna Deavere Smith.

As Katie Miller. Photograph Adger W. Cowans. Photograph courtesy of Anna Deavere Smith.

media (**see figure 6.24**). *Fires in the Mirror* deals with the confrontation among African-Americans, Jews, and the police in Brooklyn in 1991; *Twilight Los Angeles* with the riots in Los Angeles that followed the acquittal of the policemen who beat **Rodney King**. Smith develops her performances out of in-depth interviews she makes with many who were involved in the events. Smith studies the body language, gestures, and vocal patterns of ordinary people in the street, victims, accused, community and political leaders, and academic pundits. The result is something more than imitation or impersonation. Smith's own body-spirit becomes a site for the playing out of many of the conflicts troubling American society, especially those about race, ethnicity, and neighborhood. Smith is actually very like a dhalang. Like a dhalang, Smith takes into herself the events of the community. She gives back to the community both the facts and her own inimitable interpretation. We witness her struggling to take it all in and make sense of it all. Sometimes she "fails" to make a smooth performance. Smith is to some degree possessed by those she represents. By carefully juxtaposing one character, one incorporation, to another, she opens Brechtian spaces for humor, irony, and social dialogue.

Rodney King (1966–): African-American motorist who in 1991 was chased down a highway, taken from his car, and beaten by four Los Angeles policemen. Even though he did not resist, King was struck more than 50 times with metal batons. From a nearby apartment, George Holliday videotaped the beating – Holliday's videotape was repeatedly broadcast on television. In April 1992, after a trial in California State Court and despite the graphic evidence, three of the policemen were acquitted (no verdict was reached on the fourth). The acquittals ignited rioting in Los Angeles. Fifty-three people died, 7,000 were arrested, and property damages totaled more than 1 billion dollars. In 1993 a US Federal Court found two of the four policemen guilty of violating King's civil rights. They served two years in prison.

Performing in everyday life

How different is performing in "real life" from acting in a play? Sometimes performing in everyday life is casual, almost unnoticeable, as when a person slightly adjusts an aspect of the presentation of self or personality – a change of clothes, a tone of voice – to impress someone else. If this is carried to an extreme, one might say, "Sally is showing off." Some everyday-life performances are so subtle and informal that you don't even know that someone is performing – for example, when a parent "talks down" to a small child or the child raises the pitch of his voice in order to ask for ice cream. On the other hand, many everyday-life performers – such as clergy, nurses, and police – are clearly marked by special clothes and insignia, prescribed tones of voice and professional vocabularies, and the visible exercise of authority (**see figure 6.25**). Other performances in everyday life are very like stage dramas. The actions of prosecutor, defense, judge, and jury at a high-visibility criminal trial, the behavior of doctors at work when a life is at risk, or the public appearances of a head of state during a national crisis. All are inherently dramatic because the stakes are high and the behavior of the participants is so well established that it is as if a script is being enacted. That is why these situations are favored subjects from *Oedipus* to *ER*. *Oedipus* combines the plight of a head of state in crisis, a detective story, a trial, and a shamanistic exorcism.

fig. 6.25. A British policeman leads a young boy away from a demonstration where things are turning violent. Photograph by Homer Sykes. Copyright Camera Press, 1982, London.

In Chapter 5, I discussed performing in everyday life as it relates to performativity, especially the constructions of gender and race. Here I will elaborate on the subject not from the perspective of speech acts or poststructuralism, but from the vantage of Erving Goffman's work (**see Brissett and Edgley box**). The theorists discussed in Chapter 5 begin with language. Even when dealing with behavior they take a language-centric position. For them, behavior – indeed all culture – is to be "read" as complex, interacting texts. Goffman, on the other hand, approaches social life as theatre, an interplay of behaviors where players with different motives rehearse their actions, maneuver to present themselves advantageously, and often perform at cross purposes with one another. Where the adherents of the two approaches agree is in the assertion that people are performing all the time whether or not they are aware of it (**see Goffman box 1**).

Dennis Brissett and Charles Edgley

Goffman's reality

Goffman's insistence that social life can be understood as a series of performances was tied to an understanding that still strikes many people as strange and contradictory: that the most revealing insights to be gleaned about human beings lie simply in a close look at what is right on the surface. Appearance is real. [. . .] Appearance can never be destroyed by "reality," but only be replaced by other appearances. [. . .] So Goffman wrote about guises, semblances, veneers, surfaces, illusions, images, shells, and acts. He was not, as most scholars pompously try to bill themselves, about substances, things, facts, truth, and depths. But more importantly, Goffman's argument dissolves the very distinction between the merely apparent and the fundamentally real in social life. Life to him appeared to consist of various levels of understanding and awareness, not of layers covering a fundamental core which could be duly revealed by proper scientific work. As a result, he appeared to reverse the order of everything. The theatre of performances is not in people's heads, it is in their public acts. People encounter each other's minds only by interacting, the quality and character of these interactions comes to constitute the consequential reality of everyday life. In everyday life things really are as they seem to be; but "how they seem to be" is ever changing.

1990, "The Dramaturgical Perspective", 36–37

Erving Goffman

Performances of everyday life

The legitimate performances of everyday life are not "acted" or "put on" in the sense that the performer knows in advance just what he is going to do, and does this solely because of the effect it is likely to have. The expression it is felt he is giving off will be especially "inaccessible" to him. But as in the case of less legitimate performers, the incapacity of the ordinary individual to formulate in advance the movements of his eyes and body does not mean that he will not express himself through these devices in a way that is dramatized and pre-formed in his repertoire of actions. In short, we act better than we know how.

1959, *The Presentation of Self in Everyday Life*, 73–74

All actors are performers, but not all performers are actors. In theory, one can specify the difference between actors and performers. But in practice these differences are in the process of collapsing. Stage actors enact roles composed by others, repeat these roles on a regular basis before audiences who know that the actors are pretending to be who they enact. In spectator sports, the situation is complicated. Athletes are not pretending, but they are performing. They focus on accomplishing tasks specific to particular sports ("ball play," "fighting," "racing," "jumping," "weight lifting," etc.) at the same time as they display themselves publicly. The build-up to a big game is part of the whole event. And although athletes are not pretending to be anyone, the more famous an athlete becomes, the more her actions in certain ways approach those of the stage actor. The exercise of skills remains the core performance, but the bigger the star, the more the presentation of self becomes character acting. Performing in everyday life involves people in a wide range of activities from solo or intimate performances behind closed doors to small group activities to interacting as part of a crowd. Sometimes performing in everyday life uses consciously enacted conventional behaviors, as at a formal dinner party or a funeral; sometimes the scenario of everyday life is loose, as when you are walking down the street in casual conversation with a friend. Most of daily living is taken up by performing job, professional, family, and social roles. Each of these, in every culture, comes equipped with ways of behaving and interacting. Everyone masters to some degree or another the social codes of daily life. Rebels intentionally break the rules; revolutionaries want to change them permanently.

To what degree is human social life an unending stream of performances? George Washington, the first American president, was no stranger to the eighteenth-century equivalent of a "photo op" or to carefully crafting his persona along theatrical lines (**see Marshall box**). Staging key life moments go back a lot further than the American Revolution. According to the Roman historian **Suetonius**, Emperor **Caesar Augustus** on the day he died called for a mirror, instructed servants to comb his hair and fix in place his slackened jaw, and then assembled his courtiers. "Have I played the comedy of life well?" Augustus asked. He didn't wait for their answer, but replied himself, "Since I've played my part well, all clap your hands and dismiss me from the stage with applause." Shortly after, Augustus died. The emperor's deathbed scene is not as extraordinary as it may at first appear. Before the era of nursing homes and mechanically extended lives, carefully staged deathbed scenes were common. In some cultures they still are. But even at less momentous times, theatre haunts everyday life. "You acted bravely," a mother might say in praise to her daughter who stood up to a bullying aunt. This same mother at supper might rebuke her daughter, "Don't stuff your mouth, act more grownup!" Both the praise and the admonition refer to behaviors that are decided and definite, that have a clear shape. We can easily picture such actions in our mind's eye. The words "act" and "action" are citations of not-so-hidden social scripts. Such social scripts permeate daily life. Although social scripts vary from culture to culture and epoch to epoch, there are no cultures or historical periods bereft of social scripts.

Suetonius (*c.* 70–*c.*130): Roman historian, author of *Lives of the Caesars* (*c.* 110).

Caesar Augustus (63 BCE–14 CE): first emperor of Rome. Presided over the expansion of the Roman Empire across Europe and northern Africa.

Increasingly in America, after the 1848 Women's Rights Convention in Seneca Falls, New York and the 1850 First National Women's Right's Convention in Worcester, Massachusetts, women demanded rights equal to those accorded men. But equality did not come fast or without struggle; and still today women – in the USA and elsewhere – are discriminated against because of their gender. In mid-nineteenth-century America, some regarded the very act of speaking publicly outside the home without the "guidance" of men as "brazen" and wrong. One reaction against this first wave of feminism was the appearance of manuals such as Emily Thornwell's *The Lady's Guide to Perfect Gentility* instructing women on how to "behave properly" (**see Thornwell box**). The feminists proposed one script and Thornwell's guide another. As discussed in Chapter 5, manuals such as Thornwell's – as well as many other "how to behave" articles and books from her day to ours – can be analyzed from the point of view of the construction of gender. But why stop with gender? Social behavior is constructed. The matter is complicated because the assertion, "Now I am performing" is often met by another equally insistent assertion, "The role I am playing is me." So where or who is the "real me"? The rules of behavior are obvious with

Joshua Micah Marshall

General George Washington plays his role

As scenes of heroism go, it was an odd one. In the third week of July, 1776, only days after Thomas Jefferson's Declaration of Independence was approved by the Continental Congress, His Excellency General George Washington, commander-in-chief of the Continental Army, was involved in a fastidious exchange with his British counterpart, Lord Richard Howe. [Howe] dispatched a [. . .] letter addressed to "George Washington, Esq." [. . . Washington's staff] rebuffed him, declaring there was "no person in our army with that address." Three days later, Howe's emissary returned with a new copy of the letter – this one addressed to "George Washington, Esq., etc. etc." – only to receive the same rebuff. Finally, Howe sent to inquire whether General Washington would agree to receive a new emissary, Lieutenant Colonel James Paterson [. . .]. After an exchange of pleasantries, Paterson placed on the table before Washington the same letter [. . .]. Washington refused to acknowledge it. Hoping to move the conversation along, Paterson pointed out that the "etc. etc." implied everything that might follow. "Yes, it does," Washington replied, "and anything." [. . .] Washington engaged in this brief drama not only to let Howe know whom he was dealing with but to show his men that he could stand up to anybody George III sent against them. [. . .] Washington [. . .] was never more completely himself than when he was acting. [. . .] From an early age, he submitted his entire persona to the most rigorous discipline, shaping everything from his physical bearing to the degree of intimacy that he allowed himself with friends and associates. By the time he took command of the Army, outside Boston, in July, 1775, there was little about him that was not the product of years of conscious artifice. [. . . H]e was finally handed the role for which he had been preparing all his life: himself.

2005, "National Treasure," 87–90

Emily Thornwell

How a lady ought to behave in public

Propriety of movement and general demeanor in company. To look steadily at any one, especially if you are a lady and are speaking to a gentleman; to turn the head frequently on one side and the other during conversation; to balance yourself upon your chair; to bend forward; to strike your hands upon your knees; to hold one of your knees between your hands locked together; to cross your legs; to extend your feet on the andirons; to admire yourself with complacency in a glass; [. . .] to laugh immoderately; to place your hand upon the person with whom you are conversing; to take him by the buttons, the collar of his cloak, the cuffs, the waist, and so forth; to seize any person by the waist or arm, or to touch their person; [. . .] to rub your face or your hands; wink your eyes; shrug up your shoulders; stamp with your feet, and so forth; – all these bad habits, of which we cannot speak to people, are in the highest degree displeasing.

1856, *The Lady's Guide to Perfect Gentility in Manners, Dress, and Conversation*, 87–88

regard to established roles such as "mother," "doctor," "teacher," "child," and so on. The specific gestures, tones of voice, costume, and such, appropriate to many social roles are well known. But the roles and the rules vary from place to place, circumstance to circumstance. For example, the roles of "bus driver" or "hairdresser" may be well known in one society and unknown in another; and the appropriate behavior for "bus driver," "hairdresser," etc., may vary from one society to another. But whatever the roles, disrupting accepted codes of behavior will meet with reprimands ranging from "Go to your room!" to "You are in contempt of court", and more." Serious violations can get a person excommunicated, ostracized, jailed, or executed. Role-specific and situation-specific behaviors govern all social interactions. Sometimes the scripts are relatively loose, as in conventions; sometimes fairly strict, as in rules; and sometimes very strict, as in laws. But however strictly or loosely determined, social behavior is never free and unbound. The lived details of the expected behaviors constitute the performances of social life.

But what happens in less guarded moments, when people are "off duty" – when the judge is not judging, the teacher not teaching, the parent not parenting? During these times, the performance aspect of ordinary behavior is less obvious, but not absent. One sets aside formal enactments to play roles that allow more leeway in behavior, that are less like scripted dramas and more like loose improvisations. People become "just friends," the judge shows that he is "an ordinary Joe like me," the house-cleaner sits down with the house-owner for a cup of tea. But "friend" and "ordinary Joe" are also roles – ones that blend into the background of ongoing social life rather than stand out as highly marked. Goffman felt that all social encounters were theatre-like because "life itself is a dramatically enacted thing" (**see Goffman box 2**).

One might say that the more public and "larger than life" the social role, the more it is like theatre. The American

Erving Goffman

Is all the world a stage?

It does take deep skill, long training, and psychological capacity to become a good stage actor. But this fact should not blind us to another one: that almost anyone can quickly learn a script well enough to give a charitable audience some sense of realness in what is being contrived before them. And it seems this is so because ordinary social intercourse is itself put together as a scene is put together, by the exchange of dramatically inflated actions, counteractions, and terminating replies. Scripts even in the hands of unpracticed players can come to life because life itself is a dramatically enacted thing. All the world is not, of course, a stage, but the crucial ways in which it isn't are not easy to specify.

1959, *The Presentation of Self in Everyday Life*, 71–72

president adheres to a tightly scripted schedule, reads speeches written for him, and follows strictly enforced protocol. He even memorizes the apparently impromptu answers given to reporters or the adlibs shouted to the crowds who greet him as he travels around the country. Of course, the monarch of England has long been more a theatrical role than an actual decision-making one. But the pomp and circumstance, the stuff of royal ritual, has a big effect on political and social life. The membrane separating what "appears" and what "is" is very thin and porous.

In the theatre, the actor and the audience both know that the actor is "not" who she is playing. But in "real life" a person is simultaneously performing herself and being herself. The matter is, of course, nicely complicated because in some methods of realistic acting, actors are taught how to use their own selves to construct theatrical roles. This technique of "pretending to be really myself" or "building the character from myself" has permeated society, and not only in the West. Through the media and more recently by means of the internet, people in everyday life play many roles, have access to numerous avatars. Advertising encourages people to believe that by means of cosmetics, surgery, mood-altering drugs, exercise, diet, hairstyle, and clothes one can radically change personality. Who "I am" is no longer a given, if it ever was. As the number of available "new selves" increases weekly, the media emphasize that no self need be permanent. Continuous alteration is possible. This promise of mutability entices people into playing more and more roles, discovering as many variations of themselves as possible. As never before, people are performing their multiple selves all day, every day.

Trials and executions as performance

Courtroom trials are inherently dramatic. The "crime drama" presents contested versions of what happened; the "courtroom drama" pits the prosecuting attorneys against the defense attorneys with the judge as referee (**see Harbinger box**). The jury decides who wins, who loses. Prosecution and defense construct contradictory narratives from evidence and testimony. The crime drama nested inside the courtroom drama consists in molding the forensic evidence and witness testimony into two mutually contradictory narratives forcing the jury to decide which story is "the truth" – or, in the American system, to determine if guilt has been proven "beyond a reasonable doubt." In the process, each side tries to undermine the opponent's narrative. Truth in a trial is not so much what "really happened" as it is a test of which side is more adept at using the law and shaping the data – at "building a case." The judge keeps the attorneys in line, interprets the law to the jury, and maintains order in court. High-visibility trials of famous persons, trials depicting horrendous crimes, and trials of political importance attract multiple audiences arranged in concentric circles. The outermost circle of spectators can sometimes be in the millions. But it all starts at the local level. Jury trials feature an inner circle of judge, defendant(s), and attorneys – with the jury as participant observers. The next circle consists of the "interested parties" – relatives and friends/enemies of the defendant or the victim(s). Most trials also receive at least a few people who cruise courthouses in search of entertainment. This entertainment interest is fueled by the media. **Court TV** broadcasts a stream of trials, sensational and mundane, enhanced by legal reporting and analysis by day and trial-based dramas and programmings at night. Viewers regard trials as reality television or a kind of sports show. If a case involves a celebrity or is for other reasons of general interest, the courtroom space becomes crowded; the press acts as a surrogate audience reporting to the public who isn't able to be present in person. Important trials attract viewers removed in time as well as space – people who find out what happened via news broadcasts or the papers and magazines. Finally, come historians, professors, and students studying trials centuries or even millennia later as with the Inquisition's treatment of Galileo or the trial of Socrates. On the flip side are daytime television shows such as *Divorce Court* or *Judge Judy* which exploit the theatricality of trials.

Court TV: an American cable channel seen in 83 million homes that – in its own words – is the leader in the investigation genre, providing a window on the American system of justice through distinctive programming that both informs and entertains. Court TV telecasts high-profile trials by day and original programs like *Forensic Files*, *Psychic Detectives*, *Masterminds*, and *Impossible Heists* in primetime. [. . .] Trial coverage, the cornerstone of Court TV's daytime programming, focuses on newsworthy and controversial legal proceedings, delivering powerful, real-life drama that provides a window on the justice system (adapted from www.courttv.com/about/). Obviously, Court TV intentionally blurs the boundary between the legal system and entertainment.

"Show trials" are so named because the outcome is determined in advance (as in a play) and the trials are designed to show the power of the state and, sometimes, to terrify the public. "Killing a chicken to scare the monkeys," goes an old

Richard Harbinger

Trial by drama

An adversary trial is a dramatic thing put to legal use. [. . .] When one observes an adversary trial, he sees a play; when he observes a while longer, he perceives a play within the play. This is the essential, ineluctable form of the adversary trial: a "play without" and a "play within." And from this form all else naturally proceeds: double plots, double casts, double settings, double audiences, and double effects. [. . .]

A "play within a play" is [. . .] a crime drama within a courtroom drama. [. . .] People v X is the archetype of a million murder trials – past, present, and future. [. . .] The courtroom drama ("the play without") stages the legal combat between the prosecuting attorney and the defense attorney. [. . .] The "play within" tells the story of the alleged killing by the defendant. [. . .] A courtroom drama stars the prosecuting attorney and the defense attorney, and the title page of the transcript gives them top billing. The starring attorneys get most of the dialogue and the action and they do most of the emoting and agonizing. It is only in a legal sense that the people win or lose; in a dramatic sense the attorneys win or lose. The crime drama, on the other hand, stars the defendant, and sometimes the victim. [. . .] The drama of the courtroom takes place in the courtroom, while the drama of the crime takes place elsewhere.

1971, "Trial by Drama," 122–24

Chinese proverb. The Moscow trials of 1936–38 eliminated rivals real and imagined of dictator **Joseph Stalin**. Every detail of the trials was predetermined – the accusations, the confessions, and the sentencing. No one was acquitted, most were executed. The Moscow trials were accompanied by a government-orchestrated massive propaganda campaign. Show trials can sometimes be on the "good side" – for example, the **Nuremberg Trials** of Nazi war criminals after World War II or the war crimes trial against **Slobodan Milosevic** begun in 2002. While on trial, Milosevic died of natural causes in his jail cell. Although such trials are not entirely scripted, people know how they will turn out. Many feel that Milosevic – like Hermann Goering, the Nazi bigwig who committed suicide in his cell – cheated justice. At one level, all trials are show trials demonstrating the authority of the convening power – a single nation, a consortium of victors, or the United Nations – and the viability of a society's justice system. Sometimes, however, what a show trial shows is the opposite of what the rulers intend.

The first trial broadcast on television was that of the Nazi Adolf Eichmann who in 1961 was tried and condemned to death by an Israeli court in Jerusalem for his leading role in the Holocaust. During the trial, Eichmann was kept in a bulletproof glass box where he could be safe from harm, displayed, and morally quarantined (**see figure 6.26**). The 1995 murder trial of former football and movie star **O. J. Simpson** was watched live by millions. Winning acquittal

Joseph Stalin (1879–1953): Communist ruler of the Soviet Union from 1928 until his death. Stalin – "man of steel" – was the name he chose for himself (born "Dzhugashvili"). Once in power, Stalin ruthlessly disposed of his rivals in the Great Purge of the 1930s. During World War II, he allied the USSR with the Western powers. After Germany and Japan were defeated in 1945, the alliance disintegrated and the Cold War ensued. Under Stalin, the USSR became a superpower, but the brutality of his rule was repudiated by Nikita Kruschchev in 1956.

Nuremberg Trials: from 1945 to 1949 in twelve separate trials, over 100 top Nazi leaders, lesser government officials, judges, doctors, soldiers, and industrialists were tried in tribunals convened by the victors – the USA, UK, USSR, and France. Most of the accused were convicted, 25 were executed, and a few acquitted. Several defendants cheated the gallows by committing suicide, including Field Marshal Hermann Goering.

Slobodan Milosevic (1941–2006): Serbian leader who in the 1990s used "ethnic cleansing" – a genocidal policy directed against non-Serbs, especially Muslims – in Bosnia and then in Kosovo, both regions of the former Yugoslavia. Defeated in elections in 2000, but at first refusing to leave office, Milosevic was arrested in 2001 and turned over to the war crimes tribunal in The Hague. He died before his trial was concluded.

fig 6.26. Adolf Eichmann, the Nazi overseer of the Holocaust, on display in a glass box during his trial in Jerusalem, 1961. Eichmann was executed in 1962. Photograph reproduced on the internet at http//remember.org/eichmann/eich1.htm.

O. J. Simpson (1947–): American football star and then movie actor, television commentator, and pitchman who was tried in 1995 for the murders of his former wife Nicole Brown Simpson and her companion Ron Goldman. Simpson was acquitted, but later Nicole's family won a large award in civil court.

Johnnie Cochran (1937–2005): the American lawyer who successfully defended O. J. Simpson on murder charges. Before defending Simpson, Cochran had a long and successful career – but the Simpson trial made Cochran a national figure. After the acquittal, Cochran hosted his own Court TV show and appeared as a guest on many talk shows. Cochran wrote two books: *Journey to Justice* (1996) and *A Lawyer's Life* (2002).

for his client turned defense attorney **Johnnie Cochran** into a star in his own right. Because of the enormity of his crime, and the newness of using television in this way, the Eichmann trial was treated with respect. But by the time of Simpson's trial, there had been a plethora of TV pseudo-trials as entertainment. The Simpson trial combined Hollywood, big-time sports, miscegenation, jealousy, and murder. Although he played innocent (and was acquitted), Simpson was widely regarded as guilty. There was something bigger than life about the trial that fascinated Americans. Simpson's story, like that of the great theatrical murderers – Oedipus, Hamlet, Clytemnestra, Othello – could not be resolved by the jury's verdict of "innocent". The "whole truth" may never be known, cannot be reduced to the "facts". But, finally, rather than rising to Shakespearean heights, the Simpson trial was soap-opera melodrama. Soon after the trial, a four-videotape documentary made from the trial went on sale. More videos followed. It's not the search for truth that attracts audiences to such trials. The Simpson trial was about much more than who murdered Nicole Brown Simpson and Ronald Goldman. It was about race relations in the US, the lifestyle of the rich and famous, sex, jealousy, and the kind of justice money can buy. And what does it say about the public imagination that Googling "Adolf Eichmann" in June 2005 came up with 188,000 sites versus 610,000 for "O.J. Simpson," and 1,340,000 for "Johnnie Cochran"?

After a guilty verdict comes the sentencing and punishment. As noted in Chapter 4, executions have long been theatrical spectacles. In medieval and Renaissance Europe, both the condemned and spectators prepared for the big event. Before mounting the scaffold, the condemned delivered orations while spectators picnicked. Even Christ's Crucifixion was poeticized as theatre (**see Herrick box**). In many parts of the world, the death penalty has been outlawed. But where it persists people pay attention. The condemned's "last meal" and "final words" are reported.

Robert Herrick

Jesus Christ, actor

Put off Thy Robe of Purple, then go on
To the sad place of execution:
Thine houre is come; and the Tormentor stands
Ready, to pierce Thy tender Feet and Hands.
[. . .]
The Crosse shall be Thy Stage; and Thou shalt there
The spacious field have for thy Theater.
Thou art that Roscius, and that markt-out man,
That must this day act the Tragedian,
To wonder and affrightment: Thou art He,
Whom all the flux of Nations comes to see;
Not those poor Theeves that act their parts with Thee.
[. . .]
Why then begin, great King! ascend Thy Throne,
And thence proceed, to act Thy Passion
To such an height, to such a period rais'd,
As Hell, and Earth, and Heav'n may stand amaz'd.

1956 [1647], "Good Friday: *Rex Tragicus*" in *Poetical Works*, 398–99

Robert Herrick (1591–1674): English poet and cleric whose 1648 collection Hesperides contained 1,200 poems. Herrick wrote about both scared and secular subjects. Herrick's most famous poem, "To the Virgins, To Make Much of Time," begins with the lines: "Gather ye rosebuds while ye may,/ Old time is still a-flying:/ And this same flower that smiles to-day/ Tomorrow will be dying."

When in June, 2001, the Oklahoma City bomber **Timothy McVeigh** was executed by lethal injection, nearly 300 persons – relatives of some of the 168 persons killed in the bombing – watched the execution via closed-circuit television. There was a call to broadcast McVeigh's death on public television or over the internet, but the government denied the requests. Persons gathered near the prison where McVeigh died, some to celebrate the death of a mass murderer and others to protest capital punishment.

Timothy McVeigh (1968–2001): American terrorist convicted and executed for planning and carrying out the bombing in 1995 of the Oklahoma City Federal Office Building. One hundred and sixty-eight persons died in the blast and hundreds more were wounded.

Surgery as performance

Trials put lives at risk and executions take lives. Medical practices – from shamanism to surgery – save lives. I wrote about shamanism earlier in this chapter. I will now discuss aspects of allopathic medicine. The body-in-medicine has long been a biological performative and an artistic subject. An experienced doctor performs his anatomical and diagnostic knowledge when dissecting a cadaver or diagnosing a patient before an audience of fellow doctors or medical students (**see figure 6.27**).

Consider also a surgeon performing in the operating theatre of a teaching hospital. Surgery in a teaching hospital brings into play the concept of "performance" in at least two of its meanings: a showing of a doing and an activity demanding the coordinated efforts of a team working together at an extremely high level of skills. Nurses hover about performing necessary tasks.

The anesthesiologist monitors the patient's breathing and life signs. Let us suppose that also present are interns in training to become surgeons. The surgeon and her team perform on the patient and for the interns. A star surgeon points out what she is doing and why. In addition to its meliorative function, the surgery is a medical performance used for teaching. In some hospitals, a spectators' gallery overlooks the operating room. Some pioneering operations

fig 6.27. Medical procedures, then and now.

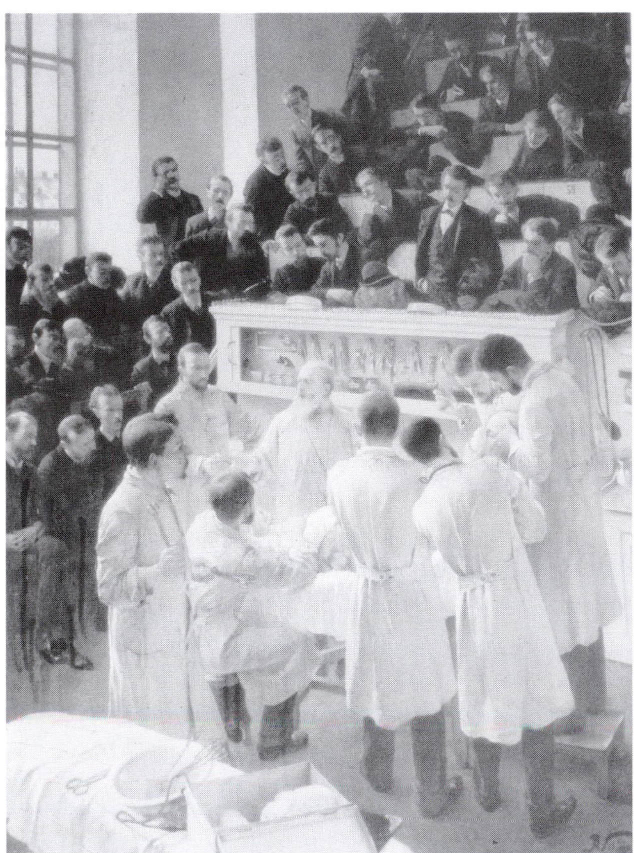

An amputation being performed in the operating theatre of old St. Thomas's Hospital, London, in 1875–76. Note the observers in the gallery. Copyright St. Thomas's Hospital Archive.

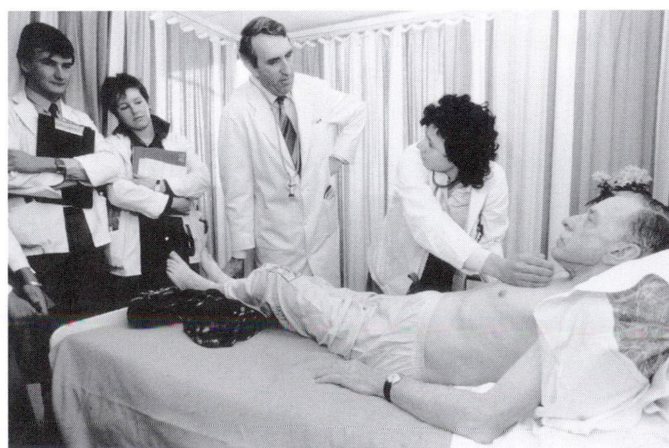

Above, medical students examining a patient under the eyes of a supervising physician in a contemporary teaching hospital. Photograph Homer Sykes. Copyright Camera Press.

are broadcast over closed-circuit television so that doctors in remote locations can watch. This kind of medical performance is nothing new, even if the techniques of dissemination have been enhanced.

Furthermore, isn't the operating theatre similar to the aesthetic theatre in its architecture, roles, costumes, and scripts? The operating room is flanked by backstage areas and dressing rooms where both the patient and the medical team prepare. Different roles are marked by distinctive costumes separating doctors from nurses from patient. Guiding the procedure are sets of known gestures and rituals. A successful operation is one where there is little need for improvisation. But when unpredictable occurrences call for improvised responses, these are based on bits of rehearsed behavior because delays and mistakes can be fatal. What role does the patient play in all this? For the patient, the surgery is a performance in which he is not present at the level of ability to interact consciously. Is the patient a star or a prop? Even before being put under anesthesia, the patient is stripped of key elements of his daily self. He is wrapped in hospital garb, the site of the surgery tightly framed and well lit, discolored by antiseptic, and drawn on with indelible ink. The patient is reduced to the object of the surgical procedure at hand. The real star of the performance is the surgeon. And like the shaman, the surgeon and his helpers battle against an adversary to be excised/exorcised – a tumor or appendix, etc. – or a "condition" to be fixed, a clogged artery or faulty heart valve, etc.

Belief in the role one is playing

To what degree does a person believe her own performance? Goffman noted that self-belief spans a continuum with the tendency to accept ourselves "as performed" (**see Goffman box 3**). Long before Goffman, Nietzsche made a more radical suggestion – that "great deceivers" are so entrancing as performers that they convince themselves of the truth of what they perform. Only when they are saturated with the self-confidence resulting from the power of their own performing are they able to draw others into their magic circle (**see Nietzsche box**). Nietzsche says this is so of the founders of religions, as surely it is of Hitlerian dictators, Churchillian prime ministers, and master hucksters of every kind. We may ask, if the deception is complete, if everyone believes it, is it a lie? Theoretically, if no one stands outside the magic circle, there is no way to measure the veracity of what is declaimed.

It was this kind of monstrous "total theatre" that the Nazis staged inside Germany. **Adolf Hitler**'s frenetic yet

Erving Goffman

Believing the role one plays

At one extreme, one finds that the performer can be fully taken in by his own act; he can be sincerely convinced that the impression of reality which he stages is the real reality. When his audience is also convinced in this way about the show he puts on – and this seems to be the typical case – then for the moment at least, only the sociologist or the socially disgruntled will have any doubts bout the "realness" of what is presented.

At the other extreme, we find that the performer may not be taken in at all by his own routine. This possibility is understandable, since no one is in quite as good an observational position to see through the act as the person who puts it on. [. . .] When the individual has no belief in his own act and no ultimate concern with the beliefs of his audience, we may call him cynical. [. . .] It should be understood that the cynic [. . .] may obtain [. . .] pleasures from his masquerade, experiencing a kind of gleeful spiritual aggression from the fact that he can toy at will with something his audience must take seriously. [. . .] Perhaps the real crime of the confidence man is not that he takes money from his victims but that he robs all of us of the belief that middle-class manners and appearance can be sustained only by middle-class people. [. . .]

These extremes are something a little more than just the ends of a continuum. Each provides the individual with a position which has its own particular securities and defenses, so there will be a tendency for those who have traveled close to one of these poles to complete the voyage.

1959, *The Presentation of Self in Everyday Life*, 17–19

Friedrich **Nietzsche**

The power of believing in the self one is performing

Even when in the deepest distress, the actor ultimately cannot cease to think of the impression he and the whole scenic effect is making, even for example, at the burial of his own child; he will weep over his own distress and the ways in which it expresses itself, as his own audience. [. . .]

If someone obstinately and for a long time wants to appear something it is in the end hard for him to be anything else.

[. . .] With all great deceivers there is a noteworthy occurrence to which they owe their power. In the actual act of deception, with all its preparations, its enthralling voice, expression, and gesture, in the midst of the scenery designed to give it effect, they are overcome by belief in themselves: it is this which then speaks so miraculously and compellingly to those who surround them. The founders of religions are distinguished from these great deceivers by the fact that they never emerge from this state of self-deception: or very rarely they experience for once that moment of clarity when doubt overcomes them; usually, however, they comfort themselves by ascribing these moments of clarity to the evil antagonist. Self-deception has to exist if a grand effect is to be produced. For men believe in the truth of that which is plainly strongly believed.

1986 [1878], *Human, All Too Human*, 39–40

well-prepared orations, the pageantry of mass rallies, and the parades of the armed forces were as important to the Nazi state as the terror of the Gestapo. The massive Nuremberg rallies of the 1920s and 1930s solidified the party faithful. In 1936, 100,000 Nazi officers assembled in the outdoor site, flanked by a "cathedral of light" made by powerful anti-aircraft searchlights aimed directly up into the night sky (**see figure 6.28**). At Nuremberg, and in other Nazi shows, theatre went beyond the theatre. **Albert Speer**'s lights, the massed military cohorts carrying thousands of flags and other Nazi paraphernalia, the Hitler-adoring roars of "Heil!" and the Führer's cadenced, shrill oratory combined to enact a fantasy of the "thousand-year Reich" played by "pure-Aryan German *volk*" (folk, people, community). The Gestapo terror eliminated Hitler's enemies, while the pageantry solidified his popular support. This total theatre drew on the "movement choirs" of **Rudolf von Laban**, who staged displays for the 1936 Berlin Olympics and the lighting, and architectural designs of Speer (**see Speer box**). The ideas of Laban and Speer were to some degree derived from the work of two important performance personages, theatre-design visionary **Adolphe Appia** and the founder of eurhythmics, **Emile Jaques-Dalcroze**. Appia and Dalcroze worked with each other before the First World War and Laban was one of Dalcroze's students. In other words, it's

Adolf Hitler (1889–1945): Austrian-born dictator of Germany from 1933 to 1945. In 1921 Hitler became the Nazi leader; by 1932 the Nazis were Germany's largest party. Hitler became Chancellor in 1933, re-titling himself "Führer" (Leader). By ordering the invasion of Poland in 1939, Hitler started World War II. A virulent anti-Semite, Hitler set the highest priority on the "final solution," the Holocaust. When he faced total defeat, Hitler committed suicide. Author of *Mein Kampf* (*My Struggle*, 2001 [1925–26]).

Albert Speer (1905–81): Hitler's architect and later director of war industries during the 1940s. For the Nazi Nuremberg Rally of 1936, Speer designed a "cathedral of light" by aiming batteries of anti-aircraft searchlights directly up. Convicted of war crimes, Speer served 20 years and was released in 1966. Author of *Inside the Third Reich* (1997 [1970]).

Rudolf von Laban (1879–1958): German dance pioneer whose work included movement choirs, expressionist dance, and the development of a system of movement notation still widely used today. Laban for a time willingly worked for the Nazis until he was "dismissed" in 1936 because of his "decadent choreography."

fig 6.28. A night-time rally of Nazis in Nuremberg, 1935. Note the "cathedral of light" formed by aiming hundreds of anti-aircraft searchlights straight up. Spectacle and invented rituals helped the Nazis arouse and control their adherents. Copyright Corbis.

Albert Speer

A rally of the Nazi party at Nuremberg

Every year a rally was held at the Zeppelin field for the assemblage of middle and minor party functionaries [. . .]. I explained my plan to the organization leaders of the Party Rally. The thousands of flags belonging to all the local groups in Germany were to be held in readiness behind the high fences surrounding the field. The flag bearers were to divide into ten columns, forming lanes in which the Amtsverwalter [party officials] would march up. Since all this was to take place at evening, bright spotlights would be cast on these banners and the great eagle crowning them all. That alone would have a dramatic effect. But even this did not seem sufficient to me. I had occasionally seen our new anti-aircraft searchlights blazing miles into the sky. I asked Hitler to let me have a hundred and thirty of these. [. . .]

The actual effect far surpassed anything I had imagined. The hundred and thirty sharply defined beams, placed around the field at intervals of forty feet, were visible to a height of twenty to twenty-five thousand feet, after which they merged into a general glow. The feeling was of a vast room, with the beams serving as mighty pillars of infinitely high outer walls. Now and then the clouds move through this wreath of lights, bringing an element of surprise to the mirage. I imagine that this "cathedral of light" was the first luminescent architecture of this type, and for me it remains not only my most beautiful architectural concept but, after its fashion, the only one which survived the passage of time.

1997 [1970], *Inside the Third Reich*, 58–59

Adolphe Appia (1862–1928): Swiss visionary opera and stage designer who was particularly fascinated by the possibilities of "living light." He also advocated abstract rather than romantic or naturalistic stage settings. His practical work and theories have had a deep impact on modern theatre lighting and stage design. Many of his important ideas are contained in *Adolphe Appia: Texts on Theatre* (1993).

Émile Jaques-Dalcroze (1865–1950): Swiss educator and originator of "eurhythmics," a system combining music, rhythm, and movement. The goal of Dalcroze's method is to integrate all the senses in the service of aesthetics. Dalcroze's method continues to be widely practiced and influential.

not possible to sift out "art" from "politics." The two were profoundly intermeshed then and now – as the mobilization of public opinion (directly or via media) constitutes a decisive base of political, military, state, and economic power.

On a more quotidian level, a person's sense of self is very much tied to her ability to believe in the roles she plays. The matter is complicated because the roles are not played by a single, stable self. The self is created by the roles even as it plays them – a psychological mobius strip keeps turning outside into inside and inside into outside. Nor are all social roles played equally well. How well a person plays a social role usually depends on how much the person believes in the role. In ordinary life, a person plays to two audiences at the same time: oneself, and the social audience. "Insincerity" as an experience is the interior mode of "hypocrisy" as a social fact. The question remains, to what audience ought

Henry David Thoreau (1817–62): American writer who championed peaceful "civil disobedience" as a way to protest oppressive or illegal acts by the government. He also cherished the "simple life" as detailed in his best-known work, *Walden* (1854).

a person pay more attention? Should we, as **Henry David Thoreau** advised, listen to our own internal drumbeat; or ought we tune ourselves to the demands of social life? There is no correct answer. There are only varying degrees of response. History offers plenty of examples on both sides of the case, ranging from martyrs who died for their beliefs to monarchs who adapted in order to save their crowns.

How realistic is realistic acting?

Ever since Charles Darwin published his *The Expression of Emotions in Man and Animals* in 1872, scientists have proposed behavior as part of the evolutionary development of the human species. Ethology, sociobiology, and kinesics are based on the assumption that behavior has evolved in a way analogous to the evolution of human anatomy. Behavior is very complex, ranging from simple motor activities like grasping, running, and jumping to the expression of emotions and intentions by means of facial displays, body gestures, tone of voice, and so on. The term "body language" refers to these expressions. **Paul Ekman** proposes that the facial displays of six "target emotions" (happiness, sadness, anger, fear, disgust, and surprise) are recognizably similar in all cultures. Long before Darwin, actors knew that emotional expression could be codified. As noted earlier in this chapter, two millennia ago Bharata set down in the *Natyasastra* the details of a codified system of emotional expression strikingly similar to Ekman's (**see figure 6.29**). In the West in 1839, **François Delsarte** began his *cours d'esthétique appliqué* (course in applied aesthetics), a system coordinating gestures, voice, and emotional expression (**see Stebbins box**).

What is the relationship between the "natural" displays studied by Darwin and Ekman and the codified aesthetic

Paul Ekman (1934–): American psychologist. Leading authority on the expression of emotions by the human face. Ekman has tried to prove that these emotional expressions are universal. Among his many books: *Unmasking the Face* (1975, with Wallace V. Friesen), *Emotion in the Human Face* (1982), *Telling Lies* (1985), *The Nature of Emotion* (1994, with Richard J. Davidson) *Emotions Revealed* (2003), and *What the Face Reveals* (2005, with Erika L. Rosenberg).

Genevieve Stebbins

The Delsarte system

A perfect reproduction of the outer manifestation of some passion, the giving of the outer sign, will cause a reflex feeling within. [. . .] Certain attitudes, by extending or contracting the muscles, by compelling the breath to come and go more rapidly, by increasing the heart-beats, cause physical interior sensations which are the correspondences of emotion. [. . .] In emotion, if the hand seeks the chin, vital instincts predominate: namely, appetites, passions; while if the hand seeks the forehead, the mental instincts predominate; if the hand touches the cheeks, the moral instincts; that is, the affections, predominate. [. . .] Excitement or passion tends to expand the gesture; thought or reflection tends to contract gesture; love or affection tends to moderate gesture. Thus, passion tends to extreme expansion of the muscles; thought tends to extreme contraction of the muscles; affection tends to a happy medium of activity of the muscles. [. . .]

1977 [1902], *Delsarte System of Expression*, 141, 217–18, 258–59

François Delsarte (1811–71): French teacher of acting and singing. Originator of a complex system coordinating facial displays, hand gestures, movements, and voice to express specific emotions. His ideas are summarized in Genevieve Stebbins' *Delsarte System of Expression* (1977 [1902]).

systems proposed by Bharata and Delsarte? All we can be sure of is that both ordinary behavior and aesthetic behavior are codified. Ordinary behavior does not appear to be codified because people perform ordinary behavior day in, day out – it's as "natural" to them as speaking their mother tongue. Are ordinary behaviors as culturally distinct as spoken languages? The answer is both yes and no. Whole suites of gestures, signs, inflections, and emphases are culture-specific. At the same time, even when persons can't converse in a spoken language, gesturing gets meanings across. Some expressions and gestures – the happy smile, lifting the nose in disgust, the wide eyes of surprise, bringing the hands to the mouth signalling the desire for food – occur in many if not all human cultures. Perhaps the physical displays are universal, while meanings vary from culture to culture and even

fig 6.29. A comparison of performances of the rasas, or basic emotions as described by Bharata in the *Natyasastra* and identified as universal by Paul Ekman. Ekman photographs from *Unmasking the Face* (1975) courtesy of Paul Ekman and Wallace V. Freisen. Rasa photographs courtesy of Phillip Zarrilli.

Natyasastra

Ekman

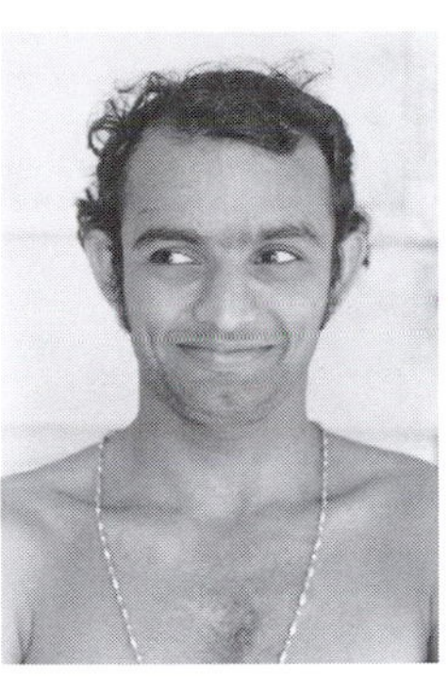

Sringara: love, happiness

Happiness

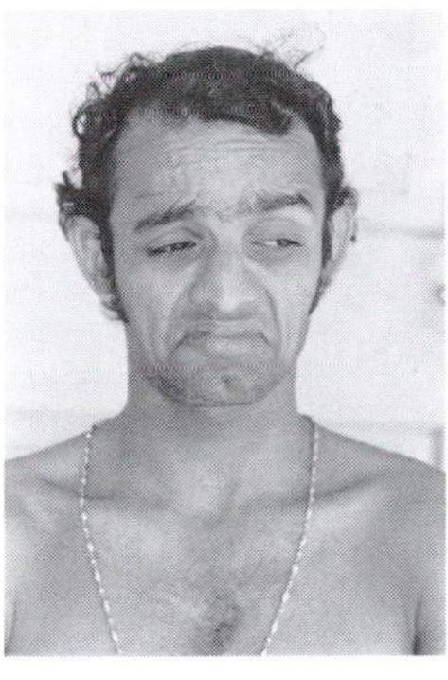

Hasya: mirth, but also impudence

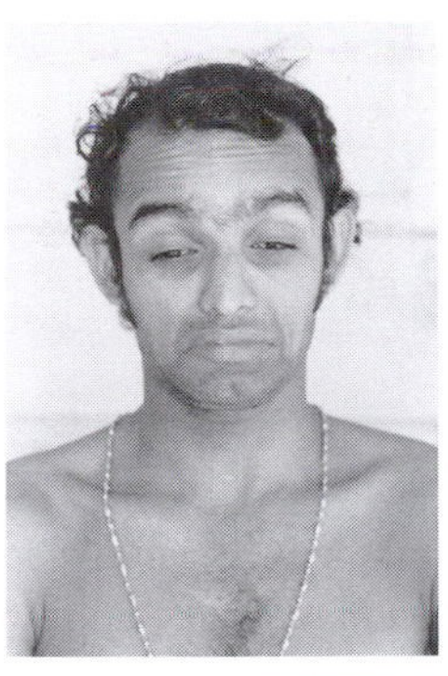

Karuna: sadness

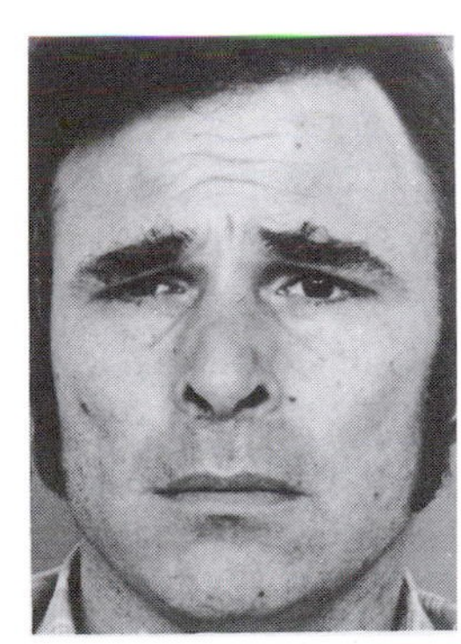

Sadness

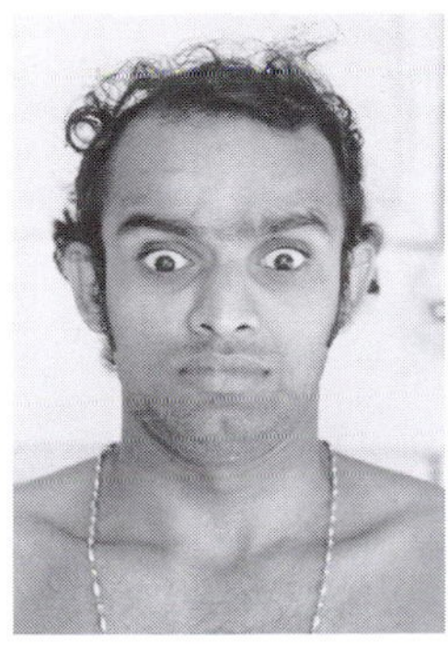

Raudra: anger, violence

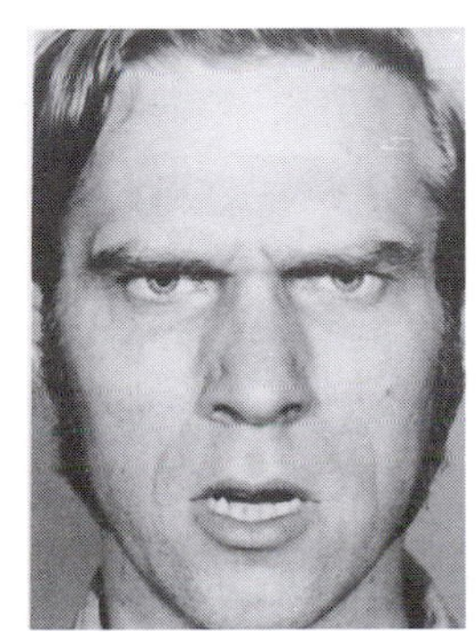

Anger

Natyasastra

Ekman

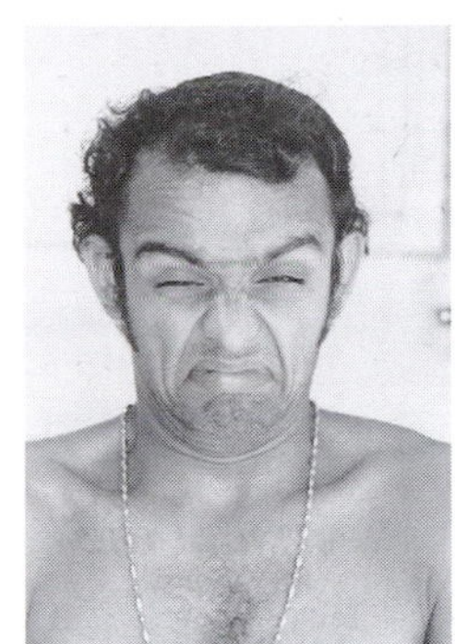

Bibhatsa: disgust

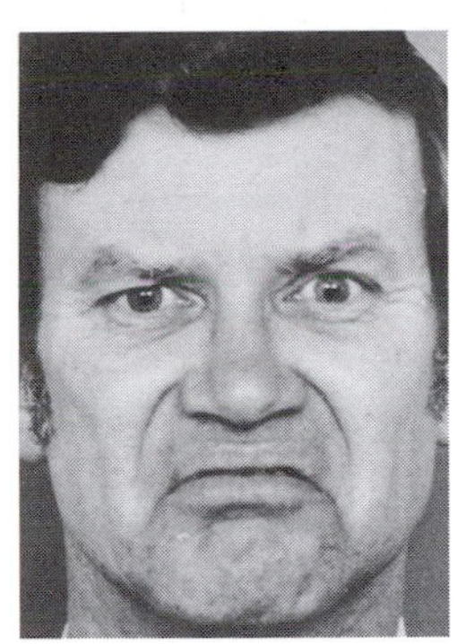

Disgust

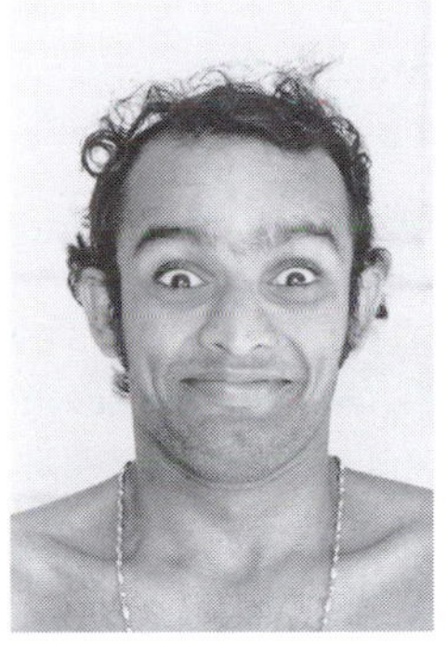

Adbhuta: surprise, excitement

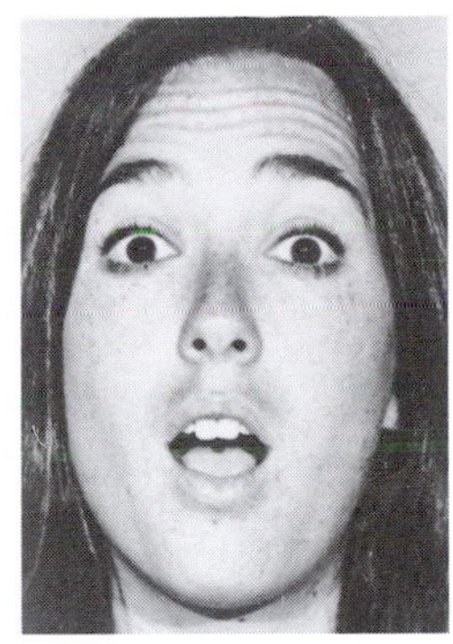

Surprise

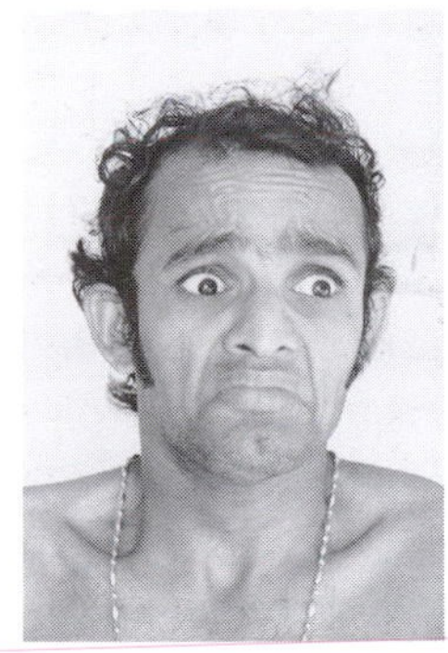

Bhayanaka: fear, guilt

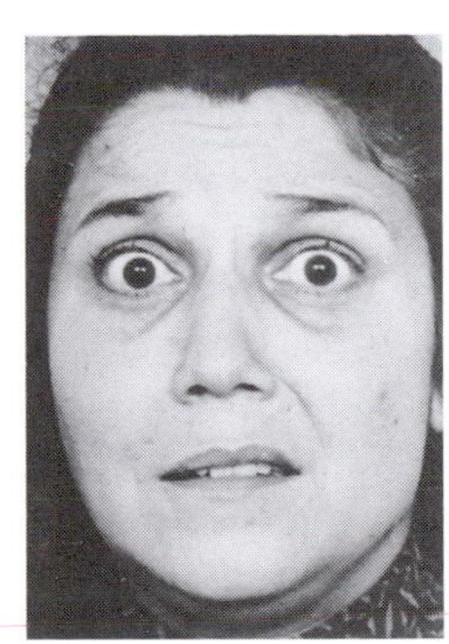

Fear

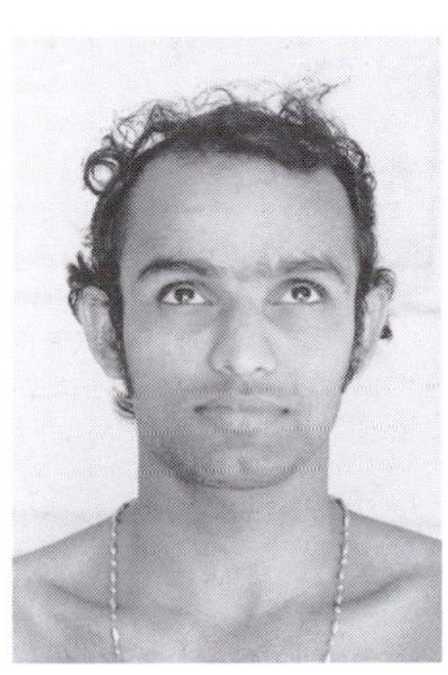

Shanta: peace, meditation

circumstance to circumstance. Not all happy smiles signify happiness. As Goffman was quick to point out, people are always putting on shows, hiding feelings, dissembling.

In any case, even realistic acting is codified. Realistic acting appears natural because it is based on behaviors people learn from infancy. Realistic acting may not look realistic to a person from another culture. Japanese realistic acting may appear understated and codified to an Italian, while Italian realistic acting might appear bombastic and codified to a Japanese. What about the codified acting of kabuki or Delsarte's exercises? Because this behavior is "natural" to no one, whoever sees it will recognize it as codified. But a person who knows kabuki or any other codified genre well will follow the action easily and not regard it as strange or "foreign."

Conclusion

An actor on the stage, a shaman, or someone in trance stands for or is taken over by someone else or something else. This "else" may be a character in a drama, a demon, a god, or a pot. On the other hand, a performer in everyday life is not necessarily playing anyone but herself. Paradoxically, this self can be known only as it is enacted. The non-stage roles of ordinary life are many, ranging from the highly formalized performances of government and religious leaders to the semi-fixed roles of the professions, to the more easy-going improvisations of informal interactions.

The two kinds of performing encounter each other when an actor studies a person in ordinary life in order to prepare a role for the stage. But this mimesis is actually not of "real life" but of a performance. There is no such thing as unperformed or naturally occurring real life. The object of the actor's "real life study" is also performing, though she may not be fully aware that her behavior is codified. All behavior is "twice-behaved," made up of new combinations of previously enacted doings. A wholly conscious performer, if such a person exists, is one who twice-performs twice-behaved behaviors.

TALK ABOUT

1. What is meant by saying that the "performances of everyday life are as codified as ballet"? Is such an assertion useful? Does it help you grasp more effectively what's going on in "real life"? How helpful in this regard is the concept of the "restoration of behavior"?
2. What are the most salient differences between the performing of a shaman in trance, the acting of a realistic movie actor such as Robert De Niro, and a mother chiding her daughter for really bad behavior?

PERFORM

1. Stage a scene from a realistic play by Henrik Ibsen, David Mamet, or Arthur Miller – in a totally non-realistic manner. Is your scene successful? If so, why; and if not, why not? Discuss how the text of a drama does or does not determine the style of acting.
2. Make a Happening. Be certain that all the performing in it is "nonmatrixed."

READ

Belo, Jane. *Trance in Bali*. New York: Columbia University Press, 1960.

Blair, Rhonda. "Reconsidering Stanislavsky: Feeling, Feminism, and the Actor." *Theatre Topics* 12, 2 (2002): 177–90.

Brecht, Bertolt. "A Dialogue about Acting." *The Performance Studies Reader*, Henry Bial, ed.: 185–88. London and New York: Routledge, 2004.

Grotowski, Jerzy. "The Actor's Technique." *The Performance Studies Reader*, Henry Bial, ed.: 189–94. London and New York: Routledge, 2004.

Harding, Frances. "Presenting and Re-presenting the Self: From Not-Acting to Acting in African Performance." *The Performance Studies Reader*, Henry Bial, ed.: 197–214. London and New York: Routledge, 2004.

Kirby, Michael. "Acting and Non-Acting." *A Formalist Theatre*: 1–20. Philadelphia, Pa.: University of Pennsylvania Press, 1987.

Strasberg, Lee. "A Dream of Passion." *The Performance Studies Reader*, Henry Bial, ed.: 195–96. London and New York: Routledge, 2004.

7 PERFORMANCE PROCESSES

The earliest performances?

Events that can be designated "performance" – dance, music, and/or theatre – occur among all the world's peoples and date back as far as archaeologists, anthropologists, and historians can go. In Chapter 3, I discussed "cave art" and performance in relation to ritual. Let me continue now with that discussion concentrating on what kind of performances took place in these ancient sites. Evidence indicates that people were performing in caves at least 30,000 years ago. What kinds of performances? The words "dance," "theatre," and "music," or their linguistic equivalents, are not universal, but the behaviors are. Of course, such behaviors vary from place to place, culture to culture, and epoch to epoch. But surviving cave art and prehistoric artifacts indicate that rhythmic movement (dancing), beating of bone-to-bone drums and flute sounds (music), wearing masks and/or costumes while impersonating other humans, animals, or supernaturals (theatre) were going on (**see Wilford box**). No one knows if these paleolithic performers were acting out stories, representing past events, experiences, memories, dreams, or fantasies. I would like to think they were; that making what we would call theatre–dance–music is co-existent with the human condition. That this kind of activity is an important marker of what it means to be human. Supposing that such performances were happening, no one can answer the chicken-or-egg question, "Which came first, ritual or entertainment?" Answering that question depends as much on definitions as on archaeological evidence. What exactly is "ritual," what "entertainment"? In earlier chapters I have offered some definitions, while insisting that all performances are to some degree both ritual and entertainment. In prehistoric times, most probably even more than today, performances were both ritual and entertainment. In historical times, for many centuries, in many societies, religious rituals and state ceremonies have entertained vast numbers of participating believers and citizens. Conversely, in today's world, more than a few aesthetic performances, popular entertainments, and sports events have been ritualized.

John Noble Wilford

Prehistoric dancing

No one will ever know when someone first raised arms into the air, pivoted and took a few steps this way and that – and danced. [. . .] Archeologists are at a loss to know the origins of dancing in prehistory because they lack direct evidence, nothing comparable to the art of Altamira or Lascaux. [. . .] An Israeli archeologist now thinks he has pieced together a significant body of evidence for dancing, if not at its beginning, at least at a decisive and poorly understood transitional stage of human culture.

Examining more than 400 examples of carved stone and painted scenes on pottery from 140 sites in the Balkans and the Middle East, Dr. Josef Garfinkel of Hebrew University in Jerusalem has established what he says is an illustrated record of dancing from 9,000 to 2,500 years ago. This record, apparently the earliest of its kind, coincides with the place in time hunters of wild game and gatherers of wild plant food first settled into villages and became pastoralists and farmers.

Some show only stick figures with triangular heads, and some headless, in highly schematic scenes that appear to be dances. Others include figures in a dynamic posture, usually with bent arms and legs. Several scenes depict people in a line or completely circling an illustrated vessel, their hands linked. There is some resemblance here to current folk dancing or even a Broadway chorus line. [. . .] The prevalence of what appear to be dancing scenes in the earliest art from the ancient Middle East, Dr. Garfinkel said in a recent interview, suggests the importance of the dance in these preliterate agricultural communities. "Dancing was a means of social communication in prestate societies," he said. "It was part of the ritual for coordinating the community's activities." [. . .]

In his research, Dr. Garfinkel found the earliest examples of the dancing motif in art from two 9,000-year-old sites in the Middle East. Engraved on a stone basin, excavated at Nevali Cori in southeastern Turkey, were three human figures in a line, faces forward, legs wide and arms bent upward. The two outer figures are larger than the central one, suggesting a scene of two dancing men flanking the woman. Only in a few cases, mainly in art from early Egypt, Dr. Garfinkel said, are both sexes seen dancing together. At Dhuweila, a small campsite in Jordan, rock carvings depict a row of four human figures holding hands. They have elongated necks and heads that appear to be nonhuman. Dr. Garfinkel thinks they're wearing masks, evidence for which has been found at other sites.

In later millenniums, most of the dance art has been found painted on pottery, usually small vessels for eating and drinking. As Dr. Garfinkel observed, the scenes emphasize dancing as a community activity. The focus is on a line or circle of identical figures moving in the same direction, indicating the importance of the group over the individual. "Dance is thus an activity through which society instills collective discipline in its members," he concluded.

The dances also appear to take place in the open; in the few examples where some architectural elements are visible, the dance seems to be outside them. And since most of the dancing figures appear as silhouettes, it is possible the dance is being performed at night. Dr. Garfinkel expressed surprise that no musical instruments are seen in the motifs.

2001, "In Dawn of Society, Dance Was Center Stage," 1

How can we in the twenty-first century relate to what took place 30,000 years ago? We do not even know if the works preserved in the caves of southwest France and northern Spain are unique. Similar, if less sophisticated, prehistoric "art" has been found in Africa, Asia, the Americas, and Australia. Because this art is hidden in caves difficult to access (the discovery of the European materials was accidental), there is no saying whether other similar troves exist. Or if there were outdoor sculptings and paintings long destroyed by weather. Performing is much more ephemeral than painting, sculpting, pottery, and architecture. Performing leaves no direct traces. The surviving paintings, sculptings, illustrated pottery, and bones that might have been used to make music point to rich prehistoric performance traditions (**see Brazil box**). The sophistication of the surviving artworks makes it logical to assume that the associated performances were not spontaneous but consisted of traditional gestures, utterances, and musics that were the result of forethought and preparation requiring training and rehearsing. Exactly what constitutes training and rehearsing is one of the subjects of this chapter.

As for precisely what was going on at these sites, we know next to nothing. Scientists are not even in agreement concerning when our species "began," with dates ranging from several hundred thousand years to 2 million years ago. Within this time scheme, the "cave art" of paleolithic Europe, dating from 15,000 to 30,000 years ago, is recent. But this art is very distant when measured against historical traces of "civilizations" that go back only to 5,000 to 10,000 years ago. The origins of theatre and dance in China can be dated to about 4,000 years ago, in Greece to about 2,600 years ago. That the peoples of Africa, Native America, and elsewhere were performing is evident – but exactly what these performances were like, we are not likely ever to know with any finality.

Nevertheless, it seems clear that the paleolithic cave art of France and Spain was not meant to be viewed as in a museum, but to surround or be part of performing (**see figure 7.1**). Perhaps the images were a kind of "action painting/sculpting" nested within encompassing ceremonial activities. The acts of making the paintings and sculptings may in themselves have been performances. Residues of ashes and, in one case, footprints in a circular pattern indicate long-burning fires and dancing. It is unlikely that the people danced in silence, so singing and other kinds of music are inferred. These earliest of theatres are hidden deep in the earth. Most of the "galleries" are difficult to get to. Today, flashlights and even electricity illuminate the cave walls. But in the period when the art was being made – and evidence indicates continuous usage over a period of centuries and in some cases

Mark Brazil

Ancient, really ancient, music

I am writing this while listening to a swan sound [. . .] And it is the first time I have ever heard it. The sounds made the backdrop to a fascinating exhibition [. . .] of the world's oldest flute – made from a swan's wing bone. [. . .] But more incredible than just seeing the flute was hearing the haunting sound it produces; an achingly beautiful and echoing tone – part flute, part whistle – that was heard and enjoyed around 35,000 years ago. [. . .]

That tiny [swan's bone] flute [. . .] is not even a hand's span in length (at just 126.5 mm long). [. . .] Yet this small, unpretentious artifact with three finger holes, which was pieced together from 20 fragments from one wing bone of a Whooper Swan, raises so many questions. How did its makers hunt swans? How long had they followed a tradition of making musical instruments? Were they modern humans, or were they Neanderthals? Why does it produce seven notes? And what was those people's music like? [. . .]

Bird bones were particularly effective as musical instruments, since they generate expressive melodies, but they were not the only suitable material, as archaeologists have shown with their finds of a similarly aged flute made from mammoth ivory and pieced together from 31 fragments.

Although the physical remains of the instruments exist, and the notes they produce are clear, we can only imagine what kind of music was performed on them – whether, for example, it was for entertainment, or ritual. [. . .]

2005 "Ancient Birds, Stone Age Music," *Japan Times* 17 March.
http://search.japantimes.co.jp/print/features/enviro2005/fe20050317mb.htm

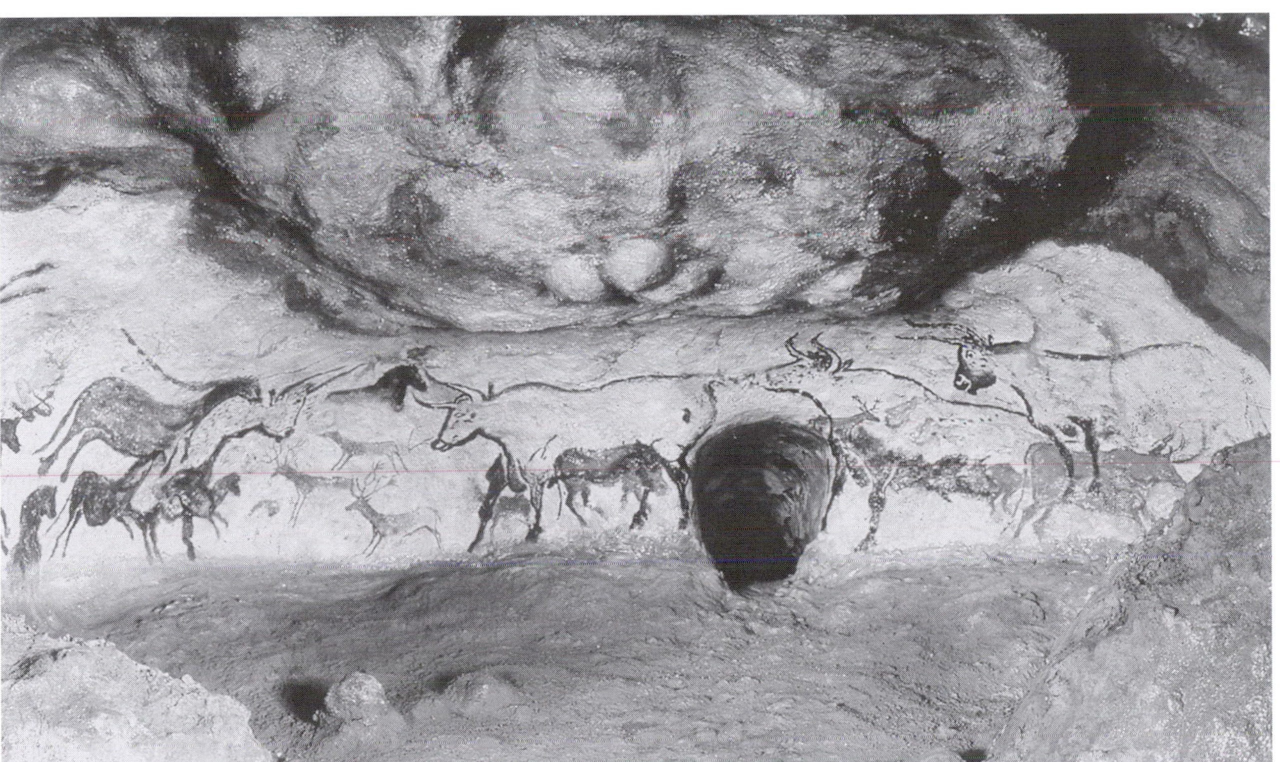

fig 7.1. The cave-theatre of Lascaux, southwest France. In paleolithic times the only light in the caves came from fires or torches. Under the warm colors and flickering flames, the images and sculptings would appear to move. Photograph courtesy Commissariat Général au Tourisme, France.

millennia – torches or fires would have provided the only light. Moving, singing, and dancing – not viewing – would be the best explanation of how the caves were used.

Because so many of the paintings and sculptings are of animals, the performances probably concerned hunting and/or fertility. It is clear why the two are associated. Until recently, among the Kung! hunter-gatherers of the Kalahari Desert in southern Africa, for example, when an animal was killed, a ritual entreated the gods for replenishment of the life taken. But it was not only animal fertility that Stone Age humans celebrated. Figures, carvings, paintings, and symbols depict human fertility as well. The most ancient sculptures are those of women with enlarged vulvas, milk-laden breasts, and massive thighs and buttocks – such as the "Venus" of Willendorf, dated at about 24,000 years before the present (**see figure 7.2**). Somewhat later come phallic symbols, cylindrical rocks worn smooth by touching. Many centuries later, in the tenth to eleventh centuries, the Chandela dynasty of central India built the Khajuraho temples adorned with many sculptures whose erotic poses are also dance steps frozen in stone (**see figure 7.3**).

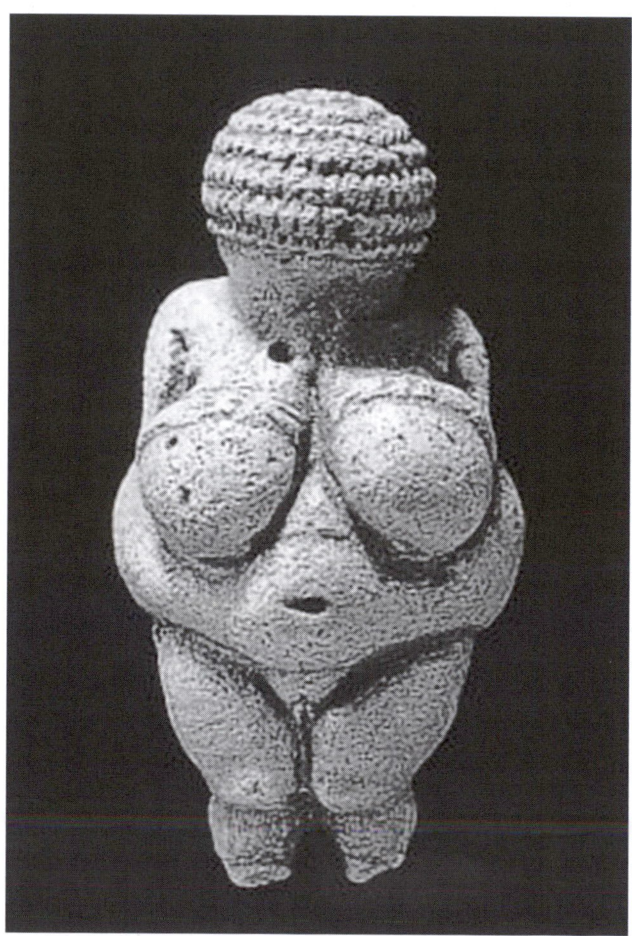

fig 7.2. One of a number of female figures from paleolithic times, this "Venus" of Willendorf is perhaps the best known. This photograph appeared on the internet at www.aeiou.at/aeiou.encyclop.data.image.v/v136200a.jpg

fig 7.3. At the temple complex of Khajuraho in India, the sculptings are often both erotic and dance-like – for example, this *apsara*, a divine nymph, on the outer wall of the tenth-century Parasvanath temple. http://community.webshots.com/photo/261789447/261793537bChGnR

What actually went on in the paleolithic caves, or in aboveground sites, we may never know with any assurance. But is it not logical to assume that there were performances associated with the paleolithic art, as there were with Khajuraho? Before writing existed in the alphabetic sense, performances were ways of enacting, reliving, remembering, and passing beliefs and knowledge through time. Some caves were in use over a period of millennia, indicating that whatever was going on in them was traditional, linking generation to generation. Whatever performances took place were not isolated instances but activities woven into a complex of phenomena. The art on the walls is what remains of an entire system that was trans-personal and abiding, belonging to communities rather than to individuals. This system comprised not only painting and sculpting, but also trans-personal ceremonies, incantations, gestures, and dance steps. Taken as a whole, these were the means of transmitting the collective knowledge of the tribe, group, or community. In order to assure that the correct gestures were made, the right songs sung and dances danced, performance knowledge was transmitted body to body. These prehistoric performances were part of a larger, inclusive process that included training, performing, remembering, and transmitting the whole system from generation to generation.

Performance process as a time–space sequence

The performance process is a time–space sequence composed of proto-performance, performance, and aftermath. This three-phase sequence may be further divided into ten parts:

Proto-performance
1. training
2. workshop
3. rehearsal

Performance
4. warm-up
5. public performance
6. events/contexts sustaining the public performance
7. cooldown

Aftermath
8. critical responses
9. archives
10. memories.

This process applies to all kinds of performances – the performing arts, sports and other popular entertainments, rituals, play, and the performances of everyday life. Understanding this time–space sequence means grasping how performances are generated, how they are staged in a focused manner, how they are nested within larger events, and what their long-term effects are. The model is not prescriptive. I intend it to be an aid to understanding, not a straitjacket.

Performances have both a short-term impact and a longer aftereffect, leaving traces in the bodies of the performers and participants spectators, in archives, and in traditions. Performance processes can be studied from the point of view of actions enacted, of the spaces in which a performance takes place, of the temporal structure of a performance, and as events surrounding and succeeding the performance, both affected by it and affecting it.

Performance processes can also be studied as interactions among four types of players:

1. sourcers (authors, choreographers, composers, dramaturgs, etc.)
2. producers (directors, designers, technicians, business staff, etc.)
3. performers
4. partakers (spectators, fans, congregations, juries, the public, etc.).

Sourcers find, compose, devise, or invent the actions to be performed. Producers work with the performers and sourcers to transform the sources into publicly performed events. Performers play the actions. Partakers receive the actions and sometimes participate in them. The first three types of players – sourcers, producers, and performers – often work together. Producers and performers almost always work together. Partakers usually take part in the process after much of the prepatory work has already been done. These categories are not mutually exclusive. Over time, many individuals perform in all the categories. In any given instance, an individual may perform in more than one, and even all, of the categories. A group may collectively devise or enact all of these processes.

Let me now discuss this system in more detail.

Proto-performance

The **proto-performance** (or "proto-p") is what precedes and/or gives rise to a performance. A proto-p is a starting point or, more commonly, a bunch of starting points. Very few performances start from a single source or impulse. A proto-p may be a legal code, liturgy, scenario, script, drama, dance notation, music score, oral tradition, and so on. It may even be a certain way that a performer makes her body into something "not ordinary," something special for performing – what Eugenio Barba calls the "pre-expressive" (**see Barba box and figure 7.4**). Many proto-ps exist outside the written realm altogether – as plans, drawings, paintings, diagrams, manifestos, or ideas. A proto-p may be a group of people who want to stage a performance. A proto-p may be an upcoming date that requires a performance – a birthday, Christmas party, or initiation rite – the list of date-driven proto-ps is very long. A proto-p may also be a

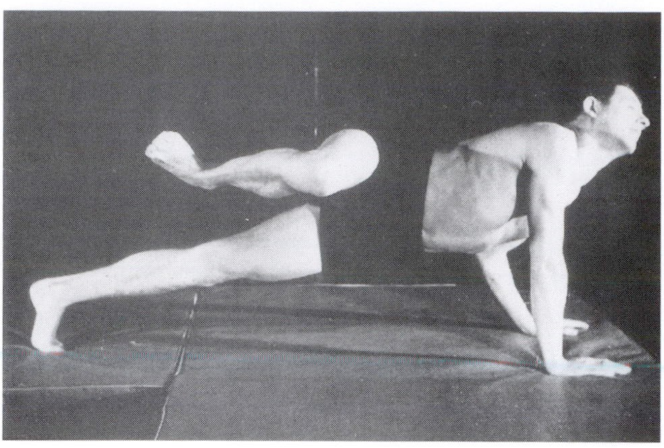

fig 7.4. An actor in Jerzy Grotowski's Polish Laboratory Theatre in the early 1960s doing "the cat," an exercise designed to help performers train their pre-expressive skills. Photograph courtesy of Eugenio Barba.

prior performance, revived, revised, or reconstructed or simply used as a model or starting point for a performance-to-be. The performances of classics as well as the enactment of rituals are always more or less driven by prior performances.

proto-performance (proto-p): a source or impulse that gives rise to a performance; a starting point. A performance can (and usually does) have more than one proto-p.

Eugenio Barba

Pre-expressivity

Widely known and practiced throughout Asia, martial arts use concrete physiological processes to destroy the automatisms of daily life and to create another quality of energy in the body. It is this very aspect of martial arts, that is, their use of acculturation technique, which has inspired codified theatre forms. The legs slightly bent, the arms contracted: the basic position of all Asiatic martial arts shows a decided body ready to leap and to act. This attitude, which could be compared to the plié in classical ballet, can be found in the basic positions of both Oriental and Occidental performers. It is nothing more than a codification, in the form of extra-daily technique, of the position of an animal ready to attack or defend itself.

1991, *A Dictionary of Theatre Anthropology*, 197

One may think of the proto-p as a "pretext," something that not only comes before the performance but is also a strategy of concealing from the audience significant portions of the performance process. Rehearsals and preparations are usually closed. Even during the performance itself, the audience is let in on only some of what's happening. Not only are backstage activities hidden, but the master performer reveals only some of what she is able to do. The sense that there is much more in reserve adds immeasurably to a performance's impact. Just as an iceberg is three-fourths submerged, so a strong performance is largely concealed. This the Japanese noh master **Zeami Motokiyo** knew well, advising actors to show audiences only 20 percent of what they knew, holding the other 80 percent in reserve.

Zeami Motokiyo (1363–1443): Japanese actor and playwright, the foremost figure in the history of noh theatre. His plays still form the core of the noh repertory; and his ideas on acting remain extremely influential. His treatises on acting, which at one time were secret, have now been published – see *On the Art of the No Drama: The Major Treatises of Zeami* (1984).

What is this hidden portion of a performance? It is what the performer has learned, not only about the specific role being enacted – the particular pretext that informs a given performance – but also about the whole craft, the years of knowledge standing behind each enactment. Being confident of a base of knowledge applies not only to the performing arts but across a wide range of professions. It is also related in each particular performance to what Stanislavsky called the "subtext" – the ongoing yet largely internal or hidden driving life force of a scene that exists behind the spoken words and the visible gestures. In this way, pretexts operate secretly, concealed deep within the performance.

In the performing arts, rituals, sports, and in many trades and professions such as lawyer, doctor, carpenter, teacher, the proto-p is worked out in three phases: training, workshop, and rehearsals. These sometimes go by other names such as "apprenticing," "interning," "on-the-job training," and so on. But whatever the name, learning what to do and practicing it under supervision is analogous to what goes on in the performing arts. Obviously, not all arts, rituals, sports, trades, and professions emphasize all three of the proto-ps. Identifying what is emphasized and what is omitted is important to understanding both the performance process and the social world which contains and is also shaped by particular performances.

A note on "text"

Before discussing performance processes in more detail, I want to say something about the notion of "text." Post-structuralists such as Derrida and interpretive anthropologists such as Geertz consider culture itself as a text that can be read. This approach has permeated cultural studies and performance studies. **Susan Foster**'s influential *Reading Dance* is but one example of many that examine performances and proto-performances as texts. Terms such as "dramatic text" and "**performance text**" are commonly used. In earlier writings I also used these terms. I choose not to use them here because although "text" can be understood dynamically, as an action, it is in current use tightly linked to writing both in a specific literary sense and in its extended Derridean meaning.

Susan Foster (1949–): American dancer, choreographer, and scholar. Author of *Reading Dance* (1986), *Choreographing History* (1995), *Corporalities* (1996), *Decomposition: Post Disciplinary Performance* (with Sue-Ellen Case and Philip Brett, 2000), and *Dances That Describe Themselves* (2002).

performance text: everything that takes place on stage that a spectator experiences, from the movements and speech of the dancers and/or actors to the lighting, sets, and other technical or multimedia effects. The performance text is distinguished from the dramatic text. The dramatic text is the play, script, music score, or dance notation that exists prior to being staged.

At the same time, I recognize that text has multiple meanings. In everyday usage, people think of a text as words inked or printed on paper or pixeled on a computer screen. But, etymologically, text is related to "textile" and "texture," suggesting the action of weaving, the feel of fabric and other materials. Text enters English via French from the Latin *texere*, which means to weave or to compose. The Latin is related to the Greek *techne*, meaning skill and artfulness (thus the group of words including "technique" and "technical"), and *tekton*, carpenter or builder. The Indo-European root is *tekb*, to plait, wind, or twist several into one. Thus in its earliest and most active meanings, a text is the product of a skilled joining of different materials to make single, supple, whole, and strong stuff. Those who make texts are both artists and crafts persons. In fact, in early usage there is scant distinction between art and craft. Although today text implies writing, the earlier meanings continue to operate subtextually, behind the scenes, as it were. Texts are synthetic, constructed, crafted, made up, invented: sites of interpretation and disagreement, not fixed canons.

Texts can be inscribed on stone, inked on vellum, printed on paper, punched into cell phone keyboards (as in texting a message), or etched on silicon chips. Texts can also be neural engrams or a dancer's body memory, a painting or architectural plan – and many other techniques of remembering, describing, representing, initiating, or repeating events. Texts can be "read" as coherent systems of communication – writing, visual art, music, theatre. Even a city or a historical epoch may be read as a coherent text. Semioticians argue for a very broad definition of text (**see De Marinis box**). In fact, during the past half-century the concept of text has been greatly expanded without entirely losing touch with the earliest meanings of the word.

Marco De Marinis

What is "text"?

From a semiotic standpoint, the term /text/ designates not only coherent and complete series of linguistic statements, whether oral or written, but also every unit of discourse, whether verbal, nonverbal, or mixed, that results from the coexistence of several codes (and other factors too [. . .]) and possesses the constitutive prerequisites of completeness and coherence. According to this understanding of textuality, an image, or group of images, is, or can be, a text. A sculpture, a film, a musical passage, or a sequence of sound effects constitute texts also, or rather they can be considered as such. Clearly, therefore, even the units known as performances can be considered as texts, and can thus become the object of textual analysis [. . .].

1993, *The Semiotics of Performance*, 47

Understood performatively, texts are transformable and pliable sign and/or symbol systems. Every text invites being remade into new texts. This proves to be the case, especially with regard to texts used in or as performances. For example, Shakespeare's *Hamlet* has been the pretext for any number of productions. *Hamlet* has even been deconstructed into new playtexts such as **Heiner Müller**'s *Hamletmachine*, itself a gloss on Shakespeare's play, a playtext in its own right, and a proto-p for many widely stylistically variant productions.

Heiner Müller (1929–95): German playwright and director. From 1992 until his death, Müller was artistic director of the Berlin Ensemble – the theatre founded by Brecht in 1949. Many of Müller's writings have not yet been translated into English, but among those that are: *Hamletmachine and Other Texts for the Stage* (1984), *Shakespeare Factory* (2 vols., 1985–89), *Explosion of a Memory* (1989), and *A Heiner Müller Reader* (2001).

Training

Training is that phase of the performance process where specific skills are learned. Training is logically if not always experientially the first step of the proto-performance. Training may be either informal or formal (**see Okpewho box**). In informal training, the novice acquires skills over time by absorbing what is going on. Mistakes are corrected as part of daily life. This training method can be very effective because what is learned is integrated into the student's overall life. This is the way infants learn to speak. This is how most people learn how to "fit in" to their families and social groups. In much of the world, training for a wide variety of occupations was or is informal, and extremely effective. Much of childplay is a kind of training for both social and technical skills that will be useful later in life. A lot of performance training is informal. Many persons who have never taken a class are excellent social dancers. In Bali, trance dancers who have never been formally trained perform simple, precise movements (**see Covarrubias box**). Apprenticeship is somewhere between informal and formal training. The apprentice watches, helps, and learns on the job. But sometimes the apprentice is given formal lessons.

Formal training comes in a variety of methods. Classroom schooling is the prevalent kind of formal training today. But there is also apprenticeship and one-on-one teaching. Formal training became increasingly necessary with the advent of industrialization, which displaced work from the home, farm, and village to factories and cities. The increasingly technical quality of life – from science and economics to law, medicine, and computers – demands formal training. Some performing arts – such as filmmaking, and interactive telecommunications – require formal technical training. But even arts that at one time were taught exclusively through apprenticeship are now taught in school. The school approach to learning assumes a systematic progression through different "grades" of knowledge and the division of knowledge into "subjects." Informal training is more holistic.

Isidore Okpewho

Formal and informal training

Two kinds of training are involved in the development of the African oral artist: informal and formal. Informal training entails a kind of loose attachment whereby the future artist happens to live or move in an environment in which a particular kind of oral art is practiced and simply absorbs the skill in it as time goes on. [. . .] It is reasonably clear what goes on in informal training. First, the future artist must be a person blessed with a considerable amount of natural genius who possesses an interest in the kind of oral literature that is practiced around him or her. Second, since no formal coaching is involved, these novices must look and listen closely and in this way absorb the ideas, the idioms, and the techniques peculiar to the art. [. . .] And finally, the process of learning entails that the novices use their imagination to select the relevant materials from the large amount they may have acquired and to increase their store of knowledge as time goes on. Very much the same things happen in the formal kind of training, except that the process is better organized and the relationship between the trainee and the teacher properly established. [. . .]

Formal training is particularly useful for the more complex kinds of oral literature – e.g., some forms of ritual poetry and performances involving the accompaniment of music – on which the future artist could depend as a major source of livelihood. [. . .] The state may recognize both the cultural value and the popularity (especially with foreigners) of a category of oral traditions and so set up a "school" where young men can be taught the skills of that art – not only to preserve the culture but also to promote the tourist economy.

1992, *African Oral Literature,* 21–25

Miguel Covarrubias

Training for trance dancing in Bali

Two little girls, trained to go into a trance, are chosen from all the girls of the village for their psychic aptitudes by the temple priest. [. . .] Choruses of men and women are formed and the training begins. Every night, for weeks, they all go to the temple, where the women sing traditional songs while the men chant strange rhythms and harmonies made up of meaningless syllables, producing a syncopated accompaniment for the dance that the little girls, the *sanghyangs*, will perform. By degrees the little girls become more and more subject to the ecstasy produced by the intoxicating songs, by the incense, and by the hypnotic power of the *pemanku* [priest]. The training goes on until the girls are able to fall into a deep trance, and a formal performance can be given. It is extraordinary that although the little girls have never received dancing lessons, once in a trance they are able to dance in any style, all of which would require ordinary dancers months and years of training to learn. But the Balinese ask, how it could be otherwise, since it is the goddesses who dance in the bodies of the little girls.

1972 [1937], *Island of Bali*, 335–36

Informal training is deemed successful when the trainee begins to practice on his own. Formal training often concludes with an initiation rite – graduation ceremonies where diplomas are conferred amidst festivities that bring family and friends together to witness the change in status of the graduates. Some great artists have been trained informally, others formally. Frequently, formal and informal training co-exist. In medicine, for example, once school is over, the neophyte doctor joins a hospital as an intern under the supervision of resident and senior physicians. Specialist designations take even more training.

In the arts and sports especially, one continues training as long as one performs, even through one's entire life. At this level, training comprises "keeping in shape" perhaps even more than acquiring new skills. In the physical arts – dancing and sports – the older one gets, the more a person needs to sustain her or his training. Although acting is not as physically demanding as dancing or sports, many successful actors feel the need to take classes.

Sometimes apprenticeship training is combined with classroom training. At the Kathakali Kalamandalam in Kerala, southwest India, some boys begin training at eight years of age. No one over the age of fourteen is accepted. (That is, no Indian over that age. Some adult foreigners are admitted – but I know of no case where a foreigner has undergone the full seven to eight years of continuous training that the Indians undertake.) Trainees rise before dawn during the rainy season of July–August for eight hours of intense psychophysical training embedded in a 13-hour day that also includes text analysis and lessons in Indian philosophy (**see figure 7.5**). The prerequisite for more detailed training of the hands, eyes, feet, and torso is a demanding program of physical exercise (**see figure 7.6**). The flexibility and turnout needed to perform kathakali is molded into the young bodies of the trainees by means of massage administered by older students or their teachers.

In their performance classes, the trainees practice gestures and movements identical to, or based on, what they will actually use later when publicly performing kathakali. In their academic classes, they learn the history of kathakali and the performance theory underlying its practice. The practical learning is by immersion and imitation. There is no improvisation or what in the West might be called "free, creative work." Over time, the training goes into their bodies – the students are transformed both physically and mentally into kathakali performers. Later in life, some performers – recognized by their peers and by connoisseurs of kathakali as "masters" – will improvise – not in rehearsals but in public performances – making changes in the scores they learned as students or after. These changes, if appreciated by knowing spectators and admired by fellow performers, will become part of a particular performer's style. He will then pass these nuanced changes on to his students, who will imitate the master who once himself was a student learning by imitation. In this way, kathakali both maintains and develops its performing tradition.

But the kathakali training system is not the only way to acquire performance knowledge. Learning how to perform the ritual dances of the Yoruba of southwest Nigeria is done in a different manner (**see figure 7.7**). After a long period of training that involves rote learning, intense concentration, and practice, the Yoruban performer is set free to improvise. The same pattern occurs elsewhere in West Africa (**see figure 7.8**). Training includes not only instruction in how to perform in public, but also the memorizing and interpreting of sacred oral texts. These texts are learned from a ritual specialist to whom the neophyte is apprenticed. Specific techniques are passed down, but the Yorubans believe that the

fig 7.5. Three young students in the 1980s at the Kalamandalam, Kerala, India, in kathakali's basic stance, knees akimbo, back arched, the weight on the outside of the foot. This position is the first thing students learn. Photograph courtesy of Eugenio Barba.

fig 7.6. A kathakali student makes a stupendous leap as part of his basic training at the Kalamandalam, Kerala, India 1976. Note the glistening of the bodies – this is because they are thoroughly oiled to make the muscles more limber. Photograph by Richard Schechner.

fig 7.7. Diviner Kolawole Oshitola drums while four neophytes in ritual dress and Oshitola's three apprentices complete the liminal stage of the Itefa ritual that establishes the personal destiny of each initiate into Ifa divination practice and initiates them as "new men." Yoruban region, Nigeria, 1986. The ritual performance is at once an initiation and a training ground. Photograph by Henry and Margaret Drewal, courtesy of the Henry Drewal and Margaret Thompson Drewal Collection.

fig 7.8. Two identical female Gelede dancers facing each other as they interpret the rhythms of the drums. The crowd controller in the foreground with a long stick keeps the dance space open. Much of the actual performing is improvised. Benin, 1971. Photograph by Henry and Margaret Drewal, courtesy of the Henry Drewal and Margaret Thompson Drewal Collection.

performances need always to be changing. For the traditions to remain meaningful they must adjust to new circumstances and realities (**see Drewal box**). Thus the Yorubans train their performers to be alert for opportunities to improvise, to apply the traditional knowledge to immediate contingent circumstances, to make performances that are both old and new at the same time. Given the successive impact of colonialism, modernization, and globalization on many Third World cultures, this ability to integrate the new with the given, to improvise creatively, has proven invaluable. In Africa and in the African diaspora, the penchant for combining rigor with improvisation is expressed in a total and precisely embodied performance knowledge (**see Thompson box**). This can be seen in genres as different as jazz and hip-hop.

Margaret Thompson Drewal

Training a ritual specialist in Nigeria

Acquiring techniques for producing ritual action is mostly a rote exercise demanding sustained effort and concentration. Oshitola [a ritual specialist] described to me how his grandfather used to make him sit attentively for hours at a time studying the oral texts of divination and ritual processes in action. Some techniques require more effort than others to master. To acquire such techniques – in other words, to know how something is accomplished, particularly if it can be picked up easily – without simultaneously learning the values and ethics operating behind that knowledge can lead to misuse and even abuse. This is particularly critical in rituals performed to effect change, as in rites of passage, divination, and healing. [. . .] What distinguishes ritual specialists from each other, and from charlatans, are their particularized ritual roles, which they have often inherited and for which they have been specifically selected and trained. It is the transformative power of this kind of sustained experience that is essential, which is why Oshitola often voiced to me his concern that "you can't learn everything in a day," in response to my persistent questioning. The fact is nobody can witness a Yoruba performance in its entirety, not even ritual specialists themselves. This is true not only because of the exclusivity of many ritual segments, but because of the simultaneity of ritual action generally. [. . .] If I could observe every aspect of a ritual firsthand, or any other kind of performance for that matter, I would have observed undoubtedly more than any other participant.

1992, *Yoruba Ritual*, 24–25

Robert Farris Thompson

The vital aliveness of African dance

African dance is seen in the eyes of its performers as an instrument of strong expression. The dancer must be strong. He must shake his being with vigor, creating a vision "terrible to watch" in the words of a Bangwa hunter. Vital aliveness, high intensity, speed, drive – these are some of the facets of artful muscularity and depth of feeling that characterize the dances of this continent. The concept of vital aliveness leads to the interpretation of the parts of the body as independent instruments of percussive force. [. . .] The dancer must impart equal life, equal autonomy, to every dancing portion of his frame. [. . .] Thus one Yoruba talked about *making* the shoulders, with forcefully marked activations, a Banyang mentioned his father playing his toes, and an Ejagham remarked on dancing "with the things where they *make 'em*," i.e., the transformation of upper and lower parts of the body into zones of independently enlivened motion.

1974, *African Art in Motion*, 9

Imitation as a way of acquiring performance knowledge

What about learning by imitation in the West? At the end of the nineteenth century, Stanislavsky was struggling against mechanical and declamatory acting. He, along with others, found in realism an access to the "truth" and "spontaneity" of everyday life which they wanted to bring into the theatre. Today, people recognize that realism and naturalism are styles as much as kathakali or Yoruban dancing are. Realism is no more "true" than any other performance mode. As I have pointed out in previous chapters, even everyday life consists of "twice-behaved behaviors." It is also true that only a few masters will be able to formulate in words the grammar of whatever performance genre they practice, be it kathakali, ballet, rock music, baseball, noh, or shamanism. Most performers will not be able to articulate precisely what they do, even if over time they get better and better at doing it. The proper use of imitation and repetition in training is in directly transmitting performance knowledge without the need for a verbal explanation or theorizing. Such "talking about" may be very helpful at a certain stage of acquiring performance knowledge, but it can hinder such acquisition if used too early or too frequently. It is better usually to get the performance knowledge into the body on its own terms, as movement, gesture, tone of voice, facial expressions – whatever the techniques of a particular genre are. By means of imitation, learners acquire through practice an organic mastery of the craft that underlies every art. It is only after making various performance scores "second nature" in the sense of learning new ways of standing, walking, gesturing, speaking, and singing that the maturing artist earns the right to experiment and improvise within the vocabulary of the genre. Learning the history and theory of a particular genre is important if brought into play at the right time. Academic knowledge should not dominate or even determine acquiring practical, embodied knowledge. Some accomplished artists prosper as they delve into the history and theory, while others freeze up. Finding the right balance between the practical and the scholarly, and the right point in the training to learn, discuss, and debate history and theory is a skill that good teachers have. In fact, the ability to integrate all kinds of information, and to know when and how much to give individual students, is the mark of a good teacher.

When I followed well-trained kathakali actors through rehearsals into performance, I witnessed artists who were "controlled" in all their actions from the most gross to the twitching of an eye, the bending of a small finger, and the turning-up of the toes. These actors felt "free" because in performance their "second body" had become through re-shaping and practice perfectly "natural." Performers trained this way embody their training so thoroughly that they no more think of it than a native speaker thinks of grammar and vocabulary while speaking his mother tongue. During performances these artists are not in trance, but they may as well be in terms of total conformity to the rules of their genre. They express both their individual creativity – the variations mature performers are expected to introduce into their scores – and the specific cultural meanings embedded in the roles they embody.

Workshop

Workshop is the active research phase of the performance process. Some artists use workshops to explore processes that will be useful in rehearsals and in making performances. For example, in workshops I led in the 1990s at New York University, I developed the rasaboxes exercise roughly based on the eight fundamental emotions described in the *Natyasastra*, the ancient Sanskrit manual for performers, directors, playwrights, and theatre architects. The rasaboxes exercise takes place inside a rectangle of nine boxes, each of which is the "place" of a basic emotion. As performers move from one box to the next, they must instantly change their emotional expression from, say, *karuna* (sadness or compassion) to *bibhatsa* (disgust), or *raudra* (rage), or *sringara* (love) (**see figure 7.9**). But these words are not the key – each rasa is an entire range of feelings clustered around an emotional core, a flavoring and savoring of emotions rather than anything fixed or "texted." The ultimate aim of the exercise is to help performers compose, control, embody, and express emotions as nimbly as athletes are able to rest on the sidelines and then, when asked to play, plunge into the game with full intensity. Antonin Artaud once called for actors to be "athletes of the emotions," and this is what the rasaboxes exercise trains them to become.

But this kind of exploration and training is not the only thing workshops are good for. Workshops may be used to dig up materials from personal, historical, or other sources and then find ways to express these in actions and interactions. These materials may become part of the completed aesthetic or therapeutic performances. Or the materials may be useful only as workshop explorations. Sometimes workshops are an end in themselves. Workshops have become popular in business and as recreation. Some workshops, often sponsored by businesses, help people acquire certain social skills such as learning how to be at ease in public or how to assert oneself without being overly aggressive, and so on. In New Age venues such as the Esalen Institute or Naropa University, workshops focus on meditation, whole-body healing, and the integration of many different religious and philosophical systems. In the performing arts, workshops cover a very broad range of activities. Some workshops bring together persons from different cultures and/or genres to exchange techniques, ideas, and approaches. Other workshops introduce people to particular skills or techniques. What qualifies all these different activities to be called workshops is that they are used to "open people up" to new experiences, helping them recognize and develop their own possibilities. Plainly, the difference between training and workshop is blurry.

fig 7.9. The rasaboxes exercise devised by Richard Schechner and developed by Michele Minnick and Paula Murray Cole.

Cole on the left and Minnick practicing rasas in two of the boxes. Photograph courtesy of Richard Schechner.

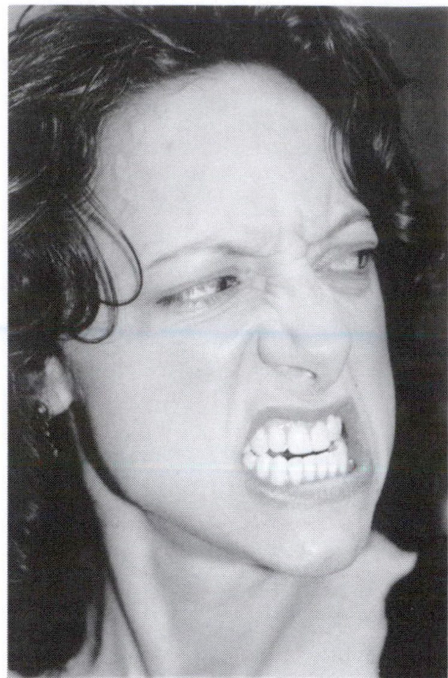

Cole demonstrating the *raudra* (rage) rasa. Photograph courtesy of Richard Schechner.

Generally, workshops look toward "the new" both personally and artistically.

Many activities are "workshopped" before they are produced. To workshop something is to produce a prototype or experimental model. This is true not only in the arts but across a wide range of activities. For example, in auto manufacturing, new car prototypes are conceived, designed, and built by teams pooling resources in an atmosphere of workshop. Designers and engineers play around with new ideas leading to the making of a single prototype vehicle. The prototype is built not on the assembly line, but on an individual basis. Of course, such a "new car" is not really wholly new. A prototype combines already proven engineering and design along with what is new. Sometimes auto companies go far out, trying to imagine what a "car of the future" would be. Such a vehicle is called a "concept car." Sometimes it is not even really finished. It may have a very advanced exterior design but no comparable motor. But by means of concept cars, auto manufacturers can familiarize themselves and their customers with possibilities. Often elements from a concept car will find their way into the prototype, which, in turn, serves as the basis for what comes off the assembly line. The process goes from workshop (concept car) to rehearsal (prototype) to production (performance). Similarly, in the performing arts, the workshop phase is where possibilities that may never be performed in public are explored. Only when a project achieves a certain level of solidity is it moved out of the workshop and into rehearsals.

Architects **Lawrence Halprin** and **Jim Burns**), working closely with Lawrence's wife, choreographer Anna Halprin, developed a collective creative workshop process they called the "RSVP Cycles" (**see Halprin and Burns box, see figure 7.10**). The RSVP Cycles are both a theory of the workshop process and a very useful technique:

Resources – all the subjective and objective material used in the creative process. These include space, people, money, things, etc.; and objectives, feelings, fantasies, open and hidden agendas, etc.

Scores – what I have termed the proto-performance: scenarios, instructions, plans. Scores can be either open or closed. A closed score controls the action; an open score allows for a variety of options.

Valuaction – where the group considers feedback about the ongoing creative process. Scores are revised on the basis of the feedback. Halprin and Burns coined the term "valuaction" to emphasize the action aspect of the feedback. Scores are revised not just by talking about what happened but by means of new actions.

Performance – the most optimal outcome possible using the scores within the given circumstances.

Lawrence Halprin (1916–): American architect who, with his wife, dancer Anna Halprin and fellow architect **Jim Burns (1926–94)**, developed a set of workshop processes known as the RSVP Cycles. Among his many projects, is the FDR Memorial in Washington, DC. His books include *Cities* (1963), *Notebooks 1959–71* (1972), *Taking Part: A Workshop Approach to Collective Creativity* (with Jim Burns, 1974), and *Sea Ranch* (with Donelyn Lyndon, James Alinder, and Donald Canty, 2004).

Lawrence Halprin and Jim Burns

The RSVP cycles

The RSVP cycles is a model of creativity that organizes and makes visible methods for people to work together in groups. The model is participatory and cyclical rather than hierarchical and linear; it emphasizes ongoingness and process, not sequence and goal attainment. It focuses on people as participants, not as mechanisms, tools, or inert recipients of products. For this reason, one step does not lead to the next. Instead, access to the cycle can occur at any point and influence the direction of change and growth.

Our concept of creativity in groups is based on the premise that people have creative potential and that, when they interact in groups, this creativity can be unleashed and enhanced. [. . .] When each facet comes into play, it is not blocked by the other three and the freedom to act remains open rather than inhibited as it usually is.

RSVP is a framework for process. It enables the process to move and action to be taken – it provides a way for many people to work together in groups productively rather than chaotically and to be aware of the process while they are involved in it. Since it is cyclical, it accepts input and change from each person rather than rejecting it if it does not fit. [. . .]

Using the RSVP Cycles permits and encourages each person to influence profoundly what happens as well as how it happens. Groups of people working with the cycles do not act out someone else's ideas or carry up pre-established intentions – they do not have a preformed goal (which is the what of things) to which they simply add their own ideas of how it should be done.

The RSVP Cycles allow people to determine what should happen, the program and objectives of actions, as significantly as how it should be accomplished. The cycles make possible the shifting and reevaluation of objectives during the process as they are influenced by events, without invalidating the process or stopping its flow. In this way process and objectives become linked and intertwined, and what happens in a group situation is affected by how it happens.

1974, *Taking Part*, 27–29

RSVP cycles: a workshop technique developed by Anna Halprin, Lawrence Halprin, and Jim Burns. RSVP is an acronym for **R**esources, **S**cores, **V**aluaction, and **P**erformance.

In the Halprin–Burns method, the RSVP cycle is repeated several times during workshops. There is no right place to start. The group may enter the cycle at any of its nodes. Nor is the performance phase necessarily a public performance. Often the performance is for members of the workshop only. At some point, a public may or may not be invited to experience the results of the workshop. This kind of workshop is not designed primarily to find materials out of which public performances are made. The primary objective of this kind of workshop is self-discovery and/or the building and solidifying of a creative group or team.

Insofar as workshops are where new ways of doing things are explored and where resistances to new knowledge are identified and dealt with, they are similar to initiation rites. As discussed in Chapter 3, Gennep called initiations "rites of passage" because by means of an initiation rite a person passes from one social identity to another. According to Gennep's theory, initiation rites consist of three phases: separation, the liminal or "in between" phase, and

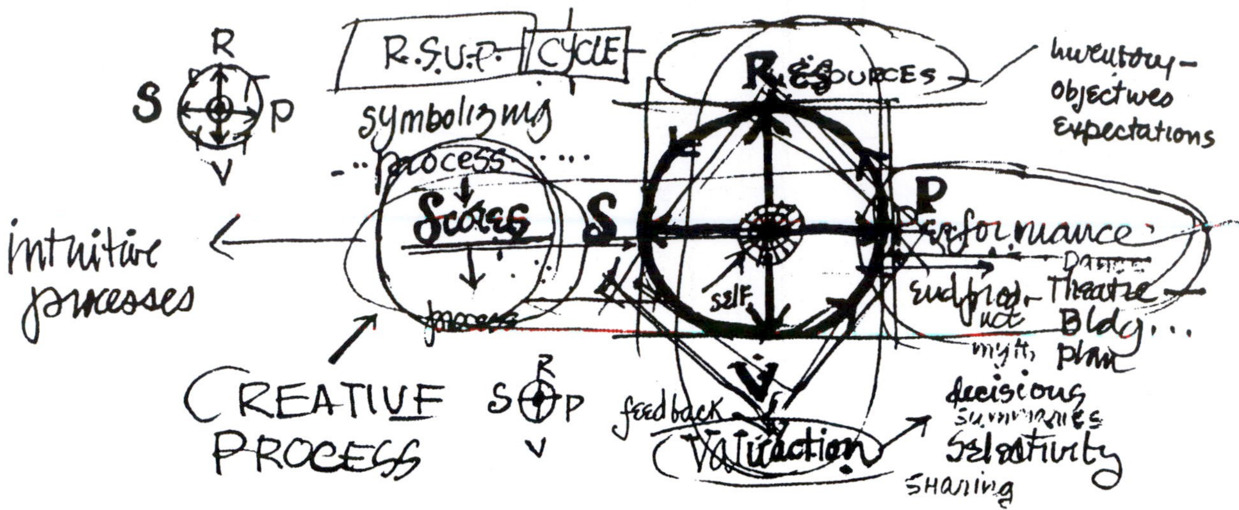

fig 7.10. An active, schematic rendition of the RSVP Cycles of Lawrence Halprin and Jim Burns. The drawing itself shows the dynamic quality of the RSVP system. Drawing courtesy of Lawrence Halprin.

reintegration. During initiations, persons leave their ordinary lives behind (separation), undergo ordeals by means of which old behaviors are erased and new behaviors and knowledge learned (liminal phase), and emerge reborn as new or at least profoundly changed beings ready to rejoin their society but with a new identity and at a new level of responsibility (reintegration). Workshop participants follow a similar path by isolating themselves from their ordinary lives, putting aside old habits, delving into themselves, and learning new ways of doing things emerging to some degree as "new persons." As in many initiations, the journey is not undertaken alone. A group sustains individual efforts just as individual contributions strengthen the group.

If a workshop is successful, participants re-emerge as changed beings. Sometimes these changes are minor, sometimes fundamental. For a workshop to succeed, the participants must do the hard work of not only mastering new skills (training) but opening themselves up to others and to new ideas and practices. This is not easy. But once participants are able to be receptive and vulnerable, they are ready to grow and change. Workshop and training may overlap in function, but they are experienced very differently. Training is a long, slow, repetitive, immersive process. Workshops are relatively brief, intense, and transformative. Some workshops use "ordeals" as a way of breaking down resistance to learning and as a way of incorporating new knowledge into the body. Fasting, long hours, strict discipline, and difficult psycho-physical exercises are just some of the techniques used to push people beyond their ordinary limits.

Rehearsal

Rehearsals operate differently and at a different level than workshops. Workshops are a way of breaking down, digging deep, and opening up. Resources are identified and explored. During the workshop phase, possibilities abound. Rehearsals are a building-up process, the phase where the materials found in workshops are organized in such a way that a performance (often a public performance) follows. Rehearsals build on, and fill in, the foundations laid down in training and the new materials uncovered and explored in workshops. During rehearsals, actions are separated into what can be used to make a performance and what must be discarded or put aside for another project. Often effective actions and meaningful insights are simply not useful for the project at hand. These are not wasted but set aside or warehoused for future use. For long stretches, rehearsals may be mostly tedious repetition and revision, a slow building-up process. But then, surprisingly and suddenly, things fall into place – an interaction, a scene, or even a whole act "makes sense" onstage for the first time (**see figure 7.11**). Or everyone experiences a "creative moment" simultaneously, adding immeasurably to the work. Even master directors such

fig 7.11. A sharp-eyed director, himself a master performer, leads a rehearsal of kathakali at the Kalamandalam, Kerala, India, in 1976. Photograph by Richard Schechner.

performance. Rehearsals are always tailored to the specific needs of the performance-at-hand, whether a wedding or a production of *A Midsummer Night's Dream*. Rehearsals reduce the "noise" in a system, creating a graceful "finished product" (**see Birdwhistell box**). Commenting on Ray Birdwhistell's observation that grace and beauty equals simplicity, ethologist Konrad Lorenz noted that when noise is eliminated from any system, the signal is less ambiguous (**see Lorenz box**). This increases the chances that whatever message is being sent will be correctly received and interpreted. If Lorenz is right, then "aesthetics," whatever other values it may have, and wherever it may occur in human life – serves an evolutionary purpose.

Both Birdwhistell and Lorenz argue for efficiency and simplicity – the "grace" of an accomplished dance. The model

Ray Birdwhistell

Graceful behavior

We have been running trajectories on dancing and other acts described as graceful behavior.

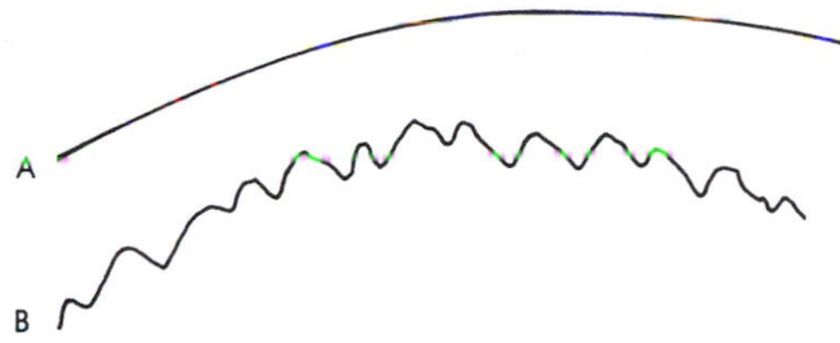

Note B and A are trajectories of an arm or leg or body. A is a smooth curve; B is the zigzag line. The sizes of the zigzags are unimportant. It is the shape of the movement with which I'm concerned. A and B express the same trajectory. However, ultimately trajectory A shows minimal variation or adjustment within the scope of the trajectory. In A there is a minimum of messages being reacted to in process. This is "grace." In B multiple messages are being introduced into the system and there is the zigzag. The things we call graceful are always multi-message acts in which the secondary messages are minimized, and there the role of the whole is maximized.

1959, *Transactions of the Conference on Group Processes of 1957*, 101–02

David Selbourne

Creative moments during rehearsals with Peter Brook

We [Peter Brook and Selbourne] also spoke of the nature of the "creative moments" in rehearsal, when a so-far fleeting sense of discovery and illumination suddenly raises the spirits, and – however briefly – suggests the ultimate possibility of exhilaration in performance. Was everyone aware simultaneously of such moments? He thought they were. For these moments, when feelings, words, and movements came together and fused into new life, depended on the "running of a current," an opening to which all present contribute. I asked him whether he thought that these and other experiences of rehearsal could be described, captured in words. "Not at all. Of course not," he replied with some asperity.

1982, *The Making of* A Midsummer Night's Dream, 39

as Peter Brook are hard-pressed to understand why these moments occur when they do or how they can be brought about (**see Selbourne box**).

Rehearsing is the process of building up specific blocks of proto-performance materials into larger and larger sequences of actions that are assembled into a whole, finished

Konrad **Lorenz**

Eliminating "noise," creating dance

[W]ith the elimination of the noise in the movement, when the movement becomes graceful, and becomes more unambiguous as a signal [. . .] the easier it is for it to be taken up unambiguously by the receptor. Therefore, there is a strong selection pressure working in the direction of making all signal movements [. . .] more graceful, and that is also what reminds us [in animal behavior] of a dance.

1959, *Transactions of the Conference on Group Processes of 1957*, 202–03

Colley Cibber (1671–1757): English playwright, actor, and Poet Laureate of Britain whose version of Shakespeare's *Richard III* held sway on stage until 1871. From 1710 to 1733, Cibber was one of three actor-managers of London's Drury Lane Theatre. His *An Apology for the Life of Mr. Colley Cibber* (1740) is an excellent account of the eighteenth-century British theatre.

Nahum Tate (1652–1715): Irish-born playwright who later became the Poet Laureate of Britain. Tate adapted a number of Elizabethan plays, including *King Lear*. In Tate's 1681 version, which ruled the English stage until the mid-nineteenth century, Cordelia survives, marries Edgar, and becomes queen of the realm.

is similar to what performance is from the business perspective – the removal of "extraneous" movements, time-and-effort efficiency and productivity. But many artworks, not to mention daily social interactions, are extremely complex, lumpy, ambivalent, and "inefficient." Many great works of art are anything but simple. The plays of Shakespeare, the spectacles of Robert Wilson, the paintings of Breughel, Yoruba Gelede masked dances, etc., are no less artistic than the plays of Beckett, the paintings of Mondrian, or haiku poetry. "Inefficient" artworks would not be any the better if made simpler and clearer. Scholars and poets have since the seventeenth century revised Shakespeare's plays for the stage removing what they felt were contradictions and morally objectionable situations (such as the "unjustified" death of Cordelia at the end of *King Lear*. **Colly Cibber**'s version of *Richard III* was the only one performed on the English stage from 1700 until 1871. From the late nineteenth century forward, directors and actors agreed that these efforts diminish rather than improve the plays. We must recognize that **Nahum Tate**'s version of *King Lear* and Cibber's *Richard III* are not adaptations or deconstructions such as *West Side Story* or *Hamletmachine*. They are misguided efforts to improve Shakespeare. But however misguided, clearly a normative, single standard for making and evaluating art is insupportable. One must always respect cultural, historical, and individual differences. These differences give works their particular heft, tones, and flavors.

The problem of "productivity" is tractable if we relocate the simplifying process from finished works to rehearsals. The question then becomes not how simple or complex a finished work is, but what happens during rehearsals. How does the production team determine which of all the things thought of and/or tried will survive into the public performance? Comparing the many possibilities that arise during rehearsals to the relatively few actions actually performed in the finished work reveals how many adjustments take place during rehearsals. The goal of rehearsing is to bring the finished product into harmony with the process that produced it. The result may be simple or complex, logical or arational, easy to follow or annoyingly difficult. But in every successful work (however that is determined), the rehearsal process will have sifted out what does not belong – will have simplified in the sense of keeping "the least rejected of all the things tried" (as Brecht once said describing the work of rehearsals). A number of supposedly unrehearsed activities – some Happenings, many common behaviors in ordinary life – are not really spontaneous and unedited. Investigating how they came to be what they are reveals extensive editing and rehearsing (either actual or in the imagination).

Furthermore, the social nature of the performing arts, sports, and rituals makes them special. Although all behavior is in some sense rehearsed and then performed, only the arts, sports, and rituals almost always rehearse in groups and present their products to a group. The performing arts are rarely a one-on-one experience. Some experimental performances have featured one-on-one interactions, but these constitute the exceptions, not the rule. Even solo performances involve more than one person during rehearsals; and of course the public performance occurs before a gathering of people. A principal task of rehearsals is to coordinate the various skills, opinions, and desires of the production team. This is true of rituals as well as other genres of performance. Among Indigenous Australians, for example, the elders will spend hours discussing, arguing, and arranging for what results in a ten-minute performance that is part of a much longer initiation rite. In sports, rehearsals are called "practice." A coach may use a chalkboard in the locker room to show how a play ought to be run, but soon enough the players are on the field and practice playing. In law, too, moot courts serve as rehearsals for future lawyers where the performance aspects of the moot court are emphasized (**see UCLA Moot Court Handbook box**).

During rehearsals proto-performances are researched, interpreted, absorbed, recomposed, and rewritten. Usually, each proto-p enters rehearsals belonging to a single person – the author, choreographer, composer, designer, or performer. Everyone brings their own agenda into rehearsals. The job of rehearsals is to sort through and transcend all this stuff – to weave disparate or not entirely understood proto-performances into a coherent public performance.

UCLA Moot Court Handbook

Performing your brief

The advocate should use his eyes, his hands, and his voice to maintain the attention of the court and strengthen the persuasive effect of his arguments. The advocate should not hesitate to use the unique advantages of his personal presence during oral argument. Good eye contact, effective gestures, and an interesting voice pattern may substantially augment the persuasive quality of a legal argument. [. . .] Looking at each member of the panel squarely in the eyes is a particularly valuable means of capturing and maintaining the undivided attention of the court. [. . .] Certain distracting habits reoccur in student arguments frequently enough to justify the following lists of Do's and Don'ts:

1. Stand straight; do not lean on the podium, slouch, or move back and forth.
2. Keep your hands at your sides or resting (not leaning) on the podium [. . .].
3. Speak in a clear audible voice; do not shout, mumble, or whisper.
4. Do not neglect to address the court. Use, "If it please the Court," "Your Honors," or "This Court;" do not address the court as "you."
5. Use affirmative language [. . .].
6. Sit up straight and listen attentively while opposing counsel or co-counsel is speaking. [. . .]
7. Dress appropriately for the occasion.
8. Introduce yourself before you speak.

A well-delivered presentation adds immeasurably to the persuasiveness of the case. It gives an air of polish and distinction to the argument.

n.d., Anonymous, *Handbook of Appellate Advocacy*, 48–49

Warm-up

On any Sunday morning at the Institutional Church of God in Christ in Brooklyn, New York, before the service really gets going, four or five children ranging in age from about eight to twelve begin playing the drums, an electric guitar, and the keyboard. Only five or six members of the congregation are in the church at that time. About 20 minutes later, as the congregation gathers, the young instrumentalists accompany the Youth Choir, who belt out a few rousing songs. Then both the Youth Choir and their backup retire in favor of more mature musicians. Those in attendance number 50 or more. Soon enough, deacons make announcements, Scripture is read, a member or two of the congregation offer testimony. More people keep entering the sanctuary. Finally, more than an hour after the children started banging the drums, the Radio Choir makes its dramatic entrance marching down the center aisle, preceded by Bishop Carl E. Williams, Sr., or his son, Bishop C. E. Williams, Jr., other preachers, and a visiting dignitary or two. The service proper is ready to begin. What went on before was warm-up.

Every performance is immediately preceded by a warm-up, some lengthy as at the Institutional Church, some brief and hardly noticeable, as when odissi dancer Sanjukta Panigrahi made a few solemn gestures to the statue of the god Jagganath – which she made certain was onstage when she danced. "I dance for Jagganath," she told me; "the rest of the world can watch if it wishes." Many actors concentrate their minds prior to stepping onstage. Singers run scales or in some other way warm up the voice. A fully costumed and masked noh actor contemplates his image in a mirror just before going onstage (**see figure 7.12**). A public speaker goes over her notes, practices a few words. Stanislavsky advised actors to prepare at length during the day of a performance. A judge will review case dockets, put on robes, and enter the courtroom on cue when the clerk announces her. A doctor will review patient records and perhaps confer with nurses or colleagues before an examination or making hospital rounds. Surgeons enact complex rituals concerning

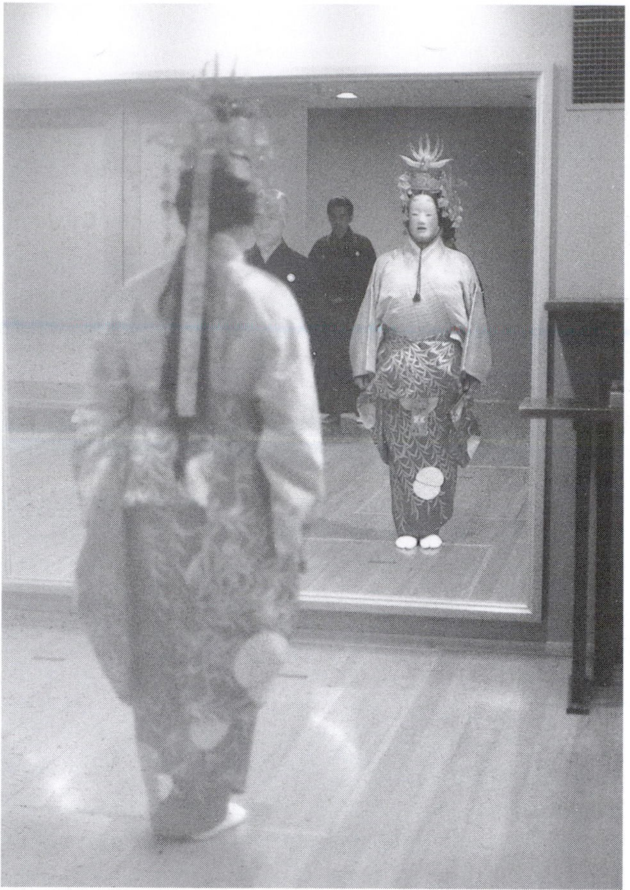

fig 7.12. Noh *shite* ("doer," the main performer) Izumi Yoshio as the heavenly maiden in *Hagoromo* by Zeami regarding his image in the mirror just before going on stage. Photograph by Monica Bethe.

their instruments, scrubbing, and other procedures before making the first incision. Athletes stretch and meditate, preparing both body and mind for the contest. Even during a game warm-ups continue. For example, a baseball pitcher will throw a few balls before each inning, or go through more extensive warm-up in the bullpen. A batter in the batting circle will swing his bat a few times before approaching the plate. A mother getting ready to scold a child may rehearse in her mind exactly what she will say and do.

The list can go on and on. There are many different kinds of warm-ups, each suiting a particular performer and performance. There is before every kind of performance – aesthetic, social, athletic, ritual, political, personal – a liminal time, sometimes brief, sometimes extended, when performers prepare to make the leap from "readiness" to "performance." This leap is decisive, a jump over a void of time–space. On one side of the void is ordinary life, on the other, performance. The warm-up takes place on the ordinary-life side, preparing the performer for the leap, giving the performer the courage to jump into performance.

In organized, ritually determined performances – the performing arts, law, medicine, religion, sports, and so on – warm-ups are often ritualized, involving specific costumes and well-known performance "faces" (attitudes, demeanors). In such cases, there may be a "pre-warm-up" where the individual performer follows her own private routine – because the ritualized genre-specific warm-up is already a performance in its own right. In other words, every performance, every entry into the enactment of a known and necessary score, demands a "time before" when the performer can ready herself for putting on/becoming the role. Shakespeare knew all about this when he penned, "The readiness is all" (*Hamlet*, 5, 2: 236–37).

Public performance

Training and workshops are where performers acquire necessary skills and find the right materials to make a public performance. Rehearsals are where the directors (choreographers, conductors, etc.) and performers construct a particular performance score. The warm-up readies performers for the leap into performing. Most of this book deals with what happens next, the vast range of public performances. Therefore, I will not linger here on what constitutes a public performance. Even in theatre there are so many different kinds of performances that at best one can refer only to a few (**see figure 7.13**). Add to these the untold other kinds of performances – and one comes up with what is, for all practical purposes, an endless list. But what is a "public performance"? A "public performance" is no easier to specify than was "is" performance in Chapter 2. I note only that a performance is whatever takes place between a marked beginning and a marked end. This marking, or framing, varies from culture to culture, epoch to epoch, and genre to genre – even, sometimes, from instance to instance. In the performing arts in mainstream Western genres, lowering the houselights and bringing the stage lights up, raising or opening curtains, and other procedures mark the start of a performance or portion of a performance. The closing or dropping of a curtain, the dimming of stage lights, the applause of spectators, and the actors taking bows mark the end of mainstream performances. At American sports events, the singing of the national anthem precedes the start of a game. For every genre, in every culture, there are usually very clear markers signaling the start and finish of a public performance.

fig 7.13. An array of different kinds of performances. This selection by no means exhausts the possibilities.

Spalding Gray as The Bishop and Joan Evans as The Penitent in The Performance Group's production of Jean Genet's *The Balcony*, directed by Richard Schechner, 1979. Photograph courtesy Richard Schechner.

Mick Jagger singing at Woodstock, 1968. Photograph by Ken Regan.

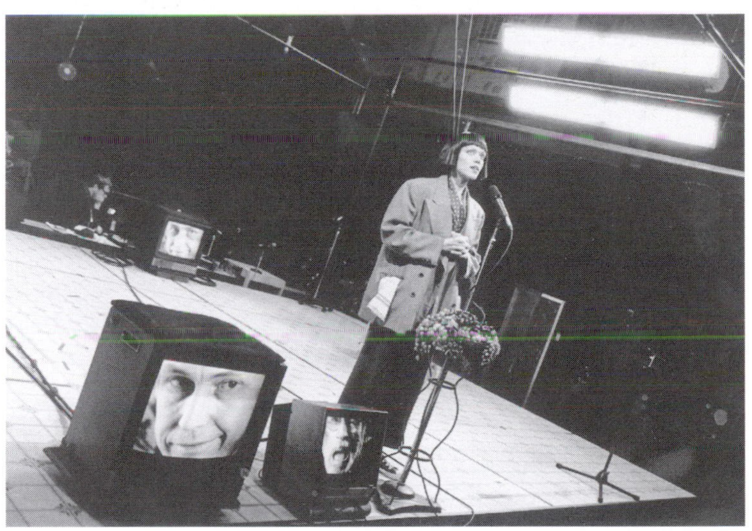

Kate Valk as the Narrator in The Wooster Group's production of *Brace Up!* based on Anton Chekhov's *Three Sisters*, 1991. Photograph by Mary Gearheart. Copyright The Wooster Group.

Sarah Bernhardt, right, as Hamlet, 1899. Most probably Ophelia is at the spinning wheel – perhaps this is the "Get thee to a nunnery" scene, act 3, scene 1. Bernhardt (1844–1923) played several male roles during her illustrious career. Photograph courtesy of Richard Schechner.

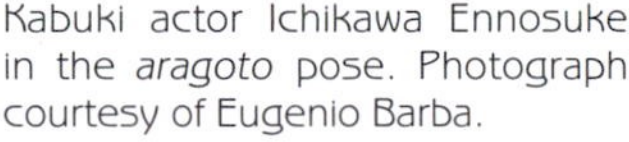

Kabuki actor Ichikawa Ennosuke in the *aragoto* pose. Photograph courtesy of Eugenio Barba.

But even these apparently definite conventions can be played with – throwing into doubt exactly what constitutes a performance. A famous example is John Cage's *4'33"* (1952). This concert consisted of pianist **David Tudor** walking onto stage, sitting down at a grand piano, and . . . not playing any music. At the start of each movement as indicated on Cage's score, Tudor shut the cover of the piano keyboard. He opened it again after a certain interval. Otherwise, Tudor sat at the keyboard, attentive but unmoving. The music Cage wanted his audience to listen to was the ambient sounds in the room over the duration of four minutes and thirty-three seconds. The theorist-composer wanted to show that there was no such thing as silence. He insisted that any period of properly marked listening was music. As the title, *4'33"*, indicates, time was measured (as music is marked by measures); what people heard within that time frame was designated by Cage as his musical composition.

David Tudor (1926–96): American pianist and composer who from the 1950s frequently collaborated with John Cage and dancer-choreographer **Merce Cunningham**. As time went on, Tudor stopped performing as a pianist and devoted himself entirely to composing electronic music both independently and as musical director of the Merce Cunningham Dance Company. Among his compositions: *Rainforest I* (1968), *Toneburst* (1974), *Webwork* (1987), *Neural Network Plus* (1992), and *Soundings: Ocean Diary* (1994).

Merce Cunningham (1919–): American dancer and choreographer who was a soloist in the Martha Graham company 1939–45 before forming his own troupe in 1953. Cunningham collaborated with John Cage from 1944 onward. Cunningham has choreographed extensively to electronic music and has often used mixed media in his works. Among Cunningham's many pieces are *Totem Ancestor* (1942), *In the Name of the Holocaust* (1943), *Suite for Five in Space and Time* (1956), *How to Pass, Kick, Fall and Run* (1965), *Video Triangle* (1976), *Roaratorio* (1983), *Ocean* (1994), and *Views on Stage* (2004).

Cage, of course, was not the only artist to challenge accepted conventions. The definition of "performance" – in the arts and beyond – has been vastly enlarged partly because of the insistence of experimental artists who actively explored new venues, new ways of performing, and new ways of receiving performances as audiences-spectators and participants (**see figure 7.14**). Today we have an enormous range of aesthetic, ritual, secular, civic, sportive, and other kinds of performances. Some are virtuosic, demanding well-trained persons; others are more ordinary, or occur within the framework of daily life and pass almost unnoticed (except by performance theorists). Some performances are polished and finished; others are intentionally "open" or unfinished. Most audiences wait until a performance is finished or nearly so before witnessing it. But many artists and groups invite people to open rehearsals. Previews followed by revisions are a necessity in commercial theatre and even with some films. The Wooster Group continues to work on its productions throughout the entire time a piece remains in the repertory. There is no formal opening of a Wooster creation. And even after a work has been reviewed, many changes will be made on a continuing basis. Revising works or changing how one performs is of course more the fact with regard to aesthetic or sports performances than with regard to rituals. But rituals do change, sometimes radically as when, starting in 1970, the Roman Catholic Church began to celebrate the Mass in vernacular languages instead of Latin. Even in everyday life, after a failed event, people revise their behavior. And in business one might say that the debut of a new product or service constitutes an "opening." Prior to the opening, test markets are used for rehearsals, with new products being changed on the basis of test market results.

Not all performances are successful. A performance can fail in two ways: if it does not please its public or if it does not accomplish most of what those making the performance intend. But even these indications of success and failure can be mistaken. Some artists are never satisfied – even with works that the public loves. Then there are those performances that more than fail to please the public or critics – shows that outrage the public. At its 1896 première in Paris, **Alfred Jarry**'s proto-surrealist *Ubu Roi* was greeted by a riot (**see Melzer box**). In 1999 and 2001, New York Mayor **Rudolph Giuliani** was so upset by paintings exhibited at the Brooklyn Museum of Art that he tried to take away the Museum's funding – and later convened a "decency commission" to recommend ways to monitor New York City's art (**see Rudolph Giuliani's "Decency Commission" box**). But history has its way of rectifying things. Naturalism, once deemed outrageous, became film and theatre's dominant style. *Ubu Roi* is still frequently performed without any disruption. What future generations will make of Giuliani's puritanical efforts remains to be seen. Often, new generations find it hard to grasp what the fuss was all about.

Alfred Jarry (1873–1907): French "pataphysicist," a term he coined. Jarry was a forerunner of the theatre of the absurd and other avant-garde movements. Best known for his "Ubu plays" – grotesque dark comedies about the petty and foolish King Ubu. The most famous of these is *Ubu Roi* (*King Ubu*, 1896).

fig 7.14. An unusual "found space" (a debris-ridden part of a New York City Park), a "site specific" setting for Grzegorz Kwiecinski's *Faustus*, a 1984 work of his Theatre of Fire and Paper. Photograph courtesy Richard Schechner.

Annabelle Melzer

Ubu Roi *opens, audience riots*

When the curtain opened before an audience of 2,500, actors [Firmin] Gemier and [Louise] Marie France were already on stage, Gemier sporting a huge belly and wearing a heavy mask which had been designed by Jarry. [. . .] Gemier opened with the play's infamous "Merdre" ["shit!"]. The resulting pandemonium has been chronicled by many critics. Laughter, hisses, cries of anger and applause vied with each other for prominence. [. . .] Tristan Bernard and Jules Renard screamed and whistled, enjoying themselves enormously in the confusion, while monocled and restrained Edmond Rostand smiled indulgently. In an effort to calm the crowd, Ferdinand Herold, in the wings (where he was responsible for the lighting), switched on the house lights. This brought only a momentary lull as members of the audience suddenly saw each other with hands raised and mouths agape. [. . .] In the days that followed the critics continued to stoke the smoldering fire of outrage. The general conclusion was unanimous, "A scandal . . . no other word will do."

1994, *Dada and Surrealist Performance*, 116–17

Rudolph Giuliani (1944–): American politician, Mayor of New York City, 1993–2001. A tough-minded public prosecutor before being elected mayor, a major objective of the Giuliani administration was to make New York a "clean and safe city." Many felt that under Giuliani the police disregarded the rights of especially the poor and the homeless. Giuliani's calm and courageous actions during and after the attacks of 9/11 won him widespread admiration both within New York and globally.

Larger events and contexts

Every focused public performance is nested in one or more larger events or contexts. These events and contexts define the limits of a performance. It may not be easy to say exactly when or where a given larger event or context ends and ordinary life begins. The focused performance is usually clearly marked at its start and its conclusion; not so the larger contexts in which a given performance is nested. Despite this blurriness, it is important to understand the larger events and contexts because these give the focused performance at least some of its meanings, channeling people, resources, and energies both to, through, and away from the performance. The larger event may be ritual, political, commercial, or social – or more than one of these simultaneously.

At the simplest level, the larger event includes everything taking place at the performance venue – the performance itself, the behavior of the audience, the backstage life, etc. – from the time a particular performance begins until it is over. This includes arriving at the performance venue, setting up, the activities in the dressing room, the box office, the lobby, and so on. It also includes shutting down the performance venue after the show is over.

Every public performance operates within or as part of a network of technical, economic, and social activities. Take an ordinary theatre, dance, or music performance. Off site, business managers, ticket and advertising agencies are running the business of the arts company, selling seats, and placing ads. Spectators have made plans and, as the event approaches, they get ready to travel to the event location. "Going to the theatre" is usually not a solitary activity. Couples and groups of various sizes attend. For some, going to the performance is a way of celebrating, a time out of ordinary time, perhaps a birthday or anniversary treat or a school project. Others are part of a theatre party or group who long before the event agreed to buy a block of tickets. On site, long before the first spectator arrives, the technical staff prepares the theatre – from cleaning the dressing rooms to making sure that all the props are ready and the stage equipment works. The box office staff is ready to honor

Rudolph Giuliani's "Decency Commission"

NEW YORK (AP) A city "decency commission," created to judge the morality of publicly funded art, will include three artists, three clergy members, Guardian Angels founder Curtis Sliwa and the mayor's own divorce lawyer.

Mayor Rudolph Giuliani, who named the panel's 20 members on Tuesday, said he had hoped they could issue a report on decency standards within three months, but they said it would likely take longer. [. . .]

The panel was created after Giuliani became incensed two months ago by a photograph at the city-funded Brooklyn Museum of Art. The 5-foot-tall photo, called "Yo Mama's Last Supper," shows a nude, black woman portraying Jesus surrounded by disciples.

Giuliani called the work "disgusting" and "anti-Catholic." The mayor used similar language in 1999 to denounce another artwork at the Brooklyn Museum: a painting of the Virgin Mary dappled with elephant dung. Giuliani halted city funding of the museum, but a federal court later ordered the city to resume it.

On Tuesday, Sliwa – who at 47 is one of the younger commission members – acknowledged that he knew little about art but believes he can contribute. "I know the difference between a Michelob and a Michelangelo," said Sliwa, who wore his trademark red beret and satin jacket. [. . .] Other members include Giuliani's attorney, Raoul Felder, and Alfred Curtis Jr., president of the United Nations Development Corp., as well as a rabbi, a bishop and an imam, a humanities professor and a free-lance news producer. The artist Peter Max declined to join after other artists criticized the panel and several news organizations reported that Max had been convicted of income tax evasion.

2001, Associated Press, "NYC Names Decency Panel"

reservations and sell tickets. The "actual performance" is nested within social, cultural, technical, and economic circumstances that extend in time, space, and kind beyond what happens onstage. Sports events are very much like the performing arts in this regard – activities heavily implicated in larger technical and economic networks. Furthermore, big-time sports – whether professional or at the college level – are enmeshed in the media, television especially, but also the internet.

What is so of aesthetic and sports performances is even truer of social, ritual, and political performances. Ritual performances involve acting out shared social values often involving the family in relation to a larger community. One can perhaps speak of "art for art's sake," but not of politics, ritual, or social events for their own sakes. These are always in the service of larger systems; and the performances always affect these larger systems. For example, a political rally brings a candidate in contact with her supporters. The whole event is staged – schoolchildren are bussed in, the media are contacted, and flags, lapel pins, and other paraphernalia are distributed. At a precise and pre-arranged moment, the Candidate Herself "appears," as if spontaneously. More seemingly spontaneous-but-carefully-scripted actions take place. Hand-shaking, baby-kissing, waving to the crowd. A speech, sometimes the often repeated "stump speech," more rarely something distinct and new, is offered to the expectant and receptive crowd. Off camera, one can see the candidate's handlers telling the crowd exactly when to cheer. The whole event is packaged for television – and, if it is successful from the candidate's point of view, 30 seconds of the rally will be seen on a number of different channels during the day, and especially on the widely watched early evening news. Now where does such an event take place? Who are its authors? Who is served by the performance?

No performance is an island. What goes on at the center – the event itself – affects and is affected by concentric circles of activities and interests. The needs and tone of these activities and interests infiltrate, contain, and shape the core event. The media clamors for news; producers demand a profit; performers want good roles, the attention of critics, and the praise of audiences. The desires and plans of allies, handlers, enemies, friends, and family sometimes clash and sometimes collaborate in shaping the core event so that it embodies and expresses certain aesthetic, political, ideological, professional, and/or religious values. Even the most apparently marginal or independent experimental performance is actually embedded in several concentric circles of activities and interests. At the very least, there is the circle of friends and associates. But operating at a slightly further distance from the center are those who will benefit from a successful performance – and who work toward making sure that the performance is successful. Emerging artists work the phones, hoping to grab the interest of critics and producers. Sports events are haunted by agents. Political upstarts seek just the right photo-op. In these and many other ways, the core event is knitted into a complex system of larger events.

Cooldown

Whatever the performance, at some point it is over. The curtain comes down, the audience leaves, the inauguration ends, the bride and groom leave the party, the dancers are in their dressing rooms changing into street clothes (**see figure 7.15**). As the performers unwind, the spectators gather their belongings, chat about what they have just seen or participated in, and go out for a bite or home to rest. Things return to "normal." This transition between the show and the show-is-over is an often overlooked but extremely interesting and important phase. If warm-ups prepare people for the leap into performance, cooldown ushers them back to daily life.

Cooldown is usually not as formal a procedure as warm-up. Part of the reason for this is that once the focused performance is over, people simply let go. But studying this "letting go" reveals a patterned activity. Informal cooldown for the active performers involves gestures that put the role to rest and reawaken the ordinary self. Actors hang up their costumes and store their masks, take off their makeup, wash, put on street clothes. Athletes visit the training room for rubdowns and attention to injuries. Often a dressing room just after the curtain comes down is relatively quiet. It takes a little bit of time to come back to oneself. When friends invade the dressing room too soon they can feel the actors' tension between wanting to be hospitable and wanting to be alone for a little while.

In ordinary social life, a party can be quite a performance for the hosts. If so, a cooldown usually takes place. After the guests leave, the hosts clean up (or decide to "leave it till morning," a way of saying, almost, that they don't want the party to end). Often, people discuss whether or not the gathering was a "success." After a date, friends ask, "how did it go?" After military action or an intelligence operation comes "debriefing," where descriptions of what happened are carefully recorded for later analysis.

On the spectator side of things, after a performance most often people go out for something to eat and drink – and to talk, not only to evaluate what they've just experienced, but

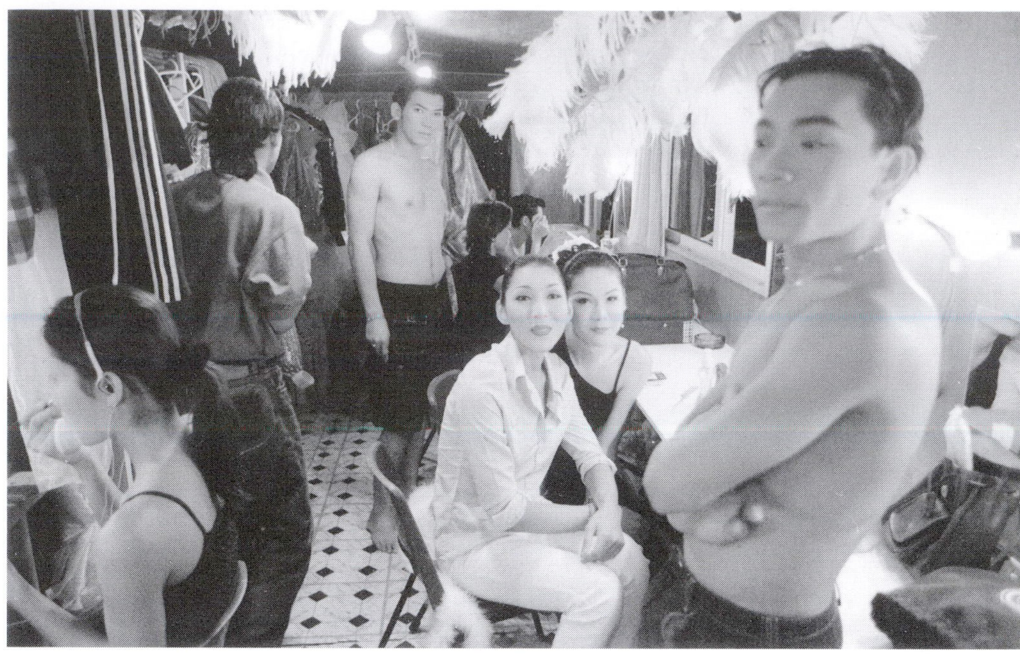

fig 7.15. The Lady-Boys of Bangkok cooling down in their dressing room after performing. Photograph by Geraint Evans. Copyright *The Independent*.

to resume authority over their own bodies and over time. Spectator behavior during a performance often demands bodily stillness and silence which leave people feeling both pent-up and empty. This physical–social paradox is fixed by talking and eating/drinking. For events such as religious services and sports matches that include active audience behavior, even sometimes the intake of food and drink, cooldown takes a different path: embraces and greetings after the service, a momentary encounter with the rabbi or minister, a family dinner – which is itself its own performance. At sports, where the generally exuberant behavior includes eating, drinking, and cheering, the cooldown consists mostly of discussing the good and bad qualities of the game just ended. This post-game activity can become a performance in its own right, a kind of continuation by means of replaying and arguing about key moments of the event. If that happens, then the post-game performance needs its own cooldown after everyone leaves the bar and goes home.

Sometimes cooldown is formal. For example, American director **JoAnne Akalaitis** gathers the actors for a specific set of cooldown exercises which includes focused breathing and a mental review of the performance just concluded (**see Saivetz box**). In Bali, after trancing, the dancers are "smoked," given incense to inhale, and sometimes a ritual sacrifice is made, all with the goal of bringing the performers back to themselves.

JoAnne Akalaitis (1937–): American theatre director and a founding member in 1970 of the Mabou Mines experimental performance collective. From 1991–93, Akalaitis was the artistic director of The New York Shakespeare Festival/Public Theatre. Currently she is Professor of Theatre at Bard College. Her productions include Samuel Beckett's *Cascando* (1975) and *Endgame* (1984), Mabou Mines' *Dead End Kids* (1980), Jean Genet's *The Screens* (1989), Georg Buchner's *Woyzeck* (1992–93), the *Iphigenia Cycle* (1997), Philip Glass' opera, *In the Penal Colony* (2000), and Harold Pinter's *The Birthday Party* (2003).

In all these cases, informal and formal, the cooldown is a bridge, an in-between phase, leading from the focused activity of the performance to the more open and diffuse experiences of everyday life.

Aftermath

The continuing life of a performance is its aftermath. This phase of the performance process may extend for years or even centuries – in fact, the duration of the aftermath is indefinite. Through various historical and archaeological research techniques a performance even thousands of years old can be to some degree reconstructed. Ironically, the more removed in time, the more important trivial or throwaway

Deborah Saivetz

The Akalaitis cooldown

In the first of the [cooldown] exercises, the actors lie on their backs with their eyes closed and their arms and legs extended. [. . .] The actors focus on their breath, inhaling through the nose and exhaling through the mouth. They allow their minds to review what they just experienced [. . .]. Akalaitis then talks the actors "through their bodies." Beginning with the soles of the feet, the actors use the breath to become conscious of and release each part of the body.

1998, "An Event in Space," 149–50

evidence becomes – pottery shards, midden heaps, snapshots, old clothing, personal letters, and so on. The aftermath persists in physical evidence, critical responses, archives, and memories. Having acknowledged the potential longevity of the aftermath, it is also true that most aftermaths are relatively brief or sequestered in personal memories. In modern times, the immediate aftermath of publicly presented performances consists of the response by the agents of official culture – reviewers and critics – plus the ever-increasing amount of photographic, video, and digital records. There are also the memories of those participating in and attending the event. And of course there is the "word-of-mouth" circuit – sometimes people who never went to an event have plenty to say about it. After a time, many of these responses come to reside in the "archive," an umbrella term that means what can be accessed by various performance-forensic means. Archival materials may include videotapes, films, digital, and sound recordings, printed matter, props or other artifacts – anything at all from or concerning the performance. In developing an archive of a particular performance, researchers read old reviews; examine photographs, films, video, and DVDs; interview surviving performers or attendees (if the performance is fairly recent); look at the scripts or scores, costumes and props; visit performance venues. In sum, do everything possible to reconstruct "what happened." This pertains not just to theatrical events, but to performances of all kinds. How many "home performances" have been reawakened by an old photograph, a pair of gloves, or a long-forgotten letter discovered in an attic or closet?

Performance itself is categorically evanescent. Even the memory of performance fades quickly. Soon enough all but the most famous performances vanish. Events that were shattering and famous in their own time are remembered only when researched. They take on a second or more lives according to who gets hold of, analyzes, and reconstructs the archival evidence. Nowadays just about every event is put onto videotape or computer disk. But what is the shelf life of these kinds of storage? Not only do the operating systems rapidly go out of date, but the attention span of most people is short-lived. There is much too much out there for most of it to be of use to anyone. Scholars dig through old newspapers or video libraries to pull out long-forgotten reviews or images.

But sometimes the aftermath of a performance is open-ended, generating many new performances that replay with a difference what the authors of the new works presumed the original event might have been. The fascination with the drama of the *Titanic*'s 1912 catastrophic collision with an iceberg in no way has abated (**see *The* Titanic *Sinks on its Maiden Voyage* box**). So many perished, famous and steerage, on the great ship's maiden voyage. *Titanic* had everything from a puffed-up name to the most modern fittings and luxuries – a swift and unsinkable microcosm of European–American society and hubris colliding with destiny and going to the bottom as the orchestra played on. Robots from another epoch dove to the seabed to photograph *Titanic* and recover unbroken dinnerware and other artifacts. Numerous exhibits, movies, websites, and written accounts continue to

The Titanic *sinks on its maiden voyage!*

Many of those who perished on the ship came from prominent American, British, and European families. [. . .] The glamour associated with the ship, its maiden voyage, and its notable passengers magnified the tragedy of its sinking in the popular mind. Legends arose almost immediately around the night's events, those who had died, and those who had survived. Heroes and heroines [. . .] were identified and celebrated by the press. The disaster and the mythology that has surrounded it have continued to fascinate millions.

2001, *Encyclopedia Britannica Online Exhibit on the* Titanic, http://titanic.eb.com/01_01.html

add to the lore. On a less grandiose scale, some artistic events also have a long and influential afterlife. *Ubu Roi* is cited as an initiator and harbinger of the twentieth-century avant-garde from surrealism to Dada, from symbolism to theatre of the absurd.

There is no fixed limit to an aftermath. In the aesthetic genres, newspaper and media reviews and word of mouth are short-term kinds of aftermath. Long-term aftermath includes self-generated documentation (photos, DVDs, artist's notes, etc.), the impact and influence a work has on other artists, and scholarly articles written about a piece. The aftermath of a work folds back into restagings of classics as well as new work that exists "under the influence of" an older work. Sometimes a particular performance style is very influential and widespread even if, at its point of origin, the artist was not well known. From the early 1960s to the late 1980s, performance artist **Jack Smith** staged irregularly scheduled amateurish "theatre evenings" in his living space. Often fewer than ten people attended. But a wide range of artists attest to the impact Smith had on their work. Smith pioneered and explored many themes including cross-dressing, queer desire, non-narrative theatre, autobiographical performance, and radical eclecticism (**see Foreman box**).

Jack Smith (1932–89): pioneering American performance artist and filmmaker. Smith performed in his loft often to an audience of ten or fewer. He intentionally blurred the boundary between art and life. His films *Flaming Creatures* (1961) and *Normal Love* (1963) featured transvestites, androgynes, and drag queens.

The aftermath can impact the performance itself, sometimes catastrophically, sometimes happily. Bad reviews can close a Broadway or West End show. Or a director may take in the reviews, have an ear tuned to the word of mouth, listen to the opinions of friends, and make adjustments in the mise-en-scène. Paradoxically, previews and out-of-town tryouts give useful "aftermath information" before a production actually opens. In all performances – social, political, and professional as well as in the arts – the aftermath records how people react to and feel about an event.

Legal systems function largely in terms of aftermath – cases are decided by "precedent": the case at hand determined on the basis of decisions made earlier in similar cases. Surgery – dramatic and highly ritualized in the operating theatre – is judged "successful" mainly in terms of its aftermath. Was the problem addressed by the operation fixed?

When things go wrong, managing the aftermath – or "spin control" – comes into play. Politicians and CEOs pay public relations people big money to manage aftermath. "Spin" is making a performance mean what the client wants it to mean rather than what an objective observer might find. Tension between handlers and the press is focused on this issue of who controls the spin, the aftermath. A lot is at stake because whoever wins the spin war has a leg up on controlling an event's long-term meaning and significance.

At another level altogether, mythic events exist almost entirely as aftermaths generating myriads of "new" performances. Literally tens of thousands of dramas, movies,

Richard Foreman

A different kind of drama

The situation in *Pearls for Pigs* is that the leading character, the Maestro, after a long career, realizes he hates the theatre. And what he hates it for is the way in which it suppresses the possibility that impulse – human impulse – might be allowed to disrupt the performance. [. . .] There is no story in my plays, because impulse is set free to deflect normal linear development. [. . .] IMPULSE, of course, need not mean hitting someone on the nose – it may also mean reaching for an unsettling idea, or letting words surface from the unconscious. The point is – ART IS THE PLACE TO ALLOW THIS, WHICH CANNOT REALLY HAPPEN IN LIFE, TO HAPPEN IN ITS FULL, RICH, RADIANT, ABUNDANT GLORY. [. . .] But – here's the important part – these manifestations of impulse are not just narrated – THE SAME IMPULSE THAT PUSHES THE CHARACTER INTO "ACTING-OUT" ALSO TWISTS AND CONTROLS THE ARTISTIC STRUCTURE, so that the form and sequencing of the play itself reflects that impulsive, usually suppressed, energy of the human mental/emotional apparatus. And it's that isomorphic relationship between form and content that often perplexes people about contemporary art. [. . .] But of course, that happens all the time in drama and film and the novel. But there now exists a large group of so-called "difficult" or transgressive artists who believe that such a strategy no longer suffices to introduce a powerful and effective "impulse" therapy to audiences desperately trying to control their own impulsive tendencies [. . .].

1998, "Program Notes on *Pearls for Pigs*," 157

paintings and sculptings, novels, and re-enactments have reconfigured events such as the American Civil War, the Passion of Jesus Christ, the Trojan War, or the conflict between the Pandavas and Kauravas as told in the Sanskrit epic, the *Mahabharata*. Once a line of performances is established, the "source" becomes not the event itself – frequently exactly what happened is in dispute or cannot be determined with any historical clarity – but other performances. The archetypal actions of a culture are burned into public memory by means of rituals, re-enactments, and iconic visual arts. "Fact" gets absorbed into collective performed memory. What do you imagine Atlanta in flames in November 1864 during the American Civil War looked like? The image that comes to mind is most likely drawn from the film, *Gone with the Wind*. Who knows what Jesus' Last Supper "really" looked like? Most people imagining that seder see in their mind's eye **Leonardo da Vinci**'s famous 1498 painting – or one of its many copies and poster prints (**see figure 7.16**).

Leonardo da Vinci (1452–1519): Italian "Renaissance man" – sculptor, painter, drawer, engineer, and scientist. Among his best-known works, *The Last Supper* (1495–97) and *Mona Lisa* (1503–06).

Rules, proto-performance, and public performance

One cannot stage anything from a play to a religious ritual to a public ceremony to a trial or a party without rules – also called conventions, precedents, liturgies, manners, etc. These rules are not the "performance itself" but guidelines connecting every performance to the past, the tradition, and to the future – performances that will occur after the one at hand is over. Rules instruct all those involved in a performance – the players, the spectators, the production team – about what can and cannot be done. Rules may be invariable or loose, leaving little or much room for spontaneity and improvisation. In sports, for example, the rules always leave plenty of room for individual prowess – although some sports encourage improvisation more than others. Basketball leaves a lot more room for creative movement than the 50-yard sprint. And of course, rules are sometimes broken – both by cheating and as a way of creating a new situation. But this "violation of the rules" does not eliminate either the need for rules or their generally prevailing force. In fact, one might say that true creativity, which is extremely rare, is a play which makes necessary a revision of the rules, not just a shrewder way to play within the rules. In the arts,

fig 7.16. Leonardo da Vinci's 1498 wall painting, *The Last Supper*. Although probably without any historical relationship to the way Jesus and his disciples actually appeared and behaved at that Passover seder, this picture has dominated the popular imagination regarding Jesus and his disciples. As displayed on the internet at www.ibiblio.org/ wm/paint/auth/vinci/lastsupp.jpg

the avant-garde defines itself as "cutting edge," as breaking rules in order to discover new ways of doing things. But a close examination of the history of the avant-garde reveals mostly replays and variations on known themes and procedures rather than actual newness.

What of free, spontaneous performances such as improvisatory theatre, music, and dance or children's make-believe games? Only a little investigating shows that even these apparently free interactions are guided by conventions and accepted procedures – including the repetition of many packaged bits and routines. In fact, every performance, indeed every social interaction, is guided by a network of expectations and obligations. Each participant expects certain things to happen and wants assurance that other things won't happen. And each participant is obligated to play by the rules – or at least to appear to do so. Spectators expect that the event will be played according to rules or conventions. Knowing the rules or conventions is how one understands and interprets the game or aesthetic performance. Dark play (see Chapter 4) is a kind of playing that subverts the rules, but even dark play obeys its own conventions. Criminal activity – a violation of the rule of law, or actions "against" the law – can be understood as a species of dark play.

The performance quadrilogue

The performance process can be studied not only as a multi-phased time–space sequence, but also as the dynamic relationship among four categories of players:

1 sourcers (authors, choreographers, composers, detectives, **dramaturges**, etc.)
2 producers (directors, conductors, coaches, judges, designers, technicians, business staff, etc.)
3 performers
4 partakers (spectators, fans, juries, the public, etc.)

dramaturge: a person who works with the director in a wide variety of ways. Dramaturgical work includes researching the historical and cultural contexts and past production history of the dramatic text, working closely with the director in interpreting the dramatic text, and writing program notes. During rehearsals, the dramaturge may offer detailed criticism of the ongoing production process.

Sourcers write, research, find, or develop the sources, the raw materials, from which the performance – a play, a personal recollection, a scenario, a courtroom case, or anything at all that is performed – is made. During the workshop and rehearsal process, sources are revised or even discarded; new sources can always be found or brought in by the producers and performers as well as by the sourcers. Producers serve as facilitators guiding the shaping of the sources into a "finished performance." Producers work most closely with the performers, but also with the sourcers and sometimes even with the partakers. Producers are "link" persons, building bridges, making connections. Performers play the actions for the public. Partakers not only receive the actions, but may also participate in the actions. If they do participate, partakers at least temporarily become performers. A person may belong to more than one of these categories. Someone checking himself in a mirror as he dresses for a date plays all four roles. A performance artist like Spalding Gray was a sourcer, performer, and producer (though Gray also worked with producers other than himself). A group may do some or all of the sourcing, performing, producing, and partaking collectively.

A courtroom trial provides an excellent illustration. The sourcers are detectives, forensic experts, and witnesses – on both sides of the case. These people provide the information to the prosecuting and defense attorneys and their teams – producers and performers simultaneously – who then mold the source material into two opposing narratives of "what happened." This building a case and developing a strategy for the defense happens before the trial begins – in the workshop and rehearsal phases where information is gathered, witnesses interviewed and rehearsed, experts hired, etc. During the trial, the performers include the accused, the victim (present in person or represented by evidence), attorneys, witnesses, and the judge – a producer who physically sits above the action both representing and enforcing the rule of law. There are also bit players/stagehands – court stenographers and bailiffs. In terms of partakers, a trial is more complex than theatre or sports where there are only three kinds of partakers – spectators/fans, the press, and those watching live on the media or later finding out what happened via news reports. A trial has five concentric circles of partakers, each capable of interacting with the others. The innermost circle, and the most constrained, is the jury. A jury is the opposite of theatre or sports audiences. Jury members are not supposed to show what they are feeling by laughing, applauding, weeping, booing, or catcalling. A jury member is not permitted to walk out if the show is boring or distasteful. A jury is expected to pay attention so that it can decide the case on the evidence – acting, finally, not only collectively but unanimously. Of course, both prosecuting and defense attorneys try to stir the jury up and unsettle hostile witnesses – but courtroom convention – enforced by the judge – demands that there be "order in the court." The second circle of partakers is the families/friends of the accused and the victim. These people can, and frequently do, make a show of themselves. Next come the press who in the courtroom maintain an appearance of objectivity – but not necessarily in their reports and stories. The fourth circle consists of ordinary spectators: the trial of a celebrity, or a particularly gruesome crime, draws overflow crowds who attend for a wide variety of reasons ranging from the salacious to law students interested in how the case is being tried. The fifth and outermost circle of partakers includes those who follow the case in the press and/or via the media where legal experts comment and opine. Star witnesses and the accused play double roles – they are both sourcers and performers. Even if the accused does not take the stand, her/his courtroom demeanor is closely watched by the jury and others for tells indicating guilt or innocence. Smirking or keeping a straight face, fidgeting or sitting still, dozing or alertness, laughing or acting in a dignified way, and so on. These are all interpretable behaviors. A witness who speaks openly, clearly, and from the heart is more likely to be believed than a confused mumbler with shifty eyes. Defendants and witnesses are carefully costumed and rehearsed. Attorneys practice their examinations, cross-examinations, and summations.

The "performance quadrilogue" can be represented as a rectangle with every point connected to every other point (**see figure 7.17**). Theoretically, all connections are given equal weight. But in actuality, each performance enacts a specific route within the performance quadrilogue. The route taken to get from point to point of the quadrilogue, and the primacy or dominance of one player category over one or more of the others, reveals a great deal about the performance process of that particular performance or genre of performance.

Take mainstream theatre, for example. This kind of theatre begins with a sourcer, a playwright whose play is selected by the producers (a stage director and/or whoever is in charge of the production). Sometimes the project begins with an investor or producer wishing to mount a production – the producer or producers search for the right "property," a play or other vehicle. Next, the producers assemble an artistic team consisting of a stage director, actors, designers, and technicians. The job of this team is to use their particular skills to "realize" the source, in this case, a play: in other words, to make a public performance. The result of this collaboration is a specific theatre event offered to the partakers – the "Z-path" around the performance quadrilogue depicted in **figure 7.18**. No direct line connects the sourcers to the performers or to the partakers or the producers to the partakers. In this kind of theatre, although the playwright is the source, and the producers bring the production into existence, the final relationship is between the performers and the partakers. The great Russian director **Vsevolod Meyerhold** visualized the Z-path as a straight line (**see Meyerhold box**). In his depiction, Meyerhold emphasized the work of the actors. Meyerhold's "theatre of the straight line" shows a process in which the play is wholly absorbed by the director who conveys his interpretation to the actors. Once this has been done, the director steps out of the way. The actors relate face to face, without interference, to the partakers, the audience. Meyerhold rarely followed his own advice. In much of his work, the director ruled.

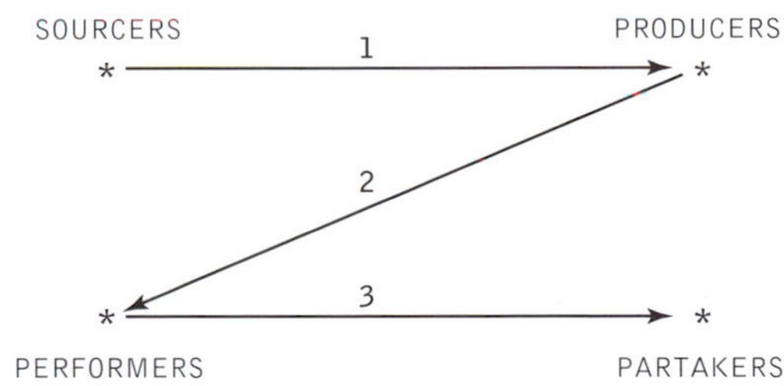

fig 7.18. The Z-path around of the performance quadrilogue signifying the way mainstream theatre works. Drawing by Richard Schechner.

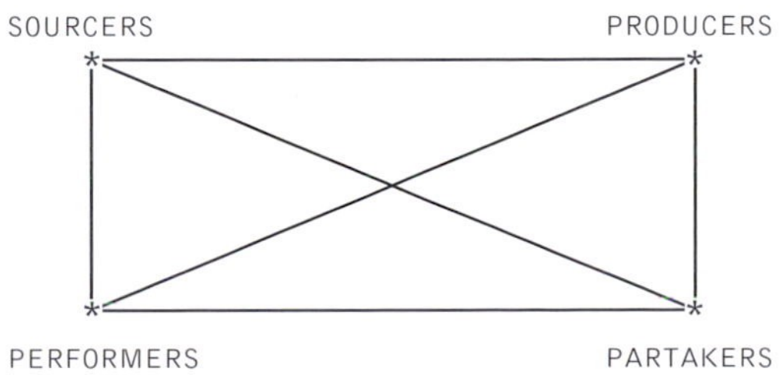

fig 7.17. The performance quadrilogue – with all connections potentially available. Drawing by Richard Schechner.

Many directors claim they follow Meyerhold's "theatre of the straight line." But in practice, directors such as Peter Brook, JoAnne Akalaitis, and **Peter Stein** work as shown in **figure 7.19**. Here the director rules. This kind of director absorbs the play or other sources and keeps control of the actors. The partakers experience the performance as interpreted by the director. Sometimes there are producers controlling the stage director because these producers are paying. But often a big-name director can get complete artistic control or serves both as producer and director. In these cases, the director is relatively free throughout the

Vsevolod Meyerhold (1874–1940): Russian director and actor. Before the Russian Revolution of 1917, Meyerhold was an actor in Stanislavsky's Moscow Art Theatre and later an independent director. Meyerhold was an enthusiastic supporter of the Revolution, attempting to apply its principles to theatre ("October in the Theatre"). He developed "biomechanics," a system of kinetic acting using highly stylized, expressive movements that Meyerhold felt perfectly suited the new proletarian age. During the 1930s, Meyerhold increasingly was regarded by Stalinists as an enemy of the state. In 1940, he was arrested and murdered in a Moscow prison by Stalin's police; his wife was murdered in their home. Meyerhold's key writings have been translated into English as *Meyerhold on Theatre* (1969).

Vsevolod Meyerhold

Theatre of the straight line

A straight, horizontal line with the four theatrical elements (author, director, actor, spectator) marked from left to right represents [. . .] what we shall call the "theatre of the straight line." The actor reveals his soul freely to the spectator, having assimilated the creation of the director, who, in his turn, has assimilated the creation of the author.

[. . .] The actor's art consists in far more than merely acquainting the spectator with the director's conception. The actor will grip the spectator only if he assimilates both the director and the author and then gives of himself from the stage.

1969 [1907], *Meyerhold on Theatre*, 50–51

Peter Stein (1937–): German theatre director whose artistic leadership of Berlin's Schaubuhne 1970–85 helped invigorate European theatre. Stein's productions include Ibsen's *Peer Gynt* (1971), Wagner's *Das Rheingold* (1976), Chekhov's *Three Sisters* (1984), and Goethe's *Faust* (2000).

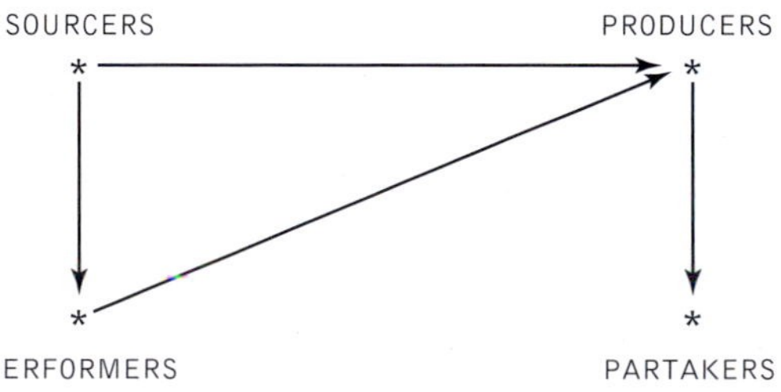

fig 7.19. The director rules configuration of the performance quadrilogue. This is the way directors such as Peter Brook, JoAnne Akalaitis, and Peter Stein work. Drawing by Richard Schechner.

process to realize her/his vision. "The director rules" kind of director works from the principle that a play cannot speak for itself (**see Carlson box**). Brook was attacked for the way he treated the Indian epic in his production of *The Mahabharata*. The attacks basically claimed that Brook did not respect the "Indianness" of his source material. Although directors frequently claim that their productions follow the author's intentions, unless the author is alive and actively involved in the rehearsal process, most directors take for themselves the right of interpretation. Of course, the public knows this. People go to the productions of specific directors to find out how an Akalaitis, a Brook, or a Stein understands and interprets certain texts and source materials.

Even more radically than the director-rules path around the quadrilogue is the "**auteur** director" path (**see figure 7.20**). An auteur director's route around the performance quadrilogue is not a "Z" as in mainstream theatre, but a gathering up of all elements into a single hand. Like painters or some filmmakers (the source of the "auteur" term), auteur directors totally control what the partakers experience.

Marvin Carlson

A play cannot speak for itself

Even today, one encounters those who urge that the theatre produce plays by Shakespeare "straight" or "as the author intended," or to "let the plays speak for themselves," as if unmediated performance were desirable or even possible. Peter Brook has responded to this common advice as succinctly as anyone. "A play cannot speak for itself," he says; one must "conjure its sound from it." Similarly Tyrone Guthrie has warned that the attempt to avoid interpretation usually results in the imitation of previous interpretations which have grown comfortably familiar. It is important to remember that the performed play, unlike the painting, comes to us not as a specific object, but only through a performance tradition.

1990, *Theatre Semiotics*, 116

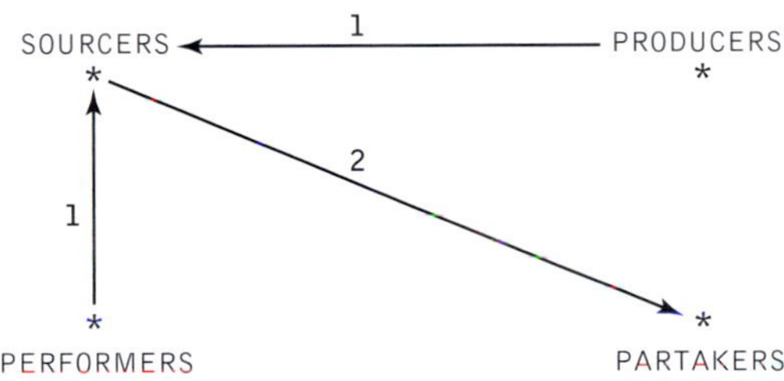

fig 7.20. Auteur-director route around the performance – the way Robert Wilson and even more so, Richard Foreman, work. Drawing by Richard Schechner.

Artists such as **Robert Wilson** and **Richard Foreman** are the auteurs of their works down to the smallest details of staging and movement, timing, set and costume design, sound, and role interpretation (**see figures 7.21 and 7.22**). Auteur directors collaborate or draw on the creative abilities of many people. But when one agrees to work with an auteur director, you know that the final word on what will be used, and how, belongs to the auteur. Wilson has had many collaborators – including composer Philip Glass and composer-performer **Tom Waits** – but Wilson's work projects a very identifiable "Wilson style." Foreman is even more singular in his control of what the partakers get. Foreman writes the plays, designs and paints the sets, produces, and directs. Everything from the program to the tiniest set detail belongs to Foreman. The costumes and set are built by others but under Foreman's strict instructions. It is Foreman's voice that is heard on tape during the performance. In his earlier work, Foreman himself ran the sound cues and placed himself in the theatre so that the audience could see him as well as the actors on stage. In recent years, Foreman has employed others to operate the technical equipment but there is no mistaking Foreman's style for anyone else's. Performers in this kind of theatre are not free agents; they may feel more like living puppets – the "über marionettes" that early twentieth-century theorist and director **Edward Gordon Craig** dreamed of for the theatre.

auteur: the French word meaning "author" used by critics to signify film directors who exercised complete control over their films comparable to the control literary authors have over their works. Auteur is a term used today to designate theatre, dance, or film artists who exercise such control.

Robert Wilson (1941–): American opera and theatre director and visual artist known for his spectacular large-scale performance pieces, including *Einstein on the Beach* (1976), *the CIVIL warS* (1984), *The Black Rider* (1990), Strindberg's *Dream Play* (1998), Buchner's *Woyzeck* (2002), Ibsen's *Peer Gynt* (2005), and the Sulawesian-Indonesian epic, *I La Galligo* (2005).

Richard Foreman (1937–): American playwright, theatre director, and theorist. Foreman has written more than 50 plays – most of which he has directed. His plays include *Sophia=Wisdom* (1972), *Rhoda in Potatoland* (1975), *Penguin Torquet* (1981), *Now That Communism is Dead My Life Feels Empty* (2001), and *The Gods Are Pounding My Head* (2005). His books include *Plays and Manifestos* (1976), *Unbalancing Acts* (1992), and *Paradise Hotel* (2001).

Tom Waits (1949–): American singer, composer, and actor whose music is edgy and political, something like Bertolt Brecht meets Bob Dylan. Waits collaborated with Robert Wilson on *Black Rider* (1990), *Alice* (1992), and *Woyzeck* (2002). Among his many albums: *Closing Time* (1973), *Heartattack and Vine* (1980), *Night on Earth* (1992), *Mule Variations* (1999), *Blood Money* (2002), and *Real Gone* (2004).

Edward Gordon Craig (1872–1966): English scene designer, director, and actor who staunchly opposed realism. Arguing for the authority of the director, Craig proposed doing away with actors, replacing them with large marionettes. Craig edited the influential journal, *The Mask* from 1908–29. Among his books are *On the Art of the Theatre* (1911, rev. edn, 1956) and *The Theatre Advancing* (1919).

fig. 7.21. Robert Wilson's *Einstein on the Beach*, 1976. This production was directed and designed by Wilson, with music by Philip Glass, and choreography by Andrew de Groat. Photo courtesy Richard Schechner.

fig 7.22. Richard Foreman's *Sophia = Wisdom*, 1972. Everything you see in this scene was conceptualized and even actually built by Foreman. The actors function to some degree as extensions of Foreman's consciousness. Photo courtesy of Richard Foreman.

Interestingly, although auteur directors are relatively rare in theatre – the director-rules model is more common – in dance, auteuring is the dominant mode. In modern dance, the choreographers are frequently also the principal dancers. The choreographer dances her own score or sets movements onto the bodies of other dancers. This is the way Martha Graham and Doris Humphrey worked – and this tradition continues today. Keeping strictly to a known score is important enough that reconstructing the choreography of dancers who have passed from the scene is common. Labanotation or other means are used to make certain that exactly the right steps are danced. In ballet, there are many dances from the repertory whose choreography was set long ago. These dances are repeated over and over with relatively little variation. Changes in the score of a **George Balanchine** ballet are likely to be less radical than what a strong conductor might do to a Beethoven symphony where the notes may remain the same, but the tempo and feel of the music will change. But when the New York City Ballet dances *The Nutcracker* – "George Balanchine's classic, a Christmas holiday tradition in New York City and one of the first ballets kids get to see" (says the NYC Ballet's website) – the company dances Balanchine's steps in the way he intended. It was just this kind of strict adherence to tradition imposed both by ballet and modern dance that postmodern dancers rebelled against. In doing so, choreographers such as **Pina Bausch** make works that are close to theatre in several key ways. Pieces are often collaboratively composed; improvisation is widely used; spoken or sung text – some of it very personal, authored by the dancers – is integrated into the choreography.

George Balanchine (1904–83): Russian-born American choreographer and dancer. After fleeing the Soviet Union in 1924, Balanchine worked widely in Europe – including with Brecht and Kurt Weil. He was brought to the USA in 1934 by arts patron Lincoln Kirstein (1907–96) to form the School of American Ballet. In 1946, Balanchine and Kirstein founded the New York City Ballet which Balanchine led until his death. His works with the NYC Ballet include *The Firebird* (1949), *The Nutcracker* (1954), *Agon* (1957), *Bugaku* (1963), *Vienna Waltzes* (1977), and *Mozartiana* (new version 1981). Over his lifetime, Balanchine choreographed 425 works including many set to the music of **Igor Stravinsky**. Balanchine also worked extensively in Hollywood and on Broadway.

Igor Stravinsky (1882–1971): radically innovative Russian-born composer whose work helped shape modernism. Leaving Russia before the First World War, Stravinsky lived first in Europe and then moved to USA in 1939. Among his many compositions are *Capricio* (1929), *Symphony in C* (1940), *Canticum Sacrum* (1955), and *Requiem Canticles* (1966). Stravinsky also composed ballets and stage works including *The Firebird* (1910), *Petrushka* (1911), *The Rite of Spring* (1913), *The Soldier's Tale* (1918), *The Rake's Progress* (1951), and *Oedipus Rex* (1927).

Pina Bausch (1940–): German choreographer whose dances cross the boundaries separating theatre from dance. Since 1973, Bausch has been artistic director of the Wuppertal Dance Theatre where she has composed works ranging from Stravinsky's *The Rite of Spring* (1975) and Brecht's *The Seven Deadly Sins of the Bourgeoisie* (1976) to *Café Muller* (1978), *Nelken* (1982), *Two Cigarettes in the Dark* (1985), *Aqua* (2001), and *Rough Cut* (2005).

Performing music spans the possibilities. Rock musicians often compose many of the songs they perform as well as stage their shows, thus combining sourcer, producer, and performer. Classical orchestral concerts, on the other hand, maintain a strict separation of tasks. The composer provides the source material. The conductor often radically interprets the score (but usually does not change the notes). Individual orchestra members are given less latitude for interpretation than actors – except for soloists who are expected to put their own stamp on the music they play. Also, composers sometimes conduct or play their own music.

Coaches of athletic teams have much less control over what happens on the field than do directors, choreographers, or conductors. After long periods of training and practicing, the actual playing belongs to the players. Single-person sports – golf, racing, singles tennis – are almost entirely in the hands of the individual athletes. Their situation approaches that of Meyerhold's theatre of the straight line. Even team sports come close to what Meyerhold wanted. Because of the adversarial nature of sports, games often go off in their own direction. Coaches try to maintain tight control – in football this has gone as far as installing small radio receivers in the helmets of quarterbacks so that plays can be sent in from the sidelines. In sports, intricate systems of "signs," codes known only to the team, convey instructions from the coaches to the players. But the unpredictability of sports often takes over. This appeals to fans because spectacular and unexpected plays, errors, willful risk-taking, and surprising moves by the other side provide many thrills.

From performance montage to desktop theatre

Montage, a powerful and widely used technique in visual media and theatre, was developed in the 1920s by filmmaker **Sergei Eisenstein**, at one time a student of Meyerhold's. A montage is a way of "speaking" with images rather than words. In a film montage many different shots are spliced together in quick sequence to form a coherent whole that is more than any of its parts. The shots used in a montage may be of different subjects and from different locations. The unity is a result of very careful editing. Thus a montage is a way of constructing new meanings from numerous disparate sources or bits. In the 1960s, Jerzy Grotowski led the Polish Laboratory Theatre in developing performance montages drawing on a wide variety of sources ranging from the personal associations of the actors to materials taken from dramas, literature, music, and the visual arts. The performance montage method is at the heart of Grotowski's best-known theatre works, *Akropolis*, *The Constant Prince*, and *Apocalypsis cum Figuris*. Even when working with a dramatic text, such as **Pedro Calderón de la Barca**'s *The Constant Prince*, Grotowski treated the play as a "scalpel" which the performers used to cut to deep levels of the self (**see Grotowski box 1**). After Grotowski, many others in theatre, dance, and performance art followed suit in using both performance montage and highly personal materials.

Sergei Eisenstein (1898–1948): Russian film director and inventor of montage editing. A former student of Meyerhold, Eisenstein secretly preserved some of Meyerhold's writings throughout the Stalinist period. Eisenstein's films include *The Battleship Potemkin* (1925) and *Aleksandr Nevskii* (1938).

Pedro Calderón de la Barca (1600–81): Spanish playwright and priest known for his highly romantic treatment of faith and loyalty to the Spanish crown. Author of many plays including *The Constant Prince* (1629) and *Life is a Dream* (1635).

Jerzy Grotowski

A great text is a scalpel

All the great texts represent a sort of deep gulf for us. Take Hamlet: books without number have been devoted to this character. Professors will tell us, each for himself, that they have discovered an objective Hamlet. They suggest to us revolutionary Hamlets, rebel and impotent Hamlets, Hamlet the outsider, etc. But there is no objective Hamlet. The work is too great for that. The strength of great works really consists in their catalytic effect: they open doors for us, set in motion the machinery of our self-awareness. My encounter with the text resembles my encounter with the actor and his with me. For both director and actor, the author's text is a sort of scalpel enabling us to open ourselves, to transcend ourselves, to find what is hidden within us and to make the act of encountering the others; in other words, to transcend our solitude. In the theatre, if you like, the text has the same function as the myth had for the poet of ancient times. The author of *Prometheus* found in the Prometheus myth both an act of defiance and a springboard, perhaps even the source of his own creation. But his *Prometheus* was the product of his personal experience. That is all one can say about it; the rest is of no importance.

2002 [1968], *Towards a Poor Theatre*, 57

In the final phase of his work during the 1990s, Grotowski adapted and applied the performance montage technique to his collaboration with Thomas Richards on "Downstairs *Action*" and the related performance that followed, "Main *Action*." The montages for these performances began with Richards linking personal associations with specific physical actions. These formed a positive feedback loop: the more clear and precise the memory, the more exact the physical action; the more precise the physical action, the more clear the memory becomes. The physical actions were then made into a precise, repeatable score. Richards subsequently taught this technique to others at the Grotowski Workcenter in Pontedera, Italy. The resulting score is more than personal because while the performers were working on personal associations they were also mastering songs and movements taken from traditional performances both ancient and contemporary – in Richards' case, songs from Haiti (which "vibrated" with Richards' Caribbean heritage). Finally, the scores of different performers are enacted simultaneously. There is give-and-take among the performers; they sing the same songs; they develop their movements in relation to each other. But they are not performing a single-sourced drama that tells a coherent story. They are each performing their own personal scores inflected with the cultural performance materials. This way of performing is personal, intense, and hermetic. Witnesses to work such as this are not usually aware of Richards' personal associations or the associations of the other performers. Those attending "Main *Action*" experience a seamless flowing of movement and song (**see Richards box**). Even Grotowski, the guiding genius behind the performance, is not present in it. The Richards group has achieved the kind of "straight-line theatre" Meyerhold envisioned.

Thomas Richards

Grotowski's system of montage

One of the differences between Stanislavsky's and Grotowski's use of physical actions lies in the technique of montage. All of my associations and actions revolved around this personal event, and that was my secret. No one who watched us do the "Main *Action*" would ever know that. They, by means of the complete montage, would receive an entirely different story. While I followed my series of physical actions related to my father, next to me an actress followed another, completely different: *her own personal story*. But, because of the precise coordination in timing and rhythm of some of our actions, and because of the proximity of her and myself, a person looking would perceive our actions as being interrelated. They would see one story which had to do with the two of us together, when in reality we were following *two completely different lines of associations and actions,* which were separate. The actress did not know the memories on which I was working, and I did not know the ones on which she was working.

From the work on this "individual structure," I discovered in practice that I should not tamper with the emotions at all. I should not even worry about them. The key to physical actions lies in the body's process. I should simply do what I was doing, and each time I repeated the "individual structure," remember more and more precisely the way in which I had done what I had done. Let the emotions be. I knelt down like this. My father was lying like this. I reached out to him and my hands were curving like this. I touched him. To massage him I have to press with my hands in a specific way. If I feel nothing, I feel nothing. My emotions are free. I would try to remember anew this way of doing each time I executed this "individual structure" in the "*Main* Action."

1995, *At Work with Grotowski on Physical Actions*, 65

When I saw it in 1999, fewer than a dozen persons were allowed to witness "Main *Action*" at any given time. These spectators sat on folding chairs in a room that could accommodate many more people. The idea was to share on an intimate scale. Although there was no audience participation in the conventional sense, there was a kind of inclusion rarely felt in orthodox Western performing arts. The mood created for experiencing "Main *Action*" was an extension of Grotowski's earlier experiments in environmental theatre (**see Grotowski box 2**). Grotowski tried any number of arrangements of space to foster different relationships between spectators and performers (**see figure 7.23**). But in his "theatre of productions" phase, Grotowski never used actual audience participation. Interacting directly with the "invited" came during later phases of Grotowski's work. These later phases will be discussed in Chapter 8. In any event, audience participation was not, of course, Grotowski's invention. Meyerhold and others experimented with it in post-revolutionary Russia. Participation was a hallmark of many Happenings and theatre events from the 1960s to the present, including some of my own environmental theatre work (**see figure 7.24**). Today's interactive installations and internet performances, where partakers are co-creators,

fig 7.23. Jerzy Grotowski experimented with different ways of having performers relate to spectators. Although in his theatre of productions phase (1957–69), he never had actual "audience participation," frequently spectators felt as if they were part of the action. Grotowski never used the orthodox proscenium stage.

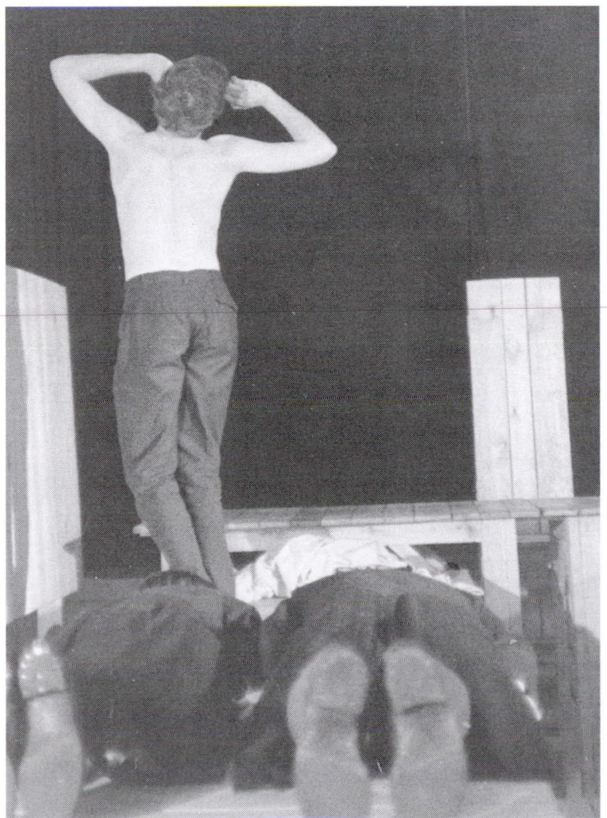

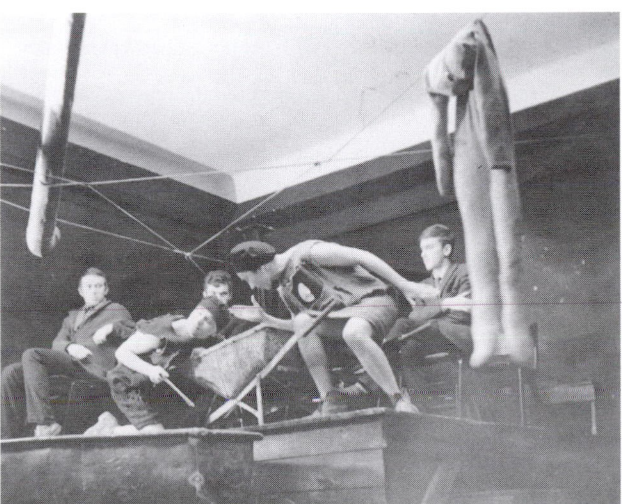

Akropolis, 1962–65, (above) went through five versions. The production was very loosely based on a play by the man who was one of the founders of modern Polish theatre, Stanislaw Wyspianski (1869–1907). The performance by the Polish Laboratory Theatre under Grotowski's direction took place all around and in the midst of the audience. Photograph courtesy of Eugenio Barba.

Dr. Faustus, 1963, (left) based on Christopher Marlowe's Elizabethan play. The scenic arrangement was two tables around which the spectators sat and on which the performers played. Photograph courtesy of Eugenio Barba.

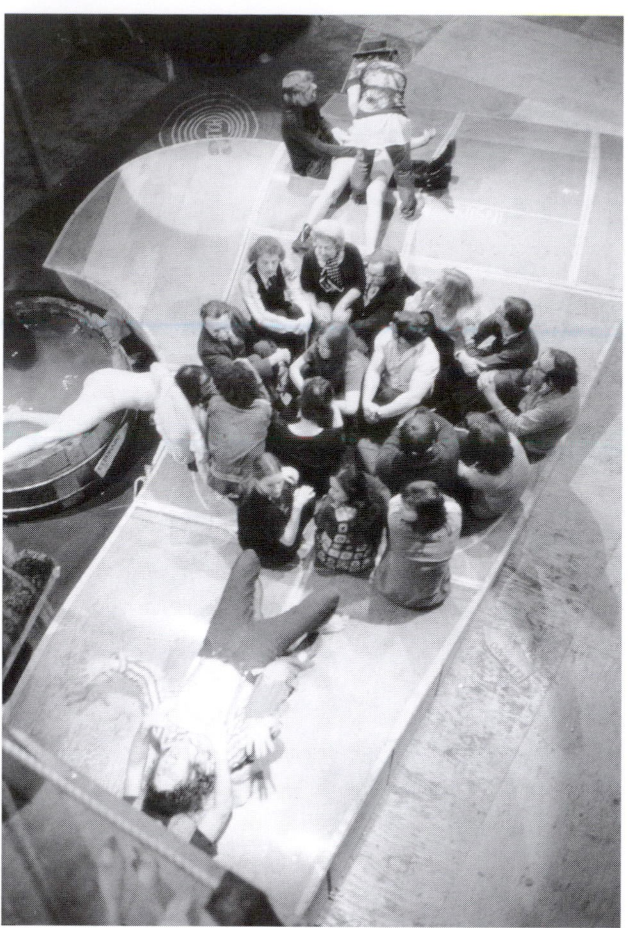

fig 7.24. Audience participation in The Performance Group's *Commune*, 1972, directed by Richard Schechner. Here a small group of spectators is "guarded" by the performers. The spectators represent Vietnamese villagers, the performers, the US military and, in the scene above, the Charles Manson commune and those Manson murdered. Photograph by Richard Schechner.

are a continuation of this tradition. One such internet performance is "Desktop Theatre," challenging many assumptions about what theatre is, how it is enacted, and who its performers are. Desktop Theatre is played by persons in far-flung locations using icons on their computer screens as characters/avatars (**see Jenik box**). Beginning with a version of *Waiting for Godot*, aptly titled *waitingforgodot.com*, Desktop Theatre has since staged its own original plays as well as initiated works involving collective creativity. This kind of work is continuing on a number of internet sites – see especially www.franklinfurnace.org.

Jerzy Grotowski

Performer–audience relationships

[F]or each production, a new space is designed for the actors and spectators. Thus infinite variation of performer–audience relationships is possible. The actors can play among the spectators, directly contacting the audience and giving it a passive role in the drama (e.g. our productions of **Byron**'s *Cain* and Kalidasa's *Shakuntala*). Or the actors may build structures among the spectators and thus include them in the architecture of action, subjecting them to a sense of the pressure and congestion and limitation of space (Wyspianski's *Akropolis*). Or the actors may play among the spectators and ignore them, looking through them. The spectators may be separated from the actors – for example, by a high fence, over which only their heads protrude (*The Constant Prince*, from Calderón); from this radically slanted perspective, they look down on the actors as if watching animals in a ring, or like medical students watching an operation (also, this detached, downward viewing gives the action a sense of moral transgression). Or the entire hall is used as a concrete place: Faustus' "last supper" in a monastery refectory, where Faustus entertains the spectators, who are guests at a baroque feast served on huge tables, offering episodes from his life. The elimination of the stage–auditorium dichotomy is not the important thing – that simply creates a bare laboratory situation, an appropriate area for investigation. The essential concern is finding the proper spectator–actor relationship for each type of performance and embodying the decision in physical arrangements.

2002 [1968], *Towards a Poor Theatre*, 19–20

Lord Byron – George Gordon Noel Byron (1788–1824): English romantic poet who died of a fever while fighting for the Greeks in their war of independence from the Ottoman Empire. Byron's most notable works include *Childe Harold's Pilgrimage* (1812–18) and *Don Juan* (1819–24). *Cain*, his only drama, was published in 1821.

Adriene Jenik

Desktop Theatre

What constitutes theatre? How might drama be expressed when separated from the body, the voice, and shared space? Can poetic speech and changes in expression or gesture attract and sustain group attention in an arena of constant distraction? What new languages exist in this forum? How might theatrical play be used to examine the striking shift in consciousness ushered in by ubiquitous computing? [. . .]

waitingforgodot.com was performed using the Palace visual chat software [. . .] that has since become the venue for most Desktop Theatre productions. The Palace is a software application that provides access to a network of servers that host individual "palaces." These palaces are in turn made up of linked "rooms" designated by 512 × 384 pixel (approximately 6 × 4.5 inches) background images that represent a room, a place, a planet, or dimension. Each of the live connected chatters is visible through a small representative image or avatar. [. . .] Avatars can be borrowed or collected from the myriad palaces built for this purpose or can be constructed and designed by the user from scratch. [. . .]

Palace culture is dynamic, ever-changing, and [. . .] largely heterogeneous. There are popular "social" palaces, which consistently host more than 200 chatters at a time, as well as adult palaces and palaces hosted by celebrities, rock groups, TV shows, and films. There are also hundreds of personal and educational palaces. [. . .] After both observing and participating in conversations with palacians in this environment, we were struck by the inherent expressive potential found in the software, but were dismayed by the level of dialogue and activity we found. [. . .] Thinking that introducing an external narrative or drama might provoke more interesting exchange, we began to develop our version of Beckett's *Waiting for Godot*. [. . .]

As we began working with the text, it proved eerily well suited to chatroom delivery. In producing *waitingforgodot.com*, our first task was to read and discuss the text, and then edit or "compress" it into a format suitable for our venue. In doing so, we tried to remain true to Beckett's overall rhythm and dramatic arc even as we cut and reformed whole sections of the text. We then fashioned simple "everyman" avatars from the basic Palace character known as the "roundhead." [. . .] We concentrated our efforts on the production values of a virtuosic cut-and-paste performance, literally copying the text from a text document, and quickly pasting it into the chat input window. Once input, the text appeared as if "spoken" from a speech bubble attached to the characters onscreen and was simultaneously "spoken" out loud, through the computer's text-to-speech capabilities. Other chatters in the room would alternately comment on our presence, leave in confusion, or join in the piece by trying to help us locate "godot" on the server. [. . .]

In another, more ambitious experiment, *INVISIBLE INTERLUDES I: Santaman's Harvest*, [. . .] we added cast members and improvisational elements. [. . .] In the largest and most tightly scripted of the scenes, there were a total of 11 actors performing at once – in four time zones! [. . .] With our avatars (even the crudely rendered 2D images we encounter on the Palace) we enter a psychic space in which we become our masks. Anyone who spends time in these parallel worlds understands, perhaps implicitly, that one makes accommodations to one's avatar. [. . .] The most recent examples of Desktop Theatre practice are activities that represent alternative models of online play. [. . .] We have begun to perform a series of "dream-plays." The practice, which can be seen as a globally experienced hybrid of sand-play therapy, charades, and surrealist games, takes place in our own "dream-room" [. . .] as well as in the public palaces with dreamers from all over the world. As we solicit dreams from passersby and act them out using available props, improvisational acting, and [computer] painting tools, we meet each other in a true exchange of deeply felt desires and fears, and share the transformative power of collective creativity.

2001, "Desktop Theatre," 96, 98–100, 107, 109

Experimental in one context, ordinary in another

What is experimental in the performing arts is commonplace in sports, pop-music concerts, and religious services. Here the partakers are very powerful event-shapers. Every athlete knows the "home-field advantage," which is not due to any difference in rules or playing surface. The roaring enthusiasm of the fans energizes the players for the home team, lifting the level of their performance. In much the same way, pop-music groups are driven by the crowds cheering, singing along, and pressing onto the stage. More informally, raves and even ordinary parties consist of multiple performances enacted by the partakers. To move from popular culture to religion, even the tamest church service includes abundant responsive reading, rising, sitting, kneeling, and embracing – actions and gestures that draw congregants into the service and closer to each other. Holiness churches go much further, with people suddenly "falling out" into trance, dancing in the aisles, or proclaiming in "tongues," a direct vocalization of the divine that has no verbatim translation. This kind of sacred performance can be viewed on television any Sunday of the year. In initiation rites and shamanic cures the partakers actively participate by laying on hands, singing, or assisting the shamans. In some cases, the participation is so total that it is difficult to distinguish performers from partakers (**see Read box**).

Trials are much tamer. As noted earlier, because the authority of the state is on display, the decorum of the courtroom is tightly monitored. Spectators are expected to hold back their reactions, which are sometimes extremely emotional. Although jurors have been known to weep and witnesses to break down on the stand, usually trials are subdued, even humdrum (the movie and media versions

Kenneth E. Read

Collective creativity in New Guinea

The house was packed to its capacity, but in the blackness I was unable to discover so much as a single feature of the man who sat beside me. Almost immediately, enveloped in disembodied voices, I felt the first stirrings of a curious panic, a fear that if I relaxed my objectivity for so much as a moment I would lose my identity. At the same time the possibility that this could happen seemed immensely attractive. The air was thick with pungent odors, with the smell of unwashed bodies and stranger aromatic overtones that pricked my nostrils and my eyes. But it was the singing, reverberating in the confined space and pounding incessantly against my ears, that rose to cloud my mind with the fumes of a collective emotion almost too powerful for my independent will. Momentarily the night vanished, and my purpose, even the circumstances of my presence in the village, were no longer important. I stood poised at a threshold promising a release from the doubts and anxieties that separate us from one another, offering, if one took the step demanded, a surety, a comforting acceptance such as those who share an ultimate commitment may experience. [. . .]

The songs followed one another without a perceptible break, a single shrill and keening voice lifting now and then to point the way to a new set. As the others joined in strongly, I felt close to the very things that eluded me in my day-to-day investigations, brought into physical confrontation with the intangible realm of hopes and shared ideas for which words and actions, though they are all we have, are quite inadequate expressions. In analytic language, the situation could be accommodated under the rubric of a rite of separation – an event by which a young girl in her father's house, surrounded by her kinsmen, was brought to the morning of the day when she must assume a new status and be transferred to her husband's people, but its quality could not be conveyed in any professional terms. While the voices swelled inside the house, mounting to a climax, the barriers of my alien life dissolved. The sound engulfed me, bearing me with it beyond the house and into the empty spaces of the revolving universe. Thus sustained, I was one of the innumerable companies of men who, back to the shrouded entrance of the human race, have sat at night by fires and filled the forest clearings and the wilderness with recitals of their own uniqueness.

1965, *The High Valley*, 251–52

being very much more melodramatic than the actual thing). However, as noted in Chapter 6, an adversary trial is the enactment of two simultaneous dramas. It is the judge's job to keep these dramas moving forward in an orderly fashion. To do so, the judge functions both as referee and as director. The jury consists of partakers of a special kind empowered by the state to pass judgment on the veracity of what they see and hear. A jury's verdict can literally dictate life or death. Even in petty cases, however, the storytelling and outcome are of extreme importance to the participants – and, as the daytime mock-courts on television show, of enormous entertainment value. A celebrity trial is always big news, often generating widespread public excitement. To make certain that a jury will not be affected by this hubbub, jurors are sometimes sequestered during trials. The more consciously formal and rule-bound a situation is, the less movement there is among the role categories of the quadrilogue.

The degree to which the operations of the performance quadrilogue are combined in a single person or group and the degree to which they are dispersed varies widely from genre to genre, culture to culture, even occasion to occasion. In everyday life the roles depicted in the quadrilogue are almost always in flux. A short social interaction around the dinner table can include people acting out all four role categories. In fact, "everyday life" might be defined as that social time when people can swiftly move from being a sourcer or producer to being a partaker or performer. Daily life is the raw material of a great deal of art. One of the differences between daily life and art is that art abstracts, simplifies, intensifies or relaxes, and organizes daily life – its actions, sights, and feelings. Art's other source of raw material is "mental life," an interior realm that ranges from imagination through fantasy to hallucination.

Conclusion

Performance processes are dynamic ways of generating, playing, evaluating, repeating, and remembering. Performance processes can be theorized as an orderly sequence of training, workshops, rehearsals, warm-up, performing, performance contexts, cooldown, critical response, archives, and memories. I have developed my basic theory of performance processes from the theatre, the performance genre I am most familiar with. Others may develop a theory based on another genre. The kind of processual analysis I have used in this chapter can be applied to other genres of performance. In theory, the three-phase, ten-part sequence is an orderly diachronic progression, proceeding from one part to the next. In practice, things aren't so neat. Not all the parts are present in every performance. Noting what is emphasized or omitted can be a powerful analytic tool in understanding specific performances. For example, in modern Western cultures drama is the domain of the playwright who parses out dialogue to individual characters who resemble "real people." In other cultures, the text of a play, though clearly indicating which words belong to which characters, is actually performed by several persons simultaneously strongly calling into question the notion that "character" = "a real individual person." Thus in Japanese noh drama, the lines uttered by a player may include description as well as dialogue; the words of the main character may be sung by the chorus in the first person (**see Brazell box**). It is hard to find this out by reading the dramatic texts. One must know the performance tradition. Another example is the passionate preaching heard in many Christian evangelical churches. When the reverend gets going, the sermon is more than said, it is sung; and the preaching is met with the

Karen Brazell

The scripts of Japanese traditional theatre

The scripts of Japanese traditional theater are not solely, or even primarily, concerned with reproducing ordinary dialogue. That is, in addition to dialogue, they also include descriptions of and commentary on the setting, the stage actions, and the characters. The lines may be in poetry or metered prose and may be sung, chanted, or spoken, often with patterned intonation. The words uttered by a particular actor are not limited to lines that his character might "logically" or "naturally" speak; that is, the actor is not restricted to remaining "in character." Moreover, a chanter or chorus may recite large parts of a play, including the first-person utterances of the characters, in which case the reciter(s) may momentarily take on the voice of one or another character. These reciters, however, are never personified storytellers; the noh chorus is not a group of

> townspeople commenting or elaborating on the action [. . .]. Rather they are stage figures voicing the text, a text that is not limited to creating naturalistic characters or sustaining fixed points of view. [. . .] This fluid narrative stance is exploited in both verbal and visual enactments of theatrical texts. Moments occur [. . .] when the text speaks without apparently being spoken; that is, the words are voiced by the performers, but no character or clearly defined narrator is speaking them. Released from the limitations of direct mime and defined narrative voice, playwrights and/or actors can manipulate the presentation of the text for aesthetic effects and practical purposes.
>
> 1998, *Traditional Japanese Theater*, 24–25

cadenced responsive shouts of the congregation, which uplift and drive the preacher. In this kind of service, the warm-up takes place as part of the sermon, the performance swells until it fills the whole space, and the aftermath lives in the spirit the congregants take with them when church is over. Often, the formal service leads to and blends in with a church lunch or other social activity. These are but a few of countless examples of how the performance processes are adapted and shaped to suit particular occasions.

If performance processes can be understood as a ten-part sequence, they also can be understood as a complex relationship among four types of "players" – sourcers, producers, performers, and partakers. Sourcers write, research, or in other ways make or find the actions to be performed. Producers guide the shaping of the actions into something suitable for a performance. Performers enact the actions. Partakers receive and/or interact with the actions. A single person may belong to more than one of these categories; a group may do the sourcing, performing, producing, and partaking collectively. The possibilities are without end.

TALK ABOUT

1. Recall a performance in which you were a producer or performer. Explain what you did or saw in terms of proto-performance, performance, and aftermath. If you have enough information, discuss the performance process in terms of training, workshop, rehearsal, warm-up, public performance, context, cooldown, critical response, archiving, and memories.
2. How might expanding the idea of the performance process to include the whole sequence discussed in this chapter enhance your understanding of social and political events? Discuss this in relation to a campaign for political office, a courtroom trial, and a medical procedure.

PERFORM

1. Begin to stage a scene from a drama or a performance from everyday life such as getting ready for a date, a supper party, or going to a doctor. Invite your audience to one or two rehearsals. Discuss the "workshop phase" and/or the "rehearsal process." How does it differ from a "finished performance"?
2. Using only "aftermath information" – newspaper accounts, scholarly articles, reviews, opinions of people who have attended the event, photos, videotapes, etc. – reconstruct and perform a scene. Do you think such a reconstructed scene is an accurate rendition of the "original"? If so, why? If not, why not?

READ

Barba, Eugenio. "The Deep Order Called Turbulence: The Three Faces of Dramaturgy." *The Performance Studies Reader*, Henry Bial, ed.: 252–61. London and New York: Routledge, 2004.

De Marinis, Marco. "The Performance Text." *The Performance Studies Reader*, Henry Bial, ed.: 232–51. London and New York: Routledge, 2004.

Meyerhold, Vsevolod. "First Attempts at a Stylized Theatre." *The Performance Studies Reader*, Henry Bial, ed.: 217–25. London and New York: Routledge, 2004.

Okpewho, Isadore. "The Oral Artist: Training and Preparation." *The Performance Studies Reader*, Henry Bial, ed.: 226–31. London and New York: Routledge, 2004.

Read, Kenneth E. "Asemo." *The High Valley*: 129–40. New York: Scribner, 1965.

Zimmerman, Mary. "The Archaeology of Performance." *Theatre Topics* 15, 1 (2005): 25–35.

8 GLOBAL AND INTERCULTURAL PERFORMANCES

Globalization's throughline

Globalization's throughline (to use Stanislavsky's term for the overall intention or objective of a drama) is to integrate all systems – information, economic, military, ideological, social, political, and cultural – along the lines of "high performance." If successful, the result will be a worldwide network of maximum productivity. While globalization allows, even encourages, "cultural differences" at the level of daily behaviors, spoken languages, foods, clothes, lifestyles, artistic works, and so on, its underlying system is unified and transcultural – and its underlying goal is to bring all subsystems into harmony and under control. Whether this is good for most of the world's people in terms of eliminating poverty, disease, overcrowding, wars, resource depletion, and the other threats to the planet is, of course, debatable. Globalization's supporters argue that only through systematic integration can most of the world's peoples achieve a high standard of living, however painful the process in the short run. Globalization's opponents argue that systematizing means that power (and profits) will remain in the hands of a few with gross inequities – increasing numbers of nomads and exploited workers – a permanent condition.

globalization: the increasing interconnection and interdependency of systems: information, economic, social, cultural, technical, and ideological. Full globalization would mean total connectivity.

Intercultural performances are best studied in relation to globalization. Frequently, intercultural performances arise as responses to and in some cases as protests against an increasingly globalized world. Both globalization and intercultural performance have historical antecedents: Globalization in colonialism and imperialism, intercultural performance as an outcome of "contact" among the world's peoples. Clearly, these phenomena are linked. Intercultural performances range from the Olympics to rap and rock, from tourism to the performances of everyday life resulting from the rapid global circulation of news, styles, foods, musics, media, and more. Even world-scale intercultural social dramas such as the struggle between **Al Qaeda** and the USA and its allies can be studied "as performance." Considering aesthetic performances and performance research only, there are four kinds of international work:

intercultural: between or among two or more cultures. Intercultural performances may emphasize what connects or is shared or what separates or is unique to each.

1. Research into artistic processes which can be either "vertical" or "horizontal." The goal of **vertical research** is to discover performances or performance fragments that have survived from very early times. This research occupied Jerzy Grotowski during the last 25 years of his life. **Horizontal research** compares the codified or "extra-daily" practices of contemporary performances in order to identify what is general or universal. This is the aim of Eugenio Barba's International School of Theatre Anthropology (ISTA).
2. Hybrids and fusions that intentionally combine diverse cultural elements. Here the colonial horror of "impurity" or "mixing" is subverted, overturned, and developed. A large and increasing number of artists are doing this kind of postcolonial, postmodern work, which ranges from the respectful to the ironic and parodic. Popular music is a powerful example of hybridity as are the theatres of **Ariane Mnouchkine** and **Ong Keng Sen**.
3. Tourist shows that simultaneously preserve, distort, and display traditional performances, daily life, or anything else that may be packaged and sold to an ever-increasing audience of world travelers.
4. Community-based performances emphasizing local challenges to globalization. This kind of work activist **Suzanne Lacy** calls "new genre public art."

vertical/horizontal intercultural research: vertical research seeks "original" or "true" universal performances in the convergence of past cultural practices with individual "deep" experiences. Horizontal research locates transcultural or universal "truths" in similarities among contemporary cultures.

Al Qaeda: literally, "the base," an organization formed by **Osama bin Laden** in 1988 to fight the Soviets occupying Afghanistan (**figure 8.1**). Guerrilla soldiers from many countries but mostly from Islamic populations helped the Taliban force the Soviets out of Afghanistan in 1989. Since then, Al Qaeda continues to fight the Western, especially American, presence in the Islamic world and Islamic regimes bin Laden considers corrupt (such as in Saudi Arabia). Al Qaeda is also extremely anti-Israeli, viewing the Jewish state as an intrusion. Al Qaeda is a global, sophisticated, flexible network moving money and people, disseminating information and propaganda, training militants, and staging attacks. The attacks include the 1998 bombing of the US embassies in Kenya and Tanzania, the 2000 assault on the American warship *Cole* in Yemen, and the September 11, 2001 air strikes on New York and Washington. Al Qaeda's headquarters are presumed to be in the mountainous Afghan–Pakistan border region.

fig 8.1. Osama bin Laden, with a rifle behind him, speaks to a selected group of reporters in mountains of Helmand province in southern Afghanistan Photo: Rahimullah Yousafzai. Copyright AP/EMPICS.

Osama bin Laden (1957–): a member of one of Saudi Arabia's wealthiest families and founder in 1988 of the Al Qaeda ("the base") terrorist network. Bin Laden is believed to mastermind and finance terrorist actions including the 2001 attacks on New York's World Trade Center and Washington's Pentagon. In 1998, he issued an edict to his followers: "Kill the Americans and their allies, civilians, and military." He is vehemently anti-American, anti-Western, and anti-Israeli. Bin Laden's headquarters were in Afghanistan where he enjoyed the protection of the Taliban regime. His present whereabouts are unknown but probably in Afghanistan or Pakistan.

In this chapter, I will discuss these different kinds of intercultural performance in their own terms and in relation to each other.

Ariane Mnouchkine (1939–): French director, founder in 1964 of the Théâtre du Soleil. Productions include *Les Clowns* (1969–70), *1789 and 1793* (1970–73), *Les Shakespeare Cycle* (1981–84), *Sihanouk* (1985), *L'Indiade* (1987–88), *Les Atrides* (1990–93), *Tartuffe* (1995–96), and *Le Dernier Caravanserail (Odyssées)* (2003).

Ong Keng Sen (1963–): artistic director of Theatre Works Singapore, Ong has directed, taught, and curated performance in Asia, Europe, Africa, Australia, the Middle East, and the Americas. In 1994, his Flying Circus Project embraced hybridity by engaging the encounter between contemporary urban arts and traditional performance. An example of his intercultural directing is the trilogy performed in Asia, Australia, and Europe inspired by Shakespeare and performed in several languages: *Lear* (1997), *Desdemona* (2000), and *Search:Hamlet* (2002). *Search:Hamlet* was Ong's first collaboration using both Asian and European artists who together created what Ong calls "a coherent universe of difference on stage." This continued with *The Global Soul* (2003) inspired by the travels of Buddha and Pico Iyer's book of the same title. Ong's *The Continuum: Beyond the Killing Fields* (2001) seen in Cambodia, Singapore, and various European cities featured a 75-year-old Cambodian classical dancer.

Suzanne Lacy (1945–): conceptual/performance artist who addresses social issues such as racism, homelessness, aging, and violence by engaging local people in site-specific work. Editor of *Mapping the Terrain: New Genre Public Art* (1995).

The intercultural performances of everyday life comprise a vast panoply of styles, habits, mixes, hybrids, and fusions inhabiting the way people dress, talk, eat, interact, worship, celebrate, and are entertained. Some cite this hybridity as evidence of Western and especially American cultural imperialism and/or as a negative outcome of colonialism (**see Chin box**). Others see it as an opportunity for creativity and dynamic growth. But whether one regards what's happening as positive or negative, there is no place on earth not being influenced and changed by activities going on elsewhere. Some places and people may appear "far away" or "other" from the vantage of the metropolis. But networked communications, the circulation of material goods and techniques, curiosity about the way "other" people live, fascination with novelty, and, of course, global popular culture are omnipresent.

Daryl Chin

The duplicity of interculturalism

The idea of interculturalism is one which is, in a sense, duplicitous. One question which must be addressed is the presence of a dominant power structure, and the presumptions of that power structure. In the context of the United States, the cultural power structure is one which is dominated by the ideology of a specifically white, Eurocentric, specifically capitalist establishment. In addition, all questions regarding interculturalism must be complicated by the pervasiveness of a commercialized popular culture. For those who have grown up with the artifacts of the American cultural establishment, the effects have become endemic, pervasive, and all encompassing. [. . .]

Interculturalism hinges on the question of autonomy and empowerment. To deploy elements from the symbol system of another culture is a very delicate enterprise. In its crudest terms, the question is: when does that usage act as cultural imperialism? Forcing elements from disparate cultures together does not seem to be a solution that makes much sense, aesthetically, ethically, or philosophically. What does that power prove: that the knowledge of other cultures exists? That information about other cultures now is readily available?

1991, "Interculturalism, Postmodernism, Pluralism," 87, 94

Scenarios of globalization

If globalization were treated "as" performance, what kind of performance would it be? There are competing storyboards (**figure 8.2**). The boosters of globalization envision a Hollywood production full of high-tech special effects starring American super-heroes who dissolve national, cultural, and economic boundaries as they spread free-market corporate capitalism, individual entrepreneurship, and democracy to every corner of the world (see **Friedman box**). Another scenario retells the David versus Goliath story as the struggle of millions of individuals using the internet as a global participatory forum creating new cultural myths battling against corporate conglomerates determined to privatize culture and copyright ideas (**see Jenkins box**).

The detractors of globalization see it increasing Western, and especially American, power and hegemony militarily, economically, politically, and culturally (**see Gómez-Peña box 1**). Opponents to globalization regard the fancy talk about "technology transfers," "free trade," and "democracy" as a show staged to distract attention from what's really happening: an ongoing process of accumulating and centralizing wealth and power. For example, aid to

fig 8.2. Globalization – good or bad? www.perfectworld productions. com/education/portfolio/clc-globalization.html

Thomas Friedman

Globalization = integration

The globalization system [. . .] has one overarching feature – integration. The world has become an increasingly interwoven place, and today, whether you are a company or a country, your threats and opportunities increasingly derive from whom you are connected to. This globalization system is also characterized by a single word: the Web. [. . .]

The driving idea behind globalization is free-market capitalism – the more you let market forces rule and the more you open your economy to free-trade and competition, the more efficient and flourishing your economy will be. Globalization means the spread of free-market capitalism to virtually every country in the world. [. . .]

Unlike the Cold War system, globalization has its own dominant culture, which is why it tends to be homogenizing to a certain degree. [. . .] Culturally speaking, globalization has tended to involve the spread (for better and for worse) of Americanization – from Big Macs to iMacs to Mickey Mouse.

Globalization has its own defining technologies: computerization, miniaturization, digitization, satellite communications, fiber optics, and the Internet, which reinforce its defining perspective of integration. Once a country makes a leap into the system of globalization, its elites begin to internalize this perspective of integration, and always try to locate themselves in a global context. [. . .]

Today, more than ever, the traditional boundaries between politics, culture, technology, finance, national security, and ecology are disappearing. You often cannot explain one without referring to the others, and you cannot explain the whole without reference to them all. [. . .]

I believe that this new system of globalization – in which walls between countries, markets, and disciplines are increasingly being blown away – constitutes a fundamentally new state of affairs.

2000, *The Lexus and the Olive Tree*, 8–10, 20, 23

Globalization 1.0, 2.0, and 3.0

[T]here have been three great eras of globalization. The first lasted from 1492 – when Columbus set sail, opening trade between the Old World and the New World – until around 1800. [. . .] In Globalization 1.0 the key agent of change [. . .] was how much brawn – how much muscle, horsepower, wind power, or, later, steam power – your country had and how creatively you could deploy it. [. . .]

The second great era, Globalization 2.0, lasted roughly from 1800 to 2000 [. . .]. In Globalization 2.0 the key agent of change [. . .] was multinational companies [who] went global for markets and labor [. . .]. In the first half of this era, global integration was powered by falling transportation costs, thanks to the steam engine and the railroad, and in the second half by falling telecommunications costs – thanks to the diffusion of the telegraph, telephones, the PC, satellites, fiber-optic cable, and the early version of the World Wide Web. It was during this ear that we really saw the birth and maturation of a global economy. [. . .]

Around the year 2000 we entered a whole new era: Globalization 3.0. Globalization 3.0 is shrinking the world from a size small to a size tiny and flattening the playing field at the same time. And while the dynamic force in Globalization 1.0 was countries globalizing and the dynamic force in Globalization 2.0 was companies globalizing, the dynamic force in Globalization 3.0 – the thing that gives it its unique character – is the newfound power for *individuals* to collaborate and compete globally. [. . .]

But Globalization 3.0 not only differs from the previous eras in how it is shrinking and flattening the world and in how it is empowering individuals. It is different in that Globalization 1.0 and 2.0 were driven primarily by European and American individuals and businesses. [. . .] Globalization 3.0 is going to be more and more driven [. . .] by a much more diverse – non-Western, non-white – group of individuals. Globalization 3.0 makes it possible for so many more people to plug and play, and you are going to see every color of the human rainbow take part. [. . .]

[But] it's not only the software writers and computer geeks who get empowered [. . .]. It's also al-Qaeda and other terrorist networks. The playing field is not being leveled only in ways that draw in and superempower a whole new group of innovators. It's being leveled in a way that draws in and superempowers a whole new group of angry, frustrated, and humiliated men and women.

2005, *The World Is Flat*, 8–10

Thomas Henry Jenkins

Participatory culture on the internet

One of the real potentials of cyberspace is that it is altering the balance of power between media producers and media consumers, enabling grassroots cultural production to reach a broader readership and enabling amateurs to construct websites that often look as professional and are often more detailed [. . .] than commercially-produced sites. In such a world, the category of the audience, as a mass of passive consumers for pre-produced materials, may give way to the category of cultural participants, which would include both professionals and amateurs. [. . .]

Grassroots groups are seizing the potential of the internet to transmit their materials, to reach a much larger public with their ideas, and they are thus making their own cultural appropriations and productions more visible than ever before. [. . .] Such an argument rejects the idea of a definitive version produced, authorized, and regulated by some media conglomerate. Instead, it pushes towards a world where all of us can participate in the creation and circulation of central cultural myths. [. . .]

We are on a collision course between technologies that encourage collaboration and full participation in cultural production and economic and legal structures which are pushing to further privatize our culture. [. . .] We are going to be watching increasingly bloody fights about intellectual property rights in digital media over the coming decade and those fights are going to determine – in part – the cultural logic that will structure the 21st century.

1998, "The Poachers and the Stormtroopers"

developing nations takes the form of loans from the World Bank, the International Monetary Fund, etc., structured so that the poor nations subsidize the rich ones by paying interest on debts they can never retire. Furthermore, many of the projects supported benefit mostly large contractors and the elites of the receiving nations. Resistance to globalization is dealt with both softly, by means of public relations and political manipulation, and harshly, using economic pressure, the police, and the military.

The result is extreme inequity on a global scale. As of 2004, the per capita annual income of a person living in one of the "most developed countries," Europe, North America, Japan, Australia, and New Zealand, was more than twenty times that of someone living in one of the LDCs, "least developed countries," the euphemism for the poorest of the poor. As goes income, so goes literacy, longevity, and general well-being (**see Human Development box**). Be shocked but not surprised by these deadly disparities. Globalization thrives on inequities of wealth, power, information, and access. To win the game of globalization, those who control the game advertise "unlimited opportunity" while making sure there's no actual "level playing field." Manufacturing is located where labor is cheapest; consumption takes place where wealth is concentrated. Efficient communications and transportation ensure that orders, goods, and capital flow seamlessly. Disparities exist within as well as between countries. For example, young women flock to the sweatshops of Shenzhen, just over the border separating Hong Kong from the rest of China, because the pay in Shenzhen's factories is far better than what these women can earn on the farm –

Guillermo Gómez-Peña

Globalization's dark side

Phase one of the much-touted project of globalization has now been thoroughly completed: macro-economic communities such as the European Union and NAFTA have replaced the "dated" functions of the nation state. Politicians are now "trading partners," and their religious dictum is called transnational "free trade" ("free" meaning that it benefits only those who have the power to determine its terms). The "information superhighway," the Internet, e-commerce, cable TV, and "smart" tourism have ideologically narrowed the world and the word. Effectively, "the world" is now "at our fingertips," or at least that's how we're invited to (mis)perceive it so long as we are members of that elite micro-minority which stands on the benign side of globalization. The dark side of this project, however, is implacable. Entire Third World countries have become sweatshops, quaint bordellos, and entertainment parks for the First World and for the inhabitants of the Southern Hemisphere the only options for participating in the "global" economy are as passive consumers of "global" trash, or providers of cheap labor or materia prima. Those excluded from these "options" are forced to become part of a transnational economy of crime (sex, drug and organs trafficking, child labor, kidnappings, fayuca [smuggled goods], etc. Many will cross the border North in search of the source of the rainbow, only to find racial hatred and inhumane working conditions.

Now that humanistic concerns are perceived as passé, U.S., European, and Asian corporations and governments are no longer accountable to anyone. The "global" goal is to add several zeros to their accounts by simply pressing a button. It is savage capitalism at its most efficient and diabolical: virtual operators discretely trading capital, products, weapons, and hollow dreams; and starving or killing their inconsequential victims in the ether of virtual space, a parallel "world" devoid of ethical or ideological implications, of tears and blood. It's economic-darwinism.com. Only the digitally fit will survive. [. . .]

Compassion and philanthropy aren't part of the "global" agenda. In fact, governments and corporations (increasingly more intertwined with and indistinguishable from one another) have effectively designed a high-tech prison industrial complex to keep the excluded from bothering us and at the same time to make money off of them. In the U.S., not coincidentally, the prison population is disproportionately black and Latino. This mega-industry has an intricately symbiotic relationship with other equally macabre "industries" such as law enforcement, the border patrol, gun manufacturers, the courts, and of course, the media, where "bad guys," cops, lawyers, and judges all get to have their own TV shows and entertain America.

2001, "The New Global Culture," 9–10

Human Development Reports

Global inequities

Life expectancy: Japan and Sweden over 80 years; Zambia and Sierra Leone under 35 years. The average of the "most developed countries," 78 years. The average of the "least developed countries," 51 years.

Literacy: 19 countries 100%, all but Japan, Georgia, Australia, and New Zealand in North America and Europe. 18 countries under 50%, all but Pakistan, Bangladesh, Nepal, Bhutan, and Vanuatu in Africa.

Annual per capita income: Most developed countries, $29,000. Least developed countries, $1,307.

Composite human development index measuring longevity, health, education, and standard of living: Of the 25 countries with an index of 0.90 or above, all but Australia, New Zealand, Japan, Israel, and China-Hong Kong are in Western Europe or North America. Of the 35 countries with an index of 0.50 or less, all but Pakistan, Timor-Leste, and Haiti are in Africa. The average for "most developed countries" is 0.935; the average for "least developed countries" is 0.446. The world average is 0.729.

2004, Data culled from the United Nations Human Development Reports, http://hdr.undp.org/hd/

yet only a fraction of what workers in the US, Australia, New Zealand, or Europe are paid for comparable labor. Most of the goods made in Shenzhen are exported, a very large proportion to America, generating enormous profits for oligarchs and corporations. It can't go on forever because when companies outsource manufacturing, white collar, and technical work, the number of jobs and the earnings of American workers fall. But the globalizers hope that by the time the USA is no longer the best market, the internal Chinese market will have evolved – or some other region will be ripe. Meanwhile, prosperity is spotty. Even as a bustling and ambitious middle class is emerging in many parts of the world, billions of people and entire regions are left out. These poor are everywhere, inhabiting the LDCs, living in rural areas and in slums within or surrounding burgeoning cities. Even the richest nations encompass archipelagos of poverty. The indigenous poor are supplemented by "guest workers," "migrant laborers," and "illegal aliens," nomads who are often little more than indentured servants or worse. Labor and sex slavery is far from extinct. Over the past thirty years, many outspoken artists such as Nigerian **Wole Soyinka** and Kenyan **Ngũgĩ wa Thiong'o** were forced into exile, the public spaces of more than a few postcolonial states closed to them.

Wole Soyinka (1934–): Nigerian writer-in-exile and winner of the 1986 Nobel Prize for Literature. Author of the plays *The Swamp Dwellers* (1959), *Kongi's Harvest* (1965), and *Death and King's Horseman* (1976). Soyinka's books include *Myth, Literature, and the African World* (1976), *The Open Sore of a Continent: A Personal Narrative of the Nigerian Crisis* (1996), *Arms and the Arts – A Continent's Unequal Dialogue* (1999), *Climate of Fear: The Quest for Dignity in a Dehumanized World* (2005).

Ngũgĩ wa Thiong'o (1938–): Kenyan writer and political activist. In the 1970s, he was a key member of the Kamiriithu Community Center and Theatre, a collective effort to develop an authentic Kenyan peoples theatre in the Gikuyu language. In 1977, Ngũgĩ's *Ngaahika Ndeenda* (*I Will Marry When I Want*) was performed in Kamiriithu's open-air theatre. After being imprisoned, Ngũgĩ was driven into exile and the Kamiriithu theatre was literally leveled by the government in 1982. A novelist, essayist, playwright, and filmmaker, Ngũgĩ's works include *Petals of Blood* (1977), *Detained: A Writer's Prison Diary* (1981), *Decolonising the Mind* (1986), *Moving the Centre* (1993), *Penpoints, Gunpoints, and Dreams* (1998), *Murogi wa Kagogo* (2004), and *Ngũgĩ wa Thiong'o Speaks* (2005).

Cultural impositions and appropriations

Which scenario is being enacted? No definitive answer can be given. The disadvantage of scenarios is that they are extremely reductive. However one approaches the question of globalization, it's not as simple as one culture imposing itself on the others. One must remember that the USA is itself increasingly multicultural. The fastest growing population in the USA is the Latin one. But Latinos are themselves a very mixed group, combining indigenous, African, Caribbean, and European peoples. In America, before the mid-twenty-first century, the so-called white majority will be a minority. "So-called" because, as Adrian Piper so dryly proves in *Cornered*, the concept of race is culturally constructed: a social circumstance, not a genetic fact. Therefore, questions of race, ethnicity, the inflow of new citizens, and the performance of various cultural norms are tightly related to each other. How will American society – and other societies also – accept/reject, integrate/isolate multiculturals in terms of languages, religions, histories, races, lifestyles, ethnicities, economic opportunity, political liberty, and social justice?

Furthermore, many American cultural exports are already intercultural. For example, American pop music is thoroughly Africanized, its theatre heavily influenced by Asia. Because so many different kinds of people live in the USA, Americans are relatively open to assimilating cultural practices. One might even go so far as to argue that there is no American culture comparable to French or Japanese cultures, for example. This very emptiness accounts for America's cultural accessibility, porosity, and exportability. It is one of the reasons why American culture, which does not exist, is so active globally.

The situation in Europe is somewhat different. Millions of South Asians are citizens of the UK. France has a rising population of Arab North Africans as well as large numbers of sub-Saharan Africans. Many Turks live in Germany. Add these "outsiders" to the circulation within the European Union and one detects a great mixing of East and West, South and North. But because so many Europeans experience their cultures as distinct – French, German, Spanish, Italian, and so on – tensions are rising concerning what it means to be a "real" European. On top of all this, radical Islamic "terrorism" and the Western counteraction to the attacks are here to stay. The Cold War was a fifty-year struggle marked by an arms race, economic and diplomatic maneuvers, and "limited wars." Yet, as the name signifies, there was no general conflagration comparable to the two world wars. Terrorism and "the war on terror" are different because they are taking place in many parts of the world simultaneously without involving a general military mobilization. This kind of protracted engagement involving both overt and covert actions complicates matters enormously, reminding some of the long struggle from the seventh to the sixteenth centuries between Islam and Christendom.

Jihad/terrorism as performance

To those who oppose them, **mujahideen** are terrorists. To themselves, they are combatants in an epic battle of good against evil. Though some forms of **jihad** are non-violent, the kind that grabs today's headlines involves suicide bombers whose devices have killed thousands. If what I wrote in Chapter 2 is correct – that "anything can be studied 'as' performance" – then jihad/terrorism comprises an important subject. I am not advocating terrorism, or any violence for that matter (though sometimes violence may be necessary as a last resort). My intention is to understand how terrorism works, how it functions in a globalized world, and why its effects are far in excess of its actual death or property toll.

Take the UK as an example. During World War II, the Blitz wreaked tremendous damage on people and property (**see figure 8.3**). Far from defeating the British, the Blitz galvanized society, uniting the people in the war effort. At the present time, a relatively few attacks with relatively little damage and death (compared to the Blitz) frightens some while mobilizing others who recall or, if they were too young, cited Britain's brave behavior during the Blitz. But the situations are not comparable. All Britons knew that Germany was the enemy and from which direction the planes and rockets would come. The war involved nation-states. Although there was a "fifth column," the most deadly attacks came from outside the British Isles. But today, the anonymity of the terrorists, their statelessness, their presence among ordinary citizens, and their ability to engage in deadly dark play arouses suspicions and fears directed not only against an alien enemy but also aimed at native-born Britons.

fig 8.3. St Paul's Cathedral seen through the fire and smoke of the Nazi bombing of London during World War II. Copyright EMPICS.

Terrorism is a new kind war suited to globalization. It is difficult to combat terrorists because nations as such do not have either the conceptual or actual equipment to move against stateless adversaries whose weapons are as much performative as they are explosive. Just as corporations have learned how to outsource and function from dummy states, so mujahideen exploit the global banking and free-trade system, the lowering of national territorial barriers, and the ubiquity of the internet and other digital media. Terrorists move stealthily from nation to nation. Or moles reside for years in a place awaiting their marching orders. Attacks occur anywhere against a wide variety of targets – some "hard" and obvious such as warships, the Pentagon, or guerrilla attacks in Iraq or Afghanistan, others "soft," designed to frighten ordinary citizens and disrupt economies: tourist hotels in Bali and Egypt, public transportation in Madrid and London, the attack on New York's World Trade Center. There are no "fronts" or "lines." What is consistent is that the mujahideen have ideological goals that cannot be realized or defeated by means of traditional military action. Those opposing the terrorists are hard pressed to design strategies even to recognize who is an enemy and who not without at the same time undermining the very freedoms of movement and free speech that Western democracies cherish. "Profiling" is rampant even when officially denied. "Is that person just an Arab-looking individual wearing a backpack on his stomach, or is he a terrorist?" The

jihad and mujahid (plural, **mujahideen**): from the Arabic meaning to exert utmost effort, to strive, to struggle. Jihad connotes a range of meanings from an inward spiritual struggle to attain perfect faith to a political or military campaign furthering an Islamic cause. Muslims classify jihad into two forms: *Jihad Al-Akbar*, the greater jihad, an internal struggle with one's soul; and *Jihad Al-Asgar*, the lesser jihad, an external fight using physical force. Jihad engages all dimensions of human thought and action in a cosmic battle of good against evil spanning time and space. A *mujahid* – a striver, struggler – is a person who engages in any form of jihad. Adapted from http://en.wikipedia.org/wiki/Jihad#Different_usages.

Mark Danner

Terror as a kind of horrible advertisement

Al Qaeda controlled no state, fielded no regular army. It was a small, conspiratorial organization, dedicated to achieving its aims through guerrilla tactics, notably a kind of spectacular terrorism carried to a level of apocalyptic brutality the world had not before seen. Mass killing was the necessary but not the primary aim, for the point of such terror was to mobilize recruits for a political cause – to move sympathizers to act – and to tempt the enemy into reacting in such a way as to make that mobilization easier. [. . .] Standing between the more radical Salafi groups and their goal of a conservative Islamic revolution are the "apostate regimes," the "idolaters" now ruling in Riyadh, Cairo, Amman, Islamabad and other Muslim capitals. [. . .] Many of the Salafists, however, see behind the "near enemies" ruling over them a "far enemy" in Washington, a superpower without whose financial and military support the Mubarak regime, the Saudi royal family and the other conservative autocracies of the Arab world would fall before their attacks. [. . .] But how to "re-establish the greatness of this Ummah" – the Muslim people – "and to liberate its occupied sanctities"? On this bin Laden is practical and frank: [. . ."T]o initiate guerrilla warfare."

Such warfare, depending on increasingly spectacular acts of terrorism, would be used to "prepare and instigate the Ummah." [. . .] The notion of "instigation," indeed, is critical, for the purpose of terror is not to destroy your enemy directly but rather to spur on your sleeping allies to enlightenment, to courage and to action. It is a kind of horrible advertisement, meant to show those millions of Muslims who sympathize with Al Qaeda's view of American policy that something can be done to change it. [. . .] The asymmetric weapons that the 19 terrorists used on 9/11 were not only the knives and box cutters they brandished or the fuel-laden airliners they managed to commandeer but, above all, that most American of technological creations: the television set. On 9/11, the jihadists used this weapon with great determination and ruthlessness to attack the most powerful nation in the history of the world at its point of greatest vulnerability: at the level of spectacle.

2005, "Taking Stock of the Forever War," 48, 50.

mujahideen succeed not only in scaring people, but in dividing the population. It's a war of appearances and performances maybe even more than it is one of bullets and bombs (**see Danner box**).

The mujahideen want not only to destroy, frighten, and destabilize but also to perform bin Laden's **fatwa**, a declaration of war without boundary or end (**see bin Laden box**). The fatwa nicely suits the counter-message of the Americans that they are engaged in a "global war on terror" also known as "a global struggle against violent extremism" (**see Schmitt and Shanker box**). Both sides agree on a narrative that depicts a "civilizational war" involving not only arms but also economic, ideological, religious, and political weapons. In one way, this epic struggle has no fixed geography, timetable, or objective beyond the destruction of the other. However, within this global struggle are the ongoing engagements in Iraq and Afghanistan taking place in specific theatres of war pitting conventional armies against guerrilla forces. The stated American and British reasons for the 2002 invasion of Iraq – weapons of mass destruction,

fatwa: an Islamic religious-political pronouncement based on the Qur'an that carries the authority of law. However, because there is no single Muslim superstate – as there was in the days of the **Caliphate** and **Saladin** – fatwas can be in conflict with each other. There is an ongoing struggle among Islamic authorities concerning which fatwas are legitimate and which are not.

Caliphate and **Saladin:** in the two centuries after the death of the Prophet Muhammad in 632, the Muslims rapidly expanded their domain. These territories were ruled by a line of "caliphs" (from the Arabic *khalifah*, "successors"). Caliphs were both political and religious leaders – in fact, the State and Islam were one. At its height in the ninth–tenth centuries, the Caliphate included what today are called Spain and North Africa, Saudi Arabia, Jordan, Syria, Israel-Palestine, Iraq, Afghanistan, and Pakistan. Internal struggles led to the decline of the Caliphate which ceased to exist when the Mongols destroyed Baghdad in 1258. Though not a Caliph, **Saladin (1137–93)** was the greatest of Muslim military heroes. He defeated the Crusaders, capturing Jerusalem in 1187. Saladin ruled Egypt, Syria, Yemen, and Palestine.

Osama bin Laden/World Islamic Front

Fatwa: Jihad against Jews and Crusaders

Praise be to Allah, who revealed the Book, controls the clouds, defeats factionalism, and says in His Book: "But when the forbidden months are past, then fight and slay the pagans wherever ye find them, seize them, beleaguer them, and lie in wait for them in every stratagem (of war)"; and peace be upon our Prophet, Muhammad Bin-'Abdallah, who said: I have been sent with the sword between my hands to ensure that no one but Allah is worshipped, Allah who put my livelihood under the shadow of my spear and who inflicts humiliation and scorn on those who disobey my orders. [. . .]

Despite the great devastation inflicted on the Iraqi people by the crusader–Zionist alliance, and despite the huge number of those killed, which has exceeded 1 million, despite all this, the Americans are once against trying to repeat the horrific massacres, as though they are not content with the protracted blockade imposed after the ferocious war [of 1990–91] or the fragmentation and devastation. So here they come to annihilate what is left of this people and to humiliate their Muslim neighbors. [. . .]

If the Americans' aims behind these wars are religious and economic, the aim is also to serve the Jews' petty state and divert attention from its occupation of Jerusalem and murder of Muslims there. The best proof of this is their eagerness to destroy Iraq, the strongest neighboring Arab state, and their endeavor to fragment all the states of the region such as Iraq, Saudi Arabia, Egypt, and Sudan into paper statelets and through their disunion and weakness to guarantee Israel's survival and the continuation of the brutal crusade occupation of the Peninsula.

All these crimes and sins committed by the Americans are a clear declaration of war on Allah, his messenger, and Muslims. And ulema [scholars] have throughout Islamic history unanimously agreed that the jihad is an individual duty if the enemy destroys the Muslim countries. [. . .] On that basis, and in compliance with Allah's order, we issue the following fatwa to all Muslims:

The ruling to kill the Americans and their allies – civilians and military – is an individual duty for every Muslim who can do it in any country in which it is possible to do it, in order to liberate the al-Aqsa Mosque and the holy mosque [Mecca] from their grip, and in order for their armies to move out of all the lands of Islam, defeated and unable to threaten any Muslim. This is in accordance with the words of Almighty Allah, "and fight the pagans all together as they fight you all together," and "fight them until there is no more tumult or oppression, and there prevail justice and faith in Allah." [. . .] We – with Allah's help – call on every Muslim who believes in Allah and wishes to be rewarded to comply with Allah's order to kill the Americans and plunder their money wherever and whenever they find it. We also call on Muslim ulema, leaders, youths, and soldiers to launch the raid on Satan's U.S. troops and the devil's supporters allying with them, and to displace those who are behind them so that they may learn a lesson. [. . .]

Almighty Allah also says: "O ye who believe, what is the matter with you, that when ye are asked to go forth in the cause of Allah, ye cling so heavily to the earth! Do ye prefer the life of this world to the hereafter? But little is the comfort of this life, as compared with the hereafter. Unless ye go forth, He will punish you with a grievous penalty, and put others in your place; but Him ye would not harm in the least. For Allah hath power over all things." Almighty Allah also says: "So lose no heart, nor fall into despair. For ye must gain mastery if ye are true in faith."

1998, www.fas.org/irp/world/para/docs/980223-fatwa.htm

strong links to Al Qaeda – were bogus. So why did the "coalition of the willing" (a weird phrase coined by the Bush team) invade? To show Islam some muscle? To finish the job of removing **Saddam Hussein**? To implant democracy and free markets in the Arab heartland? To lay hands on vast oil reserves? Iraq sits atop the world's second largest oil reserves (after Saudi Arabia) and is geopolitically the lynchpin of the Middle East. Afghanistan has long been astraddle the road connecting East and West. Whatever the reasons, soon enough Al Qaeda took advantage of the opportunity for a face off. Today and for the foreseeable future, in Iraq, Afghanistan, and elsewhere, Al Qaeda and its allies are combating the

Eric Schmitt and Thom Shanker

"The global struggle against the enemies of civilization"

The Bush administration is retooling its slogan for the fight against Al Qaeda and other terrorist groups, pushing the idea that the long-term struggle is as much an ideological battle as a military mission. [. . .] In recent speeches and news conferences, Defense Secretary Donald H. Rumsfeld and the nation's senior military officer have spoken of "a global struggle against violent extremism" rather than "the global war on terror," which had been the catchphrase of choice. [. . .] General Richard B. Myers, chairman of the Joint Chiefs of Staff, told the National Press Club on Monday that he had "objected to the use of the term 'war on terrorism' before, because if you call it a war, then you think of people in uniform as being the solution." He said the threat instead should be defined as violent extremists, with the recognition that "terror is the method they use." Although the military is heavily engaged in the mission now, he said, future efforts require "all instruments of our national power, all instruments of the international communities' national power." The solution is "more diplomatic, more economic, more political than it is military," he concluded. [. . .] Mr. Rumsfeld described America's efforts as it "wages the global struggle against the enemies of freedom, the enemies of civilization." The shifting language is one of the most public changes in the administration's strategy to battle Al Qaeda and its affiliates, and it tracks closely with Mr. Bush's recent speeches emphasizing freedom, democracy and the worldwide clash of ideas. [. . .]

By emphasizing to the public that the effort is not only military, the administration may also be trying to reassure those in uniform who have begun complaining that only members of the armed forces are being asked to sacrifice for the effort. New opinion polls show that the American public is increasingly pessimistic about the mission in Iraq, with many doubting its link to the counterterrorism mission. So, a new emphasis on reminding the public of the broader, long-term threat to the United States may allow the administration to put into broader perspective the daily mayhem in Iraq and the American casualties.

2005, "New Name for 'War on Terror' Reflects Wider U.S. Campaign," section A: 7.

Americans and their allies. These forces are enacting two conflicting theories of how to organize the world. Bush's Americans push for globalization and democracy. Bin Laden's Al Qaeda wants the rule of Wahhabi Islam (also known as Salafi or Muwahiddun Islam), a fundamentalist version of the faith that, in the late eighteenth century, emerged in what is today named Saudi Arabia.

Although globalization and democracy are secular, the civilizational war deeply involves religions and cultures: Wahhabian Islam versus fundamentalist Christianity. Key strategists on both sides imagine today's struggle as a continuation of an ancient social drama between the world's two most vehemently proselytizing religions – a struggle for nothing less than the souls of humankind. Taking a long view, Christian fundamentalists believe they have since the time of Christ been destined, indeed ordered by God, to convert the Jews and the pagans – all who do not accept Jesus Christ as their savior. The arrival of Islam in the seventh century signaled a contradictorily different revision within the "religions of the Books." For Muslims, Mohammed and the Qur'an are primary, even as they accept the Old Testament prophets and the New Testament's Jesus as a prophet (but not the son of God). Some Wahhabians – those who support Al Qaeda – believe they are instructed by Allah to "purify" Islam and to convert and/or conquer the infidels – everyone who is not a Muslim.

Saddam Hussein (1937–): leader of the Ba'ath party and dictator of Iraq from 1979 until 2003 when he was overthrown by the American invasion. A brutal ruler, Saddam used poison gas against Iraqi Kurds, executed many political enemies, and waged a bloody war against Iran, 1980–88. In 1990, Saddam's army invaded neighboring Kuwait. In 1991, American and British forces responded, routing Saddam's army but not removing him from power. In the interim between the two Iraq wars, America accused Saddam of developing weapons of mass destruction – a charge that has since proven false. After his defeat in the war of 2003, Saddam fled and was later captured. As of 2006, he is a prisoner on trial for crimes against humanity.

These radicals are a small minority of the world's Muslims, but in executing dramatic and frightening attacks and by knowing how to use the media, they wield power and influence far in excess of their numbers. In fact, the "war on terror" and the "jihad against Jews and Crusaders" are often made for the media. This does not trivialize the war/jihad, but feeds them, giving them enormous strength. Today's media – from tabloid journalism to internet **blogs** – is a reverberation machine structured to amplify events that are swiftly narrativized in order to capture the broadest attention. "News" is whatever gets people's attention – more likely to be an attack or threat than an in-depth analysis. Once a "story" is taken up by the media, it is dramatized and played over and over again. Certain core images – the World Trade Center swathed in smoke and flames, the wreckage of a London double-decker bus – are rebroadcast so many times that they become iconic. This is especially true of American and British media which, for better or worse, set the world standard. Furthermore, what analysis there is casts individual events as parts of an all-encompassing world social drama.

blog: a "we**blog**" or chronicle posted on one's own web page. A blog can take anything as its subject, from intimately personal diaries to political opinions and media promotions. Blog formats range widely from simple text to complex intermedia presentations.

Although an over-simplification, this social drama gives shape to today's struggle. The struggle is armed – as in the "war against terror" and the jihad against Jews and Americans; but it is also economic and cultural. In fact, the military, economic, and cultural warfare blend into one another. Each military action or terrorist attack – because of the density and totality of media – immediately impacts publics around the world. Economics is obviously important. But the cultural actions of broadcasts, newspapers, books, plays, movies, religious observances, and so on are equally if not ultimately more decisive. People actually respond and act according to the dictates of their roles within the social drama rather than coolly according to their economic or political interests (**see Trofimov box**). But the social drama narrated by media may not be the true story. Some argue that at least on the Anglo-American side the ideological and cultural struggle is a mask hiding territorial and economic goals: follow the oil. That may be, but even geopolitical aims cannot be accomplished without successful economic and cultural policies – which means an effective deployment of media and other cultural weapons.

The media is the stage where many dramas concerning the global civilizational struggle are played out. It is not simply that terrorist acts and responses by whoever is attacked are made for the media. Or that the internet is home to thousands of sites proclaiming, analyzing, arguing, and strategizing the multiple perspectives of the struggle. As with the global genome discussed earlier, the struggle has both a material and an informational presence. Things happen – but reporting and displaying the events and their aftermaths feed back into the events themselves. A mujahideen attack anywhere is immediately present everywhere. If one train is bombed all trains suddenly appear to be unsafe. The devastation is multiplied by being rebroadcast. It appears as if there is no safe place, nowhere to hide, and that so many people might be dangerous. In this regard, the exploding planes that brought down the World Trade Center towers in New York on September 11, 2001 was the mother of all terrorist actions. The aftermath has changed not only the way things are but the way they appear and the ways people behave. Around New York are posted signs that instruct, "If you see something, say something." Cameras are everywhere. Privacy dissolves in the acid of paranoia. Of course, a population afraid depends on its police, its governmental leaders, its counter-terrorist operations. The result is that rights hard won over centuries are set aside in the interest of "homeland security." All this functions within an atmosphere of a global performance, a clash of civilizations – an epic movie or, rather, serial thriller. Violence and the threat of violence are used both as instruments of war and as symbolic performances.

Although terrorism has been practiced for more than a century, the 9/11 attacks on New York and Washington were different because of their magnitude, the intention to humiliate and destabilize the world's superpower, and the extraordinarily performative quality of the attacks. Two thousand, five hundred and ninety-five people were killed when two hijacked commercial airliners – the largest suicide bombers in history – were crashed into New York's World Trade Center (**figure 8.4**). Another hijacked plane ploughed into Washington's Pentagon building, the headquarters of the US Defense Department, and a third plane whose destination was probably the US Capitol or the White House was brought down in Pennsylvania through the determined intervention of passengers who refused to let the aircraft be used as a bomb.

In October 2001, in order to reassure the American public, to avenge the deaths and damage, and to show American "resolve," President **Bush** and his advisors orchestrated a war in Afghanistan against the Taliban Islamic fundamentalist government and the Al Qaeda terrorist network. They prepared for war against Iraq which came in 2002 (for the second time in a decade). The Taliban were

Yaroslav **Trofimov**

What some Iraqis think of America

Sheikh Qutaiba Ammash was one of the main Sunni religious leaders in Iraq. [. . .] I asked him what he thought about America's promises to instill democracy in Iraq. "America?" he laughed. "We only believe in American technology. We don't believe in American democracy because the Americans themselves don't have any." Chuckling, Ammash excused himself: it was time for a sermon. An Al Jazeera crew was on hand to transmit his words across the Arab world. [. . .] He started out by praising anti-American insurgents, including the man who would be buried after the prayer. "The brave men of Mohammed's nation are protecting our sanctities. They will earn a place in the books of the great, with their names written in gold" [. . .].

[Later] I spent more than an hour chatting with Sheikh Majid al Saadi [. . .] one of the prayer leaders at the Kadhimiye shrine. [. . .] As Saadi went on talking, I noticed that his worldview went beyond the familiar vision of Islam clashing with the infidel West. [. . .] America was not just the enemy of Islam: it was the enemy of mankind. "Look at the three countries that are occupied – Palestine, Afghanistan, Iraq. Why them?" he wondered. "In Iraq, seven thousand years ago, we invented mathematics, geography, law. We taught civilization. In Palestine, the Christian Messiah was born. And in Afghanistan, the Buddhist religion was rooted. [. . .] Because of their deep history, all these people have a deep faith – and this angers America, which wants the entire world to become like it." To the sheikh, this was a doomed enterprise. "America? They don't have any history longer than two hundred years. They're ignorant. They have no idea how to manage countries. There, the people come from many nations and have many religions, but they have no relationship with the land and with their faith." [. . .]

It was disheartening to see how America was reduced, in the minds of these clerics, and the mobs who hang on their every word at packed sermons, to a confused caricature of a soulless vampire state. But I could see why such paranoia was flourishing. [. . .] It would become even harder to argue about Western values of freedom once the iconic photos of naked Iraquis tortured by American soldiers at Abu Ghraib prison became, for many, the most memorable symbol of America's effort to spread democracy in the lands of Islam.

2005, *Faith at War*, 183–86

ousted from Kabul but remain entrenched in outlying districts. Bin Laden eludes capture. Occupied, Iraq is the scene of a bloody insurgency. The social drama involves stupendous role-playing on both sides. Bush appears at rallies before a backdrop of American flags proclaiming "We're making steady progress. A free Iraq will mean a peaceful world. And it's very important for us to stay the course, and we will stay the course." Bin Laden releases videotapes insisting "The enemies of God are aware that this war is a turning point in the world, that it is a choice between an absolute control by the infidel West, its culture, and way of life and the Islamic renaissance which is coming, God willing."

George W. Bush (1946–): forty-third president of the United States and the eldest son of the forty-first president, George Herbert Walker Bush. George W. was born in Connecticut but raised in Texas where he worked in the oil business before becoming in 1989 a co-owner of the Texas Rangers baseball team. In 1995, Bush was elected governor of Texas. He won the presidency in 2000 only after the intervention of the United States Supreme Court which stopped the recounting of ballots in Florida (whose governor is Jeb Bush, George W.'s brother). In 2001, he led America into war in Afghanistan and in 2002, in Iraq. Bush was elected to a second term as US president in 2004.

Both bin Laden and Bush reduce the complexities of the situation to a performative either/or by casting the other side as "evil." Categories such as "good" and "evil" and terms such as "tragedy" and "jihad" invoke a highly theatrical protagonist–antagonist conflict. No doubt it is easier to mobilize popular support – on Main Street America and on the streets of the Third World – by means of theatre than by employing nuanced analyses. In the American media, the destruction of the World Trade Center brought forth repeated allusions to "tragedy." But does this classical category fit what happened (**see Taylor box 1**)?

The attacks on New York and Washington were shocking not only because of their audacity and precision but also because the effects were immediate and enormous. America

fig 8.4. New York's World Trade Center under attack, 11 September 2001. Photograph by Robert A. Patrick.

was hit simultaneously in its capitalist and military heart. Air traffic was halted nationally, the vice-president was removed to a "safe location" in case the president was killed, and the president himself was shuttled aloft for a number of hours to avoid being a sitting target. Almost as if to perform the difference between secrecy and display, thousands of American flags were flown all over the country. If capitalism and the "American way of (relatively carefree) life" were their targets, the terrorists scored bull's-eyes. In the months that followed, a new cabinet-level Department of Homeland Security was formed; the "Patriot Act" – sharply increasing surveillance and curtailing many previously accepted civil liberties – was passed by Congress. People were arrested in Iraq, Afghanistan, and elsewhere and held in prison camps

Diana Taylor

A different kind of tragedy

When I saw the north tower in flames – about five minutes after the first plane hit – I thought, "God, it's going to take a lot of time and money to fix that." A small community of watchers gathered in the street. [. . .] Others joined us. "Were there people trapped inside?" it finally occurred to us to ask. Traffic stopped. Then the second plane. Another explosion. More people. Even then we didn't start speculating about deliberate terrorists attacks. That happened only after word of the Pentagon filtered onto the street. We stood transfixed, watching, witnesses without a narrative, part of a tragic chorus that stumbled onto the wrong set. The city stopped. The phones went dead, cars vanished, stores closed, the towers folded. [. . .] Some hours later I heard that the attack that we had witnessed was now being called "war," albeit a "different kind of war." The world was suddenly being re-shuffled into those who stood by "us" and those who turned against "us."

Tragedy, as an aesthetic category, turns around the challenge of containment. Can Oedipus curb the tide of devastation that has wrecked Thebes? Hamlet's inability to act decisively leads to generalized death and the loss of the kingdom. Yet, tragedy is not just about containment, it functions as a structure of containment. [. . .] The massive potential for destruction depicted in tragedy is contained by the form itself – for tragedy delivers the devastation in a miniaturized and "complete" package, neatly organized with a beginning, middle and an end. Ultimately, tragedy assures us, the crisis will be resolved and balance will be restored. The fear and pity we, as spectators, feel will be purified by the action.

The events of September 11th, however, make me think that we're not only looking at a different kind of war but also a different kind of tragedy. When people refer to the "September 11th tragedy," they usually refer to that awesome spectacle of pity and fear so brilliantly executed by the suicide pilots and so efficiently delivered nationally and globally by the U.S. media. They refer to the hijacked planes and the thousands of victims, whose smiling faces and life-stories appear on Xeroxed sheets taped to phone booths, mailboxes, and hospital walls. President George W. Bush, hastily re-cast as a leader with a definable moral character, sets out to set time right. All of these events are certainly tragic in the popular understanding of the term, and it offers us a language to talk about them. Yet, I think that using tragedy in its aesthetic connotation not only "structures" the events but also blinds us to other ways of thinking about them.

Take tragedy's organizational timetable: beginning, middle and end. Did the tragic action really start on September 11th? Some might argue that we were hijacked long before September 11th, maybe starting in the fall of 2000 when the elections were pulled off course. Important items on the American national agenda, such as improving education and health-care, for example, went up in smoke. The victims from that catastrophe remain uncounted, although they are certainly identified. New victims are created daily as anti-terrorist legislation, anti-immigrant sentiment, and corporate welfare packages wind their way through the House and Senate. Others might point out that we have been on a seemingly inevitable collision course with Islamic, oil-producing nations for decades. Should the civilian losses they have sustained figure in among the victims? As for the ending, nothing seems certain except that it won't be speedy, make sense, or bring purification and release. [. . .]

September 11th created a revealing paradox. This was an event that, because of the time lag between the first hit and the fall of the last tower, produced a huge number of eyewitnesses. Moreover, they responded as citizens, who wanted to help their fellows by giving blood or volunteering. It soon became clear that their protagonism was not needed. Bush and Giuliani asked people to respond as consumers by visiting malls and attending Broadway plays. When witnesses visited ground zero to commemorate the loss, the Mayor accused them of "gawking." We should, it seems, know these events only through the media. In other words, this is an event that has banished and blinded the witnesses, even as it created them. Will purification and release come from participating in polls asking whether we support war efforts?

Talk of "tragedy", like talk of "war," in relation to the September 11th attacks gives the events a sense of clarity, directionality, and moral purpose that they do not have. I only wish they did.

2002, untitled entry in "A Forum on Theatre and Tragedy in the Wake of September 11, 2001," 95–96.

without recourse to the constitutionally guaranteed American legal process. In the most notorious of these camps at Guantanamo Bay, Cuba and Abu Ghraib prison in Baghdad, prisoners were "forcefully" interrogated and tortured. Sometimes, interrogations take the form of theatrical dark play, threatening but not using physical violence (**see Lelyveld box**). The practice is not unlike that of the **Inquisition** when confessions could often be procured simply by showing the accused the "instruments of torture." Photos of prisoners being humiliated and harassed by smiling American soldiers were broadcast globally, further degrading public opinion regarding the American "mission" in Iraq (**see figure 8.5**). But why were these pictures taken in the first place? Many resemble "bragging" photos showing dominance over an animal, a difficult mountain climb, or in a more touristy vein, simply, "Look what I'm doing!" Like photos of lynchings that an earlier generation of Americans made and sent as postcards to friends, the Abu Ghraib shots

fig 8.5. A human pyramid of Iraqi prisoners held in Abu Ghraib prison, 2004. Behind the prisoners stand grinning American soldiers. This humiliating treatment of prisoners by their American captors was part of the systematic use by US forces of psychological and physical torture.

Photo (a) US Army Specialist Charles Graner, one of the torturers.

Photo (b) copyright unknown.

Joseph Lelyveld

Like actors inhabiting their roles

When the prisoner is important enough and the interrogator has time to invest in the subtle task of undermining his resolve, the best practitioners perform like accomplished actors fully inhabiting their roles. Recounting their successes, they show some of the same dramatic flair. Chatting in a lounge of a Tel Aviv hotel, a former chief interrogator of the Israeli security agency, Shin Bet, briefly acted out his part in order to make the point that violence was seldom necessary. It can be enough to just lay the latest Amnesty International report on the table, he said, drumming his fingers in pantomime on the imagined document. "Have you read this?" he said as if speaking to a detainee. "It tells the sort of things we can do." Dramatic pause.

"And it doesn't include the answers of those who were afraid to speak to Amnesty International." *Second dramatic pause, meaningful stare, husky whisper.* "Or answers of those who can no longer speak."

In the telling of the former chief interrogator – who insisted that he be identified only by his initials, H.B.A. – an interrogation was a contest of brains, of personalities. An unequal contest, by definition: one party determines the rules and may change them at any moment – manipulation in pursuit of a moral end, saving lives (even if an archly implied threat is, strictly speaking, illegal under international law that's formally accepted by both Israel and the United States).

2005, "Whether We Like It or Not, Detainees in the War on Terrorism Will Be Subjected to Lies, Threats, and Highly Coercive Force," 40

Inquisition: a judicial arm of the Roman Catholic Church instituted in the thirteenth century to combat heresy, sorcery, alchemy, and witchcraft. Inquisitors' methods ranged from interrogation to torture resulting in death. Some historians believe that the Spanish Inquisition, not supressed until 1834, was so virulent because church authorities feared Islam and Judaism whose presence was palpable in Iberia. In 1908, the Church dropped the word "Inquisition" but continued the work. In 1965, the office was named the Congregation for the Doctrine of the Faith – headed by Cardinal Joseph Ratzinger from 1981 until his election as Pope Benedict XVI in 2005.

say more about the photographers and guards than about the prisoners. Once these photos hit the internet, the American "mission" in Iraq took on a whole new, disturbing, and sadistic aspect.

The media amplified many of these effects. With regard to the Twin Towers, surely the sudden loss of so many lives is a terrifying event, but within recent times the world has suffered many atrocities of much greater magnitude which the media has paid much less attention to. The fact that 9/11 was "an American tragedy" guaranteed its immediate translation into a global spectacle of awesomely televisable clips. This specularity was no accident, either on the part of the hijackers or of the media. The photos of Abu Ghraib may not have been meant for general consumption when snapped, but once the media grabbed them, their global distribution was no accident. Another face of America was disseminated and in the battle of images, a lot of the sympathy generated by 9/11 was cancelled.

In the Twin Towers attack, the world was given free tickets to a real-life made-for-media movie (**see Gabler box**). The footage of exploding, burning buildings uncannily resembled *The Towering Inferno* and other catastrophe films where terrified, panicked crowds flee down the canyons of Manhattan ahead of fire, smoke, and debris. Although the Pentagon was also hit, and one of the hijacked planes crashed in Pennsylvania, New York took center stage. It was not only the site of the most destructive attack, but also in itself an almost made-for-media "Gotham" or "Metropolis," capital of the West. The networks contained, packaged, labeled, and made money on the attacks and the wars that followed. News programs – their commercials rampant – were titled as if they were mini-series: "War on Terror," "America's New War," "Target Terrorism," "America Rising," and the most ironic of all, CNN's and NBC's "America Strikes Back," calling to mind the second of the *Star Wars* movies, *The Empire Strikes Back*. Are we now waiting for the sequel, *Return of the Jihad*?

Ironically, even as mujahideen oppose globalization, they are creatures of globalization. Without integrated systems of banking, communications, media, and transportation, organizations such as Al Qaeda cannot function. The sternest messages of Wahhabian fundamentalism are delivered via videotape and disseminated by means of satellite. The fact is that West no longer equals West, South no longer equals South, East no longer equals East. Globalization is more than a system of dominance, it is a network dissolving boundaries, subverting nations, mixing up populations, and taking strategic advantage of available technologies. Significant pockets of "West" exist everywhere; and equally significant cultural presences of "non-West" thrive in the West. In fact, "West," "East," and similar designations have become cultural rather than geographical terms.

Is globalization good or bad?

Finally, in the light of all that we are learning, is globalization "good" or "bad"? Good for what, bad for whom? Kenyan playwright and novelist Ngũgĩ wa Thiong'o accuses the West, and especially the USA, of dropping a "cultural bomb" on the struggling peoples of the world, destroying indigenous languages and practices, making it much more difficult, if not impossible, for these peoples to fulfill what **Frantz Fanon** called their "passionate search for a national culture" (**see**

Neal Gabler

Terrorism with an audience in mind

Over and over Tuesday [11 September 2001], after the planes tore through the World Trade Center towers and then the Pentagon, benumbed spectators said the same words: "It was like a movie."

Which was to say they had seen it before in countless disaster movies. The explosion and fireball, the crumpling buildings, the dazed and panicked victims, even the grim presidential address assuring action would be taken – all were familiar, as if they had been lifted from some Hollywood blockbuster. [. . .]

None of this could have been lost on the perpetrators of this tragedy. American films [. . .] now reach every corner of the world and their images colonize the imaginations of virtually everyone – one reason Muslim fundamentalists so hate America. They certainly understand the power of those visuals. So in attacking the symbols of American finance and American security, it may have been no accident that they chose the language of American movies. [. . .] You have to believe at some level it was their rebuff to Hollywood as well as their triumph over it – they could out-Hollywood Hollywood.

Consider the timing. When the first plane hit the World Trade Center, presumably there would be no camera ready. So the terrorists provided a second attack at a decent interval that they knew would be captured on film or video, and then repeated from many different angles – a montage of death and destruction. It was terrorism with an audience in mind.

2001, "This Time the Scene Was Real," 1.

Fanon box and Ngũgĩ box). Discovering, making, or reawakening a national culture means resisting alien cultural practices first imposed by colonialism and then seductively proffered by globalization. But specifying such resistance is far from easy. Take **hip-hop**. Its origins, if one can meaningfully use that term in this context, are African. But hip-hop took its particular tone in the USA as it was articulated and performed by African-Americans (**see figure 8.6**). Can African-Americans be considered a "diasporic" people? If so, pretty much the whole non-Native American population of the New World is diasporic. And, as noted in Chapter 5,

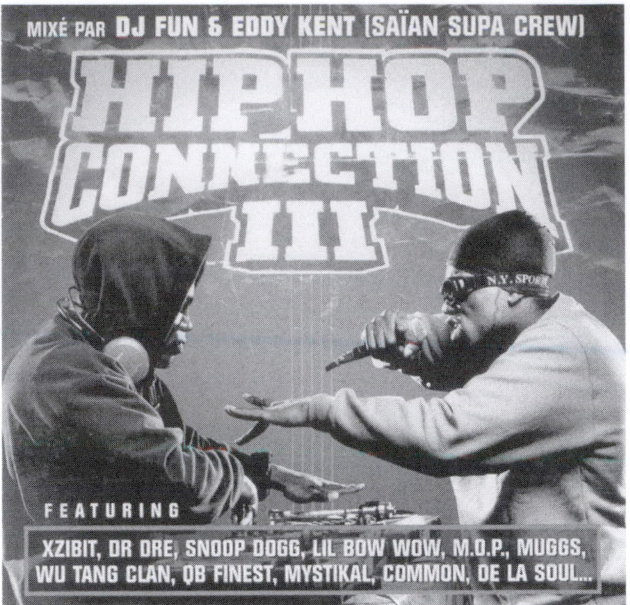

fig 8.6. *Hip-Hop Connection III* magazine cover – from Tunisia. http//tunisiano1981.free.fr/images/hiphop%20connect

people in the Americas are hybrids genetically and culturally. In Africa, should hip-hop be resisted because it is an American cultural bomb or welcomed as the return home of a distinctly Africanized music? And what about the rest of the world? Music through digitization and the internet travels swiftly and saturates the globe. In evaluating these musics should one consider the music in itself, who produces it, where it is produced, who owns the means of its production, and how it is disseminated? These questions overlap. Furthermore, rock and other music stars are not only famous the world over, but some actually influence social, economic, and political policies. The band U2's Bono (born Paul Hewson in 1960) has met many world leaders ranging from UN Secretary General Kofi Annan to the presidents and premiers of the UK, USA, Germany, and France. Bono leads DATA – the acronym stands for Debt, AIDS, Trade, Africa – a powerful advocate for debt relief and aid for Africa (**see Traub box**). U2's and Bono's popularity and global profile give him access and, in addition, his organizational skills have parlayed fame into policy clout.

hip-hop: an African-American cultural style that spans rap music, break-dancing, graffiti art, fashion, and hip-hop theatre. Hip-hop artists and their lyrics are often politically savvy, pointing up the racism of American society. Though African-American in origin, style, and themes hip-hop is performed in many parts of the world. Hip-hop appeals to a very wide cultural and racial range of youthful audiences.

Frantz Fanon

On national culture

[T]his passionate search for a national culture which existed before the colonial era finds its legitimate reason in the anxiety shared by native intellectuals to shrink away from that Western culture in which they all risk being swamped. Because they realize they are in danger of losing their lives and thus becoming lost to their people, these men, hotheaded and with anger in their hearts, relentlessly determine to renew contact once more with the oldest and most pre-colonial springs of life of their people. [. . .]

Colonialism is not simply content to impose its rule upon the present and the future of a dominated country. Colonialism is not satisfied merely with holding a people in its grip and emptying the native's brain of all form and content. By a kind of perverted logic, it turns to the past of the oppressed people, and distorts, disfigures, and destroys it. [. . .] The effect consciously sought by colonialism was to drive into the natives' heads the idea that if the settlers were to leave, they would at once fall back into barbarism, degradation, and bestiality. [. . .]

We have noticed, on the eve of the decisive conflict for national freedom, the renewing of forms of expression and the rebirth of the imagination. There remains one essential question: what are the relations between the struggle – whether political or military – and culture? Is there a suspension of culture during the conflict? Is the national struggle an expression of a culture? [. . .] In short, is the struggle for liberation a cultural phenomenon or not?

We believe that the conscious and organized undertaking by a colonized people to re-establish the sovereignty of that nation constitutes the most complete and obvious cultural manifestation that exists. It is not alone the success of the struggle which afterward gives validity and vigor to culture; culture is not put into cold storage during the conflict. The struggle itself in its development and in its internal progression sends culture along different paths and traces out entirely new ones for it. [. . .] This struggle which aims at a fundamentally different set of relations between men cannot leave intact either the form or the content of the people's culture. After the conflict there is not only the disappearance of colonialism but also the disappearance of the colonized man.

1963, *The Wretched of the Earth*, 210–11, 245–46

Frantz Fanon (1925–61): Martinique-born anti-colonial theorist who lived mostly in France but concentrated his attention on Africa. His books include *Black Skin, White Masks* (1952, Eng. 1967) and *The Wretched of the Earth* (1961, Eng. 1965).

On another level of global circulation and interaction, to whom do genetic materials or body parts "belong"? To the individual or culture from which the genes or organs were "harvested"? Does a person own her own genes? There is an active trade in body parts and genes are being patented. The genetics trade is abetted by the fact that genes/genetic codes are both material substances and digitized information residing in computer simulations. For the most part, the advantage in these global trades goes to the strongest, most efficiently organized – that is, to global corporations. These corporations are still predominantly Western owned and operated. But at the very least India, China, and Brazil are

Ngũgĩ wa Thiong'o

The cultural bomb

Imperialism, led by the USA, presents the struggling peoples of the earth and all those calling for peace, democracy, and socialism with the ultimatum: accept theft or death. The oppressed and the exploited of the earth maintain their defiance: liberty from theft.

But the biggest weapon wielded and actually daily unleashed by imperialism against that collective defiance is the cultural bomb. The effect of a cultural bomb is to annihilate a people's belief in their names, in their languages, in their environment, in their heritage of struggle, in their unity, in their capacities and ultimately in themselves. It makes them see their past as one wasteland of non-achievement and it makes them want to distance themselves from that wasteland. It makes them want to identify with that which is furthest removed from themselves; for instance, with other peoples' languages rather than their own. [. . .]

The real aim of colonialism was to control the people's wealth: what they produced, how they produced it, and how it was distributed; to control, in other words, the entire realm of the language of real life. [. . .] Economic and political control can never be complete or effective without mental control. To control a people's culture is to control their tools of self-definition in relationship to others.

For colonialism this involved two aspects of the same process: the destruction or the deliberate undervaluing of a people's culture, their art, dances, religions, history, geography, education, orature and literature, and the conscious elevation of the language of the coloniser.

1986, *Decolonising the Mind*, 3, 16

James Traub

Bono: The one-man state on the world stage

At 1:45 in the morning one day this pasty July [2005], Bono, the lead singer for U2 and the world's foremost agitator for aid to Africa, was in a van heading back to his hotel in Edinburgh from Murrayfield Stadium; he had just performed in, and expounded at, a concert designed to coincide with the beginning of the summit meeting of the major industrialized nations, held nearby at the Gleneagles resort. [. . .] The summit meeting's final communique offered significant pledges on aid and debt relief for Africa, as well as new proposals on education and malaria eradication. Bono's own embrace of the package was treated with a solemnity worthy of a Security Council resolution. [. . .] Bono had moved the debate on Africa, as five years ago he moved the debate on debt cancellation. [. . .] He's a strange sort of entity, this euphoric rock star with the chin stubble and the tinted glasses – a new and heretofore undescribed planet in an emerging galaxy filled with transnational, multinational, and subnational bodies. He's a kind of one-man state who fills his treasury with the global currency of fame. He is also, of course, an emanation of the celebrity culture. But it is Bono's willingness to invest his fame, and to do so with a steady sense of purpose and tolerance for detail, that has made him the most politically effective figure in the recent history of pop culture.

2005, "The Statesman," 82

entering the global markets. As the twenty-first century proceeds, the loci of corporate, transnational power may not be described by the standard geographical metaphoric divide of East/West or North/South. In terms of the organ trade, rich individuals wherever they reside seek organs from wherever they can be obtained.

Increasingly, resisting cultural impositions means confronting hard questions. Can there be a "national culture" without a nation? Doesn't globalization eat away at the very basis of nationhood? Is nationhood essential for the existence of local or indigenous cultures? Resistance to the global is not easy, especially when giving in is a way not only of earning necessary hard currencies such as American dollars or Japanese yen but also of participating in the good life that the upbeat propounders of globalization promise. Defending against the cultural bomb takes many forms. In Japan, traditional arts such as noh and kabuki are designated "national treasures," their master artists awarded the title of "living national treasures." These arts and artists receive substantial subsidies. In the developing world, where money is hard to come by, the options are stark: the dumbing-down and selling of traditional arts and practices as tourist attractions, giving up indigenous cultural practices altogether in favor of rapid globalization, which most often means Westernization or some kind of "world culture" as with hip-hop, or extinction.

But it is not only, or even mostly, the arts that are under pressure. In fact, a number of governments and foundations find ways to preserve what are deemed to be very important national, regional, or local traditional arts. The practice of everyday life is something else: for example, the wearing of traditional clothes. It seems the more global the location, the more Western the dress. In Tokyo, Shanghai, or Singapore, few wear kimonos or traditional Chinese or Malay clothes. This garb is reserved for ceremonial or religious occasions. Worldwide, where the weather permits, young children wear short pants or dresses. Older kids and youths put on jeans, T-shirts, and blouses. Even in India, in the cities especially, *saris*, *dhotis*, and *lunghis* are giving way to Western-style clothes. In Africa, there is a wide variety of dress, from *dashikis* to Levi's. Food habits as well are changing in accord with global tastes. The ubiquity of McDonald's tells the story. Then there is the question of language, with English becoming the world's lingua franca. This has led to an explosion of literature in India, Anglophone Africa, and the Caribbean that is English but not British. Although most European languages, Chinese in its several variants, Indian languages, Arabic, Japanese, and other tongues are thriving, vast numbers of people find it necessary to acquire English in order to participate in the global multilogue. And a number of languages are in danger of extinction. Many Native American languages are gone or nearly so. The same is true in Africa. How much will the extinction of several hundred or even thousands of languages impoverish the human imagination?

By far the most pervasive cultural aspect of globalization is the media – movies, television, radio, digitized music, and the internet. There are three levels of culture. At the most local level, distinct habits, foods, dialects, and other cultural markers thrive. At a second level, certain local practices and items enter the global marketplace materially and/or culturally. At the most general level, people everywhere attend the same movies, watch the same television programs, acquire the same DVDs, listen to the same music, and cruise the internet. The question is whether or not the third most general level is swelling at the expense of the first, most distinctively local level. Local media adopt global styles so that wherever produced the products are similar. The impact of especially American films and television is strong. Whether dubbed or subtitled, the programs retain their Americanness. But it is too easy to rage against impositions when the situation is much more complex. New styles of music, food, films, and the like regularly sweep the world, but without the older "classical" musics disappearing. Also there is an abundance of local and regional music performed and broadcast. The interaction of the global and the local – as well as the emergence of unique "glocal" styles combining global and local – is robust. In terms of music, scanning the air with shortwave, AM, and FM, at any given time one can listen to everything from The Beatles to Puff Daddy, ragas to Beethoven, chutney soca to the chanting of the Qur'an.

In the future, the internet may prove to be the most influential medium because it is both widespread and difficult to control. This is becoming increasingly so as the internet merges with and captures other kinds of communications such as cell phones and television. The rise of blogs and **podcasts** are harbingers of paradoxical kinds of media that are global, personal, commercial, and hybrid. But before we celebrate this diversity, we need to recognize that at present, and for a longer time than its promoters allow, the internet and wireless communications are not universally or evenly available. The advantage goes to people living in the West, Japan, China, India, Australia, and New Zealand along with those living in large cities anywhere. However, even though relatively few individuals living in rural Africa and Asia can afford to be online on an individual basis, most villages have at least one computer and/or cell phone linked to the World Wide Web. Television and film are very widespread if not universal. The trend is strongly to more and more connectivity. Putting it all together, the question remains whether or not cultural globalization – the hybridities and "world styles" – are really global – the result of contributions made by many individuals and many cultures – or are they a sign of the increasing hegemony of the West, more specifically of the USA? And if so, is there anything that can or should be done about it? Al Qaeda, for all its hatred of Western values, uses the media. Does that mean that the media qua media is "value free"?

podcast: podcasting makes audio files easily downloadable for listening whenever one wants to on a portable player such as the popular iPod. Podcasting enables both established and independent producers to create "radio shows" that are heard at the listener's convenience.

Some believe globalization is the inevitable next step in human social evolution on the way toward the emergence of a single world system. What kind of system? Economic, surely. Possibly political too because "free-market capitalism" and "democracy" go hand in hand. This scenario supposes the ultimate defeat of fundamentalists of different religions – Islamic, Christian, Hindu, Jewish – who advocate theocracies or religious superstates. These opponents to democracy number in the hundreds of millions, if not billions. Their leaders know very well how to use the most up-to-date media and internet techniques. Thus, even if a world system emerges, it may resemble more a caliphate than a global democracy. Or the world may share media and advanced science while struggling for centuries over economic, political, religious, and cultural values. Neither in the near term or the long range is there a guarantee of a world system founded on what Westerners and their allies call "human rights." Finally, it is doubtful that there will be a single world religion despite what some fundamentalists want. But what about world popular culture? And even if people everywhere listen to the same music, wear the same clothes, and watch the same movies, will this result in any improvement in their daily material, political, or spiritual lives? Or will the ongoing culture wars waged globally result in ever-tightening interlocked surveillance and control systems? Will the firewalls and passport controls of the future block not only computer viruses and unwelcome aliens but also ideas? The advocates of the internet argue that the web is uncontrollable, a self-generating global agora. But at the same time, new techniques of control – some subtle and invisible, some heavy-handed involving intimidation, imprisonment, torture, and assassination – are also afoot. It is not clear if the world is headed toward a liberation or neo-medievalism. Or maybe none of my scenarios will come to pass. Perhaps the future is unimaginable. Whatever the case, an important part of the work of performance studies is to project various possibilities.

Colonial mimicry

Globalization, if not the heir of colonialism, owes a great deal to the earlier historical period. During colonial times, and even after, a complex kind of intercultural performance occurred when "natives" took, or were afforded the "privilege" of acquiring, the language, dress, habits, religion, and social values of the colonial rulers. These performances were imperfect simulations, non-Europeans almost but not quite passing for European. As culture theorist **Homi K. Bhabha** put it, the **colonial mimic** became as if European; Anglicized, not British (**see Bhabha box**). But what kind of failed performance was this? The colonial subject often acted more British than the British. The failure to pass was enforced by the colonial rulers who made the racial difference, not the acquired behaviors and skills, the basis upon which to make the final judgment of who was and who wasn't accepted as "one of us." The rulers could not bear to be perfectly replicated because that would deny them the difference upon which their authority was ultimately based. By means of snubs, slights, discrimination, and outright violence, the rulers reminded the subjects that no level of mastering the "parent culture" could wash out the racial stain. Of course, the rulers' own "racial purity" was an illusion, as is the whole notion of race at the genetic level. It is worth noting that colonial mimicry also can go the other way. In these cases, the ones who passed were sometimes honored by the colonial power, as was **T. E. Lawrence** (of Arabia), and sometimes

colonial mimicry: a performance of everyday life in which colonized persons adopt in part or wholesale the culture of their colonizers.

Homi K. Bhabha (1949–): Indian cultural theorist, a leading figure in postcolonial studies. His works include *The Location of Culture* (1994), the edited volume *Nation and Narration* (1990), and *Edward Said: Continuing the Conversation* (2005).

T. E. Lawrence, "Lawrence of Arabia" (1888–1935): Welsh soldier and author who served as British liaison to the Arabs during their revolt against the Turkish Empire (1916–22). Lawrence gave his account of that revolution in *Seven Pillars of Wisdom* (1935).

Homi K. Bhabha

Colonial mimicry

Within the conflictual economy of colonial discourse which Edward Said describes as the tension between the synchronic panoptical vision of domination – the demand for identity, stasis – and the counter pressure of the diachronic of history – change, difference – mimicry represents an ironic compromise. [. . .] Colonial mimicry is the desire for a reformed, recognizable Other, as a subject of difference that is almost the same, but not quite. Which is to say, that the discourse of mimicry is constructed around an ambivalence; in order to be effective, mimicry must continually produce its slippage, its excess, its difference. [. . .] The menace of mimicry is its double vision which in disclosing the ambivalence of colonial discourse also disrupts its authority. [. . .] Almost the same but not white: the visibility of mimicry is always produced at the site of interdiction. It is a form of colonial discourse that is uttered inter dicta: a discourse at the crossroads of what is known and permissible and that which though known must be kept concealed; a discourse uttered between the lines and as such both against the rules and within them. [. . . T]he difference between being English and being Anglicized.

1994, *The Location of Culture*, 86, 88–90

disparaged for "going native." In still another kind of mimicry, many anthropologists who use the "participant observation" method of research wholeheartedly take part in the daily life of the people they are studying. These anthropologists also "almost, but not quite" become who they imitate.

There is more. As with gays recuperating the term "queer," more than a few radicals used colonial mimicry to subvert, challenge, and overthrow the authorities. Many anti-colonial leaders were educated in the very countries against whom they battled. But to be educated "in" does not determine the uses to which an education is put. Some leaders, after a period of performing the culture of the colonial power, rejected it and flaunted it simultaneously. Two figures of the Indian independence struggle provide illuminating examples. Few English could act more British than India's first prime minister, **Jawaharlal Nehru**. Nehru was tutored in India as a child by a Britisher; he matriculated in England at Harrow and Cambridge. He mastered English thought, language, and social mien. He became close friends with **Earl Louis Mountbatten**, the last British Viceroy of India. With his aristocratic bearing and lucid intellect, Nehru could (and did) outdo the British at the banquet table, the debate lectern, and the negotiating chamber. But Nehru's colonial mimicry did not in the least deter him from his life's task. He was a relentless, intrepid battler for Indian independence. As prime minister, Nehru led the "non-aligned" nations of the world – those that favored neither the USSR nor the USA during the Cold War.

Jawaharlal Nehru (1889–1964): a revolutionary founder of modern India, Nehru served as the nation's first prime minister from Independence in 1947 until his death. Nehru was a key leader not only of India's independence struggle against Great Britain but of the unaligned nations of the Third World. His books include *An Autobiography* (1936) and *The Discovery of India* (1946).

Earl Louis Mountbatten (1900–79): last British Viceroy of India, he turned authority over to the leaders of India and Pakistan in August 1947. During the Second World War, Lord Mountbatten headed the Allied Southeast Asian Command.

No one could be less like Nehru in appearance and style than his closest ally in the struggle, **Mohandas K. Gandhi** whose traditional Indian garb of dhoti and walking stick was his signature look. But at the start, Gandhi was an excellent colonial mimic. He took his law degree from the Inns of Court in London, and when he arrived in South Africa in 1893 to practice law, he looked every inch an Englishman (**see figure 8.7**). But despite looking and acting properly British, Gandhi was humiliated and physically abused because he was an Indian. This led him to a profound change of heart. Gandhi learned that "performing British" was not in the interest of truth, Indian independence, his own dignity, or that of the Indian people. A deep pattern of his life took the shape of "performing not British." His campaigns against colonial rule were exercises in "non-cooperation" – boycotting or rejecting British goods, courts, schools, dress, bureaucracy, food, legislatures, and religion. This did not stop him from using the ideas of Leo Tolstoy, **John Ruskin**, and others when they suited him. And Gandhi's values and political strategies profoundly influenced non-Indians, **Martin Luther King** especially. Gandhi brought his life-style, appearance, and behavior into harmony with his values and beliefs. He was from boyhood a strict vegetarian. He grounded his actions in Indian religious and philosophical texts, the *Bhagavad Gita* in particular, with its teaching of engaging fully but without hatred in the necessary wars of life. He intentionally made a spectacle of himself by leading marches, going on hunger strikes, challenging the British to jail him, and dressing only in homespun cloth, *khadi* (**see figure 8.8**). Gandhi's Indianness contrastively staged British colonialism before a world audience. His *satyagraha* (non-violent struggle) was both actual and symbolic, consisting of "demonstrations" – embodied proofs. For example,

fig 8.7. Mohandas K. Gandhi the proper British lawyer in South Africa in the 1890s. Photo courtesy of www.mahatma.org.in

fig 8.8. Mohandas K. Gandhi striding through Bengal wearing a traditional Indian dhoti, 1946. Photo courtesy of www.mahatma.org.in

in the 1930 protest against the British salt tax, Gandhi led a 241-mile march from Ahmedabad to Dandi on the Arabian Sea coast, where he and his followers gathered sea salt (no tax on that). This symbolic act ignited a general protest against British colonial rule resulting in the jailing of Gandhi and more than 60,000 others. The jailings, far from being a defeat for Gandhi's movement, was convincing proof of its mass appeal and deeply rooted strength. Gandhi's performances won the respect of some of his British adversaries and the scorn of others. He pretty well drove them all crazy. But to hundreds of millions of ordinary Indians, Hindus and Muslims alike, this trained lawyer, strong negotiator, non-violent warrior, and great performer was, simply, *mahatma*, the "great soul."

Mohandas K. Gandhi (1869–1948): Indian political and spiritual leader advocating non-violent resistance to British colonial authority. In January 1948, Gandhi was assassinated by a Hindu fundamentalist. His writings include *Autobiography: The Story of My Experiments with Truth* (1954) which Gandhi updated several times.

John Ruskin (1819–1900): English essayist whose *Unto This Last* (1862), a critique of capitalism, influenced Gandhi during his formative years in South Africa.

Martin Luther King, Jr. (1929–68): African-American religious and civil rights leader, winner of the 1964 Nobel Peace Prize for his efforts to end racial discrimination in the USA. King was assassinated by a white racist in April 1968 in Memphis, Tennessee.

Tourist performances: Leisure globalization

Tourism is no simple matter. To satisfy an enormous and still rapidly growing market of intercultural, international, intracultural, and intranational tourists, performances of all kinds have been found, redesigned, or invented. There are many kinds of tourism – culture, sports, sex, wildlife, historical, etc. – where at the destination the tourist witnesses or, increasingly, takes part in a performance of one kind or another. While on safari, for example, tourists become hunters-with-cameras, living in a refurbished and toileted "wild." Sports tourists at the Olympics or the Superbowl more than watch athletes. They party, sightsee, vicariously take part in the competition while identifying with their heroes and their city or nation. These tourisms, for we must use the plural to describe them, can transport people to distant places or back in time by means of restorations and re-enactments.

It is common wisdom to disparage tourism and tourist performances as shallow and tawdry, a pastime for the rich and an exploitation of "native" or "local" peoples, their beliefs, and skills. Tourists yearn for the "authentic" and the "real," even as most of them know they are being fed the ersatz and the invented. Although all this is too often true, it is not always the case, nor is it the whole story. In Bali very similar performances may be part of a temple ceremony in one instance and presented in unconsecrated space for tourists at another time. The quality suffers, but not as much as those who condemn tourism say. *Ketchak* – the "monkey chant-dance" which re-enacts an episode from the *Ramayana* – is performed by the Balinese both in their own ceremonies and as a big tourist attraction. Ironically, ketchak began in the 1920s as a tourist performance.

There are performances not made for tourists which attract them in droves all the same. Many religious observances are open to visitors – sometimes in the hopes of proselytizing, or to earn money, or just to be hospitable. When tourists enter churches, temples, synagogues, shrines, or mosques are they enjoying (and paying for) an entertainment or experiencing the sacred? Need one strictly separate these orders of experience? And insofar as the tourists are present at the "real thing," what adjustments are made in the performances to accommodate the outsiders? The answer cannot be given briefly or definitively because the changes may be subtle and slowly transformative.

There is virtual and media tourism – film and television are so enormously popular partly because they give people a chance to experience "the other" without leaving home. Brazilians watching reruns of *Seinfeld* or Americans watching a *National Geographic Special* (or any number of programs on the Discovery Channel) are virtual tourists. Surfing the web yields similar opportunities for experiencing the far away. Does virtual tourism create a pressure for the places depicted to attempt to live up to their media images?

When tourism involves actual travel, this can take many forms. Pilgrimages, popular the world over, and undertaken by poor and rich alike combine religious devotion and tourism. Hindus are continually in circulation around India, visiting literally thousands of *tirths* (pilgrimage spots) – temples, caves, mountains, rivers. Multitudes journey to performances such as the Raslila at Mathura or the Ramlila at Ramnagar. At Raslila Krishna, and at Ramlila Rama, are manifest. People come from far and near to have *darshan* – a vision or view – of the gods who the devoted believe are incarnate in the guise of young boys. In 1978 at Ramnagar, I met a man who had been carrying his mother around India in a basket for two years so that she could visit as many pilgrimage sites as possible (**see figure 8.9**). Millions of Muslims make the Hajj to Mecca at least once in their lives (**see figure 8.10**). Places sacred to Christianity abound,

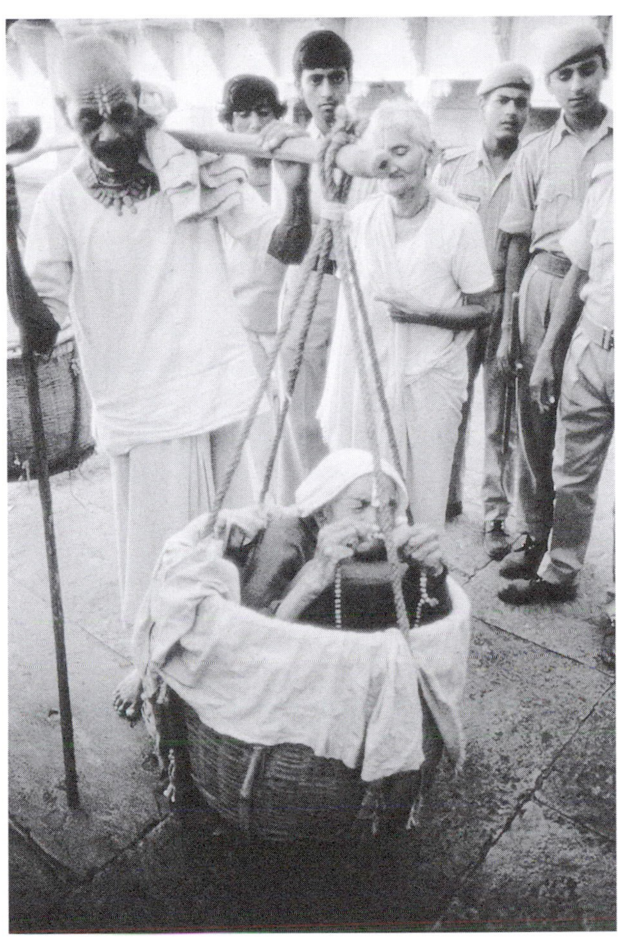

fig 8.9. A devoted son carrying his mother to important pilgrimage centers in India. The journey was to take more than two years. As shown here in 1978 they have arrived at the Ramlila of Ramnagar. Photograph by Richard Schechner.

Geoffrey Chaucer (1342–1400): English poet, best known for *The Canterbury Tales*, written between 1386 and 1400. In this poem, persons old and young, women and men on a pilgrimage to Canterbury, England, tell stories to pass the time.

fig 8.10. The Hajj during prayers at sunset on 27 February 2001. Nearly one million pilgrims are facing the Kaaba – a granite cube draped in black silk – located inside the Masjid al Haram in Mecca, Saudi Arabia. Photograph Adrees Latif/Reuters.

attracting tourists to the Holy Land and to miracle shrines in Europe and the Western Hemisphere. People make these journeys not only to fulfill a religious obligation but also to see the world, sharing in the camaraderie that "going away" enlivens – a liminal time–space well known to poet **Geoffrey Chaucer** as recounted in his *Canterbury Tales*.

Tourism within nations is at least as big a business as travel among nations. Protecting local peoples, practices, wildlife, or landscapes can turn into selling them, or imitations of them, to tourists. In India, city-dwelling Rajasthanis flock to a specially built "authentic" village to view craftspeople at work and to enjoy music, dance, and supper. The tourists sit on the floor of a large thatch-roofed house eating traditional foods dished onto banana leaves by young women dressed in "traditional" garb. As Jaipur's Rex Tours puts it, "Take a peek into the lives of rural folk, their abodes, social set up, religious beliefs, and innovative cuisine" (**see figure 8.11**). The night I was there most of the tourists were visibly middle class. My hunch was right that at least some of the visitors were returning to a sanitized version of their own past. "This is very authentic," a man told me. "It is just like the village my parents came from." So why didn't he simply make a trip back to his parents' village? Tourism simplifies, idealizes, and packages. When the show is over, you can wash your hands of the whole thing. The actual village may have been far away or held some disturbing reminders – or even relations to whom he would be obligated. Or maybe his own village had changed so much that the tourist village was a better representation of his past. But most probably, seeing his own experience reified gave him a sense of mastery over his past. He could literally purchase his past. Tourism does that – allows the tourist to purchase the other, the past, the exotic, the sexy, the exciting . . . whatever is up for grabs. And if "purchase" means to buy with money, it also means to get a hold on, to grasp firmly, to be in charge.

fig 8.11. A Rajasthani family as portrayed in a tourist brochure seeking business from Indian as well as foreign tourists. Photo courtesy Richard Schechner.

fig 8.12. Maasai men dancing at Mayer's Farm, a tourist destination in Kenya, in 1983. Although Mayer's Farm has closed, tourist photographers still aim their cameras at the Maasai. Too often, the tourists and tour managers treat "native people" as another form of wildlife – this is an attitude deeply founded in colonialism. Photograph by A. Kent Christensen.

In Kenya, Mayer's Farm – a homestead owned by white settlers – attracted tourists who wanted to experience "authentic" colonial life including members of the Mayer family and Maasai employees all playing their colonial roles. So for the "eternal past" of the tourist experience, the vanished world was back in place, if only in the realm of the performative make-believe. Mayer's Farm no longer exists – but the Maasai continue to be exploited by hordes of camera-toting tourists who treat them as little more than part of the area's wildlife (**see figure 8.12 and Maimai box**). What about the economics of this kind of tourism? Much tourism feeds on the needy and, like globalization generally, depends on a sharp imbalance of economic opportunity. The tourist is free-floating, a consumer with a lot of cash (relatively speaking) who could in theory go anywhere.

Kakuta Ole Maimai

Commercial photographers in the Maasai region

The Maasai people are among the indigenous people hunted by photographers who found free access into a land filled with exoticism, wildlife, and tribal people, where the law to protect indigenous people remains scarce. Some western photographers are stepping over boundaries; they are not being sensitive to our culture and way of life. They are invading and exploiting our people and culture for profit purposes.

Here are some questions to ask yourself, when looking at a portrait book with Maasai images: Who is this person in the picture? What is her name? How does she feel being in a portrait book? Does she know that her picture is being sold in the Western world? Did she receive anything in return? Has the photographer obtained a letter of consent from this person or from the community? Now look at a portrait book, or magazine, with images of Western people. Repeat the same questions stated above.

It appears that a wild animal is given a better recognition than a Maasai person. When you visit a zoo [. . .] the keeper will present that animal to you by its name. Why can't a photographer name a Maasai if s/he can name a wild animal? A Maasai is not less of a human being. Recently, we came across images of a circumcision event, a sacred rite of passage that is not intended for the public. This discovery was shocking, sad, and disappointing to us, as this is a personal and sacred rite of passage that should have not been photographed, published, and sold to the public.

The photographers must stop invading the privacy of the Maasai people, community, and culture. There are other ways to take images of the people without humiliating, invading, and exploiting the culture. Photographers can make profits without disrespecting the culture. On the other hand, the reader/viewer can learn about Maasai culture without supporting a disrespectful photographer. The reader has the power to change this behavior of a misbehaving photographer. [. . .] Do not buy books with nude images of indigenous people. [. . .] Encourage your bookseller to buy books that are culturally sensitive to indigenous cultures. [. . .] Write to the photographer and encourage her/him to give something back to the community in which s/he photographed. [. . .]

It is important to make clear that we are not opposed to ordinary and respectful photographers. A tourist, for example, is free to take family pictures, as s/he wishes, so long as s/he has obtained a consent from the individual. Also, we are not opposed to learners who wish to understand the Maasai culture. In fact, we are glad to learn that people from all corners of the world are willing to learn about our culture. What we are opposed to is commercial photography obtained without consent. [. . .] We respect other cultures and their way of life. As such, we expect the outside world to respect us in return. What might be accepted in your culture might not be accepted in our culture. Cultural boundaries must be obeyed. Our culture must be represented in a respectful manner.

2005, http://maasai-infoline.org/index.html

The international tour agency has access to local operators who, in turn, organize the "workers," the Maasai or whoever are the destination objects. As in globalized industries, the money is unevenly distributed: the agency and local operators take the lion's share. The Maasai – and their case is not unusual – get less than 10 percent of the tourists' dollars. They are in effect working in a sweatshop.

Visiting the "eternal past" is not just an overseas thing. The Rajasthanis seeking a replica of their own village are matched in the USA by a host of historical re-enactments, theme parks, and restored villages. "**Living museums**" such as Plimoth Plantation in Massachusetts and Colonial Williamsburg in Virginia pride themselves on the historical verisimilitude of their environments. Because no houses survive from the seventeenth-century pilgrim settlement, Plimoth is not a restoration but a "re-creation." And the location of the present-day plantation is about a mile from the original site. The "interpreters" – the word "actor" is shunned because of the association with theatrical inauthenticity – are dressed in period costumes and coached in the language and manners of the New England pilgrims or the Virginia planters. Interpreters not only improvise dialogue with tourists, but

Phineas Pratt
'FEHNYERZ PRUHT'

PERSONATION BIOGRAPH

Dialect Speciman:
'Right there, through those there trees, I seein' the red Devils'
'ROIT THUHR, DREW THUHZUHR DREEZ OI ZEEN THUR RID DUHFILZ'

Signature: Phinehas Pratt.

Wardrobe Design:

Dialect Region: Southern Code 6

Current Wealth:

Friends, Associates:
ms Jn. Winslow & bros.
Eliz & Jn. Howland
Eliz & Mary Warren
ms Jn. Alden
Capt. Myles Standish
Marriageable and manageable visiting lasses.

Syllabus: Smith: Sea Grammer P. Pratt: Narrative
Wood: N.E.'s Prospect
Manten: 'Free Trade' Paper
Morton: N.E. Canaan
Dobbs: The Great Fur Opera
Hobbs: Stage Fight
Travers: Happy Blunderbi
The Book of Rates, Debts hopeful etc.
Plentitudinous Howard, Leiber etc.

\- Notes -

plimoth plantation

P. Pratt is a man of Character;* he cannot Lie, nor bear nor suffer one heard — Quicker Master P. would unscabbard his Temper a'la Sword than tolerate a false-hood or an dissembilating Man. Nor ought he, by his own Code of Good Word & Valiant Deed. One doesn't find him continually Defending his or others verity, however, for the same disposition which causeth him to believe in his own Truth-telling, causeth him to trust the truth of Others — unless he find ample cause to Doubt. To some, therefore, for all his catholic interest in the Ways of men of all nations, Salvages & Beasts indiscriminant, he seemeth an over-Credulous man. He has lived as close to the red men — ffriends & ffoes — as anie English Man & accepted — nay, even adopted to his open ways, their customs & beliefs — but his animated telling of the Sagacities & civilities of The Beaver causes some of the more canny & doubtful of the community to wince at 'Finyuz's acceptance of what they deem heathen apocrypha.

Still, his wide portalled hearth of mind, has opened, (in its unprejudiced consideration), Phinheas's awareness of points of view & economical & cosmological standpoints that the most learned of N. Plimmoth's planters fail to cognize. This may be caused by his relative Lack of Religious instruction as opposed to Scientifick & mathmatical tutoring — or it may be, as wise Wm Brewster asserts, that Mr Pratt is a special Work of the Lord to Provender the Colonie with rarer Arts than purely homely Men oft devise.

R. M.

* Everything : ms Kempton pretended to be.

fig 8.13. A "personation biograph" of Phineas Pratt used by an "interpreter" at Plimoth Plantation in the 1980s. The actor is called an interpreter in order to distance his "historical reenactment" from theatre because theatre is tainted "untruth." Photo courtesy Plimoth Plantation.

enact specific persons and scenes. At Plimoth, interpreters study "personation biographs" written out in colonial English script describing the settler to be enacted along with a full body portrait (**see figure 8.13**). The interpreter is expected to develop an in-depth characterization and maintain it at all times while on site during the hours that the public is admitted. Needless to say, there are slips and even larger difficulties. Similar to living museums are many "historical re-enactments" researched, costumed, and staged by amateur adepts. For example, American Civil War buffs reenact with meticulous detail hundreds of different events from the bloody battle of Gettysburg in 1863 to the surrender of Confederate General Robert E. Lee at Appomattox Courthouse, Virginia, ending the war in 1865 (**see Wisconsin Historical Society box**). Re-enactments are simulations, reconstructions, popular entertainments, living histories, and commercial ventures all rolled up into one package. There are hundreds if not thousands of other kinds of re-enactments ranging from fanciful medieval fairs to famous courtroom trials.

living museums: also called "living history" museums, these are historical and/or tourist sites where a specific historical period is recreated in architectural, behavioral, and physical detail. Living museums are often constructed at or near the place where the events reenacted took place – as at Plimoth Plantation in Massachusetts or Colonial Williamsburg in Virginia.

Wisconsin Historical Society

Fifteenth Annual Civil War Weekend

In what has become the biggest and best Civil War reenactment in Wisconsin, Confederate and Union armies set up camp on the sprawling, wooded grounds of Wade House State Park. Visitors meet and mingle with the troops as well as civilian sutlers – civilian merchants who follow troop movements and sell Civil War-era merchandise. The event's emphasis for 2005 is civilians and medicine helping to save lives. Each afternoon at 2 o'clock the opposing armies clash in a full-scale historic battle reenactment featuring cavalry, infantry and artillery duels.

Ticket Info: Adults $10; children (5–12) $5; family (two adults and two or more dependent children 5–17) $27. Horse-drawn transportation on the site included in ticket cost.

2005, www.wisconsinhistory.org/wadehouse/events.asp?id=203

Plimoth Plantation had a "problem" with how to represent the Wampanoag Native Americans who in colonial times occupied the land near the Pilgrim settlement. Most tourists come for the pilgrims, and just as in the colonial past, the natives are pretty well pushed out of the picture. Their "summer settlement" consists of a few tepees. One peculiar detail. A brochure informs visitors that the Wampanoags are "staffed by Native Americans." Why tell us this? Those who interpret the pilgrims are not advertised as descendants of white Britishers (which most probably most of them aren't). There is both an intercultural apology and a bragging about authenticity encoded in detail about the "natives." The brochure goes on to invite tourists to "meet the Native American people who have lived for centuries along the New England coast." But are these interpreters from coastal tribes? And what difference would that make when there is no engagement with the circumstances of native "removal" – the wars, the European diseases, and the general decimation of both cultures and peoples that took place? Tourist pleasure trumps historical accuracy even in a museum site that exults in its accuracy. Something similar haunts Colonial Williamsburg.

When Colonial Williamsburg began in 1926, and for many years thereafter, it was a white-only living museum recreating the life of the eighteenth century. African-Americans were present, of course, but behind the scenes, mostly as menial laborers. No African-Americans were allowed onto the premises as visitors during the period of segregation. But from the 1960s onward, things changed. Yet it was one thing to admit African-Americans as tourists, another to integrate their history into a site that depended on slave labor for its very existence. African-American interpreters performed certain aspects of enslavement – working the fields, plantation servants (**see figure 8.14**). Then in the 1990s, it was decided to enact a slave auction. Some of the African-American actors, though recognizing the need for the depiction, felt demeaned and humiliated. But they persevered because they believed that only by performing the auction could people really understand the abomination of African slavery in America.

fig 8.14. The "Slave Quarters" at Colonial Williamsburg as depicted on its official site, http://history.org/ in 2005.

The Olympics: Globalism's signature performance

The modern Olympic Games are the most popular performance event in history, a truly global phenomenon. More than 4 billion people watched some portion of the 2004 summer Olympics at Athens. Several million attended the Games in person. The 2004 Games featured 11,099 athletes from 202 nations competing in 300 events of 28 sports. By comparison, the United Nations in 2005 had 191 member nations. In addition to athletes, many thousands are involved as press, dignitaries, officials, technicians, snack and souvenir sellers, janitors, housekeepers, performers and other artists, scientists, and commercial exhibitors. Building arenas for the competitions and for housing athletes involves reconstructing large sections of cities, laying down roads and infrastructure, and uprooting neighborhoods. The new construction has reinvigorated urban areas. But the displacements and profiteering have also evoked strong protests. It all adds up to billions in investments and, during the Games, the spending of even more money by the media, sponsors, and those attending the Games.

The first modern Olympics took place in 1896 in Athens. The brainchild of **Pierre de Coubertin**, those first modern Games featured 245 white male amateur athletes from 14 European nations, the USA, Canada, and Australia. They competed in 45 events of nine sports ranging from racing and weight-lifting to swimming, tennis, and fencing (where a professional was allowed to compete). In the present-day Olympics, about 40 percent of the athletes are women, people from all over the world compete, and the distinction between professional and amateur has all but vanished because every athlete is either paid or sponsored. When the Games are over, many can look forward to lucrative careers built on their Olympic triumphs. This "impurity" is nothing new. Whatever the rhetoric of the founders, from the start, the modern Olympics combined sport, spectacle, ritual, festivity, performing arts, economics, and politics.

Pierre de Coubertin (1863–1937): founder of the modern Olympics movement and president of the International Olympic Committee from 1896 to 1925.

And although the International Olympic Committee (IOC) says it wants to keep the Games "above" politics, rifts in the global political landscape are played out at the Olympics. The Games were cancelled three times because of war: in 1916, in 1940, and in 1944. Ironically, the 1916 Games were scheduled for Berlin, the 1940 for Tokyo, and the 1944 for London. At Munich in 1972, terrorists murdered eleven Israelis. At the 1976 Montreal Games, 20 teams from Africa (plus Iraq and Guyana) withdrew to protest the New Zealand rugby team's tour of South Africa during the height of apartheid. Taiwan withdrew because it was not allowed to play under the banner of the "Republic of China." The USA and four other nations boycotted the Moscow Games of 1980 to protest the Soviet invasion of Afghanistan. The USSR retaliated by leading 14 nations in a boycott of the 1984 Los Angeles Games.

Despite all this, the Games keep growing in general popularity and national participation. The opportunity to use the Olympics as a showcase is too much to resist. The media event is too popular to forego. Although the original idea was for individuals not nations to compete, the flying of flags, the playing of anthems, the jockeying over where the Games are held, and the keeping of records proclaiming which nation has won the most medals focus attention on national accomplishment.

The modern Olympics were meant to rekindle the spirit of the ancient Olympiads (776 BCE–369 CE), themselves a kind of recreation of the funeral games honoring the slain Patrocolus described by **Homer** in book 23 of the *Iliad*. A key goal of the Olympics, modern and ancient, is to transcend the local and emphasize the "global" (however that is conceived). In ancient times, warfare was suspended for the games, in modern times, the games were suspended for war. The underlying Olympic ideal is for nations to put aside their differences and sublimate their rivalries on the fields of play. But "the world" of 2004 and beyond is not the world of 1896 no less that of the ancient Greco-Roman civilizations. At the end of the nineteenth century, the world was controlled by Europe and the European diaspora. But over time, with the end of colonialism and the emergence of multiple players on the world stage, more and more nations joined the Olympic movement.

Homer (eighth or ninth century BCE): the legendary blind Greek poet, putative composer of the seminal epic poems, the *Odyssey* and the *Iliad*. Most scholars believe that Homeric tradition is oral. Only long after Homer's time were his poems set in writing.

fig 8.15. Crowds in Beijing celebrating the International Olympic Committee's selection of their city as the site of the 2008 Games.

In terms of the participating athletes and media spectators, the Olympics are a truly global event. However, at the organizational and structural levels the Eurocentricity of the Games remains intact. First, the IOC continues to be led by Europeans or North Americans. Second, although people everywhere run, jump, swim, play fight, and so on, the Olympic sports based on these activities are European. No effort is made to include non-European sports such as sumo wrestling, Trinidadian stick fighting, or the kind of mixed-terrain long-distance running enjoyed by the Tarahumaras of northwest Mexico. Third, venues remain overwhelmingly Western. Only Seoul in 1988 lay outside the West (if one considers Sydney culturally a Western city). Mexico City, host to the 1968 Games, is both Western and Third World; Moscow, site of the 1980 Games, is a European city even if, at that time, it was capital of the USSR. The 2004 Games returned to Athens and the 2008 Games will be in Beijing.

When in July 2001 the IOC selected Beijing, the decision was televised on large screens in China and more than 100,000 persons poured onto the streets of Beijing shouting, waving flags, and setting off fireworks (**see figure 8.15**). The joyous celebration was by far the largest free-flowing mass in the streets of the Chinese capital since the Pro-Democracy movement of May–June 1989. The Pro-Democracy demonstrators were shot, beaten, and crushed as the Chinese army used troops and tanks to clear Tiananmen Square. Clearly the crowds celebrating the Olympics had the blessing of the authorities. What were they and Chinese officials so happy about? As *The New York Times* put it: "Winning the Olympic bid is much more than a matter of civic or even national pride for people here. [. . .] As host to the Games, China believes it will stand as a respected member of the world community, a position it has long felt the West has denied it." Wanting to be a "respected member of the world community" is to enact a concept made real by globalization.

Aside from the sports competition, the Olympics have always featured sheer spectacle. The first modern Games commenced on Easter Sunday with Athens adorned in colorful bunting, streamers, and green wreaths inscribed with the letters "O.A." (the Greek initials for the games) and the dates "776 B.C." and "A.D. 1896" connecting the ancient to the modern. After the Greek **King George I** (1845–1913) opened the modern Olympic era, cannons were fired, pigeons released, and the Olympic hymn sung. The present era features the arrival of the Olympic torch, elaborate opening-day ceremonies, raising the national flags of winning athletes, playing national anthems, and the constant media drumbeat.

King George I of Greece (1845–1913): born William, Prince of Denmark, and proclaimed King of Greece in 1863. In 1896, George I inaugurated the first modern Olympics, hoping to restore some glory to Greece.

The Olympics are a lot more than a sports competition. Surrounding the Games are all kinds of celebrations, artistic events, and commercial operations. The 1984 Los Angeles Olympics spawned the "Cultural Olympics," which in turn morphed into the Los Angeles Festivals of 1987 and 1990. The vast conglomeration of performances and exhibitions in 1990 included 550 events in 70 venues with more than 1,400 artists from 21 Pacific Rim countries. Although the 1990 LA Festival may have been the biggest, there have been many similar festivals around the world modeled on the Olympics and on similar gatherings: world's fairs and expositions. All of these super-conglomerations import, package, and stage events performed by persons from a variety of nations and cultures; they also display the latest scientific achievements and commercial products. The goal – sometimes stated, sometimes implicit – is to assemble, own, and display the largest quantity and widest diversity of peoples performing either culture-specific (the expositions and fairs) or "universal" activities (the Olympics).

What kind of performance are the Olympics? The Games can't be subsumed under a single category. According to anthropologist **John J. MacAloon**, the Olympics are a complex interplay of spectacle, festival, ritual, and play (**see figure 8.16 and MacAloon box**). The largest, most inclusive category is spectacle (**see Debord box**). The global spectacle of the Olympics is crystallized in the opening-day show, which features thousands of performers, music, dance, and special effects. Spectacle both generates and is

John J. MacAloon (1947–): American anthropologist and foremost scholar of the Olympic Games. Author of *This Great Symbol* (1981) and *Brides of Victory: Nationalism and Gender in Olympic Ritual* (1997); editor of *Rite, Drama, Festival, Spectacle* (1984).

John MacAloon

Genres of performance in the Olympics

The genres [. . .] spectacle, festival, ritual, game by no means exhaust the roster of performance types found in the Olympic Games. But they are semantically and functionally the most significant. The order in which they are discussed reflects a passage from the most diffuse and ideologically centrifugal genres to the most concentrated and ideologically centripetal. Spectacle and game appeared earliest, festival and ritual consolidated later, in Olympic history. [. . .] These genres are distinctive forms of symbolic action, distinguished from one another by athletes, spectators, and officials alike. While certain features are shared between genres, others are in tension or in opposition, both categorically and in context. [. . .] At the same time, the Olympic Games form a single performance system. The genres are intimately and complexly interconnected on all levels: historically, ideologically, structurally, and performatively. Thus we are forced to recognize that the Olympic Games represent a special kind of cultural performance, a ramified performance type, and we are forced to seek for new models and methods of analysis that will allow us to understand the relationships between the various forms of symbolic action without losing sight of their distinctive properties. [. . .]

By the late 1920s and early 1930s, cultural history had, so to speak, caught up with the Olympic movement. Until that time, the semantic boundary "This is play" had remained more or less intact around the games of the Olympic Games. In turn, this protected the festival frame as well, and it afforded Olympic rituals a certain serenity within which to condense and elaborate. But largely due to the success of the Olympics themselves, a mass efflorescence of organized sport, first in Euro-American cultures, then worldwide, drew down upon the Games of the 20s and 30s ideological, political, and commercial interests of every sort. [. . .]

The professionalization of sports and the transformation of athletes into celebrities, the growing number-fetishism and specialization in athletics, the increased role of technology and hyperextended training periods [. . .], the growth of athletic bureaucracies, the recognition of sport's importance and the incorporation of sports success by the dominant world ideologies, the takeover of the selection, preparation, and financing of the teams by national governments and corporate interests, the counting of medals as propaganda and ersatz warfare, the attempts to co-opt the Games for chauvinistic purposes by host nations, and their use as a stage for "jock-strap diplomacy," saber rattling, regime building, and, finally, terrorism by insiders and outsiders alike: these developments represent in a general way the penetration of the "stuff of ordinary life" into the public liminality of the Games. And as ordinary life has changed, so have the Games been forced to change.

1984, "Olympic Games and the Theory of Spectacle in Modern Societies," 242, 258–59, 262–63

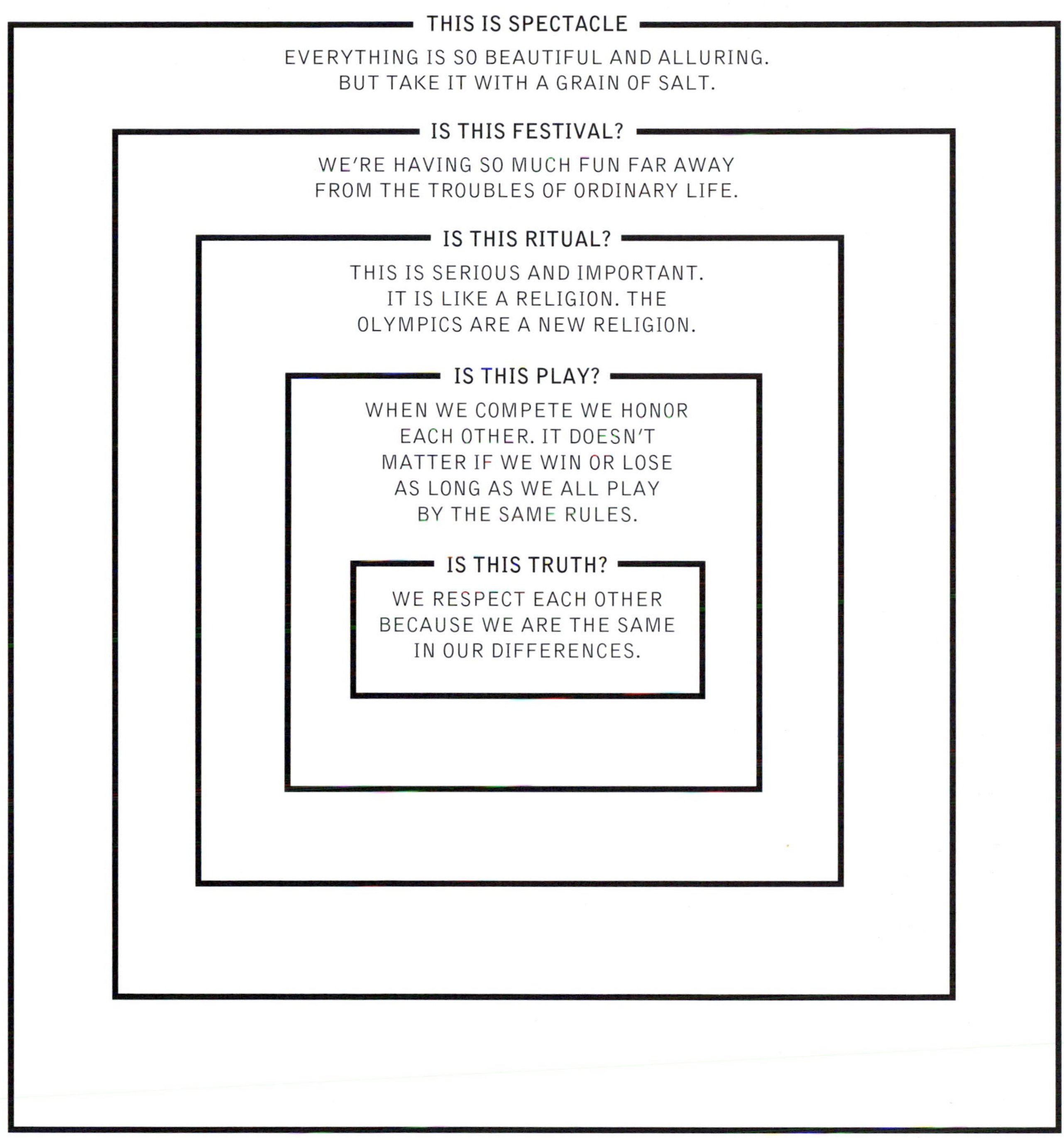

THIS IS SPECTACLE
EVERYTHING IS SO BEAUTIFUL AND ALLURING.
BUT TAKE IT WITH A GRAIN OF SALT.
IS THIS FESTIVAL?
WE'RE HAVING SO MUCH FUN FAR AWAY
FROM THE TROUBLES OF ORDINARY LIFE.
IS THIS RITUAL?
THIS IS SERIOUS AND IMPORTANT.
IT IS LIKE A RELIGION. THE
OLYMPICS ARE A NEW RELIGION.
IS THIS PLAY?
WHEN WE COMPETE WE HONOR
EACH OTHER. IT DOESN'T
MATTER IF WE WIN OR LOSE
AS LONG AS WE ALL PLAY
BY THE SAME RULES.
IS THIS TRUTH?
WE RESPECT EACH OTHER
BECAUSE WE ARE THE SAME
IN OUR DIFFERENCES.

fig 8.16. Each frame contains all the others within it. The entire Olympics are a spectacle inside which is a festival inside which are rituals inside which are the competitive sports inside which is a presumed "core truth." The frames signify mostly a conceptual arrangement, but also to some degree the actual uses of space. That is, the spectacle is everywhere, the festival moves in and out of the various venues and permeates the city beyond. Rituals are enacted side by side with spectacles and competitions. The sum total is supposed to be a liminal time of communitas where differences and sameness occupy the space simultaneously.

The question marks represent the change from the founders' desire to enact a truth by means of sports, ritual, and festivity. What has occurred is that only the spectacle – in Debord's sense – continues unquestioned. The other objectives of the Olympics system have been called into question. However, this interrogation has not undermined the Olympics as an event of global magnitude. On the contrary, the questions have only served to enhance the Games because they enact both what they claim they are and what their detractors say they have become.

Adapted from John MacAloon's "Olympic Games and the Theory of Spectacle," 1984: 258, 262.

Guy Debord

Spectacle, society's real unreality

The whole life of those societies in which modern conditions of production prevail presents itself as an immense accumulation of spectacles. All that was once directly lived has become mere representation. [. . .] The spectacle is not a collection of images; rather, it is a social relationship between people that is mediated by images. [. . .] Understood in its totality, the spectacle is both the outcome and the goal of the dominant mode of production. It is not something added to the real world – not a decorative element, so to speak. On the contrary, it is the very heart of society's real unreality. In all its specific manifestations – news or propaganda, advertising or the actual consumption of entertainment – the spectacle epitomizes the prevailing model of social life. [. . .]

The unreal unity the spectacle proclaims masks the class division on which the real unity of the capitalist mode of production is based. What obliges producers to participate in the construction of the world is also what separates them from it. What brings together men liberated from local and national limitations is also what keeps them apart. What pushes for greater rationality is also what nourishes the irrationality of hierarchical exploitation and repression. What creates society's abstract power also creates its concrete unfreedom.

1994 [1967], *The Society of the Spectacle*, 12–13, 46

part of the overall festivity permeating the Games. Although this festivity is centered in the Olympic city, it extends to many parts of the world, where groups assemble to root for their national heroes. Then come the many rituals of the Olympics. On opening day there are the declaration that the Games are open, the arrival of the Olympic torch from Greece, and the parade of athletes. After each event, the winners are displayed before the crowds as the flags of their nations are raised and their anthems played. The Games close with more rituals and the promise of another Olympiad four years hence. At the center of all this are the games themselves. In appearance these maintain a relative purity determined by the rules. However, because of the intensity of the competition and the huge rewards awaiting both individuals and nations, performance-enhancing drugs and other manipulations are rampant. The ideal of free competition has been corrupted by the demand for victory at any cost. Additionally, all else aside, athletes from poorer nations are at a disadvantage because they cannot afford the kind of training or facilities used by athletes from richer countries.

Vertical transculturalism

Nothing could be further from the global spectacle of the Olympics than the transcultural explorations of Jerzy Grotowski. Except for one period from the mid-1970s to the early 1980s, he never showed his work to large numbers. But despite this, Grotowski's work is influential globally with adherents in all continents. His methods of textual and scenic montage, actor training, staging, vocal work, and using materials from cultures both ancient and contemporary have influenced a great many in theatre, dance, and performance art – some directly and even more by means of diffusion.

From the very start of his career, Grotowski made connections across cultures and back in time seeking what he believed were deep universal human truths. In 1956, while still a student, Grotowski made his first trip to Asia. Upon his return to Poland, he lectured on yoga and Chinese philosophy. He broadened his interest to include the sacred knowledge of many cultures, ancient and contemporary. What he learned inflected his theatre work throughout his "poor theatre" phase, 1957–69. Then, at the end of the 1960s, he stopped directing plays. From 1969 to 1983 Grotowski devised paratheatrical experiments, face-to-face encounters between members of the Polish Laboratory Theatre and outsiders some of whom were well-known artists and others students and ordinary persons from many nations. Finally, these investigations ran out of energy.

At that point, Grotowski narrowed his focus. He concentrated his work on a few traditional ritual performance specialists from Asia and the Caribbean. This work culminated in Grotowski's 1983–86 "Objective Drama" project housed at the University of California-Irvine. Grotowski wanted to find specific elements of performance that transcended the particular cultures in which they were embedded. In order to do this, he brought traditional performance specialists from Colombia, Korea, Bali, Taiwan, Haiti, and India to work with students. One of these students was Thomas Richards, the young American to whom Grotowski entrusted his most precious performance secrets. Richards heads up the Workcenter of Jerzy Grotowski and Thomas Richards with its headquarters in Pontedera, Italy – where Grotowski spent his last years.

The underlying assumption of Objective Drama and Grotowski's final phase, "Art as Vehicle" (1986–99) is that there is an intersection where the most intimate-personal meets the most objective-archetypal. Locating that intersection demanded what Grotowski called "rendering," used both in its sense of an artist's prepatory sketch (also the Zen "art of the beginner") and in the sense of the distillation of substances into their essences. The substances to be rendered were traditional performances yielding "vibratory songs" and movements and performers yielding their innermost associations. The result was the formation of the Performer performing the *Action* – an attempt to recreate the "origin" of performance (**see Grotowski box**).

One can readily see how Grotowski's ideas are related to globalization. Both are universalistic; both are utopian; both depend on the acceptance of certain **transcultural** assumptions and methods. Neither could occur except in a period of advanced communications and travel. Globalization at the popular-culture level imposes (or seduces people into) a similarity in styles and tastes; at the technical level, requires the use of standardized hardware and software; at the business level, demands adherence to the rules of various world-trade protocols. Grotowski's project also leads to standardization embodied by the adherence to a specific kind of training and the nearly absolute dedication to the work. The result is *Action*, an archetypal, ahistorical, finely executed performance.

transculturalism: working or theorizing across cultures with the assumption that there are cultural "universals" – behaviors, concepts, or beliefs that are true of everyone, everywhere, at all times.

But there is a big distance separating Grotowski's from other kinds of globalization. Grotowski's reach is vertical, fetching back in time rather than stretching horizontally across cultures. Grotowski assumes a coincidence of origin and finality. This lack of historicity is the Achilles' heel of Grotowski's work, especially his final phases. Nevertheless, Art as Vehicle is proving influential. Even though *Action* and

Jerzy Grotowski

Discovering the beginning

Performer, with a capital letter, is a man of action. He is not somebody who plays another. He is a doer, a priest, a warrior: he is outside aesthetic genres. Ritual is performance, an accomplished action, an act. Degenerated ritual is a show. I don't want to discover something new but something forgotten. Something so old that all distinctions between aesthetic genres are no longer of use. [. . .]. Essence interests me because nothing in it is sociological. It is what you did not receive from others, what did not come from outside, what is not learned. [. . .]

One access to the creative way consists of discovering in yourself an ancient corporality to which you are bound by a strong ancestral relation. [. . .] Starting from details, you can discover in you somebody other – your grandfather, your mother. A photo, a memory of wrinkles, the distant echo of the color of the voice enable you to reconstruct a corporality. First, the corporality of somebody known, and then more and more distant, the corporality of the unknown one, the ancestor. Is it literally the same? Maybe not literally – but yet as it might have been. You can arrive very far back, as if your memory awakes [. . .] as if you recall Performer of the primal ritual. [. . .] With the breakthrough – as in the return of an exile – can one touch something which is no longer linked to beginnings but – if I dare say – to the beginning? I believe so.

1997 [1988], "Performer," 374–77

the performances that arose out of it are played for only a handful of people at a time, over the long haul many hundreds have experienced *Action* – especially younger persons not only from theatre but from a diversity of fields. The most recent activity of the Grotowski Workcenter is *Tracing Roads Across* (2003–06) (**see Workcenter of Jerzy Grotowski and Thomas Richards box**).

Workcenter of Jerzy Grotowski and Thomas Richards

Tracing Roads Across

Performance craft, artistic know-how and creative witnessing, traveling across the European cradle. [. . .] In *Tracing Roads Across* we have articulated all elements of our present research at the Workcenter of Jerzy Grotowski and Thomas Richards, from the practical to the theoretical. Herein we trace links with those outside the work through open events, exchanges of work, meetings, etc.; and also trace links inside the group – there where the content of the work goes toward what is more essential in us and between us; and address a question for the individual: the development of the craft for the human being and the human being in the craft. There is an inner-place, yes, a kind of inside place, that, when unearthed, is longing to be filled, and in a subtle way, completed. Over and between us, there is a source that is looking to flow in, and into life, to nourish and be nourished. Through doing and through craft, we are looking to remember, and to trace roads across.

2003, www.tracingroadsacross.net

Those who are attracted to Richards' work are impressed by the dedication, the precision of the performances, and the felt presence of the performers, especially Richards and his long-time partner at the Grotowski Workcenter, Mario Biagini. People are also excited by the Workcenter's utopian spirit. In this regard, Grotowski's late work is analogous to the utopian speculations of Victor Turner at the end of his life. Like Grotowski, Turner sought an "objective" basis for ritual – not in survivals of ancient performances but in brain structure and function. Turner dreamed of a "global population of brains," an organic network that included not only human beings but the whole planet (**see Turner box**). Both Turner and Grotowski saw the best human endeavors as Janus-like, the Roman god who looks back to the "most ancient" and forward to "the newest" at the same time.

Victor Turner

A global population of brains

I am really speaking of a global population of brains inhabiting an entire world of inanimate and animate entities, a population whose members are incessantly communicating with one another through every physical and mental instrumentality. But if one considers the geology, so to speak, of the human brain and nervous system, we see represented in its strata – each layer still vitally alive – not dead like stone, the numerous pasts and presents of our planet. Like Walt Whitman, we "embrace multitudes." [. . .] Each of us is a microcosm, related in the deepest ways to the whole life-history of that lovely deep blue globe swirled over with the white whorls first photographed by Edwin Aldrin and Neil Armstrong from their primitive space chariot, the work nevertheless of many collaborating human brains.

1983, "Body, Brain, and Culture," 243

Horizontal interculturalism

Grotowski's project essentializes. *Action* simultaneously enacts the intimate and the "origin" – what in Indian philosophy (certainly an influence on Grotowski's thought) is the union of atman (the kernel of absolute in each person) and brahman (the universal absolute). Eugenio Barba – who in the 1960s assisted Grotowski and kept in close contact with him since – has from at least 1980 onward developed a particular aspect of the Grotowski work, answering the question: Where does a performer's "energy" and/or "presence" come from? Barba investigates this not only with his own group, Odin Teatret, but also in the sessions of the International School of Theatre Anthropology (ISTA). ISTA is not a usual school, nor is Barba's "anthropology" the conventional brand.

At ISTA sessions, which last from a few days to a month, Barba brings together a team of performers and performance theorists to advance and demonstrate to a wider public his basic thesis: that there are movements, stances, and rhythms employed by the most accomplished performers in all cultures (**see Barba and Savarese box**). These constitute the "pre-expressive" patterns of "extra-daily" behavior that spectators respond to as the performer's "presence" or "energy."

What are these pre-expressive behaviors? Barba seeks the answer by investigating mostly Asian classical performances. He concentrates not on finished products but on how accomplished performers train and display their bodies. Although he refers to non-Asian genres and performers – ballet, Meyerhold, Stanislavsky, the mime of **Etienne Decroux**, the energetic style of **Dario Fo** – these serve mostly as confirmation of principles Barba derived from working very closely with Asian collaborators such as odissi dancer Sanjukta Panigrahi and buyo dancer Azuma Katsuko (both of whom died relatively young). For example, Barba claims that the pre-expressive principle of "opposition" is embodied in Indian dance's *tribhangi* ("three arches") position, where the body is bent at three places (neck, torso, hips) to form a figure "S." Barba then illustrates the wide distribution of tribhangi-like poses with photographs of ancient Greek and Renaissance statues, the Aztec goddess Macuilxochitl, ballet dancer **Natalia Makarova**, actor **Igor**

Eugenio Barba and Nicola Savarese

Theatre anthropology

Theatre anthropology is the study of the behavior of the human being when it uses its physical and mental presence in an organized performance situation and according to principles which are different from those used in daily life. This extra-daily use of the body is what is called technique.

A transcultural analysis of performance reveals that the performer's work is the result of the fusion of three aspects which reflect three different levels of organization: (1) The performers' personalities, their sensibilities, their artistic intelligence, their social personae: those characteristics which make them unique and once-only. (2) The particularities of the traditions and socio-historical contexts through which the once-only personality of a performer is manifest. (3) The use of physiology according to extra-daily body techniques. The recurrent and transcultural principles on which these techniques are based are defined by Theatre Anthropology at the field of pre-expressivity.

The first aspect is individual. The second is common to all those who belong to the same performance genre. Only the third concerns all performers from every era and every culture: it can be called the performance's "biological" level. The first two aspects determine the transition from pre-expressivity to expression. The third [. . .] does not vary; it underlies the various individual, artistic, and cultural variants. [. . .]

Applied to certain physiological factors (weight, balance, the position of the spinal column, the direction of the eyes in space), these principles produce pre-expressive organic tensions. These new tensions generate a different energy quality, render the body theatrically "decided," "alive," and manifest the performers "presence," or scenic bios, attracting the spectator's attention before any form of personal expression takes place. [. . .] ISTA's field of work is the study of the principles of this extra-daily use of the body and their application to the actor's and dancer's creative work. [. . .]

Theatre anthropology postulates that there exists a basic level of organization common to all performers and defines this level as pre-expressive. [. . .] Theatre anthropology postulates that the pre-expressive level is at the root of the various performing techniques and that there exists, independently of traditional culture, a transcultural "physiology." In fact, pre-expressivity utilizes principles for the acquisition of presence and the performer's life. The results of these principles appear more evident in codified genres where the technique which puts the body in form is codified independently of the result/meaning.

Thus theatre anthropology confronts and compares the techniques of actors and dancers at the transcultural level, and, by means of the study of scenic behaviour, reveals that certain principles governing pre-expressivity are more common and universal than would first have been imagined.

1991, *A Dictionary of Theatre Anthropology*, 7, 187–88

fig 8.17. The *tribhangi* position as exemplified in both Asian and Western, high art and popular culture contexts. Shown here are Indian odissi dancer Sanjukta Panigrahi and ballet dancer Natalia Makarova, top row, and Russian actor Igor Ilinsky and an unnamed fashion model, bottom row. Photos courtesy of Eugenio Barba.

Ilinsky, and a 1960s fashion model (**see figure 8.17**). But most of these similarities can be explained by cultural diffusion. There is no need to assert the existence of a universal.

Etienne Decroux (1898–1991): French performer considered "the father of modern mime." Decroux's techniques have been very influential in both dance and theatre.

Dario Fo (1926–): Italian satirical communist playwright, actor, and director, winner of the 1997 Nobel Prize in Literature. His plays include, in English translation, *The Accidental Death of an Anarchist* (1970), *We Won't Pay, We Won't Pay* (1974), *The Pope and the Witch* (1989), and *The Devil With Boobs* (1997). Actress and author Franca Rame (1929–) joined Fo's theatre in 1951 and they married in 1954. Rame has contributed greatly to Fo's achievements.

Natalia Makarova (1940–): Russian-born dancer who performed with Russia's Kirov Ballet and later with the American Ballet Theatre.

Igor Ilinsky (1901–87): Russian actor and comedian who worked closely with Meyerhold in developing biomechanics. Ilinsky played Bruno in Meyerhold's production of Fernand Crommelynck's *The Magnanimous Cuckold* (1922).

More importantly, the dialogue concerning universals would be radically different if Barba paid as much attention to African and African-diaspora performers as he does to Asians. Are the principles of pre-expressivity embodied by Gelede dancers of Nigeria, sambaistas of Brazil, or Trinidad carnival dancers the same as those of odissi and bharatanatyam in India or buyo in Japan? If so, in what particular way? Is the tribhangi employed? And why stop there? If one wants universals, then examples must be drawn from the widest possible range of cultures. It is not possible to universalize on the basis of a relatively small sampling of examples hand-picked to make a point. This is not to deny that Barba's work is extremely stimulating – and has already proven of great value to theatre artists in various parts of the world. At the same time, the ISTA work is culturally specific. At heart, it exemplifies the Western and now global project of taking from, adapting, generalizing, and exporting the "results" of an analytic process.

Finally, at a theoretical level, the search for universals of performance ancient or contemporary, finished or in formation, transcultural or intercultural, is dubious. Neither Grotowski's performance archaeology in search of practices older and "deeper" (in both senses of that word) than today's practices nor Barba's comparative analysis of Asian and Western genres is likely to come up with anything other than preferences for, and techniques to acquire, specific styles of performing. These may be of artistic merit, but they are not universal in themselves or founded on universal aesthetic principles. Aesthetics, like other aspects of human life, is culture-specific. That having been said, Barba is hardly unique. He is part of a long tradition reaching back more than a century. Many visionary Western theatre artists have, and continue to, look East: Antonin Artaud, Vsevelod Meyerhold, Bertolt Brecht, **Paul Claudel**, Peter Brook, **Lee Breuer**, Ariane Mnouchkine, and **Julie Taymor** to name just a few from a long list.

Sometimes the encounter with another culture, though brief and partial, is decisive, as was Artaud's experience of Balinese dance-theatre in Paris in 1931. Or it snaps into focus a theory already in formation as it did for Brecht who in Moscow in 1935 watched Mei Lanfang demonstrate, without costume, lighting, or makeup, a *dan* (female) role

Fernand Crommelynck (1886–1970): Belgian playwright who specialized in farces where ordinary failings become irrepressible obsessions. Among his best known works are *The Magnificent* [or *Magmanimous*] *Cuckold* (1920) and *A Woman Whose Heart is Too Small* (1934).

Paul Claudel (1868–1955): French playwright, poet, essayist, and diplomat who spent many years in China and Japan. Claudel not only had a deep interest in Japanese noh theatre but wrote noh plays himself. Among his better known works: *Tidings Brought to Mary* (1912) and *The Satin Slipper* (1924).

Lee Breuer (1937–): American director and writer and a co-founder in 1970 of the experimental theatre company, Mabou Mines. Breuer's many productions include the *Animations* series (1970–78), *Gospel at Colonus* (1983), *Epidog* (1996), *Peter and Wendy* (1996), *Ecco Porco* (2000), and *Red Beads* (2005).

Julie Taymor (1952–): American theatre and film director, designer, and puppeteer. Taymor studied mime in Paris and puppetry in Indonesia, where in the 1970s she started her own group, Teatr Loh. Her work integrates live actors, puppets, and performing objects. For the stage Taymor's work includes *Juan Darien* (1988), Stravinsky's *Oedipus Rex* (1992), *The Green Bird* (1996), and *The Lion King* (1997). Her films include Shakespeare's *Titus Andronicus* (1999), a life of artist Frida Kahlo, *Frida* (2002), and *Across the Universe* (2006).

from the Chinese theatre, embodying in a definitive way what Brecht called *Verfremdungseffekt* ("alienation effect"). Some artists thoroughly metabolize what they learned in and from Asia, as in the grand spectacles of Mnouchkine's Théâtre du Soleil or the puppet work and visual imagination of Taymor (**see figure 8.18**). Are these activities "Orientalist"? Certainly most of them would not have occurred except under the aegis of colonialism or its aftermath (even when the artist was actively anti-colonialist). Brook's *The Mahabharata* (1985), an attempt to stage the vast Sanskrit epic, and Mnouchkine's *l'Indiade* (1987), a panoptic performance of a culture and subcontinent, bespeak both the artistic-cultural ambition of these individuals and a more general tendency to control or own the Other that is specific to Orientalism (**see figure 8.19, Carlson box, and Mnouchkine box**). But the process is far from a one-way street (**see Latrell box**). I will discuss these questions further shortly.

fig 8.18. Rafiki watches a herd of gazelles stampede across the African savannah in Julie Taymor's *The Lion King* (1997). Photo by Joan Marcus and Marc Bryan-Brown, courtesy of Julie Taymor.

fig 8.19. Le Théâtre du Soleil's *L'Indiade* (1987) with Andrés Perez-Arya as Mahatma Gandhi. Photo by Michèle Laurent.

Marvin Carlson

Brook's transnational theatre

In fact, Brook's *The Mahabharata* is absolutely faithful to his entire experimental enterprise, which has been much more directly involved with cultural questions than Mnouchkine's more directly political theatre, but which has from the beginning sought expression which could most properly be characterized not as intercultural but as transcultural. Brook has often spoken of his "international theatre," whose goal is "to articulate a universal art, that transcends narrow nationalism in its attempt to achieve human essence." The fact that nineteen nations are represented by the actors of *The Mahabharata,* Brook sees as both a metaphorical and physical indication of the international voice of his theatre. "The truth is global," Brook has observed, "and the stage is the place where the jigsaw should be played." The intention and the strategy are clear, even if the result may be a layering on of cultures rather than a transcendence of them. One Sanskrit scholar, a warm supporter of Brook on the whole, called the idea of an international cast charming, but noted that when one hears a Japanese with a French accent pronouncing an English transliteration of a Sanskrit name, it is hardly surprising that the effect is rather that of a one-man Tower of Babel. [. . .]

The search for the transcultural theatrical experience has occupied Brook's Centre International de Création Théâtrale since its inception [1970]. Indeed it may be said to have been the basic concern of Brook himself for almost two decades, inspiring the research into universal language reflected in *Orghast* and the innumerable performances in remote villages with different cultural backgrounds in many parts of the world. [. . .]

In sum, both *The Mahabharata* and [Mnouchkine's] *L'Indiade* may be seen less as attempts to deal specifically with India or even what the concept of India means to us in terms of difference or otherness than as attempts to utilize images drawn from the Indian experience to construct a theatrical celebration of human brotherhood, either metaphysical or political. Both are appeals to what is imagined to unite all cultures, and this common vision is presented as necessarily positive and grounded on the same bases which ground traditional Western liberal humanism. A potential Otherness of the Indian cultural is absorbed in the universal. For this purpose, the specificity of India itself is not important – China, Southeast Asia, Nigeria, or American Indian myth and history could have served a similar purpose, since the ultimate goal is not to confront the alien element in these cultures but to utilize them as external markers to our own culture upon which to ground a final synthesis. To criticize such productions for failing to speak with the authentic voice of India, as a number of critics have done, is thus to place upon them an expectation quite incompatible with their goals, which are clearly seen by their creators as transcultural rather than intercultural in aim.

1996, "Brook and Mnouchkine," 88–90

Ariane Mnouchkine

My source is Asia

Everyone has their sources, that is to say something that sets their imagination to work. In the West we have classical tragedy and the commedia dell'arte, which in any case comes from Asia. As far as I am concerned, the origin of theatre and my source is Asia. The West has led us towards realism, and Shakespeare is not realist. For actors who want to be explorers, the Asian tradition can be a base to work from. [. . .]

I do not believe in starting with a clean slate. I don't deny my influences: but you have to know how to choose them if you can.

1996, "The Theatre is Oriental," 96

Craig Latrell

Interculturalism is not a multi-way street

We tend to think of "intercultural transfer" or "artistic borrowing" primarily as a one-way phenomenon, something done "by" the West "to" other cultures. Much of the critical rhetoric surrounding this phenomenon has [. . .] an accusatory tone, with Western popular culture pictured as a sort of juggernaut, rolling over helpless local cultures, taking what it wants and in the process ruining fragile indigenous art forms and homogenizing all culture, turning the world into a lowbrow combination of Baywatch and Disney. [. . .]

Interculturalism is portrayed as something that can only be "explained" by inequities of power between East and West [. . .]. The idea that artists in other societies might be using elements of Western culture for their own reasons is rarely entertained. But why should we deny to other cultures the same sophistication and multiplicity of responses to "foreign" influences that we grant to ourselves in viewing non-Western works? Why should we assume that intercultural transfer is primarily a politically based, one-way phenomenon? [. . .] Why not start with the assumption that other cultures are not just passive receivers of Western ideas and images, but active manipulators of such influences, and that intercultural borrowing is not simply a one-way process, but something far more interestingly dialogic? [. . .]

The Minangkabau traditional music ensemble at the tourist center in Bukittinggi, West Sumatra, casually includes in its program a version of a British disco hit (the ever popular *River of Babylon* by Boney M) played on the gongs, considerably altering the disco beat to fit conventional Minangkabau rhythms. In doing so, the musicians are in effect changing the borrowed Western form of disco music as much as they are being changed by it; the resulting hybrid contains elements of both Western disco and Minangkabau traditional music [. . .]. Far from abandoning or tainting formerly pure local forms, the Sumatran musicians are assimilating new influences, and in the process interpreting what they borrow. Such complicated interactions between borrower and borrowed are the rule rather than the exceptions, and narratives of passivity and neocolonialism have little place in this kind of creative activity.

2000, "After Appropriation," 44–47

Integrative interculturalism

Grotowski's and Barba's work are but two examples of the rich variety of intercultural performances (**see Pavis box**). Intercultural performances come in at least two varieties: integrative and disruptive. The integrative is based on the assumption that people from different cultures can not only work together successfully but can also harmonize different aesthetic, social, and belief systems, creating fusions or hybrids that are whole and unified. This is not a question of one culture or performance genre absorbing or overwhelming others (as in the "cultural bomb" Ngũgĩ deplores), but of evolving something new from a basis of mutual respect and reciprocity. What Barba attempts at the level of the pre-expressive, the integrators work with at the level of public performance. With regard to rituals and the performances of everyday life, integrative **hybrid performances** spread on the wings of colonialism, commerce, religion, and the migration of populations.

Integrative ritual hybrids are so common that they are the dominant mode of actual worship. Even the relatively conservative Roman Catholic Church welcomes elements absorbed over time from a variety of cultural sources. Contemporary Catholic worship in many parts of the world actively includes and integrates local rituals and deities (often transmuted into saints). The Yaqui Waehma is a syncretic ritual drama integrating Native American and Roman Catholic practices. Another example would be the Carnivals of Trinidad or Rio de Janeiro. These integrate African, New World, and European masking, music, dance, and beliefs. Trinidad Carnival also has strong South Asian qualities expressed in music, masking, and dancing. Hinduism has long been receptive to integrating gods and ritual practices ranging from local spirits and holy places to giving a place to Christian and Old Testament figures. Gandhi was fond of making room for Allah. What is going on in this kind of intercultural performance is a negotiation whereby ideas and practices from both "inside" and "outside" a culture are sorted through, evaluated, interpreted, and reconfigured to suit complex, dynamic situations. The resulting hybrids embody new meanings even as they create new ways of worship and new aesthetics. The process is open-ended; change is always occurring.

hybrid performances: performances which incorporate elements from two or more different cultures or cultural sources.

A clear example is the Mami Wata (mother water) worship widespread in sub-Saharan Africa (**see Henry John Drewal box**). This practice mediates between the African and what came to Africa from overseas, transforming aspects of colonial imposition and foreign trade into something positive. When European colonists and Indian merchants moved into Africa, they brought with them new technologies, materials, gods, ritual practices, and beliefs. These fused with indigenous African water spirits. The resulting Mami Wata is a deity who is simultaneously foreign and African, quite literally free-floating, like many of the foreigners in Africa. Mami Wata has no family or social bonds. She rules the waters which surround Africa and articulate the land as rivers and lakes. Mami Wata demands much from her adepts but promises wealth in return. Her worship incorporates African, Indian, and European images and activities – from mermaids to trance possession to Hindu deities, especially Lakshmi, goddess of wealth. Mami Wata manifests herself in dancing,

Patrice Pavis

What is intercultural theatre?

From our Western perspective, Peter Brook's dramatized adaptation of the epic *Mahabharata* which primarily employed Western performance techniques might be called "intercultural." So might the dramatic and scenic writing of [Hélène] Cixous and [Ariane] Mnouchkine in their staging of Indian history (*L'Indiade*), in which simulated corporeal and vocal techniques were supposed to represent diverse ethnic groups in the Indian subcontinent. Or Barba's rereading of *Faust* for Japanese or Indian dancers. From the perspective of the non-Western other, on the contrary, one might examine the ways in which a Japanese director like Suzuki stages Shakespeare or Greek tragedy, using gestural and vocal techniques borrowed from traditional Japanese forms. Or **butoh**, with its debt to German expressionist dance. Although such relationships seem inextricably entangled, there can be no sense in which Asian perspectives are always reversible and symmetrical with those of the West – as a purely functionalist use of the hourglass, turned over and over ad infinitum, might lead us naively to believe. Indeed it is perhaps Eurocentrist to imagine that a Japanese perspective, whether that of shingeki ["new" or modern theatre] at the beginning of the [twentieth] century, or that of Suzuki or [butoh pioneer] **Hijikata Tatsumi [see figure 8.20]** more recent times, also implies the imitation and borrowing of elements from outside its own culture in order to further affirm and stabilize it. [. . .]

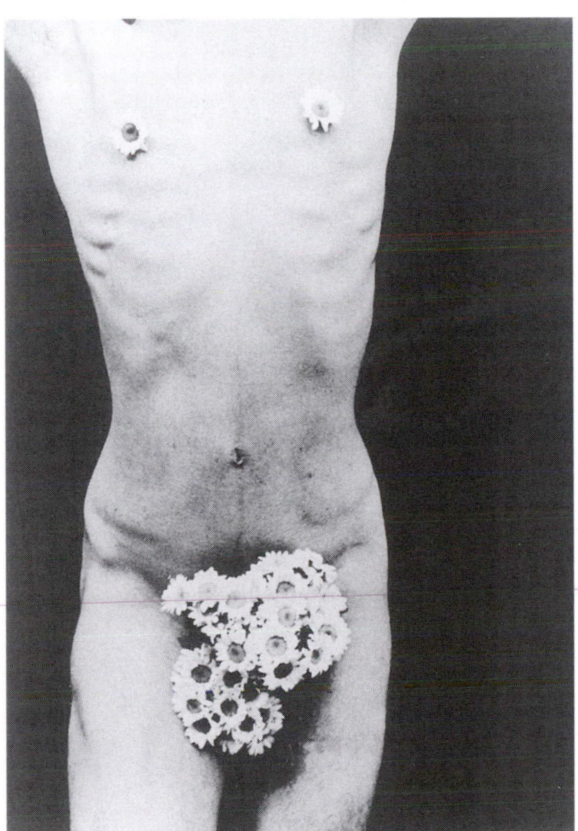

fig 8.20. Photo staged by Eikoh Hosoe, in his studio, of the principle expressed by Butoh pioneer Tatsumi Hijikata [Hijikata Tatsumi] in *Dance Experience*, a pamphlet (1960). Hijikata wrote: "You have to pull your stomach up high in order to turn your solar plexus into a terrorist." Photo by Eikoh Hosoe, 1960.

"Intercultural" does not mean simply the gathering of artists of different nationalities or national practices in a festival. In this banal sense of international (or cosmopolitan), one might say that contemporary theatrical choreographic production has become international, often for simple economic reasons. [. . .]

It is necessary [. . .] to envisage every sort of configuration [. . .] of theatrical interculturalism. Six varieties may be distinguished.

Intercultural theatre. In the strictest sense, this creates hybrid forms drawing upon a more or less conscious and voluntary mixing of performance traditions traceable to distinct cultural areas. The hybridization is very often such that the original forms can no longer be distinguished. [. . .]

Multicultural theatre. The cross-influences between various ethnic or linguistic groups in multicultural societies (e.g. Australia, Canada) have been the source of performances utilizing several languages and performing for a bi- or multicultural public. This sort of exchange is only possible when the political system in place recognizes, if only on paper, the existence of cultural or national communities and encourages their cooperation, without hiding behind the shibboleth of national identity.

Cultural collage. If the intercultural theatre claims to be concerned with the cultural identities of the forms it utilizes [. . .] certain artists, like Robert Wilson [. . .], cite, adapt, reduce, enlarge, combine, and mix various elements without concern for a scale of importance or value. The intercultural becomes the unexpected and quasi-surrealist encounter of cultural debris or – more positively – of cultural material that has been repressed or discredited. [. . .]

Syncretic theatre. [. . .] The creative reinterpretation of heterogeneous cultural material, resulting in the formation of new configurations (for example, the theatre of **Derek Walcott** or Wole Soyinka).

Postcolonial theatre. This takes up elements of the home culture (that of ex- or neo-colonization) and employs them from its indigenous perspective, thereby giving rise to a mixture of languages, dramaturgies, and performance processes.

Theatre of the Fourth World. Created by authors or directors belonging to pre-colonization cultures, which have often become minority cultures in relation to that of the colonizers (e.g. the Maoris in New Zealand, Aborigines in Australia, or Indians in Canada and America).

1996, "Introduction: Towards a Theory of Interculturalism in Theatre?" 1–2, 8–10

trance, ventriloquism, and snake charming. Some of her followers dress in combinations of Western, African, and Indian garments, while others present themselves in the lotus position sitting on Muslim prayer rugs signing *mudras* (**see figure 8.21**).

butoh: literally, "stamping dance." The first butoh performance was *Kinjiki* (1959) choreographed by Hijikata Tatsumi who, along with **Ohno Kazuo** founded butoh. Hijikata called his dancing *ankoku butoh* or "dark dance." The dark side of butoh is based on a nonrational collision of images and sounds. After Hijikata and Ohno, many individuals and groups, both Japanese and non-Japanese, have performed butoh. Butoh's intense performance style and underlying philosophy draw on Japanese martial arts and classical dance, German expressionist dance, Shinto, shamanism, and Zen. At present, butoh is both very Japanese and part of the global culture of experimental performance.

Hijikata Tatsumi (1928–1986): the dancer-choreographer who, along with Ohno Kazuo, invented butoh. Hijikata's dances were extremely intimate and violent, shocking many who saw them. Over time, his work was accepted. Hijikata's works include *Kinjiki* (*Forbidden Colors*, 1959), *Gibasan* (1972), *Hosotan* (*A Story of Small Pox*, 1972), *Hitogata* (*Human Mold*, 1976), *Taka Zashiki* (*Hawk Parlor*, 1984), *Tohoku Kabuki Kekaku 1* through *4* (*Tohoku Kabuki Project*, 1985).

Ohno Kazuo (1906–): a founder, performer, and theorist of butoh. Ohno's work is known for its intensity and delicacy. His written work in English includes: "Selections from the Prose of Kazuo Ohno" (1986), "Performance Text *The Dead Sea*" (1986), and *Kazuo Ohno's World* (with Yoshito Ohno, 2004).

Derek Walcott (1930–): West Indian playwright and poet, 1992 winner of the Nobel Prize for Literature. Author of *Dream on Monkey Mountain* (1970), *The Odyssey: A Stage Version* (1993), *The Prodigal* (2004), and *Another Life Fully Annotated* (2004).

Such a large number of dance, music, and theatre artists make integrative intercultural performances that it would be impossible to list them all. Three of the better known are Suzuki Tadashi from Japan, **Chandralekha** from India, and Philip Glass from the USA. African-American choreographer **Ralph Lemon** went on an actual and spiritual journey to Africa and then Asia seeking points of contact out of which to make his *Geography* trilogy (1997–2004). In a scene from *Tree*, Part 2 of the trilogy, a Japanese dancer, not young by any means, sits listening to a tape of American

Chandralekha (1929–): Indian dancer-choreographer widely known for her experimental and intercultural reinterpretations of traditional forms. Her works include *Angika* (1985), *Bhinna Pravaha* (1993), and *Sharira* (1997).

fig 8.21.

Syncretizing images from a variety of sources, a devotee creates the appearance of Mami Wata by using a black wig, a Western-style dress of imported fabric with a sari-like sash over her left shoulder, an Indian bindu on her forehead and feet, a brace snake in her right hand and holding a trident in her left. The jewelry symbolizes Dan, the celestial serpent. She is seated on a traditional African sacred stool placed on a Muslim prayer rug. Togo, 1975. Photograph by Henry John Drewal.

A formal portrait of a Mami Wata devotee signing an Indian mudra as he sits in a lotus position on a Muslim prayer rug. Togo, 1975. Photo courtesy of Henry John Drewal.

Henry John Drewal

Dynamic hybridity in Africa

In their religious practices involving the water spirit Mami Wata, African peoples from Senegal to Tanzania take exotic images and ideas, interpret them according to indigenous precepts, invest them with new meanings, and then re-create and re-present them in new and dynamic ways to serve their own aesthetic, devotional, and social needs. In so doing, they evaluate and transform external forces, using them to shape their own lives. [. . .] Mami Wata, Pidgin English for "Mother of Water," refers to an African water spirit whom Africans regard as foreign in origin. Africans use the pidgin term to acknowledge the spirit's otherness as well as to indicate its incorporation into the African world. [. . .]

A Yoruba print seller in Togo dramatically illustrates how meanings are constructed and how Mami Wata ritual practices evolve and spread. He uses books on Buddhism, Hinduism, and Occultism as references for his synthesis of foreign and indigenous divinities and the paraphernalia necessary for their worship. [. . .] Since about the First World War, when Indian merchants established firms along the west coast, Africans have been observing their ways, especially Hindu devotions. Many of these rituals are based on the practice of Gujaratis, who predominated among Indian merchants in Africa and were devotees of Lakshmi, the Hindu goddess of wealth [. . .]. Like Mami Wata devotees, Gujaratis place their account books or ledgers on their shrines as objects of veneration. [. . .] These observations and others have resulted in specific ritual practices among Mami Wata worshippers. In Nigeria and Togo, devotees light candles and burn incense during consultation with the spirit called "meditations." One Mina Mami Wata priest displays a photograph of himself taken during his initiation in which he is seated on a Muslim prayer mat in lotus position wearing a turban and signing a *mudra*.

1988, "Performing the Other," 160, 174–76

blues and ballad singer **Leadbelly**. Immersed in Leadbelly's deep baritone, the Japanese man begins to tap his hand on his thigh, then move his feet. Over the next five minutes, he improvises a dance that is both/neither Japanese nor African-American, yet perfectly whole. Lemon intended his work to bridge and fuse cultures but his journeys brought him face to face with unexpected difficulties and discoveries (**see Lemon box**).

The Flying Circus Project of Singapore director **Ong Keng Sen** is specifically designed to integrate performance genres/styles from different Asian cultures (**see Ong box and figure 8.22**). Ong's project is fully comprehensible in terms of where and what Singapore is: at the crossroads of trade routes linking Asia, Australia, Africa, and Europe; a city-state consisting of Chinese, Malay, Indian, Indonesian, and European peoples, languages, religions, and aesthetic traditions. Singaporeans are highly conscious of their multiculturality, celebrating rather than denigrating it. They see their ways of handling cultural and technological inputs as a model for future global development elsewhere. Many Singaporeans are also aware of, and not happy with, their authoritarian government. At the same time, they will tell you that this regimented way of life is the price paid for economic success.

Ralph Lemon (1952–): American choreographer and dancer whose *Geography* trilogy – *Geography* (1997), *Tree* (2000), and *Come Home Charley Patton* (2004) – explores multicultural and intercultural themes, performers, musics, and dancing. Earlier works include *Joy* (1989) and *Persephone* (1991). Lemon chronicles his experience on Parts 1 and 2 of *Geography* in his book *Tree: Belief/Culture/Balance* (2004).

Leadbelly (1885–1949): born Huddie Ledbetter, this legendary African-American blues and ballad composer and singer was a pardoned murderer and the master of the twelve-string guitar.

Ralph Lemon

How mysterious we are to each other

Geography, premiered in 1997, featured dancer/musicians from the West Coast of Africa. Fed by West African traditions, religions, and modern sensibilities, the all-male cast performed a passionate theatrical piece that, by conception, explored the nature of race, and unexpectedly evolved into a highly integrated work of spirituality. The performers from Africa fluidly, boldly brought traditions of prayer and "cleansing" to the everyday process of my formal experiments. They did not share my issues with race as an African-American.

After the completion of *Geography Part 1*, I extended my exploration to Asia in search of a perceived belief system. [. . .] I traveled through India, Indonesia, China, and Japan, following the geographical map of Buddhism to Zen, collaborating and sharing questions with performers and musicians contacted throughout the map – a parallel search for diverse but communicable art languages. [. . .] I discovered that the belief systems that I encountered stemmed from the ritual of the art itself, the discipline, the form, thus giving rise to a new exploratory dilemma: How to reconcile ancient traditions with the potential irreverence of [post]modernity dominating a shrinking world? [. . .]

I'm licking my wounds from the amazing onslaught of being in far away places for the past 5 years, experiencing how little of my art past is relevant to the world, and how I can never know another language or culture deeply. But also how essential and common are bodies moving together and laughing.

I found little "spirituality" as theme in *Tree* [Part 2 of *Geography*, 1999], which was supposed to be about spirit. [. . .] I find the process is about people, just people. And how mysterious we are to each other.

1999, "Director's Notes," Program for *Tree*, 9

fig 8.22. Othello (Madhu Margi) performs the role of the puppeteer manipulating Desdemona (Claire Wong) in Ong Keng Sen's *Desdemona* in the version presented at the Adelaide Festival in 2000. Photograph courtesy of Ong Keng Sen.

Ong Keng Sen

Making intercultural theatre

My sojourn as a creator, for the past six years [1996–2001], of intercultural projects bringing together traditional Asian arts and contemporary interdisciplinary expression has only just begun. The Flying Circus Project is at the root of my thinking. The Project is an ambitious large-scale laboratory that brings together diverse Asian artists – documentary filmmakers, drag queens, visual artists, rock and computer musicians, disk jockeys, modern dancers, and actors, as well as ritualists, and other traditional performers. For four weeks, different cultures, aesthetics, disciplines, and of course, individual personalities encounter each other in a series of training classes, workshops based on improvisation and reinventing traditional art forms, discussions, and lectures. Thus far, three laboratories have brought together 150 artists from India, Korea, China, Tibet, Taiwan, Vietnam, Cambodia, Laos, Thailand, Myanmar, Japan, Indonesia, the Philippines, Malaysia, and Singapore in a process that I call "cultural negotiation," with no view to end product or final presentation. The Project has also included a few "guests" from Europe and the USA. The question posed by the Flying Circus Project is, "Can we, as artists from Asia, bring another perspective and forge a different relationship to intercultural performance than what has developed in the United States, for instance?"

In March 2000 I directed *Desdemona* in which 10 artists – actors, musicians, designers, video/installation artists – from India, Korea, Myanmar, Indonesia, and Singapore worked together on stage. Desdemona premiered at the Adelaide Festival and then went on to the Munich Dance Festival and the Singapore and Hamburg Festivals. In 2001 it metamorphosed into a visual arts exhibition/performance/outreach program at the Fukuoka Asian Art Museum. [. . .] I wanted to move away from earlier interpretations of Othello, especially the obsessive stereotyping of black machismo. What if Othello was played by a woman or by a slight, slender boy? Finally, I cast two Indian performers in this role, a man and a woman: Madhu Margi, a kutiyattam actor, and Maya Rao, a modern theatre actress also trained in kathakali. [. . .]

I wanted to harness a wide range of "contemporary" arts in *Desdemona.* I wanted the contradictions of traditional and contemporary exposed rather than glossed into unity. Maya Rao hinted at Othello, his father, the female within him, and much more. Maya wanted a flow between male and female. Opposed to narrow portrayals of gender that would reinforce stereotypes, she was not costumed/made up to look like a man. Rather than play two characters, she represented the male and female aspects in Othello.

My method of constantly creating different performance drafts, turning written scenes on their heads, developing extensive performance texts, multiple focal points and multiple realities, parallel texts of music and visual arts was difficult for the traditional artists. [. . .] But I was intent on driving a dense, intense, stream of consciousness into the psyche of the two central characters. This required multiple layering, quick shifts into surrealism, abstraction, symbolism, the fracturing of self into different parts and nonlinearity. [. . .] Ultimately, *Desdemona* is a cultural study about a group of Asian artists looking at themselves and rethinking the ways in which Asia has been represented on the stage in the past.

2001, "Encounters," 126–29

Ong's project is an example both of Barba's investigations into Eurasian performance and of Singapore playwright **Kuo Pao Kun**'s proposal for an "open culture" (**see Kuo box**). The workshops and productions of Flying Circus aim toward but do not achieve seamless integration. As Ong himself notes, "the contradictions of traditional and contemporary are exposed rather than glossed into unity." It takes a longer time and the practice of many artists for whom the hybrid genre is "natural" for there to be unity. Such is the case of butoh, which combines traditional Japanese approaches to the body, movement, and meditation with impulses drawn from Western modern dance and experimental performance. Similarly, jazz and blues are musical genres with deep roots in Africa and the African diaspora played on Euro-American instruments sung in vocal styles that draw on African and Euro-American traditions. Trinidad's rich musical expression includes "chutney soca," soul-calypso played/sung to a South Asian beat.

Kuo Pao Kun (1939–2002): Chinese born, multilingual Singapore playwright, director, and theorist. In 1965 he and his wife Goh Lay Kuan founded the Practice Performing Arts School. Kuo was imprisoned for his leftist views from 1976 to 1980. In 1990, he was awarded Singapore's Cultural Medallion; and in 2002 the Excellence for Singapore award. From 1989 to 1995, Kuo headed Singapore's Substation performance center. Kuo's plays include *The Coffin Is Too Big For The Hole* (1984), *Descendants of the Eunuch Admiral* (1995), *Mama Looking for Her Cat* (1988), *The Spirits Play* (1998), and the multilingual *Sunset Rise* (1998).

Border wars

Intercultural performances need not aim for integration. Many artists want to expose the difficulties and explore the creative possibilities of playing across national, cultural, artistic, and personal borders. This brand of intercultural performance refuses utopian schemes, uncloaks and parodies power relations, and promotes critical ideological perspectives. At present, there is no better exemplar both practically and in enunciating its theory than Guillermo Gómez-Peña. Working both solo and in collaboration, Gómez-Peña probes the ambivalences, fears, disruptions, and hilarities occurring when and where cultures collide, overlap, or pull away from each other (**see Gómez-Peña box 2**).

Since the late 1970s, Gómez-Peña has created hybrids made from (in his own words) Mexican carpa (urban popular theatre), magical realism, kabuki, and US multimedia with the goal of demolishing monoculture. Gómez-Peña's

Kuo Pao Kun

Open culture – the global perspective

Open Culture proposes that the fundamentals of the nurturing process no longer be racially based. Not even bi-culturally and bilingually. A quantum leap must be made onto the global level. Instead of *Multiculturalism* (the twin of *Multiracialism* in Singapore), Singapore's education should begin actively evolving a global awareness. However, while the vision reaches for the global, the footing remains rooted in Indian, Chinese, Malay, European cultures as its primary base or launching point. This will be necessary as a general policy until the people are ready to collectively, and individually, choose otherwise. Shifting to a global perspective would make it necessary for every student to internalize an overview of the *cultures of the world*. [. . .] This requires an institutional shift in syllabus and allocation of resources to a global perspective. Similarly, the choice of third and fourth languages and cultures must become more open – until it reaches the full spectrum of world cultures. [. . .]

Open Culture is based on several fundamentals: First, every individual should be deeply rooted in at least one culture. Second, every individual should be given the choice to begin one's opening up by first deepening the organic culture one is living by, that is, one's parent culture. Third, the cultural development of the individual should be de-linked from the racial and linguistic origin of the individual. Fourth, every student should be exposed, generally, to an overview of the cultures of the world and, specifically, to at least two cultures in depth. Fifth, the state should recognize culture as a primary, core area of study [. . .]. In short, *Open Culture* contemplates a transcendence of the individual from race and tradition-bound communities to embrace a diverse global community. [. . .]

It is mainly in the realm of culture – especially in intellectual explorations and artistic creations – that the deeper human issues and problems can be identified, analyzed, debated, explored, experimented with, and resolved. For, metaphorically, culture is a huge laboratory and a vast *Play Space* where current ideas and practices are challenged, classical models are re-examined, gut impulses are articulated, fantastic imaginations are exploded, outrageous proposals are tested, and new ways and means are explored. [. . .] *Open Culture* provides resources and provokes dynamic interaction; it is the necessary ambience for enhanced creativity. This very openness, however, also makes it impossible to predict results. *Open Culture* begets Open Futures.

1998, "Contemplating an Open Culture," 57–60

Guillermo Gómez-Peña

I carry the border with me

I am a nomadic Mexican artist/writer in the process of Chicanization, which means I am slowly heading North. My journey not only goes from South to North, but from Spanish to Spanglish, and then to English; from ritual art to high technology; from literature to performance art; and from a static sense of identity to a repertoire of multiple identities. Once I get "there," wherever it is, I am forever condemned to return, and then to obsessively reenact my journey. In a sense, I am a border Sisyphus. [. . .]

I make art about the misunderstandings that take place at the border zone. But for me, the border is no longer located at any fixed geopolitical site. I carry the border with me, and I find new borders wherever I go. [. . .]

When I am on the East Coast of the United States, I am also in Europe, Africa, and the Caribbean. There, I like to visit Nuyo Rico, Cuba York, and other micro-republics. When I return to the U.S. Southwest, I am suddenly back in Mexamerica, a vast conceptual nation that also includes the northern states of Mexico, and overlaps with various Indian nations. [. . .]

The work of the artist is to force open the matrix of reality to introduce unsuspected possibilities. Artists and writers are currently involved in the redefinition of our continental topography. We see through the colonial map of North, Central, and South America, to a more complex system of overlapping, interlocking, and overlaid maps. Among others, we can see Amerindia, Afroamerica, Americamestiza-y-mulata, Hybridamerica, and Transamerica – the "other America" that belongs to the homeless, and to nomads, migrants, and exiles.

1996, *The New World Border*, 1, 5–6

early performance world was populated by Mister Misterio, a Mexican detective/poet, Misterio's friend, the burned-out ballerina Salome Zentit, a wrestler shaman, a multimedia *pachuco*, an Aztec princess working as a cabaret chanteuse, and an androgynous Maori warrior opera singer. For some performances, Gómez-Peña constructed multimedia altars with a video monitor as the main icon. Before performing, Gómez-Peña and his co-performers made elaborate rituals to reach a trancelike state – it is not clear if they actually did so or parodied such rituals. But can the distinction between the "real" and the "parody" be definitively made? Later Gómez-Peña figures include Border Brujo, El Warrior Gringostroika, Humble Mariachi Player, and El Mad Mex (**see figure 8.23**). In all these guises and enactments, Gómez-Peña and his colleagues combine parody, irony, ritual, popular arts, and social commentary.

Gómez-Peña is a performance artist, critical theorist, poet, and provocateur. He enacts his belief that nomadism and migration are the central experiences of our epoch. In the mid-1980s, Gómez-Peña was a founder of the Border Arts Workshop/El Taller de Arte Fronterizo. One of BAW/TAF's actions was placing a table on the beach at Tijuana–San Diego where Mexico and the USA meet. At first the Mexicans sat in Mexico, the North Americans in the USA. Then they "illegally" held hands and passed food across the border; then they rotated the table so that each group sat in the national territory of the other. Whose border is it, anyway?

From 1988 to 1990 Gómez-Peña was possessed by Border Brujo, a figure of fifteen personae each speaking a different "border language" such as Spanish, English, Spanglish, and tongues. According to Gómez-Peña, Border Brujo was a character, a performance artist, an alternative chronicler of community life, a cultural prisoner, a homeless shaman, and the village fool. He appeared in galleries, community centers, migrant-worker camps, political rallies, museums, and theatres. Border Brujo taught Gómez-Peña how to cross the borders of cultures, communities, institutions, and territories. Increasingly, he enacted a radical and experimental hybridity (**see Gómez-Peña box 3**).

Guillermo Gómez-Peña

Hybrid culture is experimental and radical

My version of the hybrid is cross-racial, polylinguistic, and multicontextual. From a disadvantaged position, the hybrid expropriates elements from all sides to create more open and fluid systems. Hybrid culture is community-based yet experimental, radical but not static or dogmatic. It fuses "low" and "high" art, primitive and high-tech, the problematic notions of self and other, the liquid entities of North and South, East and West.

An ability to understand the hybrid nature of culture develops from an experience of dealing with a dominant culture from the outside. The artist who understands and practices hybridity in this way can be at the same time an insider and an outsider,

fig 8.23. Some of Guillermo Gómez-Peña's many guises. All photographs courtesy of Guillermo Gómez-Peña.

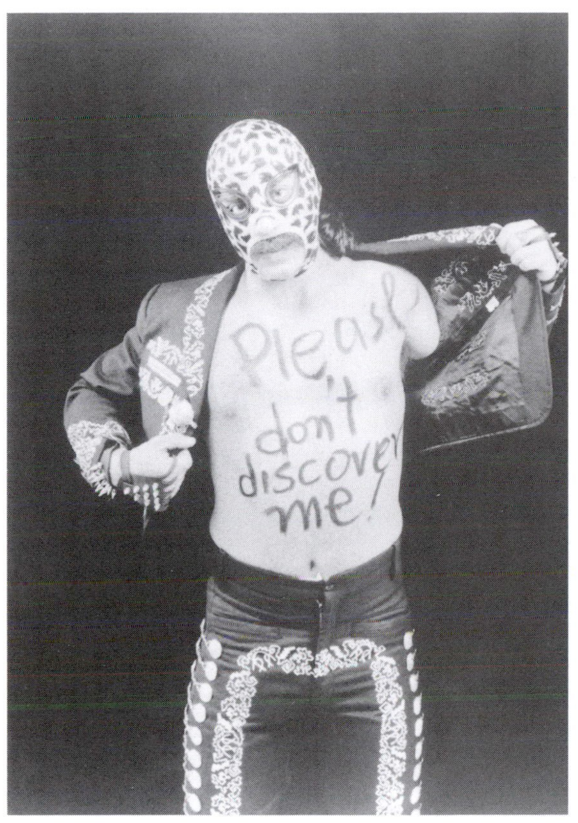

El Warrior Gringostroika in his wrestler's mask. Photograph by Eugenio Castro.

Border Brujo and "Aztec" Carmel Kooros draw their weapons.

A Humble Mariachi Player shakes hands with a NAFTA diplomat (Roberto Sifuentes).

El Mad Mex. Photograph by Eugenio Castro.

an expert in border crossings, a temporary member of multiple communities, a citizen of two or more nations. S/he performs multiple roles in multiple contexts. At times s/he can operate as a cross-cultural diplomat, as an intellectual coyote (smuggler of ideas) or a media pirate. At other times, s/he assumes the role of nomadic chronicler, intercultural translator, or political trickster. S/he speaks from more than one perspective, to more than one community, about more than one reality. His/her job is to trespass, bridge, interconnect, reinterpret, remap, and redefine; to find the outer limits of his/her culture and cross them.

1996, *The New World Border*, 12

In 1992–93, in response to the many mainstream celebrations of the 500th anniversary of **Christopher Columbus**' "discovery" of the "New World," Gómez-Peña and Coco Fusco devised a performance that parodied how "exotic peoples" were (and sometimes still are) exhibited by and to Europeans and Euro-Americans (**see Fusco box**). Displayed as just-discovered "primitive" Amerindians from an island in the Gulf of Mexico, Fusco and Gómez-Peña lived for three days in a 12-foot square golden cage in Madrid's Columbus Plaza (**see figure 8.24**). After Madrid, the exhibit was seen in London, Sydney, several locations in the USA, and Buenos Aires. The "Guatinauis" carried on their daily lives under the gaze of spectators: sewing voodoo dolls, reciting stories in gibberish, watching TV, lifting weights, and working on a laptop computer. The Guatinauis posed for Polaroid photos. For a small donation, Fusco danced to rap music. At

fig 8.24. Guillermo Gómez-Peña and Coco Fusco as "newly discovered Amerindians" on display in Madrid in 1992. Photograph by Nancy Lytle courtesy of Coco Fusco.

New York's Whitney Museum, a glimpse of "authentic Guatinaui male genitals" cost five dollars. A handout pinpointed on a map the couple's home island, explaining in ethnographic style who the "specimens" were, their height and weight, what they ate (Diet Coke and burritos), their place in the Guatinaui social hierarchy ("His frequent pacing in the cage leads experts to believe that he was a political leader on his island," "Her facial and body decorations indicate that she has married into the upper caste of her tribe"), and their personalities ("quite affectionate in the cage, seemingly uninhibited in their physical and sexual habits"). Two guards led them on leashes to the toilet and fielded questions from viewers because the "natives" knew no European languages. Many persons knew this was a politically savvy performance, but a surprising number did not – believing that "real natives" were on display. And why not? Exhibiting the "exotic other" is well documented in the colonial archive.

Christopher Columbus (Cristoforo Colombo) (1451–1506): Italian explorer who in 1492, while searching for a westward passage to Asia under commission from Queen Isabella of Spain, "discovered" the Americas by landing on several Caribbean islands. He claimed the "new" lands he touched for the Spanish crown and inaugurated the modern colonial period.

Coco Fusco

Two Undiscovered Amerindians Visit . . .

Our plan was to live in a golden cage for three days, presenting ourselves as undiscovered Amerindians from an island in the Gulf of Mexico that had somehow been overlooked by Europeans for five centuries. [. . .] Our project concentrated on the "zero degree" of intercultural relations in an attempt to define a point of origin for the debates that link "discovery" and "Otherness." We worked within disciplines that blur distinctions between the art object and the body (performance), between fantasy and reality (live spectacle), and between history and dramatic reenactment (the diorama). The performance was interactive, focusing less on what we did than on how people interacted with us and interpreted our actions. Entitled *Two Undiscovered Amerindians Visit . . .*, we chose not to announce the event through prior publicity or any other means when it was possible to exert such control; we intended to create a surprise or "uncanny" encounter, one in which audiences had to undergo their own process of reflection as to what they were seeing, aided only by written information and parodically didactic zoo guards. In such encounters with the unexpected, people's defense mechanisms are less likely to operate with their normal efficiency; caught off guard their beliefs are more likely to rise to the surface.

Our performance was based on the once popular European and North American practice of exhibiting indigenous people from Africa, Asia, and the Americas in zoos, parks, taverns, museums, freak shows, and circuses. While this tradition reached the height of its popularity in the 19th century, it was actually begun by Christopher Columbus, who returned from his first voyage in 1492 with several Arawaks, one of whom was left on display at the Spanish court for two years.

1995, *English is Broken Here*, 39–40

The performance subverted the already blurred boundaries between ethnography, art, and tourism. Reactions were extremely varied. Even those who knew this was an "art performance" readily played the role of colonizer – gazing, probing, objectifying. Some who were taken in tried to free the imprisoned natives; others complained to museum or gallery administrators about the horror of such an exhibition. Many simply enjoyed the exhibit at face value: "interesting, unusual, and rare natives on display." Some wanted to have sex with the Guatinauis. A few thought they were actors working for other artists who conceived the performance but would not participate in it. At the University of California-Irvine, the Environmental Health and Safety Office worried that the excrement of "real aborigines" in the gallery would be a health hazard. The performance exposed uncomfortable parallels between international arts festivals, colonial expositions, museum displays, and tourist expeditions.

If *Two Undiscovered Amerindians Visit . . .* played on the trope of colonial curiosity, objectifying the Other, and the pleasures/horrors of exploitation, the Gómez-Peña–**Roberto Sifuentes** 1994–96 collaboration, the *Temple of Confessions*, conflated ethnographic and religious dioramas with people's real desire for spiritual experience. Gómez-Peña and Sifuentes displayed themselves in Plexiglas boxes as scientific specimens of the last two living saints from a "border region." Spectators were invited not only to gaze on these exotic beings but to confess their "intercultural fears and desires" to them.

Roberto Sifuentes (1967–): Chicano interdisciplinary performance artist from Los Angeles now based in New York. Sifuentes collaborated with Guillermo Gómez-Peña on several works including *The Temple of Confessions* (1994) *Techno-Dioramas* (1999). Sifuentes' own work includes *Undermining the Machine* (2001) and *The Virgin of Perpetual Security* (2003).

Gómez-Peña and Sifuentes were not prepared for the reception they got when the exhibit premiered at the Scottsdale Center for the Arts near Phoenix, Arizona. Hundreds thronged the exhibit to confess (in Gómez-Peña's words) "their innermost feelings, fantasies, and memories of Mexico, Mexicans, Chicanos, and other people of color." As the *Temple of Confessions* toured Mexico and the USA, the reactions varied from fascination to anger to sharing innermost secrets. The performance itself changed to suit particular circumstances. Gómez-Peña's trademark cultural pastiche style was in full force: on his ghetto blaster he mixed Gregorian chants with rap, circus music, Mexican waltzes, and Indian blues. He and Sifuentes shared their Plexiglas booths (reminiscent of television quiz shows, Eichmann on trial, church relics, and museum exhibit cases) with roaches, crickets, an iguana, fake "tribal" musical instruments, and various other items eclectically assembled. But, as Gómez-Peña notes, from a distance the pair looked "authentic." "I could have been an indigenous shaman in a diorama sponsored by the *National Geographic*." Only close up did people see that these performers were Benetton advertisement primitives, more MTV than . . . but who is to say that MTV isn't authentic? Despite this, throughout the two-year life of the performance, Gómez-Peña wrote,

> Visitors attempted to establish a personal 'spiritual' connection with me. Their eyes looked desperately for mine. If I decided to engage in a personalized relation with them (mainly through eye contact, symbolic hand motions or subvocalizing), emotions began to pour from both sides: vulnerability, guilt, anger, tenderness. Some people cried, and in doing so, they made me cry. Some expressed their sexual desire for me, and I discreetly reciprocated. Others spewed their hatred, their contempt and their fear, and I willingly took it. At least a third of the visitors eventually decided to kneel and confess (*Dangerous Border Crossers*, 38).

From the glocal to social theatre

The real feelings evoked by the ersatz *Temple of Confessions* reveal a need for living contact and interaction, a counterforce to the alienation and homogeny of globalization. Globalization is opposed on many fronts. Political demonstrators disrupt meetings of the WTO and other gatherings of the world's economic masters. Artists expose the contradictions between globalization's hype and the exploitation, displacement, and impoverishment that are what globalization has delivered to so many of the world's poorest poor. Whether this descent into misery is the dark before dawn as the boosters of globalization claim or a nightmare of indefinite duration remains an open question.

For all the demonstrations against globalization, there is also a resigned desperation: globalization, like industrialization in the nineteenth century, is not going away. More positive responses to globalization have been the growth of community-based, identity-based, and minoritarian performances. Many of these are expressions of the **"glocal"** – a combination of the global and the local. This kind of activity goes under several names. In the Third World there is "theatre for development," some organized by governments, some by NGOs. Theatre for development helps people cope with, and where possible take advantage of, the changes being wrought by globalization. Augusto Boal's Theatre of the Oppressed is another response to globalization.

glocal: according to the website that claims to have invented the term, "The word '**GLOCAL**' originally derived from the combination of the words '**GLO**bal' and 'lo**CAL**'; and, by definition, it refers to the individual/group/division/unit/organization/community, who is willing and is able to ***'think globally and act locally.'*** Indeed, how could one realistically think of being global without first being local? To meet the challenge of today's business environment, we need a synergy between vision and action and a well balanced focus on both, the global and local environments" (www.geocities.com/rija_ rasoava/def_glocal.htm). This is one of 339,000 sites turned up by a Google search of "glocal."

Performance artist Suzanne Lacy has from the early 1970s addressed social issues by devising site-specific performances with local people. In *Whisper, the Waves, the Wind* (1984) 154 older women dressed in white sat at white-cloth-covered tables on the beach at La Jolla, California talking to each other about their lives and especially how it felt to grow old (**see figure 8.25**). Their conversations, microphoned and mingled with the sounds of wind and ocean, were overheard by spectators standing above the beach. Three years later, in *The Crystal Quilt*, Lacy arranged a similar performance after-hours in a Minneapolis department store, where 430 older women dressed in black sat and spoke to each other. The purpose of these performances was to give voice to people and communities often ignored. Over the years, Lacy and other artists have developed ways to involve themselves in different communities. In these involvements, artists can assume several personae: as experiencer, reporter, analyst, and activist (**see Lacy box**).

Suzanne Lacy

From private to public artist

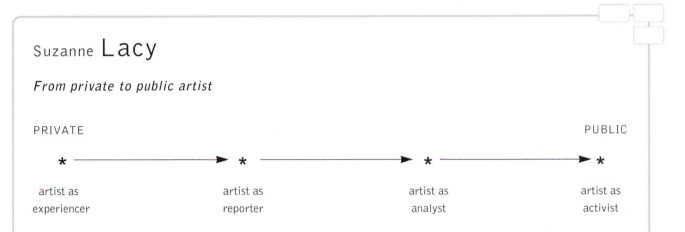

Experiencer. [. . .] In August 1991, I sat for seven days in an abandoned hospital room at Roswell Park Cancer Center in upstate New York, charting the private conversations I had with patients, nurses, doctors, scientists, and administrators. The artwork was located in the interaction between myself as artist and the members of the community, framed by the hospital room and fueled by the human need to reflect on the meaning of one's life and work. [. . .]

Reporter. In the role of the reporter, the artist focuses not simply on the experience but on the recounting of the situation; that is, the artist gathers information to make it available to others. She calls our attention to something. [. . .] Reporting might be compared to aesthetic framing. [. . .] Reporting involves a conscious selection, though not necessarily an analysis, of information. [. . .]

Analyst. From reporting, or presenting information, to analysis is a short step, but the implied shift in the artist's role is enormous. [. . .] As artists begin to analyze social situations through their art, they assume for themselves skills more commonly associated with social scientists, investigative journalists, and philosophers. [. . .] When an artist adopts the position of analyst, the visual appeal of imagery is often superseded by the textual properties of the work, thus challenging conventions of beauty. Their analysis may assume its aesthetic character from the coherence of the ideas or from their relationship to visual images rather than through the images themselves.

Activist. The last step along the proposed continuum is from analysis to activism, where art making is contextualized within local, national, and global situations, and the audience becomes an active participant. In seeking to become catalysts for change, artists reposition themselves as citizen-activists. Diametrically opposed to the aesthetic practices of the isolated artist, consensus building inevitably entails developing a set of skills not commonly associated with art making. [. . .] Entirely new strategies must be learned: how to collaborate, how to develop multilayered and specific audiences, how to cross over with other disciplines, how to choose sites that resonate with public meaning, and how to clarify visual and process symbolism for people who are not educated in art.

1995, "Debated Territory: Toward a Critical Language for Public Art," 174–77

fig 8.25. Suzanne Lacy's *Whisper, The Waves, The Wind* (1984). Photographs by John Warner. Photos courtesy of Suzanne Lacy.

An overview of the beach and tables where the women sat and talked.

One table with four older women conversing.

The movement from the personal to the local to the global and back again, the glocal, is a well-trod path (**see Lippard box**). A large number of community-based performances are based on the premise that what is specific to a place and a community is also generalizable. On one level, it is necessary to preserve the local in the interest of cultural diversity – both actual and virtual diversity. Increasingly in the twenty-first century with its plethora of wars, displacements, and migrations – a fluidity never before experienced – a new category of performance, "social theatre," is growing in importance (**see Thompson and Schechner box**). Social theatre covers a wide range of activities – from interventions in war-torn regions such as Sri Lanka or Kosovo to work in prisons or refugee camps to the many local outposts of Augusto Boal's Theatre of the Oppressed. Inherent in such activities is a utopian, democratic ideal: "the people" have stories to enact and these stories are embedded within living traditions that are worthy of preservation, dissemination, and further development. It is not that aesthetic performance is dying so much as it is a question of recognizing the great variety of possibilities offered by the performing arts, from individual and group therapy to political action, from enhancing group solidarity to uncovering, enjoying, and sharing the vast resources of what Clifford Geertz terms "local knowledge."

Some minoritarian performances involve "world-making," inventing creative alternatives to mainstream media, values, laws, and styles (**see Muñoz box**). Cultural

Lucy R. Lippard

The local is the global

National, global, collective narratives are especially accessible through one's family history – by asking simple questions about why we moved from one block or city or state or country to another, gained or lost jobs, married or didn't marry whom we did, kept track of or lost track of certain relatives. A starting point, for example: simple research about the place where you lived or were raised. Who lived there before? What changes have been made? have you made? [. . .] What Native peoples first inhabited it? [. . .] Do any animals live there? And on a broader scope, are you satisfied with the present? If not, are you nostalgic of the past or longing for the future? And so forth.

Questions like these can set off a chain of personal and cultural reminiscences and ramifications, including lines of thought about interlinking histories, the unacknowledged American class system, racial, gender, and cultural divisions and common grounds, land use/abuse, geography, environment, town planning, and the experience of nature that has made a "return" to it so mythical. When this kind of research into social belonging is incorporated into the interactive or participatory art forms, collective views of place can be arrived at. It provides ways to understand how human occupants are also part of the environment rather than merely invaders (but that too). [. . .] As we look at ourselves critically, in social contexts, as inhabitants, users, onlookers, tourists, we can scrutinize our own participatory roles in the natural processes that are forming our futures.

1995, "Looking Around," 115–16

James Thompson and Richard Schechner

What is "social theatre"?

Social theatre may be defined as theatre with specific social agendas; theatre where aesthetics is not the ruling objective; theatre outside the realm of commerce, which drives Broadway/the West End, and the cult of the new, which dominates the avant-garde. Social theatre takes place in diverse locations – from prisons, refugee camps, and hospitals to schools orphanages, and homes for the elderly. Participants have been local residents, disabled people, young prisoners, and many other groups often from vulnerable, disadvantaged, and marginalized communities. Or even with individuals who have lost touch with a sense of groupness, who are internally as well as externally displaced and homeless. Social theatre often occurs in places and situations that are not the usual circumstances of theatre, turning "nonperformers" into performers. Social theatre practitioners are "facilitators" [. . .] helping others to perform as much as performing themselves. Social theatre activists often are artists, but they need not be.

Social theatre draws on theory that pertains to the particular locations where the projects happen. So, for example, theatre in schools has used educational theories to interrogate its work; theatre for development has used development theory to guide its analysis; theatre in prisons has used different models of criminology or rehabilitation theory to explain its practice. The act of applying theatre to the issue or situation at hand means that the social theatre worker enters a practical and discursive space already full of psychological and/or sociological reference points. [. . .]

The view that social theatre is simply a matter of taking theatre to sites that have no theatre or where theatre has been disrupted or destroyed needs to be challenged by the argument that the practice of social theatre is a complex process of interdisciplinary performance. From the performance studies perspective, "non-theatre" venues are in fact sites of multiple performances. Prisons, refugee camps, hospitals, etc., are not empty of theatre nor do they only experience the theatrical when a social theatre project is staged. These locations are arenas rich in performance moments – sometimes small and subtle and at other times huge and obvious. These places and the regimes of knowledge and practice that operate within them are performed. The dress, demeanor, and responses of people are performed – even more so in institutional and highly controlled situations such as prisons, hospitals, schools, and refugee camps. Social theatre uses one set of performance processes to make new sets at sites already full of performances.

2004, "Why 'Social Theatre'," 12–13

José Muñoz

Mapping alternative worlds

Minoritarian performance labors to make worlds – worlds of transformative politics and possibilities. Such performance engenders worlds of ideological potentiality that alter the present and map out a future. Performance is thus imbued with a great deal of power. But what is meant [. . .] by "worldmaking"? The concept of worldmaking delineates the ways in which performances – both theatrical and everyday rituals – have the ability to establish alternate views of the world. These alternative vistas are more than simply views or perspectives; they are oppositional ideologies that function as critiques of oppressive regimes of "truth" that subjugate minoritarian people. Oppositional counterpublics are enabled by visions, "worldviews," that reshape as they deconstruct reality. Such counterpublics are the aftermath of minoritarian performance. Such performances transport the performer and the spectator to a vantage point where transformation and politics are imaginable. Worldmaking performances produce these vantage points by slicing into the facade of the real that is the majoritarian public sphere. Disidentificatory performances opt to do more than simply tear down the majoritarian public sphere. They disassemble that sphere [. . .] and use its parts to build an alternative reality. Disidentification uses the majoritarian culture as raw material to make a new world.

1999, *Disidentifications*, 195–96

diversity must be thought of in lifestyle as well as ethnic and religious terms. On another level, giving voice to local issues – such as opposition to a dam that will flood out the farms and homes of thousands, or demanding a boycott of products made by sweatshop or slave labor – transforms the personal into the political as the particular engages global issues. From AIDS activists and Greenpeace staging guerrilla theatre to Palestinians mounting a drama about the destruction of their village by the Israeli army to Northern Irish parading for or against the British presence, performance is a way to embody concerns, express opinions, and forge solidarity. How the environment is managed, wars prevented, occupying armies expelled, or pandemics treated are questions inextricably enmeshed in the globalization process.

Conclusion

How should artists respond to globalization? Should they cut back on intercultural activities? Or is this troubled epoch precisely the time when such works are most needed? And even if artists wanted to work in isolation or in a condition of cultural purity, how could they in a hybridizing world of ever-increasing movement and exchange of people, goods, and ideas? But having noted this, we can ask artists – non-Western as well as Western – to be mindful and careful about from whom they borrow, what use they make of the arts and rituals of other cultures, and how individual works might exacerbate or ease global imbalances. Should artists boycott international festivals and tourist performances? Ought the rules governing borrowings differ depending on whether one is a Western or non-Western artist, an urban or rural artist? Most of the heat has been applied to white Western artists such as Peter Brook, Ariane Mnouchkine, Philip Glass, and so on. But what ought one to say to artists of color who are also Western? Can choreographer Ralph Lemon do what Mnouchkine cannot? Is playwright **Suzan-Lori Parks** exempt from restrictions binding Peter Brook? What about Gómez-Peña, whose work depends upon borrowing, parodic distortion, and making art in the interstices separating/joining Mexican, gringo, and Hispanic cultures? Is there a way of achieving equilibrium in intercultural exchanges (**see Bharucha box**)?

Rustom Bharucha

The possibilities of equilibrium

What concerns me are not the realities of appropriation but the possibilities of equilibrium, of maintaining and sustaining some kind of balance in what could be called the ecology of cultures. Rivers are said to be in a state of equilibrium when their "load" (of materials) is in direct proportion to their carrying capacity as determined by their speed, volume, and depth. Truly, nature's secrets for sustaining its variable balances are elusive. It is we who destroy these secrets in our zeal to "know," to "develop," to "trade," to "plunder." Indeed, it is with some sadness that I inscribe this process of disruption in my own discourse in order to acknowledge that we are living today with the most acute disequilibrium of cultures. To a large extent, it has materialized thorough the overload of materials from First World economies, which have been indiscriminately imposed on ongoing processes of culture, particularly in those parts of the world and among those indigenous communities who are not in a position to negotiate their increasingly vulnerable positions in the larger context of globalization, the marketing and patenting of biodiversity, and the homogenization of diverse cultural identities.

Can we restore, or more accurately, can we begin to invent a sense of balance in our perception and uses of each other's cultures? If our faith in the dominant mechanisms and institutions of cultural exchange has declined over the years, what are the new agencies of negotiating the transportation and translation of cultures? How do we sensitize ourselves to new principles of vigilance in regulating processes of appropriation and piracy? Can we envision a new ethics of respecting differences in theatre?

1997, "Negotiating the 'River'," 32–33

Suzan-Lori Parks (1964–): African-American playwright whose works include *Imperceptible Mutabilities in the Third Kingdom* (1989), *The America Play* (1993), *Venus* (1996), *In the Blood* (2000), *TopDog/UnderDog* (2001), and *Getting Mother's Body, A Novel* (2003).

Those opposing intercultural works condemn Western artists for using non-Western ideas and techniques to make signature "original," "innovative," "avant-garde" works, which define the world's arts markets, both economically and conceptually. In other words, the colonial cycle is enacted in the arts market: raw material from the colonies at a cheap price; manufactured items back to the colonies at a high price. But it is not only Western artists who participate in this cycle. Nor are all the "foreign" materials from outside an artist's own region.

Artists residing in Third World metropolises such as São Paolo, Kolkata, Mexico City, Cairo, Johannesburg, Jakarta, and many other cities are hooked into global circuits from which they take both foreign and local materials – sometimes freely, sometimes in accord with local restrictions. It is increasingly difficult to assign areas or nations to one "world" or another. Shanghai is in some ways more First World than New York, but rural China is far behind both cities; ditto for Mumbai and rural India. Even in apparently tightly regulated or oppressive societies, such as Iran or Nigeria, artists find ways to communicate with like-minded people around the world. The internet is a main avenue, but there are other ways too, some of them secret. In more open societies, the play of differing values and materials is stupendous, operationally infinite.

For example, Japan is culturally "Japan," while also being part of global culture, and I don't mean just economically. Ever since the **Meiji Restoration** in 1868, a key question faced by the Japanese is how to be Japanese and up-to-date simultaneously. At present, the avant-garde not only thrives alongside noh, bunraku, and kabuki but also draws on these traditional forms. Japan also boasts world-class Western-style performing arts such as modern theatre, ballet, and classical music. Many Japanese artists explore and deepen their Japaneseness even as they are busy using materials from other parts of Asia, the West, Africa, and Latin America (**see Martin box**). Butoh mines traditional Japanese dance and theatre, Zen, and Shinto along with elements derived from, or influenced by, German expressionism and American and European experimental performance. Suzuki Tadashi's world-renowned training method is based on traditional Japanese martial arts and dance. Suzuki uses this training in his productions, several of which have been of Greek tragedies. Many other Japanese artists approach their work interculturally – and what's happening in Japan is also taking place throughout the rest of the world. Cultural fluidity and hybridity is the driving force globally of both the avant-garde and popular arts.

In terms of performance studies, the "intercultural question" involves valuing embodied and digital as well as written and archived knowledge. For the most part, at least until the advent of performance studies, Western modes of knowing privileged the written over the enacted, in Diana Taylor's terms, the archive over the repertory. However, increasingly the embodied – the performed – is recognized as its own domain of knowledge and experience. It used to be that such a domain existed only during face-to-face contact. But the internet and the digital sharing of performances are changing that. Intercultural performances take place both digitally and in person by means of various exchanges, festivals, and scholarly meetings. Digital knowledge and experience is not a settled category. From one perspective, it appears archival; from another, very "live." Chatrooms, streaming video, instant messaging, live telecasting, pod-casting, and the like create an expanding, dynamic space between face-to-face presence and "finished" works.

Under these circumstances, there is no such thing as cultural purity. All cultural practices everywhere – from religion and the arts to cooking, dress, and language – are hybrids. Cultural purity is a dangerous fiction because it leads to a kind of policing that results in apparent monoculture and actual racism, jingoism, and xenophobia. The "natural" proclivity of humankind is promiscuity – which results in an always changing, if sometimes unsettling, diversity. The ongoing work of performance studies is to explore, understand, promote, and enjoy this diversity.

It would be satisfying to end this book here. But it's not triumphally simple. We live in a world awash in horrors that are played out daily in our faces thanks to an always turned on media and internet. As noted earlier in this chapter, the work of social theatre is to ameliorate these horrors, to bring concerned individuals and organizations into close, enabling, and healing contact with those who suffer. But there is the opposite tendency also, very much present in fanatical jihadism and the equally venomous response to it, the "War on Terror." Facing the unsettling and volatile global situation, what should artists do? Not everyone wants to engage in social theatre. When confronted with violence and criminal acts – many committed by nations and transnational corporations as well as by stateless, nomadic "fundamentalists" – are artists best advised to be onlookers and witnesses? But what kind of witnesses? Do we join in condemning composer **Karlheinz Stockhausen** for his widely publicized statement after 9/11 that the attack was "the greatest work of art imaginable for the whole cosmos" or do we agree with Dario Fo who

Meiji Restoration: in 1868, young modernizers overthrew the feudal Tokugawa shogunate returning power to the emperor. Meiji ruled until his death in 1912. The 1890 constitution established a legislature, prime minister, and cabinet. At the same time, the emperor was regarded as divine, a status he held until after World War II. During Meiji's rule, Japan transformed itself into a modern industrial and military power.

Carol Martin

Japaneseness in the glocal world

Until relatively recently, the political and aesthetic focal point of postwar Japanese performance was fixed on ideas about premodern Japanese aesthetics, modernization, and Westernization. After World War II, the subject of modernization got mixed, sometimes in reactionary ways, with how to restore "Japaneseness" to Japanese aesthetics. This project was undertaken against the background of Japan having been both an extreme aggressor and a victim in the war: The "rape of Nanjing" and "comfort women" [Korean women forced into having sex with Japanese soldiers] stood in contrast to the fire bombings of Tokyo and the mushroom clouds rising over Hiroshima and Nagasaki. Reconstructing the sensibility of premodern Japan that was so much a part of HijikataTatsumi's butoh and even Suzuki Tadashi's avantgarde theatre [. . .] has since the immediate postwar era morphed into another project. The lingering heat of the idea of a local premodern Japaneseness is evaporating into a staging of the presence of the most profound absence.

This shift is partly attributable to [. . .] a new cultural force in which the economic sphere is global while the cultural sphere is parochial. It is part of Japan's most influential artists' response to globalization. The apprehension created by participation in globalization while maintaining local culture and politics has altered our sense of history, identity, and aesthetics. The proliferation of new-millennium identities and epistemologies obliges scholars to know the local in the context of the global and the global in the context of the local. Looking at Japanese performance as one crucible of globalization makes the difficulty of this task apparent. [. . .]

Unlike conventional Western drama, which re-creates history or actuality, noh actors represent precisely that which cannot ordinarily be seen. Noh's *hashigakari* (the bridge that leads from offstage onto the stage) is the path from the visibility of the green room where the actors regard themselves in a mirror to the invisibility of the stage [, . . .] the place where the actor is visible to the spectators as he enacts beings that erupt from an invisible world, but no longer visible to himself as a mirror image. The opulent material beauty of the noh masks and costumes help perform the paradoxical task of representing invisibility through fantastic visual effects.

Noh is consciously preserved as a tradition, an example, a remnant of a certain era of Japanese aesthetics. It would not continue to exist without intervention. But as the intervention is in the interest of present notions of past Japan, it necessarily erases the past while attempting to preserve it. In this way, noh participates in its own disappearance.

2006, "Lingering Heat and Local Global J Stuff," 47–49

said, "Big speculators joyfully splash about in an economy that lets millions of people die every year in misery. What are 20,000 dead [*sic*] in New York by comparison? [. . .] Regardless of who carried out the massacre, this violence is the legitimate daughter of the culture of violence, hunger, and inhumane exploitation" (both Stockhausen's and Fo's statements can be accessed at: www.osborne-conant.org/documentation_stockhausen.htm)? Stockhausen was savagely criticized. On the defensive, Stockhausen soon backpedaled, claiming he was misquoted (he wasn't). But no one cried out against Fo. The difference in reactions can be explained by realizing that Fo's statement was boilerplate anti-American rhetoric, while Stockhausen cut much too close to the bone.

Karlheinz Stockhausen (1928–): German avant-garde composer known for his serial and electronic compositions. In some works, Stockhausen gives freedom to performers to play his music in a variety of ways – scores read backwards or upside down, for example. His music has influenced a broad range of artists from The Beatles to Stravinsky. Among his major works: *Kontrapunkte* (*Counterpoint*, 1953), *Gruppen* (*Groups*, 1958), *Mikrophonie* (*Microphones*, 1964), *Zodiac* (1975–76), and the seven-part opera, *Licht* (*Light*, 1977–2002).

I saw the second airplane crash into the World Trade Center. Then joined by a few neighbors (after fetching my daughter from school), we took our places on my penthouse balcony less than 1.5 miles from the catastrophe. I was very aware that we were spectators. I was less certain concerning what we were seeing. History, tragedy, art, human suffering, chaos, the humiliation of a great power, a carefully planned spectacle, warfare, heroism, payback . . . some undefinable conglomeration? Soon enough, I recognized that the attacks were designed by Al Qaeda to be seen globally, the mother of all reality shows, a theatre of extreme cruelty. In 1937, Picasso painted *Guernica*, a horrific vision of the fascist bombing of a Spanish-Basque town during the civil war (**see figure 8.26**). *Guernica* is art though what it depicts is not.

fig 8.26. Picasso's *Guernica* (1937) regarded by many as a great anti-war painting. It protests the bombing on 26 April 1937 of the small town of Guernica by the Germans who were assisting Franco's forces during the Spanish Civil War. Madrid, Museo Nacional Reina Sofia. Copyright Succession Picasso/DACS. Photo: akg-images/Eric Lessing.

fig 8.27. The smouldering wreckage of New York's World Trade Center. Images like these became instant iconic metaphors both for the attack and the resiliency of New York City and its people.

Today, for better or worse, the ubiquitous cameras, the narrations and commentaries, and the countless replays of iconic digital images and film clips frame events as they are happening, alienating them in the Brechtian sense, presenting them as a kind of art. Long ago **Marshall McLuhan** theorized that media was cool, training viewers to regard events as if they are happening at a distance. The attack of 9/11 photographed from all angles, reported as a real-life drama, emanated an artlike aura transforming 9/11 into a living-yet-mediatized multifaceted *Guernica*. What began as news almost instantly became a ritualized worldcast. The performance and re-performance of these images made them iconic: part real-life, part artlike spectacle (**see figure 8.27**). Similarly, "embedded" journalists (in bed with, ideologically speaking) transform war itself into war games and war movies. I say "artlike," wanting to distance myself from Stockhausen's absolute assignment of genre, while acknowledging that the thinnest, almost wholly dissolved, membrane separates art from artlike. If performance studies can study anything "as performance," how can the 9/11 attack, and untold other violent acts past and ongoing, and whatever is still to come, be studied? I have tried to explore some of the ways. At the very end of this book, I know that many questions are unanswered. Asking them is what performance studies is all about.

Marshall McLuhan (1911–80): Canadian visionary communications theorist known for his aphorism, "the medium is the message." McLuhan forecast the enormous impact of television and the internet. He theorized the transition from print-based individualized culture to media-based collective or neo-tribal culture – a new social reality McLuhan called the "global village." McLuhan's books include *The Mechanical Bride* (1951), *The Gutenberg Galaxy* (1962), *Understanding Media* (1962), and *War and Peace in the Global Village* (1968).

TALK ABOUT

1. Has globalization affected you personally? If so, are these effects good or bad?
2. From the point of view of the majority of the world's peoples, do you believe globalization is good or bad? Whatever your answer, what can you do performatively either to advance or to stop globalization?
3. Have you ever had an "intercultural moment," when you have miscommunicated or been misunderstood because of a difference in cultures? What did you do in that situation? What should be done in such circumstances?

PERFORM

1. After reading Turner's "Performing Ethnography," use it as a guide to making your own ethnographic performance. How did acting as if you were of another culture help you understand that culture differently than if you just read about it? Did the superficial quality of your enactment actually further distort your understanding of "the other"?
2. Stage a "border scene" in the style of Gómez-Peña. Do it twice, once in class; once in a public space.

READ

Barba, Eugenio. "Theatre Anthropology." *The Secret Art of the Performer*, Eugenio Barba and Nicola Savarese, eds: 8–9. London: Routledge, 1991.

Bhabha, Homi. "Of Mimicry and Man." *The Performance Studies Reader*, Henry Bial, ed.: 279–86. London and New York: Routledge, 2004.

Gómez-Peña, Guillermo. "The New Global Culture." *TDR: The Drama Review* 45, 1 (T169) (2001): 7–17, 23–30.

Marlin, Robert O. IV, commentator. *What Does Al-Qaeda Want?* Berkeley, Calif.: North Atlantic Books, 2004: 1–17, 44–47, 56–74.

Pavis, Patrice. "Introduction." *The Intercultural Performance Reader*: 1–21. London and New York: Routledge, 1996.

Riverbend. *Baghdad Burning*. New York: The Feminist Press at the City University of New York, 2005. Read any 50 pages from this book of a blog.

Turner, Victor, with Edie Turner. "Performing Ethnography." *The Performance Studies Reader*, Henry Bial, ed.: 265–78. London and New York: Routledge, 2004.

REFERENCES

Aeschylus. *Aeschylus*, vols 1 and 2. Chicago, Ill.: University of Chicago Press, 1953-56.

——. *Aeschylus II: The Suppliant Maidens*; *The Persians*; *Seven Against Thebes*; *Prometheus Bound*. Chicago, Ill.: University of Chicago Press, 1991.

Adorno, Theodor. *Prisms*. London: Spearman, 1967.

——. *Dialectic of Enlightenment* (with Max Horkheimer). New York: Herder & Herder, 1972.

——. *The Philosophy of Modern Music*. New York: Seabury Press, 1973.

——. *The Authoritarian Personality*. New York: Norton, 1982.

Alland, Alexander. "The Roots of Art." *Ritual, Play, and Performance*. Richard Schechner and Mady Schuman, eds. New York: Seabury Press, 1976.

Allen, James. *Without Sanctuary: Lynching Photography in America*. Santa Fe, N. Mex.: Twin Palms, 2000.

Amalarius. *Amalarii Episcopi Opera Liturgica Omnia*. Studi e Testi, 138–40. Città del Vaticano: Biblioteca Apostolica Vaticana, 1948–50.

Ancelet, B. J. "Falling apart to stay together: deep play in the Grand Marais Mardi Gras." *Journal of American Folklore* 114, 452 (2001).

Anderson, Laurie. *United States*. New York: Harper & Row, 1984.

——. *Strange Angels* (sound disk). Burbank, Calif.: Warner Bros. Records, 1989.

——. *Life on a String* (sound disk). New York: Nonesuch, 2001.

Anisimov, A. F. "The Shaman's Tent of the Evenks and the Origin of the Shamanic Rite." *Studies in Siberian Shamanism*, Henry N. Michael, ed.: 84–123. Toronto: University of Toronto Press, 1963.

Anonymous. *Complete Rules of Etiquette and Usages of Society*. New York: Dick & Fitzgerald, 1860.

Anonymous. "Handbook of Appellate Advocacy of the UCLA Law School." nd.

Appia, Adolphe. *Adolphe Appia: Texts on Theatre*. London and New York: Routledge, 1993.

Aristotle. *The Poetics of Aristotle*. Chapel Hill, NC: University of North Carolina Press, 1987.

Artaud, Antonin. *The Theater and Its Double*. New York: Grove Press, 1958.

Associated Press. "NYC Names Decency Panel." 4 April 2001.

Auslander, Philip. *Liveness*. London and New York: Routledge, 1999.

Austin, J. L. *How to Do Things with Words*. Cambridge, Mass.: Harvard University Press, 1962.

——. "Pretending." *Philosophical Papers*. Oxford: Oxford University Press, 1979.

——. "*How to Do Things with Words*: Lecture II." *The Performance Studies Reader*, Henry Bial, ed.: 147–53. London and New York: Routledge, 2004.

Bakhtin, Mikhail. *Rabelais and His World*. Cambridge, Mass.: MIT Press, 1968.

——. *The Dialogic Imagination: Four Essays*. Austin, Tex.: University of Texas Press, 1981.

Banes, Sally. *Terpsichore in Sneakers: Post-Modern Dance*. Boston, Mass.: Houghton Mifflin, 1980.

Barba, Eugenio. *The Paper Canoe*. London and New York: Routledge, 1995.

——. "The Deep Order Called Turbulence: The Three Faces of Dramaturgy." *The Performance Studies Reader*, Henry Bial, ed.: 252–61. London and New York: Routledge, 2004.

Barba, Eugenio and Nicola Savarese. *A Dictionary of Theatre Anthropology: The Secret Art of the Performer*. London: Published for the Centre for Performance Research by Routledge, 1991.

Barba, Eugenio and Ferdinando Taviani. *The Floating Islands*. Gråsten: Drama, 1979.

——. *Beyond the Floating Islands*. New York: PAJ Publications, 1986.

Bateson, Gregory. *Naven*. Cambridge: Cambridge University Press, 1936.

——. *Trance and Dance in Bali* (film with Margaret Mead and Jane Belo). New York: NYU Film Library, 1951.

——. *Steps to an Ecology of Mind*. New York: Ballantine Books, 1972.

——. *Mind and Nature*. New York: Dutton, 1979.

——. "A Theory of Play and Fantasy." *The Performance Studies Reader*, Henry Bial, ed.: 121–31. London and New York: Routledge, 2004.

Baudrillard, Jean. *Simulations.* New York: Semiotext(e), 1983.

——. *The Illusion of the End.* Stanford, Calif.: Stanford University Press, 1994.

——. *Selected Writings.* Cambridge: Polity, 2001.

Beauvoir, Simone de. *The Second Sex.* New York: Knopf, 1953.

——. *The Mandarins.* Cleveland, Ohio: Meridian Books, 1960.

——. *Force of Circumstance.* New York: Putnam, 1965.

Beckett, Samuel. *Waiting for Godot.* New York: Grove Press, 1954.

——. *Endgame and Act Without Words.* New York: Grove Press, 1958.

——. *Happy Days.* New York: Grove Press, 1961.

Bell, Catherine. *Ritual Theory, Ritual Practice.* New York: Oxford University Press, 1992.

——. "Performance and Other Analogies." *The Performance Studies Reader*, Henry Bial, ed.: 88–96. London and New York: Routledge, 2004.

Bell, John. "Performance Studies in an Age of Terror." *TDR* 47, 2 (2003): 6–9.

Belo, Jane. *Trance in Bali.* New York: Columbia University Press, 1960.

——. *Traditional Balinese Culture Essays.* New York: Columbia Universty Press, 1970.

——. *Bali: Rangda and Barong.* New York: AMS Press, 1986.

Benjamin, Walter. *Illuminations.* New York: Harcourt, Brace, and World, 1968.

——. *Understanding Brecht.* London: NLB, 1973.

——. *Reflections: Essays, Aphorisms, Autobiographical Writing.* New York: Schocken Books, 1986.

Bentham, Jeremy. *Panoptican Writings*, London: Verso, 1995.

——. *An Introduction to the Principles of Morals and Legislation.* Oxford: Oxford University Press, 1996.

Berger, Maurice. "The Critique of Pure Racism: An Interview With Adrian Piper." *Afterimage* 18, no. 3 (1990).

Bhabha, Homi K., ed. *Nation and Narration.* London and New York: Routledge, 1990.

——. *The Location of Culture.* London and New York: Routledge, 1994.

——. "Of Mimicry and Man." *The Performance Studies Reader*, Henry Bial, ed: 279–86. London and New York: Routledge, 2004.

——. *Edward Said: Continuing the Conversation.* With W.J.T. Mitchell, co-editor. Chicago, Ill.: University of Chicago Press, 2005.

Bharata. *The Natyasastra.* New Delhi: Munshiram Manoharlal Publishers, 1996.

Bharucha, Rustom. *Theatre and the World: Performance and the Politics of Culture.* London and New York: Routledge, 1993.

——. "Somebody's Other: Disorientations in the Cultural Politics of Our Times." *The Intercultural Performance Reader*, Patrice Pavis, ed.: 196–212. London and New York: Routledge, 1996.

——. "Negotiating the 'River': Intercultural Interactions and Interventions." *TDR* 41, 3 (1997): 31–38.

Bial, Henry, ed. *The Performance Studies Reader.* London and New York: Routledge, 2004.

Birdwhistell, Ray L. "Graceful Behavior". *Transactions of the Conference on Group Process of 1957*, B. Schaffner, ed.: 101–2. New York: Josiah Macy, Jr. Foundation, 1959.

——. *Kinesics and Context: Essays on Body Motion Communication.* Philadelphia, Pa.: University of Pennsylvania Press, 1970.

Birnbaum, Cara. "How to Wow Anyone You Meet." *Cosmopolitan*, June 2001.

Blair, Rhonda. "Reconsidering Stanislavsky: Feeling, Feminism, and the Actor." *Theatre Topics* 12, 2 (2002): 177–90.

Blau, Herbert. "Thinking History, History Thinking," *Theatre Survey* 45, 2 (2004): 257.

Boal, Augusto. *Theatre of the Oppressed.* New York: Theatre Communications Group, 1985.

——. *Games for Actors and Non-Actors.* London and New York: Routledge, 1992.

——. *Legislative Theatre: Using Performance to Make Politics.* London and New York: Routledge, 1998.

——. *Hamlet and the Baker's Son: My Life in Theatre and Politics.* London and New York: Routledge, 2001.

Bourdieu, Pierre. *Outline of a Theory of Practice.* Cambridge: Cambridge University Press, 1977.

——. *Practical Reason: On the Theory of Action.* Stanford: Stanford University Press, 1998.

——. *Masculine Domination.* Stanford: Stanford University Press, 2001.

Brazell, Karen and James T. Araki. *Traditional Japanese Theater: An Anthology of Plays.* New York: Columbia University Press, 1998.

Brecht, Bertolt. *Brecht on Theatre.* New York: Hill & Wang, 1964.

——. *Plays.* London: Methuen, 1987.

——. *The Rise and Fall of the City of Mahagonny*; and, *The Seven Deadly Sins of the Petty Bourgeoisie.* New York: Arcade Publishing, 1996.

——. "A Dialogue about Acting." *The Performance Studies

Reader, Henry Bial, ed.: 185–88. London and New York: Routledge, 2004.

Brentano, Robyn. "Outside the Frame: Performance, Art, and Life." *Outside the Frame: Performance and the Object: A Survey History of Performance Art in the USA Since 1950*. Robyn Brentano ed.: 31–61. Cleveland, Ohio: Cleveland Center for Contemporary Art, 1994.

Breucer, Lee. *Animations: A trilogy for Mabou Mines*. New York: Performing Arts Journal Publications, 1979.

——. *The Gospel at Colonus*. New York: Theatre Communications Group, 1989.

Brissett, Dennis and Charles Edgley. "The Dramaturgical Perspective." *Life as Theater: A Dramaturgical Sourcebook*, Dennis Brissett and Charles Edgley, eds.: 1–46. New York: Aldine de Gruyter, 1990.

Brook, Peter. *The Empty Space*. London: MacGibbon & Kee, 1968.

——. *The Shifting Point: 1946–1987*. New York: Harper & Row, 1987.

——. *The Open Door*. New York: Theatre Communications Group, 1995.

——. *Threads of Time*. Washington, DC: Counterpoint, 1998.

Brown, Patricia Leigh. "This Is Extremely Sporting." *The New York Times*, 13 August 2000. Section 4: Week in Review: 2.

Buber, Martin. *Eclipse of God: Studies in the Relation between Religion and Philosophy*. New York: Harper, 1952.

——. *I and Thou*. New York: Scribner, 1958.

——. *The Origin and Meaning of Hasidism*. New York: Horizon Press, 1960.

Burghardt, Gordon M. *Foundations of Comparative Ethology*. New York: Van Nostrand Reinhold, 1985.

——. *The Cognitive Animal*. Cambride, Mass.: MIT Press, 2002.

——. *The Genesis of Animal Play*. Cambridge, Mass.: MIT Press, 2005.

Burnham, Linda Frye. "An Unclassified Number" (an interview with John Fleck). *TDR* 35, 3 (1991): 192–98.

Burns, Elizabeth. *Theatricality: A Study of Convention in the Theatre and in Social Life*. London: Longman, 1972.

Butler, Judith. "Performative Acts and Gender Constitution: An Essay in Phenomenology and Feminist Criticism." *Theatre Journal* 40, no. 4 (1988): 519–31.

——. *Gender Trouble*. New York: Routledge, 1990.

——. "Imitation and Gender Insubordination." *Inside/Out Lesbian Theories, Gay Theories*, Diana Fuss, ed. New York: Routledge, 1991: 13–31.

——. *Bodies That Matter*. New York: Routledge, 1993.

——. *Excitable Speech*. New York: Routledge, 1997.

——. "Performative Acts and Gender Constitution: An Essay in Phenomenology and Feminist Theory." *The Performance Studies Reader*, Henry Bial, ed.: 154–66. London and New York: Routledge, 2004.

Butt, Gavin. "The Paradoxes of Criticism." *After Criticism*. Gavin Butt, ed.: 1–19. Malden, Mass.: Blackwell Publishing, 2005.

Byron, George Gordon. *The Major Works*. Oxford and New York: Oxford University Press, 2000.

Cage, John. *Silence: Lectures and Writings*. Middletown, Conn.: Wesleyan University Press, 1961.

——. *A Year From Monday; New Lectures and Writings*. Middletown, Conn.: Wesleyan University Press, 1967.

Caillois, Roger. *Man, Play, and Games*. New York: Schocken Books, 1979.

Calderón de la Barca, Pedro. *Six Plays*. New York: Las Americas Publishing Co., 1961.

——. *Eight Dramas of Calderón*. Urbana, Ill.: University of Illinois Press, 2000.

——. *Life's a Dream*. Boulder, Co: University Press of Colorado, 2004.

Calvin, Jean. *Institutes of the Christian Religion*. Chicago, Ill.: Encyclopedia Britannica, 1990.

Carlson, Marvin. *Theatre Semiotics: Signs of Life*. Bloomington, Ind.: Indiana University Press, 1990.

——. "Brook and Mnouchkine: Passages to India?" *The Intercultural Performance Reader*. Patrice Pavis, ed.: 79–92. London and New York: Routledge, 1996.

——. *Performance: A Critical Introduction*. London and New York: Routledge, 1996, 2nd edn, 2004.

——. "What Is Performance?" *The Performance Studies Reader*, Henry Bial, ed.: 68–73. London and New York: Routledge, 2004.

Carroll, Noel. "Performance." *Formations* 3, no. 1 (1986): 63–81.

Carse, James P. *Death and Existence: A Conceptual History of Human Mortality*. New York: Wiley, 1980.

——. *Finite and Infinite Games*. New York: Free Press, 1986.

——. *Breakfast at the Victory: The Mysticism of Ordinary Experience*. San Francisco, Calif.: Harpers, 1994.

Certeau, Michel de. *The Practice of Everyday Life*. Berkeley, Calif.: University of California Press, 1984.

Chaikin, Joseph. *The Presence of the Actor*. New York: Atheneum, 1972.

Chaucer, Geoffrey. *The Canterbury Tales*. New York: Modern Library, 1994.

Chin, Daryl. "Interculturalism, Postmodernism, Pluralism."

Interculturalism and Performance, Bonnie Marranca, and Gautam Dasgupta, eds: 83–95. New York: PAJ Publications, 1991.

Chute, Marchette Gaylord. *Shakespeare of London*. New York: Dutton, 1949.

Cibber, Colley. *A Critical Edition of An Apology for the Life of Mr. Colley Cibber, Comedian*. New York: Garland Publishing, [1740] 1987.

Claudel, Paul. *The Tidings Brought to Mary*. New Haven, Conn.: Yale University Press, 1916.

——. *The Satin Slipper*. New York: Sheed and Ward, 1945.

Clurman, Harold. *On Directing*. New York: Macmillan, 1972.

Cochran, Johnnie L., with Tim Rutten. *Journey to Justice*. New York: Ballantine Books, 1996.

——, with David Fisher. *A Lawyer's Life*. New York: Thomas Dunne Books/St. Martin's Press, 2002.

Colborn-Roxworthy, Emily. "Role-Playing Training at a 'Violent Disneyland': The FBI Academy's Performance Paradigms." *TDR* 48, 4 (2004): 81–108.

Conquergood, Dwight. "Rethinking Ethnography: Towards a Critical Cultural Politics." *Communications Monographs* 58, June (1991): 179–94.

——. "Performance Studies: Interdisciplinary Interventions and Radical Research." *TDR* 46, 2 (2002): 145–56.

Cornford, Francis Macdonald. *The Origin of Attic Comedy*. London: E. Arnold, 1914.

Covarrubias, Miguel. *Island of Bali*. Kuala Lumpur: Oxford University Press, 1972 [1937].

Craig, Edward Gordon. *The Theatre–Advancing*. Boston, Mass.: Little, Brown, & Company, 1919.

——. *On the Art of the Theatre*. New York: Theatre Arts Books, 1956.

Critical Art Ensemble. "Recombinant Theatre and Digital Resistance." *TDR* 44, 4 (2000): 151–66.

Crommelynck, Fernand. *The Theater of Fernand Crommelynck: Eight Plays*. Selinsgrove, Pa. and London: Associated University Presses, 1998.

Csikszentmihalyi, Mihaly. *Beyond Boredom and Anxiety*. San Francisco, Calif.: Jossey-Bass, 1975.

——. *Flow: the Psychology of Optimal Experience*. New York: Harper & Row, 1990.

——. *Creativity: Flow and the Psychology of Discovery and Invention*. New York: HarperCollins, 1996.

——. *Good Business Leadership, Flow, and the Making of Meaning*. New York: Viking, 2003.

Danner, Mark. "Taking Stock of the Forever War." *The New York Times Magazine*, 11 September 2005: 44–53, 68, 86–87.

D'Aquili, Eugene G., Charles D. Laughlin Jr., and John McManus. *The Spectrum of Ritual*. New York: Columbia University Press, 1979.

Darwin, Charles. *The Origin of Species by Means of Natural Selection*. New York: Modern Library, 1998.

——. *The Expression of the Emotions in Man and Animals*. New York: Oxford University Press, 1998.

Dasgupta, Gautam. "The Mahabharata: Brook's Orientalism." *Interculturalism and Performance*, Bonnie Marranca and Gautam Dasgupta, eds: 75–82. New York: PAJ Publications, 1991.

De Marinis, Marco. *The Semiotics of Performance*. Bloomington, Ind.: Indiana University Press, 1993.

——. "The Performance Text." *The Performance Studies Reader*, Henry Bial, ed.: 232–51. London and New York: Routledge, 2004.

Debord, Guy. *The Society of the Spectacle*. New York: Zone Books, 1994.

Deleuze, Gilles and Félix Guattari. *Anti-Oedipus: Capitalism and Schizophrenia*. New York: Viking Press, 1977.

——. *A Thousand Plateaus: Capitalism and Schizophrenia*. Minneapolis, Minn.: University of Minnesota Press, 1987.

Deren, Maya. *Divine Horsemen: The Living Gods of Haiti*. London and New York: Thames & Hudson, 1953.

Derrida, Jacques. *Of Grammatology*. Baltimore, Md.: Johns Hopkins University Press, 1976.

——. *Writing and Difference*. Chicago, Ill.: University of Chicago Press, 1978.

——. "Signature, Event, Context" (excerpt). *Margins of Philosophy*, Alan Bass, tr.: 325–27. Chicago, Ill.: University of Chicago Press, 1982.

——. *Limited Inc*. Evanston, Ill.: Northwestern University Press, 1988.

——. *The Derrida Reader: Writing Performances*. Lincoln, Nebr.: University of Nebraska Press, 1998.

——. *Who's Afraid of Philosophy?* Stanford, Calif.: Stanford University Press, 2002.

——, with Peter Dreyer. *On Touching*. Stanford, Calif.: Stanford University Press, 2005.

Drewal, Henry John. "Performing the Other: Mami Wata Worship in Africa." *TDR* 32, 2 (1988): 160–85.

Drewal, Margaret. *Yoruba Ritual*. Bloomington, Ind.: Indiana University Press, 1992.

DuPlessis, Rachel Blau and Ann Snitow, eds. *The Feminist Memoir Project*. New York: Three Rivers Press, 1998.

Durkheim, Émile. *The Elementary Forms of the Religious Life*. New York: Free Press, 1965.

Durland, Steve. "An Anarchic, Subversive, Erotic Soul"

(an interview with Tim Miller). *TDR* 35, 3 (1991): 171–78.

Ehrmann, Jacques. "Introduction." *Yale French Studies*, no. 36–37 (1966): 5–9.

Eibl-Eibesfeldt, Irenäus. *Ethology, the Biology of Behavior*. New York: Holt, Rinehart & Winston, 1970.

Einstein, Albert, Max Born, and Hedwig Born. *The Born–Einstein Letters 1916–1955*. London: Macmillan, 1971.

Eisenhower, Dwight D. "Farewell Address to the American People." *Public Papers of the Presidents of the United States, Dwight D. Eisenhower 1960–61*: 1035–40. Washington, DC: Government Printing Office, 1999.

Ekman, Paul. *Emotion in the Human Face*. Cambridge: Cambridge University Press, 1982.

——. "Autonomic Nervous System Activity Distinguishes among Emotions." *Science* 221 (1983): 1208–10.

——. *Telling Lies: Clues to Deceit in the Marketplace, Politics, and Marriage*. New York: Norton, 1985.

——. *Emotions Revealed.* New York: Times Books, 2003.

Ekman, Paul, and Richard J. Davidson. *The Nature of Emotion*. New York: Oxford University Press, 1994.

Ekman, Paul, and Wallace V. Friesen. *Unmasking the Face: A Guide to Recognizing Emotions From Facial Clues*. Englewood Cliffs, NJ: Prentice-Hall, 1975.

Ekman, Paul, and Erika L. Rosenberg. *What the Face Reveals.* Oxford: Oxford University Press, 2005.

Emigh, John. *Masked Performance: The Play of Self and Other in Ritual and Theatre*. Philadelphia, Pa.: University of Pennsylvania Press, 1996.

Euripides. *Euripides*, vols 1, 3, 5. Chicago, Ill.: University of Chicago Press, 1955–59.

Evreinoff, Nicholas. "The Never Ending Show." *Life As Theater*, Dennis Brissett and Charles Edgley eds.: 419–23. New York: Aldine de Gruyter, 1990.

Faber, Alyda. "Saint Orlan: Ritual as Violent Spectacle and Cultural Criticism." *The Performance Studies Reader*, Henry Bial, ed.: 108–14. London and New York: Routledge, 2004.

Fabian, Johannes. "Theatre and Anthropology, Theatricality and Culture." *The Performance Studies Reader*, Henry Bial, ed.: 175–82. London and New York: Routledge, 2004.

Fanon, Frantz. *The Wretched of the Earth*. New York: Grove Press, 1965.

——. *Black Skin, White Masks*. New York: Grove Press, 1967.

Finley, Karen. *A Different Kind of Intimacy.* New York: Thunder's Mouth Press, 2000.

Fischer, Roland. "A Cartography of the Ecstatic and Meditative States." *Science* 174 (1971): 897–904.

Fleck, John. "BLESSED Are All the *Little* FISHES." *TDR* 35, 3 (1991): 179–91.

Fo, Dario. *We Won't Pay! We Won't Pay!: A Political Farce*. North American version. New York: Samuel French, 1984.

——. *Plays*. London: Methuen, 1997.

——. *The Pope and the Witch*. London and New York: Samuel French, 1997.

Foreman, Richard. *Plays and Manifestos*. New York: New York Univesity Press, 1976.

——. *Unbalancing Acts*. New York: Pantheon Books, 1992.

——. "Program Notes for *Pearls for Pigs*." *TDR* 42, 2 (1998): 157–59.

——. *Paradise Hotel*. Woodstock, NY: Overlook Press, 2001.

Foster, Susan Leigh. *Reading Dancing: Bodies and Subjects in Contemporary American Dance*. Berkeley, Calif.: University of California Press, 1986.

——. *Choreographing History*. Bloomington, Ind.: Indiana University Press, 1995.

——. *Corporealities: Dancing, Knowledge, Culture, and Power*. London and New York: Routledge, 1996.

——, with Sue-Ellen Case and Philip Brett. *Decomposition: Post-Disciplinary Performance*. Bloomington, Ind.: Indiana University Press, 2000.

——. *Dances that Describe Themselves: The Improvised Choreography of Richard Bull.* Middletown, Conn.: Wesleyan University Press, 2002.

Foucault, Michel. *Madness and Civilization: A History of Insanity in the Age of Reason*. New York: Pantheon Books, 1965.

——. *The Order of Things*. London: Tavistock Publications, 1970.

——. *The Archeology of Knowledge*. New York: Random House, 1972.

——. *Discipline and Punish: The Birth of the Prison*. London: Allen Lane, 1977.

——. *The History of Sexuality*. New York: Pantheon Books, 1978.

Friedman, Thomas L. *The Lexus and the Olive Tree*. New York: Anchor Books, 2000.

——. *The World Is Flat*. New York: Farrar, Straus, & Giroux, 2005.

Fusco, Coco. *English Is Broken Here: Notes on Cultural Fusion in the Americas*. New York: The New Press, 1995.

——. *Corpus Delecti: Performance Art of the Americas*. London and New York: Routledge, 2000.

——. *The Bodies That Were Not Ours.* London and New York: Routledge, 2001.

Fusco, Coco and Brian Wallis. *Only Skin Deep: Changing*

Visions of the American Self. New York: International Center of Photography with Harry N. Abrams.

Gabler, Neal. "This Time, The Scene Was Real." *The New York Times*, 16 September 2001, News of the Week in Review. Op-Ed, electronic archive.

——. "Life the Movie." *The Performance Studies Reader*, Henry Bial, ed.: 74–75. London and New York: Routledge, 2004.

Gandhi, Mohandas. *Autobiography: The Story of My Experiments With Truth*. Washington, DC: Public Affairs Press, 1954.

Geertz, Clifford. *The Interpretation of Cultures*. New York: Basic Books, 1973.

——. *Negara: The Theatre State in Nineteenth-Century Bali*. Princeton, NJ: Princeton University Press, 1980.

——. *Local Knowledge*. New York: Basic Books, 1983.

——. *Available Light: Anthropological Reflections on Philosophical Topics*. Princeton: Princeton University Press, 2000.

——. "Blurred Genres: The Refiguration of Social Thought." *The Performance Studies Reader*, Henry Bial, ed.: 64–67. London and New York: Routledge, 2004.

Genet, Jean. *Our Lady of the Flowers*. Paris: Morihien, 1949.

——. *The Maids and Deathwatch*. New York: Grove Press, 1954.

——. *The Balcony*. New York: Grove Press, 1958.

——. *The Thief's Journal*. Paris: Olympia Press, 1959.

——. *The Blacks*. New York: Grove Press, 1960.

——. *The Screens*. New York: Grove Press, 1962.

Gennep, Arnold van. *The Rites of Passage*. Chicago, Ill.: University of Chicago Press, 1960.

Goethe, Johann Wolfgang von. *Goethe's Collected Works*. Cambridge, Mass.: Suhrkamp/Insel Publishers, 1983–89.

Goffman, Erving. *The Presentation of Self in Everyday Life*. Garden City, NY: Doubleday, 1959.

——. *Behavior in Public Places*. New York: Free Press, 1963.

——. *Interaction Ritual*. Chicago, Ill.: Aldine, 1967.

——. *Frame Analysis*. Cambridge, Mass.: Harvard University Press, 1974.

——. "Performances: Belief in the Part One Is Playing." *The Performance Studies Reader*, Henry Bial, ed.: 59–63. London and New York: Routledge, 2004.

Golub, Spencer. *Evreinov, The Theatre of Paradox and Transformation*. Ann Arbor, Mich.: UMI Research Press, 1984.

Golding, William. *Lord of the Flies*. London: Faber & Faber, 1954.

Gómez-Peña, Guillermo. *Warrior for Gringostroika*. St. Paul, Minn.: Graywolf Press, 1993.

——. *The New World Border*. San Francisco, Calif.: City Lights Books, 1996.

——. *Dangerous Border Crossers: The Artist Talks Back*. London and New York: Routledge, 2000.

——, with Enrique Chagoya and Felicia Rice. *Codex Espangliensis: From Columbus to the Border Patrol*. San Francisco, Calif.: City Lights Books, 2000.

——. "The New Global Culture." *TDR* 45, 1 (2001): 7–30.

——, with Elaine Peña. *Ethno-Techno: Writings on Performance, Activism, and Pedagogy*. London and New York: Routledge, 2005.

Goodall, Jane. *In the Shadow of Man*. Boston, Mass.: Houghton Mifflin, 1971.

——. *The Chimpanzees of Gombe*. Cambridge, Mass.: Belknap Press of Harvard University Press, 1986.

Goodall, Jane with Dale Peterson. *Visions of Caliban: On Chimpanzees and People*. Athens, Ga.: University of Georgia Press, 2000.

Gould, Richard A. *Yiwara: Foragers of the Australian Desert*. New York: Scribner, 1969.

Gray, Spalding. *Swimming to Cambodia*. New York: Theatre Communications Group, 1985.

——. *Sex and Death to the Age of 14*. New York: Vintage Books, 1986.

——. *Gray's Anatomy*. New York: Vintage Books, 1994.

——. *Morning, Noon, and Night*. New York: Farrar, Straus, & Giroux, 1999.

——. *Life Interrupted*. New York: Crown Publishers, 2005.

Grimes, Ronald L. *Readings in Ritual Studies*. Upper Saddle River, NJ: Prentice Hall, 1996.

Grotowski, Jerzy. *Towards a Poor Theatre*. London and New York: Routledge, 2002.

——. "Performer." *The Grotowski Sourcebook*, Lisa Wolford and Richard Schechner, eds.: 376–80. London and New York: Routledge, 1997.

——. "The Actor's Technique." *The Performance Studies Reader*, Henry Bial, ed.: 189–94. London and New York: Routledge, 2004.

Habermas, Jürgen. *Theory and Practice*. London: Heinemann, 1974.

——. *The Theory of Communicative Action*. Boston, Mass.: Beacon Press, 1984–87.

——. *The Future of Human Nature*. Cambridge: Polity, 2003.

——, with Jacques Derrida and Giovanna Borradori. *Philosophy in a Time of Terror*. Chicago, Ill.: University of Chicago Press, 2003.

Hafner, Kate. "A Beautiful Life, an Early Death, a Fraud

Exposed." *The New York Times*, 31 May 2001, sec. Circuits.

Hallett, Garth and Ludwig Wittgenstein. *A Companion to Wittgenstein's "Philosophical Investigations"*. Ithaca, NY: Cornell University Press, 1977.

Halprin, Anna. *Moving Toward Life*. Middletown, Conn.: Wesleyan University Press, 1995.

Halprin, Anna and Seigmar Gerken. *Returning to Health with Dance, Movement, and Imagery*. Mendocino, Calif.: Life Rhythm Books, 2002.

Halprin, Lawrence. *Cities*. New York: Reinhold Publishing Corporation, 1963.

——. *Notebooks 1959–71*. Cambridge, Mass.: MIT Press, 1972.

—— with Donelyn Lyndon, James Alinder, and Donald Canty. *Sea Ranch*. New York: Princeton Architectural Press, 2004.

Halprin, Lawrence and Jim Burns. *Taking Part: A Workshop Approach to Collective Creativity*. Cambridge, Mass.: MIT Press, 1974.

Hamisi, Katuka Ole Maimai. "Western Paparazzi in the Maasai Region." http://maasai-infoline.org/index.html, 2001.

Handelman, Don. "Rethinking 'Banana Time'." *Urban Life* 4, no. 4 (1976): 33–48.

——. "Play and Ritual: Complementary Frames of Metacommunication." *International Conference on Humour and Laughter: It's a Funny Thing, Humour*, Antony J. Chapman and Hugh Foot, eds: 185–92. Oxford and New York: Pergamon Press, 1977.

Handelman, Don and David Shulman. *God Inside Out: Siva's Game of Dice*. New York: Oxford University Press, 1997.

Hanisch, Carol. "The Personal Is Political." *Feminist Revolution*, Kathie Sarachild, ed.: 204–05. New York: Random House, 1978.

——. *Frankly Feminist*. Port Ewan, NY: Truthtellers, 1997.

——. "Two Letters from the Women's Liberation Movement." *The Feminist Memory Project: Voices from Women's Liberation*, Rachel Blau Duplessis and Ann Snitow, eds: 197–207. New York: Three Rivers Press, 1998.

Harbinger, Richard. "Trial by Drama." *Judicature* 55, no. 3 (1971): 122–28.

Harding, Frances. "Presenting and Re-presenting the Self: From Not-Acting to Acting in African Performance." *The Performance Studies Reader*, Henry Bial, ed.: 197–214. London and New York: Routledge, 2004.

Hardison, O. B. *Christian Rite and Christian Drama in the Middle Ages*. Baltimore, Md.: Johns Hopkins University Press, 1965.

Harrison, Jane Ellen. *Themis: A Study of the Social Origins of Greek Religion*. Cambridge: Cambridge University Press, 1912.

——. *Ancient Art and Ritual*. London: Williams & Norgate, 1913.

Havel, Vaclav. *Selected Plays 1963–83*. London: Faber & Faber, 1992.

——. *Selected Plays 1984–87*. London: Faber & Faber, 1994.

Hein, Norvin. *The Miracle Plays of Mathura*. New Haven, Conn.: Yale University Press, 1972.

Heisenberg, Werner. *Physics and Philosophy: The Revolution in Modern Science*. New York: Harper, 1958.

Heraclitus. *Fragments: The Collected Wisdom of Heraclitus*. New York: Viking, 2001.

Herrick, Robert. *Poetical Works*. Oxford: Clarendon Press, 1956.

Hess, Linda. "Ram Lila: The Audience Experience." *Bhakti in Current Research, 1979–1982*, Monika Thiel-Horstmann, ed. Berlin: D. Reimer Verlag, 1983.

Hitler, Adolf. *Mein Kampf*. Boston, Mass.: Houghton Mifflin, 2001.

Hobsbawm, E. J. and T. O. Ranger. *The Invention of Tradition*. Cambridge: Cambridge University Press, 1983.

Homer. *The Iliad* and *The Odyssey*. Chicago, Ill.: Encyclopedia Britannica, 1990.

Hooks, Bell. *Yearning: Race, Gender, and Cultural Politics*. Boston, Mass.: South End Press, 1990.

Horace. *The Art of Poetry*. Albany, NY: State University of New York Press, 1974.

Horkheimer, Max. *Eclipse of Reason*. New York: Oxford University Press, 1947.

——. *Critical Theory: Selected Essays*. New York: Herder & Herder, 1972.

——, with Theodor Adorno. *Dialectic of Enlightenment*. New York: Herder & Herder, 1972.

——. *Between Philosophy and Social Science*. Cambridge, Mass.: MIT Press, 1993.

Hughes, Holly. "The Lady Dick." *TDR* 35, 3 (1991): 199–215.

—— and David Roman, eds. *O Solo Homo: The New Queer Performance*. New York: Grove Press, 1998.

Huizinga, Johan. *Homo Ludens*. New York: Harper, 1970.

——. "The Nature and Significance of Play as a Cultural Phenomenon." *The Performance Studies Reader*, Henry Bial, ed.: 117–20. London and New York: Routledge, 2004.

Huntsman, Jeffrey F. "Native American Theatre." *American Indian Performance: A Reader*. Hanay Geiogamah and Jaye T. Darby, eds: 81–113. Los Angeles, Calif.: UCLA American Indian Studies Center, 2000.

Hurston, Zora Neal. *Mules and Men*. New York: Harper, 1990.

Hutcheon, Linda. *Narcissistic Narrative: The Metafictional Paradox*. Waterloo, Ont. Wilfrid Laurier University Press, 1980.

——. *A Theory of Parody*. New York: Methuen, 1985.

——. *A Poetics of Postmodernism*. London and New York: Routledge, 1988.

——. *The Politics of Postmodernism*. London and New York: Routledge, 2002.

Huxley, Julian. *Evolution, the Modern Synthesis*. London: Allen & Unwin, 1942.

——. *Essays of a Humanist*. New York: Harper & Row, 1964.

Ibsen, Henrik. *The Complete Major Prose Plays*. New York: New American Library, 1978.

Jackson, Shannon. "Professing Performance: Disciplinary Genealogies." *The Performance Studies Reader*, Henry Bial, ed.: 32–42. London and New York: Routledge, 2004.

Jakobson, Roman. *Fundamentals of Language*. Linguarum, No. 1: Gravenhage: Mouton, 1956.

——. *Studies in Verbal Art*. Ann Arbor, Mich.: Dept. of Slavic Languages and Literature, University of Michigan, 1971.

——. *Main Trends in the Science of Language*. London: Allen & Unwin, 1973.

Jameson, Fredric. *The Political Unconscious: Narrative As a Socially Symbolic Act*. Ithaca, NY: Cornell University Press, 1981.

——. *Postmodernism, Or, The Cultural Logic of Late Capitalism*. Durham, NC: Duke University Press, 1991.

——. *A Singular Modernity*. London and New York: Verso, 2002.

Jarry, Alfred. *The Ubu Plays*. London: Nick Hern Books, 1997.

Jenik, Adriene. "Desktop Theatre." *TDR* 45, 3 (2001): 95–112.

Jenkins, Henry. "The Poachers and the Stormtroopers." http://commons.somewhere.com/rre/1998/The.Poachers.and.the.Sto.html, 1998.

Jones, Amelia. *Body Art/Performing the Subject*. Minneapolis, Minn. and London: University of Minnesota Press, 1998.

Josephson, Michael S., Kenneth Klenberg, and Franklin Tom, eds. *Handbook of Appellate Advocacy*. Los Angeles, Calif.: UCLA Moot Court Honors Program, nd.

Joyce, James. *Finnegans Wake*. London: Faber & Faber, 1968.

——. *Ulysses*. New York: Random House. 2002.

Kant, Immanuel. *Critique of Pure Reason*. New York: Barnes and Noble Books, 2004.

——. *Critique of Practical Reason*. Mineola, NY: Dover Publications, 2004.

——. *Critique of Judgment*. New York: Barnes and Noble Books, 2005.

Kaprow, Allan. *Assemblage, Environments, and Happenings*. New York: H. N. Abrams, 1966.

——. "The Real Experiment." *Artforum* XXII, no. 4 (1983): 36–43.

Kaprow, Allan and Jeff Kelley. *Essays on the Blurring of Art and Life*. Berkeley, Calif.: University of California Press, 2003.

——. *Childsplay: The Art of Allan Kaprow*. Berkeley, Calif.: University of California Press, 2004.

Kawai, Norie, Manabu Honda, Satoshi Nakamura, Purwa Samatra, Ketut Sukardika, Yoji Nakatani, Nobuhiro Shimojo and Tsutomu Oohashi. "Catecholamines and Opioid Peptides Increase in Plasma in Humans During Possession Trances." *Cognitive Neuroscience and Neuropsychology* vol. 12 no. 16, November (2001): 3419–23.

Kendall, Laurel. *Shamans, Housewives, and Other Restless Spirits: Women in Korean Ritual Life*. Honolulu, Hawaii: University of Hawaii Press, 1987.

Kirby, E. T. "The Shamanistic Origins of Popular Entertainments." *TDR* 18, 1 (1974): 5–15.

Kirby, Michael. *Happenings*. New York: Dutton, 1965.

——. *A Formalist Theatre*. Philadelphia, Pa.: University of Pennsylvania Press, 1987.

Kirshenblatt-Gimblett, Barbara. *Destination Culture*. Berkeley, Calif.: University of California Press, 1998.

——. "Performance Studies." *The Performance Studies Reader*, Henry Bial, ed.: 43–55. London and New York: Routledge, 2004.

——. "Playing to the Senses: Food as a Performance Medium." *Performance Research* 4, no. 1 (1999): 1–30.

Kolankiewicz, Leszek, ed. *On the Road to Active Culture*. Wroclaw: Instytut Laboratorium, 1978.

Kuczynski, Alex. "On CBS News, Some of What You See Isn't There." *The New York Times*, 12 January 2000, sec. Business: 1–4.

Kuo, Pao Kun. "Contemplating an Open Culture: Transcending Multiracialism." *Singapore Re-Engineering Success*, Arun Mahizhnan and Tsao Yuan Lee, eds: 50–61. Singapore: Oxford University Press, 1998.

La Barre, Weston. *The Ghost Dance: Origins of Religion*. New York: Dell, 1972.

Lacan, Jacques. *Écrits: A Selection*. London: Tavistock Publications, 1977.

——. *The Four Functions of Psychoanalysis*. New York: Norton, 1978.

Lacy, Suzanne. "Debated Territory: Toward a Critical Language for Public Art." *Mapping the Terrain: New Genre Public Art*, Suzanne Lacy, ed.: 171–85. Seattle, Wash.: Bay Press, 1995.

Lakoff, George. *Don't Think of an Elephant*. White River Junction, Vermont: Chelsea Green Publishing Company, 2004.

Langer, Susanne K. *Philosophy in a New Key*. Cambridge, Mass.: Harvard University Press, 1942.

——. *Feeling and Form: A Theory of Art*. New York: Scribner, 1953.

——. *Problems of Art*. New York: Scribner, 1957.

Lanham, Robert. "Wearing Nothing but Attitude." *The New York Times*, 1 May 2005, sec. Style: 15.

Latrell, Craig. "After Appropriation." *TDR* 44, 4 (2000): 44–55.

Lawrence, T. E. *Seven Pillars of Wisdom: A Triumph*. Garden City, NY: Doubleday, 1935.

Leach, Jerry W. and Gary Kildea. *Trobriand Cricket* (video). Port Moresby, Papua New Guinea: Office of Information, Government of Papua New Guinea, 1973.

Lee, Du-Hyun. "Korean Shamans: Role Playing Through Trance Possession." *By Means of Performance*, Richard Schechner and Willa Appel, eds: 149–66. Cambridge: Cambridge University Press, 1990.

Leffingwell, Edward, Carole Kismaric, and Marvin Heiferman, eds. *Flaming Creature Jack Smith, His Amazing Life and Times*. New York: Lookout Book/The Institute for Contemporary Art, 1997.

Lelyveld, Joseph. "Whether We Like It or Not, Detainees in the War on Terrorism Will Be Subjected to Lies, Threats, and Highly Coercive Force." *The New York Times Magazine*, 12 June 2005: 36–43, 60 ff.

Lemon, Ralph. "Director's Notes." Program for *Tree*, Yale Repertory Theatre (1999).

——. *Tree: Belief/Culture/Balance*. Middletown, Conn.: Wesleyan University Press, 2004.

Lepecki, André. "Skin, Body, and Presence in Contemporary European Choreography." *TDR* 43, 4 (1999): 128–40.

Lévi-Strauss, Claude. *Structural Anthropology*. New York: Basic Books, 1963.

——. *The Savage Mind*. Chicago, Ill.: University of Chicago Press, 1966.

——. *The Elementary Structures of Kinship*. Boston, Mass.: Beacon Press, 1969.

——. *The Raw and the Cooked*. New York: Harper & Row, 1969.

——. *Look, Listen, Read*. New York: Basic Books, 1997.

Lewis, I.M. *Ecstatic Religion: An Anthropological Study of Spirit Possession and Shamanism*. Harmondsworth: Penguin Books, 1971.

Lewis-Williams, David. *The Mind in the Cave*. London: Thames & Hudson, 2002.

Lippard, Lucy R. "Looking Around: Where We Are, Where We Could Be." *Mapping the Terrain: New Genre Public Art*, Suzanne Lacy, ed.: 114–30. Seattle, Wash.: Bay Press, 1995.

Liptak, Adam. "When Is a Fake too Real? It's Virtually Uncertain." *The New York Times*, 28 January 2001, sec. 4, Week in Review, Ideas & Trends: 3.

Loizos, Caroline. "Play Behaviour in Higher Primates: A Review." *Primate Ethology*, Desmond Morris, ed.: 226–82. Garden City, NY: Anchor Books, 1969.

Longman, Jere. "Someday Soon, Athletic Edge May Be from Altered Genes." *The New York Times*, 11 May 2001, SEL. A, D: 1, 5.

Lorca, Federico García. *Collected Plays*. London: Secker & Warburg, 1976.

Lorenz, Konrad. "The Role of Aggression in Group Formation." *Transactions of the Conference on Group Processes of 1957*, B. Schaffner, ed.: 202–03. New York: Josiah Macy, Jr. Foundation, 1959.

——. *On Aggression*. New York: Harcourt, Brace & World, 1966.

——. *The Foundations of Ethology*. New York: Springer-Verlag New York, 1981.

Lyall, Sarah. "A 'Swan Lake' with Male Swans Is a Hit in London," *New York Times*, C13 and C20, 8 October 1996.

Lyotard, Jean-François. *The Postmodern Condition: A Report on Knowledge*. Minneapolis, Minn.: University of Minnesota Press, 1984.

——. *The Differend: Phrases in Dispute*. Minneapolis, Minn.: University of Minnesota Press, 1988.

——. *Peregrinations: Law, Form, Event*. New York: Columbia University Press, 1988.

MacAloon, John J. *This Great Symbol: Pierre De Coubertin and the Origins of the Modern Olympic Games*. Chicago, Ill.: University of Chicago Press, 1981.

——. "Olympic Games and the Theory of Spectacle in Modern Societies." *Rite, Drama, Festival, Spectacle*, John J.

MacAloon, ed.: 241–80. Philadelphia, Pa.: Institute for the Study of Human Issues, 1984.

——. *Brides of Victory: Nationalism and Gender in Olympic Ritual*. Oxford: Berg Publishers, 1997.

Mamet, David. *American Buffalo*. New York: Grove Press, 1977.

——. *Glengarry Glen Ross: A Play*. New York: Grove Press, 1983.

——. *House of Games: A Screenplay*. New York: Grove Press, 1987.

——. *Oleanna*. New York: Pantheon Books, 1992.

——. *The Old Neighborhood: Three Plays*. New York: Vintage Books, 1998.

——. *The Spanish Prisoner and The Winslow Boy: Two Screenplays*. New York: Vintage Books, 1999.

——. *Romance*. New York: Vintage Books, 2005.

Mao Zedong (Tse-Tung). *Selected Works of Mao Tse-Tung*. New York: Pergamon Press, 1961.

——. *Mao Tse-Tung On Literature and Art*. Peking: Foreign Languages Press, 1967.

——. *Poems*. Peking: Foreign Languages Press, 1976.

——. *On Guerilla Warfare*. Urbana, Ill.: University of Illinois Press, 2000.

Marcuse, Herbert. *Eros and Civilization*. Boston, Mass.: Beacon Press, 1955.

——. *One Dimensional Man*. Boston, Mass.: Beacon Press, 1964.

——. *Negations: Essays in Critical Theory*. Boston, Mass.: Beacon Press, 1968.

——. *Towards a Critical Theory of Society*. London and New York: Routledge, 2001.

Marlin, Robert O. IV, commentator. *What Does Al-Qaeda Want?* Berkeley, Calif.: North Atlantic Books, 2004.

Marlowe, Christopher. *The Complete Works of Christopher Marlowe*. Cambridge: Cambridge University Press, 1973.

Marshall, Eliot. "DNA Studies Challenge the Meaning of Race." *Science* 282, no. 5389 (1998): 654–55.

Marshall Joshua Michah. "National Treasure." *The New Yorker*, 23 May 2005: 87–90.

Martin, Carol. "Lingering Heat and Local Global J Stuff," *TDR* 50, 1 (2006): 46–56.

Mason, Michael Atwood. "'The Blood that Runs Through the Veins': The Creation of Identity and a Client's Experience of Cuban-American *Santeria Dilogun* Divination." *The Performance Studies Reader*, Henry Bial, ed.: 97–107. London and New York: Routledge, 2004.

Maxwell, Ian. "Learning at the Department of Performance Studies." www.arts.usyd.edu.au/Arts/departs/perform/Learning%20at%20Perf%20Studies.html, 2005.

McGrath, John. "Trusting in Rubber: Performing Boundaries During the AIDS Epidemic." *TDR* 39, 2 (1995): 21–38.

McKenzie, Jon. *Perform Or Else: From Discipline to Performance*. London and New York: Routledge, 2001.

——. "The Liminal-Norm." *The Performance Studies Reader*, Henry Bial, ed.: 26–31. London and New York: Routledge, 2004.

McKinley, James C. Jr. "It Isn't Just a Game: Clues to Rooting." *The New York Times*, 11 August 2000, sec. Sports.

McLuhan, Marshall. *The Mechanical Bride*. New York: Vanguard Press, 1951.

——. *The Gutenberg Galaxy*. Toronto: University of Toronto Press, 1962.

——. *Understanding Media*. New York: McGraw-Hill, 1964.

——. *War and Peace in the Global Village*. New York: McGraw-Hill, 1968.

Mead, Margaret. *Coming of Age in Samoa*. New York: W. Morrow, 1928.

——. *Growing Up in New Guinea*. New York: W. Morrow. 1930.

——. *Sex and Temperament in Three Primitive Societies*. New York: W. Morrow, 1935.

——. *And Keep Your Powder Dry: An Anthropologist Looks at America*. New York: W. Morrow, 1942.

——. *Male and Female: A Study of the Sexes in a Changing World*. New York: W. Morrow, 1949.

Mei Lanfang. "Reflections on my Stage Life." *Peking Opera and Mei Lanfang*, Huang Zuolin, Mei Shaowu, and Wu Zuguang, eds.: 30–45. Beijing: New World Press, 1981.

Melvin, Sheila and Cai Jindong. "Why this Nostalgia for Fruits of Chaos?" *The New York Times*, 29 October 2000, sec. Arts & Leisure: 1, 31.

Melzer, Annabelle. *Dada and Surrealist Performance*. Baltimore, Md.: Johns Hopkins University Press, 1994.

Merback, Mitchell B. *The Thief, the Cross, and the Wheel*. Chicago, Ill.: University of Chicago Press, 1999.

Meyerhold, Vsevolod. *Meyerhold on Theatre*. Trans. and ed. Edward Braun. New York: Hill & Wang, 1969.

——. "First Attempts at a Stylized Theatre." *The Performance Studies Reader*, Henry Bial, ed.: 217–25. London and New York: Routledge, 2004.

Miller, Arthur. *Arthur Miller's Collected Plays*. New York: Viking Press, 1957–81.

——. *Broken Glass*. New York: Penguin Books, 1994.

——. *The Theatre Essays of Arthur Miller*. New York: De Capo Press, 1996.

——. *The Ride Down Mt. Morgan*. New York: Penguin Books, 1999.

——. *Resurrection Blues*. Minneapolis, Minn.: Guthrie Theatre, 2002.

Miller, Tim. "Stretch Marks." *TDR* 35, 3 (1991): 143–70.

——. *Body Blows: Six Performances*. Madison, Wisc.: University of Wisconsin Press, 2002.

Mnouchkine, Ariane. "The Theatre is Oriental." *The Intercultural Performance Reader*, Patrice Pavis, ed.: 93–98. London and New York: Routledge, 1996.

Montelle, Yann-Pierre. *Paleoperformance: The Emergence of Theatricality in the Deep Caves of the Upper Paleolithic*. Providence, RI: Brown University doctoral dissertation, 2004.

Moore, Sally Falk and Barbara G. Myerhoff. *Secular Ritual*. Assen: Van Gorcum, 1977.

Müller, Heiner. *Hamletmachine and Other Texts for the Stage*. New York: Performing Arts Journal Publications, 1984.

——. *Shakespeare Factory* (2 vols). Berlin: Rotbuch Verlag, 1985–89.

——. *Explosion of a Memory*. New York: PAJ Publications, 1989.

——. *A Heiner Müller Reader: Plays, Poetry, Prose*. Baltimore, Md.: Johns Hopkins University Press, 2001.

Muñoz, José Esteban. *Disidentifications*. Minneapolis, Minn.: University of Minnesota Press, 1999.

Murray, Gilbert. "Excursus on the Ritual Forms Preserved in Greek Tragedy." *Themis: A Study of the Social Origins of Greek Religion*, Jane Ellen Harrison, ed. Cambridge: Cambridge University Press, 1912: 341–63.

——. *Five Stages of Greek Religion*. New York: Columbia University Press, 1925.

Nehru, Jawaharlal. *Jawaharlal Nehru, An Autobiography with Musings on Recent Events in India*. London: John Lane, 1936.

——. *The Discovery of India*. New York: The John Day Company, 1946.

Nelson, Steve. "Broadway and the Beast: Disney Comes to Times Square." *TDR* 39, 2 (1995): 71–85.

Newton, Isaac. *The Principia*. Amherst, NY: Prometheus Press, 1995.

Ngũgĩ wa Thiong'o. *Petals of Blood*. London: Heinemann, 1977.

——. *Detained: A Writer's Prison Diary*. Nairobi: Heinemann, 1981.

——. *Decolonising the Mind*. London, Portsmouth, Nairobi, Harare: James Curry (London), EAEP (Nairobi), Heinemann (Portsmouth), Zimbabwe Publishing House (Harare), 1986.

——. *Moving the Centre*. London, Nairobi, Portsmouth: James Currey (London), EAEP (Nairobi), Heinemann (Portsmouth), 1993.

——. *Penpoints, Gunpoints, and Dreams: Toward a Critical Theory of the Arts and the State in Africa*. Oxford and New York: Oxford University Press, 1998.

——. *Murogi wa Kagogo*. Nairobi: East African Educational Publishers.

——. *Ngũgĩ wa Thiong'o Speaks*. Trenton, NJ: Africa World Press, 2005.

Nicoll, Allardyce. *Masks, Mimes, and Miracles*. New York: Cooper Square, 1963.

Nietzsche, Friedrich Wilhelm. *Philosophy in the Tragic Age of the Greeks*. South Bend, Ind.: Gateway Editions, 1962.

——. *Human, All Too Human*. Cambridge: Cambridge University Press, 1986.

——. *Beyond Good and Evil*. New York: Penguin Books, 1990.

——. *Thus Spake Zarathustra*. Mineola, NY: Dover Publications, 1999.

——. *The Birth of Tragedy*. Oxford and New York: Oxford University Press, 2000.

Northrup, F. S. C. "Introduction." *Physics and Philosophy* by Werner Heisenberg. New York: Harper, 1958.

O'Flaherty, Wendy Doniger. *Dreams, Illusions, and Other Realities*. Chicago, Ill.: University of Chicago Press, 1984.

Ohno, Kazuo. "Performance Text: *The Dead Sea*." *TDR* 30, 2 (1986): 170.

——. "Selections from the Prose of Kazuo Ohno." *TDR* 30, 2 (1986): 156–62.

Ohno, Kazuo and Yoshito Ohno. *Kazuo Ohno's World*. Middletown, Conn.: Wesleyan University Press, 2004.

Okpewho, Isidore. *African Oral Literature*. Bloomington, Ind.: Indiana University Press, 1992.

——. "The Oral Artist: Training and Preparation." *The Performance Studies Reader*, Henry Bial, ed.: 226–31. London and New York: Routledge, 2004.

Ong, Keng Sen. "Encounters." *TDR* 45, 3 (2001): 126–33.

Oohashia, Tsutomo, Norie Kawaic, Manabu Hondae, Satoshi Nakamurae, Masako Morimotoh, Emi Nishinai, Tadao Maekawaj. "Electroencephalographic Measurement of Possession Trance in the Field." *Clinical Neurophysiology* 113 (2002): 435–445.

Ortolani, Benito. *The Japanese Theatre From Shamanistic Ritual to Contemporary Pluralism*. Princeton, NY: Princeton University Press, 1995.

Osinski, Zbigniew. "Grotowski Blazes the Trails." *The Grotowski Sourcebook*. Lisa Wolford and Richard Schechner, eds: 383–98. London and New York: Routledge, 1997.

Palladio, Andrea. *The Four Books on Architecture*. Cambridge, Mass.: MIT Press, 1997.

Park, Robert Ezra. *Race and Culture*. Glencoe, Ill.: Free Press, 1950.

Parker, Andrew and Eve Kosofsky Sedgwick. "Introduction: Performativity and Performance." *Performativity and Performance*, Andrew Parker and Eve Kosofsky Sedgwick, eds: 1–18. London and New York: Routledge, 1995.

——. "Introduction to *Performativity and Performance*." *The Performance Studies Reader*, Henry Bial, ed.: 167–74. London and New York: 2004.

Parks, Suzan-Lori. *The America Play, and Other Works*. New York: Theatre Communications Group, 1995.

——. *Imperceptible Mutabilities in the Third Kingdom*. Los Angeles, Calif.: Sun & Moon Press, 1995.

——. *Venus*. New York: Theatre Communications Group, 1997.

——. *In the Blood*. New York: Dramatists Play Service, 2000.

——. *Topdog/Underdog*. New York: Theatre Communications Group, 2001.

——. *Getting Mother's Body, A Novel*. New York: Random House, 2003.

Pavis, Patrice. "Dancing with Faust: A Semiotician's Reflections on Barba's Intercultural Mise-en-Scene." *TDR* 33, 3 (1989): 37–57.

——, ed. *The Intercultural Performance Reader*. London and New York: Routledge, 1996.

——. "Introduction: Towards a Theory of Interculturalism in Theatre?" *The Intercultural Performance Reader*. Patrice Pavis, ed.: 1–21. London and New York: Routledge, 1996.

Pelias, Ronald J. and James VanOosting. "A Paradigm for Performance Studies." *Quarterly Journal of Speech* 73 (1987): 219–31.

Phelan, Peggy. "Money Talks, Again." *TDR* 35, 3 (1991): 131–42.

——. *Unmarked: The Politics of Performance*. London and New York: Routledge, 1993.

——. *Mourning Sex*. London and New York: Routledge, 1997.

——, with Helena Reckitt. *Art and Feminism*. London and New York: Phaidon, 2001.

Phelan, Peggy. "Marina Abramovic: Witnessing Shadows." *Theatre Journal* 56, 4 (2004): 569–77.

Phelan, Peggy and Jill Lane, eds. *The Ends of Performance*. New York: New York University Press, 1998.

Piper, Adrian. "Passing for White, Passing for Black." *Out of Order, Out of Sight Volume 1: Selected Writings in Meta-Art, 1968–1992*: 275–307. Cambridge, Mass. London: MIT Press, 1996.

Piper, Adrian, Maurice Berger, and Jean Fisher. *Adrian Piper: A Retrospective*. Baltimore and New York: Fine Arts Gallery, University of Maryland, Art Publishers, 1999.

Pirandello, Luigi. *Naked Masks: Five Plays*. New York: Dutton, 1952.

Plato. *The Republic*. Mineola, NY: Dover Publications, 2000.

Rappaport, Roy A. *Pigs for the Ancestors*. New Haven, Conn.: Yale University Press, 1968.

——. *Ecology, Meaning, and Religion*. Richmond, Calif.: North Atlantic Books, 1979.

——. *Ritual and Religion in the Making of Humanity*. Cambridge: Cambridge University Press, 1999.

Read, Kenneth E. *The High Valley*. New York: Scribner, 1965.

——. *Return to the High Valley*. Berkeley, Calif.: University of California Press, 1986.

Redstockings. *Feminist Revolution*. New Paltz, NY: Redstockings, 1975. Reissued in an abridged version with Kathie Sarachild/ Redstockings listed as authors. New York: Random House, 1978.

Richards, Thomas. *At Work With Grotowski on Physical Actions*. New York: Routledge, 1995.

Riverbend. *Baghdad Burning: Girl Blog from Iraq*. New York: The Feminist Press at the City University of New York, 2005.

Rodrick, Stephen. "Michael Winterbottom Gets Naked." *The New York Times Magazine* 3 July 2005: 22–27.

Roth, Moira, ed. *The Amazing Decade: Women and Performance Art in America, 1970–1980*. Los Angeles, Calif.: Astro Artz, 1983.

Rothstein, Edward. "A Jewish Canon, Yes, But Not Set in Stone." *The New York Times*, 24 February 2001, sec. Arts & Ideas: B7, B9.

Rouget, Gilbert. *Music and Trance*. Chicago, Ill. and London: University of Chicago Press, 1985.

Ruskin, John. *"Unto This Last": Four Essays on the First Principles of Political Economy*. London: Smith, Elder & Co, 1862.

Sainer, Arthur. *The New Radical Theatre Notebook*. New York: Applause, 1997.

Saivetz, Deborah. "An Event in Space: The Integration of Acting and Design in the Theatre of JoAnne Akalaitis." *TDR* 42, 2 (1998): 132–56.

Santino, Jack. "Performative Commemoratives, the Personal, and the Public: Spontaneous Shrines, Emergent Ritual." *Journal of American Folklore* 117 (2004): 363–72.

Sarachild, Kathie, ed. *Feminist Revolution*, New York: Random House, 1978.

Saussure, Ferdinand de. *Course in General Linguistics*. New York: Philosophical Library, 1959.

Schaller, George, B. *The Mountain Gorilla*. Chicago, Ill.: University of Chicago Press, 1963.

——. *The Serengeti Lion; a Study of Predator-Prey Relations*. Chicago, Ill.: University of Chicago Press, 1972.

——. *The Last Panda*. Chicago, Ill..: University of Chicago Press, 1994.

Schechner, Richard. *Environmental Theater*. New York: Hawthorn Books, 1973.

——. *The End of Humanism*. New York: PAJ Publications, 1982.

——. *Between Theater and Anthropology*. Philadelphia, Pa.: University of Pennsylvania Press, 1985.

——. *Performance Theory*. London: Routledge, 1988, revised edition 2003.

——. *The Future of Ritual*. London: Routledge, 1993.

——. "Performance Studies: The Broad Spectrum Approach." *The Performance Studies Reader*, Henry Bial, ed.: 7–9. London and New York: Routledge, 2004.

Schechner, Richard and Willa Appel, eds. *By Means of Performance*. Cambridge: Cambridge University Press, 1990.

Schechner, Richard and Mady Schuman, eds. *Ritual, Play, and Performance*. New York: Seabury Press, 1976.

Schmitt, Eric and Thom Shanker. "New Name for 'War on Terror' Reflects Wider U.S. Campaign." *The New York Times*, 26 July 2005, sec. A: 7.

Schneemann, Carolee, with Bruce R. McPherson. *More Than Meat Joy: Performance Works and Selected Writings*. Kingston, NY: McPherson & Co., 1997.

Schneider, Rebecca. "Solo Solo Solo." *After Criticism*. Gavin Butt, ed: 23–47. Malden, Mass.: Blackwell Publishing, 2005.

Schneider, Rebecca and Jon McKenzie. "Keep Your EYES on the FRONT and WATCH YOUR Back." *TDR*: 48, 4 (2004): 5–10.

Schopenhauer, Arthur. *The World as Will and Representation*. New York: Dover Publications, 1969.

Searle, John R. *Speech Acts: An Essay in the Philosophy of Language*. Cambridge: Cambridge University Press, 1969.

——. *Expression and Meaning: Studies in the Theory of Speech Acts*. Cambridge: Cambridge University Press, 1979.

——. *The Construction of Social Reality*. New York: Free Press, 1995.

——. *Mind, Language, and Society: Philosophy in the Real World*. New York: Basic Books, 1998.

——. *Rationality in Action*. Cambridge, Mass.: MIT Press, 2001.

——. *Mind: A Brief Introduction*. Oxford and New York: Oxford University Press, 2004.

Selbourne, David. *The Making of* A Midsummer Night's Dream. London: Methuen, 1982.

Shakespeare, William. *The Complete Works*. Oxford: Oxford University Press, 1988.

Shephard, William Hunter. *The Dionysus Group*. American University Studies. New York: Peter Lang, 1991.

Shirokogoroff, S. M. *Psychomental Complex of the Tungus*. London: Kegan, Paul, Trench, Trubner, 1935.

Smith, Anna Deavere. *Talk to Me: Listeninng Between the Lines*. New York: Random House, 2000.

——. *House Arrest*. New York: Anchor Books, 2004.

Smith, Craig S. "Joyous Vindication and a Sleepless Night in China." *The New York Times*, 14 July 2001, sec. Sports.

Sophocles. *Sophocles*, vols 1 and 2. Chicago, Ill.: University of Chicago Press, 1954–57.

——. *The Theban Plays: Oedipus the King, Oedipus at Colonus, Antigone*. New York: A. A. Knopf, 1994.

Soyinka, Wole. *Collected Plays*. Oxford: Oxford University Press, 1973.

——. *Death and the King's Horseman*. London: Methuen, 1975.

——. *Myth, Literature, and the African World*. Cambridge: Cambridge University Press, 1976.

——. *The Open Sore of a Continent: a Personal Narrative of the Nigerian Crisis*. New York: Oxford University Press, 1996.

——. *Arms and the Arts – A Continent's Unequal Dialogue*. Cape Town: University of Cape Town, 1999.

——. *Climate of Fear: The Quest for Dignity in a Dehumanized World*. New York: Random House, 2005.

Spariosu, Mihai. *Dionysus Reborn: Play and the Aesthetic Dimension in Modern Philosophical and Scientific Discourse*. Ithaca, NY: Cornell University Press, 1989.

——. *The Wreath of Wild Olive: Play, Liminality, and the Study of Literature*. Albany, NY: State University of New York Press, 1997.

Speer, Albert. *Inside the Third Reich: Memoirs*. New York: Simon & Schuster, 1997.

Sprinkle, Annie. *Post-Porn Modernist*. San Francisco, Calif.: Cleis Press, 1998.

——. *Hardcore from the Heart: The Pleasures, Profits, and Politics of Sex Performance*. London and New York: Continuum, 2001.

——. *Dr. Sprinkle's Spectacular Sex*. New York: Jeremy P. Tarcher, Penguin, 2005.

Squier, Susan Merrill. *Liminal Lives*. Durham, NC and London: Duke University Press.

Stanislavsky, Konstantin. *My Life in Art*. Boston, Mass.: Little, Brown, 1924.

——. *An Actor Prepares*. New York: Theatre Arts, 1936.

——. *Building a Character*. New York: Theatre Arts Books, 1949.

——. *Stanislavsky on the Art of the Stage*. London: Faber & Faber, 1950.

——. *Creating a Role*. New York: Theatre Arts Books, 1961.

Stebbins, Genevieve. *Delsarte System of Expression*. New York: Dance Horizons, 1977.

Stern, Carol Simpson and Bruce Henderson. *Performance: Texts and Contexts*. London and New York: Longman, 1993.

Strasberg, Lee. "Working with Live Material." *TDR:* 9, 1 (1964): 117–35.

——. "A Dream of Passion." *The Performance Studies Reader*, Henry Bial, ed.: 195–96. London and New York: Routledge, 2004.

Strasberg, Lee and Robert H. Hethmon. *Strasberg at the Actors Studio: Tape Recorded Sessions*. New York: Viking Press, 1965.

Strasberg, Lee and Evangeline Morphos. *A Dream of Passion: The Development of The Method*. Boston, Mass.: Little Brown, 1987.

Suetonius. *Lives of the Caesars*. Oxford: Oxford University Press, 2000.

Sutton-Smith, Brian. *Play and Learning*. New York: Gardener Press, 1979.

——. *Toys as Culture*. New York: Gardner Press, 1986.

——. *The Ambiguity of Play*. Cambridge, Mass.: Harvard University Press, 1997.

——. "The Ambiguity of Play: Rhetorics of Fate." *The Performance Studies Reader*, Henry Bial, ed.: 132–38. London and New York: Routledge, 2004.

—— and Diana Kelly-Byrne. *The Masks of Play*. New York: Leisure Press, 1984.

Suzuki, Tadashi. *The Way of Acting*. New York: Theatre Communications Group, 1986.

Tate, Nahum. *The History of King Lear* (a 1681 version of Shakespeare's play). Lincoln, Nebr.: University of Nebraska Press.

Taylor, Diana. *Theatre of Crisis: Drama and Politics in Latin America*. Lexington, Ky.: University Press of Kentucky, 1991.

——. *Disappearing Acts: Spectacles of Gender and Nationalism in Argentina's "Dirty War"*. Durham, NC: Duke University Press, 1997.

——. "Translating Performance." *Profession* 2002, 1 (2002): 44–50.

——. Untitled entry in "A Forum on Theatre and Tragedy in the Wake of September 11, 2001," *Theatre Journal* 54 (2002): 95–96.

——. *The Archive and the Repertoire*. Durham, NC: Duke University Press, 2003.

TDR: Offensive Plays, 35, 3 (1991): 131–220. Including Tim Miller, "Stretch Marks"; John Fleck, "BLESSED Are All the *Little* FISHES"; Holly Hughes "The Lady Dick." Also: Peggy Phelan, "Money Talks, Again" and interviews with the playwrights.

Thompson, James and Richard Schechner. "Why 'Social Theatre'?" *TDR* 48, 3 (2004): 11–16.

Thompson, Robert Farris. *African Art in Motion*. Los Angeles, Calif.: University of California Press, 1974.

Thoreau, Henry David. *Walden*. Boston, Mass.: Beacon Press, 1997.

Thornwell, Emily. *The Lady's Guide to Perfect Gentility in Manners, Dress, and Conversation*. New York: Derby & Jackson, 1856.

Tolstoy, Leo. *War and Peace*. New York: Knopf, 1992.

——. *Anna Karenina*. Oxford: Oxford University Press, 1999.

Toro, Fernando de. *Theatre Semiotics: Text and Staging in Modern Theatre*. Frankfurt am Main, Madrid: Vervuert Verlag, Iberoamericana, 1995.

Traub, James. "The Statesman." *The New York Times Magazine*, 18 September 2005: 81–89, 96–97.

Trofimov, Yarolsav. *Faith at War*. New York: Henry Holt, 2005.

Turner, Edith L. B. *Experiencing Ritual: A New Interpretation of African Healing*. Philadelphia, Pa.: University of Pennsylvania Press, 1992.

——. *The Hands Feel It: Healing and Spirit Presence among a Northern Alaskan People*. DeKalb, Ill.: Northern Illinois University Press, 1996.

Turner, Victor. *The Forest of Symbols: Aspects of Ndembu Ritual*. Ithaca, NY: Cornell University Press, 1967.

——. *The Ritual Process: Structure and Anti-Structure*. Chicago, Ill.: Aldine Publishing Company, 1969.

——. *Dramas, Fields, and Metaphors*. Ithaca, NY: Cornell University Press, 1974.

——. *From Ritual to Theatre: The Human Seriousness of Play*. New York: PAJ Publications, 1982.

——. "Body, Brain, and Culture." *Zygon* 18, no. 3 (1983): 221–45.

——. *On the Edge of the Bush: Anthropology As Experience*. Tucson, Ariz.: University of Arizona Press, 1985.

——. *The Anthropology of Performance*. New York: PAJ Publications, 1986.

——. "Liminality and Communitas." *The Performance Studies Reader*, Henry Bial, ed.: 79–87. London and New York: Routledge, 2004.

Turner, Victor with Edith Turner. "Performing Ethnography." *The Performance Studies Reader*, Henry Bial, ed.: 265–78. London and New York: Routledge, 2004.

Ueda, Makoto. *Literary and Art Theories in Japan*. Cleveland, Ohio: Western Reserve University Press, 1967.

Vyasa. *The Bhagavad Gita*. New York: Bantam Books, 1986.

Walcott, Derek. *Dream on Monkey Mountain and Other Plays*. New York: Farrar, Straus & Giroux, 1970.

——. *The Odyssey: A Stage Version*. London, Boston, Mass.: Faber & Faber, 1993.

——. *The Prodigal*. New York: Farrar, Straus, & Giroux, 2004.

——, with Edward Baugh and Colbert I. Nepaulsingh. *Another Life Fully Annotated*. Boulder, Col.: Lynne Rienner Publishers, 2004.

Waldrop, M. Mitchell. "Do-It-Yourself-Universes." *Science* (1987): 845–46.

Wilford, John Noble. "In the Dawn of Society, Dance Was Center Stage." *The New York Times*, 27 February 2001, sec. Science: 1–5.

Willett, John. *The Theatre of Bertolt Brecht*. New York: New Directions, 1960.

Williams, Francis Edgar. *Drama of Orokolo: The Social and Ceremonial Life of the Elema*. Oxford: Clarendon Press, 1969.

Wilmoth, Charles M. "The Archaeology of Muff Diving." *TDR* 35, 3 (1991): 216–20.

Wilson, Edward Osborne. *Sociobiology: The New Synthesis*. Cambridge, Mass.: Harvard University Press, 1975.

——. *On Human Nature*. Cambridg, Mass.: Harvard University Press, 1978.

——. *Consilience: The Unity of Knowledge*. New York: Knopf, 1998.

Wilson, R. Rawdon. *In Palamedes' Shadow: Explorations in Play, Game & Narrative Theory*. Boston, Mass.: Northeastern University Press, 1990.

Winkelman, Michael. "Shamanism as the Original Neurotheology." *Zygon* 39, 1 (2004): 193–217.

Winnicott, Donald Woods. *The Child and the Family; First Relationships*. London: Tavistock Publications, 1957.

——. *Playing and Reality*. London: Tavistock Publications, 1971.

Wittgenstein, Ludwig. *Philosophical Investigations*. Oxford: Blackwell, 1953.

Wojtyla, Karol Jozef (Pope John Paul II). *The Collected Plays and Writings on Theater*. Berkeley, Calif.: University of California Press. 1987.

Wolford, Lisa and Richard Schechner, eds. *The Grotowski Sourcebook*. London and New York: Routledge, 1997.

Worthen, W. B. "Disciplines of the Text: Sites of Performance." *The Performance Studies Reader*, Henry Bial, ed.: 10–25. London and New York: Routledge, 2004.

Wu Tsu-kuang, Mei Shao-wu, Huang Tso-lin, and Mei Lanfang. *Peking Opera and Mei Lanfang: A Guide to China's Traditional Theatre and the Art of its Great Master*. Beijing: New World Press, 1981.

Zarrilli, Phillip. "For Whom Is the 'Invisible' not Visible?" *TDR*: 32, 1 (1988): 95–106.

——., ed. *Acting (Re)Considered*. London and New York: Routledge, 1995, 2nd edition, 2002.

——. *When the Body Becomes All Eyes*, New Delhi: Oxford University Press, 1998.

——. *Kathakali Dance Drama*, London and New York, Routledge, 2000.

Zeami Motokiyo. *On the Art of the No Drama*. Princeton, NY: Princeton University Press, 1984.

Zimmerman, Mary. "The Archaeology of Performance." *Theatre Topics* 15, 1 (2005): 25–35.

INDEX

Related titles from Routledge

The Performance Studies Reader

Edited by Henry Bial

'A collection of this type has been needed for a long time.'

Sally Harrison-Pepper, *Miami University*

'Clearly an important collection of essays that will provide an excellent resource for levels II and III specialist courses.'

Nick Kaye, *Exeter University*

The Performance Studies Reader is a lively and much-needed anthology of critical writings on the burgeoning discipline of performance studies. It provides an overview of the full range of performance theory for undergraduates at all levels, and beginning graduate students in performance studies, theatre, performing arts and cultural studies.

The collection is designed as a companion to Richard Schechner's popular *Performance Studies: an Introduction* but is also ideal as a stand-alone text. Henry Bial collects together key critical pieces from the field, referred to as 'suggested readings' in *Performance Studies: an Introduction*. He also broadens the discussion with additional selections. Featuring contributions from major scholars and artists such as Richard Schechner, Eugenio Barba, Marvin Carlson, Judith Butler, Jon McKenzie, Homi K. Bhabha, Eve Kosofsky Sedgwick and Jerzy Grotowski, this important collection offers a wide-ranging introduction to the main areas of study.

ISBN10: 0-415-30240-4 (hbk)
ISBN10: 0-415-30241-2 (pbk)

ISBN13: 0-415-30240-1 (hbk)
ISBN13: 0-415-30241-8 (pbk)

Related titles from Routledge

Performance: A Critical Introduction 2nd Edition

Marvin Carlson

Performance: A Critical Introduction was the first textbook to provide an overview of the modern concept of performance and its development in various related fields. This comprehensively revised, illustrated edition discusses recent performance work and takes into consideration changes that have taken place since the book's original publication in 1996. Marvin Carlson guides the reader through the contested definition of performance as a theatrical activity and the myriad ways in which performance has been interpreted by ethnographers, anthropologists, linguists, and cultural theorists.

Topics covered include:

- the evolution of performance art since the 1960s
- the relationship between performance, postmodernism, the politics of identity, and current cultural studies
- the recent theoretical developments in the study of performance in the fields of anthropology, psychoanalysis, linguistics, and technology.

With a fully updated bibliography and additional glossary of terms, students of performance studies, visual and performing arts or theatre history will welcome this new version of a classic text.

ISBN10: 0-415-29926-8 (hbk)
ISBN10: 0-415-29927-6 (pbk)

ISBN13: 978-0-415-29926-8 (hbk)
ISBN13: 978-0-415-29927-5 (pbk)